Visual Basic 3

By EXAMPLE

que

D.F. Scott
Eric Bloom

Visual Basic 3 By Example

©1994 by Que® Corporation

Library of Congress Catalog Number: 94-65324

ISBN: 1-56529-724-5

96   95   94   6   5   4   3   2   1

Interpretation of the printing code: The rightmost double-digit number is the year of the book's printing; the rightmost single-digit number, the number of the book's printing. For example, a printing code of 94-1 shows that the first printing of the book occurred in 1994.

Publisher: *David P. Ewing*

Associate Publisher: *Michael Miller*

Managing Editor: *Michael Cunningham*

Marketing Manager: *Ray Robinson*

Publishing Director
Joseph B. Wikert

Product Development Specialist
Bryan Gambrel

Production Editor
Lori Cates

Copy Editors
Lynn Northrup
Elsa Bell
Charles Hutchinson
Andy Saff
Jeanne Lemen

Technical Editor
Russell Jacobs

Book Designers
Amy Peppler-Adams
Paula Carroll

Cover Designer
Jean Bisesi

Production Team
Cameron Booker
Ayrika Bryant
Karen Dodson
Joelynn Gifford
Carla Hall
Michael Hughes
Greg Kemp
Joy Dean Lee
Beth Lewis
Tim Montgomery
Shelly Palma
G. Alan Palmore
Caroline Roop
Dennis Sheehan
Susan Shepard
Michael Thomas
Tina Trettin
Susan VandeWalle
Johnna VanHoose
Mary Beth Wakefield
Dennis Wesner
Donna Winter
Lillian Yates

Editorial Assistant
Michelle Williams

Composed in *Palatino* and *MCPdigital* by Prentice Hall Computer Publishing

About the Authors

D. F. Scott is an independent technical author, artist, musician, and poet. He was Technical Editor of *The Computer Street Journal*, Contributing Editor of *ANALOG Computing* and *ST-Log* magazines, and a contributor to *Computer Monthly*. His insights and observations on alternative computing appeared in *Computer Shopper* from 1985 to 1990, during which time he also served as moderator of the Computer Shopper Information Exchange. He is the author of *Visual Basic for MS-DOS* and *Programming Illustrated* from Que; *Extending Visual Basic for Windows* and *Visual Basic for Windows Developer's Guide* from Sams Publishing; and *WordPerfect 6 for Windows HyperGuide* from Alpha Books.

Eric Bloom is a principal consulting manager with Fidelity Investments, an adjunct faculty member at Boston University, and the author of various other computer-related books.

Trademarks

All terms mentioned in this book that are known to be trademarks or service marks have been appropriately capitalized. Que cannot attest to the accuracy of this information. Use of a term in this book should not be regarded as affecting the validity of any trademark or service mark.

Visual Basic is a registered trademark of Microsoft Corporation.

Screen Reproductions in this book were created using Collage Complete from Inner Media, Inc., Hollis, New Hampshire.

We'd Like to Hear from You!

In a continuing effort to produce the highest-quality books possible, Que would like to hear your comments. As radical as this may sound for a publishing company, we **really** want you, the reader and user, to let us know what you like and dislike about this book, and what we can do to improve this book and future books.

In order to provide the most service to you, Prentice Hall Computer Publishing now has a forum on CompuServe (type **GO QUEBOOKS** at any prompt) through which our staff and authors are available for questions and comments. In addition to visiting our forum, feel free to contact me personally on CompuServe at 70714,1516. Or send your comments, ideas, or corrections to me by fax at (317) 581-4663, or write to me at the address below. Your comments will help us to continue publishing the best books on the market.

Bryan Gambrel
Product Development Specialist
Que
201 W. 103rd Street
Indianapolis, IN 46290

Overview

Introduction 1

I The Visual Basic Environment

1 What a Program Is 11
2 The Workspace 21
3 Grammar and Linguistics 37
4 The Development Process 51

II Values and Variables

5 Using Variables 65
6 Arithmetic Formulas 75
7 Logic and Number Systems 85
8 Alphanumeric Strings 99
9 Array Variables 111
10 Value Declaration 121

III Instructions and Groupings

11 Phrasing 137
12 Conditional Clauses 143
13 Loop Clauses 155
14 Arbitrary Instruction Clusters 167
15 The Module Hierarchy 179
16 Parameter Passing 195

IV Designing for User Interaction

17 Control Identification and Contents 203
18 Design and Layout 217
19 The Window as Form 229
20 The Window as Document 245
21 The Window as Panel 257

V Graphic Objects and Controls

22 Menus and Options 267
23 Managing List Boxes 281
24 Storage and Printer Controls 297
25 Shape and Line Controls 309
26 Scroll Bars 317

27 The Timer 323
28 The Keyboard 327
29 The Pointer as Device 339
30 Dragging the Controls 349
31 Grids and Tables 365
32 Object Variables 379

VI Arithmetic Functions

33 Classifications 395
34 Conversion 401
35 Practical Math 411
36 String Functions 417
37 Time and Date 433
38 The Random Number Generator 441

VII Text

39 Conventional Output 449
40 Text Properties 463
41 The Printer and Sound Output 479

VIII Bitmapped Graphics

42 Picture and Image Boxes 485
43 Plotting 493
44 Image Integrity and Scaling 511

IX Error Trapping and Debugging

45 Registering Errors 521
46 Debugging Techniques 527

X Physical Data

47 Sequential Access 537
48 Random and Binary Access 553
49 Data File Attributes 563
50 Formal Records 575
A ASCII/ANSI Code Chart 599
B Answers to Review Questions 609
C Complete Source Code Listings of Major Applications ... 627
Index 647

Contents

Introduction   **1**

Overview 2

Who Should Use This Book 4

Conventions Used in This Book 4

Pseudocode 5

More Conventions 6

Part I The Visual Basic Environment

1 What a Program Is   **11**

A Programmer's Credo 11

Fundamental Terminology 13

The Visual Basic Interpreter 14

The Process of Interaction 15

The Computing Environment 17

Summary 18

Review Questions 19

2 The Workspace   **21**

The Visual Basic Project 21

Graphic Objects 25

Properties 30

The *.Name* Property 31

Saving Your Work 33

Summary 34

Review Questions 34

Review Exercise 35

3 Grammar and Linguistics   **37**

Modern Syntax 37

Expressions 39

Intrinsic Functions 40

Program Components 41

More on Program Components 45

Visual Basic Symbols 47

Summary 50

Review Questions 50

Contents

4 The Development Process   **51**

Entering Applications from Listings 51
Building an Application 52
Making the Expressor 53
Building Your Program 56
Summary 61
Review Questions 62

Part II Values and Variables

5 Using Variables   **65**

Declaring Variables 65
Degrees of Precision 69
Memory Conservation 71
Summary 72
Review Questions 73
Review Exercises 73

6 Arithmetic Formulas   **75**

The Purpose of Formulas 75
The Order of Evaluation 76
The Use of Parentheses 77
Summary 82
Review Questions 83
Review Exercise 83

7 Logic and Number Systems   **85**

Boolean Logic 85
Higher-Level Comparisons 87
Using Logic 89
Boolean Operators 90
Number Systems 93
Summary 97
Review Questions 97

8 Alphanumeric Strings   **99**

String Values 99
ANSI, ASCII, and Other Acronyms 101
Summary 109
Review Exercise 110
Review Questions 110

9   Array Variables   111

The Purpose of Arrays 111
Dimensioning Variables 112
Regulating Arrays 115
Establishing Bounds 117
Counting from 0 or 1 117
Summary 118
Review Questions 119
Review Exercise 119

10   Value Declaration   121

Structured Programming 121
A Variable's Scope of Existence 123
Constants 128
The Composition of Variables 130
Summary 133
Review Questions 134
Review Exercise 134

Part III Instructions and Groupings

11   Phrasing   137

Statements and Functions 137
Program Remarks 139
Summary 141
Review Questions 141
Review Exercise 141

12   Conditional Clauses   143

The Construction of a Clause 143
If-Then as a Two-Sided Argument 147
The *Select Case* Statement 148
Summary 153
Review Questions 153
Review Exercise 154

13   Loop Clauses   155

The *Do-Loop* Clause 162
Summary 164
Review Questions 165
Review Exercises 165

Contents

14   Arbitrary Instruction Clusters   167

Branching 167
Program Context 173
The Subroutine 173
Sequential Branching 175
Summary 176
Review Questions 177
Review Exercise 178

15   The Module Hierarchy   179

The Origin of Modules 179
The Order of Execution 183
The Form Module 186
The *Sub Main ()* Procedure 187
The *DoEvents* Statement 188
The *End* Statement 189
Summary 192
Review Questions 193

16   Parameter Passing   195

Parameter Passing Order 198
Summary 200
Review Questions 200

Part IV Designing for User Interaction

17   Control Identification and Contents 203

Clarifying the Graphic Object 203
Using Aliases 204
Control Array Indexing 206
Object Events 207
What the User Can and Cannot Edit 209
When Is a Command a Command? 212
Summary 214
Review Questions 215

18   Design and Layout   217

The Twip Coordinate System 217
Positioning and Sizing Controls 218
Design-Aided Computing 221
Using Tabs..222
Monitoring Activity 224
Using Color 225

Summary 227
Review Questions 228

19 The Window as Form   229

Where Your Forms Are 229
Transition between States 231
Knowing the Names of the Controls 233
The Anatomy of a Form 233
State Determination 240
Summary 242
Review Questions 243

20 The Window as Document   245

Worlds within Worlds 245
Parent Forms 246
Rearranging Windows 253
Summary 255
Review Questions 255

21 The Window as Panel   257

Boxes versus Panels 257
The Input Box 261
Summary 262
Review Questions 263

Part V Graphic Objects and Controls

22 Menus and Options   267

The Menu 267
Menu Production 269
Grouping Controls in a Form 274
Grouping Controls in the Source Code............................277
Summary 279
Review Questions 279

23 Managing List Boxes   281

Using Visual Basic Controls 281
List Boxes and Combo Boxes..282
Multiple-Choice Selection 291
Summary 294
Review Questions 295
Review Exercise 295

Contents

24 Storage and Printer Controls **297**

Directory Assistance 297
A File Selector Box Application 299
Offshoots from the _Change_ Event 302
Common Dialog Boxes 302
Summary 307
Review Questions 307

25 Shape and Line Controls **309**

Shapes and Lines 309
Object-Oriented Graphics 314
Summary 316
Review Questions 316

26 Scroll Bars **317**

The All-Purpose Range Finder 317
Summary 321
Review Questions 322

27 The Timer **323**

An Experiment in Real Time 323
Summary 326
Review Questions 326

28 The Keyboard **327**

Substituting Buttons for Keys 333
Assigning Keystrokes to Buttons 335
Summary 336
Review Questions 336

29 The Pointer as Device **339**

When Is a Move a Move? 345
The Appearance of the Pointer 345
Summary 347
Review Questions 348

30 Dragging the Controls **349**

Lock and Key Example 357
Moving Controls 360
Summary 363
Review Questions 364
Review Exercises 364

31 Grids and Tables   365

Anatomy of the Grid 366
Putting the Grid to Work 371
Other Grid Properties 375
Summary 376
Review Questions 377

32 Object Variables   379

Putting Several Name Tags on the Same Item 382
Giving Focus to an Object 383
Indirect References 385
Arbitrary Object Variables 387
Summary 390
Review Questions 391

Part VI Arithmetic Functions

33 Classifications   395

Redeclaration 396
Pinning down the Variants 397
Summary 399
Review Questions 399

34 Conversion   401

String Conversions 403
ASCII Conversion 404
Summary 409
Review Questions 410

35 Practical Math   411

More Math Functions 413
Summary 414
Review Questions 415

36 String Functions   417

The `String$()`, `LCase$()`, and `UCase$()` Functions 424
In the Midst of Strings 426
Summary 431
Review Questions 432

Contents

37 Time and Date   **433**

Times and Dates as Text...437
How Dated Are Your Variants?..................................439
Summary 440
Review Questions 440

38 The Random Number Generator   **441**

Summary 444
Review Questions 445

Part VII Text

39 Conventional Output   **449**

Formatting Textual Output 454
Summary 461
Review Questions 461

40 Text Properties   **463**

Font Characteristics 463
Tailoring Text to Fit Controls, and Vice Versa 464
True/False Font Properties..465
The Technique of Text Trapping 466
Making It All Fit 473
Selection and the Grid 474
Summary 476
Review Questions 477

41 The Printer and Sound Output   **479**

Font Selection...480
Sound 481
Summary 482
Review Questions 482

Part VIII Bitmapped Graphics

42 Picture and Image Boxes   **485**

Persistent Bitmaps..489
Summary 492
Review Questions 492

43 Plotting   **493**

Coordinate Systems 493
Windows inside Windows 494

The Color Scheme 495
Plotting Lines 500
Line Thickness and Fill...502
Summary 508
Review Questions 509
Review Exercises 509

44 Image Integrity and Scaling   511

Integrity Properties 511
Rescaling...513
Summary 517
Review Questions 518

Part IX Error Trapping and Debugging

45 Registering Errors   521

Error-Trapping Routines...522
Summary 526
Review Questions 526

46 Debugging Techniques   527

Using Watch Expressions 530
So What Is Debugging? 532
Summary 533
Review Questions 533

Part X Physical Data

47 Sequential Access   537

Sequential Data as Pages...549
Summary 550
Review Questions 550
Review Exercises 551

48 Random and Binary Access   553

Records versus Data 559
Summary 561
Review Questions 562

Contents

49   Data File Attributes   563

Data Process Control 566
Unformatted Data Input 568
System Clipboard Management 570
Summary 573
Review Questions 574

50   Formal Records   575

Making NameForm Work 575
Placing the End in the Middle 581
A Procedure of Sorts 594
Algorithmic Logic 597
Summary 597
Review Questions 598

A   ASCII/ANSI Code Chart   599

B   Answers to Review Questions   609

**C   Complete Source Code Listings
of Major Applications   627**

The Expressor—Textually-Assisting Calculator 628

Index   647

Introduction

Welcome to the art of programming. The majority of your time working on a microcomputer thus far may have been spent writing documents and composing spreadsheets. Up to now, you have interacted with programs in the role of *user*. As such, you have acted out a role, literally, in a script. Each program has given you choices of actions and, for the most part, you've composed the data you've entered. Yet your personal interaction with the program has been scripted, planned, and plotted well in advance by programmers. This interaction is, in essence, a dialog between you and the computer, which uses data as its medium of communication.

Microsoft Windows is an elaborate stage for the production and presentation of programs. Windows' visual resources—the various buttons, gadgets, and pointers—are the props for this stage. Naturally, the program itself is the play. The purpose of the program—whether to balance the corporate account or to give the user a few moments of stress relief—is the *theme*.

In the same way that no great play can be written without a strong underlying theme, no computer program can be conceived without a strong underlying purpose or objective. This book cannot give you an objective for your program any more than a book on 20th century playwrights can supply you with a theme for a play. Yet this is the very thing other books on the subject of programming try to do: They tell you what to write, rather than how to write it.

Visual Basic 3 By Example shows you various techniques for writing working programs, allowing you to develop your own style. Programming is not just a method for translating everyday procedures into logical code; it's also a means of expression. To be a user of applications, you assume the role of an actor on a stage. As a programmer, however, you set the stage, conceive the dialog, and in a somewhat detached fashion, direct the user.

To better understand the role of programmer, imagine the elements of a program—the various modules, procedures, routines, and clauses—as if they were the supporting characters of a play. In other words, the part of the program that figures the totals, the part that draws the lines on the graph, the part that recalls the name of your client, and the part that checks to see if the user pressed a button are all supporting characters, different in purpose although equal in treatment.

The user, however, has the lead role in this production. The dialog between the lead and the rest of the cast comprises the body of the play. If the characters don't interact with each other, their individual identities aren't apparent to the audience, and the message in the play doesn't come through. Likewise, without a high degree of coordination and data exchange between the elements of a program and the user, the program doesn't flow, and its objective may not be completed with ease. Like the confused, disgruntled patron of a theater who walks out in mid-scene, the user may choose to quit your program early.

So, you can see that your role as programmer is similar to both playwright and stage director. No programming environment to date more closely resembles a stage than Visual Basic—there are platforms, props, gadgets, and in a sense, choreography. You arrange and assemble the stage for each program on-screen. The production itself, however, is still a script, meticulously executed and thoroughly rehearsed.

Visual Basic 3 By Example explicitly and exhaustively demonstrates the development of programs and program modules from the perspective of the programmer, showing you what decisions are made—both necessary and arbitrary—that lead to a well-planned, perfectly executed production.

Overview

First you need to comprehend the mechanics and characteristics of the stage where you will produce your programs. In Part I, "The Visual Basic Environment," you take a guided tour of the workspace where you will construct your programs. Once you're comfortable in your new workspace, you begin to concentrate on your main objective: learning what a program is and how a Visual Basic program differs from a conventional BASIC program or even a C program.

Part I

In Part I of the book, you see example programs and program modules in various stages of construction and get some practice constructing your own modules for real-world purposes. Instead of just showing you a working program, Chapter 4, "The Development Process," takes you step-by-step through the construction of a small Visual Basic application, concentrating on what goes through the mind of the programmer and what type of goals programmers set for themselves. No program, regardless of the language, manifests itself in complete, flawless source code. Most good programs are the result of bursts of inspiration, separated by several hours of error-trapping and debugging.

Part II

When you're comfortable with the setting and the process of programming, you start to examine the verbal and graphic elements of Visual Basic piece-by-piece. As visually comprehensive as Visual Basic is, a novice programmer might be led to believe there is little or no arithmetic left in the programming process. Such is not the case; arithmetic logic and procedural algebra still comprise the basis of all programming; so in Part II, "Values and Variables," you are introduced to arithmetic logic and procedural algebra using tangible, real-world terms and analogies.

Part III

In Part III, "Instructions and Groupings," you examine Visual Basic's "parts of speech." Visual Basic instructions have their own grammar, much like English-language sentences; as a result, you, the programmer, will be able to better comprehend the structure of Visual Basic, using a structure that's at least partly familiar to you. Throughout the programming process, you'll write descriptions of the work process that your program is designed to perform. This part of the book demonstrates how the overall job assigned to a Visual Basic program is divided and delegated to the various modules and constituent procedures.

Part IV

One of the skills you'll develop as you program for the Windows environment concerns the fine art of designing screens, dialog boxes, and menus. You will find this process to be very similar to that of a graphic artist designing a magazine page or printed advertisement. You'll understand more about this skill in Part IV, "Designing for User Interaction."

Part V

The Visual Basic language contains dozens of reserved terms for handling graphic elements and user interaction processes. Each of them is covered in Part V, "Graphic Objects and Controls."

Part VI

Part VI turns to the subject of "Arithmetic Functions." You use mathematical formulas in Visual Basic, although not in the same way as you use them with a spreadsheet package. On a spreadsheet, a formula contained within a cell always has a fixed, predictable result. With programming languages, values (as opposed to cells) are in transition. Rather than fixed results, you deal with variables.

Parts VII and VIII

In addition to the graphical controls covered earlier in Part V, the two other primary forms of data output are through standard text and through bitmapped graphics panes. These output methods are covered, respectively, in Part VII, "Text," and Part VIII, "Bitmapped Graphics."

Part IX

The Visual Basic interpreter offers a trial-and-error environment for testing programs. It is natural for programs to exhibit errors in the early stages of their development; working through such errors is a major part of writing and perfecting a program. Part IX, "Error Trapping and Debugging," introduces you to the art of correcting yourself—which is probably what you spend half your time doing as a programmer, even after you become an expert.

Part X

Comparisons are continually drawn between Visual Basic and graphical database management systems such as PerForm and Oracle. Despite all the enhancements, the VB methodology for handling data in the form of records—such as records of your clients or of items of inventory—is still rooted in the old BASIC dialects. The subject is covered in detail in Part X, "Physical Data."

Who Should Use This Book

This book assumes that you have already used Windows enough that you understand the principles of icons, buttons, and pulldown menus. It also assumes that you have already fully installed Visual Basic, and that it is operating normally. The book does not assume, however, that you have prior knowledge or experience with BASIC unless stated otherwise.

Conventions Used in This Book

From time to time throughout the book, a specific keyword from the Visual Basic vocabulary is featured. Most keywords in Visual Basic are like the subject of an English-language sentence. Once you invoke a keyword in an instruction, several rules dictate how you can phrase that instruction. This book demonstrates these rules by displaying each instruction in a "syntax block," which is a grouping of the keyword along with other terms that symbolize how that keyword should appear in the midst of the program. The following is an example syntax block:

```
[Static] Function procedure_name ([[ByVal] argument1[()]
   [As type], [ByVal] argument2[()][As type]. . . ])
    instruction_block1
    procedure_name = expression1
    [Exit Function]
    [instruction_block2]
    [procedure_name = expression2]
End Function
```

This syntax for the keyword Function is one of the larger syntax blocks you'll see in the book. Keywords here are identified in monospace type. Monospace italic type is used here to denote terms used in the context of the syntax block to stand in place of other terms or instructions. For instance, procedure_name appears in three places on the preceding syntax, and stands for whatever arbitrary name you give this procedure. GetHelp is a good name for a procedure; it makes the purpose of that procedure obvious to the reader. For a procedure with that name, you enter GetHelp in place of procedure_name in all three cases.

Wherever you see a term or group of terms appearing between regular square brackets, as in [Static], the brackets denote that the contents therein are optional. The Function statement works with or without Static, although adding Static changes the meaning of the keyword. You don't actually type the square brackets when you choose to include Static. The use of square brackets in syntax blocks is conventional in computer books; however, the Visual Basic 3 interpreter now uses square brackets for its own purposes. So in syntax blocks, where you are supposed to type the square brackets into the interpreter, they are printed in **boldface** type.

In other syntax blocks, when two or more terms within braces are separated with a vertical line—as in {either ¦ or}—only one of the terms within the braces appears in that position. In the example syntax of a clause, *vertical ellipses* (three dots, each on its own line) stand in place of any number of interpretable instructions. Keep in mind that you do not type certain punctuation—such as brackets ([ ]), braces ({}), or ellipses (. . .)—in the VB instruction or clause.

Pseudocode

One of the tools this book uses to show you how the Visual Basic language works is *pseudocode.* In essence, a paragraph of pseudocode states in English what the program instructions do. Pseudocode is identified with the "light bulb" icon shown next to italicized text. Following are two samples: the first is written in pure Visual Basic, and the second is a pseudocode sample that explains the function of the code fragment that precedes it.

```
For C = 1 to 5
     Form1.Print C
Next C
```

Start counting from 1 to 5.
 Print the number you just counted.
Go back to where you started counting and repeat
 yourself until you reach 5.

The preceding pseudocode segment is a bit verbose, but its purpose is not only to show you what the Visual Basic source code is trying to state for the interpreter, but also at what point in the code it is stated.

Next to many working example program modules and fragments in this book is an icon representing the difficulty level of the example. A module's size is no measure of how confusing it can be. These icons should reassure you that when a particular module is difficult, it was meant to be. The following is a list of the icons used for this purpose:

Level 1

Level 2

Level 3

Throughout this book, you occasionally encounter a Visual Basic instruction that is too long for the typesetters to fit it all on one line. In such cases, a rightward-sweeping arrow before a line indicates that the line is the continuation of the previous one, as in the following example:

```
Declare Function GetSystemDirectory Lib "Kernel" (ByVal
➥lpBuffer As String, ByVal nSize As Integer) As Integer
```

Margin notes emphasize important new terms and concepts.

To make every inch of this book useful, information has been included in the margins. If an important new term is introduced, a definition for that term appears in a *margin note*.

At the end of most chapters is a short series of review questions and, where applicable, exercises that should challenge your comprehension of the information in that chapter. The difficulty-level symbols appear here too, indicating the difficulty of the questions. The answers to the review questions are in Appendix B.

More Conventions

A few items concerning English-language syntax are worth noting before you proceed. From time to time, however, Visual Basic is abbreviated as *VB;* and where necessary, the abbreviation *VB3* is used to refer specifically to version 3.

In this book, certain keywords are preceded by punctuation that is normally used within VB instructions to identify their purpose. When you see references to the _Load event, to the .Count property, or to the Sub Form1_Click () procedure, the _, the ., and the () are all elements of Visual Basic punctuation that help distinguish the keywords' identity and purpose.

The screen shots depict Microsoft Windows running on a standard VGA monitor at 1024×768 resolution. Due to slight variations in Windows video display drivers, especially in varying resolutions, your screen may appear slightly different from the ones shown in this book.

Before Windows-based programming, you could print a few pages of source code—pure text and numbers—type it all, and you would have a working program. Times have changed, and now you do not entirely *type in* a Visual Basic program. The positioning and characteristics of graphic objects are determined with the mouse; you now practically *draw* controls within windows. Whenever you see a complete source code listing in this book, you also see a table showing the names of the important graphic objects used in the program, along with the properties or characteristics—such as position, size, color, and index number—that have been changed from their default settings. You can then assemble your control form manually using the table as a guide.

A programmer writes programs with the aid of Visual Basic, although Visual Basic is itself a program. This could cause some confusion if you see the phrase "the Visual Basic program" without knowing specifically whether it refers to the program written in the VB language or to Visual Basic the program. Therefore, this book refers to the programs you write using the VB language as "Visual Basic applications." This book uses "the Visual Basic program" to refer to the software you bought in the white box.

With respect to the actions a user makes when operating a program in a graphical environment, the usage of individual verbs for specific actions is standardized. Thus, a menu item is *selected,* an entry from a list box is *chosen,* data in a form or window is *indicated,* and a button is *clicked.* Further, a setting, property, or file name typed manually into a text field is a *designation,* and a setting or attribute chosen from a list box is an *assignment.* This choice of terms is consistent throughout the book to reduce confusion.

The standard mouse button used for indicating objects on the screen is the left button; however, Microsoft Windows enables its left-handed users, through the Control Panel, to reconfigure the mouse so that the right button acts as the left. Because the right button can be the left button if you want, this book uses the term *index button* to refer to the mouse button that is used to indicate objects.

This text refers to the *cursor* as the blinking vertical line or block that denotes on-screen where text is to appear when it is typed from the keyboard. By contrast, the *pointer* is the arrow or symbol that the mouse moves.

Now that the stage is set, it's time to raise the curtain on Act I.

Part I

The Visual Basic Environment

CHAPTER 1

What a Program Is

In this chapter you learn about the concept of a program, with respect to both Visual Basic and the art of computing as a whole. This chapter explains what you must know about the behavior of programs in a computer and covers the elementary concepts of programming with a high-level language. If you're already familiar with what such a language is and what it does, you can skip to Chapter 2.

A Programmer's Credo

The objective of all programming is to model or simulate some process that can be rationally described—in the real world or imaginary—as a logical and arithmetic procedure. These processes can be completely mathematical as in accounting, geometrical as in floor planning, or recreational as in game playing. If you understand the principle behind the process, you already know what your computer program should contain. You must reconstruct and reorganize this process as a mathematical model. In other words, you must find a way to describe absolutely every part of the process mathematically.

Everything about a computer is logical and is composed of numbers and mathematical methods. Therefore, conceiving an accounting program is relatively easy because the process of accounting is composed of numbers and numerical methods. Consider, however, a program that renders floor plans and landscaping plans. There geometry plays a role, and some processes that at first may not be viewed as numerical—such as drawing where the trees or shrubbery are to be planted—are simulated with program instructions.

Now consider a program that makes routine medical diagnoses for doctors. The part of the program that maintains a list of symptoms, causes, and medications would be the easiest part to create; you might call this portion the database

A *database* is a collection of organized records. A *database manager* is the program that maintains database information.

manager. A *database* is a collection of organized records (such as a doctor's list of patients). A *database manager* is the part of a program that maintains the database information.

Simulating the decision-making process is more difficult than maintaining the lists of symptoms and medications. If the person writing this program is not already a doctor, he would need to talk with medical doctors extensively and study the concepts and procedures of diagnosis. The programmer would have to read all the introductory material as if he were a medical student. It is important for a doctor to rely to some degree on his or her gut feelings and intuition when making a clinical diagnosis. Keeping this in mind, the programmer must simulate the diagnosis with a machine that has no intuition. This task is not impossible. You can let the program simulate just the "memory" functions and let the doctor provide the intuition.

Consider writing a chess program. You probably know from experience that a computer *appears* to play chess very well, and grand masters such as Gerry Kasparov can appreciate how well these programs play the game (although Kasparov still beats them constantly). What you may not know is that no chess program conceives its own strategy for winning the game. The program reevaluates the board after every move, and it generally discards the evaluation results after each move is made. When you play chess against a computer, you play human strategy versus a bunch of math. The job of a chess game programmer is to conceive the math. Programming a chess game does not require a mastery of chess; however, it does require a mastery of math. The programmer should probably be a reasonably good chess player, but he couldn't program his own strategies into the game because chess programs don't think. Instead, he defines methods for the proper position of the knight 10 moves ahead with respect to all other squares that could be in check by that time.

When conceiving a program that performs work that would otherwise be performed by a human being, you should thoroughly comprehend the fundamentals of the work process and the principles, laws, and mathematics governing that process. Mastering the process itself is not necessary. In other words, you don't need to be an accountant to write an accounting program or an M.D. to write a clinical diagnosis program. Simply review the fundamentals of the process and look up the details when you need to. You should, however, comprehend the jobs of the professionals who will use your program to a degree that they won't be insulted or aggravated by that program.

When a program is applicable to your business task, that program is an *application*. Visual Basic is a tool for the development of applications. When you use it, keep in mind that your objective is *automation*—taking the logical and arithmetic part of a real-world job, such as record keeping or data analysis, and delegating to the computer some responsibility for it. If the applications you write merely invent more work for their users, automation doesn't take place and people will not want to use the applications. An application should take a load off somebody's shoulders or at least distribute the weight more evenly in the way a word processor organizes documents or a database management system handles records.

Fundamental Terminology

A *program* is the symbolic form of a task.

To comprehend Visual Basic requires more than a little effort; you are trusted to have mastered the mental concept of a program. To start you toward this level of mastery, here is a new, broader, but fitting definition for the term *program* in this context: A program is the symbolic form of a task or work process. It is any computing process that is described logically using a fundamental code that is interpretable by both the person reading it and the computer processing it.

Source code is the written text of a program in its native language.

Notice that in the preceding definition I did not use the term *language*. Computer programs are generally written using languages. Visual Basic programs are no exception. The written text of a program is called its *source code.*

An *instruction* is any complete directive made within a program.

The source code of a program consists of *instructions* that are executed in sequence. This sequence is not necessarily top-to-bottom or beginning-to-end, but there is a sequence nonetheless. Because the instructions of a Visual Basic program appear to have sentence structure and because the sequence of those instructions in a program communicates the purpose of that program to its human reader in a manner more like human language than machine language, Visual Basic is a *high-level* programming language. Machine or assembly languages, by contrast, are called *low-level* languages because they more closely resemble the logic of the computer than the reasoning of the mind.

Although you use a language to program a computer, the act of programming is not like a conversation or giving orders to an employee or crew member. Unlike communication with a knowledgeable human being, you cannot expect an unprogrammed computer to *intuit* the meaning behind a complex instruction or have any processing capability ahead of time that is related to the task you instruct it to perform. If a computer came to you "out of the box" with the capability to do whatever you asked it to do, there would be no need for packaged software.

A *low-level* programming language "talks" directly to the computer in machine code.

When you program a computer using the most rudimentary symbols recognized by its central processing unit (CPU), the program is written in machine language and the symbolism constitutes a low-level program. As a low-level programmer, you could feed your computer instructions such as 24, 62, 47.... Imagine how difficult it would be for you to have to interpret the meanings behind these digits day after day.

A *high-level* programming language resembles written words and must be translated into machine code.

This is why there is a BASIC programming language. People should program computers using something more closely resembling human language. BASIC and its descendant Visual Basic both use words as symbols rather than numbers or mnemonics to represent electronic operations logically. This is one reason BASIC is a high-level language.

The Visual Basic Interpreter

An interpreter translates high-level linguistic code into low-level numeric code.

An *interpreter* is a program that continually breaks down a program's high-level linguistic symbols into low-level arithmetic symbols. A computer doesn't execute code until it has been broken down to its lowest level; language of any form is beyond the capacity of a central processing unit to interpret for itself. Visual Basic is an interpreter that continually breaks down source code into instructions the CPU can recognize, because BASIC instructions must be reinterpreted into machine language before they can be executed.

If you've programmed a computer using the GW-BASIC or QBasic interpreters supplied with your copy of DOS, you're familiar with the conventional concept of the interpreter. Normally, you supply the BASIC interpreter with a list of instructions using a built-in editor, and the interpreter processes each instruction while the program is being executed. With other interpreted languages, the program is translated into machine language one line at a time as the program runs.

Visual Basic interprets the program as it is written.

On the surface, the Visual Basic interpreter appears to be no different from a standard interpreter, except for the fact that it performs the interpretation process while the program is being entered into the editor.

Figure 1.1 illustrates the differences among these processes.

Figure 1.1

Three forms of program generation compared.

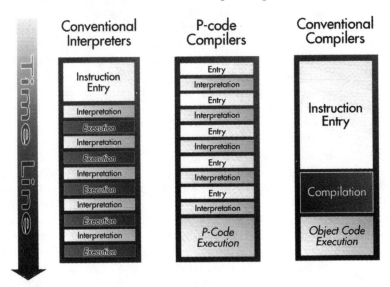

Visual Basic does not actually interpret the program fully while you are writing it. The code that Visual Basic generates internally (which you never see) is called *intermediate code* or *p-code*. This code rests in memory, awaiting the execution call from the user or programmer. The p-code is then reinterpreted—or interpreted the rest of the way—until it becomes *object code* for the CPU. This code is then executed but is not retained in memory. Instead, the interpreter reinterprets more p-code.

Object code (machine code) is composed of CPU instructions that are not symbolized in any way for human interpretation.

Visual Basic source code executes quickly in comparison to a standard interpreter because half the interpretation process is already done by the time you give the order to run the program. Still, another program is required at all times for the intermediate p-code to be executed, whether that program is the main Visual Basic interpreter or a special, smaller interpreter program without the editor. This program is shipped with every copy of Visual Basic and is freely distributable with permission of Microsoft. At the time of this writing, this runtime interpreter is called VBRUN300.DLL.

A *compiler* produces a stand-alone executable program file.

In contrast to an interpreter, a *compiler* is a program that takes high-level instructions and translates them all at once into a machine-language executable code file. A C compiler produces object code that is executable (able to be run) without the aid of the C compiler, comprising a stand-alone program. When you run a compiled program, there is no interpretation process; the compiler has already completely broken the source code into object code. Most programs or applications you'll ever buy or use are compiled this way.

Although compilers give you the benefit of generating pure object code without having to supply an interpreter of some form with your programs, the act of programming with a compiler generally gives you no room for trial and error. If there's an error in your program, execution generally stops, and that's that. Modern compilers such as those currently sold by Microsoft and Borland have eliminated this problem by including with their editors separate p-code interpreters (also called *p-code compilers*) that work in much the same way Visual Basic works. This way, you can test your source code to make sure the program works properly before compiling it into pure object code. The standard Visual Basic package does not include an object code compiler.

You can use the Visual Basic control program or editor to produce a file with the extension EXE, although this file is not executable by the DOS definition. The "compiled" program file produced by Visual Basic is in fact the preinterpreted high-level p-code that the editor program would normally generate while the VB application is entered into the editor. All Visual Basic programs, even if they have an EXE extension, must be run with the VB interpreter—either the main interpreter or the VBRUN300.DLL interpreter.

The Process of Interaction

Information is any symbol or message that is meaningful to people. *Data* is the carrier of information within a computer.

Earlier, you read that computing is an *interactive* process. Generally, this term implies the exchange of information between parties. You often hear the misstatement that information can be shared between a person and a computer. It's important that you draw a vital distinction between the terms *information* and *data.* The formal definition of *information* is any symbol or message that conveys meaning to a person or to people. A computer cannot be informed of anything; it's not intelligent, and it cannot be taught. Information is imparted from one party to another through a medium. In the field of computing, *data* is this medium. A computer stores and retrieves only data, which may or may not impart meaning to you or anyone else. Data cannot impart meaning to the computer because the computer does not reason.

The exchange that takes place between a person and a computer may be informative, and it may even be conversational. Note, however, that this conversation does not really take place between the computer and the user; it is between the *programmer* and the user. The conversation is merely indirect, the symbols used in the conversation are limited, the topic is chosen in advance, and the responses as delivered by the program are, in effect, prerecorded. In the way syllables convey meaning when utilized in a conversation between people, instructions and data convey meaning to the person using an application.

To be more specific, compare real-world, person-to-person interaction with person-to-computer interaction. Assume you own a small-business. You deliver your company's financial data to a professional accountant (or CPA) and give her instructions about what to do. You perform the same role as the user of an accounting program—supplying the raw data and initiating the process. You wouldn't tell the CPA *exactly* what to do; you would assume her training has prepared her to know what to do.

Switch sides now and assume you're the CPA. Your training is based on years of learning and reviewing accounting principles. Along with that, you've gained much business experience. You know the process of recording this small business' account information after you receive this mountain of data because your experience guides you. The more experienced you are with figuring numbers as an accountant, the more skilled you become.

Still, as a CPA you do not perform the role of a computer accounting program. The computer is not an instrument that acquires skill over time or with constant use. The computer's "understanding" of what to do with all this data is constructed beforehand as its program, long before the data is created. The difference between giving a person instructions and giving a computer instructions is that a person has numerous faculties available for deducing the proper process. By contrast, you instruct the Visual Basic interpreter using only mathematics, logic, formulas, and comparisons. You cannot construct an accounting program by taking existing business financial data, feeding that data into the program, and having the computer generate formulas from it. Unlike the way people reason, the computer cannot deduce the process that leads to particular results based on the values of those results.

You can, however, take existing business information as an example for yourself and reasonably deduce the formulas that a CPA would use to analyze and record this data. You would, however, remove any part of those formulas that makes them specific to a particular business at a particular time. You replace these specifics with vague references to unknown or arbitrary values, called *variables*. In other words, you remove everything absolute from the example process, leaving in its place only the algebra.

The Computing Environment

The *control program* of a computer provides the resources that a program needs to run.

Almost all computers run more than one program at a time. In the history of computing, when the job of computer control was first removed from the human operator and handed over to software, as many as two real programs were in operation in a computer system at any one time. The *control program* (the operating system of the computer) provided input/output, memory, and storage services to the *user program.* In your computer system running Visual Basic today, there can be six levels of program operation at any one time, with the program at a lower level providing services to the program above it.

Figure 1.2 depicts the structure of all programs in a computer system at all times while Visual Basic runs. The arrows in this figure depict the provision of services from one level of program to the one above it. The resulting strata of environments forms a sort of computing "atmosphere," in which the richest elements shared between tiers in the structure rise to the top.

Figure 1.2

The Visual Basic "computing atmosphere."

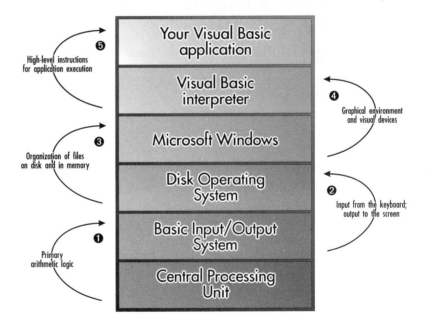

A *pixel* is the smallest point that can be plotted on-screen at any given resolution.

At the bottom of this structure is the CPU, the core element of any computer system. The primary arithmetic logic of the computer is literally etched into this unit like a drawing. The CPU provides services to the Basic Input/Output System (BIOS), which is officially the lowest-level program in a microcomputer. This part tells your computer that it is a computer, and its job is to *poll* (make a request of) the keyboard and other devices for user input and to display characters or pixels on-screen as output.

The job of collecting all the characters, pixels, and bytes registered from the BIOS as actual files is delegated to the *disk operating system*. In this particular system, this is some form (or clone) of MS-DOS or PC DOS. Microsoft Windows relies for the most part on DOS to provide it with file-handling services; at times, however, Windows 3.1 does assume responsibility for these services. For now, Windows acts as a "visual overlay" on top of DOS that makes DOS easier to use, until Windows is developed into a fully-capable operating system.

An *environment* acts as the graphical mediator between the user and the program.

Microsoft calls its Windows product a *graphical environment*, which means that it provides facilities and resources for other programs to operate, cooperate, and share data. Windows provides the *environment* for Windows applications such as Excel, CorelDRAW!, and Visual Basic.

The facilities and resources Windows provides Visual Basic are significant. Most obviously, the appearance and function of graphic objects such as buttons, menus, and scroll bars are defined for Visual Basic by Windows. Furthermore, the visual display drivers, special considerations for different fonts and type styles, and the drivers for individual printers are all regular provisions of the Windows environment. Visual Basic as a program must concentrate only on its main objective as an interpreter of a programmer's instructions.

At the top of the heap, the Visual Basic application is granted use of the resources given to the VB interpreter by Windows. This way, you can specify the presence, location, and purpose of a button, a drop-down list box, or one of the other Windows graphical controls without having to program the mechanics of that control from scratch. As a Visual Basic programmer, you will spend less time drawing controls and more time conceiving instructions and organizing information as data. The remainder of this book is organized proportionally with respect to what you as a Visual Basic programmer will do with your time and effort.

Summary

The purpose of programming can either be the automation of a real-world process or the simulation of a new process. A Visual Basic program is a mathematical model of a task that people could most likely perform using pencil and paper in the "old world." If the program is no easier to operate than pencil and paper or if the program does not add some measure of functionality to the process, the objective of the program hasn't been fulfilled.

To achieve automation of a work process within a program does not require you to master this process in the real world; in other words, if you are the author of a legal assistance database manager, you do not need to be a lawyer. If you can model just the fundamental principles of a real-world process, that alone will help professionals in their daily business.

The written form of a program is called *source code*. The individual directives within this source code are called *instructions*. A low-level program instruction makes sense to the computer almost instantly, although a high-level program instruction, as in Visual Basic, must first be translated into intermediate instructions or p-code before it can be executed. This is why Visual Basic is called an *interpreted language.* Unlike a conventional interpreter, however, VB source code is completely interpreted prior to the program's execution. In other words, the program is compiled to memory.

All programs exchange data with their users, although a good program exchanges more information with its user using less data. In information theory, data is seen as the carrier of information, just as a sound wave over a phone line is seen as the carrier of the message. A mathematical process cannot be described to the interpreter by example or inference—it can be described only through algebra. The form of a Visual Basic program certainly doesn't resemble conventional algebra, although its processes are said to be algebraic. The interpreter makes no assumptions as to how any real-world process works. That process must be described using the vocabulary of Visual Basic before the program's execution.

An operating environment provides services, functions, and facilities to its programs. Microsoft Windows gives Visual Basic access to its graphic control resources. Visual Basic recognizes the primary Windows graphic controls and enables you to place these controls into a form. Visual Basic receives your language-form instructions concerning how to operate these graphic controls and interprets these instructions on behalf of Windows.

Review Questions

1. Why is BASIC considered a high-level language?

2. What is a "sentence" within a program's source code called?

3. What is the primary low-level language of any computer called?

4. Which program in your computer provides services to Microsoft Windows?

CHAPTER 2

The Workspace

In this chapter, you are introduced to the methodology by which Visual Basic programs are organized visually. A VB application contains many on-screen elements called *controls,* around which the linguistic components of the program are constructed. Each control has its own procedure, which is a part of the overall program. The more linguistic elements are discussed in Chapter 3; for now, discussion concentrates on the structural and graphical composition of the Visual Basic project.

The Visual Basic Project

Now you're ready to dive into the Visual Basic environment. Figure 2.1 shows the Visual Basic workspace as it generally appears at startup.

Figure 2.1

The Visual Basic environment in its natural state.

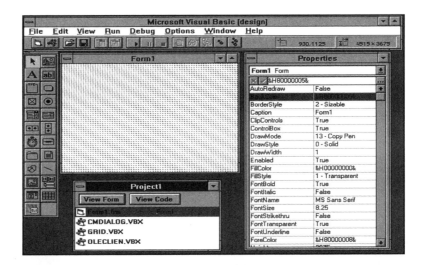

The old-style BASIC interpreter's READY prompt is not used in VB. Instead, the majority of the tools you need to program are laid out before you as if they are on a drafting table. At the center of this table is Form1, which currently represents the site of the main input/output panel for your future program.

Generally, each Windows application is given its own self-contained window, and all the tools you need to operate that application are placed within that window. Visual Basic violates this law of organization entirely because it has no primary window of its own. Actually, this is for a good reason: The applications you develop should follow the rules of Microsoft Windows, which state that each program has one primary window. To make this feasible, Visual Basic has to step outside the main window of the application you're developing, because you shouldn't have two main windows active at the same time.

A *project* consists of all the files that collectively make up a Visual Basic program.

While a Visual Basic program is under construction, it is called a *project* because the source code of a VB program can be distributed among more than one physical file stored on disk. A VB project may consist of three types of files:

◆ The *form module,* which contains the graphic elements of the VB application along with the instructions

◆ The *general module,* which contains general-purpose instructions that do not pertain to anything graphic on-screen, and global variable definitions

◆ The *extension module,* which contains non-Visual Basic code that extends the features of the interpreter

The *form* is the input/output window for Visual Basic applications.

On startup, Visual Basic displays a blank project by default. At the center of the screen is Form1, which is the primary window for your VB application. Each form in a VB project, including this one, has a physical file to itself. Stored in this file is all the information concerning the appearance, contents, and characteristics of the form, along with the VB instructions for operating each graphic object that is a part of the form.

In figure 2.1, notice that there are two other windows to the right of the blank Form1 window. These windows were brought into the workspace using Visual Basic's Window menu. At upper right is the Project window, which contains a list of all files that are part of the project currently being constructed. This list itself makes up a file, the name of which appears as the title bar of the Project window. When saved to disk, this title becomes the project file name. The example in figure 2.1 shows the default file name for the project, which is Project1.

Below the Project window is the Properties window. Its purpose is to enable you to set the initial conditions of the various graphic objects—buttons, lines, list boxes, and so on—that you put into the form or forms, as well as set the conditions of the form itself. If you place a button on a form, for instance, the Properties window shows you where the button is in relation to the form, what the button is supposed to say, whether the button can be pressed when the application starts up, whether this is the default button, and a long list of other characteristics that distinguish this device.

While you program in Visual Basic, you do basically two things: type instructions for the program and draw the control forms on-screen. While you do the latter, the VB interpreter helps you with the former by preparing in advance the framework for procedural modules for each graphic object you add to the form.

As you continue this guided tour of the visual part of the VB environment, you can follow along on your computer as you read how to invoke certain facilities and windows. You should already have started Visual Basic, and your screen should look similar to figure 2.1. A blank form is in the center of your screen. Visual Basic reserves a space for the entry of program instructions regarding only this form. The area in which you enter code is called the *procedure window*.

To examine the instructions pertaining to this form, double-click anywhere within the form window. The procedure window appears, as shown in figure 2.2.

You enter code for your Visual Basic program into a *procedure window*.

Figure 2.2

The first blank procedure window.

The *procedure* is the core program component of Visual Basic. Each time you add a graphic object to a form, the VB interpreter creates a new set of procedure frames. These frames may later contain instructions defining what the graphic object makes the program do whenever anything important happens with respect to that object—for instance, the user clicking it or the arrow pointer entering it.

A Visual Basic *procedure* defines what should happen when an event takes place, such as clicking a button.

Immediately following the addition of a graphic object to the form, without you having to press a key, Visual Basic prepares the *frames* of formal procedures pertaining to that object, such as the one appearing in figure 2.2. This frame awaits further instructions from you. The opening and closing statements have already been entered into the procedure; the blank line between them denotes where you will type new instructions.

An *event* is some action caused by the user that results in a programmed response.

You invoked this procedural frame by double-clicking within the area of the blank form; as a result, the procedure Sub Form_Load () was called. In object-oriented syntax, _Load is an *event* that acts in this instruction as a verb to the noun Form. The _Load event is the first event that the Visual Basic interpreter recognizes for this procedure window. Any instructions you type into this procedure frame are executed whenever the form—or more to the point, the background area within the form window—first appears within the VB workspace.

Example

As a test, type the following on the blank line between `Sub Form_Load( )` and `End Sub`:

```
Form1.Show
Form1.Print "Hello, world!"
```

Remember to type a carriage return between these two lines. You have set up a response to an event; namely, whenever the interpreter recognizes the existence of Form1 (and by default, it has to), the text within the quotation marks is printed to that form. Written as pseudocode, here's how your first procedure might appear:

Start this procedure whenever this form first appears.
Show Form1 in the workspace.
Print "Hello, world!"
* to the first available space in Form1.*
End this procedure.

The *toolbar* contains buttons that double for often-used menu commands.

Although you can have several forms on-screen at one time (Form2, Form3, and so on), you can work on only one Visual Basic project at a time. A project within the VB workspace is in one of three states: *design* (the startup state), *run*, or *break* (or temporary suspension). To see the current project in its running state, follow this procedure.

To run the current VB program (yes, you've just written a program): At the bottom of the Visual Basic control window (currently marked `Microsoft Visual Basic [design]`) is a long, gray *toolbar*. In the middle of the toolbar is a button containing a right-pointing arrow, like the one next to this paragraph. Click this button once to run the program.

> **Note:** If you're a veteran of 1970s BASIC interpreters, such as GW-BASIC or BASICA, clicking the Run button is the modern equivalent of typing **RUN** at the **READY** prompt. Alternatively, to run a VB program that is currently being edited, you can also press the F5 key.

When a Visual Basic program runs within the interpreter environment, any windows or palettes that are currently open in the workspace disappear, leaving only the control window. The startup form window is redrawn without its spotted grid. The title bar of the VB control window now reads `[run]` rather than `[design]`.

As a test, click once within the area of Form1. Your screen now should look like figure 2.3. You should notice your message in the top left corner of the form.

To end program execution at any point: Another button appears in the toolbar containing just a black square, like the button pictured next to this paragraph. Click this button to end the program and return the interpreter to `[design]` mode.

Figure 2.3

The first running
program.

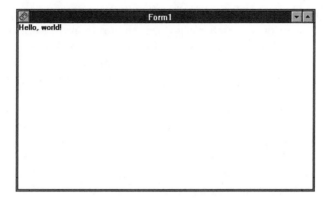

After you compile your completed Visual Basic application, you can assign an icon to it and install it into the Windows Program Manager as though it were a standard Windows application.

Graphic Objects

As discussed in Chapter 1, the Visual Basic interpreter gets its instructions on how to handle graphic objects from Microsoft Windows. One such object is the button, which is the gray, bevel-edged device that you generally find within dialog boxes and usually contains OK, Cancel, or some similar directive. Having received instructions from Windows, VB can then "hand" you a button from inside its toolbox and let you place that button anywhere on the form.

In version 3.0 of Microsoft Windows, buttons were given an animated effect. When pressed, they look as if they recede slightly into the framework of the window in which they appear. With Visual Basic, whenever you need a button for a control panel or dialog box, you can click the button tool in the VB toolbox with the mouse, draw the perimeter of the button on the input form, and give it new contents by immediately typing its new caption. Visual Basic thereafter understands that there is a button in this form window and treats it as a graphic object with all the attributes and animation generally given a Windows button.

You do not have to tell Visual Basic how the button recedes into the framework when the user indicates it with the mouse. In other words, you don't have to tell VB to plot a separate image of the button two pixels to the right and two pixels down to give it the appearance of sinking. Microsoft Windows already knows how to animate a button, and Visual Basic knows how to engage that animation.

Several years ago, if you wrote a program in BASIC, you might have had to write a routine yourself to perform this animation because there wasn't a Windows environment to perform it for you. Moreover, you probably would have had to write a routine that defined a "button" for the sake of your program alone. Every time you wrote a new program, you'd need to integrate your old button routines into the new contexts.

Part of the beauty of Visual Basic is that you have easy access to the most often-used graphic elements of Windows. You can lift those elements from a toolbox with the mouse and place them on the input panel at the points where the user will operate them. This process is far less tedious than plotting the identity and coordinates of each element by number.

Visual Basic has a toolbox, which generally appears to the left of the Form, containing columns of graphic control tools from which the programmer retrieves graphic objects and adds them to the form. Each tool within this toolbox is represented by a button. Most of the tools here are symbolic representations of resources you commonly use in Windows; you've probably already spotted the scroll bar tools and list boxes. The primary tool is in the top left corner of the box; the left-pointing arrow is the primary indicator of graphic elements already residing on the form. When you want to point to an existing element of the form, you use this tool.

The graphic controls available from the Visual Basic standard edition toolbox are shown in table 2.1.

Table 2.1. The contents of the Visual Basic toolbox.

Icon	Item	Definition
	Picture box	Used to display any images, containing pictures or text or both, that are interpretable graphically rather than as text.
	Text box	A field for the entry and editing of text.
	Label	A field for the display of noneditable text.
	Frame	Groups related objects together, such as two check boxes.
	Command button	"Depresses" when clicked. Enables the user to give directives to the VB application, such as OK, Cancel, or Options >>.

Icon	Item	Definition
	Check box	Used to represent the active or "on/off" state of a single item.
	Option dot	Used in a multiple-choice situation to represent the currently active choice.
	Combo box	Gives the user the option of choosing from the list or entering an option of his or her own within the attached text box.
	List box	Used to present a fixed list of choices to the user.
	Horizontal scroll bar	Used to represent any numeric selection within a range.
	Vertical scroll bar	Used to represent any numeric selection within a range.
	Timer	Allows the form to be timed using a real-time clock. Does not display on a form when the program is run.
	Drive list box	Displays a list of the user's active storage devices, such as disk drives, RAM disks, CD-ROM drives, and network drives.
	Directory list box	Displays a list of a device's directories.
	Files list box	Displays a list of the user's files within a directory.
	Shape	Displays a simple rectangle or circle.
	Line	Displays a line that you can use as a separator or internal border.

continues

Table 2.1. Continued

Icon	Item	Definition
	Image box	Displays a bitmapped image that you can use as a backdrop or decorative element.
	Grid	Allows tables of related data to be displayed in a row/column format, like a spreadsheet.
	Common dialog	Allows you to display standard Windows common dialog boxes.
	Data control	Provides access to databases via the MS-Access data drivers and bound controls.
	OLE Client	Allows for the display of data, text, or images being supplied to the VB application by another Windows application.

Note: The Grid control is provided to the Visual Basic toolbar by means of a separate file, GRID.VBX. The OLE Client control is provided by means of OLECLIEN.VBX. When your VB project shows either of these controls available in the toolbox, their associated VBX files are included as a listing in the Project window. If you do not intend to use either control in your current VB project, you can remove them from the toolbox by indicating the VBX file in the Project window and selecting Remove File from the VB File menu.

Example

After the first test program's initial run has ended and the control window reads [design], the next order of business is to add a graphic object to this form—namely, a button that invokes a small procedure. To add a button to a form, follow these steps:

1. Indicate the command button tool in the toolbox. The button you just clicked will stay receded; you don't need to hold down the mouse index button.

2. Move the mouse pointer to the form window, and click and hold down the index button on the point that is to be one corner of the button control.

3. With the index button held down, drag the pointer to the opposite corner of the button control area.

4. Release the index button. The button control appears in the form.

At this point, the VB interpreter has already prepared several frames for procedures relating to this button. The most useful of these procedures, obviously, is the one that is invoked when the button is clicked during runtime. To bring up this procedure frame, double-click on the button control in the form.

> **Note:** The terms *control* and *graphic object* refer to the same thing, in two different capacities. The graphic object is the element addressed by the *programmer* as a part of the Visual Basic application; the control is the graphic object acting in its role as a device that the *user* manipulates in the course of operating the VB application.

Visual Basic uses procedure names made up of the object name, an underscore, and the event name.

Visual Basic buttons are said to direct commands to the application; thus, they are named Command1, Command2, and so on, by default. The procedure frame showing now is `Sub Command1_Click ( )`, which contains the instructions to be executed whenever the button is clicked during runtime. The VB interpreter derived the name for this procedure by combining the button's name with the name of the event to which this procedure pertains, joined with the underscore (_) character.

To test this procedure, type the following line into the procedure frame:

```
Form1.Print "You clicked on the Command1 button."
```

Using the steps you learned earlier in this chapter, run your program. Notice that when you click the button, the message reads You clicked on the Command1 button.. When you are done, end the program by selecting **E**nd from the **R**un menu, or by selecting the stop button from the toolbar.

An *event* triggers the execution of a procedure.

These test programs may not be exciting, but they demonstrate the most important feature that distinguishes Visual Basic from its predecessors: The VB language is almost entirely *event-driven,* in that most of its procedures are not executed until the user gives the computer some sign, signal, or other form of input. This sign can be a waver of the mouse, a press of a key, or perhaps the act of making the computer wait for five minutes doing nothing. An *event* is a unit of user input from any of the available devices attached to the computer system that triggers the execution of a procedure in response.

Visual Basic already knows how to wait for an event and also how to discern one event from another. All you have to tell VB is what to do to respond to these events. Event-driven procedures comprise the majority of almost every Visual Basic program you write.

As a test, bring up the procedure window again for Sub Command1_Click () by double-clicking the Command1 button. The window for a graphic object's procedure appears. Below its title bar is a control bar that contains two drop-down list boxes. Click on the down arrow for the list box on the right, which is marked *Proc*. A list of events attributable to a command button appears, as shown in figure 2.4.

You can write procedures to be executed on the occurrence of each of these events. Choosing one of these events from the list brings up its event procedure in the code window below. You could say the procedures for all the associated events for each object virtually exist, although they remain codeless until you give them instructions.

Figure 2.4

Some of the events for a command button.

The leftmost list box in the procedure window, marked *Object*, displays the names of all the graphic objects belonging to the current form. The form itself is included because Visual Basic considers it a graphic object as well. After you choose a different object from this list, a new set of recognized events is loaded into the *Proc* list. Think of the object list in the procedure window as a display of everything within the form that can have something done to it, and the procedure list beside it as a display of everything that can be done. The object is the recipient of the action in Visual Basic, just as it is in English grammar. Now you have an idea of the general concept of "object-oriented" syntax.

Properties

A *property* is an attribute of a graphic object that is accessible by name and can be described by a value or term.

Much of the Visual Basic programming process is accomplished through graphical inference. A button is not placed on a form by you typing its coordinates into the source code of the program, but by drawing the button on the form with the mouse. Visual Basic interprets the act of drawing the button as a directive to the program being constructed. The position, size, and contents of the button are all defined by Visual Basic, for the program, as *properties*.

You can declare these properties using written Visual Basic instructions. The VB environment also lets you place a graphic object on the form by pointing to its location and drawing its outline. The position and size of this object instantly become two of its properties. By using the controls located in the VB Properties window, as shown in figure 2.5, you can access each property of a graphic object by name and assign or change its value, setting, or description.

Figure 2.5

The Properties
window.

The *.Name* Property

The *.Name* property
is used to identify
an object by name
in the program
source code.

Perhaps the most important property of any graphic object is its *name*. In all cases, the `.Name` property of a graphic object and the `.Caption` or `.Text` contents of that object on-screen are separate from one another. This is important, even though the `.Name` of a button and the `.Caption` of that button are often set to the same contents. For instance, a command button marked *OK* is often named OK, although that is not a prerequisite.

If you look at the Properties window in figure 2.5, you see that the first line beneath the title bar shows the current name and identity of the button you placed on the form earlier in this chapter. This line is the top of a drop-down list box; clicking on the down-arrow to the right displays a list of all objects contained in the current form, headed by the name and identity of that form.

To change the name of a control, follow these steps:

1. Indicate the button that is to have its name changed by clicking once on that button. Eight *indicator nodes* surround the button; these are used as handles for resizing the button.

2. In the VB Properties window, use the scroll bar at the right to manipulate a list of all properties recognized for the control whose name currently appears at the top. Use this scroll bar to locate the item Name in the left column of this two-column list.

3. Below the upper list box is another list box (or combo box) that acts as the actual device with which you set the property you just accessed. Click once on the Name row to bring the current name property setting into this list box, or click twice on the Name row to bring it into the list box and indicate its entire contents for immediate replacement.

4. If the possible property settings for the chosen property were multiple-choice, you could click on the down-arrow button and see a list of those settings. In the case of the `.Name` property, the name you give a control is arbitrary, so there is no such list. Your only job is to type a new name in this text box. While the mouse pointer is in the area of this text box, its form becomes an I-beam, indicating that you can use it to place the cursor in this box. If no text is currently indicated, you can place the cursor in this box by clicking once while the pointer looks like an I-beam.

5. Type the replacement caption. As you type, the text is echoed into the button control.

6. To complete the entry, either press Enter or click the Checkmark button to the left of the text-entry box. At this point, the `.Name` property is set and a new blank procedure has been created, wiping out any previous one.

7. To cancel an entry in progress, click the Cancel button.

The `.Caption` property is used to change the text displayed on an object.

Again, it's important to note that changing a button control's contents (the `.Caption` property) does not change the name (the `.Name` property) with which that button is addressed throughout the source code. Command1 is both the default control name and default caption for the first button in a form. Changing one does not change the other. To change the button's contents from Command1 to Setup, use the method described previously, but choose the property `.Caption` rather than `.Name`.

Whenever you change a control's `.Name` property, its name in the VB procedure frames in the source code is changed automatically. Say, for example, you use the preceding process to rename button Command1 to MainButton. Notice immediately that the `_Click` event procedure for the former Command1 immediately reads `Sub MainButton_Click ()`. You may change the name of a graphic object at any time. When renamed, events that contain VB code (for example, `_click`), are saved in the "General" object section of the form. Object events that do not contain any VB code are automatically deleted. In either case, VB automatically creates a new list of associated procedures. By contrast, changing a button's caption does not result in any alteration to procedure code.

The full name of a property is made up of the name of its object, a period, and the name of the property.

Notice that in the terms discussed thus far, an event is separated from an object by an underscore character, as in `MainButton_Click`, whereas a property is separated from its object by a period, as in `MainButton.Caption`. This punctuation helps identify the attribute of the object preceding it as an event or a property.

You can use the Properties window, among other purposes, to designate the size of a control by number, to set the color of a control or its background, or to change the font for included text. Throughout this book, you will be continually setting the attributes of properties, setting the stage—at least visually—for each full project you produce. Later, you'll read about the more conventional predeclaration of values, variables, and functions for the computational portion of the programs, all of which is done with instructions.

> **Note:** Although the job of creating controls and designating their properties can be considered *programming* in the context of Visual Basic, the act of property setting is not instructional and is therefore not reflected in the source code of the program being constructed. When the source code is executed, the VB interpreter expects many of the initial properties of the graphic objects referred to in the program to be set beforehand. If you're a BASIC veteran, this may make reading the source code of the program a bit confusing. Most programmers who have worked with BASIC for a long time have grown accustomed to modeling all the characteristics of a program with written instructions and reading those characteristics as instructions. This habit may be difficult to break.

Saving Your Work

The following is the procedure for saving your project to disk for safekeeping.

1. From the VB toolbar, click on the button containing a floppy disk; or from the File menu of the control window, select Save Project. You can alternatively select Save Project As if you want to specify a different file name for the project.

2. If the elements of the VB application as they appear in the Project window haven't been given formal file names, file selector panels appear for each element, enabling you to designate the file name of your choice. The state of a form, along with its associated procedure code, is saved in a file with the extension FRM. You can type a file name for each element or accept the default file name supplied by VB. Click OK.

3. Finally, a file selector panel appears, asking you to designate a file name for the project itself. Project file names carry the .MAK extension. Either designate a file name or accept the default and then click OK. The project is saved.

Use the preceding method to save the single-button form project to disk, accepting the default file names MODULE1.BAS and FORM1.FRM for the two project elements and designating TEST1.MAK as the project file name.

One way to save the project as a file independent of the VB control program is to compile it into a separate intermediate p-code file. This way, you can install the file into the Windows Program Manager and run it from there by double-clicking on its icon or by double-clicking its file name in the Windows File Manager. This p-code file is not a stand-alone program; the VBRUN300.DLL program needs to coexist with the p-code file in the same directory, although it does not need to be installed into the Program Manager.

To make a distributable p-code file from a VB project, follow these steps:

1. Save the VB project to disk using the preceding method.

2. From the **File** menu, select **Make EXE File**. A file selector box appears.

3. Type the eight-letter file name for the p-code file into the text line marked `Filename`. VB automatically attaches the EXE extension to the file. This file does not overwrite any other file pertaining to the project.

4. To give this application a formal title for the Program Manager, click on the text box marked `Application Title` and type a new name—the default is Project1.

5. To give this application its own icon, choose one from those already applied to the `.Icon` properties attributed to the various forms in those projects.

6. Click OK. You now have an intermediate p-code file, which you can execute from the Program Manager.

Summary

Visual Basic considers the forms and procedure modules collectively as a project. You do not need to give the Visual Basic interpreter extensive instructions for the display and handling of graphic controls. When these controls are placed in the control form, you need only tell the Visual Basic interpreter how to respond to the input events attributed to those controls. Each possible event for a graphic object has its own virtual procedure in a VB application. Each object in a VB form, including the form itself, has properties attributed to it, the characteristics of which you can set in advance using the Properties window without specifying any instructions in code.

Review Questions

1. In what type of file does Visual Basic store a collective list of forms and their controls, and modules and their procedures?

2. During the runtime of your VB application, commands are passed to the application through what graphic control?

3. In a term that joins the object `ClickHere` and the event `DblClick`, what item of punctuation is used between them?

4. In the procedure heading `Sub Form4_Click ()`, what term represents the event?

5. Where do you look on-screen to determine whether your Visual Basic application is running?

6. In what mode is the interpreter when you are creating a VB application?

7. What is the three-letter extension of the name of a file that contains the property settings for a form?

Review Exercise

1. Write a procedure that prints the line Something has happened! into a form called Form7 whenever a button called BobTheButton is clicked.

CHAPTER 3

Grammar and Linguistics

In this chapter, you study the terminology of the Visual Basic application—how its terms and keywords are organized and expressed within the source code. You then study the composition of more complex examples of programs than those you've seen developed thus far. You learn about instructions and how they are constructed. You then learn how instructions are executed, organized, grouped, and modularized.

The topics introduced here are covered in greater detail in later chapters. This chapter presents the major concepts of program construction so that you can see how these concepts relate to each other.

Modern Syntax

A *variable* represents a unit of data that can be altered.

At the heart of every program you write are logical comparisons between known and unknown numeric values. Whatever overall objective you have in mind for your VB application, the primary business of that application—the stuff that keeps your program busy—is the manipulation of values in memory. As in algebra, unknown values are represented within the Visual Basic syntax by variables. A *variable* is an arbitrarily named term that represents a unit of data in memory that the program can alter.

A value is assigned to a variable with an equality statement, such as a = 1 or items = 27, on a line by itself. When a Visual Basic instruction can be placed on one line, that instruction is called a *phrase*, partly because the syntax of the instruction resembles that of an English-language phrase or a complete sentence. For example, you can deduce the syntax of the instruction

```
If a = 1 Then GoTo More_Help
```

by using some rules of the English language. This instruction can rightfully be considered a phrase.

Each Visual Basic instruction has a component structure, in much the same way an English sentence can be divided into component phrases. The instructional phrase

```
If a = 1 Then GoTo More_Help
```

A *statement* is an instruction that specifies a change or deviation in the operating status of the program.

consists of three statements, all of which rest on one line. Therefore, this phrase is called a *compound instruction*. A mathematical expression is included in one of the statements: a = 1. The words If, Then, and GoTo are some of the primary keywords in all BASIC programming languages. If-Then and GoTo are considered *statements* because they specify changes in the state of operation of the program. Their use is demonstrated later in this chapter. For now, concentrate on the fact that a statement in programming is a directive made to the interpreter that tells it how things are changing.

In Visual Basic, what appears to be an order or directive to change the state or value of something is actually interpreted as a statement of fact and a report of the current operating status of the program. In the statement GoTo Away, the line marked Away is someplace else in the program. Telling the interpreter to go to that part in the program, from the interpreter's point of view, is as good as saying it is at that point in the program now. You've written what looks like a command, but from the standpoint of the logic of the computer, you've made an unconditional statement.

Suppose, however, that you add a condition to that statement. Assume, for instance, the VB interpreter encounters the following phrase:

```
If num > 1000 Then GoTo Away
```

Here num is a variable or symbol that represents a numeric value and stands in place of that value in the text. For this example, the interpreter first evaluates the variable num to determine whether its value is greater than 1000. The two parts of this phrase If and Then constitute one statement, which is called the If-Then statement. It tells the interpreter to make an evaluation—in this case, to see if the value represented by the variable num is greater than 1000. The result of this evaluation is logically considered to be *true* or *false*. In pseudocode, the statement's general framework might appear as follows:

If what's being said here is True, then execute the statement immediately thereafter.

In this case, if the expression `num > 1000` evaluates True, the interpreter suspends execution and then resumes at the point of the program marked `Away`. The phrase `GoTo Away` is interpreted as a statement only if the expression is True. Otherwise, the interpreter never sees the statement. `If-Then` in this instance appears to be a command. In earlier versions of BASIC, it was categorized as such. Yet given the understanding that commanding the interpreter to do something is really a way of stating that it is done already, realistically you must consider `If-Then` and `GoTo` as statements.

A *binary state* is the minimum unit of value in a computer and can be described as either *True* (–1) or *False* (0).

All computer processes are the result of logical evaluations. Such evaluations are called *binary* because their results can have one of two states: `True` or `False`, or in Visual Basic values, –1 or 0. The purpose of logical evaluation in the real world is to eliminate "gray areas." Nothing, once it is logically evaluated, is "for the most part true." Within the computer, there are no gray areas to begin with. Absolutely everything retained in memory, stored on disk, or undergoing processing within some evaluator chip can be described in its rudimentary form or forms as a *binary state.*

Because there is no "in-between" state in a logical evaluation and because logical evaluation is all the computer actually does, the computer cannot understand "change." The concept of one state becoming another state is foreign to the computer; there is simply no logical way to represent it, just as in real-world evaluation there is no way to represent gray logically. The Visual Basic language makes it appear that you are telling the interpreter to change something by giving it instructions that appear to be commands, when in fact you are actually restating the operating conditions for the computer at the present time. The syntax of the language gives you a more tangible and perhaps more realistic method of communication with the computer. In the real world, things change all the time, so it might help you to understand what's happening in the computer if things appear to change. If you were a computer, however, you would believe that nothing ever changed.

Expressions

The computer can only "think" using on/off binary states, represented by ones and zeroes.

In the preceding example, one of the statements within the `If-Then` compound instruction was an expression: `num > 1000`. This expression compared an unknown value to a known value and evaluated the result of that expression. Logically, there can be only two possible results, which can be expressed only as binary states.

Whenever an unknown value or variable is compared to a known or unknown value—as in `num > 1000` or `liquidity_ratio = (assets / liabilities)`—the statement of that comparison is called an *expression.* An expression is any of the following:

♦ An arithmetic comparison between two values, having a result that is expressed logically as a binary state

◆ One or more values or variables arithmetically joined by functions or functional operators

◆ An assignment of value to a variable using another value, variable, or another expression

An *expression* is the assigning of or the comparison between two variables.

Under the first definition, `num > 1000` is an expression of comparison. If `num` is greater than `1000`, a Boolean value of `True` (–1) is returned to the interpreter that may trigger the execution of a process. Under the second definition, `a + b * c` and `4 * (n - 3)` are expressions of combination, resulting in a numeral value that can be assigned to a variable. Also under the second definition, `6` is officially an expression—a rather boring one, but an expression nonetheless. Under the third definition, `x = a + b * c` and `liquidity_ratio = (assets / liabilities)` are expressions of assignment, in which the results of the arithmetic combinations are actually stored as variables.

An *equation* is a statement of equality that assigns a value to a variable.

You could place `liquidity_ratio = (assets / liabilities)` on a line by itself, in which case the expression is both a statement and an *equation* that assigns the value of `assets` divided by `liabilities` to the variable `liquidity_ratio`. You then say the preceding expression assigns a value to the variable `liquidity_ratio` using two other variables.

In the preceding equation, the virgule (`/`) is used as an *operator* designating division between the two values it separates. Operators are used within BASIC expressions like the function buttons on a calculator.

A *binary operator* is a symbol that represents a mathematical function combining, comparing, or equating two values.

When an equality expression is listed on a line by itself, that expression is considered by the interpreter as an assignment of value to a variable. The equal sign in that statement is considered the *assignment operator*. If you were to state on a line by itself `x = 6` and then later invoke the statement `Text.Print x`, the number `6` would appear in the text. By contrast, when an expression is part of an instruction—as in `If x = 6 Then...`—that expression is treated as a comparison of `6` to `x`, the result of which is a Boolean value of `True` (–1) or `False` (0). The equal sign in a comparison is, naturally, the *comparison operator*. The negative sign preceding the 1 is called a *unary operator* because it concerns only one value rather than two.

Intrinsic Functions

A *function* returns a value in a single variable.

For arithmetic operations that cannot be described by symbols or operators, Visual Basic maintains a broad vocabulary of intrinsic functions that perform arithmetic operations on values or expressions enclosed in parentheses. A *function* is an arithmetic operation performed on a value, variable, or expression, resulting in an explicit value returned within a single variable.

A function in Visual Basic has the following syntax:

```
Function_name(expression)
```

The expression in parentheses is evaluated first so that the function can operate on one rational value—something more closely resembling 67.5 than (x + 6). More than one expression can be within the parentheses; in such cases, they are separated from each other by commas. The specified function is then performed on the value or values between the parentheses.

An *intrinsic function* is a term that is built into the Visual Basic vocabulary (in other words, a *keyword*). You can program other functions and add them to the functional vocabulary within the scope of a VB project.

An intrinsic function is one that is built into Visual Basic.

Intrinsic functions are actually quite simple. For instance, Sqr(9) represents the square root of 9, so the function is said to *return* a value of 3. The function Int(3.1415927) returns the value of the expression in parentheses converted to an integer by rounding to the nearest whole number—in this case, 3 again. If the variable g has the value 6, the function Abs(g - 10) returns the value 4. Because g is 6, 6 - 10 = -4, the absolute value of –4 is 4, and thus Abs(-4) = 4.

Program Components

Over the decades that the BASIC programming language has been developed and redeveloped, those who have been part of the development process have also managed to break BASIC constructs into an increasing number of parts. There are more parts, or divisions of instruction groups, to a Visual Basic application than perhaps any other BASIC application.

Figure 3.1 depicts the hierarchy of divisions and subdivisions of a Visual Basic application.

A module is a complete set of procedures stored within a single file.

The entire source code of a VB application is the *program*. The first division of a program is the *module,* at least one of which is always attributed to a form window.

In any VB application, there can be three types of modules:

♦ A *form module* pertains to the objects and contents of a particular form window or to the main window of a Multiple Document Interface (MDI) form set.

♦ A *general module* contains the procedures that exist independently of forms or other graphic objects. The general module may contain declarations of variables and structures that pertain to the program as a whole, thus specifying the context of the entire program.

♦ An *extension module* consists of non-Visual Basic code compiled in such a way that it is accessible through the Visual Basic interpreter by way of the toolbox or by addressing its code as if it contained Visual Basic procedures.

Because a module is by definition a set of procedures, it naturally follows that the program component on the next lower level is the procedure. A *procedure* is the core component of a Visual Basic application. The purpose of a procedure is to logically describe or model at least one task or mathematical function and pass its results to some other component.

Figure 3.1

The divisions of a Visual Basic application.

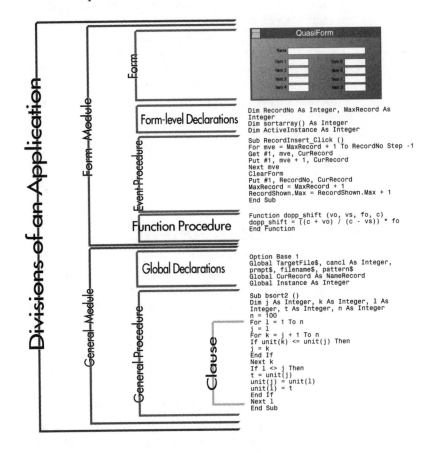

When you edit a form or general module using the code editor window, you look at only one procedure at a time. The name of that procedure appears within the window's heading, generally beside the term Sub. As such, the name also appears in the editor window control bar, in the list box marked Proc. The Sub statement as a whole is called a *procedure declaration* because it not only defines the procedure for the rest of the program, but it also helps define the *context* of that procedure—what values and variables are shared with the rest of the program. The context of a procedure is the understanding the interpreter has of which variables and functions pertain only to the procedure, which values and variables are exchanged between this procedure and the one that called it, and which variables and functions pertain to the program as a whole.

A *procedure* is Visual Basic's core program component.

The *context* of a procedure defines its relative pertinence to the rest of the program.

A *parameter* is a value or variable passed to a procedure.

The way a Sub procedure is structured enables it to accept variables and values as input from the body of the program that called it (in Visual Basic, another procedure) and perform computations using those values. These passed values are called *parameters*.

Any variables created or declared during the procedure are specific to that procedure alone, unless otherwise specified with statements. In other words, each procedure has a variable context all its own, called the *local context*. When the procedure is exited and some other procedure is being executed, the variables within the local context are deallocated.

Example

The following procedure draws an unfilled rectangle on-screen, given four parameters.

```
Sub Rect_Draw (x As Integer, y As Integer, w As Integer,
➡h As Integer)
    Line (x, y) - (x + w, y)
    Line (x + w, y) - (x + w, y + h)
    Line (x + w, y + h) - (x, y + h)
    Line (x, y + h) - (x, y)
End Sub
```

So that you can get a better feel for what the program does, here is the preceding procedure translated into pseudocode:

Procedure for drawing a rectangle with its top left
corner at (x,y), a width of w, and a height of h:
  Draw a line from the top left to top right corners
  of the rectangle.
  Extend the line to the bottom right corner.
  Extend the line to the bottom left corner.
  Extend the line back to the origin point.
End of procedure.

The coordinates for the top left corner of the rectangle are accepted as x and y. The width and height of the rectangle are accepted as w and h. The following procedure's sole purpose is to call procedure Sub Rect_Draw ().

```
Sub Form_Click ()
    Rect_Draw 10, 10, 500, 500
End Sub
```

Notice that the four variables mentioned previously don't exist within the context of procedure Sub Form_Click (). Instead, four explicit integral values are designated in the same order as the variables listed as parameters for Sub Rect_Draw (). These values are passed to the procedure Sub Rect_Draw (), which accepts them as parameters in the order in which they were given, and uses them within its own context. This way, variable w can refer to "width" in the context of Sub Rect_Draw (), and perhaps to "water level" within some other procedure. When Sub Rect_Draw () is exited, variables x, y, w, and h no longer exist. But if the user clicks on Form1, the rectangle remains.

A variable's *scope* is its pertinence to the rest of the program.

Within the preceding procedure, the individual variables invoked pertain only to that procedure. The way it is written now, when the procedure is exited, the values of x, y, w, and h are discarded. The names can be used again when the procedure is reentered. This is one example of a set of variables with *local scope*; their meaning pertains only to their local procedure. The scope of a variable is the degree to which that variable can be used throughout your application. For example, a variable's scope could be a single procedure, an entire module, or if defined as Global, your entire VB application.

Example

Another form of procedure is the Function procedure, which is structured like a Sub procedure, except it passes a value back to the procedure that called it. The following function finds the future value of an annuity, given three parameters:

```
Function Fvalue (pvalue, interest, nperiods As Integer)
    Fvalue = pvalue * ((1 + interest) ^ nperiods)
End Function
```

Notice how Fvalue is not only the name of the Function procedure, but also a variable to which the computed value is assigned. Here, pvalue is the present value of the annuity or loan, interest is the rate of interest per annum, and nperiods is the number of payment periods remaining. The following procedure calls this function:

```
Sub Future_Click ()
    FutVal1.Print Fvalue(1000, .1, 3)
    FutVal2.Print "Computation complete."
End Sub
```

Here is the procedure written in pseudocode:

*Procedure for clicking on the **Future** button:*
  *Execute the procedure **Fvalue** for a $1000 annuity
  paid off with a 10 percent interest rate over three
  years, and print the result within the picture box
  called **FutVal1**.*
  *Print the message "Computation complete." within
  the picture box called **FutVal2**.*
End of procedure.

In Visual Basic, a picture box can contain text as well as graphics; you use the .Print method to place text into a picture box. For a button having the control name Future and for two picture boxes with control names FutVal1 and FutVal2, procedure Sub Future_Click () places the future value of a $1000 annuity at 10 percent interest over three years—assuming annual payment periods—into picture box FutVal1. The call to Fvalue looks and acts like an intrinsic function in the regular Visual Basic vocabulary.

Note that function Fvalue is executed in its entirety before the instruction to print the message in picture box FutVal2 is executed. This is an example of program control being passed between procedures. Further execution of procedure Sub Future_Click () is suspended when the call to Fvalue is made. After Fvalue is done, execution of Sub Future_Click () resumes with the instruction immediately following the call.

More on Program Components

Informally, a grouping of instructions from a procedure is called a *routine*. On occasion, this text may use as an example a portion of a large procedure without the headings. If the instructions within that portion perform some whole function or task, the excerpt is referred to as a routine.

In the previous two examples, you saw program control being passed from procedure to procedure. As I've noted before, instructions within modules are not necessarily executed from top to bottom. Within the confines of a procedure, program control can be commanded to branch to another point designated by a *label*. A label is a noninstruction on a line by itself and followed by a colon (on the same line). The label designates a branching point.

Formally, a *subroutine* is a series of instructions within a procedure—especially a long one—that can be branched to by calling its label by name. A subroutine allows for automatic branching back to the instruction that follows the one calling the subroutine.

A long instruction broken apart and distributed over several lines is called a *clause*. A clause is a compound instruction containing one or more subordinate instructions. Generally, the instructions within a clause appear indented in order to distinguish the clause's borders within the source code.

The following is an example of a small clause:

```
If a = 1 Then
    GoTo More_Help
Else
    HelpBlock.Text = "Click on OK to continue."
    a = 0
End If
```

To be honest, there really is more than one instruction here. All three lines that are inset a few spaces are legitimate instructions themselves. At the same time, they are part of a greater conditional instruction that tells the VB interpreter, "Either execute this group of instructions or else execute that group." These inset phrases are called *nested* instructions. The act of embedding instructions within a clause in this manner is called *nesting*. Still, `If-Then...Else...End If` is treated as a single instruction and more categorically as a statement.

The next most common type of clause is the loop clause. A *loop* is a sequence of instructions that is executed repetitively either for a specified count or until a condition is evaluated True.

> A *loop* is a sequence of instructions that is repeated either a specific number of times or until a condition is True.

Example

Often, you find you need to execute a set of instructions a certain number of times or, to evaluate functional series, you need to accumulate values using a loop clause. The following loop uses an array variable and uses its own running count to create an exponential series:

```
For num = 1 To 5
    ExpTotal = 3 ^ num
    Output1.Print ExpTotal;
Next count
```

Count from 1 to 5, and for each count, do the following:
 Assign the value of 3 raised to the power of the count to the
 stated variable.
 Print the value of this variable within this output region.
Count the next number and execute all instructions between the
 beginning and end statement of the loop.

The primary loop clause statement in any BASIC language is the `For-Next` loop. Within it, the variable `num` is created and its value is initially set to 1. The program continues execution in sequence. First, the value of `3 ^ 1` (three to the first power) is evaluated and stored in the variable `exp`. The value of the variable `exp` is then printed to the output region named `Output1`. On reaching the instruction `Next num`, the interpreter increments (adds 1 to) the `num` variable and branches back to the instruction following the `For` statement.

This repetition continues until `num` equals 5 and `Next num` is reached. At that point, `num` is no longer to be incremented, and execution continues with the instruction following `Next num`. The result is a text region that contains the exponential series 3, 9, 27, 81, and 243.

Visual Basic Symbols

The primary difference between a program written in the original BASIC and one written in a modern dialect such as Visual Basic is that the older program is more textual, whereas the newer one is more graphical. For instance, a program written in the 1964 edition of BASIC might ask, `"HOW WIDE IS THE WOODEN BEAM?"` or `"WHAT IS THE INTEREST RATE PER ANNUM?"` to obtain values for a formula. This question could only be posed at a specific time, under specified conditions. The programmer therefore needed to consider the user input process chronologically. What time was the right time to pop the question? In the old conversational usage model of the program, it was the programmer's job to write the script for all user interaction. In a conversational mode, a BASIC program could be executed step-by-step, in a totally predictable manner. From the programmer's point of view, the only unknown element in such a program would be the answers to these questions. You could argue that it was simpler to program in the era of conversational programs, because the programmer didn't have to consider very deeply what the user intended to do with the program.

Figure 3.2 depicts the on-screen appearance of two simple programs from two different eras, but with exactly the same purpose. They calculate the zone of a sphere—or the measure of the area of a strip along the surface of a sphere. The sphere is divided by two parallel planes. Where those planes meet with the surface of the sphere, they form the boundaries of the zone. These two programs calculate the area of the zone. The formula is described mathematically as

```
z = 2Πrh
```

in which P is the symbol for the constant pi, r is the radius of the sphere, and h is the distance separating the two planes.

Figure 3.2

The zone formula, then and now.

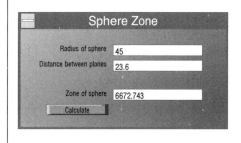

```
WHAT IS THE RADIUS OF THE SPHERE
?> 45

WHAT IS THE DISTANCE BETWEEN PLANES
?> 23.6

THE ZONE AREA IS:  6672.743

READY
>_
```

Sphere Zone

Radius of sphere 45
Distance between planes 23.6

Zone of sphere 6672.743
Calculate

1970s

1990s

Imagine zoning off and measuring the area of the earth's crust between 20 and 30 degrees north latitude, and you'll get a picture of this formula in your mind.

Now compare the source code of both these programs. The older, conversational program uses the ANSI standard BASIC adopted in the 1970s. The newer program is written in Visual Basic. So that you can see the simple structure of both programs, this fragment does not include the error-trapping code that good programmers generally include. First, here is the old BASIC program:

```
10 REM +++ FORMULA FOR ZONE OF A SPHERE +++
20 CLS
30 INPUT "ENTER THE RADIUS OF THE SPHERE";R
40 INPUT "ENTER THE DISTANCE BETWEEN BISECTING PLANES";H
50 Z=(2*3.1415927)*R*H
60 PRINT
70 PRINT "THE ZONE AREA IS ";Z
80 END
```

It's easy to spot in the preceding source code which instructions perform the role of conversing with the user; they're marked with the term INPUT. This term is not a part of the Visual Basic vocabulary. Because typed data in VB is entered into predrawn form fields rather than in response to input prompts, the INPUT statement has faded into history, along with the MAT statement and line numbers.

Now look at the modern code. Because the following source code is its own procedure, it may be called as needed from various places within your VB application.

```
Sub ZoneCalc_Click ()
' Formula for Zone of a Sphere
    r = Val(Radius.Text)
    h = Val(PlaneDist.Text)
    z = (2 * 3.1415927) * r * h
    ZoneSphere.Text = Str$(z)
End Sub
```

Procedure for calculating the area of a sphere zone:
  *Retrieve the value of **r** from a text box **Radius**.*
  *Retrieve the value of **h** from a text box **PlaneDist**.*
  Calculate the sphere zone using the classic formula.
  *Output the results in a text box **ZoneSphere**.*
  End of procedure.

Knowing what you know about properties, you should be able to identify .Text as a property by looking for the period that separates the property from its graphic object. Radius, PlaneDist, and ZoneSphere are three text boxes in the form. The textual contents of these boxes are addressed by adding .Text to their names.

If you compared the mathematical formula for the area of a sphere zone to either of the two programs, you probably located the basic form of the formula. Notice that it doesn't appear much different from the algebraic form of the formula—which is partly why the theory of high-level programming is called *procedural algebra*. In both programs, letters represent values; so as in algebra, you call these letters *variables*. In Visual Basic, you can use entire words as variables, as long as these words aren't recognized by VB as instructional terms.

In the first (old BASIC) program, the values for the formula are put into variables that are declared following the INPUT statements. In the second (Visual Basic) program, text is extracted from the two input text boxes in the form and translated into values that are used in the formula. The result of the formula is translated back into text and placed in the output text box of the form. Remember that this procedure is not executed until the button named ZoneCalc is clicked.

The sphere zone formula itself is the one part of both programs that has kept its syntax over time, partly because procedural algebra is resistant to change. More obviously, there are no line numbers in Visual Basic programs, and lowercase is now prevalent. However, the methodology of user interaction with the BASIC program has changed drastically. As a result of this change, Visual Basic is a different language from ANSI Standard BASIC, BASICA, GW-BASIC, or even Microsoft QuickBasic. Note also that the pseudocode element provided applies equally to both examples.

The linguistic portion of Visual Basic is loosely based on the first 1964 Kemeny/Kurtz edition of BASIC—the If-Then, GoTo/GoSub, and For-Next statements still abound in VB, although Microsoft has greatly reshaped them to fit their modern roles. With the advent of Visual Basic, Microsoft has introduced object-oriented syntax to the BASIC dialect. Using this syntax, a graphic object, such as a text box or a button, has its own "noun," and processes related to that object (such as printing or resizing) have their own "verbs." An earlier edition of BASIC might express the measurement of whether a mouse button was pressed within an instruction as follows:

```
IF MOUSE(0)=1 THEN PRINT AT 15,15;"You pressed the mouse button."
```

In Visual Basic syntax, the value of a pressed mouse button is implied, not expressed directly, as in the following example:

```
Sub Form_Click ()
    Form1.Print "You pressed the mouse button."
End Sub
```

Even if you're a novice programmer, you can tell from the preceding comparison that Visual Basic bears a loose resemblance to its progenitors. If you're a veteran of older BASICs, you probably also noted how the simple process of printing in the event of a mouse-button click has been elevated in stature from a mere clause to a subprogram module.

Summary

A large percentage of all instructions within the source code of a Visual Basic program consists of comparisons between known and unknown values. The unknown values are represented, as in algebra, by variables. The instruction that compares such values can be classified, among other instructions, as a statement.

The phraseology of a BASIC-language statement is borrowed from English syntax, although more from the syntax of an English command than an English statement. A Visual Basic statement may appear to be a command to the computer to change some value or some operating component of the program; from the point of view of the interpreter, the would-be command states the present value of a variable or the present state of the component. For this reason, directive instructions are called statements.

The portion of a statement that actually compares the two values to each other is called an expression. The interpreter arithmetically reduces an expression to the most fundamental logical value in computing, that being a True or False binary state. A complex statement that assigns a value to a variable is a formula. Within formulas, common arithmetic functions can be symbolized by VB function terms, which contain an abbreviation of the function's name followed by a value or expression on which the function operates.

A Visual Basic project consists of at least one module. A form module pertains specifically to one (parent) form in the project. A project may also contain one or more general modules that don't relate to a form. Within each module are procedures, which are the core components of all VB programs. A procedure describes or models at least one work task, or performs at least one mathematical function.

Within the boundaries of a procedure, a subroutine in Visual Basic is a set of instructions that can be executed repetitively. This repetition is accomplished by branching to that set and then branching back to the instruction following the one that called the subroutine. A more common method of repetitive execution is the loop clause.

Review Questions

1. What part of the instruction If f = 6 Then GoTo Outahere is an *expression*?

2. What part of the instruction Total = Int(a + b + c) is a *function*?

3. What part of the instruction If quality > 10 Then good = 1 is an expression of assignment?

4. If x = 5 and y = 2, what integral value does the function Sqr((x - y) ^ 3) return?

5. The instruction If coins >= too_many Then Return ends what type of instruction grouping?

CHAPTER 4

The Development Process

The objective of this chapter is to give you a tour through the conception and development of a Visual Basic application. First, it's necessary to go over a few points concerning how this book presents Visual Basic applications.

Entering Applications from Listings

In just about every other book on programming, it would be easy for the author to give you a source code example and ask you to type it verbatim, from front to back. In most high-level programming languages such as C or standard BASIC, the source code sequence of any program can be written out all on one spool from beginning to end. C is a modular programming language, and sometimes the order of its modules is arbitrarily defined by the programmer—but at least the order is defined.

A Visual Basic application, regardless of its proclaimed modularity, is in many ways structured like the water system of a major city. Given the blueprints, not even an engineer could decisively tell you where the system begins and ends. When you ask the VB interpreter to list the current project for you—the modern equivalent of the LLIST command in the old Microsoft interpreters—the interpreter starts by displaying a rendition of the main or startup form, followed by a listing of all properties belonging to that form, in a format you don't really even have to use to build a form. Later, the interpreter lists the actual source code for the VB application.

In this book, applications are presented first by listing only the properties that belong to a form and its graphic objects that have changed from their default values.

Properties, you remember, are descriptive elements of graphic objects, defining some manner in which the objects appear or behave. Among the properties displayed are the objects' contents and names.

To enter property settings from the listings, follow these steps:

1. If a window for the form mentioned in the "Object type" column is not present, select New Form from the File menu. This places a new form into the workspace and gives it a temporary title in the Project window.

2. For each graphic object not currently displayed that is a part of the form, click the VB toolbox button associated with the object type listed. Draw or place the object somewhere within the form for the moment (preferably not overlapping another object).

3. Find and choose each property for the form or object listed in the book's "Property" column, from the leftmost drop-down list box in the VB Property window. To bring the property title into the window's selector bar, click on the row containing the property title.

4. Enter the setting for that property into the selector bar of the Properties window. If the setting is textual, type it directly in the box. If the down-arrow button is available (if the arrow is black rather than gray), click on it to see the list of current setting choices for that property. If an ellipsis (. . .) appears in place of the down arrow, click on it to see a file selector box from which you can select the file name that acts as the property setting, such as an icon's ICO file name. If the setting is True/False, double-clicking on the property title in the window reverses the current setting. If the setting is an entry in a list of possible settings, double-clicking on the property title in the window changes the setting to the one in the list immediately following the current setting.

With regard to the way source code is listed in this book, because Visual Basic programs are not executed along a concrete path, it becomes necessary to seek another rational path of explanation. This book presents procedures in the order in which the programmer might most reasonably conceive them.

Building an Application

An application is built in stages and written in layers, with the heart of the program—the calculation part—written first and the various frills and eccentricities added to it later. You may not yet understand many of the structural details of programming; the rest of this book is devoted to that subject. Still, to understand what you're learning, you need to see a program being built.

Programming is a science to the extent that it is studied, analyzed, and theorized on. Programming can be an art inasmuch as it can be practiced, cultivated, and appreciated. You are about to witness a Visual Basic application under construction. By observing the principles of the programming process being applied, you may be able to obtain a greater understanding of the meaning behind each individual part of the program when you study it in detail.

Making the Expressor

To give you an idea of how the Visual Basic programming process works, here's how the author programmed a special type of scientific formula calculator (called the Expressor). This application simulates a scientific and financial hand-held calculator from which you can retrieve a formula; type the variables into specific windows that show not only each variable typed, but what it represents with respect to the formula; and see the result of the formula in a separate window. Generally, when you operate most scientific and financial calculators, by the time you've reached the result of your formula, you've lost track of your input parameters because you can't see them anymore.

All calculators have a storage bank of "memories" that holds values you've typed at one time or another. The Expressor has five of those "memories" visible, set apart from the main register, and labeled with terms that relate them to the formula on which you're working. This enables you to calculate the values for the memory parameters independently from the main formula calculation. One input parameter, for instance, may be the sum of several items. With the Expressor design, you can calculate the inputs separately and let the Expressor take care of the main formula.

Programming is a process of trial and error. Many books paint a picture of a rosy world in which you can compile and execute programs on the first try. This viewpoint is simply unrealistic; the better you are at programming, the more errors you will make per program. This is because the better you are, the bigger and more cumbersome your programs become.

Figure 4.1 is a sketch of the Expressor in its conceptual stage.

Here's how the Expressor works: The calculator portion of the program behaves like a standard RPN four-function calculator. If the user presses one of the arrow buttons, the value currently appearing in the readout is copied into the "memory slot" next to the button. Suppose the user wants to solve a formula for a set of given values. The user selects the name of a formula from a list in the bottom left corner of the device. On doing so, the names of various parameters for this formula appear beside each memory slot. Values can then be copied into the memory slots by making the input parameters appear in the readout, either through calculation or direct entry, and then clicking the arrow button beside the appropriately labeled slot.

Figure 4.1

A sketch of the Expressor.

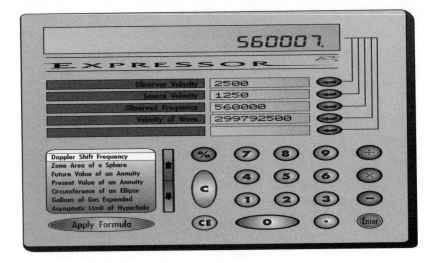

When the text for the parameters accurately describes the values that have been inserted into the slots, the user clicks the Apply Formula button. The Expressor then immediately solves the formula for the parameters given and displays the result in the main readout. This method of entry reduces the possibility of error and makes the entry process more efficient.

The most difficult part of writing a program is in the act of translating those first ideas into logic. Instead of first imagining the first line of source code, I visualize a potential end product. When I've decided on a partway-feasible goal, the final part of the conception process is in creating the beginning of the program.

For the Expressor, I decided my goal would be to write a program the user could operate like a hand-held device. One of the goals of Microsoft Windows is to provide an environment in which programs appear to operate like real-world devices with buttons and gadgets. It is tempting at this point in the Visual Basic programming process to start drawing buttons and gadgets on the screen—to first plot how the user sees the program and later decide how the computer will see the program. To construct a program in any language, you do not organize the user control elements (the shell) first and try to fill that shell with the yolk of the program later. Your first task as a programmer is to determine which elements of the program can be represented numerically as values.

When looking at the Expressor sketch, what do you see beneath the obvious that can be represented numerically as values? If you've ever used a programmable calculator, you know that the specific key you press—whether a numeral or function key—is represented numerically. A calculator arithmetically combines the value previously entered into its main window with the one currently being entered, so two important values are there. The number being typed is different from the one that is entered into the arithmetic combination, so there is a third important value. The number of digits appearing in the main window is another important value because you can't enter a number of characters that flow past the left edge of the display.

For the sake of the Expressor, five "memory" values are held in separate text boxes for use later as parameters for the chosen formula. The formula name appears in a drop-down list box. Which formula is chosen also can be considered a value. The VB interpreter "thinks" in terms of numbers, not gadgets or things. So when you plan a program, you too should think in terms of numbers.

In effect, a Visual Basic form appears to be a series of objects on-screen that react to events in a programmed way. At the core of the system, however, an object has properties that are described numerically; beneath that surface, events are merely the results of continual comparisons of numbers to each other until an expected result is reached. These numbers concern the position of the object, the position of the pointer with relation to the object, the color values within the object, and so on. Objects are not the quanta—or indivisible constituent units—of Visual Basic any more than atoms—as learned from the discoveries of subatomic particles and quarks—are the building blocks of matter.

After you determine what can be represented as values, your next step is to estimate which values will be important throughout the entire program. Your Visual Basic program will be made up of numerous procedures, such as those that respond to the user pressing a button, those that apply arithmetic functions to the input values, or the one that stores a displayed number in a "memory slot." Each procedure awaits a certain event that triggers its execution. When the procedure starts, it must be shown the values that are important to its operation. Otherwise, the procedure doesn't know what's going on in the program. Think of each procedure as being asleep until an event wakes it. When the procedure is awake, it suffers from "amnesia" until it has a chance to be briefed concerning the current status of the program.

The value of a *global variable* is maintained throughout the entire program.

So that the program never forgets its purpose, the most important values the program uses throughout are declared as *global variables*. These declarations are made in the general section of a module named EXPRESOR.BAS. Figure 4.2 shows where the listing for the global module appears in the Visual Basic Project window and shows the global module window itself. The project has been saved to disk, so each element of the project has been given its official file name.

Figure 4.2

The Expressor's main variables in the global module.

The three variables that are pertinent to the program are the current value in the window, the value with which it is combined, and the number of digits in the "readout" window. These variables were named arbitrarily, as every BASIC programmer has the right to do. The window where the main number appears is called the *readout*, rather than the *window* or the *display*—two words with synonyms that may be confusing. I decided to call the values I attributed to the readout readout_value and combine_value. The underscore character is not part of a Visual Basic convention, but it is instead a replacement for a space, making the variable name easier to read.

In determining which values are global and which are local, one consideration is what values comprise the objective of your program—the sum totals, the statistics concerning the records being kept, and the product of the analysis. Another consideration is which values, unseen by the user, are most likely to be shared among several procedures. For the Expressor, the number of digits in the readout is one such value. Its variable is named ready because it refers both to the readout and to the state of readiness for the readout to receive more digits from the button panel.

The value of a *local variable* is remembered within the procedure that invoked it.

The size of the global module shown in figure 4.2 is an indication of how small this program is. Throughout the book, more instructions and procedures are added to the Expressor program, improving its performance and giving it more capabilities.

Building Your Program

When you write a program from the beginning, you do not foresee the modular interrelationship, draw the framework of that interrelationship into the program, and fill that framework with immaculate source code. The technique I use is to select some procedure of the program that I know is within my ability to create now, make that procedure work well, and then orient the rest of the procedures around that one. This procedure might not necessarily be the main or startup procedure of the program, although it can be.

When planning your program, start with the most important *operational* elements.

The Expressor's digit buttons were made operational first. The formula-solving routines could have been written instead, but to test them in their running state would require a number entered into the readout. One rule of thumb is that the most important *purposeful* elements of a program are not necessarily the most important *operational* elements. Each procedure of a program is like the gear of a mechanism, such as a watch. When you lay out a program using the layered technique, the main gear is "wound" first. This becomes the "engine" of the program. When the engine is running, it provides the power for the rest of the program, including the gears that perform the true purpose of the program.

The Expressor project is a good example of this principle in action because the actual formula-solving part of the program was added toward the end of the project. The first stage in the process was to make the digit buttons work. I chose in the beginning to draw the first 11 buttons (digits 0 through 9, and the decimal point), write the procedural source code for one button that would echo its contents into the readout, and copy that code into the procedures for the remaining buttons. I wrote the code for the 7 button and then copied it into the other procedures, replacing 7 with the appropriate digit. Here's how the procedure looks:

```
Sub Button7_Click ()
If ready > 0 Then
    Readout.Caption = Readout.Caption + "7"
Else
    Readout.Caption = "7"
End If
ready = ready + 1
End Sub
```

Here's the preceding procedure explained as pseudocode:

> *Procedure for clicking on the 7 button:*
> *If the tally of digits in the readout is one or more,*
> *   Add a "7" to the end of the readout,*
> *Otherwise,*
> *   Make the readout just say "7" and nothing else.*
> *End of condition.*
> *Add 1 to the number of digits in the readout tally.*
> *End of procedure.*

Notice that this procedure starts to mimic the way a pocket calculator works. When clear, the readout always reads 0, and the first digit typed always replaces that 0—unless you type a decimal point or press the 0 key. In the process of writing a program, you gradually realize what all the exceptions are and add them layer by layer as you go.

The second major principle you learn—and continue to learn—as a programmer is that the simplest code to produce is not necessarily the most efficient. The most efficient BASIC code is generally the most compact. The preceding source code example may look compact, but if you multiply it by 11, you may begin to wonder whether one big gear runs better than a handful of smaller ones.

A *control array* is a group of similar graphic objects addressed jointly within a single procedure.

Visual Basic enables you to establish a single structure of related graphical controls, called a *control array*. Such an array can contain several controls, each of which is accessed using the same control name, and all of which are referenced within the same Sub procedure. Each control in an array, however, is distinguished by its .Index property. To initiate a control array, you start by placing the first object of the array in the form. After indicating that object and selecting **C**opy from the **E**dit menu, Visual Basic responds by asking if you want the copies of this object to form a control array. You respond by clicking the Yes button. At that point, VB sets the original object's .Index property to 0, and each clone thereafter to 1, 2, 3, and so on.

The .Index property of elements of a control array is a number. The purpose of each button in this particular array is to pass a digit—which is a number—to the readout. If that number is always a single digit, you can write a generic procedure for the entire control array. The procedure passes some distinct value, whatever it is, to the readout when one of the buttons in the array is pressed. You don't need several separate-but-equal procedures to define the pressing of buttons when one procedure does the job just as well. The one element of distinction here is the .Index property of each button, so if each .Index is made equal to the number being passed, the procedure can be programmed to pass the .Index to the readout.

The third thing you learn to do as a programmer is to say, "On second thought…" often. As stated earlier, the 0 and decimal point buttons operate differently on a calculator than the rest of the digit keys, so you can't include these two wayward buttons in the control array. The 1 through 9 buttons are functionally identical, however; so the buttons with positive-valued indices can be included in a control array. Here's the code for the new procedure, rewritten from the 7-button version presented earlier:

```
Sub ButtonPos_Click (Index As Integer)
If ready > 0 Then
    If ready < 20 Then
        Readout.Caption = Readout.Caption + Right$(Str$(Index),
1)
        ready = ready + 1
    End If
Else
    Readout.Caption = Right$(Str$(Index), 1)
    ready = 1
End If
assess_readout
End Sub
```

Notice how this procedure has evolved. Because this procedure belongs to a control array rather than to one control, the Index of that control is automatically passed to the procedure through the parentheses within the initial Sub statement. Index is the parameter passed to the procedure when the user clicks on a positively numbered button. Think of the parentheses within the Sub and Function statements as a slot through which values—here called *parameters*—are passed.

The function Right$(Str$(Index), 1) converts the numeric value of Index to textual contents. Visual Basic stores alphanumeric text and real numbers differently; the text may have numbers in it, but VB still cannot evaluate that text. To give numeric text value, it must be converted to a value using the function Str$(). The Right$(..., 1) function, which encloses the Str$() function, in this instance removes the leading space character—another bit of alphanumeric text.

Here are the instructions for the new and improved procedure, written as pseudocode:

> *For all positively numbered buttons, receive the index for the*
> *particular button pressed.*
> *If the tally of digits in the readout is one or more,*
> > *Then if this tally is less than 20,*
> > > *Add the numeric form of the index to the readout*
> > > *and add one to the tally of digits.*
> > *End of this condition.*
> *Otherwise (if there's only one digit in the readout),*
> > *Place the numeric form of the index into the*
> > *readout and make the tally equal 1.*
> *End of the main condition.*
> *Execute the procedure that assesses the readout value.*
> *End of procedure.*

Within the "memory bank" portion of the Expressor form, the groups of five value registers, descriptive text boxes, and value-loading buttons were each created as control arrays.

The four-function calculator portion of the Expressor was programmed using Reverse Polish notation (also called H.P. or Hewlett Packard notation) primarily because it is easier to implement. If you've ever used a Texas Instruments (T.I.) calculator or one that uses T.I. notation, you know that you enter each element of an arithmetic expression the way it would appear on paper in algebraic notation. Thus, *two times three divided by six* is entered in T.I. notation as 2 * 3 / 6, in which * is the multiplication operator and / is the division operator.

The downside of T.I. notation is that the previous arithmetic function is implemented whenever the next one is entered. For instance, in 2 * 3 / 6, 2 is actually multiplied by 3 when the division key is pressed. Subsequently, the division operation takes place when the = key is pressed. To implement this notation in a Visual Basic program, the previous arithmetic function must be remembered—which means creating another variable and giving each function its own arbitrary index.

For Reverse Polish notation, you enter the same formula as 2 [Enter] 3 * 6 /. This looks backward on paper—thus the name *Reverse*—but it's easier to implement in a program. Each arithmetic operation takes place at the time its operator is pressed. You can then program the Expressor's function buttons to execute the operation the moment the button-pressing event is triggered.

Here's the source code for the procedure that handles the pressing of the multiplication button:

```
Sub Times_Click ()
assess_readout
readout_value = readout_value * combine_value
combine_value = readout_value
Readout.Caption = Str$(readout_value)
ready = 0
End Sub
```

Here is the same procedure written in pseudocode:

Procedure for clicking on the "Times" button:
Execute the procedure that assesses the value of the number in
the readout.
Multiply that assessment by the combination value—previous
value entered into the readout.
Make the combination value the current value, in the event of
future button presses.
Place the textual form of the mathematically combined value into
the readout.
Pretend there are no digits in the readout so that the next digit
button pressed will clear it.
End of procedure.

Notice the next-to-last statement in the source code of the procedure. The way the digit buttons work, a digit replaces the contents of the entire readout if the register of the number of digits, ready, is equal to 0. You know that the solution value in the readout is not likely to be 0. You also know, however, that the next digit button pressed should not add a digit to the solution but should instead replace it. The digit-number tally is set to 0. The real-world term for this form of process-triggering is *lying*.

I admit that I am a "code-as-you-go" programmer. I don't devise the inner schematics of my BASIC programs beforehand. In fact, most of my grand solutions to procedural dilemmas come to me by accident. The setting of ready to 0 when there were clearly digits in the readout is one case in point. I could have prepared another variable to act as a register that sets itself to 1 whenever a function button is pressed and then had the digit button procedures check to see if register = 1 before proceeding. I would, however, have had to add another comparison to my conditional statements. Furthermore, why make two registers perform similar purposes when one does the job just as well, if not better? When programming, be prepared to abandon at any time whatever process or method you originally thought would work in favor of a better way. This really is the way to program.

> **Note:** The Visual Basic programmer's choice of names for graphic objects is entirely arbitrary. In its current Programmers' Guide, Microsoft suggests that you give graphic objects' `.Name` properties prefixes that help identify the type of object. In an attempt to prevent the imposition of too many arbitrarily determined "standards" on the programmer, this book chooses to leave the naming conventions up to the reader.

Summary

Here is an outline of the principles of programming introduced in this chapter, which are used throughout the book:

- ◆ When conceiving a program in your mind, start with the end product and work backward toward the beginning.

- ◆ Your first task as a programmer is to determine which elements of the program—graphical or logical—can be represented numerically as values.

- ◆ The second task is to determine which values are important to the entire program and which are necessary only within their own local procedures.

- ◆ Make one whole procedure of the program work first and then write the other procedures to work around it.

- ◆ The most compact code may be the most difficult for a person to read—or, for that matter, write—but it is probably the most efficient code for the interpreter to execute.

- ◆ Prepare to rewrite entire procedures as you discover new methods that work better. You will probably keep less than 30 percent of the original draft of your source code, regardless of how well-written it is.

- ◆ Accept new solutions that come to mind along the way.

The Expressor program is far from complete at this point in the development process. In upcoming chapters, the programming process continues, as well as the revision process. The complete source code for all versions of the Expressor used in this book appears in Appendix C.

Review Questions

1. In the Expressor program, why were the 0 and period keys not part of the same control array as keys 1 through 9?

2. Why is Reverse Polish notation easier to implement than T.I. and other "fringe" notations in a computer program?

Part II

Values and Variables

CHAPTER 5

Using Variables

In this chapter, you are introduced to the concept of the variable, which is the logical container for values and text. You learn the different categories of variables and experiment with placing values within each type. You also construct mathematical expressions using variables as components.

Every Visual Basic instruction you write manipulates the contents of the computer's memory in one way or another. Even the instruction `Stop`—which suspends the program's execution—alters the contents of memory. The `Stop` statement, however, does not tell its human reader what contents are being altered at the time. The programmer, therefore, manipulates the computer indirectly. The user sees only the cause of the program's suspension—the "command" `Stop`—and its seemingly immediate effect. What the user doesn't see, however, is the manipulation of all the values in memory. Because of this manipulation, the VB application appears to stop. The `Stop` command actually starts many internal processes—for instance, processes that give back control to the VB environment.

> *A variable represents a unit of data.*

A direct statement such as `Stop` is, in fact, an indirect method of manipulating values in memory. In Visual Basic, the direct method of manipulating values in memory is to represent those values as variables. A *variable* is an arbitrarily named term that represents a unit of data in memory that that program can alter.

> *A formula states the relationship between known and unknown quantities.*

A *formula*, such as $E=mc^2$, is an algebraic expression of equality that states the relationships among values, quantities, or other known or unknown values.

Declaring Variables

Visual Basic recognizes variables as unique combinations of alphanumeric characters up to 40 characters long. (You rarely need to use a 40-character variable.) When the Visual Basic interpreter starts executing a program, no variables exist for that program. The interpreter maintains several values for the program, although you have not yet explicitly claimed any of them. To claim a variable using the informal method, you use that variable for the first time in a mathematical *expression* of equality.

An expression is any of the following:

An *expression* can be a comparison between values, a formula, or an assignment of value to a variable.

♦ An arithmetic comparison between two values, having a result that is expressed logically as a binary state

♦ One or more values or variables arithmetically joined by functions or functional operators

♦ An assignment of value to a variable by way of another value, variable, or expression

In BASIC, a variable is *declared* when it is first used within the source code.

Whenever a variable is used for the first time within a program, that variable is *declared*. The declaration of a variable is the first statement in a program to assign a legitimate value to that variable.

Example

Here is perhaps the simplest variable declaration:

```
x = 1
```

This is a mathematical expression that creates the variable x and assigns to it the value 1. From this point on, whenever x appears in the program, the interpreter evaluates it to be 1 until some instruction explicitly changes the value of x to something else.

The best way to experiment with variables is to bring up the *immediate pane* of Visual Basic's Debug window, as shown in figure 5.1. This lower portion of the Debug window contains a command-line interpreter—a prompted line like the DOS prompt, on which you type direct statements as commands. This is the descendant of the READY prompt from the old BASIC interpreters.

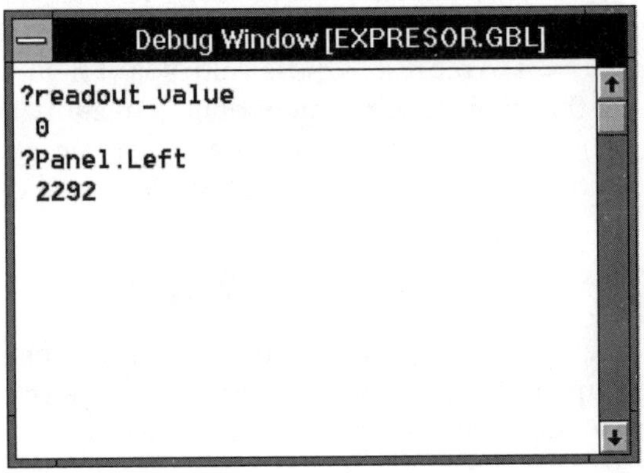

Figure 5.1

The Debug window showing the immediate pane.

Debug Window [EXPRESOR.GBL]
?readout_value
0
?Panel.Left
2292

To access the immediate pane without loading a program, perform the following steps:

1. From the VB **F**ile menu, select **N**ew Project. A blank Form1 window appears.

2. Click the Run button in the VB toolbar. For a moment, the Form1 window disappears and then reappears without the grid.

3. Click the Break button. The Debug window appears. At this point, the immediate pane takes up the majority of this window. If the Debug window is used to monitor the current running application, the status is displayed in the immediate pane.

4. Click once anywhere within the immediate pane to begin operating it. A blinking cursor appears there.

The *command-line interpreter* parses (analyzes) your commands as they are entered and responds instantly.

Each instruction you enter into the immediate pane is interpreted immediately. To test the effectiveness of the immediate pane, enter Print x at the prompt. If x has previously been set to a value of 1, the *command-line interpreter* (CLI) will respond with a 1 on a line by itself. Likewise, if you enter Print y, the CLI should respond with a blank line, because no real value has yet been loaded into the variable y. All variables that have not been assigned a value are equal to 0. In other words, if a variable is invoked in a formula and has no assigned value, that variable is evaluated as nothing, or is "null."

The statement x = 1 is an *expression of assignment*, in that the value 1 is assigned to x. The statement also says that x exists only if the expression is the first instruction within the VB program to use x.

As stated earlier, an expression of equality—an *equation*—specifies the relationships between values as well as their proportions, ratios, and limits. The Visual Basic application is, in the purely logical sense, a mechanism that uses equations as instructions for the construction and assembly of a product. This product is not the program, but the data "manufactured" by that program. This data is always, in its root form, a set of numbers.

If you're beginning to get the impression that all a computer program does is take one group of numbers and reconstitute it with formulas so that it becomes another group of numbers, you're beginning to think like a programmer.

Example

Here's an example of this principle. Suppose you use a formula in your business to determine whether you are charging too much for an item. You figure your cost for the item is equal to its actual wholesale cost (the price you paid for it), plus your costs for shipping, employee time, and time the item spent on your shelf. This formula is fixed, but your percentage of markup over your costs varies, perhaps daily.

Your formula might appear as follows:

```
Sub Analyze_Markup (sale_price, shipping, manhours,
➥shelf_time, markup_ceiling)
total_cost = shipping + manhours + shelf_time
ratio = (sale_price / total_cost - 1) * 100
If ratio > markup_ceiling Then
      too_high = 1
End If
End Sub
```

Following is the task the VB interpreter is instructed to perform, written as pseudocode:

Procedure for analyzing the fairness of the markup value, taking into account the current sale price, costs for materials, shipping, production hours, shelf time, and the current markup ceiling:
Calculate the total cost of producing the item as equal to the shipping cost for raw material, plus the number of production hours, plus the time the item will be on the shelf.
Calculate the percentage ratio of sale price to this total cost.
If this ratio is higher than the maximum allowable markup ceiling, then
  Set the "too high" flag.
End of condition.
End of procedure.

There are three value assignments in the preceding procedure. You add all the operating costs and expenditures to calculate the total cost per item. The next procedure is a formula that determines the percentage of price markup. The third procedure, which is executed conditionally, is the simplest of all. It assigns a value directly to a variable, as a flag, in case the markup is too much.

Suppose that before you execute this procedure, instead of acquiring inputs from a form, you *seed* (assign initial values to your variables) the formula with the following statements that appear in another procedure:

```
   .

   .

   .
shipping = 2.90
manhours = (av_salary / no_boxes) * 8
shelf_time = .25 * no_days
```

```
markup_ceiling = 33
        .
        .
        .
```

You can interpret these statements as a sort of parts list for the "assembly manual" that is `Sub Analyze_Markup ()`. These statements, or some such assignment of value to these variables referred to in `Sub Analyze_Markup ()`, are essential to the operation of the program; otherwise, Visual Basic cannot execute the procedure. The `total_cost` variable cannot equal 0; the interpreter "errors out" if it attempts to divide another value by 0.

Because some of the preceding ingredients are formulas, you can take this seeding process one step further with the following initial statements:

```
av_salary = 6.50
no_boxes = 1300
no_days = 5
```

The programming process sometimes works best backward. Direct assignment statements act as the fuel for the arithmetic engine of the program. As the programmer, you can easily change the values within these statements.

Degrees of Precision

A *byte* is made up of eight bits, or binary digits.

When the Visual Basic interpreter sees a variable for the first time, it allots a space for that variable in memory. Computers do not "think" in terms of decimal numbers (numbers in the base 10 numeral system). Therefore, the VB interpreter does not place into memory numbers like the kind you are used to using. A unit of memory is a *byte*—the primary memory storage unit for all forms of data in a computer system. A byte is made up of eight binary digits (bits).

Each eight-bit byte can hold any absolute integral value between 0 and 256 and any signed value between –128 and 127.

Variables can have fractional values. Bytes, however, do not have fractional values; so when it apportions space for a variable that may at some time become fractional, the Visual Basic interpreter, by default, allots extra memory for both fractional and whole-number values to be maintained for each variable.

A *floating-point* value may or may not be fractional.

In fractional value storage, the interpreter maintains a separate register for each value that could possibly be fractional. This register specifies the placement of the decimal point in the binary, or base 2, form of the number. The whole-number and fractional parts of the number are then translated into base 10 separately. This type of number is called a *floating-point* number. The term *floating-point* refers to the storage format for a value that is possibly fractional, in which the position of its decimal point is stored as a separate value.

Table 5.1 shows the five numeric precision types and the two alphanumeric types that Visual Basic supports, along with the number of bytes set aside for each type. In addition, the table displays the special characters used for addressing these different classes. These characters are placed immediately after the variable name to indicate the variable's precision type throughout the source code. The table also shows the keywords used in formal declarations when new variables are created.

Table 5.1. Visual Basic variable types.

Variable Type	Symbol	Keyword	Memory Usage
Integer	%	Integer	2 bytes
Long integer	&	Long	4 bytes
Single-precision floating-point	!	Single	4 bytes
Double-precision floating-point	#	Double	8 bytes
Currency	@	Currency	8 bytes
Alphanumeric	$	String	Number of characters in the string
Indefinite or unspecified	(none)	Variant	Apportioned as necessary

Table 5.2 lists the maximum and minimum values of the various variable types.

Table 5.2. Ranges of the Visual Basic variable types.

Variable Type	Range
Integer	–32,768 to +32,767
Long integer	–2,147,483,648 to +2,147,483,647
Single-precision	
Positive numbers	1.401298E–45 to 3.402823E+38
Negative numbers	–3.402823E+38 to –1.401298E–45
Double-precision	
Positive numbers	1.797693134862332E+308 to 4.94065645841247E–324

Variable Type	Range
Negative numbers	–4.94065645841247E–324 to –1.79769313486232E+308
Currency	–922337263685477.5808 to 922337263685477.5807
Alphanumeric	0 to approximately 65,500 bytes

Keep in mind that a *kilobyte* (K) is equal to 1,024 bytes and a *megabyte* (M) is equal to 1,024 kilobytes. Because installed computer memory is commonly measured in megabytes rather than in multiples of 16K, to consider conserving memory for variable usage two bytes at a time might seem outdated. However, it's always a good idea to do as much as you can with as little memory as possible.

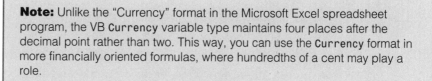

Note: Unlike the "Currency" format in the Microsoft Excel spreadsheet program, the VB `Currency` variable type maintains four places after the decimal point rather than two. This way, you can use the `Currency` format in more financially oriented formulas, where hundredths of a cent may play a role.

Unless you specify otherwise, the interpreter considers each new variable as having a *variant type*. While a VB application is running, if you assign a value—any value—to a variant or undeclared variable, it takes the form of a four-byte, floating-point value even if the value you assigned to it is a whole number. If, in the application, the contents you assign to a variant are alphanumeric—that is, something like `Hello World` rather than the number `149.95`—the variable is considered a *string variable,* having no mathematical value. `Hello World` has no mathematical value, but `149.95` does.

However, if you break a running VB application and ask the interpreter the value of a variant or undeclared variable, rather than the response of "0" characteristic of older versions of BASIC, Visual Basic 3 responds with a blank line. A variant that is not used by the running application has no identity. It takes on whatever form you choose to give it.

Memory Conservation

Why declare variables as having any specific type in the first place? One good reason is to allow for the conservation of memory. Furthermore, if you've ever tried to write a book using a huge word processor while testing programs with a high-level interpreter and also running background utilities all in the same environment, you most likely appreciate small, efficient programs.

One way to tighten the object code or threaded p-code of a program is to eliminate the "trailing zeros" from unnecessarily decimalized *integers*, or eliminate whole numbers with two or four bytes of decimal values all set to zero. Another way might be to determine which variables will always be described as whole numbers—for instance, the number of manhours in the earlier example—and declare those variables as integers rather than as floating-point (possibly fractional) variables.

> An *integer* is any whole number that has no fractional value.

Example

Following is the last group of assignment expressions, edited to specify their new variable type:

```
av_salary@ = 6.50
no_boxes& = 1300
no_days% = 5
```

For values you know will never be fractional—for instance, any variable that represents a number of units—consider using the % integer symbol. This symbol instructs VB to use two bytes for the variable rather than four, or optionally, the & long integer symbol, for anything you keep in stock that may number in the billions.

Summary

All computer programs manipulate values in memory. The result of this value manipulation is the production of data. In the Visual Basic language, values used within a program that are not subject to change are represented using numerals and are called constants. Values that are subject to change are represented using alphanumeric characters and are called variables.

In Visual Basic, once a variable is invoked within a program, a value is automatically assigned to it, even if that value is zero. When a variable is formally declared, its initial value is zero. A variable may be informally declared by using the variable within a formula. Such a formula assigns a specific value to a variable by direct assignment or calculation.

The primary program element used to assign a value to, or assess the value of, a variable is the expression. In an expression, a variable on the left side is compared to a variable or value on the right side. If one value is compared to another within an expression for equality, the equal sign is used between the two.

Review Questions

1. What values does VB return as the result of a logical comparison?

2. Under what category of instruction does the `Print` instruction to the immediate pane of the Debug window fall?

3. If one instruction sets the value of `y` to `12`, what type of instruction is required to set it to some other value?

4. How many binary digits (bits) are in a long integer variable?

5. Why can an unsigned byte hold a value between 0 and 255, but a signed byte can hold a value between –128 and 127? Why can't a signed byte hold a value between –256 and 255? Why is the positive maximum value odd?

Review Exercises

1. Write five instructions that set the variables `prime1`, `prime2`, and so on equal to the first five prime numbers.

2. Write expressions of assignment for arbitrarily named variables. Assign the following values to those variables. Use symbols for the variables that direct the interpreter to allocate the least number of bytes feasible for each value.

   A. 17.725

   B. 1 3/8

   C. –16

   D. 0.176470588235294

   E. $56.25

   F. 152,587,890,625

CHAPTER 6

Arithmetic Formulas

In this chapter, you experiment with equations and formulas that involve values and arithmetic functions. You learn how values are derived from elsewhere in the program and assigned to a variable with an expression of assignment. You also study the order in which BASIC evaluates simple arithmetic functions, and begin to incorporate more complex Visual Basic functions into formulas.

The Purpose of Formulas

Although Visual Basic uses procedural algebra to encode its own applications, it really doesn't use algebra to its full extent to evaluate mathematical expressions. Algebraic equations deal primarily with unknown values. As you learned in the preceding chapter, no variable in Visual Basic has an unknown value. Even if a variable was never declared and you ask the interpreter to print its value to a form, VB responds with a blank line, because it has never seen the variable.

If you've studied algebra, you know that each algebraic statement is an equation. Likewise, each statement of value assignment in Visual Basic is an equation. An *equation* is a statement of equality that assigns a value—either numeric or arithmetically derived—to a variable.

> An *equation* is a statement that assigns a value to a variable.

The elementary syntax of a Visual Basic equation is as follows:

```
variable = value1 [[operator1] [value2]...]
```

When you assign a value to a variable—through either direct specification (as in x = 1), or indirect reference by way of other variables (as in x = y + 1)—you use an equation. Here are some valid Visual Basic equations:

```
a = n + 1
lifeboats = crewmen / 15
Energy = mass * light_speed ^ 2
sphere_volume = (4/3) * 3.1415927 * r ^ 3
```

Notice that these equations always show a single variable on the left side and the arithmetic function on the right. Therefore it would be invalid to state n + 1 = x / 6 and expect the interpreter to solve for n. Although Visual Basic uses algebraic notation, it is not so figurative in its evaluation. The interpreter does not simplify algebraic terms the same way, for example, that the equation $6y^2 = 3y$ simplifies to $2y = 1$ and then to $y = 1/2$.

> **Note:** The solution to a Visual Basic equation is always a known value and is always assigned to a single variable on the left side of the equation.

An *operator* is a symbol (+, −, *, /) that represents a mathematical function.

In the previous sample equations, the variables and numbers are separated by arithmetic symbols. Some of these symbols you know, but some you may not recognize if you're a newcomer to BASIC. Arithmetic symbols are called *operators*, and their purpose is to represent simple arithmetic functions. A *binary operator* is a symbol that represents a mathematical function that combines, compares, or equates two values.

Table 6.1 lists operators used in Visual Basic expressions. The third column of this table lists solutions to the expression 2 *operator* 3, in which *operator* is replaced with the specific arithmetic operator in the first column.

Table 6.1. Arithmetic functional operators.

Operator	Function	2 operator 3
^	Exponentiation (raising to a power)	8
*	Multiplication	6
/	Division	.66666666
+	Addition	5
-	Subtraction	-1

The Order of Evaluation

In Table 6.1, the operators are listed in the order of their evaluation in a formula. When you type numbers and functions into a pocket calculator, the evaluation generally takes place as you press each button, so the order of evaluation—also called the operator *precedence*—is generally front-to-back.

Example

With Visual Basic, the entire expression is stated within an instruction before evaluation takes place. A Visual Basic expression is in many ways a restatement of an algebraic formula or equation. To better understand the order of evaluation in VB, examine the following equation, stated first in pure algebraic notation, then as an equivalent Visual Basic expression:

$$c = y^3 + \frac{5y^2}{4}$$

```
c = y ^ 3 + 5 * y ^ 2 / 4
```

In algebra, a variable raised to an exponent—such as y^3—is considered one term rather than a function relating y to 3. Thus, if the entire equation is solved rationally, "y to the third" is solved first. If the term is multiplied by a whole number, that number is the term's coefficient. In algebra, "5 y squared" is rarely stated as "5 times y squared," although it would be correct to do so. Multiplication of this nature is generally presumed in algebra to exist almost by default, so the function has taken on a virtual priority just below exponentiation.

In the preceding algebraic equation, "5 y squared over 4" is considered a fraction. Fractional values in Visual Basic are stated as functions of division, as in "5 times y raised to the power of 2 *divided by* 4." Nonetheless, a fractional term in algebra is one term, rather than two terms separated by a division symbol. Therefore, to maintain the algebraic hierarchy, division operations are performed at the same time as multiplication.

Addition and subtraction symbols separate terms in algebraic notation, so these functions are evaluated last. To understand why, examine the first part of the preceding Visual Basic equation: `c = y ^ 3 + 5 . . . .` The solution for this part of the equation should be the same if you state it as `c = 5 + y ^ 3 . . . .` If addition is performed first rather than exponentiation, 3 + 5 would be evaluated first. The solution for the first three VB terms would be the value, algebraically speaking, of y^8 rather than y^3—y to the eighth power (the `3 + 5` power) rather than y to the third.

In the second example (`c = 5 + y ^ 3 . . .`), if addition is evaluated first, the solution would reflect the value of $(5+y)^3$ rather than $5+y^3$. In other words, y and 5 would be added and then the result would be cubed, instead of the cube of y being added to 5. There would be a discrepancy of 120 in the final solution.

The Use of Parentheses

A *delimiter* separates elements of an expression.

To evaluate the value of 5 + y added and cubed, place parentheses around the part of the expression you want the interpreter to evaluate first: in this case, `(5 + y) ^ 3`. In such an expression, the parentheses act as delimiters for the interpreter. A *delimiter* is a punctuation mark used to distinguish or separate elements of an expression.

Example

Here's an example of a real-world formula in which parentheses are necessary. A formula for depreciation of the monetary value of an asset over a given period follows:

```
dep@ = ((init_value@ - prior_dep@) * factor%) / life%
```

Figure 6.1 shows a "parenthetical mountain" for this formula. At its summit is the smallest enclosure of terms within parentheses. Evaluation of this formula starts at the summit and works its way toward the foot of the mountain. Notice that the type designators (such as @ and %) are shown beside each variable, so that the formula consumes less memory.

Figure 6.1

A mountain of depreciation.

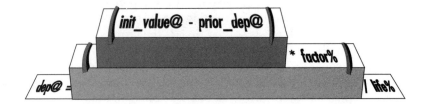

The first order of business for this formula is to subtract any depreciation of the asset `prior_dep@` from the initial value of that asset `init_value@`. The remainder is multiplied by the variable `factor%`, which represents the rate at which the balance is declining, before it is divided by the life span of the depreciation in equivalent periods `life%`. The solution is rendered to the depreciation variable `dep@`. Variable `dep@` is obviously a currency value, so the result is limited to four decimal places.

Here is an example session—a "conversation"—using the immediate pane of the Debug window. You can test this formula without devising an entire project for it. The last line represents the immediate response from the interpreter.

```
init_value@=2400
prior_dep@=500
factor%=2
life%=12
dep@=((init_value@-prior_dep@)*factor%)/life%
?dep@
 316.6667
```

Occasionally, you use the VB immediate pane to test formulas. BASIC formulas have been tested and proven this way for years. The spaces between terms, operators, and delimiters are left out in the preceding code. Visual Basic does not require these spaces, especially within the immediate pane.

The first four lines seed the variables for the formula in the fifth line. The statement `?dep@` is on the sixth line. Here, the `?` is an abbreviation for the `Print` statement. Since the 1970s, `?` has stood in place of `Print`, primarily because in conversations with the *command-line interpreter* (CLI), `?` is easier to type when you're in a hurry and you're "quizzing" the interpreter. From this point on, the immediate pane is referred to as the CLI.

The *CLI* (*command-line interpreter*) is available through the immediate pane of the Debug window.

In the first six lines of the conversation, the CLI does not type a response. Only after the quizzing statement does the CLI respond with `316.6667`. In the text of such conversations, the CLI adds a leading space to distinguish its responses from your statements.

Example

For the next example, you construct a working Visual Basic project that concerns coordinate geometry. Its objective is to enable you to figure the distance between two points with Cartesian (x, y) coordinates—such as (0, 0) or (16, 5)—on a plane. Figure 6.2 shows the form for the two-dimensional Cartesian calculator.

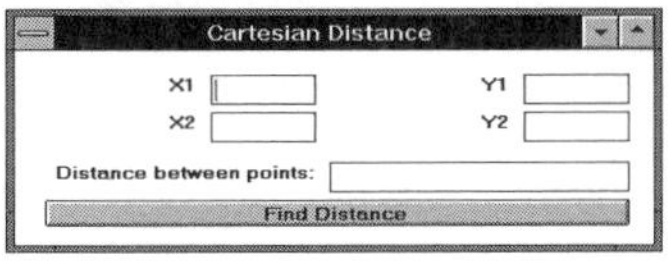

Figure 6.2

The Cartesian calculator.

To add controls and graphic objects to a form, click the symbol button for that object on the toolbox and move the pointer to the form area. Click and hold the index button, and drag the pointer from one corner of the control to the opposite corner. After you release the button, the object appears on the form. You can alter its shape or position by dragging any of the eight indicator nodes that surround it. You can change properties such as textual contents using the combo box in VB's main properties bar.

Using figure 6.2 and the following table as guides, draw five text boxes, five labels, and one command button on the form. Change the properties of each object as indicated in the following table. The following is the extended listing for the two-dimensional calculator:

Two-Dimensional Cartesian Coordinates Calculator

Project name: 2D_DIST.MAK
Constituent files: 2D_DIST.FRM

Object Type	Property	Setting
Form	.Width	5265
	.Height	2280
	.Caption	Cartesian Distance
Text box	.Name	Box_x1
	.Text	(blank)
	.TabStop	True
	.TabIndex	0
Text box	.Name	Box_y1
	.Text	(blank)
	.TabStop	True
	.TabIndex	1
Text box	.Name	Box_x2
	.Text	(blank)
	.TabStop	True
	.TabIndex	2
Text box	.Name	Box_y2
	.Text	(blank)
	.TabStop	True
	.TabIndex	3
Text box	.Name	Distance
	.TabStop	True
	.Text	(blank)
Label	.Caption	X1
	.Alignment	1 - Right Justify
Label	.Caption	Y1
	.Alignment	1 - Right Justify
Label	.Caption	X2
	.Alignment	1 - Right Justify

Object Type	Property	Setting
Label	.Caption	Y2
	.Alignment	1 - Right Justify
Label	.Caption	Distance between points:
	.Alignment	1 - Right Justify
Button	.Name	Go
	.Caption	Find Distance

To enter the following procedure, double-click the Go command button in the newly drawn form and type the following:

```
Sub Go_Click ()
    x1 = Val(Box_x1.Text)
    x2 = Val(Box_x2.Text)
    y1 = Val(Box_y1.Text)
    y2 = Val(Box_y2.Text)
    d# = Sqr(((x2 - x1) ^ 2) + ((y2 - y1) ^ 2))
    Distance.Text = Str$(d#)
End Sub
```

To help you understand what's going on, here is the preceding procedure written in pseudocode:

Procedure for clicking on the Go button:
Retrieve the four values from their respective
text boxes.

.

.

.

Calculate the zone of the given sphere using the
specified coordinates.
Place the result in the text box called Distance.
End of procedure.

Like the sphere zone calculator in Chapter 3, this program has only one formula to maintain and one procedure to execute. After you click the Find Distance button (with the control name Go), the alphanumeric contents of the four text boxes are converted to real numbers using the Visual Basic function Val(). Four variables are derived from this process and are referenced in the formula for variable d#. The formula solves for d#—a double-precision floating-point number. The solution is then converted back to text using the VB function Str$(). The string is placed in the text box named Distance.

When examining a formula with multiple sets of parentheses, in the previously shown `Go_Click` subroutine, try to imagine it in three dimensions, like a terraced platform seen from above. Visualize each parenthesis as a stairstep, with the left parenthesis leading up toward you and the right one leading down away from you. If you can visualize a complex formula in this way, the parts of the formula that solve first should telescope themselves toward you.

Look at the preceding Cartesian distance formula. The two expressions `(x2 - x1)` and `(y2-y1)` solve first because they appear to jut out furthest toward you. Geometrically speaking, these two expressions represent the difference between coordinates along one axis. So the difference between the x-coordinates and the difference between the y-coordinates are solved separately. The solutions to those two expressions are squared and then added to each other in the part of the equation that solves next. *Squaring* a value gives it form or dimension.

Along the final tier, the base platform of the equation, the sum of the two squares is then "rooted" once more back to a linear value, using the square-root function `Sqr()`. This value is the distance between two points along a Cartesian grid, which is assigned to the double-precision variable `d#`.

You can use the distance-finding formula for the coordinate systems of any two points appearing on a map. Compare the Visual Basic version of the formula to the algebraic version that appears here:

$$D = \sqrt{(x_2 - x_1)^2 + (y_2 - y_1)^2}$$

Summary

Values are assigned to variables in Visual Basic by way of equations. In equations that arithmetically combine values, simple arithmetic functions are represented by operators and complex functions are evaluated using intrinsic Visual Basic function terms. A Visual Basic equation is an expression of assignment, and therefore has only one term on the left side of the equation. This term is the variable that receives the solution value to the equation. The solution is always a known value.

The simple arithmetic functions in Visual Basic equations have a natural order of evaluation that is based on the way terms are evaluated in algebra. You can override this natural order through the use of parentheses as delimiters in an equation. These delimiters reestablish the precedence of the evaluation of terms; offsetting an expression in parentheses raises its precedence.

Review Questions

1. Predict the solution values to the following equations:

A. $x = 4 + 6 \wedge 2 / 5 * 6$

B. $x = (4 + 6) \wedge 2 / (5 * 6)$

C. $x = (4 + 6 \wedge 2) / 5 * 6$

2. Convert the following algebraic expressions to Visual Basic equations:

A. $v = \dfrac{1}{3} \pi r^2 h$ (where $\pi = 3.1415927$)

B. $P = \dfrac{F}{(1 + i)^n}$

Review Exercise

Using 2D_DIST.MAK as a framework, revise the project so that it displays the distance between coordinates in three-dimensional space. As a guide, here are the formulas for distances in two-dimensional and three-dimensional space:

$$D_2 = \sqrt{(x_2 - x_1)^2 + (y_2 - y_1)^2}$$

$$D_3 = \sqrt{(x_2 - x_1)^2 + (y_2 - y_1)^2 + (z_2 - z_1)^2}$$

CHAPTER 7

Logic and Number Systems

In this chapter, you dive directly into the heart of all computer operations. First, you explore the functions that result in True or False (–1 or 0) values. You see how logic constitutes every part of a computer's operation, both numerically and mechanically. Next, you construct expressions of comparison that have solutions which are True or False values. I then introduce Boolean logical operations, which separate "black" from "white," using truth tables.

Later, you gain further insight into how a computer counts, thus becoming reacquainted with the number systems of mathematics. You construct an application that uses the primary principles of number systems to convert any decimal number to a system of anything from base 2 to base 36.

Boolean Logic

The only thing a computer does is compare two binary digits and render the state of that comparison as another binary digit. This is the basis of all logic. As stated in Chapter 2, the logic of a computer can only interpret states—in other words, it evaluates the presence or absence of electrical current in its own integrated circuits. A binary state represents the presence or absence of current as the simplest digit within a computer—a bit. The term *bit* is short for *binary digit,* which is the elementary unit of value within a computer. The bit represents a logical state of True (1 or ON) or False (0 or OFF).

A current, electrically speaking, is a constant change or flux. The computer does not know this, however, because it looks only for the presence of this flux. This presence is treated as if it were a physical object in the machine.

Imagine the central processor of the computer as a converted upright pachinko machine, with slots for eight marbles positioned along a horizontal chute at the top of the machine. In this model, a lever is pulled which releases the marbles from the chute all at once. As they drop, they hit various pins, dampers, and levers, which flip up on one end as marbles strike them on the opposite end. The moved levers can cause other marbles to change course and fall in some other direction. When struck, some levers open gates through which other marbles can pass. Others open traps that cause marbles to become stuck. At the bottom of the machine is a series of collector slots that catch the marbles that have survived the obstacle course.

Suppose the operator of this machine loads marbles into the top eight slots at random. She may fill some slots and leave others blank as she wishes. In other words, she selects the pattern in which the marbles are loaded into the chute. After the marbles are released, she keeps track of which marbles are accumulated in the slots at the bottom. Assume the following conditions:

♦ The pachinko machine remains upright at all times.

♦ The machine is bolted to something firm.

♦ The marbles have identical mass, shape, and weight.

♦ The various levers and gates are all set to their starting positions.

♦ Gravity remains a constant.

It should follow that for each random marble-loading pattern, there should be one predictable falling pattern as a result. To restate, as long as you maintain identical conditions for the machine, each loading pattern must result in only one falling pattern.

A common byte is made up of eight bits.

Suppose the person at the pachinko machine attributes a specific number to each pattern. There is an easy way to do this: Each slot in the loading chute either contains a marble or it doesn't; the same is true of the accumulator at the bottom. Each slot can therefore be described by a binary digit—1 for presence and 0 for absence. The opening chute and closing slots can thus be described by eight-digit binary numbers—in other words, by bytes. In computing, a *byte* is the primary memory storage unit for all forms of data in a computer system, and is comprised of eight binary digits (bits).

Here's how each pattern is enumerated: You're familiar with the decimal system of numbers (also called base 10), in which digits from 0 through 9 each have their own place—or slot—in the number. The value of each place is described by increasing powers of 10 (10^0, 10^1, 10^2, 10^3, and so on). Thus, there is the *ones* place followed by the *tens* place, *hundreds* place, *thousands* place, and so on.

There are 10 digits in the decimal system, thus the alternate name *base 10*. In the binary number system—or base 2—there are two digits (0 and 1). Each place is described by increasing powers of 2 (2^0, 2^1, 2^2, 2^3, and so on). Thus there is the *ones* place, followed by the *twos* place, the *fours* place, the *eights* place, and so on by powers of two.

Figure 7.1 depicts a potential marble-loading pattern, represented as an eight-digit binary number. The powers of two for each place are listed beside each slot so that you can better comprehend the arithmetic behind the conversion of a binary number to a decimal number.

Figure 7.1

A potential marble-loading pattern represented as an eight-digit binary number.

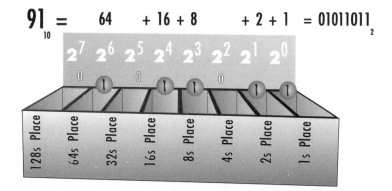

Suppose the person loading the marbles pays careful attention to the starting position of the devices—the pins, levers, gates, and traps—before loading marbles into the chute. She could give each setting pattern its own number as well. Conceivably, therefore, for each particular pattern of loaded marbles and for each particular pattern of device settings, there is one predictable fallout pattern of marbles in the bottom accumulator. Resetting the devices' loading positions by their pattern numbers would have a direct, perhaps measurable, effect on the outcome of the fallout pattern. The term for this type of device-resetting by pattern number is *programming*.

Basically, you have just witnessed what a computer and its programmer actually do—except that the marbles are really electric currents, the various devices are actually logic gates, and both the loading chute and the fallout accumulator can be described as memory. An instruction in machine language is literally a device-setting pattern. The sequence of these patterns is a program. If you consider patterns to be instructions and you give each pattern a number corresponding logically to the construction of that pattern, every logical arrangement of those patterns yields a predictable result. This is how a computer works.

Higher-Level Comparisons

In Visual Basic, the results you have in mind for your program are complex. The tools you use to achieve those results are complex as well. This complexity makes it possible for you to program with instructions like If-Then rather than 00101101. Still, the most fundamental tools of programming—logical comparisons between two states—are at your disposal in the Visual Basic language.

Visual Basic assumes True to be equal to –1 and False to be equal to 0.

Arithmetic operators are symbols used in expressions of comparison to derive logical results. Think of these operators as the high-level language version of pins, traps, gates, and levers. As you've learned, Visual Basic recognizes the values –1 and 0 to be True and False, respectively. An expression of comparison always results in a True or False value.

Table 7.1 shows the logical operators of comparison in Visual Basic. Beside each operator is the logical solution to the expression 6 *operator* 3.

Table 7.1. Comparison operators.

Operator	Function	6 operator 3
=	Equal to	0 (False)
>	Greater than	-1 (True)
<	Less than	0 (False)
>=	Greater than or equal to	-1 (True)
<=	Less than or equal to	0 (False)
<>	Not equal to	-1 (True)

The order of the symbols in both <= and >= can be swapped as you enter them, although the interpreter immediately rearranges their order to one of the styles shown in table 7.1.

Example

 For the first example of comparison operators in action, let's go to the VB command-line interpreter (CLI) in the Debug window. The following example conversation evaluates the logic of b = 4. After the value of 4 is assigned, variable b takes on the form of a single-precision floating-point variable, even though the value itself is a whole number. The response from the CLI in the immediate pane is shown in boldfaced type:

```
b=4
?b=4
-1
```

It might seem odd at first to use the equality operator = in an expression that is not an equation, but you'll soon get used to it. After b was set to 4, I quizzed the CLI whether b = 4. The CLI's response was -1, which means that it is True.

Suppose we quiz the CLI whether b < 3. Here is its response:

```
?b<3
0
```

Zero is the response for *False* or *no*.

Understand that –1 and 0 are not just the CLI's way of saying yes and no. They are, in fact, the evaluated values of the expression, and they are real numbers. Thus the following dialog results:

```
?(b=4)-1
 -2
```

Now, -2 is not a symbol for more True than True. By subtracting 1 from –1—the value of (b = 4)—you've made the expression part logical and part arithmetic. The parentheses in this expression are important. Look at what would happen if you removed them:

```
?b=4-1
0
```

The CLI evaluated 4 - 1 first, derived 3, and compared b to 3 rather than to 4. The traps were set in the wrong order.

While we're on the subject of order of evaluation, can truth be evaluated for the presence of truth? The following dialog proves that it can be done. Remember that b = 4.

```
?b=4=-1
 -1
```

Yes, there can be two equality operators within a single expression, as long as you realize it's not an equation. The value of b = 4, which you already know to be –1, was compared to –1 for equality. Naturally, the result was nothing but the truth: -1. Suppose you change the order of evaluation, however, by placing the latter comparison in parentheses, as in the following:

```
?b=(4=-1)
0
```

The first thing the CLI did this time was compare 4 to -1 for equality. The result was 0, which was compared to the value of b (4) for equality, and that too was False.

The preceding comparison of 4 to -1 is not something you'd ever want to write during the course of a real program. However, it does prove the point about the importance of ordinance in a compound logical comparison. If you ever used the expression b = (c = d) in a program, and c = 4 and d = -1, the result of that expression would still be 0. I simplified this expression by using real numbers so that you can understand the role of the operators in the instruction.

Using Logic

In Visual Basic, you use comparison expressions most frequently within the If-Then comparison clause statement. Here, an expression is evaluated for truth. A set of instructions following the term Then will be executed if the result of the expression is logically True. Alternatively, another set of instructions that may follow the term Else can be executed if the result of the expression is logically False.

Example

You study the construction of conditional clauses in greater detail in Chapter 12, "Conditional Clauses." For now, concentrate on the logical part of the If-Then statement. Assuming b is still equal to 4, give a conditional instruction to the CLI, as in the following:

```
if b=4 then ?"Hello There."
Hello There.
```

The bottom line is the CLI's response to the instruction on the top line. First, the interpreter evaluates the expression b = 4 for truth. As you've already learned, the value of that expression at present is -1. The interpreter will execute the instruction following the term then if the result of the expression is -1. This is proven by the following test instruction fed to the CLI:

```
if b=3 then ?"Probably won't see this line again."
```

The prediction is correct because, as you can see, the CLI did not make any visible response to this instruction.

Boolean Operators

A Boolean operator compares one binary value to another.

The second category of logical operators in Visual Basic is *Boolean operators*. These are terms used to compare one binary value to another, and to derive a single binary value as a result.

The purpose of Boolean operators is to evaluate expressions comparing two values that are already binary in nature. For instance, -1 AND -1 = -1, whereas -1 AND 0 = 0. Here, AND is the Boolean operator. The result of the expression x AND y will be True if, and only if, x is True and y is True—otherwise the result is logically False.

Note: VB3 recognizes the following terms to represent −1 and 0:

−1	0
True	False
On	Off
Yes	No

Example

As an example, here is yet another dialog with the command-line interpreter:

```
x=3
y=5
?x=3 AND y=5
-1
```

First, variables x and y were seeded with the nonbinary values 3 and 5, respectively. On the third line is the compound logical comparison. Here, the values of x = 3 and y = 5 are obtained first. They are both -1, which satisfies the conditions for the AND comparison to equal -1, as printed on the fourth line by the CLI. In the preceding quizzing statement, it is important to leave spaces around the Boolean operator so that the interpreter won't confuse it with just another variable.

Example

Assuming you leave x and y as they are, you can apply the preceding compound logical expression in a conditional execution clause:

```
If x = 3 AND y = 5 Then
      Form1.Print "It's True"
Else
      Form1.Print "It's False"
End If
```

The logical expression is evaluated, and its result triggers the execution of one or the other set of instructions in the If-Then clause. If-Then really does not evaluate the expression. In truth, all it is looking for is a –1 or a 0. One way or the other, a logical expression simplifies to one of those two possible values.

By introducing the Boolean operator OR, you now can have a logical expression that has a True result (–1) if one or the other value is True.

Example

As usual, the best way to test a function is through a dialog with the CLI:

```
x=4
y=10
?x=4 OR y=9
-1
```

Obviously, the result can be True if one of the compared values is True. As a quick test, see if it works when both comparisons are True:

```
?x=4 OR y=10
-1
```

The result is still True. The only way you can get a False value is if both comparisons are False:

```
?x=3 OR y=9
0
```

Example

A related Boolean operator XOR (exclusive-or) returns a True value if one or the other comparison evaluates True, but not both. In other words, the compared values can't match. Let's leave x = 4 and y = 10 for a moment and retry a few of the preceding evaluations, using XOR rather than OR.

```
?x=4 XOR y=9
-1
?x=4 XOR y=10
0
?x=3 XOR y=9
0
```

Notice that when both comparisons evaluated True, the result of the XOR comparison was False. An exclusive-or comparison really does specify that only one or the other is True.

Example

Combining the ANDs and ORs and taking advantage of what you know about the usefulness of parentheses, let's examine a complex logical comparison, first using the CLI:

```
x=6
y=7
z=9
?(x=6 AND y=3) OR z=9
-1
?(x=6 OR y=3) AND z=9
-1
?(x=6 AND y=3) OR z=10
0
```

The values within parentheses, as always, are evaluated first. The result of that comparison is itself compared using another Boolean operator to the expression outside the parentheses. When you integrate one of these compound comparison expressions into the source code sample that you created a few pages back, you get the following:

```
If (x = 6 AND y = 3) OR z = 9 Then
      Form1.Print "It's true"
Else
      Form1.Print "It's false"
End If
```

If the two compared values of a Boolean expression are not binary, the Boolean operators will compare the bitwise values of each bit of both values in their respective places and render their results in the same place of the solution variable. In other words, the binary value of the third binary place in one variable (representing 23) will be compared to the value in the third binary place in a second variable. The binary result is rendered in the third binary place of the solution to the expression.

Number Systems

The binary system, as the Greek origin of the term indicates, deals with twos, or instances in which there may never be more than two possible values. Our common system of counting is called *decimal* because *deci-* is a Greek prefix meaning *ten*. Some people have a tendency to call fractional values *decimal numbers*, perhaps because such numbers force us to use the decimal point to divide the whole-number side of the number from the fractional side.

The number 1495 is a decimal number because we trust it to be written in base 10, and because nothing tells us otherwise. Unfortunately, as you become a programmer, you start to lose some of that trust, replacing it with a sort of natural, rational skepticism. When you regulate your skepticism, however, you'll be better able to detect how something works just from observation and logical deduction.

The Logic behind the Computer

To understand how computers count is to understand the inspiration behind their invention. Modern computing began to take shape in 1854, when British mathematician George Boole wrote a treatise called *Investigation of the Laws of Thought*. In this work, Boole attempted to equate the sciences of mathematics and psychology by theorizing that strictly binary logical processes may be the primary constituents of all reasoning in the human mind. Boole believed that absolutely all thought could be catabolized (broken down) into comparisons of one binary state to another. Boolean logic is named for him.

Charles Babbage gets credit for inventing the mechanism of the computer; however, the concept was actually brought forth in large part by a Hungarian physicist named John von Neumann. In the late 1930s, von Neumann studied Boole's works thoroughly and, employing natural skepticism, bent Boole's logic so that it applied not to mental processes, but to physical processes—as in quantum physics and mechanics. Along the way, von Neumann discovered that sequences of electrical currents—discussed earlier in this chapter—can replace mechanical devices such as wheels and levers in a calculation mechanism. The first stored-program computers, for precisely that reason, were called *von Neumann machines*.

Binary and Decimal Systems

One of the things we rely on in the everyday world is the ability to count and to know what a number means when we see it. When we write *1495*, the number is expected to mean one thousand four hundred and ninety-five. If this number is written in base 16, however, that isn't what this number means. The 9 is no longer in the tens place, but is instead in the sixteens place.

Computers have a difficult time with decimal, or base 10, numbers. This is because computers are naturally binary and have an easier time dealing with anything that is a factor or multiple of 2 and only 2. Computers have an easier time with base 16, or hexadecimal, numbers because 16 factors out to $2 \times 2 \times 2 \times 2$. A computer can easily interpret anything you can describe as a power of 2. The number 10 factors out to 5×2 and stops there, because 5 is a prime number. Computers understand only two states—0 and 1—so 5 is as much of a mystery to a computer as a 10-dimensional universe would be to us.

The number 5 is best represented within a computer as a combination of three binary states—three being the number of binary digits, or bits, required to represent 5.

When written in base 2 or binary, 5 appears as 101. In other words, there's a 1 in the fours place and a 1 in the ones place. What determines the place in any number system is the base of that number system, raised to the number of the place counting from the right toward the left, starting with the zeros place. Table 7.2 demonstrates this principle using the number 1495 (base 10).

Table 7.2. Converting a base 10 number to a base 2 number.

1495	=	1495	\	1024	=	1
− 512	=	471	\	512	=	0
	=	471	\	256	=	1
− 256	=	215	\	128	=	1
− 128	=	87	\	64	=	1
− 64	=	23	\	32	=	0
		23	\	16	=	1
− 16	=	7	\	8	=	0
		7	\	4	=	1
− 4	=	3	\	2	=	1
− 2	=	−1	\	−1	=	1

In any number system, there are as many digits as stated in the base of that system, ranging from 0 to the base minus one. In the decimal system, there are 10 digits ranging from 0 through 9. In octal (base 8), there are eight digits ranging from 0 through 7. In hexadecimal (base 16), however, there are more digits than there are numerals available. Thus the digits for 10 through 15 are represented by the capital letters A through F. Where no digit (0-9) can represent the value within a place, capital letters are used.

Base Conversion Procedure

To put what you know about number systems into action, here is a procedure that takes any base 10 number and converts it to any specified number base from 2 to 36. The number 36 was chosen because it is equal to the number of digits (10) plus the number of letters in the alphabet (26).

```
Function Convert$ (convValue, convBase)
Find_Top:
comp = convBase ^ expn
If comp < convValue Then
    expn = expn + 1
    Goto Find_Top
End If
For spot = expn To 0 Step -1
    digit% = convValue \ (convBase ^ spot)
    convValue = convValue Mod (convBase ^ spot)
    If digit% < 10 Then
        cvt$ = cvt$ + Right$(Str$(digit%), 1)
    Else
        cvt$ = cvt$ + Chr$(65 + (digit% - 10))
    End If
Next spot
If Left$(cvt$, 1) = "0" AND Len(cvt$) > 1 Then
    cvt$ = Right$(cvt$, Len(cvt$) - 1)
End If
Convert$ = cvt$
End Function
```

This is a Function procedure that accepts two values: the base 10 value being converted (convValue) and the base to which it's being converted (convBase). The converted number will be expressed as Convert$, an alphanumeric string, because it may contain "digits" such as A and F.

An *implied loop* starts at the point marked Find_Top. The purpose of this loop is to determine the number of digit places in the number convValue after it is converted to the base specified in convBase. The point of this loop is to keep adding power exponentially to the variable comp until its value becomes greater than that of the number you're converting (convValue). Each time you add power to comp, you increment (add 1 to) variable expn; so expn is counting the number of places in the converted number that will be Convert$. When comp becomes greater than convValue, you know you've gone too far and have counted enough places. You now know there are as many digits in Convert$ as have been counted by expn.

The loop that follows is a conventional For-Next loop, in which you start with the leftmost place in Convert$ and work backward (Step -1) to the right toward the ones place. The countdown is kept within the variable spot. When spot = 0, the loop is complete and the number is nearly converted. You're figuring the value of Convert$ one digit at a time, starting from the left. For the first iteration of the loop, the leftmost digit is equal to the number of times the value being converted (convValue) goes evenly into the place value being considered (convBase ^ spot). That number of times is the first digit% of Convert$.

Having converted one digit, *shave* the amount of the converted digit from convValue using *modulo arithmetic*—in other words, take the remainder from the division equation convValue \ (convBase ^ spot) and put it back into convValue. This remainder is evaluated during the next iteration of the loop. Until then, the converted digit% is made into an alphanumeric character using the function Str$(), and the leading space Visual Basic attaches to positive values is trimmed from it using the function Right$(). Both functions are covered in detail later.

As an example, assume convValue is the base 10 number 1495 from the previous table and convBase is 2—meaning that you're converting to base 2. The initial Find_Top loop will determine that the base 2 form of 1495_{10} is an 11-digit number; so at the end of that loop, the value of expn is set to 10, the power that 2 is raised to at the 11th digit. The spot loop counts down from 10 to 0. During the first iteration, spot = 10. The value of 2^{10} is 1024, and that goes into 1495 once. This makes 1 the first digit in Convert$. The remainder—471, which is equal to 1495 - 1024—is derived using the Mod modulo arithmetic function, which returns the remainder of a division—in this case, of 1495 \ 1024. The value 471 becomes the convValue for the next iteration of the loop. After the final iteration, Convert$ = 10111010111.

> **Note:** In Visual Basic, hexadecimal (base 16) values, when written into source code or displayed on-screen, are preceded by the symbol &H. Thus &HFF is equal to 255.

Summary

Logic is the basis of all computing operations. In Visual Basic, logical operations are comparisons between two binary states, the result of which is rendered as a binary state. Logical operations can be compounded with further operators and the inclusion of parentheses; however, the result of the expression of logical comparison is still a binary state.

The native number system of a computer is binary (base 2). Often certain variables used by the system are expressed as hexadecimal (base 16) because its numbers are shorter, and 16 is a multiple of 2, making conversion between the two bases easy. By comparison, conversion between binary and decimal (base 10) numbers is difficult for the computer. A representation of the digit-by-digit conversion procedure was the example program for this chapter.

Review Questions

Given x = 5, y = 9, and z = -1, assess the binary truth value of the following:

1. (x = 5)

2. (x < y)

3. ((x + z) >= y)

4. (x = 5) AND (x < y)

5. ((x < 5) AND (z < x)) OR (y = 9)

6. (x < 5) AND ((z < x) OR (y = 9))

7. ((x <= 5) AND (y = 3 ^ 3)) XOR z

Respond to the following questions using table 7.3 and the Function procedure presented in this chapter.

8. The fifth digit from the left of Convert$ represents 2 raised to what power?

9. When (convBase ^ spot) does not divide into convValue, what is the value of the digit% at the current spot?

10. If convValue is integral, will there ever be a case in which Convert$ is a fractional number?

CHAPTER 8

Alphanumeric Strings

In this chapter, you learn about string variables, which are containers for groupings of alphanumeric characters—letters, words, or entire sentences. You witness how alphanumeric contents of graphic controls are assigned to strings, using what appear to be arithmetic expressions. You then study how patterns of binary numbers form the patterns that comprise alphanumerics.

Next, you see how to use expressions to manipulate the contents of string variables by using the + arithmetic operator, as well as intrinsic Visual Basic functions. Finally, you see how properties of graphic objects in Visual Basic forms are treated as string variables.

String Values

Up to this point, this book has discussed the manipulation of data in memory as values—numbers you can use in calculations or substitute for variables in formulas. A value is one way Visual Basic translates data. As you've seen, a byte of data is, at its lowest level, just a sequence of ones and zeros. In essence, a numeric value as we think of it, such as the number 10, is a higher interpretation of data, in the way that 81 is a higher interpretation of 01010001.

A string is a sequence of alphanumeric characters.

The other common way to interpret data is as text. Text in Visual Basic is assigned to string variables. A *string* is a sequence of any number of bytes interpreted jointly as text, or alphanumeric characters.

A sequence of characters is assigned to a string variable with an expression of assignment, as in the following example:

```
a$ = "Q"
```

This statement creates the variable and assigns it the contents Q (assuming the variable a$ wasn't declared beforehand). A simple expression of assignment for a string variable is stated as an equation, using the following syntax:

```
variable$ = "alphanumerics"
```

With Visual Basic 3, the $ is no longer required in an informal declaration of a string variable.

The dollar sign ($) distinguishes string variables in the way that the percentage sign (%) distinguishes integer variables. With Visual Basic 3, the $ is no longer required in an informal declaration of a string variable; thus the following instruction would now be acceptable to the VB3 interpreter:

```
a = "X"
```

The official variable type the interpreter gives a in the preceding instance is Variant, as is the case with all informal declarations where no type distinction symbol is used. In the instruction a$ = "X", however, the official type given to variable a$ is String. In either case, the same number of bytes represents the string in memory—for just X, one byte plus those bytes that identify a$ for the interpreter.

So why use special punctuation if the interpreter ignores it anyway? Assume that the following instructions appear in your VB application:

```
city = "New York"
state = "NY"
zip = 10019
location = city + state + zip
```

The first two instructions are obviously string assignments. If the quotation marks in the second instruction are omitted from "NY", the interpreter attempts to assign the contents of a variable NY to the variant variable state. If NY hasn't been declared yet—and chances are, it hasn't—this instruction makes it exist and gives it a value of 0. After 0 is assigned to state, state also equals 0. As you know, 0 is not a state.

In the preceding code, the third instruction assigns the value 10,019 (ten thousand and nineteen) to variant variable zip. This is acceptable for now, except that later the interpreter expects 10,019 to be suited for a mathematical formula, not a ZIP code. So, when the fourth instruction is processed, the interpreter first sees city as a string, and assumes location also will be a string. Variable state is also a string. Variable zip, however, is a floating-point number—despite the fact that ZIP codes have no fractional value. When the fourth instruction is processed, a "Type mismatch error" is generated and the program stops. The following instructions, with all necessary punctuation included, generate no errors.

```
city$ = "New York"
state$ = "NY"
zip$ = "10019"
location$ = city$ + state$ + zip$
```

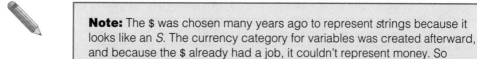

Note: The $ was chosen many years ago to represent *strings* because it looks like an *S*. The currency category for variables was created afterward, and because the $ already had a job, it couldn't represent money. So Microsoft chose the @ character to distinguish currency variables.

As you've seen, quotation marks enclose characters being assigned to string variables. These quotation marks do not become part of the string; this book uses the marks here as delimiters to mark where the string begins and ends. Note that if you want to place a quotation mark within your text, you must use the CHR() function call. The following are valid string variable assignments:

```
x$ = "Valid."
nick_name$ = "Robert " + chr(32) + "Bob" + chr(32) + " Sled"
alert$ = "RED"
full_name$ = "Hubert H. Humphrey"
sale_price$ = "359.95"
```

With this syntax, any character can be assigned as part of a string variable, except a quotation mark, which is reserved for marking the beginning and end of the string. The contents of sale_price$ appear to be numeric. Like the three examples preceding it, however, the contents are actually text. In other words, sale_price$ is six bytes long, beginning with the character representation for 3, followed by that for 5, and so on.

ANSI, ASCII, and Other Acronyms

In this book, *character representation* refers to the pattern of bits in a byte that stands for an alphanumeric character. The decision of which pattern belongs to which character is not exactly arbitrary. If this decision were left to the individual manufacturers, users would be left with dozens of incompatible codes. Imagine what would happen if Microsoft's *B* were Borland's *&*.

Some time ago, the American National Standards Institute (ANSI) devised a coding scheme for the most-used characters in computers and Teletype machines. A subset of that code exists today as the American Standard Code for Information Interchange (ASCII, often pronounced *as'-key*). The ASCII code is the most widely used method for transmitting and storing alphanumeric data in a bitwise form within or between computers.

In the ASCII code, the letter B is represented by the binary form of decimal value 80. Table 8.1 shows the word *QUANTUM* as it appears in its binary form.

Table 8.1. The mechanics of the word *QUANTUM*.

Alphanumeric Character	ANSI	Binary
Q	81	01010001
U	85	01010101
A	65	01000001
N	78	01001110
T	84	01010100
U	85	01010101
M	77	01001101

Because you're not storing a number, no consideration is made for place or value.

Notice that ASCII values have a constant number of symbols—eight. Additionally, ASCII provides for upper- and lowercase letters. Therefore, the numbers in the preceding table allude only to the uppercase version of those letters. Their lowercase equivalents would have different numbers.

A listing of the ANSI character codes used and adapted by Microsoft for use with Windows and Visual Basic is in Appendix A.

Example

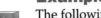

The following is a sample dialog with Visual Basic's CLI in the immediate pane:

```
quantum$="Niels Bohr"
?quantum$
Niels Bohr
```

Notice that the syntax of the ? (Print) statement doesn't really change when the reference is to a string rather than a numeric variable. The expression of assignment (also known as the Let statement) is one of few where string variables and numeric variables are interchangeable. The CLI's response to the ? on the bottom line is precisely the contents between the quotation marks in the assignment equation.

Example

Strings can also be used in place of values in equations that appear to involve addition, as shown in the following dialog:

```
first_name$="Niels"
last_name$="Bohr"
full_name$=first_name$+" "+last_name$
```

```
?full_name$
Niels Bohr
```

Concatenation is the process of joining strings together.

The third line of the preceding dialog is a formula that consists of three elements—two string variables and an explicit string consisting of one space to separate the first name from the last name. The + operator here is used for *concatenation*—joining strings together. For example, in the third line of the preceding example, `full_name$=first_name$+" "+last_name$`, the value placed in `full_name$` would be `"Niels Bohr"`. This is the only operator symbol allowed in string variable formulas. The minus sign doesn't work here because it wouldn't be reasonable to try to "subtract" the contents `Bohr` from `Niels`.

Example

The most common practical use of string variables is as containers for people's names and vital information. This test involves the skeleton of a record-entry system. A Visual Basic form acts as the receiver for the individual elements of each person's vital information.

A record-keeping system might need to sort each record by the person's last name; when you print these names to envelopes, however, the first name should come before the last name. A system that maintains such a database, by the formal definition, needs to be able to resituate data, such as the parts of a person's name, in a list or reference.

Figure 8.1 is a picture of `NameForm`, the form for the skeletal record-keeping system. For now, examine one particular procedure from this form, which is shown in figure 8.1.

Use figure 8.1 and the following table to construct the `NameForm` form. Be sure to adjust the properties of objects as needed.

Figure 8.1

The rudimentary *NameForm* form.

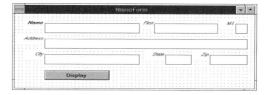

> **Note:** The `.FontSize` property sets the size of the letters that are typed into the graphic objects. Microsoft Windows uses "points" to determine the size of type styles. Because this system is not always exact, however, the font sizes displayed here might not match what is currently available from your installed font lists. Fonts rarely, if ever, change the functionality of your VB application. Choose the nearest font size and style that you can.

The attributes specified in the following table will build the window shown in figure 8.1.

Name-Only Record-Entry System

> **Project Name: NAMEFORM.MAK**
> **Constituent Files: NAMEFORM.FRM**

Object Type	Property	Setting
Form	.Left	960
	.Top	1155
	.Width	7800
	.Height	3255
	.Name	NameForm
	.Caption	NameForm
Text box	.Left	960
	.Top	360
	.Width	3015
	.Height	375
	.Name	LastName
	.Text	(blank)
	.FontSize	9.6
Text box	.Left	4440
	.Top	360
	.Width	2055
	.Height	375
	.Name	FirstName
	.Text	(blank)
	.FontSize	9.6
Text box	.Left	7080
	.Top	360
	.Width	375
	.Height	375
	.Name	MidInit
	.Text	(blank)
	.FontSize	9.6

Object Type	Property	Setting
Text box	.Left	960
	.Top	960
	.Width	6495
	.Height	375
	.Name	Address
	.Text	(blank)
	.FontSize	9.6
Text box	.Left	960
	.Top	1560
	.Width	3015
	.Height	375
	.Name	City
	.Text	(blank)
	.FontSize	9.6
Text box	.Left	4800
	.Top	1560
	.Width	855
	.Height	375
	.Name	State
	.Text	(blank)
	.FontSize	9.6
Text box	.Left	6240
	.Top	1560
	.Width	1215
	.Height	375
	.Name	Zip
	.Text	(blank)
	.FontSize	9.6
Label	.Left	360
	.Top	240
	.Width	615
	.Height	255
	.Caption	Name
	.FontItalic	True
	.FontBold	True
	.Alignment	0 - Right Justify

continues

Name-Only Record-Entry System Continued

Object Type	Property	Setting
Label	.Left	3960
	.Top	240
	.Width	495
	.Height	255
	.Caption	First
	.FontItalic	True
	.FontBold	False
	.Alignment	0 - Right Justify
Label	.Left	6600
	.Top	240
	.Width	495
	.Height	255
	.Caption	M.I.
	.FontItalic	True
	.FontBold	False
	.Alignment	0 - Right Justify
Label	.Left	120
	.Top	840
	.Width	855
	.Height	255
	.Caption	Address
	.FontItalic	True
	.FontBold	False
	.Alignment	0 - Right Justify
Label	.Left	360
	.Top	1440
	.Width	615
	.Height	255
	.Caption	City
	.FontItalic	True
	.FontBold	False
	.Alignment	0 - Right Justify
Label	.Left	4200
	.Top	1440
	.Width	615
	.Height	255
	.Caption	State
	.FontItalic	True
	.FontBold	False

Object Type	Property	Setting
	.Alignment	0 - Right Justify
Label	.Left	5760
	.Top	1440
	.Width	495
	.Height	255
	.Caption	Zip
	.FontItalic	True
	.FontBold	False
	.Alignment	0 - Right Justify
Button	.Left	960
	.Top	2160
	.Width	2055
	.Height	375
	.Name	Display
	.Caption	Display

After you enter the preceding graphic objects into the NameForm form, double-click the Display command button and type the following:

```
Sub Display_Click ()
  FullName$ = FirstName.Text + " " + MidInit.Text + " " +
  ➡LastName.Text
  StreetAddress$ = Address.Text
  Residence$ = City.Text + ", " + State.Text + "  " +
  ➡Zip.Text
  Next_Line$ = Chr$(13) + Chr$(10)
  Envelope$ = FullName$ + Next_Line$ + StreetAddress$ +
  ➡Next_Line$ + Residence$
  MsgBox Envelope$
End Sub
```

Now here is the preceding procedure rephrased as pseudocode:

*Procedure for clicking on the **Display** button:*
The person's full name is the equivalent of his first
name and a space, plus his middle initial and a
space, plus his last name.
*Take his street address out of the **Address** box.*
The location where the person lives is phrased as the
city plus a comma and space, plus the state and
two spaces, plus the ZIP code.

*The code for "next line please" is a carriage return
character plus a line-feed character.
The name that appears on the envelope is the
equivalent of the full name, next line please, his
street address, next line please, plus the place
where he lives.
Put this data in a message box.
End of procedure.*

The property .Text is applied to each text box in the form. Therefore, when you refer to the contents of a text box, the name of the box is stated first, followed by a period and the word Text. Think of this reference as pulling the text that the user typed from the form without placing it in a variable. Although it is considered a reference to an element of text in formulas, object properties such as FirstName.Text are not considered string variables. Thus, for many statements, the .Text property of an object will not suffice when an explicit string variable is required.

In the first line following the Sub statement, the string variable FullName$ is created, which contains the three parts of a person's name—assuming that all people have middle initials. These parts are added using the + concatenation operator. Notice, however, that " " spaces separate the elements. There is one space between the quotation marks so that the words in the string are set apart. Concatenated strings do not space themselves, and for good reason: Suppose that you had part1$ = "Washi" and part2$ = "ngton" in the course of a procedure. If you joined the two with +, you would not want an automatic space between them. So when you need a space, you must insert it yourself.

In Sub Display_Click (), the variable Residence$ is created on the fourth line. Notice that both a comma and a space separate the city from the state. As a result, you don't have to make a comma part of every City *datum* (unit of data) to make the address appear properly in print.

On the fifth line, Next_Line$ is created purely as a signal string to tell the interpreter to invoke the carriage return (with Chr$(13)) and to feed one line down (with Chr$(10)). The term Chr$() is an intrinsic Visual Basic function that returns the specific ANSI-code character with the number that falls between the parentheses. For example, Chr$(81) returns the letter *Q* and Chr$(51) returns the digit *3*. Chr$() follows the standard intrinsic function syntax *function(expression)*.

Control characters are handled in memory like regular letters and numbers, although their purpose is to send some signal to the computer, such as to delete the previous character or end the current line. Control characters are part of both the ANSI and ASCII codes, although Microsoft Windows doesn't use all these characters in either set, so the code is not true ASCII. Visual Basic supports the carriage-return (13) and line-feed (10) characters for some text display areas, although not all.

> **Note:** Carriage returns and line feeds work only in dialog boxes such as message boxes and Visual Basic picture boxes, which are objects capable of displaying both graphics and text. By default, carriage returns and line feeds do not work in text boxes; instead, they generate little, black blocks that return neither carriage returns nor line feeds. To eliminate this problem in text boxes, set the boxes' `.MultiLine` property to `True`.

In `Sub Display_Click ()`, the next-to-last line `MsgBox Envelope$` invokes a message box that displays the contents of `Envelope$`. A *message box* is a small window that contains just a message, often with an accompanying symbol such as a big exclamation point or question mark, and one OK button. In the procedure, `Envelope$` was created in the line above the `MsgBox` line by joining all three lines of the person's formal address and separating those lines with `Next_Line$`—the special string that forces the carriage return with the line feed.

The results of this first effort at concatenation are shown in figures 8.2 and 8.3. Figure 8.2 depicts the fully filled form, whereas figure 8.3 shows the contents of this form reorganized as they would appear printed on an envelope. This application is not extremely functional yet; later, however, you add functionality to it.

Figure 8.2
NameForm before processing.

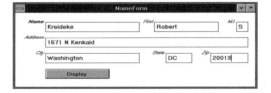

Figure 8.3
NameForm after processing.

Summary

A *string* is a group of alphanumeric characters that is considered as text instead of as a value. Characters in the computer are patterns that have code, called ANSI or ASCII code. This code consists of logically derived bitwise patterns for the most necessary 256 characters in standard communication between computers. Each character in this code is stored in one byte.

A string variable is an arbitrarily named term used to represent text groupings in an expression. The contents of such a variable are set with an equation, in which the contents to be assigned to the variable are enclosed in quotation marks. String variables are identified in source code by the symbol $, which in Visual Basic is not used to represent currency. Strings can be joined in an expression with the + concatenation operator. Textual properties from user input forms can be assigned to string variables. Names chosen for string variables must not conflict with names chosen for any other string or numeric variables in the same context of the source code.

Review Questions

Figure 8.4 shows the form from the NameForm procedure earlier in this chapter, filled with vital information for a fictitious person. Using as a guide the property table and the procedure Sub Display_Click (), which appears earlier in this chapter, determine the contents of the following:

1. LastName.Text

2. Zip.Text

3. FirstName.Text + LastName.Text

4. StreetAddress$

5. Residence$

6. Envelope$

7. FullName$ + Next_Line$ + Next_Line$ + Residence$

8. "Mr. or Ms. " + FullName$

Figure 8.4

NameForm filled with fictitious information.

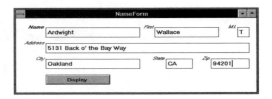

Review Exercise

Using the NameForm example program as a guide, modify the line that prints the person's name so that the last name prints first and is separated from the first name by a comma.

CHAPTER 9

Array Variables

In this chapter, you see how Visual Basic processes lists of items in the form of arrays. First you experiment with generating simple item-by-item lists. You then progress to processing values that reside in two-dimensional tables.

The Purpose of Arrays

An *array* is a list of related values that are referred to by a common variable name.

In almost every Visual Basic application you write, you compose a formula or procedure that processes a list of values that have the same purpose or fulfill the same role individually in a formula. For instance, you may have a formula that returns a value for *a1*, and then at some other time for *a2* and *a3*. Or you may be composing a record-keeping routine that tells the interpreter how and where to print the last name, the first name, and the middle initial—and there will certainly be more than one name on this list. The primary tool you use for referring to lists of values that are somehow related is the *array variable.*

As an example, one array variable may contain the names of the 50 United States in alphabetical order. You could then have us$(1) = "Alabama", us$(2) = "Alaska", us$(3) = "Arizona", and so on until us$(50) = "Wyoming". Another procedure in the program might be used to figure the state sales tax on an item on an invoice for a company that does business in all 50 states. Instead of having 50 forms, you can program one form that contains "holes" for any state's sales tax. The print line might appear as follows:

```
Form7.Print us$(state); " State sales tax:",tax_pcnt(state)
```

In effect, what you're telling the interpreter to do is this:

*Print to **Form7** the name of the state having its number
currently kept by the variable **state**, followed
immediately by the words **State sales tax:**,
followed thereafter by a tab, then that state's
sales tax value.*

A *subscript* is the position within an array that holds a particular value.

Suppose you want to put the tax percentage for Maine on this line. Maine, on the alphabetical list, is the 19th state; so, at some point in the program the value of the variable state would be set to 19. The value 19 becomes important because it now stands for Maine in any array variable within this program that pertains to the states. It is as if 19 were equal to Maine. Of course, it can't be in the logical sense, although it can in the symbolic sense. The number 19 is now representative of Maine. Representation in this manner is part of the role of an array variable's *subscript*. A subscript is an integral value or variable within an array variable that represents the place or position of a value in the array's list or table.

Dimensioning Variables

A standard variable in Visual Basic with one value can be informally declared by its mere invocation in a formula. As you've seen, you can write state = 19 and, by writing state for the first time, you've made that variable exist for the sake of the program, as what VB3 calls a *variant*. An array variable, on the other hand, cannot be invoked in this manner. Obviously, you couldn't have a statement us$(19) = "Maine" as the first instance of us$() in a program and expect the interpreter to know that you want 50 of these things.

BASIC has always handled declaring array variables with the Dim statement. Dim is short for *dimension.* To *dimension a variable* is to declare an array and thus make a unit into a list the way one makes a point into a line. In geometry, by drawing a line and understanding it as a sequence of points, you give that line dimension; likewise, extending that line into a plane gives it another dimension. Dimensioning is, therefore, used analogously in Visual Basic to add a sequential level to a variable.

The following is the conventional syntax and definition for the Dim statement:

Dim   Statement

Purpose: Variable declaration
Syntax 1 (simple):

```
Dim variable([integer])
```

Syntax 2 (complex):

```
Dim variable1([integer])[, variable2([integer])
        ...variable60([integer])][As [New] type]
```

Syntax 3 (complex):

```
Dim variable1[(integer [To integer][,integer
[To integer]])][As [New] type][, variable2
[([integer[To integer][,integer [To integer]])]
[As [New] type],,..variable60[([integer[To integer]
[,integer [To integer]])][As [New] type]]
```

The Dim statement declares at least one array *variable* to be a list or table of values or string contents that are addressable by number. This number is an *integer* (whole number), and is used as an address to represent the place of a piece of data in the list. This index number is commonly called a *subscript*. A one-dimensional array, or *list*, is generally declared using one integer (or integral expression) between the parentheses. This integer represents the highest subscript in the list. Optionally, a one-dimensional array can be declared using two integers, which represent, respectively, the lowest and highest subscripts in the list, and are separated by the term To.

A two-dimensional array, or *table*, is declared using two integers between each pair of parentheses, separated by a comma. These integers represent the references, or *axes*, of the table, as in a table's x- and y-axes. Both integers represent the highest subscripts along their respective axes, unless the term To is used to distinguish the lowest and highest subscripts along either or both axes. A three-dimensional array, or three-axis table, is declared in the same manner using three sets of integers separated by commas.

Unless otherwise specified, a variable bearing no type symbol or formal *type* qualifier beside the term As is dimensioned as a *variant*, or unknown type. Once a value or contents are assigned to this variable, the interpreter determines an unofficial type for the variable, although its official type is still Variant. You can establish an official formal type for each variable in the dimension list either by attaching a type symbol to the variable or by stating the type as an optional term following the term As.

Placement of the Dim statement is restricted to the general declarations section of a module, or to a procedure. The scope of variables declared using Dim may be modular if used in the general declarations section, or local if used within a procedure. You may declare up to 60 variables within a single Dim statement.

The New term is reserved for cases in which the Dim statement is used to declare a new instance of a graphic object. This process is described in detail later in the book.

Example

Here's how to dimension an array for the 50 states:

```
Dim us$(50)
```

The minimum address in any array dimensioned in this way is (0), so in fact, the preceding statement makes room for 51 states. Still, it might not make sense at times to refer to states 0 through 49. The programmer may choose simply to allocate strings for addresses 1 through 50 and leave address 0 blank.

Example

Here's a simple two-dimensional array being dimensioned:

```
Dim chessboard%(8,8)
```

This statement would be useful within a chess program to represent the squares on a chess board.

Example

Here's a compound declaration for a set of array variables for a BASIC game program:

```
Dim klingons(299), starfleet$(15), sector_map(7,7) As Integer
```

Perhaps the two most well-known games ever to have been originated in BASIC (or so says legend) are both called *Star Trek,* after the original television series. One version is played on an 8 × 8 grid that is sometimes called a *short-range sensor map* or a *sector map.* There are several of these maps in the game—generally 64.

This dimensioning example pays closer attention to the type of variable being declared, as well as the number of units. The variable klingons may represent the current energy level given the maximum number of enemy ships in the game—300 of them, numbered 0 through 299. When a ship's energy level reaches 0, it's considered conquered. The energy level can have fractional value. So, knowing that the default setting for a dimensioned array variable is single-precision, floating-point—just what I want—I added no extra symbols or type declarations to klingons.

The string array starfleet$ can contain the names of 16 (numbered 0 through 15) friendly starships in the game. The two-dimensional integer array sector_map is an 8 × 8 grid (again, remember the number system starts with 0) within which the identities of the individual game pieces (friendly ship, enemy ship, star, planet) are represented. This time I used the term As Integer to specify that I wanted whole numbers only; there's no need to have a variable that has a default value of roughly 0.00000000 when 0 does just as well. I could have dimensioned sector_map% instead. Using As Integer, however, you can refer to sector_map without the accompanying symbol and still have it represent an integral value.

Regulating Arrays

Consider some future possibilities for the NameForm application. Suppose that at a future date you want this program to save and load its data as disk files. When reloading a saved file into memory, you want the contents of the old file in memory to be erased. You can do this with the Erase statement.

Erase   **Statement**

Purpose: Array refresh
Syntax:

```
Erase array[, array...]
```

The Erase statement clears the values and contents of all specified arrays in the statement. Parentheses are not used in the specification. The length of each erased array previously declared with a Dim statement is not affected. The state of all erased arrays is as it was immediately following the execution of the Dim statement that originally dimensioned it.

Example

Suppose you're writing the routine in the NameForm application for loading a new file into memory. Here's how the Erase statement for that application would appear:

```
Erase LastName$, FirstName$, MdInit$, Adress$, Cty$, Stat$, Zp$
```

Now the contents are clear for entry of new data.

Next, consider the following situation: Normally when you use the Dim statement, you state between the parentheses the maximum number of elements that your array can contain. In the previous examples involving NameForm, the Dim statement was used to declare several fields for 1,000 records each. Chances are, 1,000 is a "safe number"; most likely, the length of your data file won't exceed a thousand records. The problem is that the unused record space is still allocated.

Visual Basic's solution to this dilemma is to give you a mechanism for declaring and managing *dynamic arrays,* which are arrays with no fixed maximum length. You declare a dynamic array using the Dim statement, but excluding any values between the parentheses. Later, you use the ReDim statement at one or more points in the VB application to give the array an absolute length.

ReDim   **Statement**

Purpose: Dynamic array redeclaration
Syntax 1 (simple):

```
ReDim variable(integer)
```

Syntax 2 (complex):

```
ReDim [Preserve] variable1(integer [To integer]
[,integer [To integer]])[As type][, variable2
(integer [To integer][,integer [To integer]])
[As type],...variable60(integer [To integer]
[,integer [To integer]])[As type]]
```

The ReDim statement reapportions the dynamic arrays stated for new minimum and maximum bounds, and can be used to change the storage type for the stated variables. In so doing, all values or contents within the dynamic arrays are cleared, unless the Preserve option is stated. Each dynamic array in the ReDim statement must previously have been declared using the statement Dim variable() using precisely this syntax, omitting any array boundaries between the parentheses. New boundaries can be specified at any time using ReDim. The contents of the array will be clear of any values or contents after ReDim is executed, so it can also be used in place of Erase to clear or refresh a dynamic array.

Example

Suppose you implement within the NameForm application a routine that allocates as many units for each array variable as there are records within the file being loaded into memory. This way, there aren't a bunch of null and void records residing in memory following the last one loaded. Within the general module, you would first declare the arrays in the following manner:

```
Dim LstName$(), FrstName$(), MdInit$(), Adress$(),
➡Cty$(), Stat$(), Zp$()
```

When the file is loaded into memory, the first value recognized is a value that sets the length, in records, of the entire file. This value is then assigned to the variable FileLength. The loading procedure would then contain the following statement:

```
ReDim LstName$(FileLength), FrstName$(FileLength),
➡MdInit$(FileLength), Adress$(FileLength),
➡Cty$(FileLength), Stat$(FileLength), Zp$(FileLength)
```

As a result, each array in the program would be exactly as long as the loaded file.

Establishing Bounds

One problem that might come up when you are dimensioning an array variable for a variable amount, or when you are dimensioning an array dynamically, is that a procedure may not know at any one time just where the array starts and ends. Conventionally, when a list array is dimensioned, one integer is specified within the parentheses, representing the upper limits or *bounds* of the array. The lower bounds are assumed to be 0, or 1 if the statement Option Base 1 appears at the top of the general or global module. Using the term As, two integers are declared between the parentheses, which specify both the upper and lower bounds of the array. If you allow both bounds to be variables themselves, the possibility of losing track of that array doubles.

So that you can remind a procedure how big the arrays are, Visual Basic gives you two functions suited to the purpose: LBound() and UBound().

LBound() and UBound()   **Functions**

Purpose: Array bounds acquisition
Syntax:

```
variable% = LBound(array[, dimension])
variable% = UBound(array[, dimension])
```

The LBound() and UBound() functions return the lower and upper bounds, respectively, of the specified array. If the array is multidimensional, to return the bounds for a dimensional level, the number of that level is specified as the second parameter of the function. The name of each array is stated without parentheses.

Example

Using the existing NameForm program, the following function returns the value 1000 in the variable FileMax:

```
FileMax = UBound(LastName$)
```

Counting from 0 or 1

The following statement has the sole purpose of changing the default lower-bounds address number used by array variables:

Option Base   Statement

Purpose: Array default presetting
Syntax:

```
Option Base {0 ¦ 1}
```

The Option Base statement, used within the global module or general declarations area of an application, establishes whether the starting address of an array variable is to be 0 or 1. This value is specified in the accompanying integer and can be no other value. The default lower bounds value of array variables is 0.

A good place for Option Base to appear is at the top of the general module area in the NameForm application:

```
Option Base 1
Dim LstName$(1000), FrstName$(1000), MdInit$(1000),
➡Adress$(1000), Cty$(1000), Stat$(1000), Zp$(1000)
Dim Shared RecordNo As Integer
```

This statement may come in handy if you'd like for the first element of your arrays to be element #1 rather than element #0. If you plan to use two-dimensional geometric arrays, however, in which an origin point is element (0, 0), you'll want to leave the Option Base at 0.

Summary

An array is a list or table of values or text. In Visual Basic, arrays are referred to through the use of array variables, which contain integral subscripts enclosed in parentheses. Each subscript in an array variable acts as the address for a value or string contained within the array. Each subscript in an array variable gives that array an added dimension, or an added axis of a table.

When an array is dimensioned using the Dim statement, it is given upper bounds, or the address of the highest element in the array. The lower bounds are by default assumed to be 0, unless lower and upper bounds have been specified in the dimension statement using the To term. The type of a variable can also be declared using Dim paired with the As term. The ReDim statement can be used to change the specifications of an array that has been allocated dynamically using Dim with empty parameters. The Erase statement clears the contents of a dimensioned array without changing its dimensions or type. Upper and lower bounds of a dimensioned array can be returned using the UBound() and LBound() functions, respectively. The default lower bounds of an array can be reset from 0 to 1 using the Option Base statement.

Review Questions

1. Using what you know about the structure and dimensioning of array variables, and using the first example as a guide, what are the contents of the variable us$(27)?

2. In the second example, assuming you are playing black, what piece occupies the square that has its value represented by chessboard%(6,8)?

3. Assume that the general procedure of your form contains the statement Dim GridValue(255, 400 To 1200). If GridHigh = LBound(GridValue, 2), what is the value of GridHigh?

4. Which of the following three valid statements allocates the dynamic array?

> **A.** Dim Aspen As Double
>
> **B.** Dim Aspen() As Double
>
> **C.** Dim Aspen(30) As Double

Review Exercise

Write just the procedure for the NameForm application that accepts numeric input from a text box and interprets this number to be the upper bounds of all the array variables used in the program, assuming they were dimensioned dynamically. Have the procedure redimension the array to the upper bounds specified when you click a button. If possible, reconfigure the right scroll bar so that the lowermost point of its thumb represents the upper bounds of the array.

CHAPTER 10

Value Declaration

In this chapter, you see how variables are formally declared in Visual Basic, using explicit statements rather than equations. You learn about the scope of a variable, which is the extent to which the value contained within a variable pertains to the various modules of the program. You also learn how to use Visual Basic statements to define variable scope, which defines the extent of their involvement in the application.

Next, you learn two ways to start adding your own terms to the ones Visual Basic uses. You can apply unused words to substitute for numbers by declaring them as constants. You can also create your own variable types, as composites of other types.

Structured Programming

BASIC is believed to be the first high-level programming language in which variables can declare themselves. Many times in this book, you've seen source code examples containing equations such as a = 1 where there was no a before in the code. BASIC has always been smart enough to play catch-up with the programmer; if the programmer says a not only exists but equals 1, it must exist.

The patchwork quilt that has become modern BASIC is comprised of many elements of FORTRAN, PL/I, Pascal, and C. In each of these languages, a variable is formally declared before a value is assigned to it, or before the variable is used in a formula. In other words, the variable is formally introduced to the program with a statement.

> **Note:** In BASIC, a declaration of a variable is the first statement in a program to assign a legitimate value to that variable.

For years, the only way to declare a variable in BASIC was simply to assign a value to it, as in a = 1. At first, this method of declaration was considered an advance in the art of high-level programming. As time passed and more low-level programmers added new structures to BASIC, every variable of every type could be declared before it was used.

There are certain trends in programming thought. One of these trends concerns the structure of source code. One frequent argument among programmers is whether to include comment lines. Another debate, although perhaps not as frequent, is whether to declare variables before values are assigned to them.

At this time, it is fashionable to declare variables before a value assignment, even in BASIC and Visual Basic. This does not mean you have to do it. Often when I'm writing a loop clause, I need a quick "utility variable" to keep the count from 1 to 5, so that the program performs some set of instructions five times. I don't care what the count variable is, as long as its name is not currently in use. Sometimes I give it a name from out of the blue, as in the statement For ralph = 1 To 5.

There is an instruction you can choose to use if you want to make it a *law* that all variables you create must first be formally declared: the Option Explicit statement.

Option Explicit   Statement

Purpose: Declaration stipulation
Syntax:

```
Option Explicit
```

The Option Explicit statement, when included in the declarations section of a module, places the interpreter in a mode whereby all variables included in the source code must first be explicitly declared, using the Dim or Global statement.

The advantage of using Option Explicit within a module is that it requires all variables to be declared. This forced declaration helps you find typing errors in your variable names. For example, if you accidentally typed SalesZollars rather than SalesDollars, the VB interpreter would inform you that the variable SalesZollars was not found, thus making you aware of your error. If Option Explicit was not specified, VB would assume that SalesZollars was another variable needed within your application.

A Variable's Scope of Existence

The *scope* of a variable defines at what level in the program its value is remembered.

When you create a variable by expressing it within an equation for the first time, the implied declaration for this variable gives the variable a local scope. The *scope* of a variable is the extent to which that variable applies across the various divisions of the source code of the program.

Example

A variable with *local scope* applies only to the procedure in which it is declared, whether it is a specific declaration or an inference from an equation. The following is an example from the two-dimensional distance calculator project, 2D_DIST.MAK:

```
Sub Go_Click ()
x1 = Val(Box_x1.Text)
x2 = Val(Box_x2.Text)
y1 = Val(Box_y1.Text)
y2 = Val(Box_y2.Text)
d# = Sqr(((x2 - x1) ^ 2) + ((y2 - y1) ^ 2))
Distance.Text = Str$(d#)
End Sub
```

The purpose of the five variables (x1, x2, y1, y2, and d#) invoked in the preceding example is to reach a result that could be displayed as Distance.Text. None of these variables has any purpose beyond the context of this procedure. In other words, if a larger program were to include this procedure, there's no reason why any other procedure in the application needs to access these five variables. The scope of those variables is, therefore, restricted to the local procedure.

The *context* of a body of source code describes its relationship to the rest of the program.

The concept of context is somewhat fuzzier, and is not actually defined by Microsoft (perhaps for this reason). The *context* of a body of source code is the extent to which the values generated within that body, and the statements made within that body, relate to the rest of the program.

In earlier editions of BASIC, the programmer saved the entire application to disk as one file. In Visual Basic, an application may consist of multiple modules (individual files containing separate groups of source code). The reason for this modularity is that you may want to compile several applications that use the same procedures—for instance, the same input form generator, the same graphing procedure, or the same set of arithmetic formulas. The project concept enables the programmer to choose from modules that are already programmed, which generates entirely new applications.

The key to determining how the different modules link with each other into a project, however, is to find out in advance what variables may be shared between modules. This is where the naming of variables comes into play, rather than just declaring them. Declaring a bunch of variables in one module as Global doesn't help much if those variable names do not appear in the other modules. The variables wouldn't really be global. In other words, their *scope* would be global because they're declared that way, although the *context* of the procedures containing those variables would only be modular.

Form modules and general modules are similar in that they both contain *general declarations sections* within which you can introduce the interpreter to your modular-scope variables. All the procedures within a module have access to variables declared within the module's general declarations section using the Dim statement. You may find the (general) section for a module as the top entry in the Object list in its source code window. Likewise, (declarations) appears at the top of the Proc list. Figure 10.1 shows the general declarations section for project NAMEFM2B.MAK, appearing in the proper source code window.

> Modular variables are declared in the general declarations area.

Figure 10.1

A group of variables with modular scope.

> To declare a variable with local or modular scope, use the *Dim* statement.

Within this window is a formal declaration for a variable of modular scope but of unit length—a nonarray variable. Dim Shared RecordNo As Integer creates the variable RecordNo and applies it to all procedures in the module, because the declaration appears in the general module area.

The scope of the variables declared with Dim is determined by Dim's position in the module. If Dim appears inside a Sub or Function procedure, the variables declared by Dim are assumed to have local scope. If Dim appears in the general declarations section, the variables it declares are assumed to have modular scope, and therefore apply to all procedures in the module.

Table 10.1 lists and defines the three categories of variable scope in a Visual Basic application.

Table 10.1. Scope categories of variables.

Category	Definition
Local	Pertaining only to the procedure in which the variable is first invoked or declared. Its value is cleared when the procedure is exited.
Static	Pertaining only to the procedure in which the variable is first declared, although its value is maintained after the procedure is exited in case the same procedure is called again.

Category	Definition
Modular	Pertaining to all procedures in a module by virtue of having been declared in the general module area of a form module.
Global	Pertaining to the entire source code.

Sometimes words don't do enough to describe something as geographical as variable scopes, so figure 10.2 is a map. Imagine the two large blocks are modules in a VB application, and the smaller blocks within the large ones are procedures within the modules. Within the blocks are declarative statements, along with dotted lines that act as barbed-wire fences, staking out the territory of the variables they declare.

Figure 10.2

The geographic map of VB variables.

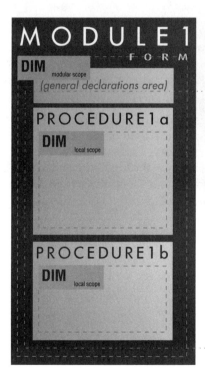
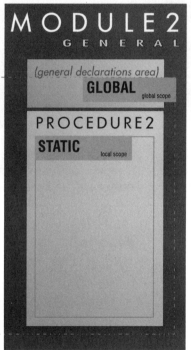

Notice how the Dim statement stakes its territory three times in the Module1 block. Inside the procedure boundaries, Dim limits its scope to their respective procedures; but outside the procedures, in the general declarations area, the Dim boundaries extend to encompass all procedures in the module.

Look now at the Module2 block, which represents a general module, as opposed to Module1 as a form module. Within the procedure there is a Static declaration that, like Dim inside procedures, limits the scope of variables to within the procedure. The difference between Static and Dim is that local variables declared with Static are maintained for whenever the procedure is entered next, whereas local variables declared with Dim are dropped on exit of the procedure.

Within the general declarations section of the general Module2 is the declaration Global. Notice how its scope extends to encompass even Module1—global variables are addressable from "foreign modules."

To declare a variable with global scope, use the Global statement.

Global   Statement

Purpose: Global variable declaration
Syntax:

```
Global variable1[(integer [To integer]
⇒[, integer [To integer]])][As [New] type], variable2
⇒[(integer [To integer][, integer [To integer]])]
⇒[As [New] type],...variable60[(integer [To integer]
⇒[, integer [To integer]])][As type]]
```

The Global statement is used to declare all unit and array variables whose values are to apply to the entire source code of the program. The scope of all variables declared using Global is considered to be global. Except for the term itself, Global's syntax is the same as the syntax of the Dim statement. Global can be used only within a general (nonform) module, and especially within one that the programmer has designated as a global module.

Example

Here again is the global module for the Expressor:

```
Global readout_value As Double, combine_value As Double
Global ready As Integer
```

What if you decide to add more modules to the Expressor to give it charting or printout capabilities? Those modules may need to access such values as the current value, the previous value, and the number of digits in the readout. For that reason, these variables are declared within the global module, even though the Expressor currently has only one module.

To declare a variable with local scope that maintains its value, use the *Static* statement.

Static variables within a procedure have local scope, for all intents and purposes. Unlike local variables declared with `Dim`, however, once the procedure is exited, the interpreter maintains the values of that procedure's variables, regardless of whether their names conflict with other variables that don't conflict in scope outside of the procedure. To declare a variable with static scope requires a special statement: the `Static` statement.

Static   Statement

Purpose: Local variable declaration
Syntax:

```
Static variable1[((integer [To integer]
➥[, integer [To integer]]))][As type][, variable2
➥[((integer [To integer][, integer [To integer]]))]
➥[As type],...variable60[((integer [To integer]
➥[, integer [To integer]]))][As type]]
```

The `Static` statement is used in place of `Dim` to declare all of a procedure's unit and array variables having values that the interpreter will maintain after the `End Sub` or `End Function` statement is executed for that procedure. Except for the main term itself, `Static`'s syntax is the same as the syntax of the `Dim` statement within a procedure. It cannot, however, include the term `Shared`.

Example

Suppose you've declared a static variable within a procedure using the following instruction:

```
Static sale_price As Currency
```

Within the boundaries of this same procedure, a `sale_price` of 149.95 is determined. Now, the procedure is exited when the interpreter finds the instruction `End Sub`. Normally, if `sale_price` were declared using `Dim`, `End Sub` would cause the variable to be dropped; instead, when the procedure is reentered, `sale_price` is equal to 149.95 rather than 0.

Example

The following procedure is from the Expressor application:

```
Sub Button_Point_Click ()
Static point_lock As Integer
```

```
If point_lock = 0 And ready < 20 Then
    Readout.Caption = Readout.Caption + "."
    point_lock = 1
    ready = ready + 1
End If
assess_readout
End Sub
```

Here, the variable point_lock was declared Static so that it will remember whether the user clicked on the decimal point button of the calculator. This way, the decimal point won't appear in the readout twice.

Constants

Throughout the source code of Visual Basic, arbitrary terms that aren't keywords or instructions can be declared as constants. A *constant* is a term that stands in place of a value in an expression. A constant's value is set only once.

The declarative statement for constants is the Const statement.

Const   **Statement**

Purpose: Constant declaration
Syntax:

```
[Global] Const name = expression[, name = expression...]
```

The Const statement is used to declare a term to represent a fixed (nonvariable) value for use in expressions. The scope of a constant is determined by the position of its declaration in the source code. A constant declared within a Sub or Function procedure will have local scope. A constant declared within the general module area of a module is said to have modular scope. A constant declared within a general module using the term Global is said to have global scope.

Example

The following is a necessary revision to the general declarations area for the Expressor:

```
Dim label$(15, 4), p(4)
Dim readout_value As Single, solution As Single
Const PI = 3.1415927
Const GRAV = 6.6732E-11
```

Here, two universally recognized constants appear: the value of Pi, and the gravitational constant GRAV that is important to Newtonian laws.

Example

Declaring constants globally may be convenient when it's easier for you to remember a word than a number. For instance, you may prefer to set some control's .BackColor background color property to MAGENTA rather than the octal number for magenta. In such a case, you can declare Const MAGENTA equal to the octal or hexadecimal number only once. As a result, you won't be looking up color tables in the middle of late-night programming.

The most efficient way to do this is with the CONSTANT.TXT file that comes with Visual Basic. CONSTANT.TXT contains a long list of constant declarations you can include within your VB application's global module for numerals that VB frequently uses for representation purposes. An error code or a color qualifies as such a numeral. These constant declarations enable you to replace the numerals—which are arguably far more difficult to remember—with universally recognized terms.

The following portion of CONSTANT.TXT deals with colors:

```
' Colors
Global Const BLACK = &H0&
Global Const RED = &HFF&
Global Const GREEN = &HFF00&
Global Const YELLOW = &HFFFF&
Global Const BLUE = &HFF0000
Global Const MAGENTA = &HFF00FF
Global Const CYAN = &HFFFF00
Global Const WHITE = &HFFFFFF
```

You can load the entire CONSTANT.TXT file into your VB application; however, it is huge, and you probably won't use one-third of the constant terms declared in even your largest application. The most efficient method of using CONSTANT.TXT is as follows:

1. Load CONSTANT.TXT into the Windows Notepad program, or some other text editor or word processor.

2. Scroll through the file, looking for the section pertaining to the subject of your constants. Each section is clearly marked with remark lines and separated from the others by blank lines.

3. Copy this section into the Windows system Clipboard and paste it into a VB BAS program module using the **P**aste command from the **E**dit menu in the VB control window.

The Composition of Variables

Microsoft uses the term *user-defined variables* to describe variable types that are defined by the programmer. Initially, this distinction does not make much sense, because the *user* is the person who operates the programs whose variables are defined (if not altogether created) by the *programmer*. This term really refers to the fact that these variables contain other variables.

A *composite variable* is a programmer-defined combination of numerals and strings that is treated as a single variable.

A *composite variable* in Visual Basic is a container for multiple numeral, string, array, or other composite variables, addressed together as one unit using a single arbitrarily defined term and invoked within an instruction using object-oriented syntax.

Suppose you use four variables throughout an application to refer to aspects of one real-world item, such as a transaction in your checkbook. Using Visual Basic's composite variable mechanism, you can declare these aspect variables to be properties of checkbook transactions. In doing so, you've rendered transactions to be virtual objects in the context of your application; thus it seems natural to use object-oriented syntax to refer to your checkbook properties, as in `Transaction.Number`, `Transaction.Recipient`, or `Transaction.Debit`.

Referring to properties this way does not, however, mean that `Transaction.` becomes an object by the formal definition of the term used in computing. If it did, you would be able to use the programming language to construct methods such as `Transaction.Record` or `Transaction.Cancel`, and call such methods as directives to your application as if they were keywords in the language vocabulary. Visual Basic does not contain facilities for programmer-defined methods; therefore, composite variables cannot be true objects—at least not in the current release.

The declarative statement used to create composite variables is the `Type-End Type` statement.

Type-End Type   **Statement**

Purpose: Composite declarative clause
Syntax:

```
Type typename
  variable1[(array_length)] As existing_type
  ➥[* string_length]
  [variable2[(array_length)] As existing_type
  ➥[* string_length]]
  .
  .
  .

End Type
```

The Type-End Type clause is used within the global module or general declarations section of an application to declare programmer-defined composite variable types for that application. The *typename* for the composite variable is arbitrarily defined by the programmer; however, it must not be a reserved keyword, a declared variable name, or a term used in the program for any other purpose.

Each variable that will make up the composite variable is listed within the clause. Listings of variables here do not count as declaratives; these variables must be declared elsewhere in the program. The invocation of each variable here is only meant as a reservation for its place within the composite variable being declared. The type of variable *existing_type* included within the composite type must be specified with the term As, and may be a composite type previously declared within an earlier clause.

If strings are being used within a composite variable, the programmer has the option of specifying the absolute length for each string in characters, by writing that length beside an asterisk * following the designation As String. Fixing the length of included strings is necessary for using Type clauses to save records to a disk-based data file.

Example

Using NAMEFORM.FRM as a guide, here is a user-defined type declaration that specifies an entire record by itself:

```
Type NameRecord
    LastName As String * 30
    FirstName As String * 20
    MidInit As String * 3
    CompanyName As String * 50
    Address As String * 50
    City As String * 20
    State As String * 5
    Zip As String * 10
End Type
```

Example

One common use for composite variables is to aid in the description of shapes, especially rectangles. Suppose the following composite declaration appears in the global module of an application:

```
Type Rectangle
    origx As Integer
    origy As Integer
    deltax As Integer
    deltay As Integer
End Type
```

The purpose of `Type Rectangle` is to describe the top left corner of a rectangle and the rectangle's length and width. The recognized property terms (`.Left`, `.Top`, `.Width`, or `.Height`) are not used as variables belonging to the composite, to help prove the point that composite variable types are defined by the programmer.

At the bottom of a test form module, a single button appears that has the caption and control name `Draw`. Within the general declarations area of this form module is the following line:

```
Dim the_box As Rectangle
```

This is the first example of actually dimensioning a variable as a composite type. The variable `the_box` can now be addressed within the source code using object-oriented syntax, as in using `the_box.origx` to refer to the origin point of the box along the x-axis.

Suppose you have the following procedure for the sole button:

```
Sub Draw_Click ()
the_box.origx = 1000
the_box.origy = 1000
the_box.deltax = 1500
the_box.deltay = 1500
display the_box
End Sub
```

There will definitely be a fixed box within this form; the application does nothing else but plot this box. Now that the box's coordinates are set, the call is placed to a procedure called Sub display (). Notice that I've created four parameters, but the only parameter passed to Sub display () is the_box.

The following is the listing for procedure display:

```
Sub display (object As Rectangle)
Line (object.origx, object.origy)-(object.deltax,
➡object.deltay), , B
End Sub
```

Notice that all four parameter names (origx, origy, deltax, and deltay) appear within this procedure, without having to appear within the parentheses of the Sub procedure declaration. The only parameter appearing there is object, which was declared to be of type Rectangle. Notice I did not call this "object" the_box. This is to demonstrate that object. now refers to the_box indirectly, in the same way that Source. in the previous examples referred to a graphic object indirectly. Another object with another name—perhaps another_box—could at some later time be passed to this procedure, and object. would refer to that object indirectly, as well. The result is that a box is plotted to the form.

Summary

A variable in Visual Basic can be declared by inference, which means stating it within an expression for the first time within the source code of the program. Variables declared by inference within a procedure are assumed to have local scope and Variant type, unless a symbol is used beside the variable denoting otherwise. Formal declaration for local variables on the procedure level, as well as for variables with modular scope, is achieved with the Dim statement. Similarly, variables with global scope can be declared with the Global statement. Variables with static scope, which are local to procedures but have values that are constantly maintained, are declared on the procedure level with the Static statement.

A constant is an arbitrarily defined term that is assigned a value only once. The constant's value does not change through the course of the program. One common purpose for declaring constants is so that a numeral used to represent an item in a list can be given a term that better represents the list item to the human reader of the source code.

A composite variable is a container for several other variables. The term for this variable is established by the programmer, as long as it does not conflict with a reserved Visual Basic keyword or another variable, graphic object, or line-labeling term currently in use within the source code. When a composite variable type is declared using the Type-End Type statement, component variables can be addressed as properties of the composite variable, as if the composite were an object.

Review Questions

1. If the instruction c = 5 appears within a procedure without variable c having been formally declared, and no other instruction in the application refers to c, what is the value of c outside the procedure?

2. If the instruction c = 5 appears within a procedure whose module contains the instruction Dim c As Integer within its general declarations section, and the entire application is just one module, what is the value of c outside the procedure?

3. If the instruction c = 5 appears within a procedure whose first declarative instruction is Static c As Integer, and the entire application is just one module, what is the value of c outside the procedure?

4. Can a composite variable include both string and value variables?

5. Composite variables use object-oriented syntax for addressing individual elements. If at one point the value of one element of a composite variable is set to the value of a regular variable, and the value of that regular variable changes later in the program, does the value within the composite variable change as well?

Review Exercise

1. Take the source code for the NameForm application (project name NAMEFORM.MAK) and list on paper each variable invoked, along with the type and scope for that variable.

Part III

Instructions and Groupings

CHAPTER 11

Phrasing

This chapter reviews Visual Basic's many "parts of speech." This review expands on many of the principles introduced in Chapter 3, "Grammar and Linguistics." You are then introduced to the principles of *object-oriented syntax*, which is relatively new to BASIC. Object-oriented syntax may not be entirely new to you, however, because you've been using it since Chapter 2.

Statements and Functions

A *statement* is an instruction that specifies a change.

A *function* is an operation that returns a single value.

An *object* is a data structure that combines the data contents and attributes with the encoded form of its function.

A *handle* is used by a true object-oriented language to manipulate objects.

The two primary types of Visual Basic instructions are statements and functions. A *statement* is an instruction that VB uses to perform a specific task, such as adding two numbers. By contrast, a *function* is an arithmetic or textual operation that is performed on a value, variable, or expression; the result is a single value.

The two types of instructions are quite distinguishable from each other. In this book, when each instruction term is introduced, its "part of speech" or type appears to the right of the instruction.

With Visual Basic, Microsoft added object-oriented syntax to the language, particularly with the wide array of graphic objects supported by the interpreter. In conventional BASIC, you make changes to a value or part of the program by stating the results of the changes as facts. In object-oriented syntax, you make changes to a part of the program by specifying the type of change.

Visual Basic is not an object-oriented language in the true sense of the word. It does give the appearance of true object orientation by using its syntax to some degree in VB instructions. Figure 11.1 depicts the interlocking nature of terms in Visual Basic's implementation of object-oriented syntax.

Figure 11.1

Object orientation
between objects
and events.

The only data objects supported by Visual Basic are graphic objects. Many people argue that these are not really objects by the definition subscribed to by the Object Management Group, a coalition of software manufacturers cooperating to define object language standards. Microsoft is a member of this group. In Visual Basic, a graphic object is a data structure that can be visually represented and that behaves like a device that receives user input, displays results, or does both.

A Visual Basic *graphic object* either receives input or displays data.

Each VB *graphic object* has a predefined set of actions, called *methods,* that can be applied toward that object.

The syntax for a method instruction follows:

A *method* is an instruction that directs the interpreter to perform a programmed action on a graphic object.

```
object.method [parameters]
```

The object is stated first, followed by a period and the name for the method. If needed, the method name is followed by the appropriate parameters.

The BASIC `Print` instruction, which is one of the language's original statements, is reborn in Visual Basic as a method, in such instructions as

```
. Form1.Print "One more method".
```

Properties are the attributes of graphic objects that can be changed.

By entering the programs listed in this book into the interpreter, you gain some experience manipulating the properties of graphic objects. A *property* is an attribute of a graphic object with values or contents that can be established or reassigned as an expression of assignment.

Here's a piece of one of the property tables from a revised version of `NameForm`:

Object Type	Property	Setting
Vertical Scroll Bar	.Top	7800
	.Left	0
	.Width	255
	.Height	2895

Object Type	Property	Setting
	.CtlName	RecordShown
	.LargeChange	10
	.SmallChange	1
	.Max	1000

These properties can also be set with source code instructions, as follows:

```
VScroll1.Top = 7800
VScroll1.Left = 0
VScroll1.Width = 255
VScroll1.Height = 2895
VScroll1.CtlName = "RecordShown"
VScroll1.LargeChange = 10
VScroll1.SmallChange = 1
VScroll1.Max = 1000
```

As you can see, the syntax of property assignments is as follows:

```
object.property = setting
```

A *setting* represents the state, appearance, or some aspect of a graphic object.

Notice that you assign strings to object properties by enclosing the string in quotation marks, as if you were assigning the contents to a string variable. The values or contents assigned here are called *settings*.

An *event* triggers the execution of a procedure.

As the recipient of user input, each graphic object can receive *events*, as they are called in object-oriented syntax. An *event* is a type of user input applied to a graphic object, which is often used to trigger the execution of a procedure.

You're familiar with the syntax for attributing an event to a graphic object:

```
object_event
```

The event is separated from the object by an underscore character, as in `Command1_DblClick`.

Program Remarks

Before you start breaking new ground again, you should know about one statement that is used primarily to add comments to a program. Note that these comments are not executed.

Rem   Statement

Purpose: Allows you to place textual comments in your source code
Syntax:

```
{Rem ¦ '} [remark]
```

When the interpreter encounters the Rem statement on a line, it ignores the remaining contents of that line and skips to the next line. This statement allows you to type anything into the source code at random, generally for use as comments to explain your code to the next person who looks at it. You can use the apostrophe (') in place of the term Rem.

Example

Remarks are often used as explanations for people who read your program code so that they can fix it or make changes. Here's a revised procedure from the Expressor:

```
Sub Times_Click ()
'Find out what the readout says.
assess_readout
'Multiply the readout by the compared value...
readout_value = readout_value * combine_value
'...and swap values.
combine_value = readout_value
'Display the result.
readout.caption = Str$(readout_value)
'Make the next digit pressed clear the readout.
ready = 0
End Sub
```

Before every instruction in the preceding code is a relatively long comment explaining what is happening. Such comments are similar to pseudocode in that they state in human language what the code is doing.

Example

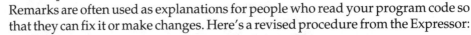

The following code shows Rem used as the anchor for a bannerhead along the top of the global module of the Expressor:

```
'------------------------------------------------------------
'¦ The Expressor                                            ¦
'¦    by D. F. Scott for Visual Basic 3 By Example          ¦
'------------------------------------------------------------
Global readout_value As Double, combine_value As Double
Global ready As Integer
```

Notice that the apostrophes, which indicate a Rem statement, appear on the far left side of the nonexecutable lines. These characters can be followed by any textual comments that you want.

Summary

In BASIC and Visual Basic, the two major types of instructions are *statements*, which operate on elements of the program, and *functions*, which operate on elements of data. Microsoft has added object-oriented syntax to Visual Basic. In the process, Microsoft classified graphic controls in VB applications as graphic objects. A stated action to be performed on a graphic object is a *method*. An attribute an object affects or changes somehow by such an action is a *property*. An element of user input involving a graphic object is an *event*. Each of these three "functions" of graphic objects is called with its own particular syntax.

Review Questions

The following questions apply to the code line that follows:

```
Let c$ = Left$("75059-0612", 5)        'Convert 9-digit to 5
```

1. Which portion of this instruction is a statement?

2. Which portion is a remark?

3. Which portion is an expression?

Review Exercise

The following is a procedure from TOUCHBAS.FRM, a more developed form of the number base-converting Function Convert$ () introduced in Chapter 7, "Logic and Number Systems." Using what you know about the various types of Visual Basic instructions, write this procedure on paper. Beside each instruction, write its type.

```
Sub Convert_Click ()
b10$ = Base10.Text
b10$ = Str$(Int(Val(b10$)))
Base10.Text = b10$
ConvValue = Val(Base10.Text)
Find_Top:
cb = Val(ConvBase.Caption)
comp = cb ^ expn
If comp < ConvValue Then
    expn = expn + 1
```

```
    GoTo Find_Top
End If
For spot = expn To 0 Step -1
    digit% = ConvValue \ (cb ^ spot)
    ConvValue = ConvValue Mod (cb ^ spot)
    total$ = total$ + d$(digit%)
Next spot
If Left$(total$, 1) = "0" And Len(total$) > 1 Then
    total$ = Right$(total$, Len(total$) - 1)
End If
Result.Caption = total$
End Sub
```

CHAPTER 12

Conditional Clauses

A *condition* is the test of whether an instruction will be executed.

In this chapter, you learn about the mechanism that makes the execution of a set of Visual Basic instructions dependent on the results of a test. The test that must be passed is called a *condition*. When the test is passed, we say the set of instructions is executed *conditionally*. The specific set of instructions that is executed based on the results of the test, or the state of some value in memory, is called a *clause*.

You construct Visual Basic clauses based on expressions of comparison, which execute sets of instructions based on the results of that comparison. The two major conditional clause statements in Visual Basic are If-Then and Select Case. You use both statements in this chapter.

The Construction of a Clause

As you become more familiar with Visual Basic, you'll grow more comfortable with the various ways of referring to sets and sequences of instructions. Visual Basic has many different conventions for referring to instruction sets, some more formal than others. A *clause* is an informal way of referring to an instruction set, although most of the source code of a Visual Basic program can be divided into clauses. A clause is any set of instructions whose execution is dependent on the value of a variable in a mathematical expression.

A *clause* is a set of instructions whose execution is dependent on the value of a variable.

When you read Visual Basic source code instructions from top to bottom and in sequence, you notice each clause is bound at its beginning and end by two parts of a clause statement. The following pseudocode shows the general construction of an ordinary clause:

> Clause statement part1 [expression]
>   Instruction1
>   Instruction2

.
.
.

*Instruction*n
Clause statement part2

The dependent instructions between both parts of the clause statement are *nested.* When *nesting* instructions within a clause, many programmers choose to indent them a few spaces or, in Visual Basic, precede them with a tab. This form of typesetting helps clauses stand out and makes them easier to identify, although the indention is not necessary for the clause to be executed. The instructions in a clause can all be flush against the left margin without affecting the program.

When the clause contains a mathematical expression for evaluation, it appears within the first part of the clause statement. Usually, expressions are stated outright, but in a few cases, parts of the expression are implied within the statement governing the clause, as you see later in this chapter.

Example

This code fragment is an example of the most basic of BASIC conditional clauses: the If-Then statement, the way it normally appears in a Visual Basic program.

```
If fingers = 5 Then
    hand_likelihood = 1
    message$ = "Five fingers. . . could be an ordinary hand."
    MsgBox message$
End If
```

The purpose of this somewhat fictitious code fragment is self-evident. Suppose you have a program that evaluates data pertaining to a living being, to determine whether it's human. The preceding fragment is a whole clause because it is bordered at the beginning and end by two parts of an If-Then statement. The mathematical expression being tested is fingers = 5, in which fingers is an arbitrarily named variable. The three dependent instructions within the clause are executed only if this being's data shows that it has five fingers. Within those dependent instructions, a flag variable is declared and a message is displayed to that effect.

If... Then... [ElseIf... Then] [Else...]... **Statement**
End If

Purpose: Conditional clause
Syntax 1:

```
If expression1 Then
    instruction block1
[ElseIf expression2 Then
    instruction block2]
```

```
        .
        .
        .
[Else
    instruction blockn]
End If
```

The If-Then statement tests a mathematical expression to see if it is true. If it is, execution continues with the first dependent instruction after the expression. If the expression is not true, execution skips to the first instruction outside the nest. If that instruction is Else, the dependent instructions following it are executed. If that instruction is ElseIf, another mathematical expression is evaluated in the same manner as the first. The clause is terminated when End If is reached.

The following is a more brief syntax for the same statement:
Syntax 2:

```
If expression Then instruction1 [Else instruction2]
```

This syntax is used for single-instruction clauses and can be written on one line. Notice that the End If is not included in this syntax.

If-Then is the fundamental conditional statement of the BASIC programming language. The statement can be described as a mechanism whose trigger is a mathematical expression. The result of this expression is a Boolean logical value somewhere in memory, which can be interpreted as True or False (–1 or 0). If the expression is true, the first set of instructions in the clause is executed in sequence.

If there is another set of instructions in the If-Then clause following the term Else or ElseIf, that set is executed in sequence if the original expression beside the term If is false.

Here is the general mechanism of a fully-developed If-Then statement written in pseudocode:

> *If this expression evaluates true, then*
> > *Execute this set of instructions;*
> *Otherwise if this other expression evaluates true, then*
> > *Execute this set of instructions instead;*
> *If all else fails to be true, then*
> > *Execute this set of instructions as a last-ditch measure.*
> *End of clause.*

The mechanism of If-Then is flexible; think of it as an adaptable, logical switch. In the conventional structure of If-Then, you can use this switch to have the program *either* perform a process *or* leave things as they are. The mathematical expression being evaluated throws this switch one way or the other. Therefore, any process of instructions that can be described as "one way or the other" or "one way or nothing at all" can be modeled by If-Then.

Example

Suppose you have an input form on your screen that contains two option buttons marked *Active* and *Inactive*, describing the state of some process. You want the users of your program to click the Active button if they want the process to take place. `If-Then` can be used to trigger a process if the Active button on the form is set. Here is how the conditional clause might appear:

```
If ActiveButton.Value = -1 Then
    process$ = "Active"
End If
```

Here, the value `-1` represents the Boolean *true* logical value as defined in Chapter 7, "Logic and Number Systems." If the `.Value` property of `ActiveButton` is set to *true* (–1), the contents of string variable `process$` are, in turn, set to read `Active`. Otherwise, execution of the program skips to the instruction following `End If`. If the variable `process$` was never formally declared before this clause was executed, and if the state of `ActiveButton` is *False* (0), `process$` will not exist as a variable. This may result in an error with any evaluation of that variable later in the program.

The `If-Then` statement itself does not recognize the complexity of the mathematical expression being evaluated. `If-Then` does not perform the actual evaluation. What the interpreter does first is take the included expression and *reduce* it logically to a –1 or 0 (True or False). Regardless of how many terms you include in your expression of comparison, `If-Then` operates as if you wrote `-1` or `0` in place of that expression.

Example

Suppose you want a list box on your form to contain a series of over-the-counter stock issues that have high price-to-earnings ratios and are worth your consideration for investment. Here's how an `If-Then` clause might appear that enters the name of an attractive company to the list:

```
If price(stock) / earnings(stock) > 10 Then
    OTCStock.AddItem ticker_symbol$(stock)
End If
```

The subscript variable `stock` is used as an index number for each informal record of stock offerings in the list. Variable `stock` is thus the *key* to each array. For instance, if you're evaluating a stock with index number 143, at some time before the execution of this clause, the value of `stock` would be set to 143. The variable is then used as an index for the three array variables in the example. Here is the clause in pseudocode:

If the price of stock #143 divided by the earnings of stock #143 is greater than 10, then add the ticker symbol of stock #143 to the list of OTC stocks under consideration.

If-Then as a Two-Sided Argument

When Else is included in an If-Then clause, it acts as a partition between the *True* part of the instruction set and the *False* part. If-Then is used in such cases so that the interpreter executes *either* one or the other set of instructions, depending on the reduced logical value of the expression (–1 or 0). Figure 12.1 demonstrates this point by breaking an ordinary clause into two "either/or" segments.

Figure 12.1

An *If-Then-Else* Example.

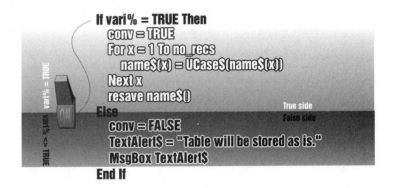

```
If vari% = TRUE Then
    conv = TRUE
    For x = 1 To no_recs
        name$(x) = UCase$(name$(x))
    Next x
    resave name$()
Else
    conv = FALSE
    TextAlert$ = "Table will be stored as is."
    MsgBox TextAlert$
End If
```

Example

Suppose there is a number box on the form and you need that number box to register a value only if the value is positive. (If the value is negative, you want the box to be left blank.) The following clause is for that purpose:

```
If balance >= 0 Then
    num_box.Text = Str$(balance)
Else
    num_box.Text = ""
End If
```

The clause sets the number box (named num_box) to the textual form of the value of the variable balance if the value of balance is greater than or equal to 0 (in other words, if balance is positive). If the expression contained in If-Then evaluates True, the expression preceding Else is executed. When Else is reached, execution skips to the instruction following End If. If the initial expression evaluates False, execution skips to the first term outside the instruction nest. In this case, that term is not End If; it is Else. This tells the interpreter that there is a set of instructions to be executed in the event of falsehood. In this case, the text of num_box is set to a null string (made blank). Graphic objects cannot receive numeric values as assignments; they can receive only text or string contents. Therefore, a numeric value must be converted to a string before it can be placed in a .Text property.

Example

The mathematical expression being tested within If-Then can be divided into parts by Boolean logical operators. As long as the expression reduces to logical True or False, any operator is allowed within the expression. For instance, imagine that your program is a game that branches to the end if the player runs out of money or if time expires. The clause that triggers that branch might read as follows:

```
If money <= 0 Or time = 0 Then
    GoTo no_win
End If
```

This clause is one example of a *conditional branch,* which skips the program to the statement beneath the label specified in the GoTo statement only if the condition evaluates True.

> **Note:** Although the clause is written like a sentence, the term If is never stated twice—so a clause such as If money <= 0 Or If time = 0 is wrong.

Example

The syntax of a mathematical expression within the first line of the If-Then clause is not restricted to an expression of assignment. The left side of the equation does not have to be a single variable; it can be an expression, as demonstrated by the following amendment to the no-more-money conditional branch:

```
If money + account <= 0 Or time = 0 Then
    GoTo no_win
End If
```

Suppose a second variable account comes into play, representing an amount the player has stashed away in savings. The player is considered bankrupt if he has no money in his pocket and no money in his account.

> **Note:** In expressions of comparison in Visual Basic, values or contents can be combined on both sides of the equation. Keep in mind that this is not true for all versions of BASIC.

The *Select Case* Statement

The If-Then statement is used frequently in this book because it makes up a large portion of all BASIC and Visual Basic programs. There is another conditional clause that is used far less frequently. This clause's form makes it especially useful in cases of *multiple* evaluated states—and not just one or two. This multiple-evaluative clause is Select Case.

Select Case... Case... End Select Statement

Purpose: Multiple-choice conditional clause
Syntax:

```
Select Case expression
   Case [Is] comparison1a [To comparison1b]
      instruction block1
   [Case [Is] comparison2a [To comparison2b]]
      [instruction block2]

         .
         .
         .

   [Case Else]
      [instruction blockn]
End Select
```

The Select Case statement compares the value or text content of an initial expression to the value of one or more other expressions for equality. The statement contains several expressions of comparison for equality, although the element being compared is written only once as the initial expression, at the front of the clause. This initial expression can consist of a variable or even a number; however, it can also contain any number of elements that are specified or implied, and combined by arithmetic operators.

For each equality comparison, in the event (or Case) one of the comparisons between expressions evaluates True, the set of instructions after Case is executed. When the next Case or End Select is reached, execution skips to the instruction immediately following End Select.

Select Case gives the program a way of assessing options. Written in pseudocode, here's the general mechanism of Select Case:

*The following clause concerns the logically reduced
value of this expression:
    In case the reduction equals this amount,
        Execute this set of instructions;
    On the other hand, in case the reduction equals
    this amount,
        Execute this set of instructions instead;
    If all else fails, and the reduction equals nothing
    mentioned thus far,
        Execute this final set of instructions.
End of clause.*

Logical reduction is the algebraic solving of an expression to its simplest terms.

The phrase *logically reduced* refers to the act of obtaining the solution value to an expression. For instance, if a equals 5, and b equals 3, the expression 5 - (a - b) logically reduces to 3. Similarly, the expression (a > b) logically reduces to -1 (True). At this time, 5 - (c - b) logically reduces to 8. This is because you haven't assigned c a value yet so c is assumed to equal 0, and 5 - (0 - b) equals 5 - (-b) equals 8. As you can see, expressions that contain variables which haven't been formally declared still reduce logically to real-number values.

> **Tip:** The *real-number value* is the logically reduced value of any validly constructed algebraic-syntax expression appearing at any time within the program.

The most common type of Select Case comparison involves an integer variable that has a value that represents one of a few possible states. This state can be as simple to understand as which button was pressed, the user's selected expert level, or which planet in the solar system is being evaluated for orbital characteristics. The sets of instructions for each option can be included within the Select Case clause, with each option specified following the word Case.

Example

For the first example of Select Case, say you're programming a board game with three expert levels (0 = novice, 1 = intermediate, and 2 = expert). You need your program to set specific conditions based on which number the user selects. Here's how the code might appear:

```
Select Case expert
    Case 0
        look_ahead = 2
        help_mode = 1
    Case 1
        look_ahead = 4
    Case 2
        look_ahead = 7
        time_stop = 300
End Select
```

There are three comparisons taking place here: expert = 0, expert = 1, and expert = 2. In each of these cases, however, the equality operator = does not appear. The Case term implies that you're comparing the value beside Case with the value beside Select Case for equality.

Example

You can also apply the same logical mechanism of Select Case to string variables. Here's an example that creates a currency conversion factor based on the contents of a string variable:

```
Select Case currency$
    Case "pound sterling"
        conv_fact = 1.76
    Case "franc"
        conv_fact = .87
    Case Else
        conv_fact = 1
        currency$ = "dollar"
End Select
```

More cases can be added; a Select Case clause can handle significantly more cases than three. The preceding clause declares by inference a currency conversion factor conv_fact and assigns to it a value based on the contents of a string variable currency$. Notice the final condition in the clause, headed by Case Else. This final case takes care of the conversion factor if the program doesn't recognize the contents of currency$. You can use Case Else for setting default values or initial conditions for your program if those conditions cannot be set or determined logically.

Figure 12.2 shows the logical mechanism of the Select Case clause. Notice how Case acts as a partition between multiple potential solutions, in the same way Else acts as a partition between the "True" and "False" sides of the If-Then clause. Recognizing the logical difference between Select Case and If-Then makes both simpler for you to use. Think of If-Then and Select Case as two different ways of posing questions, as on a written test: If-Then is like a true or false question, and Select Case is like a multiple-choice question.

Figure 12.2

The mechanism of *Select Case.*

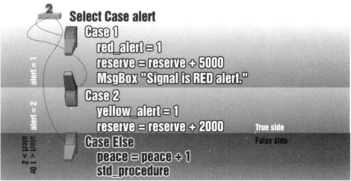

Select Case is designed so that the interpreter's mission is to compare the reduced value of two expressions for equality. We can fool this mechanism so that it evaluates one expression to see if its value is greater than or equal to the reduced value of several other expressions. Assume you have a variable fuel_level# with a value that can drop over time below three set stages, from *optimal* to *nominal*, then below *marginal*, and then below *critical*. You could establish Case ranges for which fuel levels are nominal and which are critical. For a double-precision variable, however, you would have to specify range values within 308 decimal places. In other words, we couldn't specify 0 To 299 and 300 To 499 as ranges and expect a fuel level of 299.349834923 to fall within one of those ranges. We need some way of saying "over and above *this* level" instead of merely specifying ranges and allowing for borderlines to form virtual blind spots.

Example

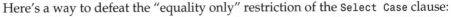

Here's a way to defeat the "equality only" restriction of the Select Case clause:

```
Select Case True
   Case fuel_level >= 1000
      alert = 0
      status$ = "Optimal"
   Case fuel_level >= 600
      alert = 1
      status$ = "Nominal"
   Case fuel_level >= 200
      alert = 2
      status$ = "Marginal"
   Case fuel_level >= 0
      alert = 3
      status$ = "CRITICAL"
End Select
```

You know Select Case compares two expressions for equality, but the depth of the expressions is unlimited. Thus True is an expression; and –1 stands for logical truth in Visual Basic. Each expression of comparison beside the Case term is reduced to a logical value of either –1 or 0. All Select Case has to do is keep making comparisons until -1 = -1—in other words, until the reduced value of the expression is equal to logical true. When that happens, the instructions following Case are executed until either the next Case instruction or End Select is reached. There are now multiple ranges with discernible borderlines; also, the equality restriction of Select Case is defeated.

You can also use an `If-Then` clause to achieve much the same results as the `Select Case` clause:

```
If fuel_level >= 1000
    alert = 0
    status$ = "Optimal"
ElseIf fuel_level >= 600
    alert = 1
    status$ = "Nominal"
ElseIf fuel_level >= 200
    alert = 2
    status$ = "Marginal"
ElseIf fuel_level >= 0
    alert = 3
    status$ = "CRITICAL"
End If
```

There's one less line in this clause, and the logical mechanism is quite similar. Theoretically, `Select Case` executes more quickly; but the difference in speed may be so marginal that it isn't noticeable. The choice of which instructions to use may be a question of style.

Summary

Sets of Visual Basic instructions can be executed conditionally by placing them within clauses. Each conditional clause is contingent on at least one expression evaluating true. Instructions that are dependent on this expression are called *nested instructions*. In the `If-Then` clause, the crucial expression is one of comparison. Such expressions logically reduce to a value of –1 or 0 (True or False). In the complex form of `If-Then`, the statements preceding `Else` are executed if the expression is True, and the statements following `Else` are executed if the expression is False.

In the `Select Case` clause, the logically reduced values of several expressions are compared with one expression for equality. Several sets of dependent instructions can be nested within `Select Case`, each set bound by a contingent expression evaluating True. Only one set of instructions is executed within a `Select Case` clause.

Review Questions

Without using your computer, execute the following code's instructions in your mind. Respond to the following questions by estimating the value or contents of the variable at the time the last instruction in the list is executed.

```
x = 15
y = 5
throughput$ = "Go"
logic = -1
If x > 8 Then
    Select Case logic
        Case (x / y) = 3
            logic = 0
            y = 3
        Case (x / y) = 5
            throughput$ = "Stop"
            x = logic
    End Select
ElseIf x > 1 Then
    Select Case y
        Case 5
            throughput$ = "Caution"
        Case 3
            caution$ = "Negative"
    End Select
End If
```

1. x

2. y

3. throughput$

4. logic

5. caution$

Review Exercise

A variable velo represents the velocity of a test rocket-powered automobile. The maximum velocity projected for this vehicle is 305 miles per hour. On the other end of the scale, the minimum safe velocity for the car at maximum power is 120 miles per hour. The Visual Basic automobile simulator lights a yellow alert light when the velocity of the car is within 20 percent of its maximum or minimum speed, and a red light when it is within 10 percent of its maximum or minimum speed. You can write alert$ = "yellow" or alert$ = "red" to stand for this light. Write a routine that sets alert$ to its proper contents for any value of velo.

Loop Clauses

In this chapter, you see how Visual Basic interprets instructions that are to be executed a set number of times with the loop clause. A *loop* is a set of instructions executed repetitively until an expressed logical condition, such as a mathematical condition, is met or until the loop is exited manually. This cycle continues from the beginning of the clause to the end of the clause and back to the beginning again, generally until some condition is met.

If the loop has no condition, execution continues in a cycle indefinitely until you stop the loop or until the program ends. By the end of this chapter, you'll understand why you might want to repeat yourself.

Some Visual Basic instructions are *not* worth executing several times in succession. Suppose that you assigned a value to a variable, as in spare_tires = 15. Making that assignment five times in succession means that the value of spare_tires would still be 15—the same as it would be if you make the assignment only once.

In cases of small clusters of instructions, don't establish loops for the sake of pure repetition. The secret to operating the loop is to repeat the same instructions, but without evaluating the same values each time. Generally, loops are constructed so that a separate variable counts the number of *iterations* made thus far in the loop.

In the For-Next loop, the enclosing statement maintains a variable that changes with each iteration. Generally, 1 is added to the variable (the variable is *incremented*) unless some other value is specified. In any event, the count variable changes. This change is reflected in the instructions in the loop. So although a For-Next loop repeats the same instructions, a For-Next loop does not make the same interpretations.

A *loop* is a set of instructions repetitively executed, and, generally, exited when a condition is met.

An *iteration* is one cycle of execution of the instructions in a loop clause.

For-Next   **Statement**

Purpose: Reiterative loop enclosure
Syntax:

```
For counter = startval To endval [Step addval]
    instruction block1
    [Exit For]
    [instruction block2]
    .
    .
    .

Next [counter]
```

The For-Next clause encloses a set of instructions to execute repetitively. At first, the variable *counter* is assigned an initial value specified by *startval*. Execution of the clause then proceeds in sequence and can be exited on reaching the statement Exit For.

At Next *counter,* a value, generally 1, is added to variable *counter*. The value is 1 unless specified as *addval* beside the optional term Step. If the augmented value of *counter* is less than or equal to the *endval* specified at the top of the clause, execution jumps to the instruction immediately following the For line. If *counter* is greater than *endval*, the loop is terminated and execution proceeds to the instruction below Next *counter*. If no For-Next clause exists in this larger For-Next clause, specifying *counter* after the term Next is optional.

The following is the general construction of a For-Next loop, expressed in pseudocode:

> Start counting between this initial value and
> this maximum value, keep track of the counter,
> and be prepared to add this amount to the counter value.
>   Execute this block of instructions.
> Now add the stated amount to the counter. If the result
> is equal to or less than the maximum value, go back
> to the beginning of the loop.

Figure 13.1 shows the For-Next statement in more visual terms.

Figure 13.1

The *For-Next* loop clause.

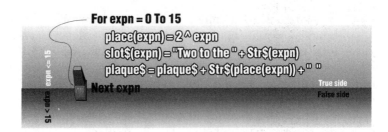

```
For expn = 0 To 15
    place(expn) = 2 ^ expn
    slot$(expn) = "Two to the " + Str$(expn)
    plaque$ = plaque$ + Str$(place(expn)) + " "
Next expn
```

Example

For the first demonstration of a loop, you see how the evaluation changes with each passing iteration, whereas the instructions remain the same:

```
For squarer = 1 To 10
    Form1.Print squarer ^ 2
Next squarer
```

This loop results in a list of the first 10 squared integers. Notice that `squarer` was referred to in the loop nest itself. Because `squarer` is continually incremented by `Next squarer`, each time the expression `squarer ^ 2` is encountered, the result is different. In almost every `For-Next` loop you write, the variable expressed just after `For` plays a role in the expressions in the nest of the clause. Note that if your program has a loop within a loop, this is called a *nested loop*.

Example

Loop clauses are perhaps most commonly used to address elements of an array in sequence. The following loop writes the contents of one array to a file one piece of data at a time:

Example

Suppose that a variable `resp()` contains one aspect of a patient's brain wave responses to stimuli over time, as shown on an EEG. Each second, a new reading was taken. These readings of responses over the passing seconds are entered into the `resp()` array. You want to plot these readings to a chart so that you can see the rises and falls in response levels.

The following loop plots these levels as vertical lines on the x-axis of the chart, representing some defined segment of time:

```
For sec = min To max
    Form1.Line (sec, 2500) - (sec, 2500 - resp(sec))
Next sec
```

Visual Basic maintains a coordinate system for graphics, although it is not pixel-oriented. Visual Basic is based on a relative scale set for each form in advance, where each unit is called a *twip*. In Windows, the twip coordinate system represents a logical arrangement of points on a graphics screen, whereas the conventional pixel system represents the physical arrangement of points.

This particular loop assumes such a coordinate system of twips exists, regardless of the actual size of the form on-screen at the time. The preceding .Line method plots a series of twips between two pairs of screen coordinates, listed in parentheses.

The preceding code fragment starts at the far left vertical twip line on the form, starting at line number sec and working line-by-line to the right. The top left corner is considered point (0, 0), so point (0, 2500) would be at the bottom left of the form. Assuming sec's initial value min is preset to 0, the loop draws lines starting at (0, 2500), working to (1, 2500), then (2, 2500), and so on, until the final value of sec reaches (sec = max).

Each new line is plotted to the right of the previous one and is drawn from the bottom (twip number 2500) up toward twip 2500 - resp(sec).

This array variable, by the way, holds the EEG response for each second of testing. Loop variable sec here establishes the relationship between the line being plotted and the response value being tested.

Example

Suppose that you want a less precise chart—perhaps a bar chart—that shows the patient's reaction over 10-second intervals. The array variable still contains reaction levels over one-second intervals. The code fragment could be modified as follows:

```
For sec = min To max Step 10
    Form1.Line (sec, 2500) - (sec + 8, 2500 - resp(sec)), , B
Next sec
```

Notice that the .Line method now draws a box (which is represented by the capital B at the end of the method). By adding Step to the end of the For instruction, you change the increment from 1—the default—to 10. Now, when Next sec is executed, the interpreter adds 10 to sec, which causes the origin point of the graph line to move 10 twips to the right rather than one. The box being plotted is eight twips wide, which accounts for the sec + 8 in the second pair of coordinates.

Example

The next example of For-Next comes from the Expressor. If you recall, this formula calculator has up to five parameter lines for formulas you select. When you choose a formula, a text line appears beside each parameter to describe its purpose in the formula. The following procedure makes those descriptor lines appear:

```
Sub CalcList_Click ()
For n = 0 To 4
```

```
      ParamText(n).Caption = label$(CalcList.ListIndex, n)
   Next n
   Clear_Params
   End Sub
```

Clicking on the drop-down list of formulas called CalcList triggers this routine. The value of the property CalcList.ListIndex represents the formula chosen, with the index of the formula name as it appears in the list.

The five descriptor lines called ParamText() in the Expressor form make up a *control array,* a sequential grouping of graphic objects with the same purpose. Graphic objects in a control array can be addressed by number, using a subscript like that in an array variable. The first object in a control array is object 0, so the loop For n = 0 to 4 starts at 0 and counts to 4. The string array variable label$ is two-dimensional; it maintains a set of parameter descriptor strings for each formula and line in the form.

When the loop instruction undergoes its first iteration, n equals 0, so the loop pertains to the first descriptor line. In the array variable label$, CalcList.ListIndex points to the chosen formula and n points to the first line (line #0). So the contents of label$, for whatever .ListIndex number, are assigned as the setting of property ParamText(0).Caption for descriptor line 0.

The last line in the procedure before End Sub is Clear_Params, which refers to yet another looping procedure:

```
   Sub Clear_Params ()
   For pl = 0 To 4
   param(pl).text = ""
   Next pl
   ClearAll_Click
   End Sub
```

At this point, you should be able to recognize the loop mechanism at work, even without indentations to mark the nest. The control array param() consists of the five parameters for the chosen formula. The property param(pl).text (not to be confused with ParamText()) refers to the textual form of the parameters, because text boxes in a form contain only what Visual Basic recognizes as text.

> **Tip:** Two quotation marks next to each other—enclosing nothing—signify a null string. Setting the textual property of a graphic object to "" clears that object of its contents.

The preceding procedure clears objects in the param control array, numbered 0 through 4, in sequence. The program then proceeds to the procedure, which clears any calculations in progress.

When you invoke a count variable for a loop clause, the name you choose for that variable is often not very important. You should, however, keep whatever name you choose consistent throughout the loop. In the preceding routine, for instance, the variable `p1` could be named something else—such as `place_where_the_numbers_will_appear`—and the operation of the routine would not be affected. For small loops, the variable name you choose can be arbitrary.

Example

A loop clause can easily be embedded in another loop clause, in which case the embedded clause is repeatedly executed. The following example creates an array that resembles a chessboard:

```
For file = 1 To 8
   For rank = 1 To 8
      chessboard$(file, rank) = man$(square_val(file, rank))
   Next rank
Next file
```

Assume `man$()` is an array that contains symbols representing chessmen. Variable `square_val()` maintains the numeric value of the chessman seated on each square in a two-dimensional array—pawns are 1s, rooks are 2s, and so on. The preceding equation assigns the symbol for each chessman to its proper position in the array `chessboard$()`. As a result, the following double-embedded loop displays a symbolic chessboard:

```
For file = 1 to 8
   For rank = 1 to 8
      Form1.Print chessboard$(file, rank); "   ";
   Next rank
Next file
```

This is perhaps the oldest way to symbolize chess pieces in computer programs, especially in machines that didn't have graphics or that used printers as their main output devices. In both preceding examples, the loop clause for variable `rank` executes eight times because it is included in the greater loop clause for variable `file`.

Example

The following example tests both the `For-Next` loop and `Select Case` clause structures. Suppose you keep records of clients sorted in order of their last names. These files will be stored on disk; however, all the records together would comprise an unmanageable file. You want to separate the records into four files, with each file designated its own quarter of the alphabet. Before you can perform an alphabetic sort, you need to assign a file division to each record and then sort each resulting file in its respective division. The following routine establishes this division:

```
For recno = 1 to maxrec
   Select Case LastName$(recno)
      Case "Aaa" To "Fzz"
         division = 1
      Case "Gaa" To "Mzz"
         division = 2
      Case "Naa" To "Szz"
         division = 3
      Case "Taa" To "Zzz"
         division = 4
   End Select
   LNDivided$(rec(division), division) = LastName$(recno)
   FNDivided$(rec(division), division) = FirstName$(recno)
   .
   .
   .
   rec(division) = rec(division) + 1
Next recno
```

Here is the preceding procedure written in pseudocode:

*Start counting from the first record to the
last record.
   For all possible cases of the current last name:
      If the name falls between A and F,
       assign the name to division 1.
      If the name falls between G and M,
       assign the name to division 2.
      If the name falls between N and S,
       assign the name to division 3.
      If the name falls between T and Z,
       assign the name to division 4.
   End of possibilities.
   Add the next last name for the previously
    assigned division to the current list for that
    division.
   Add the next first name for the previously
    assigned division to the current list for that
    division.
    .
    .
    .
   Increment the current subscript number for this
    division.
Count the next record.*

Visual Basic recognizes alphabetic ranges as valid textual expressions. Thus "A" To "F" would be a range including *Aaron*, *Ezekiel*, and *F. Fenchurch*, however, would not be included because in an alphabetic sort, *Fenchurch* falls after just plain *F*. So the ranges in the preceding code were established with lowercase a's and z's in order to include all the pronounceable proper names that may fall within the range. *Sycyznyk* would therefore fall between "Naa" To "Szz", but it would not fall between "N" To "S".

In the preceding For-Next loop clause, the variable maxrec represents the number of the final record to process. The loop counts from 1 to this number, with the count kept in the variable recno. Four files are being created in this clause, and each file has its own number addressed by the variable division. Each created "drawn and quartered" file independently counts the number of records stored in it; that number is kept in the array variable rec(). Each time a record is added to a quartered file, the independent count is incremented by 1. In the meantime, the count of records being processed by the loop clause is maintained in recno, apart from the independent counts. The statement Next recno increments that variable by 1 and sends execution to the top of the loop to process the next record in the main list.

In the Select Case clause, variable LastName$() is an array that contains the surnames of everyone in the list. Variable recno is the key variable, establishing the sole relation between LastName$() and the other similar arrays. When the contents of LastName$() fall in one of the Case ranges, a file division number is drawn from one of the four *slots*. Execution then skips, naturally, to the instruction following End Select, where the current record contents are assigned to a two-dimensional array in four partitions.

The *Do-Loop* Clause

The other form of loop clause supported by Visual Basic is the Do-Loop clause.

Do [While | Until]...Loop [While | Until]   Statement

Purpose: Conditional/unconditional loop enclosure
Syntax 1:

```
Do [{While ¦ Until} expression]
   instruction block1
[Exit Do]
   [instruction block2]
   .
   .
   .
Loop
```

Syntax 2:

```
Do
    instruction block1
[Exit Do]
    [instruction block2]
    .
    .
    .

Loop [{While | Until} expression]
```

The Do-Loop clause repetitively executes the set of instructions in it. The execution of this set may or may not depend on an optional conditional expression. If a condition is expressed, execution of the set can be terminated. If a condition is not expressed, the loop is considered endless and can be exited only with an Exit Do statement.

Under Syntax 1, a conditional expression is made at the beginning of the clause, following Do. If this expression is preceded with While, execution of the instructions in the clause proceeds in sequence, as long as the expression evaluates True. If the expression is preceded with Until, execution proceeds in sequence as long as the expression evaluates *False*—in other words, when the expression is True, the clause is terminated. If the While expression is False or the Until expression is True, execution skips to the instruction following Loop. If this is the first iteration of the loop and execution skips to Loop, the instructions in the clause will never be executed.

Under Syntax 2, a conditional expression is made at the end of the clause, following Loop. The rules governing use of While and Until are the same as for Syntax 1. Under Syntax 2, execution of the instructions within the clause proceeds following the Do statement *unconditionally*. The expression is evaluated when Loop is reached; if the loop is to proceed, execution skips to the instruction following Do. Otherwise, the loop is terminated and execution proceeds normally.

Example

Do-Loop can be used interchangeably with While-Wend; in fact, here is that implied loop from the base-conversion application in Chapter 7, "Logic and Number Systems," after being given the syntax of Do-Loop:

```
Do While cb ^ expn < ConvValue
    expn = expn + 1
Loop
```

Absolutely no logical change has been made to this clause in converting it from While-Wend to Do-Loop. The only true logical difference in syntax between While-Wend and Do While-Loop is that the Do clause has the option of being exited using the statement Exit Do. There is no equivalent "Exit While" statement.

Example

Suppose that you have a list of people or organizations who have contributed to your client's political campaign. The names are accompanied by the amount contributed, and are arranged in the order in which the contributions were made. You want to extract from this list the names of contributors of the first $25,000 to your client's campaign for inclusion in a newsletter. Because everyone contributed variable amounts, the only way your application can know when to stop extracting names is by keeping a running tally of contributions as each name is extracted and evaluating that tally each time to see if $25,000 has been exceeded.

The following routine performs the name extraction:

```
Do
    first$(listno) = contrib$(listno)
    famount(listno) = camount(listno)
    tally = tally + camount(listno)
    listno = listno + 1
Loop Until tally >= 25000
```

Here the variable `listno` maintains the current count of which record is being extracted and written to. The array `first$()` will contain the first contributors extracted from array `contrib$()`; likewise, `famount()` will contain the amounts they contributed as extracted from `camount()`. Variable `tally` contains the running amount, which is evaluated at the end of the clause to see if $25,000 has been met or exceeded.

If you're a veteran of other editions of BASIC, you may be accustomed to writing `Do` loops that end not with `Loop`, but with `Until` or `While` when conditions are expressed. In Visual Basic, the `Loop` term is mandatory when closing a `Do` loop, whether or not a condition is expressed immediately following the `Do` loop.

Summary

A clause that executes instructions repetitively is called a *loop clause.* Each repeated execution of instructions in a loop clause is called an *iteration.* The `For-Next` statement is the primary BASIC statement governing loop clauses. This statement depends on a count variable, which has its value updated each time the `Next` instruction executes. Generally, 1 is added to the count variable unless a different update value is specified beside the optional `Step` term.

Another loop clause supported by Visual Basic is `Do-Loop`. The `Do-Loop` clause can be far more versatile as a conditional loop clause, enabling conditional expressions to be evaluated either at the beginning or end of the loop, and as either true or false. The `Do-Loop` clause also enables the loop to be exited manually, if necessary, using `Exit Do`.

Review Questions

Of these types of loop clauses: For-Next, Do While-Loop, and Do-Loop Until, which is best suited for the following routines?

1. Plotting the trajectory of a moving target for each second of movement.

2. Plotting the trajectory of a moving target for each second, until the target travels beyond a specified range.

3. Plotting the trajectory of a moving target for each second, while the target travels in a specified range.

Review Exercises

Write loop clause routines that you feel would be the best-suited to perform the following jobs. Name your variables according to your personal preference.

1. Count the number of people in a list with last names that begin with *S*.

2. Tally the first 25 people in a list with last names that begin with *S*.

3. Tally the first 25 people in a list with last names that begin with *S* until no names are left in the list.

4. Tally the first 25 political contributors in a list with names that begin with *S*, as long as the total of their contributions doesn't exceed $50,000.

CHAPTER 14

Arbitrary Instruction Clusters

In this chapter, you learn more about *branching,* or how you can manually and unconditionally make a Visual Basic application's execution jump from one instruction to a distant one. You'll see how the line labeling system works and how it is used to mark the specific landing point of a manual jump. You then examine how a subroutine works and find out how Visual Basic knows to jump back to the instruction just below the one that called the subroutine.

Branching

Branching causes the program to jump to some other specified point.

When BASIC began, there were two ways to perform a direct branch: with the GOTO "command" and with the GOSUB "command." Back then, each instruction line within the entire program was given its own number in one running sequence, as you saw in Chapter 3, "Grammar and Linguistics." To *branch* is to direct the interpreter to suspend execution of the normal sequence of instructions and to resume the sequence at some other specified point. To force a branch, you would "command" BASIC to GOTO a specific line number.

Generally, a programmer numbered each line in increments of 10; so the first line might be line 10, followed by lines 20, 30, and so on. To add several lines to the middle of a program, the programmer often had to change the numbering sequence of the program entirely. If the programmer had to add one instruction between lines 17 and 18, he would have to find some way of scooting lines 18, 19, and 20 down one number. Then the programmer would have to edit all the GOTO commands that branched to line 20, making them branch instead to line 21.

In VB, line numbers have been replaced, for the most part, by *labels*. A label is a noninstruction that appears on a line by itself and is followed by a colon. The label designates a branching point. In Visual Basic, line labels are used as jumping points for branch statements.

Some people argue that, along with the passage of time, the GoTo and GoSub statements should also pass into antiquity. Indeed, there are many fully functional modern BASIC programs that contain neither statement anywhere in their source code. In the sample applications Microsoft supplies with Visual Basic, there are no GoTo (except for the error traps) or GoSub statements, nor are there line labels. The main reason for the exclusion of these once-staple elements of BASIC programs is that you can usually make execution of instructions pass seamlessly from procedure to procedure without them. Any point the interpreter might jump to is the start of a formal Sub procedure. Conceivably, every possible use for the GoTo and GoSub can be duplicated by some other clause instruction or procedural declaration.

Yet the statements remain. The role these two statements play in Visual Basic programs today is greatly reduced; they can be used only to branch execution to some other point within their own procedure and not outside of it. You may or may not choose to use GoTo and GoSub in your programs, but they still work; and people who have programmed in BASIC for decades still have a tendency to invoke these statements out of habit.

GoTo   Statement

Purpose: Branching between procedures
Syntax:

```
GoTo label
```

When it is executed, the GoTo statement causes the interpreter to suspend execution at the current instruction line, and resume with the instruction within the same procedure immediately following the specified *label*. The instruction label must appear on a line by itself and must be followed by a colon.

Example

Here's how the manual jump mechanism works. The following is a fragment from a procedure that has its initial conditions set at the beginning. The branch point for the main body of the procedure follows the setting of those conditions.

```
barrels = 3
jump_back:
For mov = 1 To barrels
    .
    .
    .
Next mov
If barrels > 0 Then GoTo jump_back
```

The preceding routine branches back to the instruction immediately following the label `jump_back` as long as there are barrels left to manipulate (`barrels > 0`).

Example

Here's another valid use of `GoTo`. This main procedure simulates the actions and conditions of a race car on a hot day in Indy. The order in which the procedures are executed is maintained within a loop clause. Execution branches to each procedure and returns from it back to the main procedure in the order specified within that loop clause. What if, however, the car stops for some reason? You need to exit the main loop and enter a damage control routine that executes corrective procedures based on the current track conditions.

But what routine do you execute? If you use the normal `Exit Do` statement for emergency exit from the main loop, regardless of the condition of the car, execution branches to only one point: the instruction immediately following the `Loop` clause-closing instruction. This is the same instruction that executes when the car comes to an intentional stop or crosses the finish line under the checkered flag; you would prefer in cases of emergency that the program go someplace else.

The following skeletal model of the main procedure concentrates on the elements of damage control and how the main loop exits conditionally:

```
Up_top:
Do
    full = Fuel_System (gas, temp, velo)
    cool = Cooling_System (water_level, temp, velo)
    intact = Body_Structure (integrity, momentum, velo)
    .
    If velo = 0 Then
        If full < 50 Then GoTo CheckFuel
        If cool > 300 Then GoTo OverHeat
        If intact < 20 Then GoTo DidWeCrash
        .
        .
        .
    End If
```

```
Loop Until miles = 500
GoTo GoodFinish
CheckFuel:
    .
    .
    .
GoTo Status
OverHeat:
    .
    .
    .
GoTo Status
DidWeCrash:
    .
    .
    .
Status:
    If okay >= 10 Then Goto Up_top
Totaled:
    Form1.Cls
    Form1.Print "Damage is beyond repair."
    .
    .
    .
    End
GoodFinish:
    Form1.Cls
    Form1.Print "You finished in ";place$(p);" place."
    .
    .
    .
    End
End Sub
```

The following is the preceding fast-paced circuit written in "encapsulated pseudocode" (EP). (In regular pseudocode, the correlation between an English-language line and a BASIC-language line is one-to-one. In EP, the correlation is more compact.)

Main procedure:
Top of main loop.
    Copy the main values from the global arrays
    into some local variables.

        .

        .

        .

    If there's no speed in this car anymore, then
        If we're low on gas, go to the fuel-checking
        routine.
        If we appear to be overheating, then go to
        the heat-checking routine.
        If we seem to be falling apart, then
        go to the crash-detection routine.

        .

        .

        .

    End of condition.
Keep up the main loop until we've gone 500 miles.
At the end, go to the Good Finish routine.
Here are the branchpoints for all those diagnostic
 routines introduced earlier.

        .

        .

        .

At the end of each diagnostic routine, go check the
 overall status.
Overall status checkpoint:
  If we're still alive, then go to the top of this
  procedure and resume execution there.
  Evidently if we're executing this instruction,
  we're dead, so clear the form.
  State the hopelessness of things.

        .

        .

        .

End of program.
Good Finish branchpoint:
    Clear the form.
    Tell us where we finished overall.

        .

        .

        .

End of program.
End of procedure.

A *routine* is any arbitrarily bounded sequence of instructions within source code.

The preceding model shows three of the many possible conditional exit points in the main Do-Loop clause that would cause execution to branch out of the loop to a specific instruction. This instruction is marked by a label that designates the beginning of the damage assessment routine. A *routine* is any arbitrarily bounded sequence of instructions within a body of source code.

There really isn't any formal structure of source code called *routine* that is maintained by the Visual Basic interpreter; when you refer to a working set of instructions, however, you may refer to it as a routine.

In the preceding skeletal model, the Do-Loop clause first places calls to Functions (not shown) that return the operating status of certain parts of the car. When these functions are executed, the If-Then clause checks to see if for some reason the speed of the car has become 0. If it has, several embedded If-Then statements check to see if any variables have fallen below the critical level, indicating a possible need for corrective action. If action is necessary, execution branches to the specified routine. You can (unofficially) refer to a portion of a procedure that is bounded by a line label and a terminating statement as a routine.

The corrective action routines fall below the Loop statement that terminates the main loop. To ensure that the interpreter doesn't execute one of these routines by accident when the car reaches the finish line (miles = 500), another GoTo statement is added that branches to GoodFinish:. Thus, you can prevent the program from diagnosing the car at the end of the race.

Each diagnostic section starts with a line label. Two of the three routines end with GoTo statements, which take the program to the label Status: that decides whether it's safe to continue running the car. DidWeCrash: doesn't need to branch to Status: because it falls immediately below it anyway. If Status: determines 10 reasons or more why it should continue—as indicated by the variable okay—execution branches to Up_top, which is the start of the main Do-Loop clause.

At the end of this procedure are two terminating routines called Totaled: and GoodFinish:, both of which end with End and together represent the extreme worst-case and best-case scenarios.

Visual Basic's syntactic structure is based not on the manual tracing of execution paths like old BASIC, but on the natural flow of data between formal procedures. When you add manual branching to a routine, you actually introduce something foreign to the scheme of things, like damming a river. When you redirect the course of the river, you suddenly become responsible for where the water goes.

> **Caution:** If you're new to programming, you may want to be cautious in your use of manual branch statements. If you're a veteran of BASIC, however, you have nothing to fear by using GoTo, because Visual Basic enables you to use it only under the confines of local procedures, anyway.

Program Context

Visual Basic is one of the first implementations of BASIC to limit the use of GoTo and GoSub to the local procedure in which they appear. In more common editions of BASIC, *procedures* are defined as routines separate from the "main body" of the program, which generally contains the primary sequence of instruction execution. In Visual Basic, there is no "main body" of the program—just a group of procedures that call one another.

The entry into and exit from each Visual Basic procedure is closely guarded; Visual Basic's procedural syntax is designed to exchange data in the way highways exchange cars at their interchanges. The Sub and Function declarations establish clear entries into these procedures, whereas End and Exit Sub ¦ Function define clear exit points. The Visual Basic interpreter can thus easily draw a map for itself, connecting all the procedures that refer to each other and designating the types of data the procedures will exchange when they meet at the intersection. To arbitrarily force branches between procedures would befuddle this roadmap.

The Subroutine

A *subroutine* is a routine which ends with a branch to the line just following the instruction that called it.

The first formal subdivision of BASIC source code was in the creation of the *subroutine*. A subroutine is a set of instructions within a procedure that is executable repetitively, can be called by name, and whose end forces a branch back to the instruction just past the one that called it.

The first subroutines in old BASIC had no absolute beginning; a branch to a subroutine was performed by addressing a line number, as in GOSUB 2900. The end of each subroutine was supposed to be more definite, defined with the RETURN "command"; however, such commands could be applied in conditional statements such as IF A > 15 THEN RETURN. As a result, subroutines had fuzzy boundaries on both sides—they had no marked point of entry and many possible points of exit.

GoSub   Statement

Purpose: Temporary branching
Syntax:

```
GoSub label
```

When the GoSub statement is executed, the interpreter branches to the instruction immediately following the specified label. While execution proceeds in sequence, the interpreter keeps track of the location of the instruction that performed the branch. When the interpreter executes the next Return instruction, it branches back to the instruction immediately following the GoSub call.

Example

 Suppose your application sends output directly to your printer. Periodically, you need the program to send the page footer and page eject code to the printer. The following shows how you can do this using GoSub:

```
Sub PrintTotals ()
Printer.Print "Monthly Totals for Period Ending ";date$
   .
   .
   .
Printer.Print "Totals thus far:        ";total(pageno)
GoSub NextPage
Printer.Print "Advertising Expense Projection"
   .
   .
   .
Printer.Print "Totals thus far:        ";total(pageno)
GoSub NextPage
Printer.Print "Maintenance Expense Projection"
   .
   .
   .
Exit Sub
NextPage:
   Printer.Print "      Page"; pageno
   pageno = pageno + 1
   Printer.NewPage
Return
End Sub
```

As you can see, you can put more than one GoSub call within the same procedure to the same subroutine. Notice that no parameters are passed; this is true for all GoSub statements. In Visual Basic (unlike some other BASIC dialects), no data is exchanged during the branch to a subroutine. Such an exchange isn't really necessary, because the context of a subroutine is identical to the procedure in which it resides—in other words, it shares variables with its procedure. Because all variables that belong to the procedure belong to the subroutine, parameter passing is entirely unnecessary.

Notice that the statement that closes the subroutine is Return.

Return

Statement

Purpose: Subroutine termination
Syntax:

```
Return
```

When the Return statement is processed, a branch is made to the instruction immediately following the most recently executed GoSub statement.

Example

Using subroutines, you can modify the Indy automotive simulator procedure so that it performs multiple diagnoses on the same accident. You can rewrite the branch statements to the diagnostic routines as follows:

```
If velo = 0 Then
    If full < 50 Then GoSub CheckFuel
    If cool > 300 Then GoSub OverHeat
    If intact < 20 Then GoSub DidWeCrash
    .
    .
    .
End If
```

Each diagnostic routine branches using a GoTo statement to a single point called Status, which may be updated as follows:

```
Status:
    If okay >= 10 Then Return
```

If something is wrong when velo = 0 (the car isn't moving), the branches to each of the diagnostic routines are all GoSub statements. The labels of the individual routines have not been altered. The end of each diagnostic routine still branches to Status: using GoTo statements. At the end of the Status: routine, however, is a Return marking the end of not only one, but *all* the diagnostic routines. The interpreter knows to branch back to the instruction following the GoSub statement that called it, wherever that is. In the case of this procedure, the Return branch could be to another conditional GoSub branch, which could start this cycle all over.

Sequential Branching

In the previous example, you saw how a single Return can cause a branch back to any of multiple calling points. Visual Basic continues to use a variation of both GoTo and GoSub for branching from the calling point to any of multiple locations specified in a sequence.

On...GoTo and On...GoSub   Statements

Purpose: Multiple-choice branching
Syntax:

> On *expression* GoTo *label0*, *label1*[, *label2*, . . .
> ➥*label255*]
>
> On *expression* GoSub *label0*, *label1*[, *label2*, . . .
> ➥*label255*]

Placing On *expression* before a GoTo or GoSub statement converts that statement into a sequential branch to any of the labels specified in the list following the keyword. Branching depends on the value of *expression*. Generally, *expression* consists of one variable by itself. The logically reduced value of *expression*, when rounded to the nearest integer, must equal between 0 and 255, inclusive. This value is equivalent to the place in the list of the *label* that will be the destination of the branch. If the statement placing the branch is GoSub, the branch will be treated as a regular call to a subroutine; on processing Return, execution proceeds to the instruction immediately following On...GoSub.

Example

You may remember seeing On...GoTo used in the Expressor application to branch to any of the five routines for processing formulas. The branch appeared within Sub ApplyFormula ():

```
On ndx GoTo f1, f2, f3, f4, f5
```

Variable ndx in this routine contains the index of a formula selected from a drop-down list box. If a formula was selected, ndx should be equal to an integer from 0 to 4. This makes the list box control a perfect candidate for being evaluated with On...GoTo. In essence, the preceding statement is like making five statements on one line: If ndx = 0 Then GoTo f1, If ndx = 1 Then GoTo f2, and so on.

Summary

Visual Basic allows for manual branching to other points in a procedure marked by line labels. Such labels are alone on an instruction line and are followed by a colon. The primary statement for performing a manual branch is GoTo. The area of instructions within a procedure that is the recipient of a branch can be called a *routine,* although no such formal structure exists in Visual Basic.

A subroutine is a portion of a procedure that is branched to using the GoSub statement. After a subroutine is completed, execution branches back to the statement immediately following the previously executed GoSub after processing the Return statement. Subroutines are informal structures and often do not have absolute beginning or ending statements. Many subroutines can be closed with a single Return statement. The instructions that make up a subroutine need not be adjacent to one another in the context of a procedure.

A conditional sequential branch is possible using On *expression* before a GoTo or GoSub statement. Such a statement branches to any label within a list delimited by commas, having a place in the list that is equal to the rounded value of the *expression* stated beside the On term.

Review Questions

1. What happens when the interpreter comes across a Return instruction in a procedure without having processed a GoSub instruction?

2. What Visual Basic loop clause structure substitutes for the conditional branch used in the following routines:

```
top_loop:
c = c + 1
.

.

.
If c < 4 Then GoTo top_loop

top_loop:
If c = 4 Then GoTo out_loop
c = c + 1
.

.

.
GoTo top_loop
out_loop:
.

.

.
```

Review Exercise

The following puzzle uses GoTo and GoSub statements. Using your mind and not the computer, follow the branching pattern of this routine. Here, line numbers are used as labels for each line of the routine. The objective is to find the final value of variable c whenever an End statement is processed.

```
1 GoTo 5
2 GoSub 4
3 GoTo 25
4 Return
5 GoSub 10
6 a = 4
7 GoTo 15
8 a = 3
10 Return
15 GoSub 8
20 GoTo 2
25 On a GoTo 30, 40, 50, 60, 70
30 b = 4
35 GoTo 80
40 Return
50 b = 3
60 b = 5
65 GoTo 80
70 b = a
80 On b GoSub 100, 110, 120, 130, 140, 150
90 Print c
95 End
100 c = 3
105 Return
110 c = b
115 Return
120 c = 6
125 Return
130 Return
140 c = a
145 Return
150 c = c
160 Return
```

CHAPTER 15

The Module Hierarchy

In this chapter, you examine the framework of a Visual Basic application in detail. Because the source code of an application is divided into modules with no obvious sequence of arrangement, it is difficult for a person reading the source code to determine the order of execution for the procedures. Understanding the hierarchical relationship between modules and procedures of an application helps you better determine the order in which the modules are executed.

Later in the chapter, you see a presentation of a quick examination of the statements that affect the execution of some defined portion of the application, or the execution of the program as a whole.

The Origin of Modules

The first BASIC programs were not divided into modules or procedures. They consisted of many pages of numbered instructions. A BASIC programmer in the 1970s didn't consider what area or region of the program a variable belonged to, because when a variable was declared—generally informally—the rest of the program had full access to that variable. Compared to the structure of Visual Basic, each old BASIC program consisted of one huge procedure.

In the 1970s and early 1980s, BASIC programmers wrote subroutines that could be used in several programs and integrated into the BASIC source code. This integration was not easy, however. First, the line numbers used by the subroutines could not conflict with any other line numbers used by the program—so programmers often numbered their reusable subroutines starting with an astronomically high number, in hopes that the main routine would stay comfortably within the four-digit range.

Second, the names of variables invoked in these subroutines could not duplicate names used in the main body of the program. Therefore, it was not generally safe to use a simple variable name like X or N for a reusable subroutine, since these variables were usually already used in the main body of the program. Imagine writing a reusable subroutine that converted radians to degrees before performing a trigonometry operation. Because your main program—to be written later— would probably use all the variables there are with meaningful names, you had to make sure your variables had meaningless names to avoid future conflicts. Programmers attempted to solve this problem by beginning all of the variables in a subroutine with a specified prefix such as "sub" (for example, subDegrees). This solution was not ideal, but it helped.

Modular programming languages such as C existed long before BASIC became modular. BASIC was originally designed for beginners. When a programmer became good enough to be concerned about variable conflict reduction, the programmer no longer needed BASIC. Yet in certain cases, it appeared C programmers were having fewer problems than BASIC programmers. It was widely agreed that a programmer should spend more time concentrating on the completion of the task at hand and less time on the maintenance of the program.

BASIC source code became much easier to manage when line numbers became optional features. The first real modular subdivision made to BASIC source code came with the introduction of *subprograms*. A subprogram was an advanced type of subroutine that existed, in a sense, in its own little world. None of the existing variable values and dimensions in the main body of the source code applied to a subprogram, except those few variables listed in a set of parentheses. Microsoft chose to mark subprograms in BASIC source code with the statement Sub. Although Microsoft doesn't use the term *subprogram* today with respect to Visual Basic, the declarative statement retains its original name.

Sub   Statement

Purpose: Nonvalued procedure initiation
Syntax:

```
[Static][Private] Sub procedure_name ([[ByVal] argument1[()]
➡[As type], [ByVal] argument2[()][As type]. . . ])
    instruction_block1
    [Exit Sub]
    [instruction_block2]
    .
    .
    .
End Sub
```

Sub is the primary procedural declarative statement in the Visual Basic vocabulary. The statement is used to enclose a procedure of a given name procedure_name. Execution can branch to this Sub statement from any point in the program if you invoke this procedure name within the source code or use the Call statement.

A Sub procedure is said to receive values from the procedure that called it, as *arguments* or *parameters* (the terms are interchangeable here). When a procedure is called from outside, the values that pertain to that procedure are listed within parentheses, separated by commas. These values are said to be passed to the procedure, and may be written as explicit numerals or represented as variables. When a procedure is declared inside, those values are received in the order in which they are passed, and are assigned to variables that have names that may not be the same as those used for the procedure call. Contents of string variables can be passed in the same manner as values of numeric variables.

If you want to ensure that a specific type of argument is passed to your procedure, an integer for example, you can place the term As type beside that argument. The contents of an entire array can be passed to a procedure as an argument, as long as the variable name of the array is identified with empty parentheses ().

Usually, any change made to the values of the arguments listed is reflected in the variables used as arguments in the procedure call. This reflection can be overridden for a specific argument by placing the term ByVal before that argument; doing so allows the variable used in the procedure call to retain its value even if the value of the variable used to receive the argument has changed in the procedure.

The instructions in a Sub procedure are executed in sequence. A Sub procedure is terminated whenever an Exit Sub or End Sub is reached during this sequence.

The values of the variables with scopes that are local to the procedure, or that have not been declared as modular or global outside the procedure, are usually nullified whenever the procedure is exited. Use of the term Static before the Sub term allows the interpreter to maintain the values and contents of variables used by the procedure after it is exited. Use of the term Private before the Sub term, if that Sub procedure appears in a general module, changes the context of the procedure from global to module-level, so that no other module may place a call to this procedure. Sub procedures declared in form modules are automatically given module-level context, and do not require the Private qualifier.

Microsoft is believed to be the originator of *user-defined functions* within BASIC source code. Initially, the definition of such a function could only be expressed on one line using the statement DEF FN (which stands for *define function*). Later, function definitions were promoted to formal clauses, and are now considered procedures in their own right. In fact, in Visual Basic, any instruction that is not a part of a Sub procedure and is not a global or modular declaration is part of a Function procedure.

Function

Statement

Purpose: Valued procedure initiation
Syntax:

```
[Static] [Private] Function procedure_name ([[ByVal]
➡argument1[()] [As type], [ByVal] argument2[()]
➡[As type]. . . ])
   instruction_block1
   procedure_name = expression1
   [Exit Function]
   [instruction_block2]
   [procedure_name = expression2]
      .
      .
      .

   End Function
```

The Function statement acts as the header for the procedures that receive arguments in the same manner as a Sub procedure, but return a single value or string. The Function statement appears to have precisely the same syntax as the Sub statement. One important difference between the syntaxes of the Function and Sub procedures is that the *procedure_name* of a Function procedure is treated like a variable in the procedure. Near the termination of the Function procedure, a validly interpretable expression is assigned to that *procedure_name* with an equation. The value of this expression is the solution or result of the function as it has been declared.

The syntax of arguments expressed within the Function statement is the same as the syntax of arguments within the Sub statement. Usually, the values of those variables that have scopes local to the procedure—or that have not been declared as modular or global outside the procedure—are nullified whenever the procedure is exited. Use of the term Static before the Function term changes the context of the procedure from standard local to static, allowing the interpreter to maintain the values and contents of variables used by the procedure after it is exited. Use of the term Private before the Function term—if that Function procedure appears within a general module—changes the context of the procedure from global to module-level, so that no other module may place a call to this procedure. Function procedures declared in the general section of form modules are automatically given module-level context, and do not require the Private qualifier.

A Sub procedure has no specific responsibility to the rest of the program to provide it with any values or results. By contrast, a Function procedure has the responsibility of providing one value or alphanumeric string as the result of the function. Within the Function procedure, between the declaration and the End Function terminator, the name of the function itself—without parentheses—is shown. The name of the function is treated like a variable. The result of the function is assigned to this apparent variable—in fact, the assignment can be made at several different points in the procedure, but it must be made at least once. This way, the function name may represent that variable value outside of the function procedure.

For instance, because twist is not a reserved Visual Basic keyword, if one procedure contains the instruction a = twist(c, d), the interpreter checks to see if twist is an array variable or a call to a function procedure. If a function declaration Function twist(x, y) exists in the program, the function procedure twist executes. Like the Sub procedure, variables x and y are treated as inputs. Unlike the Sub procedure, the Function procedure has one output; in the procedure, there must be a statement of assignment in the form twist = *formula*. Notice that twist has no parentheses in this assignment. The assignment is made as if twist were a standard variable. Like a variable, the term twist represents a value outside of the Function procedure.

The Order of Execution

Programming writers tend to say "The execution of the program proceeds in sequence." In Visual Basic, however, that sequence is not evident when you consider the important matter of which procedure comes first. For the Visual Basic interpreter, there is an absolute order for the execution of not only procedures, but declarative instructions. This order is shown in figure 15.1.

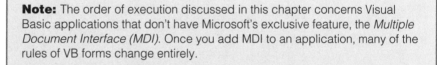

> **Note:** The order of execution discussed in this chapter concerns Visual Basic applications that don't have Microsoft's exclusive feature, the *Multiple Document Interface (MDI)*. Once you add MDI to an application, many of the rules of VB forms change entirely.

Start at the top of figure 15.1 and work your way down toward the base. The general declarations sections of all general modules in the project are executed first. This way, global variable declarations, wherever they may appear, are always executed in the beginning. The proper location for global declarations is within the general declarations section of a general (nonform) module. Because you can connect many general modules at random to the same project, each module may require its own set of uniquely named global variables; for this reason, global declarations are placed at the head of general modules.

Figure 15.1

The order of
execution.

You may decide to place global declarations in a separate *general module*. This is a general module that contains only global declarations and no procedures, so the VB interpreter does not treat it with any distinction. The order in which declarations of general modules are executed doesn't matter, because execution is complete before any of the project's primary body of instructions begin.

Visual Basic maintains many keywords, although its vocabulary is not limited to those keywords. VB allows *libraries* to be attached to the operating set of recognized instructions for an application. A library is a set of process names that are treated as procedure names by Visual Basic, but are actually calls to processes within Dynamic Link Libraries (DLL) outside Visual Basic. A DLL is a file, probably written in the C programming language, that contains functions that can be executed from within your VB program.

> A *library* is a set of procedures that supplement the Visual Basic procedures.

If you plan to extend the Visual Basic vocabulary, place the library declarations in the declarations section of a general module.

A general module does not pertain to any one form. It may contain purely mathematical or analytical functions, which have little or nothing to do with forms or graphic objects. It can, however, refer explicitly to the graphic contents of more than one form, or it can refer symbolically to contents that might appear in some form at some time. You can have a general module draw an entirely new form, and place new contents within that form. The specific instructions for that form, however, may appear in a form module for that new form.

In large applications, general modules perform the main part of the workload, whereas form modules perform the mere functions of communicating with the user. In smaller VB applications using only one form, the general procedures section of the single form module might perform the bulk of the workload as well. If your application has any procedures that do not define responses to graphical events—in other words, they're not executed because the user clicked something with the mouse or typed something on the keyboard—those procedures belong inside a general module. General modules are good places to locate Function procedures because none of the event procedures in a form module are Function procedures.

A general module is created by selecting **N**ew Module from the **F**ile menu of Visual Basic's main window. The VB interpreter gives the module its own window, with a default title of MODULE*x*.BAS. The *x* represents the order in which the module is created in the project—which has nothing to do with the order of execution. At this point, the module has no specific file name; once you enter text into this module and select **F**ile Save **A**s, you give this module a formal file name. General modules are usually given the extension BAS. You can attach an existing general module to a project by selecting **F**ile **A**dd Module and choosing the module's file name from the selector box. By default, the selector searches for files ending in BAS.

When the Visual Basic interpreter executes an application that has general modules, the file names of those general modules do not affect the execution. In other words, at run time the interpreter views all the procedures of all the general modules belonging to the project as being in a sort of conglomerated pool, unless the term Private is used in the procedure declaration to shield a procedure from any other module in the project. So, even if there are two or more general modules in a project, no two procedures in the project can share the same name unless Private is used in their declarations. In any event, no two procedures in the same module can share the same name, whether or not you use Private. If you intend to load two preexisting general modules into a project, be certain the names of the procedures won't conflict with each other.

The *startup* procedure contains the first nondeclarative instructions that are executed.

Under the default condition of the VB interpreter, no Sub or Function procedure in any general module executes unless a procedure in some form module places a specific call to that procedure. This is because the interpreter usually executes instructions belonging to the *startup* form, which is the first form module the interpreter executes. By default, this is the first form module entered into the project; it is the former Form1, whatever it may be named now.

The Form Module

A form module is divided into three sections: the declarations section, the event procedure section, and the general procedure section. Variables declared in the declarations section of a form module use the Dim statement and are considered to have modular scope—meaning they pertain to every procedure in the form module.

Following the execution of the declarations section, the interpreter looks at the event procedures section for a procedure called Sub Form_Load (). _Load is the event of loading the form into the workspace. If this procedure exists, it is executed next. After Sub Form_Load () is complete, if there are any other event-driven procedures in the form module, Visual Basic suspends execution and waits for an event to occur that activates an event procedure.

If no instructions exist in the Sub Form_Load () procedure of the startup form module, VB displays the form. This display may trigger other events in the VB vocabulary; if so, the event procedures for those events are executed. After Sub Form_Load () (if it exists) and any subsequent event procedures are executed, the VB interpreter suspends execution and waits for the user to trigger the next event. This literally means that nothing happens; the VB application is in a state of limbo. No instructions are executed during this time, although the application is officially in Run mode rather than Break mode. BASIC veterans may be confused by this suspension, because in standard BASIC, instructions are executed at all times during run time. In Visual Basic, you can run an application that does not contain any lines of source code, and still receive a form named Form1 on-screen while the interpreter waits for an event to occur—a zero-instruction program *is* a program.

The context of procedures in a form module is such that no general module can place a call to them. Specifically, you cannot *manually* trigger an event procedure from outside the form module containing that event procedure. A nonform general procedure cannot simulate a _Click or a _GotFocus. When possible, you should use the form's event procedures only to maintain the form.

The *Sub Main ()* Procedure

You may choose to have a startup procedure called Sub Main () in one of your project's general modules. Like its counterpart main() in the C programming language, Sub Main () is generally used to specify the order of execution of the other major general procedures in the project. Often this order of execution is expressed as a cycle in an unconditional Do-Loop clause. Here's an example of a Sub Main () procedure in a general module. Its sole purpose in this instance is to specify the order of execution of other procedures, in this or other general modules:

Example

This example illustrates how the main() function can be used in your application:

```
Sub Main ()
    Do
        LoadRecords()
        GetInput()
        SaveData()
    Loop
End Sub
```

In this example, there are calls to three arbitrarily named procedures that exist in this or some other general module. They are called and executed in sequence continuously until program execution stops. A project can contain more than one general module, and there is no limit to how many procedures can exist in a general module. Because a general module contains a procedure named Sub Main (), however, does not mean it is automatically recognized as the startup procedure.

To make Sub Main () the startup procedure:

1. Select **P**roject from the **O**ptions menu in the VB main window. A dialog box is displayed, containing a drop-down list box in the format of the Properties window. On the second line of the list is an item marked Start Up Form. Double-click this item to view a list of the form names of all eligible form modules in the project, plus a separate listing for Sub Main. (These names represent the .Name property settings for these forms, not their file names.)

2. If one of the general modules in your project contains a procedure named `Sub Main ()`, this procedure is also listed among the other form names, even though it is not a form. Choose it by double-clicking `Sub Main`.

Once `Sub Main ()` is made the startup form, when the VB project is executed, no form is loaded into the workspace and displayed unless a specific statement is issued to load a window.

The procedures in the general procedures section of a form module are executed only when called by name from within the form module. Likewise, every general module procedure executes only when called by name, except `Sub Main ()` if it is designated the startup procedure. You can call `Sub Main ()` directly with the instruction `Call Main`, or simply `Main`.

The VB interpreter allows you to name one of the procedures in the general procedures section of a form module `Sub Main ()`, unless you've made a `Sub Main()` procedure in one of your general modules the startup procedure. However, a `Sub Main ()` procedure in a form module differs from one in a general module in that the interpreter does not view it as a candidate for startup form, and it cannot be executed automatically.

The *DoEvents* Statement

When the Visual Basic interpreter is in the midst of a procedure, it won't consider other events (such as button clicks) until it processes an `End Sub` or `End Function` instruction. In other words, if the VB interpreter is busy, it can tell event procedures to wait in a sort of queue until the current procedure ends.

One way to alter this order of execution is by using the `DoEvents` statement, which is the only *indefinite branch* in the Visual Basic vocabulary. This statement puts the current procedure on hold, and allows the other event procedures that have been waiting for their turn to be executed in the order in which the events were generated.

DoEvents   **Statement**

Purpose: Event priority shift
Syntax:

```
[forms% = ]DoEvents[()]
```

The `DoEvents` statement suspends execution of the current procedure. This allows the VB interpreter to pass control to whatever event procedures may have been triggered by the user, awaiting execution in the event queue. The statement then enables Windows to update all graphic objects and pass control to other applications in the Windows workspace for whatever business they are waiting to perform in the background. DoEvents directs the current procedure to yield to anything else that requests permission for execution.

When phrased like a function, DoEvents() returns an integer value equivalent to the number of forms currently loaded in the workspace of the Visual Basic application to the variable *forms%*.

You've just read the general execution process for Visual Basic applications. Because this process is already defined for you by the Visual Basic interpreter, you'll find it easier to design a project with multiple modules and procedures. At first, however, the learning curve for the arrangement of modules and procedures in a VB project can best be described as a steep incline.

The *End* Statement

The *End* statement is used to end a clause or procedure.

So far, every complete procedure listed in this book closes with some form of the End statement. The statement has a few other purposes besides the more obvious ones you've already seen.

End   Statement

Purpose: Context termination
Syntax:

```
End [{Function ¦ If ¦ Select ¦ Sub ¦ Type}]
```

When invoked on a line by itself, the End statement terminates the current program, resets all declared variables, and closes all open channels to data paths, data files, or other Windows applications. There is no limit to the number of nonqualified End statements that can be invoked during an application. When used with another term, the statement specifies the closing portion of a clause or procedure. There can be only one End statement per clause or procedure.

Example

The End statement by itself does not mark the final line in the source code listing of an application; it merely symbolizes the final instruction to be executed. Suppose a dialog box is invoked, asking if the user really means to quit the application. A response code of 1 signifies that the user really means to quit. Here's how a conditional clause to terminate the application might appear:

```
If resp% = 1 Then
    End
End If
```

Note that End If is still written here, even though End may stop program execution.

One member of the original BASIC vocabulary that survives in Visual Basic is the Stop statement.

Stop   Statement

Purpose: Program suspension
Syntax:

```
Stop
```

The Stop statement suspends program execution, provoking the same response from the interpreter as if the user had selected **B**reak from the Visual Basic Run menu. The Immediate window CLI becomes available after Stop is executed. Program execution resumes at a procedure or line label specified in a statement that the user must issue through the CLI.

One of the original purposes of Stop in old BASIC was to allow programmers to insert temporary instructions—especially in error traps—that break the program in case of a bug. The Visual Basic interpreter has a more effective system of placing such gaps in programs, in the form of *breakpoints*. Any instruction in an application can be declared a breakpoint, sending the interpreter into Break mode. A breakpoint instruction is indicated in a code window by a different color of text, not by a special instruction. So although Stop is there, its duties might be handled more effectively by the interpreter's debugging system. You see breakpoints in action later in the book.

> **Caution:** All Stop instructions should be removed from an application before compilation. Because the purpose of the **Stop** instruction is to send the interpreter into Break mode, once a VB application is compiled and able to be executed without the aid of the VB interpreter, there is no longer a Break mode to be sent to. Therefore all **Stop** instructions should be removed from an application before compilation.

Because you can End a clause or procedure only once, Visual Basic gives you a sort of "back door" statement that you can use to end a particular instruction set. This statement is the Exit statement.

Exit   Statement

Purpose: Forced context abort
Syntax:

```
Exit {Do ¦ For ¦ Function ¦ Sub}
```

The Exit statement immediately stops the current procedure or loop clause. For loop clauses, execution of the program resumes with the instruction following the clause closure instruction. For Sub or Function procedures, execution resumes with the instruction following the instruction that placed the call to the procedure. If the procedure was not called by another instruction, execution is suspended pending the occurrence of a recognized user event.

Example

The following example shows the differences between the End and Exit statements, in the form of an amendment to the previous example:

```
If resp% = 1 Then
    End
Else
    Exit Sub
End If
```

Assume this clause appears in an event procedure that handles the selection of *Quit* by the user, somewhere on the form. All event procedures are Sub procedures rather than Function procedures. A response code of 1 symbolizes the user means to quit; but otherwise, there isn't much point in continuing this procedure. Whether the response code is 1 or something else, this clause is exited before End If is reached.

So why write End If in the first place? In order for the interpreter to be able to grasp this conditional clause, the clause must have a beginning and an end. Without the end, any instructions that follow—especially End Sub—will cause a context separation problem. The interpreter must be able to comprehend all the instructions, clauses, procedures, and modules in an application before it can execute the first instruction. So even though End If isn't really executed, it must be present.

Summary

The need for modular divisions in BASIC programs evolved from the conflicts that programmers faced when combining routines. These conflicts concerned distinguishing line numbers from each other and making sure variable names weren't duplicated. Visual Basic procedures eliminate both possible areas of conflict by making line numbers optional and having you state specifically which variables are to be shared between procedures.

With the exception of variable and functional declarations sections, all other executable instructions in a Visual Basic project are found in procedures. The two types of procedure declarations in Visual Basic are Sub and Function. The difference between Sub and Function is that Function returns a specific value in a variable name that doubles as the name of the Function procedure. Both Sub and Function procedures allow for input values between the parentheses of their declaration. Unlike the Sub procedure, however, a Function procedure passes a value back to the body of the program from which it was called. The values to be passed between procedures are presented as arguments in the procedure declaration and in the procedure call.

Execution of the procedures in a non-MDI Visual Basic application follows this order:

1. The global variable declarations in any general modules in the application

2. Procedure Sub Main () of any general module, if and only if it is officially declared the startup procedure

3. Any procedures in the project that are called within Sub Main ()

4. The declarations section of Form1 if that form is loaded into the workspace by Sub Main (), or of any form that has been made the startup form in place of Form1

5. Procedure Sub Form_Load () of the startup form if no Sub Main () exists, or if that form is addressed by Sub Main ()

6. Any event procedures in the startup form triggered by the initiation of graphic objects in that form

7. Any procedures called in the general procedures section of the startup form

8. The declarations section of Form2, or whatever form is entered into the project following Form1

9. Sub Form_Load () of Form2 if it is loaded into the workspace

10. Event procedures for Form2

11. General procedures for Form2, and so on

The DoEvents statement suspends the currently executing procedure to allow pending event procedures to execute. A conditional clause or procedure is terminated using the End statement. This statement acts as the bottom part of an instruction set enclosure, or nest. A loop clause or procedure is exited using the Exit statement, without having to execute the statement that closes the clause or procedure. You can suspend execution of the program at any time by using the Stop statement.

Review Questions

1. What is the difference between the End Sub statement and the Exit Sub statement?

2. What is the difference between the End statement and the End Sub statement?

3. What part of a VB project always executes first, whether or not it contains any code?

4. Assuming you've never officially set the startup form for the application, what by default is the first procedure executed if the application contains at least one dialog box?

5. What instruction from Form1 executes the first procedure of Form2?

6. Assume a VB project has no form assigned to it, only a general module. There is no Sub Main () procedure in this module. What happens when you select **R**un or **S**tart?

7. The following is a list of procedure names for a Visual Basic project, along with their locations in the modular structure of the project. This list is in random order. Reorganize the list so that it reflects the natural order of execution of these procedures.

Procedure or Region Name	Location
Function angle_over (angle, circle)	general module 1
Global declarations	general module 1
Declarations section	Form2 module
Sub Command1_Click ()	Form1 module
Sub blowed_up_good ()	general module 1
Sub Main ()	general module 1
Sub Form_Load ()	Form2 module
Declarations section	Form1 module
Sub Form_Load ()	Form1 module
Sub Main ()	Form1 module
Sub Main ()	general module 2

CHAPTER 16

Parameter Passing

In this chapter, you get more insight into the logical mechanisms that allow values to be passed and shared between procedures in a Visual Basic application. You'll understand to a greater extent why distinctions between different scopes of variables exist, and why the variables of a VB application are not simply shared among all the procedures and instructions of the program.

In the few examples you've seen of control being passed from one Visual Basic procedure to another, the call to the receiving procedure consisted of the name of the procedure being called, along with any values that procedure needs. A procedure call is actually part of a named instruction—the Call statement. The syntax of Call came from an earlier edition of Microsoft QuickBASIC; later, for efficiency as well as compatibility with C-language syntax, the verb Call was made optional.

[Call]   Statement

Purpose: Interprocedural branch
Syntax 1:

        Call *procedure_name* ([*argument1, argument2. . .*])

Syntax 2:

        procedure_name [*argument1, argument2. . .*]

When the Call instruction is processed, or when the name of a defined procedure is invoked in source code, a branch is made to the named Sub procedure. Any values to be passed to the procedure as arguments are listed beside the *procedure_name* in the order in which they are to be received by the opening statement of the Sub procedure. If values are passed to the Sub procedure, the corresponding variables listed in the procedure's opening statement receive their values. Any changes made

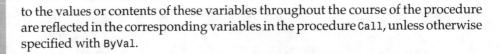

to the values or contents of these variables throughout the course of the procedure are reflected in the corresponding variables in the procedure `Call`, unless otherwise specified with `ByVal`.

> **Caution:** If the term `Call` is specified, the argument list is in parentheses. If `Call` is omitted, the argument list is not in parentheses.

Example

Assume that you have a `Sub` procedure called `tri_area` that determines the area of a right triangle given the lengths of two sides. The following two statements result in exactly the same branch to the procedure:

```
tri_area side1, side2

Call tri_area (side1, side2)
```

The procedure that solves for the area of the right triangle might appear as follows:

```
Sub tri_area (base, height)
    area = base * height / 2
End Sub
```

Arguably, this procedure could be expressed better with `Function` than `Sub`. As a result, the procedure call can be placed in the midst of a formula rather than as a statement by itself. Here's how the `Function` call and the revised procedure might appear:

```
Under_incline = tri_area (b, h)
    .
    .
    .
Function tri_area (base, height)
    tri_area = base * height / 2
End Function
```

Another reason the procedure would perform better as a `Function` than as a `Sub` is that in the `Function` syntax, a separate variable `area` need not be declared for modular scope outside of the procedure using `Dim`. This would be necessary with the `Sub` syntax, because the scope of the calculations within a `Sub` procedure are confined to that local procedure. The calculation result would have no other way to get out of the procedure except by having been declared with a scope above local.

To illustrate, for `Sub tri_area ()` to pass variable `area` in the previous example back to the calling body, the instruction `Dim area` needs to be placed in the declarations section of the module containing both the call and `Sub tri_area ()`, because area was not declared in the parentheses in the Sub procedure opening statement. However, for Function tri_area (), you're free to place the procedure in a general module completely separate from any procedure that may call it—the result is rendered in tri_area, which stands not only for the result, but for the function itself. After the instruction a = tri_area (b, h) is executed, execution proceeds from wherever the call was placed to the general module. Nonetheless, there doesn't need to be any Dim or Global declaration for a variable tri_area.

Table 16.1 shows the four variable scopes, along with the statements used to declare variables for each scope. *Scope* refers to the number of places in your program that have access to a variable's value.

Table 16.1. The four variable scopes.

Scope	*Statement*	*Definition*
Local	Dim	Pertaining only to the procedure in which the variable is first invoked or declared, and having a value that is cleared when the procedure is exited.
Static	Static	Pertaining only to the procedure in which the variable is first declared, although its value is maintained after the procedure is exited in case of possible reentry.
Modular	Dim	Pertaining to all procedures in a module by virtue of having been declared in the general module area of a form module.
Global	Global	Pertaining to the entire source code.

Notice that at the beginning of both preceding procedures, the variable names for the procedures differ from the variable names that passed those values to the procedures. This is because passing parameters is not really transferring variables from one procedure to another. Variable passes are actually methods for setting up corresponding variables between the calling and receiving bodies. Between the pass and the reception, the receiving procedure gives new identities to the values it receives.

Obviously, global variables don't have to be passed as parameters, because every procedure is entitled to know its values or contents. Yet in many applications that you write, you can declare several sets of variables to represent the same types of contents—for example, different variable sets for different customers in a mailing list, or different subatomic particles in a table. You may want a Sub or Function procedure to describe something that can be done to a particular type of variable without referring to that variable specifically.

Parameter Passing Order

In the right triangle formula, the parameter-passing order didn't really matter because the two parameters were multiplied together, anyway. For most other procedures, however, the order in which the parameters are passed is crucial.

Example

For example, take this procedure call and its formula, which calculates the area of a right-circular cylinder. This procedure call and formula were taken from the Expressor application.

```
f1:
solution = surf_area_rccyl(p(0), p(1))
GoTo display_result

Function surf_area_rccyl (r, h)
surf_area_rccyl = (2 * PI) * r * h
End Function
```

Keep in mind that routine f1: and Function surf_area_rccyl () appear in (or as) two different procedures. Notice that the input parameters for the function are stored in an array variable p(), whereas on the receiving end, their values are assigned simply to unit variables r (radius) and h (height). In geometry, these values pertain to two distinctly different aspects of the cylinder, so their order in the parentheses must be maintained. The relation between the order of parameters in the passing and receiving lists determines the purpose of those parameters.

Example

From another area of the Expressor is a call to a Function procedure that needs more parameters. This procedure contains the Doppler shift formula. This formula determines the frequency of a light or sound wave that comes from a moving source, given the observed shifted frequency of that wave and the velocities of both the wave source and its observer:

```
f5:
solution = dopp_shift(p(0), p(1), p(2), p(3))
display_result:
Readout.Caption = Str$(solution)
```

```
Function dopp_shift (vo, vs, fo, c)
dopp_shift = ((c + vo) / (c - vs)) * fo
End Function
```

The velocity of the observer of a wave is vo, vs is the velocity of the source of the wave, fo is the observed frequency of the wave, and c is the velocity of the wave (*c* generally represents the speed of light in physics equations, although the user may want to substitute the speed of sound here).

Again, the values were passed to the function with array variables, but were received by unit variables. You could use any four valid numeric variables to pass values to Function dopp_shift (), but the result of the equation would be the same. Here again, the order of the four variables within the parameter-passing sequences determines their purpose and relation to each other—not their names. This order can be arbitrarily defined when the procedure is written. After this order is defined, however, it must be maintained within every call to that procedure.

Here is the standard syntax for calls to a Function procedure:

```
variable = procedure_name (parameter1, [parameter2...])
```

The function term formed by *procedure_name*() can also be used in a formula or expression and still call the Function procedure. This is because the called procedure defines for the Visual Basic interpreter how the function term logically reduces to a real value.

Example

When passing parameters between equations, the precision of those parameters must match. Thus, a single-precision, floating-point variable must pass a value to another single-precision value in the receiving procedure. Suppose, however, for the sake of a receiving Function procedure, you need the formula to work on a rounded integer, although the original variable doing the passing may be fractional. Say that variable c is the variable to be rounded. You can write the Function procedure as follows:

```
Function wild_card (x, n, c)
c = Int(c)
.
.
.
End Function
```

Variable c is rounded inside the Function procedure. If the instruction that called it is r = wild_card(u, t, v), v will be rounded, as well as c. If you'd rather that the procedure leave the passed variable alone, this needs to be stated up front at the procedure declaration, using the qualifier term ByVal as follows:

```
Function wild_card (x, n, ByVal c)
```

The term ByVal stands for "only the value of" in this case. Including it means the rounding of c will not in any way affect the value of v in the calling procedure.

Summary

A branch to a Sub procedure is made by using a statement that may or may not contain the term Call. A branch to a Function procedure, on the other hand, is made by implication—by stating the procedure name as an element of a mathematical expression or equation.

When passing parameters between procedures, the purpose of those parameters in the procedure is determined not by the name, type, or scope of the parameter, but by the parameters' chosen order within the parameter list. The order of the list in the instruction that calls the procedure and the order of the list in the declaration of the procedure must match for the procedure to operate. When parameters are passed successfully in this manner, changes made to the variable that received the parameter value are reflected in the variable that passed the parameter value to the procedure. This reflection can be overridden in advance by using the term ByVal before the variable. The value or contents of the calling variable indicated by ByVal are left as-is.

Review Questions

1. Early in this chapter, you saw two different types of procedures—Sub and Function—perform the same type of arithmetic operation on the same parameters and yield the same results, except in different ways. Why is the instruction that calls the Sub procedure for this arithmetic operation considered a *statement*, whereas the instruction that calls the Function procedure for the same arithmetic operation is considered a *function*?

2. Syntactically speaking, why does a Call statement enclose its arguments within parentheses, whereas the same statement made without Call omits those parentheses?

Part IV

Designing for User Interaction

CHAPTER 17

Control Identification and Contents

In this chapter, you see the primary properties and events used in the processing of the most common graphic objects on a Visual Basic form. To this point, you've seen numeral values and alphanumeric contents assigned to variables, which are symbols held in memory by the VB interpreter. The user of the VB application doesn't see these symbols. To use these values and contents, they must be delivered to the user visually—in the *graphic object*.

Clarifying the Graphic Object

A *graphic object* is another name for the Image and Picture controls in the Visual Basic toolbox. When you refer to the control in your source code, you generally refer to it as an object. When you see the control in your window, you generally refer to it as a control.

Every graphic object you place on a form has a full list of characteristics, or *properties*, displayed in the Properties window, along with the properties' current settings. A *property* describes, for a graphic object, its contents, size, position, shape, operative restrictions, and any other characteristic relevant to the operation of that particular device. Not only are the contents of a form considered graphic objects, but so is the form. Most graphic objects are visible controls, although some, such as the Timer, are not seen during an application's run time; they merely add functionality to the form.

Each graphic object's properties list is unique to that control, although all graphic objects in the Visual Basic environment must share one specific property: its name.

.Name   Property

Pertains to: All controls
Representation: Title of reference
Set by way of: Properties window only

The .Name property for a graphic object, or an array of related objects, is set to an arbitrary name at design time. This property becomes the name stated to the left of the period when the graphic object is addressed within the source code of the program, using object-oriented syntax.

By default, the .Name of a form takes the syntax Form*n*, in which *n* represents the order in which the form was added to the project. At design time, when you draw a control on the form, the interpreter gives it the syntax Control*n*, where Control stands for the type of control and *n* is the accession number among controls of similar type, representing the order in which that control was added to the form. You can choose to leave these .Name properties as they stand initially, or use the Properties window; you may choose to change them to whatever seems appropriate.

The *.Name* of a graphic object cannot be set with instructions.

You can set the .Name property of a graphic object through the Properties window only. Once set, the source code of a program cannot change that name; no instruction alters the .Name of a graphic object. Any instruction that does alter the setting of a property for a named graphic object uses the following syntax:

```
[Form.][Name.]Property = setting
```

Here, the *Name* in the syntax refers specifically to the .Name property setting made at design time. If the instruction appears in a procedure belonging to the implied *Form*, you don't need to write the form name explicitly; likewise, if the instruction appears in an event procedure belonging to the implied graphic object, you don't need to write the control *Name* explicitly.

Using Aliases

You cannot have an instruction that says Control.Name = 'NewName', because the name of a control is fixed. You're probably wondering why anyone would want to change the name of a graphic object in the middle of the program, anyway. Consider the following situation: You have a form being used for many different purposes throughout the application. At one moment, it could be a "Type in your password and code number" form, and at another moment it could be a "On whose authority is this action undertaken?" form.

Obviously, this form is something of a custom dialog box. The form always contains the same three command buttons, so the same set of event procedures govern the behavior of those buttons, regardless of the purpose they're being used for at the time.

Polling means that one part of the program requests data from another part, or from the computer itself.

When the sole event procedure for the button is initiated, it needs to know its mission. It has to *poll* (request data from) some part of that button to find out what that mission is. Now the `.Caption` property is available (discussed later), so conceivably, the procedure could check the textual contents of the button (`OK`, `Cancel`, `Fire Away!`, and so on) to see what the user command truly is. Suppose, however, that the button shows the same contents all the time, regardless of its purpose?

For occasions such as these, Visual Basic provides the `.Tag` property. This property lets you give objects a second name or "alias." This property's purpose is ambiguous.

.Tag   Property

Applies to: All standard controls
Representation: Control title alias
Set by way of: Properties window, program instruction

The `.Tag` property for a graphic object is set to an arbitrary name, for a purpose that the programmer can define. For most operations, this property is largely ignored by the VB interpreter; in situations where a procedure polls the contents of an unnamed control, however, the procedure can use `.Tag` as an identifier for the control if you assigned a unique title to it. The VB interpreter does not check `.Tag` property settings to ensure their uniqueness, as it does with `.Name` settings. By default, the `.Tag` for a graphic object is a null string.

Example

Assume that a button's initial purpose in a form is to initiate the sending of password data to a security procedure. At design time, the programmer sets the `.Tag` property of a control whose `.Name` is `Go`, to `"Security"`. After the security task finishes, the `Go` button is later used in the application as an authority check. An instruction can change the `.Tag` as follows:

```
Go.Tag = "Authority"
```

With this new `.Tag` setting, the user of the application clicks the Go button (whatever its caption is at the time). In the event procedure for the button, you can now test for its purpose with the following clause:

```
Select Case Go.Tag
    Case "Security"
        .
        .
        .
    Case "Authority"
        .
        .
        .
    Case Else
        .
        .
        .
End Select
```

Here, the Sub procedure can be broken into a handful of "subprocedures" that each handle one of many changing purposes of the same button.

Control Array Indexing

Each element of a control array has an index with which it is associated.

As you saw earlier with the initial construction of the Expressor project, the nonzero buttons on the calculator panel were made part of a collective control array. To make the Visual Basic interpreter identify a group of buttons as an array, give them all the same name; but like an array variable, each element of a control array is given a subscript or an *index*.

.Index   Property

Applies to: All arrayed controls
Representation: Array element identifier
Set by way of: Order of design, Properties window

The .Index property refers to elements of a control array, especially because all elements in an array share the same .Name property. The control is referred to by its designated array name. Following that, the index of a control in an array is stated as a subscript value in parentheses. Indices for controls in an array are designated in sequence at design time. Their sequence can also be reorganized at design time using the Properties window. The index for a control is fixed throughout the run time of an application.

In the Expressor application, the 1 through 9 buttons were given captions of 1 through 9, and also corresponding indices of 1 through 9. This way, it was easy for the single event procedure for all the positively numbered buttons to determine which button was pressed by polling the value of variable Index—the standard parameter for the _Click event procedure.

Object Events

Each element of a control array has an *index* with which it is associated.

An event name such as _Click is rarely invoked in the middle of a Visual Basic instruction, except where events are manually engaged. In any event, each graphic object maintains its own list of recognized events that represent, in one sense, that object's "sensitive spots." Almost every control is sensitive to being clicked on, double-clicked on, having something dragged over it, and having the mouse pointer just pass it by. The most common event is the _Click event, which really represents the user clicking a control and, in so doing, issuing a command.

_Click   **Event**

Action: User indication
Applies to: Button, check, combo, directory, file, form, grid, image, label, list, menu, option, picture, text
Parameters: Index (control arrays only)

The _Click event for a control is recognized whenever the user presses and releases the mouse index button while the pointer is over that control.

Remember, the term *index button* here refers to the left button on desktop systems; for left-handed users, however, this could be the right button. For laptop mouse users, this could be the long button along the side of the mouse. The Sub Control_Click () event procedure is the one generally used to perform the command function associated with that control. Three other events in the VB vocabulary are associated with the act of indicating a control as a way to give a command to the application. One of them, naturally, is the double-click event.

_DblClick   **Event**

Action: User indication
Applies to: Button, check, combo, directory, file, form, grid, image, label, list, option, (not MDI), picture, text

Parameters: Index (control arrays only)

The _DblClick event for a control is recognized whenever the user quickly presses and releases the mouse index button twice while the pointer is over that control.

Two other events pertaining to mouse buttons are the _MouseDown and _MouseUp events. The _MouseDown event is recognized immediately after the index button of the mouse is pressed—it doesn't wait for the button to come up again. The _MouseUp event takes care of the release of the button. A single click, therefore, actually generates three events in the following sequence:

_MouseDown

_MouseUp

_Click

By contrast, a double-click generates *five* events in the following sequence:

_MouseDown

_MouseUp

_Click

_DblClick

_MouseUp

Event procedures are executed in their entirety, in the order in which the events are triggered.

This sequencing of events tells you two things. First, it tells you that the _MouseDown and _MouseUp event procedures can contain graphical or special effects instructions—for example, something that lights up or dims a setting, or something that engages a special animation sequence. The animation sequence for the _MouseUp event can be fully completed before the actual work ordered by the user—the contents of the _Click event procedure—begins.

Secondly, however, Windows now does not distinguish fully between a click and a double-click. Notice that in the double-click sequence, the click event was still recognized. If you've programmed for the Macintosh—especially for HyperCard— you'll notice this is different from the way Apple computers distinguish completely between clicks and double-clicks. Of course, Macintoshes use a delay following the first click to see whether the user intends to press its single mouse button a second time; on faster Macs, this delay isn't noticeable.

To make your Visual Basic application "usage-compatible" with a Macintosh application that can distinguish between clicks and double-clicks for the same control, you can consider altering the usage model (the way a user operates a program) for the VB application. You can't have the `_Click` event procedure wait for a double-click to occur, because all the instructions in that procedure will finish before the `_DblClick` event procedure begins. This is because event procedures don't necessarily start at the time the user triggers the event, although they execute in the order in which the user triggers the events.

What the User Can and Cannot Edit

For the next section, you're invited to follow along by making a simple Visual Basic form containing three objects: a label, a text field, and a command button. The label control in the VB toolbox is symbolized by a capital *A*; the text field is symbolized by a lowercase *ab* in a box. It doesn't matter precisely where you place these controls, as long as they appear as they do in the sample form in figure 17.1.

Figure 17.1

MiniForm, a model of simplicity.

These three controls are designed to represent the three things a Visual Basic form does most often. Specifically, the text field represents the location for textual data entry. The label represents a directive to the user specifying what type of data goes into the text field. Finally, the button represents the command to have the application do something with the data—most likely, file it someplace.

At first, the textual contents of the new label are "Label1," and the textual contents of the text field are "Text1." No single property pertains to textual contents; instead—for reasons you'll later come to appreciate—text properties that can be edited are distinguished from noneditable text properties.

The user can't edit *.Caption* properties; the user can, however, edit *.Text* properties.

.Caption   **Property**

Representation: Noneditable textual contents
Applies to: Label, button, check, option, form, frame, menu
Set by way of: Properties window, program instruction

The setting of the `.Caption` property for a control in a form reflects the textual contents of that control. The setting of the `.Caption` property for a form reflects the textual contents of its title bar. In each of these cases, the user cannot directly edit the textual contents within the control, although events triggered by the user can cause program instructions to change the `.Caption` property. The maximum character length of a `.Caption` property setting is 2,048 characters.

.Text   Property

Representation: Editable textual contents
Applies to: Text field, combo
Set by way of: Properties window, program instruction, user interaction

The .Text property for a control is set to its textual contents. You can change these contents at run time through direct interaction with the control. With respect specifically to combo boxes, the .Text property is set to the currently chosen item in the list, appearing in its uppermost text box. The maximum character length of a .Text property setting is 2,048 characters.

> **Note:** Modern computing terminology has treated the term *edit* rather loosely; some Visual Basic documentation calls what this book calls the *text field* the *edit box.* In general computing, the term *field* refers to any space reserved for data, whether it's visual space (such as the box on the form) or an area of memory. In Visual Basic, any field where the user can place the cursor is an editable field. Remember, the cursor and the pointer are quite different; the pointer is moved by the mouse, whereas the cursor denotes where text goes when the user types it.

The MiniForm test form is represented in figure 17.2.

Figure 17.2

Distinguishing between *.Caption* and *.Text*.

Here, two controls—the label and the button—have .Caption properties associated with them, whereas the text field—the only one in which the user can enter text—has a .Text property. When you run the MiniForm application (it still runs without instructions) without changing the default contents of any of the controls, the property setting for Label1.Caption is equivalent to Label1, the setting for Command1.Caption is equivalent to Command1, and the setting for Text1.Text is equivalent to Text1. The latter setting changes instantly whenever the user changes the contents of this text field. The VB interpreter doesn't wait to officially recognize the change after the user replaces the contents Text1 for something else—for example, Testing—but acknowledges all the changes made along the way. Backspacing over a letter, for example, is a change.

Example

Now it's time to add an instruction to start manipulating these contents. Edit the procedure framework for the _Click event to read as follows:

```
Sub Command1_Click ()
Command1.Caption = Text1.Text
End Sub
```

Run the application, enter something new into the text field, and click the command button. Instantly, the button's caption mimics at least the far left part of the text field's contents, as demonstrated in figure 17.3.

Figure 17.3

The amazing mimic button.

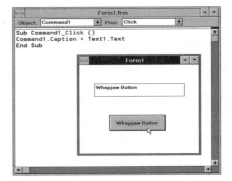

> **Note:** The width of a text field drawn in a form does not limit the length of the text entered into that field, or on the `.Text` property associated with the field. Regardless of length, the maximum number of characters a `.Text` property setting can hold is 2,048 characters. You can type that many characters, again regardless of the length of the text field, because Windows automatically knows to scroll the contents of text fields to the left to make room for newly typed characters. When the cursor leaves the text field, however (when the control loses the focus), Windows displays only the far left characters in the text field.

Picture box controls may, at some point, receive text as well, although their textual contents are not treated as properties. Text, once in a picture box, is treated as *graphics*; neither the user nor the programmer can edit it.

When Is a Command a Command?

The previous demonstration should explain that the event procedure you use to process command instructions from the user, for a button or similar device, is the _Click event procedure. Now, _Click works when the user's command is a response to an explicit *command selection*—in other words, when you placed on the form some button or label that says Proceed, Stop, Sort, or some similar directive. A selection from the menu bar works the same way. As you see later, the event procedure that handles a form's menu selections is also the _Click event procedure.

Suppose, however, the command is not the result of a selection. Suppose it is the movement of a scroll bar or, as you just saw, a verbal command typed into a field. In such cases, the Visual Basic interpreter recognizes the _Change event.

_Change   Event

Representation: Status alteration
Applies to: Label, text, picture, directory, device, list, combo, scroll
Parameters: Index (control arrays only)

The _Change event is recognized whenever the contents or status representation of the antecedent object are changed. This change may be due to the user altering the object's position or content, or because a VB source code instruction changes an object property. For a label or text field, _Change is recognized when its textual contents are altered, or when a character is added to or removed from the field. For a picture box, _Change is recognized when its graphical contents are altered. For a list box or related device, _Change is recognized when the list contents are altered or amended, or when the selection represented by that list is altered. For a scroll bar, _Change is recognized when the scroll box is moved.

Note: The "Applies to" section of an *event* description in this book lists only those graphic objects supplied with the standard edition of Visual Basic 3. If you add any more graphic objects to the toolbox later (which, of course, you can do), many of the events described in this book may apply to them as well.

Example

A Visual Basic application uses the text a user enters into a text field by assigning its textual contents to a string variable. Determining the proper time to make that assignment depends, in large part, on the construction of the form itself. For something as minimalistic as the MiniForm, however, the _Change event might be as good a time as any. The following event procedure makes the appropriate string variable assignment:

```
Sub Text1_Change ()
entry$ = Text1.Text
End Sub
```

The _*Change* event procedure is where text-parsing instructions most likely go.

This string variable assignment doesn't change the display in any way. Later, in the run time of a more complex program than MiniForm, however, the variable entry$ may be evaluated for particular contents, added to another string, or saved to a disk data file. It's important to note that both the .Text property setting and the contents of entry$ are changed by this procedure whenever the user presses a key when the cursor is in the text field. You probably wouldn't want, therefore, to include the save-to-disk routine in the _Change event procedure, because _Change is triggered many times before the user's entry into the text field is complete.

> **Caution:** After you enter instructions into the event procedure frameworks prepared for you by the Visual Basic interpreter, when you change the .Name property settings for the graphic objects those event procedures belong to, the VB interpreter automatically changes the control names in the Sub procedure headings. It does not, however, change the names of the graphic objects where they appear in the instructions between the Sub procedure headings and the End Sub closures. It is up to you to make those changes yourself, if you choose to make alterations to .Name properties while you are programming.

In the same way that the _Click event procedure is the best place for instructions that process the user's selected commands, the _Change event procedure is most likely the best place for the instructions that process the user's written commands, or data entry to the program (respectively, *directive* and *disclosure*). Depending on how the form is set up, however, you may find yourself using the _MouseUp event procedure for certain directives rather than _Click, or the _LostFocus event procedure in place of _Change—a substitution you read more about later.

The following few properties affect how a text field displays contents that extend beyond the boundaries you drew for that field in the form.

.MultiLine   **Property**

Representation: Multiple line capability
Applies to: Text
Set by way of: Properties window

The .MultiLine property setting reflects whether permission is granted to the Visual Basic interpreter to generate line feeds in a text field when its contents have exceeded its length. This way, a text field's textual contents can be broken into multiple lines using word-wrap if .MultiLine is set to logical True (or On).

.ScrollBars   Property

Representation: Scroll bar attachment permission
Applies to: Text field, grid, MDI
Set by way of: Properties window

The .ScrollBars property grants the Visual Basic interpreter permission to place scroll bars on the sides of a text box if its textual contents exceed the number of lines or columns you have set aside for it. The property is set at design time to a two-bit binary value. Bit 0 on the right (the least significant bit) is set to 1 if the horizontal scroll bar for the antecedent text box can be displayed. Likewise, bit 1 on the left (the most significant bit) is set to 1 if the vertical scroll bar for the text box can be displayed. In decimal, the value of .ScrollBars can be set to any of the following:

0   No scroll bars   (default)

1   Horizontal bar

2   Vertical bar

3   Both scroll bars

Note: The VB interpreter automatically knows to break the textual contents of labels into multiple lines if necessary, using the word-wrap technique.

Summary

A graphic object refers to the written term in source code; a control refers to the visual representation of its role on the form.

All graphic objects, including forms, receive names through the setting of the .Name property. All names must be unique and must be given at design time; any operation in which names must be changed or polled by the interpreter must be undertaken using the .Tag property, instead. The .Index property serves to identify elements of a control array that share the same .Name.

The _Click event is triggered whenever the user presses and releases the index button of the mouse. Because the event waits for the full process to occur, its associated event procedure is generally the place where command-processing instructions for its related graphic object are placed. The _DblClick event is triggered when the user double-clicks the mouse button, although Windows recognizes the _Click event first in all cases before the _DblClick event.

The .Caption property represents the textual contents of a control that the programmer determines is noneditable. The .Text property represents the textual contents of a control that the programmer determines is editable. Both .Caption and .Text settings can be made through the Properties window or set at run time.

The _Change event is triggered whenever the program or the user makes some alteration to the textual contents or to the status of a control. Its associated event procedure is the most likely place where instructions that process text entry are placed. Both the .MultiLine and .ScrollBars properties of a text field are available for cases in which the contents of that field may exceed its boundaries.

Review Questions

1. If more than one control on the same form has the same name, what distinguishes them from one another?

2. If two controls on two different forms have the same name, what distinguishes them from one another?

3. If the user is to enter a password into a text field and click a button to gain access to another form, what event procedure most likely contains the instructions that determine whether he has access?

4. If an event procedure passes control to a general procedure, and the general procedure doesn't know what control was clicked, how can the general procedure be passed the name of the control?

CHAPTER 18

Design and Layout

In this chapter, you see how the contents of a Visual Basic form are arranged and organized. You learn about the twip coordinate system that is used primarily for the positioning of elements on-screen in a device-independent manner. You also learn how graphic objects are arranged on a form so that the keyboard can be used alternately to navigate between objects in a rational manner.

The Twip Coordinate System

One of the benefits of many people using Microsoft Windows is that although they may all have different screen resolutions, they can use the same Windows applications. With release 2 of Windows, screen resolutions were somewhat fixed. If you had a computer with a monitor that was capable of higher resolutions, the control panel of your Windows applications was proportionally smaller to the degree your screen resolution was higher than the established "norm." Thus, there really were no benefits to investing in higher-resolution monitors; the better your monitor was, the smaller your applications became, and the more eye strain you had.

With Windows 3.0, the job of conforming the graphic output to the screen resolution was delegated to individual screen drivers; and Microsoft encouraged video card manufacturers to write their own screen drivers so that their brands could take advantage of Windows in unique ways. Finally, higher resolution meant greater clarity, that was further enhanced by the advent of TrueType fonts for Windows 3.1.

Programmers have grown accustomed to working with *pixels* as their standard units of graphical measurement. A pixel is a physically plotted point on any computer's screen. The higher the screen resolution for a program becomes, the smaller the pixel unit; if you choose to use pixels as standard units of measurement for Windows, you encounter the multiple-resolution problem. If a text field is 60 pixels long and 20 pixels wide, how big is that field going to be on everyone's screen? Is there a way to use a conversion factor so that the text field shows up the same size on everyone's screens, only more clearly at higher resolutions?

A *twip* is a plotting point that is considered independently from pixels. Microsoft states that there are 1440 twips to the inch.

Visual Basic's coordinate system is extraordinarily versatile. The default units of measurement that the system uses in place of pixels are actually smaller in geometric configuration space than the pixels themselves. Thus, the screen coordinate system is independent of the screen. Each point along this system is considered a *twip*. A twip is a plotting point as interpreted in memory by Microsoft Windows, within a relative coordinate system that exists independently from the physical pixel-based coordinate system of the screen.

In all graphical computers, each unit in the coordinate system is represented in memory by a certain number of bits. The combination of bits for a pixel usually represents, in binary coding, the color of the pixel at that point. This is true for most VGA graphic systems. Memory within these systems is specially apportioned for the VGA card, so that the motherboard's main memory can be used for other purposes. In the main memory, Windows maintains a representation of the screen that has a greater resolution than the actual screen. Visual Basic can allocate segments of main memory for itself to maintain images that have a greater resolution than the screen. This way, if the computer's graphics hardware changes and the screen drivers are advanced to go with it, the screen representation can be rescaled to fit the new screen without drastically altering the VB program.

Positioning and Sizing Controls

Because each control that inhabits a Visual Basic form is inherently rectangular, its twip coordinates for position and size can be set using only four properties:

.Left   Property

Representation: X-axis coordinate
Applies to: All controls, form, MDI
Set by way of: Properties window, program instruction

The .Left property of a form is set to the distance in twips (1/1440 of a logical inch) between the origin point of the form and the leftmost edge of the screen. The origin point is the first user-addressable point in the top left corner of the form; if the form has borders, they appear around the original point. The .Left property of a control is set to the distance in twips between the origin point of the control and the leftmost point on the form.

.Top   Property

Representation: Y-axis coordinate
Applies to: All controls, form, MDI
Set by way of: Properties window, program instruction

The `.Top` property of a form is set to the distance in twips between the origin point of the form and the uppermost edge of the screen. The `.Top` property of a control is set to the distance in twips between the origin point of the control and the uppermost point on the form.

.Width   Property

Representation: Rightmost boundary
Applies to: All controls, form, MDI
Set by way of: Properties window, program instruction

The `.Width` property of a graphic object is set to the distance in twips between the two vertical sides of that object. In effect, this setting establishes the x-axis coordinate of the point at the bottom right corner of the object.

.Height   Property

Representation: Lowermost boundary
Applies to: All controls, form, MDI
Set by way of: Properties window, program instruction

The `.Height` property of a graphic object is set to the distance in twips between the two horizontal sides of that object. In effect, this setting establishes the y-axis coordinate of the point at the bottom right corner of the object.

Forms in Visual Basic are not truly three-dimensional; however, when controls overlap, it's important for the interpreter to know which control will appear in front of the others. It would be nice to say that the interpreter is determining which control appears "on top," but in the VB vocabulary, `.Top` means "up," not "in front of." In this case, therefore, it is only the VB vocabulary that actually makes direct reference to a geometric axis; and it does so using the `.ZOrder` method.

> **Note:** Although the original reason why the twip scheme was invented was so that objects drawn on the Windows screen can have equivalent sizes, most objects drawn with the Visual Basic interpreter are smaller on 1024 × 768 resolution screens than they are on 640 × 480 screens—not proportionally smaller, just smaller.

.ZOrder **Method**

Purpose: Designating display ordinance
Syntax:

    [Control.]ZOrder position%

The .ZOrder method sets the plotting order of the designated *Control* within its form to the given *position%*. Those controls given a lower *position%* are plotted first; those with later numbers are plotted later. If the area occupied by a later control in the sequence overlaps any of the earlier controls, the later control appears in front of those it overlaps.

.ZOrder is a method, not a property.

The order in which the programmer places the controls at design time establishes the natural z order of controls in a form. Because .ZOrder is a method and not a property, it can only be used during an application's run time to alter the display sequence.

Example

Suppose two controls in a form overlap one another. When the user clicks one control, that control needs to be moved to the front of the display so that all of it is seen. The following procedure accomplishes this:

```
Sub Control2_Click ()
Control2.ZOrder 1
End Sub
```

In all cases, 1 is the front of the z order. If some other control has a z order of 1, after this instruction is executed, it has a z order of 2. Any other control whose z order is already 2 is bumped down to 3, and so on.

> **Note:** When two controls that are sensitive to the _Click event overlap one another, and the user clicks the area of the overlap in the form, the control with the earlier z order (the one that appears in front) is the recipient of the _Click event.

Design-Aided Computing

A representation of the MiniForm test form, introduced in the previous chapter, is shown in figure 18.1. Notice how only the form's coordinates are determined with respect to the screen as a whole, whereas all the contents of the form are coordinated with respect to the top left corner of the form, wherever that may be.

Figure 18.1

The construction blueprint for MiniForm.

Origin points

Example

You might sometimes want "occasional controls" in your form—perhaps a text field whose purpose is temporary. Instead of setting its visibility property to False and resetting it to True later, you can conceivably animate the form by bringing in that control with a "wipe" effect. Suppose your form is 5000 twips wide—in other words, its `Form1.Width` setting is set to 5000 at design time. Your text field is 3000 twips wide, but it starts off the right side of the form.

.Left and *.Top* coordinate settings for a control are not bounded by the width and height of its form.

Note that the coordinate settings for a control do not have to be within the form boundaries. The `.Left` and `.Top` coordinates may be greater than the `.Width` and `.Height` property settings, respectively, of the form itself. The control exists as far as the VB interpreter is concerned; it's invisible, and doesn't receive mouse pointer-related events, although it is there. Furthermore, you may set `.Left` and `.Top` properties to negative values if you need the control to be placed off the left side of the form.

Therefore, put the control's design-time opening position at –3000 with respect to the form. To bring it into the center of the form, its post-wipe `.Left` property needs to be 1000, leaving a margin of a thousand twips on either side of the text field. Because you need to do this with a degree of speed, have a loop clause step in increments of 50 twips. The button that starts the wipe procedure is a "Sign In" button; on the text field, the user enters a password. Here's the procedure:

```
Sub SignIn_Click ()
For wipe% = -3000 To 1000 Step 50
    PassWord.Left = wipe%
Next wipe%
PassWord.ZOrder = 1
End Sub
```

Because the control is busy processing instructions, the user can't start signing in until the text field has reached its closing position. You can remedy this by placing a `DoEvents` statement just before the `Next wipe%` instruction. Notice that any overlap over the control during the wipe is remedied after the loop clause has terminated, through the execution of a .ZOrder method.

Using Tabs

One of the most difficult adjustments a long-time computer user has to make when migrating from DOS to the Microsoft Windows environment is remembering to press the Tab key when entering text into a form with multiple fields. In most everyday DOS programs, the user can type text into a field, press Enter, and then enter text into the next field. In Windows, pressing Enter generally substitutes for clicking the default button—in many forms, the OK button. If the Windows user presses Enter, expecting the cursor to move to the next field, the Windows application might respond by assuming the entry of text for this form is complete. As a result, the form is stored as a formal record with a bunch of null fields.

In the first NameForm application listing, if you entered the text boxes into the form in the order they were presented, you should be able to enter text into one field at run time, press Tab, and proceed in sequence to the next logical field. In other words, you won't jump from the Last Name field to the ZIP code field. The Visual Basic interpreter maintains a *tab sequence* for each control. Within that sequence each control has its place.

.TabIndex   **Property**

Representation: Text entry ordinance
Applies to: All controls
Set by way of: Properties window, program instruction

The .TabIndex property for a control is set to its numerical order in the tab sequence within its associated form. By default, the tab sequence of controls in a form is established by their order of creation at design time; this sequence can be reorganized at design time or run time. By default, labels are assigned .TabIndex properties, although labels are not officially part of a form's tab sequence.

Although the .TabIndex property applies to all controls, it really works for the controls that the user can actually operate. For instance, if a label is listed as being "next" in the tab sequence, and the user presses Tab, the label is skipped, and the next editable or operable control in the sequence is indicated, generally by the Windows "hazy line." Labels and nonoperable controls are skipped in the tabbing sequence, regardless of their .TabIndex property settings. When setting the .TabIndex property, controls are automatically renumbered to reflect the change.

.TabStop   Property

Representation: Keyboard sequence enrollment
Applies to: All controls
Set by way of: Properties window, program instruction

The .TabStop property setting for a control is a True/False flag reflecting whether it is enrolled in the tab sequence. A setting of False designates that the user may not indicate the control by pressing Tab. By default, .TabStop is set to True. A control can be a tab stop like a bench can be a bus stop. To designate that the tab route does not stop at a certain control—in a sense, to remove the bench from the bus stop—set its value to False.

Figure 18.2 shows the form for the NameForm application "Mark II," along with the .TabIndex settings for each text field typed in their respective fields. All objects in Visual Basic have a .TabIndex property, even if it is not used, as in labels and command buttons. The .TabIndex settings that are "missing" from figure 18.2 are assigned to the other controls on the form.

Figure 18.2

Tab stop settings.

Suppose you want to add a field called CompanyName between the Middle Initial field and the Address field. You can easily make the form larger: scoot the Address, City, State, and ZIP code fields down and insert the Company Name field. However, the tab index for this new field is 19; this falls above the tab index for the ZIP code field of 12. Having established that the .TabIndex for the Middle Initial field is 2, you can logically reset the .TabIndex for the new Company Name field to 3. The indices for all successive controls are automatically scooted down one. The control that previously had the index of 3 is now bumped to 4. Figure 18.3 shows the amendments made to the form, along with their .TabIndex results.

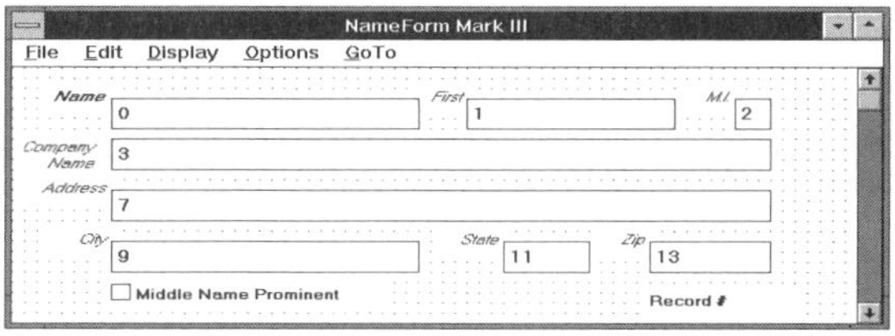

Figure 18.3

A change in plan.

Monitoring Activity

A control has the focus when it is active and awaiting user input.

Arguably, few people choose to use the Microsoft Windows environment without a mouse. However, Microsoft programmed the Windows package so that a mouse was optional rather than required. In any window that has multiple fields and controls, Microsoft allows the keyboard user to press the Tab key repeatedly until the desired control is somehow indicated on-screen. If the control is a text box, the cursor appears in that box. If the control is a visual device, an indicator box appears around its caption. In Visual Basic, a control that has the focus is the control currently indicated by a hazy rectangle, designating that the control is active or awaiting input from the user. By default, the control in a form that has the focus first is the first input-accepting control in the `.TabStop` sequence.

> **Note:** To assign an alternate keystroke (using the Alt key) to a command button, when the letter for that keystroke is part of the button's `.Caption` property, precede that letter with an ampersand (`&`).

Acquiring the focus in VB is an event comparable to intercepting a football pass; event procedures may be executed for a control when it acquires the focus.

_GotFocus and _LostFocus   Events

Action: Acquisition/forfeit of control indicator
Applies to: All controls, form (not MDI)
Parameters: `Index` (control arrays only)

The `_GotFocus` event for a control occurs whenever it acquires the focus, as a result of the user indicating it with the mouse or the Tab key, or through direct setting of the focus by the program. Acquiring the focus makes this particular control the recipient of keyboard-initiated events. Consequently, the `_LostFocus` event for a control occurs whenever it loses the focus, assuming of course that it ever had the focus.

If necessary, the program can set the focus of a control manually, thus forcing on it the role of active control.

.SetFocus   Method

Purpose: Manual indicator setting
Syntax:

> [*Control.*]SetFocus

The .SetFocus method manually appoints the antecedent control to be the active control, thus giving it the focus.

To the VB interpreter, it's entirely "legal" for a form to receive the focus. In previous interpretations of the *focus* paradigm, the control that had the focus was maintained by the form that had the focus.

In Visual Basic, an alternative to this dualism is offered. Now, the control that has the focus resides within the *active form*. This form is then said to be activated or deactivated by the user. Both of these actions can be tracked as events, and are assigned to the form as follows:

_Activate and _Deactivate   Events

Action: Form engagement
Applies to: Form (not MDI)
Parameters: None

The _Activate event for a form is triggered whenever the user indicates that form, or turns control over to it through any routine that formally loads it into the workspace. It may also be triggered by passing the form the focus, or by giving the focus to a control in that form. The _Deactivate event is triggered whenever another form inhabiting the workspace is indicated, or some activity or routine makes some other form active. It is *not* triggered for a form when that form is unloaded or hidden.

In the next chapter, you read more about the differences between loading, activating, and "unhiding" a form. They are distinctly different actions.

Using Color

When a control is first created and placed on the form, it is black on white. Described in greater detail, this is because the .ForeColor property of new controls is set by default to black, and the .BackColor property is set by default to white.

.BackColor and .ForeColor   Properties

Representation: Solid color designation
Applies to: All controls, form, Printer object (.ForeColor only)
Set by way of: Properties window, program instruction

The .BackColor property for a control reflects its current background color. The .ForeColor property for a control represents the plotting color of text and graphical elements—such as borders—within that control. Both properties are expressed as six-digit hexadecimal values. These values digitally represent the color-mixing scheme currently in use. Because all graphics cards (and thus graphics card drivers) are not alike, the colors chosen for objects on the system where the application is being programmed may not be identical (or even close) to the colors represented on some other system.

It's relatively difficult for you to express colors as six-digit hexadecimal (base 16) values—especially when you're not sure if those colors will be the same when you move your VB application to a different system. Colors across systems and across graphics cards are generally similar. Figure 18.4 shows a screen containing the Visual Basic color palette and color definition box.

Figure 18.4

The VB color palette and color definition box.

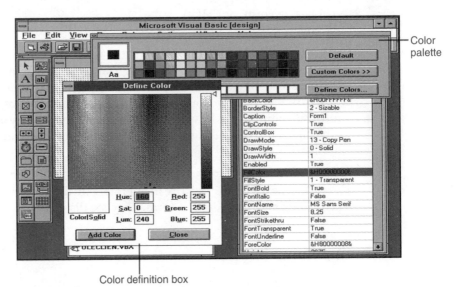

Color definition box

At the top left corner of the color palette is a small box within a big box. The color of the small box represents the current color represented by .ForeColor for the graphic object currently indicated within the VB interpreter workspace. The color of the big box that contains the small box is the current color represented by `.BackColor` for the currently active object. To set color properties for an object at design time using the color palette:

♦ Indicate the graphic object to be recolored. If this object is a form, click on any area within the form that is not inhabited by a control. The control is now surrounded by indicator nodes.

♦ To set the `.ForeColor` property for this object, click the smaller box inside the color palette once, and then choose a color from the palette by clicking that color. The color change is immediately reflected in the VB workspace.

♦ To set the `.BackColor` property for this object, click the larger box inside the color palette containing the smaller box once, and then choose a color from the palette by clicking that color. The color change is immediately reflected in the VB workspace.

Notice that in the color palette, the sample text Aa appears below the two test boxes. This test is placed there to show how text set to the two chosen colors appear within a form. In the Windows environment, regardless of how many colors are accessible from your current graphics card driver, Windows recognizes only as many as 32 actual colors for the immediate background behind text, and as many as 64 colors as mixtures for the remainder of the text area. Windows can then support as many as 256 colors for regions outside of those that are to contain text.

Summary

The twip coordinate system is used in Microsoft Windows for the sole purpose of making graphic object sizes and positions more equivalent to one another across multiple graphics platforms. The system uses a variable twip-to-pixel scale so that each Windows screen has approximately the same twip scale. Visual Basic uses the twip coordinate system by default, although other systems are available.

The `.Left` and `.Top` properties for a graphic object are used to position a form's top left corner (origin point) with respect to the screen's coordinate system. They are also used to position a graphic object with respect to its associated form's current coordinate system. The `.Width` and `.Height` properties are then used to establish the size for all graphic objects, including forms themselves, within their current coordinate systems. The `.ZOrder` property establishes the drawing order of graphic objects within a form, thus creating the illusion of one object being in front of another.

The control that is the current recipient of input from the keyboard is considered the control that has the focus. This control can be a text field or an option or command button, because they too can be operated using the Return key. The Tab key is used to traverse a set of controls whose sequence is representative of the steps the user takes when filling out a form. Each control's place in the tab sequence is maintained by the .TabIndex property setting. A form may receive a sort of focus of its own, although it is also said to be activated when it is brought into the workspace, or indicated by the user. The _Activate and _Deactivate events are triggered by such processes.

The color of a graphic object is represented in the Visual Basic interpreter by a six-digit hexadecimal value. The color value of a control's background is maintained by its .BackColor property setting. The color value of any text placed in that control is maintained by its .ForeColor property setting.

Review Questions

1. What is the foreground color of the default Windows text box?

2. In a picture box where 50 white characters are placed geometrically on a blue field, what is the .BackColor setting for the picture box?

3. Editable text is addressed using what property term?

   Using object-oriented syntax, write references for the following properties:

4. The contents of a text box called Surname

5. The tab index for an option dot called Group(1)

6. The alias for a picture called BobTheBear

CHAPTER 19

The Window as Form

In this chapter, you examine the role of the form as a graphic object. As you learned, a project can contain more than one module. When the code for that project is executed, however, not all these forms may reside in memory. Windows tends to save unused memory items to disk until they become necessary. With Visual Basic, unused forms in a project are already dispensed to disk until they are formally called. You learn more about this process in this chapter.

Later, you see the properties that relate to the appearance of a window in the Visual Basic workspace. You also see examples of these properties, as well as the other properties covered in Part V, being set with the Visual Basic design-time properties bar and with source code.

Where Your Forms Are

As discussed in Chapter 15, "The Module Hierarchy," when an application starts running, it first executes the declarations in the global module. If a general module exists in the project and contains a procedure called Sub Main (), that procedure is executed next. Otherwise, the Visual Basic interpreter loads the first form—by default called Form1 unless otherwise named—into the workspace. The *workspace* is the area of the screen where forms and Visual Basic tools reside during run time (although they do not necessarily appear there).

The *workspace* is the area of the screen where forms and tools reside.

This is the only instance where the interpreter loads a form into the workspace by itself. To better understand what is meant by "loading into the workspace," see figure 19.1.

Figure 19.1

Graphic object
states.

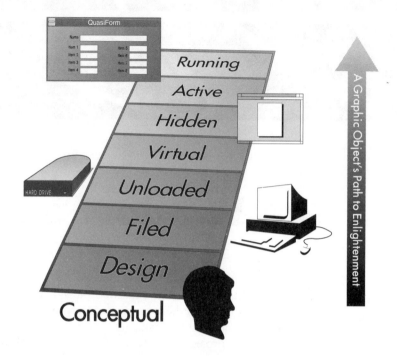

Graphic objects in Visual Basic (forms are VB graphic objects as well as controls) have different levels of existence, as figure 19.1 shows. At the base of this chart is the *design state,* or the level of a graphic object as you write the VB application. When a graphic object becomes part of a form module, it later is stored to disk as part of a file. This is the *filed state* of the graphic object—the next step up the chain.

When an application is running—whether it is a Visual Basic project or a compiled EXE file—the graphic object can be referred to by the source code. Chances are, however, that unless the object belongs to Form1, the object has not yet been loaded into memory. It exists in the middle of a running application, but it hasn't yet found its way into the RAM of the computer. In this state, somewhere along the bridge between physical and logical storage, the object is in its *unloaded state.*

When the graphic object or the form containing it is finally loaded, Microsoft Windows might consider the object to be in memory. If it isn't really in use at the time, however, chances are that the object exists in virtual memory—which is really yet another disk file waiting to be translated into RAM. This is the *virtual state* of the graphic object. When Windows considers it necessary, the file containing the virtual memory of the graphic object is at last translated into RAM and loaded into the workspace. This doesn't necessarily mean, however, that you can actually see the graphic object yet. The object may be invisible unless specifically told to appear. This invisible status is called the *hidden state.*

It takes an explicitly stated method to make the VB interpreter show this object. At last, you can say the object is in an *active state*. If the graphic object is being manipulated by the user, you can say the object is in a *running state*.

Transition between States

Regardless of the name a form receives at design time, when the project containing that form is running, the form itself can be loaded into memory—either in RAM or in virtual memory (on disk)—using the Load statement.

Load | Statement

Purpose: Object workspace enrollment
Syntax:

```
Load objectname
```

The Load statement addresses by name a graphic object belonging to the currently running application, loads it into memory and into the workspace without displaying it, and holds it in suspension until an instruction forcing that object to show is executed. If the object is a form, this statement triggers the Sub Form_Load () event procedure for that form.

Note: Remember that the Load statement loads the form and its controls into memory.

Example

If a form named Panel belongs to your application, here is the instruction that loads it into the workspace:

```
Load Panel
```

Note that the form hasn't displayed yet. To display the form, use the .Show method.

.Show | Method

Purpose: Form workspace display
Syntax:

```
[formname.]Show [style]
```

The .Show method displays a form currently in its loaded state, although not visible. If the form hasn't been loaded into the workspace yet, it loads automatically, and the Sub Form_Load () event procedure for that form, if any, is triggered. If the *formname* is omitted, the graphic form sharing the current module with the currently executing procedure shows. The optional *style* value, when set to 1 (0 is the default), makes the displayed form *modal*—in other words, no other window can accept input from the user until this form is exited.

A modal form is one that suspends the execution of all other forms until it is exited.

The two instructions previously introduced in this chapter have counterpart (opposite) instructions. They are as follows:

.Hide   Method

Purpose: Form operation suspension
Syntax:

    [formname.]Hide

The .Hide method takes a form being shown and removes it from the screen until further notice. The form still virtually occupies the same coordinates on-screen. Controls on the hidden form can still be referred to in the source code. In other words, operation of the form by the program is not suspended, but the user cannot operate the form.

Unload   Statement

Purpose: Object workspace removal
Syntax:

    Unload objectname

The Unload statement removes the loaded form or graphic object specified from the workspace, as well as from memory. The object continues to exist as a form in the project and as a stored file on disk if it ever has been stored. This statement is necessary for a compiled Visual Basic application because it will not have the services of the VB interpreter to automatically "shut down" each form once the compiled program is formally exited.

An implicit load occurs when an instruction refers to an unloaded form, causing it to display itself.

Use the Load statement or .Show method to formally load a form into the Windows workspace. However, if you have an instruction that refers to some graphic object belonging to a form that is *not* loaded into the workspace, that mere reference causes the load to happen, and most likely the show as well. Visual Basic calls this an *implicit load;* and because it is so unpredictable, it is advisable to avoid such loads as intentional processes.

Knowing the Names of the Controls

A primary intention of the creators of graphical user interfaces was that new users could deduce the meaning and function of at least some on-screen controls without referring to the instruction manual. If the creators' intentions were fully realized, those in the instruction business would be out of a job. Nonetheless, some people learned to operate the window "gadgets" and drop-down menus of Microsoft Windows without reading anything beforehand. These people have become proficient Windows users without help. Yet many people aren't sure what the individual controls and gadgets are officially called.

Some people might ask, "What does it matter what these things are called as long as we know how to use them properly?"—and with good reason. As a programmer in Visual Basic, you need to know what Microsoft calls the gadgets and controls of the individual windows because you address them by name in source code. There is no universal convention for the names of visual controls in a windowed environment. For instance, Microsoft calls the sliding gray square between the two arrows of a scroll bar the *scroll box*, and the Macintosh calls that same square a *thumb*.

The Anatomy of a Form

Figure 19.2 points out the various elements of a window with which you're already familiar, and shows Microsoft's names for those elements. At the top left corner is the window's *control box*, which, when double-clicked, closes the window. When clicked once, the control box offers options for manipulating and positioning the window, and generally offers access to the Windows Task Manager.

Figure 19.2

The parts of a Windows window.

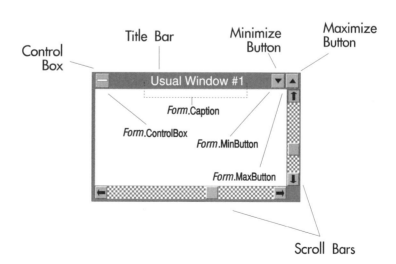

At the top right corner of this particular window, from left to right, are the *minimize* (down arrow) and *maximize* (up arrow) buttons for that window. Remember that these two buttons, as well as these two terms, are not opposite to each other in this context. To minimize a window is to suspend the application for that window and to place its icon toward the bottom left corner of the Windows desktop. Execution of the application resumes when this icon is double-clicked. By contrast, maximizing a window makes that window the same size as the screen; this process does not change the execution state of the application. When the window is maximized, the maximize button is replaced with the *restore* button, which looks like the up arrow on top of the down arrow.

You are already familiar with such commonly-used graphic controls as the title bar, which you can use to move the window as well as maximize and restore it by double-clicking it. The sliding indicator between the two arrows on the scroll bar is the *scroll box*. The arrows are called *scroll arrows*. In many applications, clicking the area between the scroll box and a scroll arrow scrolls the contents of the window in the direction of that arrow one *page,* or approximately one window-length of text or contents. Microsoft has not named the area between the scroll box and scroll arrow; for discussion, let's call this area the *paging area.*

The parts listed here are the only parts of a window provided by Microsoft. You are supposed to conceive and design any other controls to operate the window and add those controls to your Visual Basic form windows. In such cases, it is up to you to give your controls proper names.

The next few properties deal with window appearance and contents.

.ControlBox   Property

Representation: Specifies the window's control box status
Applies to: Form
Set by way of: Properties window

The .ControlBox property is set to a True or False value, reflecting whether the window's control box appears in the form for this window. By default, *form*.ControlBox is set to on. This property is reset or set only at design time, and takes effect when the application runs.

.MaxButton   Property

Representation: Maximization control inclusion
Applies to: Form
Set by way of: Properties window

The .MaxButton property is set to a True or False value, reflecting whether the window's maximize button appears in the form for this window. By default, the .MaxButton property for a new form is set to *on*.

.MinButton   Property

Representation: Minimization control display status
Applies to: Form
Set by way of: Properties window

The `.MinButton` property is set to a True or False value, reflecting whether the window's minimize button appears in the form for this window. By default, the `.MinButton` property for a new form is set to *on*.

A form in its suspended state, represented by an icon, is said to be *minimized*.

You might not want a form to have a control box or minimize and maximize buttons because some forms in a Visual Basic application serve the purpose of dialog boxes or file selectors. When you use a regular Windows application and select **O**pen from the File menu, you most likely see some kind of file selector box. Such boxes generally do not have control boxes, and never have maximize and minimize buttons, because their functions are relevant only with respect to an application's main display window. *Boxes* such as dialog boxes and file selectors are considered agents of, and therefore subordinate to, the main application window. To minimize a window generally is a directive to minimize the *application* and proceed with operating some other application active in the Windows environment.

Furthermore, because a file selector box is not officially a *task*, one usually doesn't need a control box to bring up the Task Manager by using that box. Yet you may prefer to use a control box as an alternate Cancel button for a file selector. If you set the `.ControlBox` property for a file selector box to –1 (True), most users of your application probably know the purpose you intended for that control box.

Figure 19.3
The four types of windows.

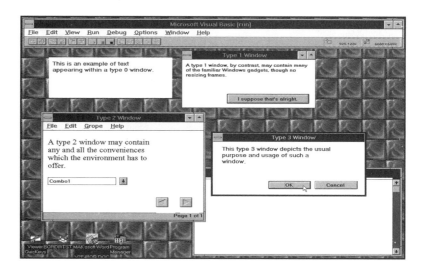

Figure 19.3 shows the four window types supported by Visual Basic.

The *type 0* window is simply a box. It can contain controls, but such a window is generally not recognized by the user as a window. You can use type 0 for temporary messages, or "blurbs," which pop up on-screen for a moment and then disappear.

Window *type 1* can contain all the controls listed so far in this chapter, but does not have the surrounding window frame the user needs in order to resize the window. Generally, a type 1 window is necessary when the window's size is critical to its operation. A type 1 window may be necessary to display graphs on a fixed-coordinate system in which rescaling the image, or changing the proportion of x- to y-axis on that image, would render it meaningless or in some way reduce its information content. In another example, if the application is a calculator, you might not want the calculator panel to be resizable.

In figure 19.3, Window *type 2* is the default window type for all forms created in the Visual Basic design area. Type 2 includes window frames with which the user can resize the form at any side or corner. *Type 3* windows are used by dialog boxes supplied by the Microsoft Windows environment. The size of a type 3 window is fixed. For that reason, it contains no window frames or maximize and minimize buttons. It can, however, contain a control box that operates as an optional Cancel button.

These four types of windows should be distinguished from each other so that the Visual Basic interpreter can have a better internal understanding of which window belongs to which application. A dialog box is not generally considered a window by the user of the application; this is probably how it should be. The Microsoft Windows environment, however, as well as Visual Basic, sees every output region as a window. From the user's point of view, it helps that the windows intended to be *boxes* are classified as such, so that the Windows environment can present such boxes to the screen more efficiently—in other words, so that each new dialog box is not interpreted by Windows as a new application.

The .BorderStyle property is used to make distinctions between window types in Visual Basic.

.BorderStyle　　　　　　　　　　　　　　　　　Property

Representation: Displayed enclosure type
Applies to: All controls, form, MDI form
Set by way of: Properties window

The .BorderStyle property represents the internal classification of a form or control maintained by Visual Basic. As long as the name of the graphic object that is the antecedent of the property is assigned through its .Name property, the VB interpreter knows whether to apply the form set or the control set of categories to the graphic object.

The ability to manipulate a window or form on the Windows screen is indicated by its border style. Setting the style of a form's border with this property simultaneously defines the operating ability—and thus, to some extent, the purpose—of that border.

The purpose and function of graphic controls are already defined, and are not affected through the setting of the .BorderStyle property.

The following table defines the border styles recognized for controls and forms.

Style	Definition
Form Border Styles	
0	No border (totally confined to its present position)
1	Fixed single border (manipulate through use of window gadgets, although not resizable at run time)
2	Framed (resizable at run time)
3	Fixed double border (not resizable, although movable and closable using the control box)
Control Border Styles	
0	No border
1	Fixed single (solid line)

Example

Here is a common use for a type 3 window: Suppose that on your main application form, you have a button called Help. You may need a dialog box to inquire about what the user needs help with. At design time, you created an all-purpose dialog box with contents and purpose that can be defined when the user clicks a button in the main form. You already gave the dialog box the .Name of Dialog and set its .BorderStyle to type 3, because you may not set this property at run time. Here is how the code for the Help button might look:

```
Sub Help_Click ()
Load Dialog
Dialog.HelpLine.Caption = "Enter a Help Subject:"
Dialog.Command1.Caption = "Index"
Dialog.Command2.Caption = "Find"
Dialog.Command3.Caption = "Close"
Dialog.Show
End Sub
```

The event this procedure answers is a single click on the Help button. The dialog box is designed to be blank so that the program can place text in it for any necessary purpose; thus the dialog box is reusable. Notice that the text property-setting instructions fall between the instructions `Load Dialog` and `Dialog.Show`. When `Dialog` is loaded into memory, the program can address the properties for all the controls, although the form is not yet visible. When the textual properties are set, the dialog box can then appear; it will seem to have a specific purpose rather than a general one.

Notice that `Dialog` is referred to by its `.Name` property setting, because this procedure belongs to a form outside of this one. When you refer to a graphic element of another form from within a form, each object is addressed by its "full name," using the syntax *Form.Object.Property*. This syntax is also used whenever a procedure in a general module addresses a graphic object within a form.

Example

Suppose that another button on your main form starts a process that searches for a certain occurrence of text in a document. Here's how the code for that button might appear:

```
Sub Search_Click ()
Load Dialog
Dialog.HelpLine.Caption = "Search for what text?"
Dialog.Command1.Caption = "Index"
Dialog.Command2.Caption = "Search"
Dialog.Command3.Caption = "Cancel"
Dialog.Show
End Sub
```

This demonstrates another advantage to using generic forms and dialog boxes: the availability of transportable code. The preceding procedure is not that much different from the one before. For the most part, you need to program the mechanics of the box display procedure only once. Then you can use **C**opy and **P**aste from the Edit menu to move the content of procedure `Sub Help_Click ()` inside `Sub Search_Click ()`; you can then edit the text and captions accordingly.

> **Caution:** Before these procedures can be executed again, the `Dialog` form must first be unloaded using `Unload Dialog`. The most convenient place for such an instruction to appear is during an event procedure such as `Sub Cancel_Click ()`, which is executed when the user exits the help or text search procedures with a button click. This way, when the instruction `Load Dialog` is executed again, a conflict does not occur.

Example

Here's an unusual type of control: Suppose that in one corner of a form, there is a clock or watch icon such as the WATCH02.ICO icon provided with Visual Basic. This procedure displays the current time whenever the mouse pointer passes over this icon. The user doesn't necessarily have to click it; he can just sweep over the icon. When the mouse pointer is over this area, the current time "floats" next to it. Here's a procedure for this odd but interesting control:

```
Sub Form_MouseMove (Button As Integer, Shift As Integer,
➥x As Single, y As Single)
If x < 1035 And y < 1215 Then
    Clock.Top = MainForm.Top + x
    Clock.Left = MainForm.Left + y
    Clock.TimeNow.Caption = Time$
    Clock.Show
Else
    Clock.Hide
End If
End Sub
```

Here is the preceding procedure written in pseudocode:

Procedure awaiting a movement of the mouse pointer:
If the coordinates of the mouse pointer are within
a given region, then
The clock form's physical top coordinate is
set to the mainform top coordinate plus
the mouse pointer x coordinate.
The clock form's physical left coordinate is
set to the mainform left coordinate plus
the mouse pointer y coordinate.
The text of the clock form should be the
current time.
Now show the clock form.
Otherwise,
Keep the clock form hidden.
End of condition.
End of procedure.

Figure 19.4 shows this procedure in action.

In this procedure, Clock. is the name of a form with its .BorderStyle set to type 0 at design time. Clock. is just tall and wide enough to fit one line, the one showing the current time. The watch icon appears at the top left corner of the main form. When the main form is invoked, its Form_Load () procedure is executed; somewhere in it is the instruction Load Clock, which brings the clock form into memory but does not display it on-screen.

Figure 19.4

The automatic
clock procedure.

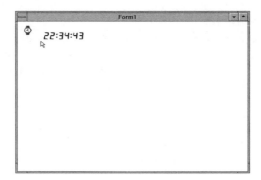

The event that triggers execution here is _MouseMove; its procedure is executed literally whenever the pointer is moved and the form containing the procedure is active. The event procedure, by nature, takes four parameters. The latter two of these parameters are the most important, because they return the mouse pointer position relative to the origin point of the *form* (not the whole screen) as integer variables x and y. When the position of the type 0 Clock. form is set, its coordinates are relative to the *screen,* not to MainForm., so the origin coordinates .Top and .Left of MainForm. (1035, 1215) are added to the x and y values returned by the mouse pointer to obtain the physical screen coordinates where VB plots Clock..

This procedure loads the Clock. form, but does not display it on-screen, yet its contents can still be set with the current time. Clock.Show, after it is executed, instantly brings those contents to the screen. If the mouse pointer is not in the stated region, the Else portion of the clause is executed, and Clock.Hide hides the form.

State Determination

When in memory, a form can be maximized, framed as a window among other windows, or minimized to an icon along the lower portion of the screen. Naturally, you may not want your application to plot anything urgent to a currently minimized form. To determine what state the form's window is in at the moment, Visual Basic offers the .WindowState property.

.WindowState   **Property**

Representation: Window operative status
Applies to: Form
Set by way of: Properties window, program instruction

The current setting of the .WindowState property is an integer that represents the operating state of the antecedent form as one of the following conditions:

0   Framed or bordered

1	Minimized; reduced to a representative icon
2	Maximized; unbordered, and allowed to fill the entire screen

Example

The .WindowState property can be used to manually set the operating state of a window from within a form or general module. It's rarely necessary to use this property to obtain information about the current form (the form in which this procedure resides). Because a form cannot wait for user events when it is minimized, it is unnecessary for an event procedure to determine for itself whether its form is not minimized. However, suppose a routine, such as the one that plotted the type 0 clock form for the preceding procedure, appears in a general module. The context of a general module is such that it cannot automatically know the current operating state of any form in the procedure. As a result, if the routine appears in a general module, it needs to be amended as follows:

```
If MainForm.WindowState <> 1 Then
    If x < 1035 And y < 1215 Then
        Clock.Top = MainForm.Top + x
        Clock.Left = MainForm.Left + y
        Clock.TimeNow.Caption = Time$
        Clock.Show
    Else
        Clock.Hide
    End If
End If
```

This way, if MainForm. is minimized, this routine does not execute.

Finally, when the .WindowState of a form is 1, by default the VB interpreter assigns the minimized window an icon representing what appears to be a blank sheet of cardboard standing upright. It represents a form for the sake of Visual Basic's form designer, but you'll probably want it to represent something else in your project.

With each copy of Visual Basic, Microsoft ships a program called Icon Works; actually, it's a VB application, supplied both in its native and compiled state (in \VB\SAMPLES\ICONWORKS). Figure 19.5 shows Icon Works with an icon drawn for the Expressor project introduced in this book. Icon Works is perhaps the most convenient program available for drawing 16×16-raster, 16-color bitmaps. Symantec also provides a nice icon-drawing program with its Norton Desktop for Windows. One of the nicest icon-drawing programs is a shareware program called Icon Designer.

Figure 19.5

Icon Works at
work.

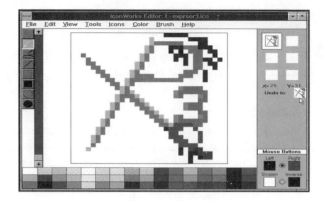

In any event, when you have an icon fully-drawn and saved to disk in Windows'
ICO format, you can assign that icon to your VB form with the .Icon property.

.Icon   **Property**

Representation: Minimized form symbol
Applies to: Form, MDI form
Set by way of: Properties window

The .Icon property for a form is set to a file name of an .ICO-format icon file,
which acts as the symbol of that form when it is minimized (.WindowState = 1).
Although no restrictions are placed on the .ICO file's location, it should be in the
same directory as the other program files. If a peculiar file path is saved along with
the icon file name, and the project is installed on a client's system after it is compiled,
that client may not have the same directory tree structure, and an error may be
generated.

Summary

When a form's design is complete and it has its .Name, the Visual Basic interpreter
executes a form as a graphic object by first loading the form into the workspace
using the Load statement and then displaying the form with the .Show method.

During the creation of a VB application, many properties of a form and its
constituent controls are set at design time. If the value or content of these property
settings is altered by the program, these properties are set at run time. Certain
properties belonging to a form represent whether its window contains minimize
and maximize buttons, as well as whether the form contains a control box in its top
left corner. Whether these property settings are available for a particular form
depends on the window type designated for that form.

A window's type can be determined by its border style. A window's type is represented in its .BorderStyle property because the border of a window generally represents its purpose in the application.

The .WindowState property represents the operating state of a window. This property can be used to set the operating state of a form manually, although its usefulness in determining the current state through inference is generally restricted to procedures outside the context of a form. The minimized icon is represented by its .Icon property setting.

Review Questions

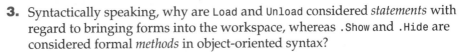

1. Do you need to Load a form into memory first before invoking the .Show method?

2. When a form is taken out of memory by using the Unload statement, does it retain its place as part of the project?

3. Syntactically speaking, why are Load and Unload considered *statements* with regard to bringing forms into the workspace, whereas .Show and .Hide are considered formal *methods* in object-oriented syntax?

State by number what window type would be the most convenient as forms for the following purposes:

4. A variable-size graph-plotting area.

5. A form made to resemble the control panel of a VCR or cassette tape player.

6. A box that displays the definition of a word when that word is clicked.

7. A window that warns the user that if he continues, vital data may be lost, and asks permission to proceed.

CHAPTER 20

The Window as Document

This chapter examines the classic construction of the Windows application and how it can be applied to Visual Basic using the Multiple Document Interface (MDI). Using MDI, a window or VB form can be made subordinate to another window or form—in other words, a Visual Basic form can now be the keeper of its own workspace, rather than just the mere inhabitant of the workspace of Windows.

Worlds within Worlds

A *document* is the primary data product of a Windows application.

Most Windows applications you use operate on the principles that data is the product of an application, that those products can be encapsulated as *documents*, and that multiple documents can be utilized at one time. Microsoft was not the originator of this concept; historically, it dates back to the mid-1970s and the Massachusetts Institute of Technology's first experiments with the early editions of X/Window, arguably the first graphical environment.

MIT originally used windowing for only one purpose: to symbolize for the user the hierarchical relationship among elements of data. For instance, a house belongs to a city, the head of the household belongs to the house, and a savings account belongs to the head of the household. To symbolize this relationship, the record of the head of the household (for example, name and personal statistics) appears in a rectangle inside a rectangle that encompasses the record of the house (street address, ZIP code, and so on), that in turn appears in the record of the city.

The *Multiple Document Interface* (MDI) is used for most applications in which windows appear in other windows.

The Microsoft scheme is somewhat simpler in its implementation, mostly due to necessary artificial limitations placed on its capability. The Multiple Document Interface represents the data products of an application as separate windows called *child windows*. The *parent window* of an MDI application is the container of the

The workspace within an MDI application is maintained in its *parent window*.

The *child window* is the container for documents in an MDI application.

workspace for that application, as the screen is the container of the Windows workspace. Each child window within an MDI parent, although it is referred to generically by Microsoft as a "document," may also be a panel or, by the broader definition, a form—a displayed record of related elements of data.

When you're using a Windows word processor, it's easy for you to consider the data product of the application as a document. To the programmer of a Windows spreadsheet program, a worksheet in memory is also considered a document. In the context of the Windows File Manager, a directory window is officially considered a document in the MDI scheme. Notice with each program category, you can open a window in the application's own workspace, minimize that window, and maximize it. Notice also that more than one window sharing the same type and layout may share the application's workspace at any one time.

The parent/child relationship of windows in an MDI application is two-tiered. There is simply one parent window and any number of identically arranged child windows, not chained to one another. This arrangement makes it simple for the programmer to symbolize a desktop-style system, with several papers of equal importance that can be shuffled about, while data may be exchanged between them.

Parent Forms

In building an MDI application using Visual Basic, you must first establish the MDI parent form. The VB interpreter views MDI forms differently than standard forms; MDI forms now have their own selection in the VB control window menu. Under normal circumstances, because the MDI parent form takes charge of most of the application's processes, it should be made the startup form. The problem is that the VB interpreter views a non-MDI form as the startup by default, so you need to manually set the parent form as the startup form.

To establish an MDI parent startup form:

1. From the VB control window's File menu, select New MDI Form. The new form's framework soon appears. Notice its background color is the same as the color that you're currently using as the Windows screen backdrop color, not the default white of standard VB forms. MDI parent forms have no .BackColor property settings; instead, they depend on the current Windows Control Panel settings. Think of this area as a void.

2. At this point, the VB application's Form1 is still the startup form. To change this, select **P**roject from the Options menu. A dialog box appears, as shown in figure 20.1.

Figure 20.1

The startup form
dialog box.

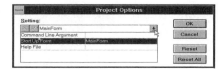

Figure 20.1

The startup form
dialog box.

3. The second line in this list is marked "Start Up Form." Click once on this line. A gray down-arrow button appears on the top line of this list.

4. Clicking the down-arrow brings down a list box that contains the current list of forms in the application, along with an entry for Sub Main (), regardless of whether you have a Sub Main () procedure in your application yet.

5. The MDI parent is represented in the list by the reference MDIForm1. Double-click this item in the list, and click OK.

> **Note:** Regardless of the nomenclature MDIForm1, there can be only one MDI parent form in a VB application.

At this point, the original standard startup form is still named Form1. If you've already planned a child form model for the application, you might want to remove Form1 now; otherwise, you might want to use Form1 as the model for the MDI child forms.

When you've enrolled a standard form as an MDI child form, the child form can make multiple appearances at any time during the application's run time. The standard form acts as the model for any number of children that may appear during run time. This may be somewhat confusing, because up to now the forms and controls you draw at design time have a one-to-one correlation with the forms and controls that appear in the application during run time. With Visual Basic's system of object declaration, it is possible to create a new instance of an undesigned form, or to create a copy of a designed form, without using the form designer portion of the VB control program.

Designing the primary layout of the MDI parent form is somewhat unusual, but not difficult. Each parent is divided into two parts. The upper part is the *control area*, and the lower part is the *application workspace*. The control area contains any buttons or graphic controls necessary for the application. Both parts extend fully from the left to right sides of the parent form. The upper part is optional, because you can conceivably place all of the MDI form's functionality within its native menu bar. The dividing line between the two is established in a slightly unorthodox manner, because the control area is actually a VB picture box.

The area where controls appear in an MDI parent form is made using a picture box.

All picture boxes in Visual Basic act as parent controls for any smaller controls that may have been initially drawn within their boundaries. What this means, among other things, is that when you move the picture box, the controls belonging to that box move with it. Frame controls are also considered parents for other controls attributed to them.

The lower part of the MDI parent is the workspace area. Notice that no standard controls can be drawn within this "void" area; you may make attempts, but controls seem to disappear. To place controls on this form, you must first build a platform for them.

To add the control area to an MDI parent form, follow these steps:

1. Click on the picture box control in the VB toolbox.

2. Proceed to draw the control area perimeter as if you were placing an ordinary picture box in a standard form; remember, however, that the control box is always as long as the parent form itself, and is always attached to the top of the form. The only parameter obtained by the interpreter through the drawing of this rectangle is the height of the control area.

3. Wherever you have drawn the rectangle, the interpreter places the control area at the top of the parent form. Its height is that of the rectangle you previously drew, although that rectangle has disappeared. The control area is indicated with the standard black nodes, although only the lower nodes can be used to resize the control area.

Figure 20.2 shows an MDI parent form just after a control area has been established for it. Notice that the background color for the control area—which is set this time through the .BackColor property—is white.

Figure 20.2

A MDI parent form.

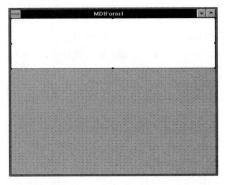

Now you can treat the control area as if it were a regular form, adding controls to the upper platform. Among these controls might be a Save button, an Import button, and—perhaps most importantly—a New Form button.

A standard VB form is made the model for an MDI child form through the setting of a single property that is available to all standard forms.

.MDIChild   Property

Representation: MDI subordinate designation
Applies to: Form
Set by way of: Properties window

The .MDIChild property for a form is set to logical true or false, representing whether that form is to be used as the model for MDI child forms to appear within the workspace of an MDI parent.

Let's use a version of the NameForm project created a few chapters back to devise a model MDI application. You must first display multiple minimizable NameForms within the same collective workspace. Once the parent form is established, to make the existing NameForm an official MDI child, it is loaded into the project using **A**dd File from the File menu. Next, the property NameForm.MDIChild is set to True through the Properties window.

Notice the Project window for this application, shown in figure 20.3. The parent form is named MULTINAM.FRM. Notice that the icon beside its listing is slightly different from the icon for a standard form; an example appears here as NAMEFM4B.FRM.

Figure 20.3

An example project file for an MDI application.

Standard forms are symbolized by a single panel; MDI forms, on the other hand, are symbolized by one big panel and one little one. The parent window is symbolized by a darker big panel and a lighter little one, whereas child windows such as NAMEFRM4.FRM are symbolized in the reverse. After you've given MDIForm1 some other .Name property setting, you'll need to refer to this set of symbols to distinguish the MDI forms from the standard forms.

Next, a command button is added to the control area of the parent form; the purpose of this form is to add another instance of NameForm into the MultiName workspace. In the previous chapter, you saw how the Load statement and the Show method are used to bring forms into active service, as well as to display them. Both of these instructions play a role in the invocation of MDI child forms, although not without help from the Dim statement, this time with an alternate syntax.

Dim   Statement

Purpose: Graphic object invocation
Syntax 4:

```
Dim objectvar1[([minobject1 To ]maxobject1)] As [New]
➥{controlname¦controltype}[, objectvar2[([minobject2
To ]maxobject2)]
➥As [New] {controlname¦controltype}. . .
objectvar60[([minobject60 To ]
➥maxobject60) As [New] {controlname¦controltype}]
```

The Dim statement can be used with its fourth syntax to declare the existence of one or more new graphic objects, thus adding them to the inventory of graphic objects currently in use by the application. The declared object may be an existing control, or a new instance of an existing control. The object is given an exclusive object variable name: objectvar. The control represented by the object variable declared with New exists in its *virtual state,* so it is not officially loaded into the Windows workspace until a specific instruction is invoked for that purpose.

If the Properties window was used during design time to create the style and layout of the control declared with the Dim statement, declaring its object variable As New controlname gives those style properties to the new control. Without the New qualifier, the new control's properties are set to their default conditions. These property settings can be changed with instructions before the new control is displayed.

Once an object variable has been declared, objectvar becomes the term used for any further reference to the object, especially in the Set, Load, and .Show instructions.

To bring into the form a new control that has not been designed in advance, its declared object variable is given a controltype. For the standard lot of Visual Basic controls, these control types are written as any of the following:

CheckBox	ComboBox	CommandButton	DirListBox
DriveListBox	FileListBox	Frame	Grid
HScrollBar	Image	Label	Line
ListBox	Menu	OptionButton	PictureBox
Shape	TextBox	Timer	VScrollBar

Custom or extension controls may use their own *controltype* terms. The New qualifier is unnecessary for declaring an object variable for a generic *controltype*, because the term always refers to a generic and undesigned control.

Once an object variable for a form is declared, and the form that it refers to is in its virtual state, it can be brought to the screen with *objectvar*.Show. Likewise, a declared control can be brought to the screen by the programmer using the Set statement, making sure to designate the form to which the new object belongs.

If Dim is invoked using Syntax 4 within a procedure, when the interpreter processes End Sub, any of Dim's declared objects brought into their running state using the As New qualifier is removed—from memory as well as from the screen. If Dim is invoked in the general declarations section of a form module, objects declared by Dim and brought to the screen are lost.

> **Note:** The Global statement can be used to declare object variables with global scope—in other words, objects that cannot be taken out of their running state without the program invoking a specific instruction to do so. Also, the Static statement may be used to declare object variables with scope that is local to a procedure. The controls to which these objects refer operate in a state of suspension while the interpreter is executing instructions outside of the object variable's native procedure.

Example

The Dim statement in this regard is quite a complex affair, but for this particular example using the MultiName application, it is simplified. Assume that a New Form button has been placed within the control area of the MultiName MDI parent form to allow the user to place a new form into the MultiName workspace. The entire procedure is as follows:

```
Sub NewForm_Click ()
Dim NameInstance As New NameForm
NameInstance.Show
End Sub
```

> **Note:** This procedure is not specific to MDI forms, although with non-MDI forms it may yield different results. If property NameForm.MDIChild was not set to True beforehand, this procedure would still invoke a new instance of NameForm and give it the object name NameInstance, although the new form would appear in the Windows workspace—not the workspace of the MDI parent form in the menu bar.

In future chapters, you see more invocations of the versitile `Dim` statement for use in declaring object variables.

An *object variable* is a composite structure in memory that refers indirectly to a graphic object.

This example shows an object variable `NameInstance` declared as having the type `NameForm`. Note that the `.Name` given the form at design time is being used here to refer to the *type* of form being added to the MDI workspace. Think of an object variable as a sort of composite variable that has been structured for you, without you having to use a `Type` clause. The object variable's components are the properties that are normally given a graphic object. (Chapter 32, "Object Variables," shows you how controls can be created, programmed, and introduced into the form entirely at run time.) For the sake of procedure `Sub NewForm_Click ()`, the new form is called `NameInstance`—*not* `NameForm`. `NameForm` is the `.Name` property setting given to the form at design time.

Example

Suppose six instances of `NameForm` are dimensioned at the beginning of the MultiName application—for example, in a general declarations section. Here's part of the global declarations section, rewritten for performing this action:

```
Global Instance As Integer
Dim NameEntry(6) As New NameForm
```

These six forms now exist; they simply aren't visible or in operation currently. It is still the job of `Sub NewName_Click ()` to bring one of these forms—now named `NameEntry()`—into the MultiName workspace. Global variable `Instance` keeps track of how many NameForms there are in the MultiName workspace. This number is vital in creating each new instance of the form, so that it can refer to itself. Because the preceding declaration has created something of a "form array," each form instance represents an element of that array.

The New Name button now must bring a form that already "exists" into the workspace. Here's the revised procedure for that purpose:

```
Sub NewForm_Click ()
Instance = Instance + 1
NameEntry(Instance).Show
End Sub
```

The new form is now visible and active. The next procedure to run is NameForm's `Sub Form_Load ()` event procedure—which applies, by the way, to all instances of NameForm that appear during the application's run time. Within NameForm's general declarations section is the following declaration:

```
Dim ActiveInstance As Integer
```

As you saw in Chapter 16, "Parameter Passing," a form module does not pass parameters to another form module in the way procedures pass parameters between each other. Because the contexts of form modules are maintained separately, it becomes necessary to declare global variables such as `Instance`, and give the value of this variable to a form-level variable when the called form starts up. Because `Sub Form_Load ()` executes first, here is where the hand-off takes place:

```
Sub Form_Load ()
    ActiveInstance = Instance
    .
    .
    .
End Sub
```

If there are ever six instances of NameForm in the MultiName workspace, there are then six versions of variable `ActiveInstance` in play at the same time, with their scopes kept separate from one another. This separation of variables is necessary so that a direct reference to the active form, phrased `NameEntry(ActiveInstance)`, refers to the specific form whose instance number is equal to the value of `ActiveInstance`.

Rearranging Windows

When an application has a handful of windows and icons in the workspace for hours at a time, you can expect a certain degree of clutter. Microsoft suggests that software authors include a **W**indow selection in their menu bars; this gives the user rearrangement functions. Sometimes windows get lost in the shuffle, and a user can't get a handle on one unless he resizes two or three others. Menu bars are discussed in Chapter 22, "Menus and Options"; for now, here is a function provided by Visual Basic that gives you access to Windows' own MDI window rearrangement functions:

.Arrange   **Method**

Purpose: MDI child regulation
Syntax:

> [*MDIparent*.]Arrange *layout*

in which *layout* may take any of the following values:

0	Cascaded, like a series of pages stacked on top of one another, and fanned downward toward the lower right, exposing the title bars of each window.

1   Tiled horizontally, so that as many windows as possible are spread out for the full width of the MDI parent window, with each child window appearing beneath the other in the chronological order of its invocation. If there are a large number of MDI child windows in the parent workspace (generally, more than 6), only the first handful of child windows are tiled, the exact number depending on the current graphics resolution and size of the MDI parent.

2   Tiled vertically, so that as many windows as possible are spread out for the full *height* of the MDI parent workspace, with each child window appearing to the right of the other in the order of its invocation. If there are a large number of MDI child windows in the parent workspace, only the first handful of child windows are tiled. The exact number of child windows tiled depends on the current graphics resolution and size of the MDI parent.

3   Reserved for cases in which child windows are minimized, this `layout` value rearranges the minimized icons along the bottom edge of the MDI parent workspace.

The `.Arrange` method rearranges the MDI child windows, in their maximized or minimized state, for the antecedent `MDIparent` form, in the style specified by `layout`.

Figure 20.4 shows an example of four NameForms on the MultiName workspace, just after being rearranged with the instruction `MultiName.Arrange 0`.

Figure 20.4

Four NameForms on the MultiName workspace.

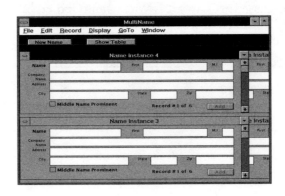

Summary

The system Microsoft Windows uses to manage applications that produce many data products at one time is called the Multiple Document Interface (MDI). In this model, a document is considered the container for the data product of the application. MDI uses a two-tiered system whereby documents are given their own windows, and documents are collected within the workspace of the application's main window. This window is called the parent window; document windows are considered child windows belonging to the parent.

To bring new copies of a designed (or undesigned) form into the parent's private workspace, the Dim statement is given a new syntax. The statement now gives new form instances their own object variables, which are manipulated in the source code like composite variables. Properties of object variables are treated like components of composite variables. The .Arrange method is used to create order out of the chaos of collected documents in the parent workspace.

Review Questions

1. For an MDI parent form named Central, what instructions bring into the parent private workspace a new instance of an MDI child form named Doc1?

2. For an MDI parent form named Central, what instructions bring into the Windows workspace a new instance of a standard form named Barometer?

3. Clicking on a standard form generally triggers the _Click event for that form. What event, if any, is triggered by clicking on the workspace of an MDI parent form?

CHAPTER 21

The Window as Panel

In this chapter, you examine the creation and display of dialog panels—brief windows the program uses to communicate with the user. Dialog panels are not forms by the Visual Basic definition; therefore, the contents of a dialog panel are defined in the source code and displayed using VB instructions.

Boxes versus Panels

Microsoft Windows refers to almost everything rectangular that is not a window as a *box*. This convention seems perfectly reasonable at first, because it is the goal of most computer literature to use common terminology rather than befuddle the text with jargon.

The problem that arises as Windows becomes further developed is that the simple terminology that once represented the meaning of a given control quite adequately becomes overused. During development of an application, several things can be described as boxes, for example. A combo box can be placed within a custom dialog box. A text box can display highlighted text using a highlight box, and show the result in another text box or place it in a picture box.

A *panel* is a supplementary window used for temporary purposes.

This revision uses new, exclusive, yet still common terminology to describe the various elements of Windows and Visual Basic. Some software and hardware manufacturers are using the term *panel* to refer to certain windows that are supplementary to the current program window, that contain controls displayed on a temporary basis for user interaction, and that generally serve a conversational purpose.

Dialog panels are generally displayed for two purposes: to determine the user's response to a yes or no question, or to warn or notify the user of some occurrence in the program. The instruction used to display such items in Visual Basic is MsgBox.

MsgBox   Function or Statement

Purpose: Standard panel display
Function Syntax:

```
response% = MsgBox (message$[, code%[, title$]])
```

Statement Syntax:

```
MsgBox message$[, code%[, title$]]
```

The MsgBox instruction, however it is phrased, displays a dialog panel containing a message that is presented as the argument *message$*. The value of the integer *code%* indicates what contents besides the *message$* appear in the dialog panel. The value of *code%* is evaluated binarily, with each bit in the binary value representing an element or style designation of the dialog panel. This is a collective value, equal to the sum of a combination of values from each of the three sections shown in the following table.

Code	Associated Feature
Button Inclusion	
0	Display OK button.
1	Display OK, Cancel buttons.
2	Display Abort, Retry, and Ignore buttons.
3	Display Yes, No, and Cancel buttons.
4	Display Yes, No buttons.
5	Display Retry, Cancel buttons.
Icon Inclusion	
16	Show red stop-sign (bad news) icon.
32	Show green question mark (query) icon.

Code	Associated Feature
48	Show yellow exclamation point (warning) icon.
64	Show blue i (information, please) icon.

Default Button Programming

256	Make second button the default.
512	Make third button the default.

If `title$` is expressed, the contents of the title bar are set to `title$`; otherwise, the title is set by default to the current name of the MAK project file in the interpreter, or to the current name of the EXE file when referring to the compiled version of the project.

If `MsgBox` is expressed as a function, the dialog panel returns a value to the variable expressed as `response%`, designating which button the user pressed in response to the dialog. This value is set by the interpreter to any of the following values:

Return Value	Button Pressed
1	OK
2	Cancel
3	Abort
4	Retry
5	Ignore
6	Yes
7	No

Example

The following instruction displays a simple dialog panel:

```
MsgBox "Project saved successfully."
```

The dialog panel resulting from this statement appears in figure 21.1.

Figure 21.1

The simplest of
dialog panels.

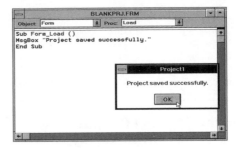

Example

Here's a more complex dialog panel, which elicits a response from the user:

```
message$ = "Proceeding will mean the contents of the
➡current form will be cleared. Proceed anyway?"
response = MsgBox(message$, 324, "Visual Basic by
➡Example")
```

This message is very long and would make the MsgBox function hard to read. In this situation, it is common to assign a string variable with the message text, then use this variable in the function. The value 324 is equal to 4 (display Yes, No buttons) plus 64 (show blue *i* icon) plus 256 (make second button the default). You could have expressed the second argument as 256 + 64 + 4 if you didn't want to strain your brain. The resulting dialog panel appears as in figure 21.2.

Figure 21.2

A slightly more
complex dialog
panel.

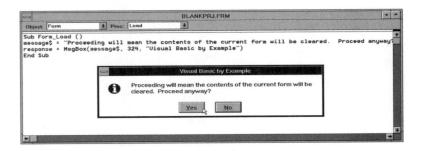

Notice that the extra highlighting appears around the No button as a result of adding 256 to the second argument of the function. If the user clicks this button or presses Enter, the value 7 is returned to the variable response.

When in use, a
modal window
suspends the
operation of every
other window in
the application.

Generally, when you place a dialog panel on-screen, your intention is to draw the user's attention to that panel only. You'd rather not let the user have access to other controls until you get an answer to your question. For that reason, a dialog panel suspends the operation of every other window in the running application until the user gives a response. Any Windows panel that suspends the operation of the other windows in the application is called a *modal window*.

By contrast, a *modeless window* enables other windows on-screen to be initiated and operated when it is active or when it has the focus. Of course, the focus passes to any other window indicated while the modeless window is active.

> **Note:** No application's modal window can suspend access to other windows currently inhabiting the Windows workspace.

The Input Box

The standard Windows dialog that receives *textual* input from the user rather than just a multiple-choice response is the *input panel*. Visual Basic supports this device with the InputBox$() function.

InputBox$()   **Function**

Purpose: Textual panel invocation
Syntax:

```
response$ = InputBox[$] (message$[, title$[, default$
➡[, xcoord%, ycoord%]]])
```

The InputBox$() function uses the message in *message$* as a prompt for a textual response, to be entered by the user on a text line appearing in the dialog panel. The contents of this line are limited to a maximum of 31 characters, and can be seeded in advance by expressing *default$*. The title of the input panel can optionally be expressed as *title$*; if the title is not expressed, the title bar is left blank.

Normally, the input panel appears in the center of the screen. If it is placed anywhere else, the origin point of the window can be expressed as coordinates *xcoord%, ycoord%*. An input box always contains two buttons: OK and Cancel. If the user clicks Cancel, the contents of *response$* remain a null string. If the user clicks OK, the contents of the text line are returned as *response$*.

> **Note:** String functions in Visual Basic use the $ string identifier optionally. The InputBox$() function can be expressed as InputBox(), and VB3 will never know the difference. For clarity, however, this book refers to string functions using the string identifier.

Example

The following function places on-screen an input box that requests a password from the user:

```
message$ = "Enter a password:"
response$ = InputBox$(message$, "", "TRIPWIRE")
```

The second parameter in the function nullifies the title of the dialog panel. The third parameter, "TRIPWIRE", places a default password in the text line. The resulting input box appears as in figure 21.3.

Figure 21.3

The password input box.

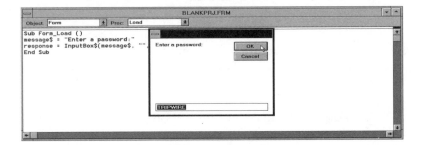

Notice the large amount of white space between the message text and the text line. The size of an input box is fixed, so this space is allotted for longer messages. Carriage return and line feed characters may be required in the message string for multiple lines.

Summary

A panel is any supplementary window whose purpose is to elicit an immediate response from the user. A dialog panel is not a form by the standard Visual Basic definition; instead, it is a temporary window that is provided as a resource of the Windows environment. The contents of this box are specified in the MsgBox instruction, along with a sum value having binary or bitwise contents that reveal what buttons and icons are found on the dialog panel.

An input panel is a type of dialog that elicits a textual response from the user. An input panel may be generated by the InputBox$() function. Visual Basic's input panels are a fixed size and always have OK and Cancel buttons.

Review Questions

1. To elicit a textual response from the user, should you use a message panel or an input panel?

2. When the VB application executes the MsgBox and InputBox$() instructions, does it display modal or modeless windows?

3. A file selector panel is used to get a file name from the user for loading or saving a particular file. Why should a selector necessarily be a modal dialog panel?

Part V

Graphic Objects and Controls

CHAPTER 22

Menus and Options

In this chapter, you examine different ways in which you can make multiple command selections available to the user. In the previous chapter you learned how to use dialog panels to get user input. However, the user doesn't necessarily respond to a dialog panel with a command. This chapter shows you some standard ways to obtain commands from the user without using panels or the standard gray command buttons.

First you learn the procedure for adding a menu bar to a form and for maintaining the menu hierarchy. You see individual menu items functioning in place of graphic controls, and examine the properties that relate to menu items. Later you learn more about control arrays and how you can use one source code procedure to direct a set of related controls.

The Menu

The menu bar is one type of control that is not available from the Visual Basic toolbox. Although Microsoft could have included a menu bar as a toolbox control, doing so would not have made much sense, because toolbox controls usually have variable positions on a Visual Basic form, and a Windows menu bar always appears at the top of the window. Instead, it makes more sense to have the Visual Basic interpreter turn the menu bar option on or off for a form.

In Visual Basic source code, menu items *are* graphic objects; you use them as though they were command buttons placed on the form, using the familiar _Click event.

The following example shows how to create a menu bar for the NameForm application. To create this menu bar, you need only NameForm by itself, without the MultiName parent form. Then you must change some of its procedures, as follows.

Here are the general declarations:

```
Option Base 1
Dim LstName$(1000), FrstName$(1000), MdInit$(1000),
➥CompanyNam$(1000), Adress$(1000), Cty$(1000),
➥Stat$(1000), Zp$(1000)
Dim RecordNo As Integer
```

Next come the event procedures:

```
Sub CompanyName_Change ()
CompanyNam$(RecordNo) = CompanyName.Text
End Sub
```

Now the array variable CompanyNam$() is a regular part of the database table and receives its contents from the text box CompanyName.

Next, CompanyName also takes its rightful place in Sub Display_Click ():

```
Sub Display_Click ()
RecordNo = RecordShown.Value
FullName$ = FirstName.Text + " " + MidInit.Text + " "
➥+ LastName.Text
WorkPlace$ = CompanyName.Text
StreetAddress$ = Address.Text
Residence$ = City.Text + ", " + State.Text + "   " + Zip.Text
Next_Line$ = Chr$(13) + Chr$(10)
Envelope$ = FullName$ + Next_Line$ + WorkPlace$ +
➥Next_Line$ + StreetAddress$ + Next_Line$ + Residence$
MsgBox Envelope$
End Sub
```

Subsequently, you add a line to Sub RecordShown_Change () to make CompanyName part of the formal record:

```
CompanyName.Text = CompanyNam$(RecordNo)
```

Menu Production

Most drop-down menus that you use in Windows applications consist of single panels that fall beneath (or above, depending on the window's position) the menu bar. Let's call the root portion of the menu bar the *base*—this is the part that is always shown. Along this base is a list of *menu categories,* and each drop-down panel contains a set of subordinate selections.

Some menu selections occasionally display a rightward-pointing arrow on the right side. Such a menu selection acts as a category. When you select an item for which the arrow is displayed, you bring down (or up) a subordinate panel that contains a separate set of selections related to the current selection. For example, if you were in a menu of a graphics program and chose Zoom from the View menu and then selected 200%, the 200% selection would appear in such a subordinate panel.

To design such a menu, you must relate its graphic objects to one another hierarchically to form a multitiered list. Unlike any other graphic object in Visual Basic, the menu bar is designed exclusively through the use of a separate modal window, as shown in figure 22.1. This window is divided into three main parts. The data fields at the top of the window allow you to enter and modify information about the highlighted menu options at the bottom of the window. In the middle of the window are three buttons and four arrows. The buttons are used to insert, delete, and select the menu options in the bottom window, and the arrow keys are used to rearrange and change the indent of the menu options. The bottom part of the window contains your defined menu structure. Note that the levels of indent in the menu definition define the menu/submenu hierarchy.

Figure 22.1

The Menu Design window at work.

To use the Menu Design window to create a menu bar for a form, follow these steps:

1. To indicate which form will contain the menu bar, make that form active by clicking on it with your mouse (giving it the focus).

2. From the Visual Basic control window, select the **M**enu Design command from the **W**indow menu, or click the Menu Design Window button in the toolbar. The Menu Design window then appears.

3. In the lower portion of the Menu Design window is a list of menu items that serves as an outline for the menu. Every addressable item in each part of the menu is listed in a hierarchical format, as shown in figure 22.1. To add a category to the base of the menu bar, type in the Ca**p**tion text box the name of the category as you want it to appear on-screen. This entry becomes the `.Caption` property setting for displaying the menu item as a graphic object.

4. You can assign a key to be paired with the Alt key as a keystroke alternative to the menu item. In the item caption that you have entered in the Caption text box, decide which character you want to pair with Alt, and then insert an ampersand (**&**) just before that character. For instance, the caption entry `&File` assigns Alt-F as the alternative keystroke to display the File menu. To assign another keystroke that involves the Ctrl and the Ctrl-Shift combinations, choose that keystroke from the **S**hortcut drop-down list.

5. In the Na**m**e text box, type the control name for this menu selection item. This entry becomes the `.Name` property setting for the menu item.

6. To set or reset any of the three True or False properties associated with this menu item, check or uncheck the **C**hecked, **E**nabled, or **V**isible options. These check boxes set the `.Checked`, `.Enabled`, and `.Visible` properties for the menu item, respectively.

7. If you want this menu to belong to an MDI parent form, a drop-down panel may have to contain a list of active MDI child windows. To place such a list on a menu panel—for instance, a panel belonging to a Window category—click the **W**indow List check box. This option in turn sets the `.WindowList` property for the menu item.

8. To enter this menu item into the list, choose the **N**ext button.

9. To designate a menu item on the list as subordinate to the category above it—as **O**pen is subordinate to File—click the right-arrow button in the window. This shifts the caption of this category four dots to the right. This designates that the item belongs to a drop-down menu for the category above it. A Visual Basic menu system can have as many as five levels of subordinate menus.

10. To delete an item from the list, select that item and choose the Delete button.

11. To open a space in which you can insert another item into the list, select the item that currently occupies the space and choose the Insert button.

12. To change the location of a menu item in the list, select the item and then click the up-arrow or down-arrow button to move the item up or down through the list.

13. To promote an item on the list to categorical rank, select the item to receive the promotion and then click the left-arrow button.

14. To add a partition to a menu, first create a menu item for the space where you want to place the partition. For the caption of the partition, type a hyphen (-). Unfortunately, you must also designate a control name for this caption, regardless of whether the partition is to be used as an actual control. An appropriate name might be hyphen1. The partition becomes a graphic object, even though it is unselectable.

15. To abort a menu bar creation, click the Cancel button.

16. When the menu bar is in an operable state and ready for testing, click OK.

Example

To experience the thrill of creating menu bars, first delete the command buttons at the bottom of the existing NameForm. You may want to resize the form so that you don't leave too much blank space at the bottom. Next, using the procedure outlined previously, enter the menu from table 22.1 into the Menu Design window.

Table 22.1. A menu to be entered into the Menu Design window.

Captions	Control Names
&File	File
....&New...	FileNew
....&Open...	FileOpen
....-	hyphen1
....&Save...	FileSave
....Save&As...	FileSaveAs

continues

Table 22.1. Continued

Captions	Control Names
&Edit	Edit
....&Cut	EditCut
....Cop&y	EditCopy
....&Paste	EditPaste
&Display	Display
&Options	Options
&GoTo	GetRecordNo

Previously this form included a button that had both a .Caption and a .Name of Display. After you delete the button and insert the preceding menu, a menu item with the same name as the button appears. Originally attributed to the button, the procedure Sub Display_Click () now automatically applies to the menu selection. In this context, Display is treated as a graphic object; however, it is not a graphic object. Figure 22.2 shows NameForm with the addition of a menu.

Figure 22.2
NameForm with the added menu.

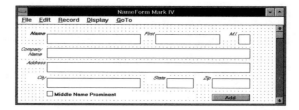

The Menu Design window lists the following three properties, designating the operative state of a control. In this case, a menu selection is a control.

.Enabled   Property

Representation: Control operability status
Applies to: All controls, menu, form
Set by way of: Properties window, Menu Design window, program instruction

The .Enabled property for a control is set to a true or false value that designates whether the control responds to user events. By default, this property is set to True. To turn off a control but allow it to remain within a form, or to "gray" a selection within a menu, you set this property to False.

.Visible   **Property**

Representation: Control display status
Applies to: All controls, menu, form
Set by way of: Properties window, Menu Design window, program instruction

The .Visible property for a control is set to a True or False value that designates whether the control can be seen. An invisible control is nonresponsive. By default, this property is set to True. To make this control disappear or to eliminate a selection from a menu temporarily, you can set this property to False. Setting the .Visible property for a form to False is virtually the same as invoking the .Hide method for that form.

.Checked   **Property**

Representation: Menu item accent
Applies to: Menu
Set by way of: Menu Design window, program instruction

The .Checked property for a menu selection is set to a True or False value (using True/False or On/Off) that designates whether a check mark appears beside the selection. This property does not change the effect of the menu or of any objects to which its event procedures may refer. It merely sets or resets a check mark beside the selection. You can use this property to help designate whether a feature of the program represented by the menu selection is currently active.

Finally, one further property setting is related to menus, affecting only menu bars that appear within MDI parent forms: the .WindowList property.

.WindowList   **Property**

Representation: MDI child listing status
Applies to: Menu
Set by way of: Menu Design window

The .WindowList property for a menu category of an MDI parent form is set to an on/off value that signifies whether the category's menu panel will display a list of all MDI child windows that are currently open. Each child window is listed by the name in its title bar. The listing for the child window that currently has the focus is automatically checked at run time.

Figure 22.3 shows a window list menu after being added to the MultiName MDI parent form introduced in Chapter 20, "The Window as Document."

Figure 22.3

A window list menu added to the MultiName MDI parent form.

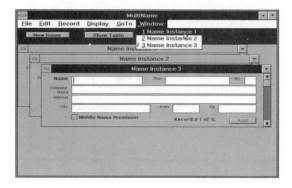

Grouping Controls in a Form

Setting an option dot beside a group of options in a form is similar to selecting a command from a menu. In both menus and option groups, multiple options are displayed and one is highlighted. The primary difference between the two types of controls is that the menu is usually reserved for user *directives*, whereas an options group enables the user to set the parameters or *characteristics* of an operation to be performed. Usually an options group offers fewer choices than a list box, which is usually reserved for elements of data. Furthermore, the number of options in a group is always fixed; you can't use the .Hide method to remove an option from a predesigned form without leaving a gap. With a menu, you can remove individual items from the visible panel and the interpreter automatically closes the gap.

You can select more than one check box at a time.

Windows has two categories of option sets. Use the common option dot set when you want to restrict the user to choosing only one unit from the set, and use the check box set when you want to give the user more than one item from which to choose. In Visual Basic's implementation, each option set is grouped within a *control array* and given a common name.

You can set only one option dot at a time.

In the case of option dots (also called *option buttons*), if one option dot is set, another option dot elsewhere on the form is reset. Check boxes are not as inter related, because you can select several boxes in a form at one time, regardless of subdivisions. Usually a check box enables the user to set the binary state of an aspect or function of the program.

Figure 22.4 shows an accessory form for an application, with three option dots on the left and three check boxes on the right. This example demonstrates the difference between the functions of option dots and check boxes. You can save a file in only one format, so you should set only one option for the Save As group. However, you can set any or all of the check boxes in the group on the right side.

Figure 22.4

Option dots and
check boxes
compared.

*A frame separates
options groups
from other parts
of a form.*

You can divide a form with a frame. A *frame* is a subdivision of a form that divides groups of elements, such as options, from groups in other such subdivisions and groups elsewhere on the form. You can place in a frame groups of options that you want to separate from other options in the form.

Adding a frame to a form is like putting one box within another and having the "child" box be subordinate to the "parent." (You'll remember this "child" and "parent" terminology from Chapter 20.) In Windows programming, frames are parent controls, and the parents' contents are child controls. Frames are not used to send user directives to the program unless another control or icon has been dragged over or on top of them. Although they are not actually operable controls, frames are nevertheless considered controls. To appear to belong together, the objects placed within a frame must fit entirely within the frame.

For a control to *belong* to a frame—or rather to be the "child" of that frame—you must take the control from the toolbox and immediately place it on the frame area. If you draw a control on the main portion of a form and then later drag the control to the area of a frame, that control would *not* belong to the frame. When you move a frame, the controls that belong to it move with it, but the controls that do not belong to the frame stay behind.

Figure 22.5 shows the option dots from the preceding form re-created as part of a frame.

Figure 22.5

Placing the control
array within a
frame.

You can add a set of option dots to the form or to another frame without having the new option dots be interrelated to those within this frame.

To determine whether an option dot is set or a check box is checked, you use the .Value property. However, when used in other situations, the keyword has other meanings.

.Value   Property

Representation: Status within a range
Applies to: Check box, button, option dot, scroll bar
Set by way of: Properties window, program instruction, user interaction

The .Value property, for an option dot, is set either to on or off. This setting specifies whether the user has chosen the option. For a check box, .Value is set to 0, 1, or 2. This setting specifies whether the box is reset, set, or dimmed (made unavailable), respectively. For a command button, .Value is set to True or False, depending on whether the user has just clicked the button. For a scroll bar, .Value returns the relative position of the scroll box along the coordinate scale set for the scroll bar.

Example

Suppose that NameForm (the form that you designed earlier in this chapter) has a string variable whose contents are set to a space when the user checks the *Spaces as tabs* check box. The following routine assigns the proper value to the string variable:

```
If Check1.Value = On Then
    sp$ = " "
End If
```

If the user does not select the check box, sp$ is left alone.

Example

Suppose that a procedure determines which option dot from the preceding frame was set by the user. When the user sets the option dot and clicks the Save button, execution branches to any of three procedures. The following procedure determines how the branching occurs:

```
Sub Save_Click ()
Select Case On
    Case Option1.Value
        Standard_Save
    Case Option2.Value
        RTF_Save
    Case Option3.Value
        ASCII_Save
End Select
.
.
.
End Sub
```

Here is this example written in pseudocode:

Procedure for clicking the Save option
dot:
In case any of the following options are set:
*   For the first option,*
*   Execute the procedure for standard saving.*
*   For the second option,*
*   Execute the procedure for RTF conversion.*
*   For the third option,*
*   Execute the procedure for ASCII conversion.*
End of cases.

.
.
.

End of procedure.

The `Select Case` clause compares all three `.Value` properties to logical truth (`On`) for equality. Only one of these values is set to `On`, because after all, these values are for option dots, and therefore only one procedure branch is possible.

Grouping Controls in the Source Code

So far, the Visual Basic interpreter sees each option dot and check box in the preceding form as a separate, individual control. Therefore, each dot and each box has its own event procedure. However, when options are closely related to each other, it may be more convenient to reduce an options group's code to one procedure. You can accomplish this by assigning each control in the options group or check box set as part of a single group that you can address with one collective name, much like an array variable. Such a group is called a control array. A *control array* is a set of similar, related controls that are in a form, are referenced together as a group, and have an operation jointly defined by a single procedure in the source code.

In a control array, the graphic objects are grouped together and given a collective name, such as `Option1()`. The parentheses denote that the control name refers to an array. A control array should consist of a group of graphic objects that look nearly alike and have somewhat related purposes.

To design a control array, follow these steps:

A *control array* is a set of similar, related controls that you reference as a group.

1. Plot to the parent a child control. This child control serves as the first element and as the model for all the controls in the array. This control should resemble the others. If the other controls are to contain different captions, you can edit them individually later.

2. Indicate the new model control by clicking it with your mouse and selecting Copy from the Edit menu.

3. Select the destination for the control array—the parent control for which the control array is to serve as a child. If the control array is to belong to the form alone, select the form by clicking its background or title bar once. If the control array is to belong to a parent control, such as a frame or picture box, select that control by clicking it once. The destination control should appear surrounded by little squares, called *indicator nodes*.

4. To add the second control to the array within the selected destination, choose Paste from the Edit menu. A dialog box appears.

5. This dialog box asks whether you want to create a control array. Respond to the dialog box by clicking OK. The control array now officially exists.

6. The second element in the array appears in the top-left corner of the parent control, and is surrounded by indicator nodes. Drag this control to its proper position within the parent. Its contents are identical to those of the copied control. Now you can edit the .Text or .Caption property for this control.

7. To add more elements to the array, choose Paste from the Edit menu and repeat the preceding step.

8. To edit the _Click event procedure for this control array, double-click any control in the array. A procedure frame appears.

Example

Instead of waiting for the user to choose the Save button, you can ensure that the procedure branch is made whenever any of the option dots are set. To do so, apply to the previous Select Case clause the procedure that creates a control array, as follows:

```
Sub Option_Click (Index As Integer)
Select Case Index
    Case 0
        Standard_Save
    Case 1
        RTF_Save
    Case 2
        ASCII_Save
End Select
End Sub
```

The event procedure is responded to as if all three controls in the array constituted one big control called Option. When the Visual Basic interpreter creates a framework for the event procedure, it automatically places Index As Integer between the parentheses as both a declaration and a passed parameter. The index of the set option dot is returned in the variable Index (note the difference between this and the .Index property term). The Select Case clause now compares Index to the three possible values (0, 1, and 2) for equality. Because you have to click the option group to execute this procedure, one of the branches must be made.

Summary

The menu bar is a container for controls that are not officially components of a Visual Basic form's background, although the interpreter considers them graphic objects. The purpose of menus is to give the user access to a list of instantaneous, perhaps hierarchical, directives to the application. You create menus with the aid of the Menu Design window.

For each group of option dots that appears in a form, only one dot can be set at one time, to designate a single selection from a list. However, the user can set many check boxes in a group within a form at one time. You can divide groups into subgroups by placing elements of those subgroups within a frame, which is a rectangular subdivision of a form. Each item in an options group has a .Value property attributed to it, which designates whether that control is currently set.

A control array is a formal grouping of controls that you address within the source code like an array variable, with a single name and a subscript index within parentheses. This type of grouping differs from a graphic or frame grouping, which you create by drawing on a frame related elements that simply rest on the frame instead of actually belonging to it.

Review Questions

1. Why didn't Microsoft include a menu bar in the standard Visual Basic toolbox?

2. What do the ellipses (…) in the .Caption of a menu command signify?

3. Can a frame control be part of a control array?

4. If you drag a control into a frame, does that control become part of a control array?

5. Can a control array exist partly within and partly outside of a frame?

6. When an event procedure applies to a button and you remove that button from the form and replace it with a menu command that has the same .Name as the removed button, where does the event procedure "go" while the replacement is taking place?

CHAPTER 23

Managing List Boxes

This chapter introduces the controls that are the standard repertoire of Visual Basic. You first learn about the properties, methods, and events that are specific to list boxes. You then see how to add items to a list box and how the operation of a list box differs from that of a combo box.

Using Visual Basic Controls

Almost every Windows application uses the same standard set of visual controls. Each Windows application is unique and must provide the user with unique options, but that does not mean that the means by which the user chooses or selects options necessarily differs from application to application. Windows works so well as an operating environment partly because the acts of rendering commands and making choices are similar from program to program.

A *control* is the visually implemented form of a graphic object, used for acquiring and displaying data.

A list should be identifiable as a list; similarly, the user should be able to set states or conditions easily with buttons. One key to good programming is to determine how many nonstandard selections or choices you can represent in the program through familiar, standardized controls, and to what extent you should represent operations graphically in unique, nonfamiliar ways, if such ways are more efficient.

Visual Basic gives programmers easy access to the most standard controls found within, and shared among, Windows applications. With extensions to Visual Basic, you can increase the amount and type of controls supported within a Visual Basic application. However, this chapter focuses on the controls that the standard Visual Basic package supports.

List Boxes and Combo Boxes

A drop-down *list box* differs from a pulldown *menu* in that the list box presents choices of data items, settings, or conditions, and the menu usually presents commands. The chosen item within a list is displayed in the highest text line of the list box that is permanently visible. A *combo box* is a version of the text box control that includes some extra device for displaying or making choices. Such a device may enable the user to type a choice within the text line, especially if the choice is not available in the list.

When you place a standard list box on a form at design time, the Visual Basic interpreter gives it the default name List*n*, in which *n* is the accession number of the list box; similarly, the interpreter gives a combo box the default name Combo*n*. Although the toolbox provides two buttons for combo and list boxes, the interpreter actually treats the two items as one type of control, the characteristics of which are distinguished by a property setting.

.Style   Property

Representation: Text box inclusion
Applies to: Combo, list
Set by way of: Toolbox, Properties window

The .Style property is set to an integer that denotes the appearance of a list on the form. Its possible settings are the following:

♦ *Drop-down combo.* This setting allows the user to enter a value using either the keyboard or a pull-down list.

♦ *Simple combo.* This setting also allows the user to enter a value using either the keyboard or a pull-down list, but in this case, the pull-down list is always automatically displayed.

♦ *Drop-down list.* This setting does not include an edit area; the user may select only the options in the pull-down list.

.AddItem   Method

Purpose: List entry maintenance
Syntax:

```
Listbox.AddItem text$ [, index%]
```

The .AddItem method places the textual contents of *text$* into the list or combo box that has the control name *Listbox*. By default, the text is placed at the end of the list. Optionally, the place of the new item in the list can be specified by number within *index%*. Items in a list are counted or indexed starting with zero; the value of *index%* must be no greater than the number of items in the list minus one. The method can add items to a list box only individually, and not by groups or arrays.

.RemoveItem   Method

Purpose: List entry maintenance
Syntax:

> *Listbox*.RemoveItem *index%*

The .RemoveItem method eliminates from the specified list or combo box the item addressed by *index%*. The method can remove items from a list box only individually, and not by groups or arrays.

A list box begins its life on the form with no items in it. It is up to the source code to feed items into the list one by one.

Example

Suppose that as a test you've placed a standard list box on a form. You want to have one button add an item to this list and another button remove that item from the list. Here is the code for both button-click procedures:

```
Sub Command1_Click ()
List1.AddItem "Test", 0
End Sub

Sub Command2_Click ()
List1.RemoveItem 0
End Sub
```

> **Caution:** If your program has a cluster of .AddItem instructions in a sequence and none of them specify a list index, by default the Visual Basic interpreter starts with item 0 and adds one item after the other to the list. If, however, you choose to specify index numbers directly with the .AddItem method, be sure you don't leave any holes in the list, as you would if you tried to add item 4 to the end of a two-item list. Such attempts generate an error.

When the items assigned to a standard list box are not more than can be displayed, the list box appears as a rectangle. However, when the list box overflows, the Visual Basic interpreter automatically adds a scroll bar to the right of the box.

A combo box at rest (with the combo list closed) on the form appears as a single line of text with a down-arrow button beside it. The list that drops below this line follows the same display rules as the standard list box.

Example

In the Expressor program that this book has periodically used as an example application, a combo box enables the user to select a formula to be solved. The following is how the formula names are added to this list:

```
Sub Form_Load ()
CalcList.AddItem "Surface Area of RC Cylinder"
CalcList.AddItem "Volume of RC Cylinder"
CalcList.AddItem "Zone Area of Sphere"
CalcList.AddItem "Force of Earth/Body Attraction"
CalcList.AddItem "Doppler Shift Transmitted Freq."
   .
   .
   .
End Sub
```

You will most likely want to place `.AddItem` instructions in the `Sub Form_Load ()` procedure. `Sub Form_Load ()` is the procedure that is automatically executed when the form is entered into memory.

Example

So far you have developed five formulas for the Expressor application. If you instead had 105, the repetitive invocations of `CalcList.AddItem` might become tiresome. Conceivably you could place each formula's text descriptions within a string array and add each string to the list in sequence, as follows:

```
Sub Form_Load ()
For place = 0 To frmulas - 1
    CalcList.AddItem frmula$(place)
Next place
   .
   .
   .
End Sub
```

The *.List()* property is one example of a Visual Basic property array.

When you add an item to a list, it is considered a property of that list, and therefore you address its contents and their aspects with property terms.

.List() — Property

Representation: List entry contents
Applies to: Combo, list
Set by way of: Program instruction

You access the .List property the same way that you access a control array; you address the contents of a list entry at a particular index as .List(*index%*). You can then treat the property just as you would an array variable. Thus, if you use .AddItem to apportion a place in the list, the text contents of the list at an index can be assigned to a string variable as follows:

```
string$ = [Listbox.]List(index%)
```

Likewise, to change the text contents of a list entry whose location is pointed to by *index%*, you reverse the order of the equation:

```
[Listbox.]List(index%) = string$
```

An instruction with the preceding syntax can be used only to change the contents of an existing list entry. You cannot use such an instruction to add an entry into a list at a nonexistent index.

> **Note:** Remember that the use of % in the preceding syntax lines has nothing to do with percentages. Instead, the symbol signifies that the value represented by *index%* must be an integer (whole number).

Example

The following instruction returns the contents of the fifth entry in the combo box CalcList, within variable ret$:

```
ret$ = CalcList.List(5)
```

Here are two property terms commonly used to determine the number of entries in a given list, and where the currently chosen item resides in that list: the .ListCount and .ListIndex properties.

.ListCount — Property

Representation: List entry amount
Applies to: Combo, drive, file, list
Set by way of: Course of program execution

The .ListCount property for a list or combo box is always set to the number of entries currently contained within it. The value of .ListCount - 1 is the index number of the last entry in the list, because the first entry has an index of 0 rather than 1.

.ListIndex   Property

Representation: Chosen entry location
Applies to: combo, drive, file, List
Set by way of: Program instruction, course of program execution

The .ListIndex property contains the index of the previously chosen item in the list. You can also use this property to compel the user to choose an item from the list. Simply assign an index value to the property with an equation, using the following syntax:

```
Listbox.ListIndex = indexno%
```

If the user doesn't choose an item, .ListIndex is set to –1 (not to be confused here with the Boolean value for True).

Example

The Expressor application uses the .ListIndex property to determine which formula the user has chosen:

```
Sub ApplyFormula_Click ()
For in = 0 To 4
p(in) = Val(param(in).text)
Next in
ndx = CalcList.ListIndex + 1
If ndx = -1 Then GoTo The_end
On ndx GoTo f1, f2, f3, f4, f5
.
.
.
End Sub
```

In the preceding code, the value of `CalcList.ListIndex + 1` is assigned to variable `ndx`. You add 1 so that the first formula addressed is item 1 rather than item 0.

Visual Basic allows entries in a list or combo box to be automatically sorted in alphanumeric order when the list or combo box is displayed.

.Sorted   Property

Representation: List sort status
Applies to: Combo, list
Set by way of: Properties Window

The `.Sorted` property for a list or combo box is set to a true or false value that denotes whether the entries contained in the list are to appear sorted in ascending alphanumeric order. When `.Sorted` is set to true, sorting of the entries takes place *before* the list box is initialized and displayed; sorting does *not* continue for the duration of the program. Therefore, if an `.AddItem` method is invoked that includes a specific index number, the item appears in the list at that location, although this may result in an unsorted list. The addition of entries to the list or the removal of entries from the list do not affect the value of the `.Sorted` property.

Example

The *Sorted* property applies to a list box only at its initiation.

The following is a sample application whose sole purpose is to test your ability to manage lists. Its startup form contains a combo box whose `.Sorted` property is preset to true at design time. Clicking a button adds an item to the list for this combo box; however, the item will be out of order. As stated previously, this does not change the `.Sorted` property for this box, so you need an algorithmic routine to tell you whether the list is actually in order.

Figure 23.1 shows this test procedure in its running state.

Figure 23.1

The list box test procedure.

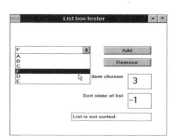

List Test Application

Project Name: LISTTEST.MAK
Constituent File: LISTTEST.FRM

Object Type	Property	Setting
Form	.Width	5130
	.Height	4725
	.Caption	List box tester
	.BorderStyle	1
Combo box	.Style	2
	.Sorted	True
Button	.Caption	Add
Button	.Caption	Remove
Text box	.Name	Chosen
	.Text	(blank)
Text box	.Name	SortState
	.Text	(blank)
Text box	.Name	Message
	.Text	(blank)
Label	.Caption	List item chosen
	.Alignment	1 - Right Justify
Label	.Caption	Sort state of list
	.Alignment	1 - Right Justify

```
Sub Form_Load ()
Combo1.AddItem "E"
Combo1.AddItem "C"
Combo1.AddItem "A"
Combo1.AddItem "B"
Combo1.AddItem "D"
End Sub

Sub Command1_Click ()
Combo1.AddItem "F", 3
SortState.Text = Str$(Combo1.Sorted)
End Sub
```

```
Sub Command2_Click ()
Combo1.RemoveItem 3
SortState.Text = Str$(Combo1.Sorted)
End Sub

Sub Combo1_Click ()
Chosen.Text = Str$(Combo1.ListIndex)
SortState.Text = Str$(Combo1.Sorted)
End Sub

Sub Combo1_DropDown ()
For amount = 1 To Combo1.ListCount - 1
    this_char$ = Left$(Combo1.List(amount), 1)
    last_char$ = Left$(Combo1.List(amount - 1), 1)
    If Asc(this_char$) < Asc(last_char$) Then
        Message.Text = "List is not sorted."
        Exit Sub
    End If
Next amount
Message.Text = ""
End Sub
```

In the Sub Form_Load () procedure, five entries are loaded into the list—obviously not in alphabetical order. When the procedure starts and Form1 appears, clicking the combo box's down arrow results in a display of a sorted list: A, B, C, D, E. The procedure Sub Command1_Click () manually adds one entry to this list, which is certainly out of order, resulting in the following list: A, B, C, F, D, E. Sub Command2_Click (), in turn, removes entry number 3 (the fourth entry) from the list. Both buttons place the textual form of the value of the combo box property .Sorted in the text box SortState.

The Sub Combo1_Click () procedure is executed whenever the user clicks the area of the list. The .ListIndex of the chosen entry is placed into the text box Chosen. and the value of the .Sorted property for the list box is placed within SortState. When F is added to the list out of order, the contents of SortState remain –1 (True) when tested; the interpreter still thinks that the list is sorted. You need to be able to tell when this list is in order and when it's not.

Here is procedure Sub Combo1_Click () written as pseudocode:

Procedure for when the user clicks a list
item in the combo box:
Place the alphanumeric form of the index of the
chosen entry in the appropriate text box.
Place the alphanumeric form of the state of the
*.**Sorted** property in its appropriate text box.*
End of procedure.

Clicking the down-arrow button of the combo box always triggers the `_DropDown` event—in this instance, `Combo1`. The event procedure `Sub Combo1_DropDown ()` is executed at that time, and it sends a message to text box `Message.` if the contents of the list are not in order. The procedure starts a loop, counting from index number 1 (the *second* item in the list) to the value of the `.ListCount` for this list—the number of entries it contains—minus 1. The result is the index number for the final entry in the list.

The pseudocode for the procedure `Sub Combo1_DropDown ()` is as follows:

Procedure for when combo box 1 drops its list:
Start counting from the index number of the second entry
to that of the next-to-last entry in the combo box.
  Extract the first character of this list entry.
  Now extract the first character of the list entry
  just preceding it.
  If this character falls beneath the order of the
  last character in alphabetic sequence, then
    Tell the user this list is not sorted.
    Get out of this procedure.
  End of condition.
Count the next entry.
Clear the text box.
End of procedure.

The variable `amount` keeps count of the index number the loop is currently processing. The first text character of this entry is compared to the first character of the *previous* list entry to determine whether it falls in sequence before the previous entry, falls after that entry, or is equivalent to that entry. The function `Asc()` derives the ASCII (actually, the ANSI) code number for the extracted characters. The code numbers are then compared to each other. If the next number in sequence is less than the previous one, the letter of the next entry in sequence must fall before the previous one. The list must therefore be out of order. In such a case, a message to that effect is delivered to text box `Message.`, and the procedure is immediately exited because it has served its purpose. If the loop completes itself totally, the list must therefore be in order, so the text contents of `Message.` are set to blank. The result of all this is that `Message.` blanks itself when the list is sorted.

The preceding procedure uses a new event, `_DropDown`.

_DropDown

Event

Action: Appearance of subordinate list panel
Applies to: Combo
Parameters: Index (control arrays only)

The _DropDown event for a combo box is activated whenever the user clicks the combo box's down-arrow button. This event is, in effect, the "click" event for the down-arrow button.

> **Note:** Because a menu bar in a form is not officially a control (only its included categories and selections are controls), the _DropDown event does not apply to menu bars.

Multiple-Choice Selection

If you've become accustomed to operating list boxes with the mouse only, you may have missed an important element of their operation. When a list box control within a form receives the focus, instead of surrounding the entire box with a second rectangle—which you could hardly see against its border—a *pre-choice indicator* surrounds one of the entries with a dotted black line, as shown in figure 23.2.

Figure 23.2

The pre-choice indicator.

Pre-choice indicator

| Force of Earth/Body Attraction |
| Doppler Shift Transmitted Freq |
| Escape Vel. of Body From Earth |
| Strength of Grav. Force |
| Simple Sine Wave |
| Parabolic Function |
| Length of Median of Triangle |

As you've learned, when you operate a form with the keyboard, pressing the Tab key moves an indicator rectangle along the planned tab stop route for that form. When the rectangle reaches the list box, it no longer selects the entire control, but instead selects a list entry in that control. Pressing the Tab key again moves the indicator to the next control; but pressing the up- or down-arrow key moves the entry indicator rectangle from one list entry to the next in sequence. In a list box, the indicator's purpose, in essence, is to help the user select an entry. If you choose to work only with the keyboard, then you press the spacebar to select your choice from the list surrounded by the pre-choice indicator. The effect of the pre-choice indicator is like moving your index finger up and down across the entries in a phone directory, browsing over each one before you finally put your finger on one of them.

List boxes may contain multiple columns, with multiple choices within those columns.

A list box can display entries in multiple columns and enable users to indicate multiple entries from one or more of those columns. To give a list box these capabilities, you must set the properties at design time.

.Columns

Property

Representation: List column inclusion
Applies to: List
Set by way of: Properties window

The .Columns property for a list box specifies the number of columns that a list box can contain, minus one. The default setting of the .Columns property is 0, denoting in effect a "false" setting for multiple columns. With the default setting, if the combined height of the entries in the list exceeds the height of the list box, the Visual Basic interpreter displays a vertical scroll bar on the right side of the list box. The scroll bar enables the user to navigate up and down the list. With .Columns set to non-zero, when the collective height of the entries exceeds that of the list, the interpreter clips the list right before the entry that falls below the lower border of the list box; the interpreter continues the list starting with this entry, at the next column to the right. A horizontal scroll bar is displayed whenever the collective width of the multiple columns exceeds that of the list box.

.MultiSelect

Property

Representation: Multiple entry choice capability
Applies to: File, list
Set by way of: Properties window

The .MultiSelect property for a standard list box or file list box is set to a value that specifies whether the user can choose more than one entry in the list, and the extent to which the user can make multiple choices. You can set the property to any of the following settings:

0   Enables the user to choose only individual entries. Choosing a second item from the same list overwrites the first choice and deselects it.

1   Enables the user to select multiple entries one at a time. The user can choose any number of items by clicking them (if you are using the keyboard, press the spacebar); no choices are overwritten.

2   Enables the user to select multiple entries with the keyboard. Choosing a single entry overwrites any existing choice in the same list, unless you hold down the Ctrl key. Choosing one entry, then choosing another while holding down the Shift key, selects both entries and all those between them.

Visual Basic programmers have become accustomed to using the .ListIndex property to determine which *single* entry from the list the user has chosen. If you have multiple entries chosen from the list box, what good is .ListIndex if it tells you the index of only the last entry chosen? What you need is an instruction that returns in a true or false value whenever the user chooses a *particular* entry. To accomplish this, Microsoft has once again become a bit liberal in its choice of object-oriented syntax.

.Selected()   Property

Representation: List entry choice status
Applies to: File, list
Set by way of: Program instruction, user interaction

The .Selected() property is actually an array of properties that pertain, by index number, to each of the entries in the antecedent list box, starting with index number zero. The property is set to a true or false value denoting whether the user has selected the subscripted list entry number. You can set the property value manually within the source code by using an instruction with the following syntax:

```
Listbox.Selected(index%) = boolean%
```

Example

Now that you have enabled the user to select multiple items from a list, what are you supposed to do with these chosen items? First, you have to determine the number of choices; next, you have to find out what the choices are; and finally, you have to create an array variable to store their contents. Here is a model procedure that does just that:

```
Sub ListOK_Click ()
For tour% = 0 To List1.ListCount - 1
    If List1.Selected(tour%) = On Then
        indic% = indic% + 1
        ReDim Preserve IndicCont$(indic%)
        IndicCont$(indic%) = List1.List(indic%)
    End If
Next tour%
End Sub
```

Suppose that within a form a list box is named List1. After the user chooses as many items from this box as he needs, he clicks a button ListOK that triggers the preceding procedure. The variable tour% counts the indices from the beginning to the end of the list. If the user has chosen the entry whose index is currently being counted by tour%, the running tally indic% of the number of entries chosen is incremented, and the length of dynamic array `IndicCont$()` is extended without losing its existing contents. Finally, the newest element of this array is given the contents of the chosen item to which `indic%` currently points.

Here is this procedure written as pseudocode:

Procedure for clicking the OK button:
Start counting from the first to last list in the list box.
 If the currently counted list entry is chosen, then
  Increment the tally of chosen entries.
  Add one element to the running array of chosen
  entry contents.
  Assign the contents of this list entry to the
  last element in the array.
 End of condition.
 Count the next list entry.
End of procedure.

After this procedure executes, you can use the string array to save items to disk, to recall a list of files, or to recall a select set of records from a data set.

Finally, the `.Clear` method clears entries from a list box:

.Clear   Method

Purpose: List box clearance
Syntax 1:

 `[Form.]Listbox.Clear`

The `.Clear` method empties the entire contents from the antecedent list box. The `.ListCount` property of the list box is reset to zero.

Summary

Visual Basic maintains provisions for list boxes and for combo boxes. Combo boxes are similar to list boxes except that combo boxes use extra graphic devices such as down-arrow buttons and often use editable text areas. To set the style of a combo box, you use the `.Style` property, which is reserved for combo boxes.

To add or remove items from a list or combo box, you use the `.AddItem` and `.RemoveItem` methods, respectively. To address the contents of items that you have added to a list, you use the property `.List`, much as you do when addressing a control array. The property `.ListCount` registers the number of items that currently inhabit a list. The property `.ListIndex` returns the index or accession number of the item that the user previously chose from the list. By presetting a list's `.Sorted` property to true, you can sort the items in the list in alphabetical and numerical order before you display them.

Review Questions

1. Suppose that it is 1959 and you have compiled a list of the 48 states of the United States within any kind of standard list box. Suddenly you receive word that two more items are to be added to the list. The `.Sorted` property for your list box is set to –1, and the list box is currently visible on-screen. When you use `.AddItem` to add Alaska and Hawaii to your list box, *without* expressing any index number, what are the indices for your two new states?

2. Suppose it is 1998 and you have compiled a list of the states of the United States within any kind of standard list box. Columbia (formerly the District of Columbia) and Puerto Rico are comfortable in their new positions as states of the union, and the President has signed the executive order officially making Guam a state as well. Sewing a 53-star flag with geometric symmetry is difficult enough; your job is to add Guam to your official list box of states. Assuming that the `.Sorted` property for your list is set to –1 and the list box is not yet loaded into memory, what will the index be for the list entry for Guam?

Review Exercise

1. Borrowing some source code from the procedures that you used in this chapter, write a procedure that informs the user whether her list is sorted whenever she clicks a button.

CHAPTER 24

Storage and Printer Controls

In this chapter, you examine Visual Basic's special provisions for directory-oriented and printer-related list and dialog boxes. Four of the buttons found in the Visual Basic toolbox are dedicated to these capabilities. Such a window (most likely type 3) is used to choose a file to load into memory, designate the directory location and file name of a file being saved to disk, or specify the location and characteristics of your printer. In this chapter, you see the development of an application using these controls.

Directory Assistance

As you've already seen, three special list box controls are available from the Visual Basic toolbar. The combined purpose of these controls is to address storage devices and their directories. The following properties pertain specifically to these controls.

.Drive   Property

Representation: Active device
Applies to: Drive
Set by way of: Program instruction, user interaction

The .Drive property for a drive list box is set to the text of its single selected entry. The syntax of the textual property setting is as follows:

```
drive:\ [volume_name]
```

The full volume name attributed to the drive device when it was last formatted appears between square brackets following the device identifier.

.Path   Property

Representation: Active file path
Applies to: Directory, file
Set by way of: Program instruction, user interaction

The .Path property for a directory list box is set to the text of its single selected
entry. The syntax for this text is as follows:

    drive:\[directory[\subdirectory. . .]\]

The textual contents of the .Path property reflect the subdirectory path where a
file resides or where a search is being conducted for a file. The text does not contain
a file name.

.FileName   Property

Representation: Chosen file name
Applies to: File list box
Set by way of: Program instruction, user interaction

The .FileName property for a file list box is set to the text of its single selected
entry. The syntax for this text is as follows:

    filename.ext

The text reflects only the name of the file itself with its three-letter extension,
regardless of the directory location of that file.

.Pattern   Property

Representation: Current search pattern
Applies to: File list box, Properties window
Set by way of: Program instruction, user interaction

The .Pattern property for a file list box is set to the current search pattern, which
each file within the currently active directory is matched against to determine
whether that file is to appear in the list. The effect is the restriction of file names
appearing in the file list box to a select group. The search pattern can—and usually
does—contain wildcard characters such as * and ? that represent any number of
characters or a single character, respectively. By default, the .Pattern property is set
to *.* (all file names).

A File Selector Box Application

The sample application for this chapter uses all three categories of directory-oriented list boxes to construct a rudimentary, yet all-purpose, file selector box. Note that this information can be obtained via the "Common Dialog" control, as you see later in this chapter. The reusable form we're aiming for is in figure 24.1.

Figure 24.1

The sample file selector box.

The Professional Edition of Visual Basic 3 comes with a control that allows Visual Basic forms to access standard Windows dialog panels, such as its own file selector panel. The Standard Edition of VB3 does not contain this extension control; so if you have the latter edition, you may find good use for your own custom file selector form, as listed here:

File Selector Box

Project name: SELECTOR.MAK
Constituent file: SELECTOR.FRM

Object Type	Property	Setting
Form	.Name	Selector
	.Caption	(blank)
	.BorderStyle	3
Drive	.Left	300
	.Top	450
	.Width	2115
	.Height	315
Directory	.Left	300
	.Top	1050
	.Width	2115
	.Height	1815

continues

File Selector Box Continued

Object Type	Property	Setting
File	.Left	2700
	.Top	1050
	.Width	2565
	.Height	1785
Text box	.Name	Filename
	.Text	(blank)
Label	.Caption	Filename
Button	.Name	OK
	.Caption	OK
Button	.Name	Cancel
	.Caption	Cancel

For the Selector to work properly, you must include the following instruction in a declarations section of a general module:

```
Global TargetFile$, cancl As Integer
```

The remainder of the Selector's listing is as follows:

```
Sub Form_Load ()
File1.Pattern = "*.*"
Filename.Text = File1.Pattern
cancl = 0
End Sub
```

The initial search pattern is set to *.* (all file names), and the text box called Filename. reflects this patterning. Global variable cancl is a flag that denotes whether the Cancel button is clicked, so the program that called the file selector will know if it is not supposed to look for a file name returned by the form. Because this is a global variable, it needs to be reset when the form starts.

```
Sub Drive1_Change ()
Dir1.Path = Drive1.Drive
ChDrive Drive1.Drive
End Sub

Sub Dir1_Change ()
File1.Path = Dir1.Path
File1_Click
End Sub
```

The _Change event occurs in the preceding cases whenever the current contents of the choice lines in the drive and directory list boxes, respectively, are altered, whether through the mouse or keyboard. Procedure Sub Drive1_Change () is invoked whenever the current choice in the drive list is changed; subsequently, it has the directory list alter itself to reflect the new drive being scanned, and tells DOS to change scanned drives as well.

```
Sub File1_Click ()
Filename.Text = File1.Filename
End Sub


Sub File1_DblClick ()
OK_Click
End Sub
```

When a file in the file list is clicked once, its name is entered into the Filename text field. The user may then click OK to choose the file. If the user double-clicks on the file, that means the file is chosen, and OK does not need to be clicked. You want to write the choice procedure only once, however, so you have procedure Sub File1_DblClick () branch to the following procedure:

```
Sub OK_Click ()
pth$ = Dir1.Path
If Right$(pth$, 1) = "\" Then
    Filename.Text = pth$ + File1.Filename
Else
    Filename.Text = pth$ + "\" + File1.Filename
End If
TargetFile$ = Filename.Text
Unload Selector
End Sub
```

The format of the .Path property can be a bit confusing. If the path being scanned is the root directory, the backslash appears at the end of the path, as in C:\. However, if the path is a subdirectory, the final backslash is omitted. Therefore, for a routine to properly assess the location and file name returned by the Selector form, a backslash must be added to the path if the path doesn't have one yet. The file name is returned to the form that called the Selector, in the global variable TargetFile$.

```
Sub Cancel_Click ()
cancl = 1
TargetFile$ = ""
Unload Selector
End Sub
```

This procedure is executed if the user clicks Cancel. The `cancl` flag (I can't write out *cancel*, because that is a reserved word in Visual Basic) is set to 1 and the file name return variable `TargetFile$` is set to a null string.

To operate this selector: the current list of accessible logical drives is available from the drive combo box, which is operated like a normal combo box. To scan a different subdirectory, double-click that subdirectory in the directory list box. To close the subdirectory being scanned, click any other directory in the list. To choose a file, either click its name in the file list and click OK, or double-click its name.

Offshoots from the _*Change* Event

Some offshoots of the `_Change` event are reserved for directory list boxes and file list boxes, as described in the following sections.

_PathChange   Event

Action: Directory path alteration
Applies to: File
Parameters: None

The `_PathChange` event for a file list box occurs whenever the path currently being scanned to obtain its contents is changed for any reason, whether by the program or by the user. The event is triggered whenever the `.Path` property is directly changed by the program.

_PatternChange   Event

Action: File search pattern alteration
Applies to: File
Parameters: None

The `_PatternChange` event for a file list box occurs whenever the pattern currently being applied against the current search path to obtain matching files is changed for any reason, whether by the program or by the user. The event is triggered whenever a change is made directly to the `.Pattern` property.

Common Dialog Boxes

As you gain experience with various Microsoft Windows applications, you will notice that virtually all of them use the same dialog boxes to save, open, and print information. These commonly used dialog boxes are provided by Microsoft for use in your applications and are called *common dialog boxes*. These dialog boxes are displayed in Visual Basic using the Common Dialog control button in the toolbox window. Below is a list of the windows that this control button can display. Included in this list are their associated .Action property values (explained later in this chapter).

Table 24.1 Available Common Dialog Boxes

Action Value	Dialog Box Name
1	Open File
2	Save As
3	Color
4	Font Type
5	Print

The Common Dialog control cannot be seen during run time, but must be placed on the form in order to call the dialog boxes listed in table 24.1. Also note that these dialog boxes do not actually open files, save files, or print data; they simply collect the information that your program needs to open, save, or print the data contained in your program. For example, the File common dialog box tells you the name of the file to be opened, but it is up to your program to actually read the file from disk.

.Action   Property

Specifies which common dialog should be displayed

Setting the .Action property does two things. First, it specifies which dialog box should be displayed. Second, it actually displays that dialog box. For example, the statement CMDialog1.Action = 1 causes the File Open dialog box to be displayed.

.ErrorCancel   Property

This property specifies whether the Err variable should be set if the user presses the Cancel button

Once a common dialog is displayed, it may be exited by pressing either the OK button or the Cancel button. If .ErrorCancel is set to True, Err is set to the numeric value 32755 (CDERR_CANCEL). If .ErrorCancel is set to False, the Err variable is not effected.

In addition to the `.Action` and `.ErrorCancel` properties, each dialog box has its own special properties. The most commonly used properties are discussed in the following section.

The File Common Dialog Box

The same File dialog box is used to open and save a file. This common dialog box is shown in figure 24.2.

This dialog box has the following associated properties.

Figure 24.2

The File common dialog box.

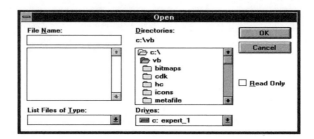

.FileName   Property

This property contains the selected file name. The `.FileName` property can be used in two ways. First, if set prior to setting the `.Action` property (before the dialog box is displayed), it specifies the initial file name that is placed in the File Name text box. Second, when the user of your program exits the dialog box via the OK button, the name of the file that the user selected is placed in the property.

.Filter   Property

This property specifies the search criteria that will be used to help the user find a file. The definition of the filter is divided into three parts. The first part is the text that you want to display in the "List files by Type" combo box, followed by the | character, followed the criteria used to fill the File Name text box. For example, the statement CMDialog1.Filter = "Text Files (*.TXT) | *.TXT) causes the words "Text Files (*.TXT)" to be displayed in the "List files by Type" combo box in the dialog box.

The following program example illustrates how to use the File common dialog box.

```
Err = 0
  CMDialog1.CancelError = True
  On Error Resume Next

  CMDialog1.Filter = "Text Files (*.txt)|*.TXT"

  CMDialog1.Action = 1

  If Err = 0 Then
    FileToOpen$ = CMDialog1.Filename
  Else
    FileToOpen$ = ""
  End If
    On Error GoTo 0
```

The preceding program begins by setting the variable Err to zero. Err is a Visual Basic reserved word that contains the numeric value of the most recently generated VB error. By setting it to zero, you can make sure that it does not contain a value caused from an earlier error. The line On Error Resume Next is telling Visual Basic to just continue to the next line if an error occurs. Remember, if pressing the Cancel button on the dialog box is going to create an error, you have to make sure that your program handles that error correctly. Then, the .Filter property is set and the File dialog box is displayed by setting the .Action property to 1. Next, if the user exits the dialog box by pressing the Cancel button, the variable FileToOpen$ is set to blank; otherwise, FileToOpen$ is set to the name entered by the user as specified in the .FileName property. Lastly, the statement On Error GoTo 0 turns off the previously executed On Error Resume Next.

The Print Common Dialog Box

The Print common dialog box is shown in figure 24.3. Remember, this dialog box does not actually print your data; it simply collects information about the printer settings, such as the number of copies to be printed.

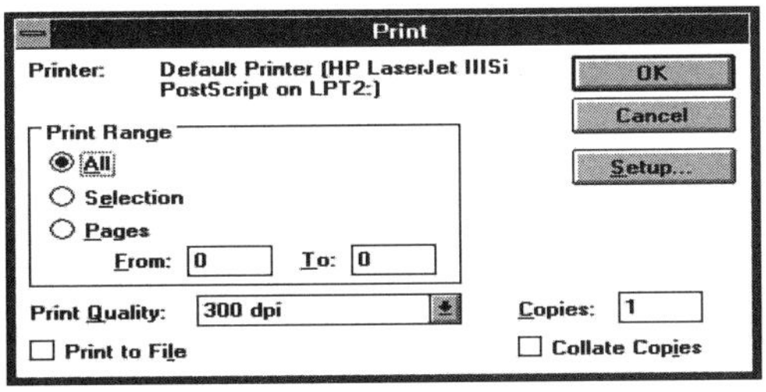

Figure 24.3

The Print common dialog box.

.Max and .Min   Properties

These properties specify the range of pages that can be printed. For example, if .Min has a value of 1 and .Max has a value of 6, the user can only print between 1 and 6 pages.

.Copies, .FromPage, and .ToPage   Properties

These properties specify the number of copies to be printed and the range of pages to be printed. For example, if .Copies has a value of 2, .FromPage has a value of 4, and .ToPage has a value of 6, your program should print two copies of pages 4, 5, and 6.

The following program example illustrates how to use the Print common dialog box.

```
Err = 0
CMDialog1.CancelError = True
On Error Resume Next

CMDialog1.Min = 1
CMDialog1.Max = 6  'in your program, replace 6 with a variable
                   'containing the maximum number of pages
CMDialog1.Action = 5

If Err = 0 Then

  TheFromPage = CMDialog1.FromPage
  TheToPage = CMDialog1.ToPage
  NoOfCopies = CMDialog1.Copies

  PrintInfo(TheFromPage, TheToPage, NoOfCopies)

End If
On Error GoTo 0
```

In the preceding programming example, I set the minimum and maximum page values and then called the Print common dialog box with the .Action property. Then, when control returns to my program, I call the print routine PrintInfo that presumably prints my information.

The Font Common Dialog Box

This Font Common Dialog Box is used to let the user select the appropriate font attributes. These attributes include the font name, size, boldfacing, and other similar attributes.

.FontBold, .FontItalic, .FontStrikeThru, and .FontUnderline **Properties**

These properties contain a True or False value and specify whether the displayed characters are bold, italic, strikethrough (a line through the middle), or underlined. Again, remember that this dialog box does not turn on or off these settings; it simply returns the user's preferences.

.FontName and .FontSize **Properties**

These properties specify the font name and font size selected by the user.

Summary

Visual Basic reserves three special types of list boxes for use in file selectors: drive or device lists, directory or path lists, and file lists. The VB interpreter automatically fills these lists with the current directory information gathered from DOS. The `.Drive`, `.Path`, `.FileName`, and `.Pattern` properties are used to direct the device controls toward specific DOS file locations. The `_PathChange` and `_PatternChange` events may be triggered if, during the use of these device controls, the current directory path and file search pattern are altered. In addition to the three special list boxes, Visual Basic also allows you to call the standard Windows common dialog boxes to gain information on what files to open or save, and user preferences on printer and font settings and options.

Review Questions

1. What type of user input is generally required to trigger the `_PatternChange` event?

2. When the user scrolls through a file list box, is a `_Change` event triggered?

3. What are the Windows common dialog boxes and how are they used?

CHAPTER 25

Shape and Line Controls

In this chapter, you are introduced to more examples of controls that don't really control anything, but add visual functionality to a form.

Shapes and Lines

A *vertex* in geometry is the end of a line or line segment.

There isn't much to tell you about lines, rectangles, and circles that you don't already know. In just about every object-oriented graphics program you've used, you've drawn lines and shapes on documents. The Visual Basic process for drawing lines is hardly different from any other process you've learned.

To draw a line within a VB form or parent object:

1. Click the Line button in the toolbar.

2. Click and hold down the index button over the point on the parent object where the first vertex of the line will appear.

3. Move the pointer to where the second vertex of the line will appear, and release the index button. The line is now plotted.

At this point, the line has four properties attributed to it. These properties represent its geometric coordinates.

.X1, .Y1, .X2, .Y2 — **Properties**

Representation: Geometric coordinates
Applies to: Line object
Set by way of: Control design, Properties window, program instruction

The .X1, .Y1, .X2, and .Y2 properties for a line object represent the geometric coordinates for the vertices of that line, with respect to the current scaling system in place for that form. The coordinate references follow the Cartesian system for vertices (x_1, y_1)-(x_2, y_2) along a two-dimensional plane.

Although lines are graphic objects in Visual Basic and have control names, they are not active controls. You cannot click on a line at run time and have an event be recognized. A line is only graphic embellishment.

The process for entering a rectangle or circle into a form is, not surprisingly, quite similar to that for entering a line.

To enter a shape into a VB form or parent object:

1. Click the Shape button in the toolbar.

2. Click and hold down the index button over the point on the parent object where one corner of the shape will appear.

3. Move the pointer to the point where the opposite corner of the shape will appear. Release the index button. A rectangle is plotted whose width and height conform to the two opposite corners you drew within the form. Note that this shape remains surrounded by eight indicator nodes.

4. In the Properties window, the .Shape property for this new object governs what shape it will finally take. At the moment, this property is set to 0 - Rectangle. You can use the Properties window to change this to another shape.

There are only a handful of basic shapes that the VB interpreter recognizes, all of which are listed in the following discussion of the .Shape property.

.Shape — **Property**

Representation: Graphical element identity
Applies to: Shape control button
Set by way of: Properties window, program instruction

The .Shape property for a graphical element drawn on a form uses the Shape control button of the VB toolbox. This property is set to a value that represents the contour currently applied to that element. The property can be set to any of the following:

0	Rectangle (default)
1	Square
2	Oval
3	Circle
4	Rounded rectangle
5	Rounded square

The property is set to zero by default. In all the preceding cases, the understood width and height of the shape control is determined by the position of the control's vertex coordinates within the form. The .Shape property affects the appearance of only the graphic element shown by that shape control. In cases 1, 3, and 5—each of which involve shape contours whose width and height appear to be equal—the actual size of the element displayed within the shape control is set to the shorter of the shape's .Height or its .Width property values, minus a few pixels for margin. In cases 4 and 5, the amount of rounding applied to the corners of the graphical element is fixed—to borrow a term from picture framing, they use uniform corner mouldings.

There are absolutely no events attributed to a shape or to a line control, although their usefulness in laying out a form is quite obvious. Figure 25.1 shows an updated form of NameForm, in which shape controls are used to help divide the contents of the form into categories. Note how the rectangle was used here to help indicate a subcategory of data along one side of the form.

Figure 25.1
The delineation of NameForm.

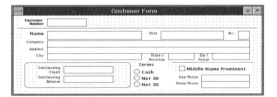

Now, if you intend to plot shapes to a form for more graphical purposes, such as charting or designing corporate logos, the shape control is certainly not what you want. Later in the book, you see several methods for plotting rectangles and ellipses to picture boxes; method-plotted shapes are far more versatile for composing charts or artistic images. Visual Basic shape controls serve quite adequately, however, as column borders and grouping elements.

There are no "fill patterns" for closed shapes; with Visual Basic, they are either filled with a solid color or are transparent. Property settings, again, determine these characteristics.

.BackStyle   Property

Representation: Solid fill state
Applies to: Shape object
Set by way of: Properties window, program instruction

The .BackStyle property for a shape object is set to a 0 or 1 value that signifies whether the shape is filled with a solid color. A value of 0 (the default) means that the area within the closed boundaries of the shape is transparent, whereas a value of 1 means that the area is filled with a color specified by the .BackColor property for the image. By default, .BackColor for a shape is set to white.

.BorderColor   Property

Representation: Contour color
Applies to: Line object, shape object
Set by way of: Properties window, program instruction

The .BorderColor property for a shape or line object is set to a six-digit hexadecimal value that represents the Windows color value of the pixels used to generate the line. You may use a decimal value within source code instructions to refer to color values; however, you might find it easier to use hexadecimal values for this purpose, because the division between the six hex digits more closely resembles the division between the six color parameters used to generate the value. When you set the .BorderColor property through the Properties window, a color palette appears below the entry line so that you can choose a proper color by sight rather than having to recall its hex number.

In Chapter 19, "The Window as Form," you were introduced to the .BorderStyle property, which simply states whether a rectangle appears around a text field; however, the .BorderStyle property does determine the style and function of windows. Regarding line and shape controls, the .BorderStyle property represents the type of "dashing," for lack of a better term, that is applied to the line or lines that make up the element.

.BorderStyle   Property

Representation 2: Line dashing mode
Applies to: Line control, shape control
Set by way of: Properties window, program instruction

The .BorderStyle property for a line or shape control, in Representation 2, reflects the current dashing that is applied to the "mark" that generates the appearance of that control. This allows for the generation of dotted or staggered lines. The marking styles representable by the .BorderStyle property appear as follows:

0		(transparent)
1	_____	(solid line, default)
2	_ _ _	(dash)
3	. . . . .	(dot)
4	_ . _ .	(dash-dot)
5	_ . . _	(dash-dot-dot)
6	_____	(inside solid)

Visual Basic treats a mark of style 0 as if it were visible, although it is actually not seen. The control is present on the form, although without apparent contents.

The interpreter considers a mark in the shape or line control as though it were being made by an ink pen. The width of the "nib" of this pen (the part that touches the page) is determined in pixels using the .BorderWidth property. For a shape control, the interpreter normally considers the mark as being made with the *innermost edge* of the nib, such that the total .BorderWidth extends *outwardly* making the shape appear to grow fatter. Setting the .BorderStyle for this control to 6 alters this process, such that the mark is extended *inwardly* as well for the same number of pixels that extend the mark outwardly. The width of the actual mark is thus doubled.

You might want to have a shape or line control be transparent (style 0) and displayed (by setting the .BorderStyle property to 1) when the user presses a button or performs some other appropriate action.

.BorderWidth was mentioned earlier and is closely related to .BorderStyle.

.BorderWidth   Property

Representation: Pixel extent of mark
Applies to: Line control, shape control
Set by way of: Properties window, program instruction

The .BorderWidth property for a line or shape control represents the length, in pixels, of the "nib" of the mark used to generate the visible image of that control. For a shape control, by default, this width is considered to be the width, in pixels, extending outwardly from the center of that control. If the .BorderStyle for the control is set to 6, this width is doubled, such that the same number of pixels extends inwardly toward the center. The .BorderWidth for a control may not be set to 0; to render a control apparently invisible (not truly invisible, for the sake of the interpreter), use a .BorderStyle property of zero.

> **Note:** The larger you make your `.BorderWidth` property, the more unlikely it is for any dashing style represented by `.BorderStyle` to show up. Extending the width of the mark used does not extend the size of the dashes or dots in a line or shape, regardless of the size of the actual control. Thus a line with a `.BorderStyle` of 3 and `.BorderWidth` of 20 may appear solid.

It's also important to note that a high `.BorderWidth` setting for a control will cause its mark to extend beyond the actual coordinate limits set for that control. It is therefore possible for a mark to actually "bleed" into the area occupied by another control. If that control is not another shape or line, the control will most likely overlap this mark. Also, as you expand the `.BorderWidth` for a line control to higher numbers, note that its ends are always rounded.

Because the `.BorderWidth` property deals with pixels and not twips—the usual coordinate system for a form—the widths of marks made to a form may not always be uniform across different graphics platforms and resolutions. A very fat line on a 640×480 VGA system, therefore, may appear somewhat thinner on a 1024×768 SVGA system. Such is part of the everyday inexactitudes one faces as a Windows programmer.

Example

Suppose a rectangle control were drawn around a list box. This control's purpose is to act as an indicator for the entire box, while the list entry indicator appears separately. By default, the `.BorderStyle` property is set to 0, denoting transparency. The following procedure makes the shape Rect appear again:

```
Sub List1_GotFocus ()
    Rect.BorderStyle = 1
End Sub
```

Object-Oriented Graphics

Object-oriented graphics (or *object graphics* from here on) comes from an entirely different school of thought than object-oriented programming. The former term is used to distinguish a type of graphical interpretation system from its more pixel-bound counterpart, raster-oriented graphics. In an object-oriented graphics system, the program that is interpreting the image understands the concept of lines being drawn between two points and of circles and rectangles. In other words, it "knows" where there's a circle in the image that you're drawing. Perhaps the most complex object graphics system employed today is PostScript, which is a language used by printing devices (and some computers) to interpret and generate images using terms. PostScript, like Visual Basic, is an interpreter.

Raster-oriented graphics, by contrast, deals with the color value of rows of pixels being plotted to the screen. In a raster system, the color value of a pixel is registered and plotted to the screen, and then the system proceeds to the pixel to the immediate right. If it runs out of space, it proceeds to the next row down. Raster graphics is the native plotting system of nearly all computers and graphics engines, including CGA, EGA, and VGA. A raster system has no idea what a circle is, because it's dealing with only a single pixel at any one time.

A *raster* in a graphics system is a row of pixels.

Certain programs and graphical environments (Windows included) can translate object-oriented graphics—such as the type produced by CorelDRAW!, Microsoft Draw, and the line and shape controls introduced in this chapter—into raster graphics that your native graphics engine knows how to plot. Not all computers, however, are raster-oriented; if you've ever played Asteroids in the arcade, you've used a *vector-graphics* computer. In such systems, the electron beam in the cathode ray tube is actually directed to go between two geometric points, instead of scanning rasters from the top down like a television set. Object-oriented graphics concepts are loosely based on vector graphics, although systems that use object graphics generally let the computer translate the images back into rasters so that you can see them.

A *metafile* is an object-oriented graphics image.

One very versatile form of object graphics that Windows uses is called the *metafile*; it is an image file that Windows translates into resizeable components. A metafile is a series of instructions to Windows for generating specific lines, shapes, and composite images. It can therefore be said that a metafile is made up of graphics objects. One program used specifically for the generation of metafiles is Microsoft Draw; however, to date, Microsoft has not sold this product separately. Microsoft Draw is generally found bundled with its major applications, such as Word for Windows. If you have Microsoft Draw installed on your system, you're in luck, because Visual Basic is capable of displaying metafiles (usually stored in the WMF format) in full color. You can use Microsoft Draw to generate backdrops or background images for a Visual Basic form.

Another definition of *object* is a data structure in memory.

Once in memory, Windows considers a metafile a type of object. In this definition, an object is a data structure that can be shared between programs and interpreted equally by those programs. Windows uses a system called *Object Linking and Embedding* (OLE) to allow one application to generate a data structure— such as a graphic image—that another application can interpret and display.

In Visual Basic, a graphic object is not necessarily graphically generated—for instance, the timer object, which appears in the VB toolbar. Objects in the Visual Basic *source code* are graphic in that the VB interpreter has found graphical means to represent them, whether directly or indirectly. You add a timer control to a form by dragging it there with the mouse. The language is then used to refer back to that graphical activity; so linguistically speaking, the VB vocabulary employs *graphic symbolism*. Thus the term "graphic object."

Summary

Line and shape controls in Visual Basic are graphic embellishments to a form that do not have any events associated with them. The positioning of a line control within a form is governed by its .X1, .Y1, .X2, and .Y2 property settings. These properties correspond to the line vertex coordinates in the Cartesian system, for the current coordinate system used within the form.

The visual appearance of a shape object is governed by its .Shape property setting. The shapes in the VB repertoire are basic rectangles, squares, ovals, and circles. Whether closed shapes are filled with solid colors is determined by the setting of the .BackStyle property. The color of the mark used to draw the line or shape is accomplished through its .BorderColor property. For line and shape controls, .BorderStyle is used to determine whether the mark is solid, dashed, or transparent. The .BorderWidth property is then used to establish the width of the mark in pixels.

Review Questions

1. Can the .BorderWidth of a mark be negative?

2. Can a line or shape be larger than the extent of the form itself?

CHAPTER 26

Scroll Bars

In this chapter, you study the operation of the independent vertical and horizontal scroll bar controls of Visual Basic. In a document-oriented application, scroll bars are generally used to scroll something. However, they can also be used to set range values in a panel or to represent a range of values.

The All-Purpose Range Finder

In Visual Basic, the relative position of the scroll box between the two arrows is represented by a coordinate value stored in the .Value property. Figure 26.1 shows how the coordinate system of a horizontal scroll bar works.

Figure 26.1

The breakdown of a horizontal scroll bar.

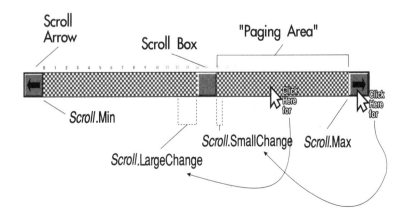

The coordinate system of a scroll bar exists without regard to its current size. Think of each scroll bar as a number line extending from one integer (generally 0) to another. The minimum and maximum values along this line are at the left and right or top and bottom points on this line. The number values at these points are assigned to properties .Min and .Max. There are (Scroll.Max - Scroll.Min) coordinate points along this line. The pixel length of a scroll bar has nothing to do with its coordinate system.

Here are the property terms that can be attributed to a scroll bar.

.Max and .Min   Properties

Representation: Extent of value range
Applies to: Scroll bar
Set by way of: Properties window, program instruction

The .Max and .Min properties of a scroll bar are set to the maximum and minimum coordinate values of the scroll box along the bar. These properties can be set to any integer between –32,768 and 32,767, inclusive, as long as .Max remains greater than .Min. When set, the length of the scroll bar is divided into (.Max - .Min) intervals. Moving the scroll box along the bar sets its .Value property equal to the interval where the box currently rests.

.SmallChange and .LargeChange   Properties

Representation: Value alteration intervals
Applies to: Scroll bar
Set by way of: Properties window, program instruction

The .SmallChange property setting for a scroll bar represents the degree of incrementation or decrementation in its represented value when one of the arrow buttons is clicked. When the user clicks the arrow button, the scroll box in the bar moves, relative to its current coordinate system of representation, toward the arrow. Similarly, the .LargeChange property setting represents the degree of incrementation or decrementation in the scroll bar's represented value when the user clicks between the scroll box and one of the arrow buttons in the direction of that arrow. This zone of the scroll bar is often called the *paging area*.

Now that you know about arrays and how items within a range are represented on-screen, let's make some changes to the NameForm application introduced in Chapter 8, "Alphanumeric Strings." The revised application can store lists of names in arrays, and uses a scroll bar to select individual names from the array range. The revised NameForm form is shown in figure 26.2.

Figure 26.2
NameForm
Mark II.

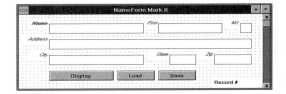

Here are the revised procedures for the application:

Name-Only Record-Entry System, Mark II

PROJECT NAME: NAMEFRM2.MAK
CONSTITUENT FILES: NAMEFRM2.FRM

```
Option Base 1
Dim LstName$(1000), FrstName$(1000), MdInit$(1000), Adress$
➡(1000), Cty$(1000), Stat$(1000), Zp$(1000)
Dim RecordNo As Integer
```

The first statement, Option Base 1, resets the system so the first address of an array is 1 and not 0. Notice that each string array variable name chosen is one letter removed from its text box equivalent on the form; this is because variable names and object names cannot match. On the lowest line, RecordNo is dimensioned as a unit integer to be Shared throughout all procedures, not as an array variable. This is part of an alternate syntax that is new to Visual Basic.

```
Sub RecordShown_Change ()
RecordNo = RecordShown.Value
If RecordNo < 1 Then
    RecordNo = 1
End If
Reg$ = "Record #" + Str$(RecordNo)
Register.Caption = Reg$
LastName.Text = LstName$(RecordNo)
FirstName.Text = FrstName$(RecordNo)
MidInit.Text = MdInit$(RecordNo)
Address.Text = Adress$(RecordNo)
City.Text = Cty$(RecordNo)
State.Text = Stat$(RecordNo)
Zip.Text = Zp$(RecordNo)
End Sub
```

The key variable here is RecordNo; it ties together all the elements of a record. If you consider the data generated by this program to be a database, RecordNo would be the sole relation in this base. The key instruction here is RecordNo = RecordShown.Value. This is where the single index to all eight string array variables below this instruction is set to the interval value of the scroll box along the bar.

The event _Change signifies a movement of the scroll bar, RecordShown, which is added to the form. This slider changes the visible record number, registered now as part of Reg$ in a new label in the bottom right corner.

Here's the general concept of this procedure, written as pseudocode:

Procedure for when the scroll bar value changes:
Change the current record number to reflect the
scroll bar value.
If the registered scroll bar value is less than 1,
then
Make the record number 1.
End of condition.
For the register, place the record number beside
the words "Record #."
Place this register in its proper position.
Change the textual contents of all the text boxes
in the form to reflect the current values of
each of their representative arrays for the
current record number.

.

.

.

End of procedure.

Here's the new Sub Form_Load () procedure for the application:

```
Sub Form_Load ()
RecordShown.Value = 1
RecordShown.SmallChange = 1
RecordShown.LargeChange = 10
RecordShown_Change
End Sub
```

In every Visual Basic application, the Sub Form_Load () procedure automatically executes once the form is invoked. The control name for the scroll bar in this application is RecordShown. Its initial .Value is set to 1, because record number 1 (not number 0) is the first to be displayed. The .SmallChange property is set to 1 (the default), which means the program moves on to the next record in the list (RecordNo + 1) if you click the down arrow, or to the previous record (RecordNo - 1) if you click the up arrow. The .LargeChange property is set to 10, which makes 10 the value of *one page* of records. The records are now said to *page down* by 10.

```
Sub Address_Change ()
Adress$(RecordNo) = Address.Text
End Sub

Sub City_Change ()
Cty$(RecordNo) = City.Text
End Sub

Sub FirstName_Change ()
FrstName$(RecordNo) = FirstName.Text
End Sub

Sub LastName_Change ()
LstName$(RecordNo) = LastName.Text
End Sub

Sub MidInit_Change ()
MdInit$(RecordNo) = MidInit.Text
End Sub

Sub State_Change ()
Stat$(RecordNo) = State.Text
End Sub

Sub Zip_Change ()
Zp$(RecordNo) = Zip.Text
End Sub
```

With these brief procedures, whenever new text is typed into any of the text boxes on the form, the contents of the string array variable for the current record number change automatically.

The way this program works now, you can set the scroll bar to any record number you choose and type a person's record for that number. You can then scroll to any other record number. When you scroll back to a filled record number, the record reappears.

Summary

A scroll bar is divided into equally spaced intervals numbered between its `.Min` and `.Max` property values. These intervals exist logically, regardless of the actual pixel length of the scroll bar in a form. The degree to which the `.Value` of a scroll bar is changed when the user clicks it is determined by the settings of its `.SmallChange` and `.LargeChange` properties.

Review Questions

1. If the .Min property setting for a scroll bar is the absolute negative of its .Max setting, where is the scroll box when its .Value property is set to 0?

2. What form of variable is the smallest form in memory necessary to represent the .Value property of a scroll bar?

3. A scroll box is positioned in a scroll bar where the represented interval between the scroll box and its maximum value is smaller than the setting of its .LargeChange property. What happens when the user clicks in the area between the scroll box and the down-arrow button?

CHAPTER 27

The Timer

In this chapter, you learn how the timer is used in Visual Basic as a control on a form to regulate *when* certain events can take place and *when* procedures can be executed. Normally, instructions in a procedure are executed once. By embedding instructions in a loop clause, or by manipulating the various branches, instructions can be executed multiple times. In Visual Basic you can program instructions to be executed continually, periodically, or after a set interval. Unlike other languages, however, Visual Basic's continual execution mechanism depends on a specific graphic object: the timer object.

An Experiment in Real Time

Each application in the Microsoft Windows environment is given a brief slice of time in which to operate, then it must yield the balance of its time to other applications or to the environment itself.

Partly because BASIC is such a popular language for programming or modeling time-intensive games, a mechanism must be maintained for keeping exact time. Yet with forms and modules in a Visual Basic application given indefinite time slices, depending on such incalculable factors as what computer the application is running on at the time, it would be difficult for the VB interpreter to keep perfect time for each running form. Therefore, Visual Basic maintains a laissez-faire attitude about timing, unless you specify otherwise. You can tell the VB interpreter directly to keep chronological (real-world) time for a particular form.

The way to do this is unusual but effective. A *timer* is assigned to a form by clicking the Timer button in the VB toolbox. The timer is then placed on the form to be timed as if that timer were a picture box. At design time, an image of a stopwatch appears where the timer is placed. At run time, however, this image is not visible; therefore, it really doesn't matter where the timer object is placed as long as it doesn't conflict with another graphic object. The user cannot operate the timer graphic object; it operates and generates an event by itself.

_Timer   Event

Action: Passing of interval
Applies to: Timer control
Parameters: None

The _Timer event takes place for a form that contains a timer control, after each passing of a certain interval of time as specified in the .Interval property.

> **Note:** The Timer() function in Visual Basic refers to the time kept by the computer system clock, and the _Timer event refers to the time maintained by VB's simulated chronological timer. These are two different timing systems.

The .Interval property is the only property that is specific to a timer control.

.Interval   Property

Representation: Timer activation value
Applies to: Timer
Set by way of: Properties window, program instruction

The .Interval property for a timer is the amount of time in milliseconds (thousandths of a second) that the form's timer counts before invoking a _Timer event. The property value ranges from 0 to 65,535 milliseconds, in which 60,000 milliseconds equal one minute. The .Interval property is often set to 1000 so that events occur every second.

Example

The most obvious use for the timer control is to have a form display the current real-world time. Assume a timer has been placed into a form. The `.Interval` property of this timer is set to 1000. The following is a procedure that displays the time as the caption of a label:

```
Sub Timer1_Timer ()
    TimeNow.Caption = Time$
End Sub
```

Example

By itself or in another procedure, the instruction `TimeNow.Caption = Time$` is executed once and displays the current time. With the preceding procedure, the `_Timer` event is generated regardless of what the user is doing at the time. The current time appears in the label `TimeNow.` once every second.

If you are more conservative with your time and want `TimeNow` to display the current time in minutes and seconds, you can reset the `.Interval` property to 60000, set the `.Enabled` property of the timer to True (–1) so that it will work, and rewrite the preceding procedure as follows:

```
Sub Timer1_Timer ()
    TimeNow.Caption = Right$(Time$, 5)
End Sub
```

Because the second hand is meaningless if the interval is set to minutes, you can use the `Right$()` function to extract the first five characters of `Time$`, leaving off the seconds digits.

Example

The `.Interval` property counts up to only one minute, five seconds, but you can keep certain elements of time independently. Suppose you have an application that maintains in memory a document that is being composed. You want this document to be backed up to disk every five minutes—regardless of what the user is doing at the moment—as a *background process.* Assuming the `.Interval` property is set to 60000 and the timer is `.Enabled`, the following procedure shows how the branch to the back-up procedure might appear:

```
Sub Timer1_Timer ()
BranchClock = BranchClock + 1
If BranchClock = 5 Then
    BranchClock = 0
    Auto_Backup
End If
End Sub
```

The pseudocode for this procedure follows:

> *Procedure awaiting a timer signal:*
> *Add 1 to the number of minutes being kept.*
> *If there are five minutes in the tally, then*
> > *Reset the tally.*
> > *Execute the backup procedure.*
> *End of condition.*
> *End of procedure.*

With the `.Interval` set to minutes, the event procedure for `_Timer` is executed every minute. Each minute, a count of 1 is added to an accumulator variable `BranchClock`. When the minutes are five, the count is reset and the branch is made to the `Sub Auto_Backup ()` procedure.

Summary

Normally, the Visual Basic interpreter doesn't time the execution of a form in a project in real-world time. To engage such timing for a form, a timer control is dragged into the form from the VB toolbox. This control is invisible at run time. When the timer is engaged by setting its `.Enabled` property to True (–1), the timer generates an event after each `.Interval` of milliseconds. An event procedure can be assigned to this event, called *Timer1*`_Timer`.

Review Questions

1. The maximum value of the `.Interval` property is equivalent to approximately how many minutes and seconds?

2. What terms, along with their delimiters (extra punctuation), are used to describe the following?

   A. The passing of the set Visual Basic interval

   B. The VB real-world chronometer

   C. The VB function that registers the passage of seconds since midnight

CHAPTER 28

The Keyboard

In this chapter, you learn how Visual Basic handles events related to the pressing and releasing of keys on the keyboard. You see how the VB interpreter processes events related to the keyboard and individual key presses. You then examine ways keystrokes can substitute for graphic control inputs.

Up to this point, you used the keyboard to generate text, which is often composed of words typed into boxes. If you ever played with Microsoft's Flight Simulator, you know that the keyboard can be programmed as an elaborate control mechanism for simulations. If you play in Piper Cherokee mode and you throttle up, you hold down the plus key on your keyboard. Likewise, you use the minus key to throttle down. The longer the key is held down, the more the throttle moves one way or the other.

With standard BASIC, it has been difficult to program the keyboard to use as such a controller. Not so long ago, programmers used the PEEK command to look into a register of memory to see whether a certain key was being held down; the *scan code* of the held down key often appeared in that memory address. This process is called *polling for keys*. Literally, this is the search for the digital form of the electrical signal generated by a key touching a metal plate inside the keyboard unit.

The problem with this polling was that the execution of these polling routines was difficult to regulate. At first, before timers and statements such as ON TIMER GOSUB, the program had to branch to the key-polling subroutine whenever it could. There was no real way to regulate the specific time the polling took place. As a result, you had no intervals. Sometimes the program branched to the key-polling subroutine by using GOSUB. To make sure that the keyboard was polled often, numerous GOSUB commands were included in the code. If you programmed a flight simulator or something like it, when the user released the key that acted as the throttle-up button, the program would not "know" that the throttle-up was released until after the next GOSUB to the key-polling subroutine. By that time, the throttle may have increased by another 10 percent; and if you're leaking fuel, another routine might generate an explosion.

Later in BASIC's history, some manufacturers used the ON KEY GOSUB statement, which forced a branch to a subroutine whenever a key was pressed. Visual Basic's solution to the key polling problem is to recognize key presses as events. The problem is that VB events "belong" to controls. If the keyboard's purpose is to operate controls on a form, it's no problem to assign a keypress event to a control. If the keypress is meant to affect some unseen value in memory, however, your objective is to determine which control or which form module processes the event.

Following are the main events recognized for keypresses, in place of the old ON KEY command.

_KeyDown and _KeyUp   Events

Action: Key activation or release
Applies to: Form, check, combo, command, directory, drive, file, grid, list, option, picture, scroll, text
Parameters: Index As Integer (control arrays only), KeyCode As Integer, Shift As Integer

The _KeyDown event for a form or control is recognized whenever that graphic object has the focus and the user presses a key on the keyboard. The _KeyDown event continues to be recognized for that control as long as that key remains pressed. Two parameters are passed to the procedure for this event: the scan code for the pressed key (not to be confused for the ASCII code value of the character the key generally represents) and an integer with a bitwise pattern that represents the depressed state of the shifting key. This integer can take any of the following values:

0	No shifting keys pressed
1	Either Shift key pressed
2	Either Ctrl key pressed
3	Control + Shift pressed
4	Alt key pressed
5	Alt + Shift pressed
6	Alt + Ctrl pressed
7	Alt + Ctrl + Shift pressed

The _KeyUp event for a graphic object is recognized whenever that object has the focus and the user releases a key that was pressed. Logically speaking, the event is recognized when the key scan code previously registered returns to 0. The procedure for the _KeyUp event is passed the same values by the VB interpreter as the _KeyDown event.

Example

Suppose that you need a quick procedure to register what the scan code is for a key, because the ASCII (ANSI) code for a character is not the same as the scan code for its corresponding key. All you need on the form is a simple text label. The following procedure returns the key scan code for any key pressed:

```
Sub Form_KeyDown (KeyCode As Integer, Shift As Integer)
Label1.Caption = Str$(KeyCode)
End Sub
```

Simply enough, the textual value of the key scan code is placed in Label1.

Suppose that you then want the contents of the label to clear when the pressed key is released. You might add the following procedure:

```
Sub Form_KeyUp (KeyCode As Integer, Shift As Integer)
Label1.Caption = ""
End Sub
```

Example

Earlier, this book discussed a set of controls for "throttling" up and down by using the keyboard. You can program such a control using the _KeyDown event and setting up a scroll bar to represent the state of the control in the form. Figure 28.1 shows this form in action.

Figure 28.1

The scroll key form.

"Scroll Key" Throttle Control Tester

Project name: SCROLKEY.MAK
Constituent file: SCROLKEY.FRM

Object Type	Property	Setting
Form	.Left	1095
	.Top	1545
	.Width	4485
	.Height	1905
Scroll bar	.Max	100
	.LargeChange	10
Label	.Alignment	2 - Center
	.FontSize	12

Event Procedures

```
Sub HScroll1_KeyDown (KeyCode As Integer, Shift As Integer)
Select Case KeyCode
    Case 48
        If HScroll1.Min <= HScroll1.Value -
            ➥HScroll1.LargeChange Then
            HScroll1.Value = HScroll1.Value -
            ➥HScroll1.LargeChange
        End If
    Case 189
        If HScroll1.Min <= HScroll1.Value -
            ➥HScroll1.SmallChange Then
            HScroll1.Value = HScroll1.Value -
            ➥HScroll1.SmallChange
        End If
    Case 187
        If HScroll1.Max >= HScroll1.Value +
            ➥HScroll1.SmallChange Then
            HScroll1.Value = HScroll1.Value +
            ➥HScroll1.SmallChange
        End If
    Case 220
        If HScroll1.Max >= HScroll1.Value +
            ➥HScroll1.LargeChange Then
            HScroll1.Value = HScroll1.Value +
            ➥HScroll1.LargeChange
        End If
```

```
End Select
Label1.Caption = Str$(HScroll1.Value)
End Sub
```

The preceding procedure is a relatively more complex Select Case clause than you saw before. The clause compares the value of KeyCode to the key scan values of the 0, –, =, and \ keys, from top to bottom. The keys perform the following functions on the scroll box:

0	.LargeChange to the left
–	.SmallChange to the left
=	.SmallChange to the right
\	.LargeChange to the right

Each Case in the clause first checks to see whether there is enough room to move the scroll box in the direction designated by the pressed key, using a subordinate conditional If-Then clause. If there is enough room, the scroll box is moved by adding the value of HScroll1.SmallChange or .LargeChange to HScroll1.Value, which represents the current scroll box position. When the Select Case clause is completed, that position is reflected in the label below the scroll bar.

You might find it easier to use ASCII codes rather than key scan codes to detect key presses. In such cases, Visual Basic supplies a key event that recognizes ASCII (ANSI) codes.

_KeyPress   Event

Action: Character recognition
Applies to: Form, check, combo, command, directory, drive, file, grid, list, option, picture, scroll, text
Parameters: Index As Integer (control arrays only), KeyAscii As Integer

The _KeyPress event for a form or control is recognized whenever that graphic object has the focus and a key is pressed on the keyboard. The _KeyPress event does not continue to be recognized by default if the key is held down; however, if key repetition is selected through the Windows Control Panel, continued depression of the key eventually causes Windows to repeat the key, making it appear to the VB interpreter that the _KeyPress event occurs repetitively. The ASCII code value of the character with its corresponding key pressed is the only parameter passed to the procedure for this event.

Example

If it's easier for you to think in ASCII, the procedure introduced previously can be modified as follows:

```
Sub HScroll1_KeyDown (KeyAscii As Integer)
Select Case KeyAscii
    Case Asc("0")
        If HScroll1.Min <= HScroll1.Value -
            ➥HScroll1.LargeChange Then
            HScroll1.Value = HScroll1.Value -
            ➥HScroll1.LargeChange
        End If
    Case Asc("-")
        If HScroll1.Min <= HScroll1.Value -
            ➥HScroll1.SmallChange Then
            HScroll1.Value = HScroll1.Value -
            ➥HScroll1.SmallChange
        End If
    Case Asc("=")
        If HScroll1.Max >= HScroll1.Value +
            ➥HScroll1.SmallChange Then
            HScroll1.Value = HScroll1.Value +
            ➥HScroll1.SmallChange
        End If
    Case Asc("\")
        If HScroll1.Max >= HScroll1.Value +
            ➥HScroll1.LargeChange Then
            HScroll1.Value = HScroll1.Value +
            ➥HScroll1.LargeChange
        End If
End Select
Label1.Caption = Str$(HScroll1.Value)
End Sub
```

This procedure is easier to implement because you can use the Asc() function to substitute for the ASCII value of the character in quotation marks; this saves you a trip to the ASCII table in Appendix A of this book. The cost of simplifying this procedure is that it now runs a bit more slowly than its key scan code process.

Substituting Buttons for Keys

Up to this point in the chapter, you used keys from the keyboard to substitute for operating graphic controls. As you might expect, Visual Basic also enables you to use graphic controls as substitutes for keys. You can do this with a statement that forces keypresses to the system as if they came from the keyboard. This statement is then issued from an event procedure for the controls to substitute for the keys.

A program with *redundant controls* offers the user many ways to enter the same commands.

Why would you want something on-screen to substitute for something else that is right in front of you? Many modern applications use *redundant controls*, or multiple ways to issue the same command to the program. In Visual Basic, as in any high-level language, you want to program an event procedure only once; however, that procedure depends solely on a single event. If you want multiple events to execute the same procedure, you may want a way to easily tie a subsidiary event to the one that contains the main body of the code. If the keyboard is more important to the particular program and graphic controls are subsidiary, keystroke substitution may be a welcome tool. Sendkeys is the statement for forced keypresses.

SendKeys   Statement

Purpose: Keypress imitation
Syntax:

```
SendKeys text$[, suspend%]
```

The SendKeys statement sends the text contained in text$ to the system, one character after the other, as if each character in text$ were typed very quickly on the keyboard. The control of the current form that has the focus will be the recipient of the text. If the cursor is in a text box, the text contained in text$ appears in that box, as if the user typed that text manually. If the value –1 is specified for suspend%, execution of the Visual Basic application is suspended until Windows processes all the keys sent and the keyboard buffer is empty.

> **Note:** The SendKeys statement sends the specific textual contents of the **text$** parameter through the event buffer. If the contents of **text$** are capitalized, the interpreter treats the key sequence as if a Shift key were being pressed.

Example

To test this statement, here is an extended version of the ScrollKey application's form with controls added to it:

"Scroll Key" Throttle Control Tester

Project name: SCROLKEY.MAK
Constituent file: SCROLKEY.FRM

Object Type	Property	Setting
Form	.Left	1095
	.Top	1530
	.Width	4485
	.Height	2505
Control array	.Name	TapeControl
Button	.Caption	<<
	.Index	0
Button	.Caption	<
	.Index	1
Button	.Caption	>
	.Index	2
Button	.Caption	>>
	.Index	3

Figure 28.2 shows the changes made to the form.

Figure 28.2

Controls that act
as keys, which in
turn act as
controls.

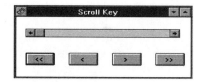

You then add the following procedure for the button control array:

```
Sub TapeControl_Click (Index As Integer)
HScroll1.SetFocus
Select Case Index
    Case 0
        SendKeys "0"
    Case 1
        SendKeys "-"
```

```
      Case 2
           SendKeys "="
      Case 3
           SendKeys "\"
  End Select
  End Sub
```

Pseudocode for the previous procedure is as follows:

*Procedure awaiting a click on the **TapeControl***
button array:
Set the focus to the horizontal scroll bar, taking it
away from any of the buttons.
  In case the first button was pressed,
    Register a "0"
  In case the second button was pressed,
    Register a "–"
  In case the third button was pressed,
    Register a "="
  In case the fourth button was pressed,
    Register a "\"
End of cases.
End of procedure.

Here, the event procedure for the control array is passed the value of the .index property of the button that was clicked. The Select Case clause then sends the appropriate key for that index, using SendKeys. The procedure doesn't need to do anything more, because the event procedure that awaits keypresses soon executes, not knowing that the ASCII code is actually being sent by Visual Basic itself, disguised as the keyboard. As a result, your redundant controls are efficient. Both keyboard objects and graphic objects perform the same events without using a branch statement or a remote procedure call from one event procedure to another.

Assigning Keystrokes to Buttons

When you operate a dialog box that contains the OK and Cancel buttons, pressing Enter generally substitutes for clicking OK, and pressing Esc substitutes for Cancel. Here, Yes and No buttons can be substituted for OK and Cancel; the two keys still perform much the same purpose. The VB interpreter cannot intuit which buttons in a form perform the yes/no functions, so property settings inform it which buttons can be assigned the Enter and Esc keystrokes.

.Default and .Cancel Properties

Representation: Acceptance/rejection of key assignment
Applies to: Command
Set by way of: Properties window, program instruction

The .Default property for a button is set to true if the user can press Enter instead of clicking that button. Generally, this button signifies that the user accepts the conditions set within the panel. Similarly, the .Cancel property of a button is set to true if the user can press Esc instead of clicking that button. Generally, this button signifies that the user rejects the conditions set in the panel.

These properties generally do not require you to write any source code. Although they can be set at run time, computing etiquette generally dictates that they be set at design time, so one default button is always the default button. For example, in the ScrollKey application, if you want the > button (the *Play* button on a VCR or tape player) to be the default, set the property TapeControl(3).Default = -1.

Summary

Visual Basic recognizes events for keypresses that occur when a graphic object running in a VB application has the focus. While that object has the focus, the VB interpreter can wait for _KeyDown, _KeyUp, or _KeyPress events for that object. The latter event recognizes the ASCII (ANSI) code for the character corresponding to the key that was pressed, whereas the other two events recognize the key scan code for the particular key pressed, as returned to Windows by your computer's BIOS.

A _KeyPress event can be forced with the SendKeys statement, which makes it appear to Windows that a key on the keyboard was actually pressed. The default and cancelling keystrokes Enter and Esc, respectively, can be assigned to individual controls on a form with property assignments.

Review Questions

The procedure Sub HScroll1_KeyDown (), presented earlier in this chapter, moved the scroll bar left or right, based on the value of the key scan code passed to that event procedure by the VB interpreter itself. Knowing what you know about Visual Basic, Microsoft Windows, and key scan codes, speculate on what might happen if the user of this test program presses at the same time two of the four keys being scanned for.

1. Windows adds the bitwise values of the two scan codes, resulting in a sum that equals none of the four codes being searched for in the `Select Case` clause. None of the `Case`-dependent instructions is executed.

2. The BIOS scans for each key code in numerical order, so that one key is considered pressed before the other key is considered pressed, because of that key's precedence in the code sequence.

3. The timing system of the computer knows that one key was really pressed before the other. So, because the computer's reflexes are faster than the user's, one key comes out in front of the other.

4. The BIOS applies priority to one key over the other, resulting in an implied hierarchy of key importance so that one key *blanks out* the other, making it more likely one key is considered "pressed" than another.

To find the answer to this question, you can add a list box to the `ScrollKey` form called `KeyPresses`. At the end of procedure `Sub HScroll1_KeyDown ()` you see this instruction:

```
KeyPresses.AddItem Str$(KeyCode)
```

Each time one of the scanned-for keys is pressed, its code is added to the list. Examine this list to determine the solution to this quandary.

CHAPTER 29

The Pointer as Device

In this chapter, you learn how Visual Basic processes events that relate to the movement and position of the mouse pointer. You're accustomed to processing a click as a quick press and release of the index button of the mouse, but Visual Basic also recognizes an event for merely pressing and holding down a mouse button; likewise, it recognizes an event just for releasing the button. You study these events, and later you work with the coordinate system for the mouse pointer itself.

In Chapter 28, "The Keyboard," you were introduced to the events the Visual Basic interpreter recognizes for the pressing of certain keys. VB also recognizes similar events for the pressing of mouse buttons.

_MouseDown and _MouseUp   Events

Action: Mouse button activation
Applies to: Directory, file, form (not MDI), grid, image, label, list, picture
Parameters: Index As Integer (control arrays only), Button As Integer,
Shift As Integer, X As Single, Y As Single

The _MouseDown event for a graphic object is recognized whenever that object has the focus and the user presses any mouse button. The Visual Basic interpreter passes four parameters to the procedure for this event. The first parameter, Button, is the state of the mouse buttons, assuming as many as three buttons for the mouse. This value can be set to any of the following:

1	Left button (default index button) pressed
2	Right button pressed
3	Left and right buttons pressed
4	Middle button pressed
5	Middle and left buttons pressed
6	Middle and right buttons pressed
7	Middle, left, and right buttons pressed

The second value passed to the _MouseDown event procedure—Shift—reflects the current state of the Shift keys on the keyboard when the mouse button registered as pressed. This value can be set to any of the following:

0	No Shift keys pressed
1	Either Shift key pressed
2	Either Ctrl key pressed
3	Shift and Ctrl keys pressed
4	Either Alt key pressed
5	Alt and Shift keys pressed
6	Alt and Ctrl keys pressed
7	Alt, Shift, and Ctrl keys pressed

The third and fourth values passed to the _MouseDown event procedure—X and Y—reflect the current mouse pointer coordinate location with respect to the graphic object to which this procedure is attributed.

The _MouseUp event for a graphic object is recognized whenever that object has the focus and the user releases a pressed mouse button. The VB interpreter passes to the _MouseUp event procedure the same values it passed to the _MouseDown event procedure.

> **Caution:** Some Windows mouse drivers do not recognize the middle button of a Logitech-brand or other three-button mouse, regardless of whether Visual Basic tries to recognize that button. As a result, a press of the middle button might not be registered by the system, so the VB interpreter would never see it.

One more important event is attributed to the mouse pointer: the event that occurs when the mouse pointer moves over a graphic object on the form.

_MouseMove   Event

Action: Pointer movement
Applies to: Directory, file box, form (not MDI), grid, image, label, list, picture
Parameters: Index As Integer (control arrays only), Button As Integer, Shift As Integer, X As Single, Y As Single

The _MouseMove event for a graphic object is recognized whenever it currently has the focus and the mouse pointer is moved when it resides over the area of that object. The _MouseMove event can occur only on a file box, a label box, a list box, a picture box, or a form. The procedure for the _MouseMove event is passed four parameters, as described previously for the _MouseDown event.

Example

To see how these events work, the following application places a large arrow at a fixed position in the form. This arrow points in the general direction that the mouse pointer moves when the pointer is over the arrow. This application's objective is to facilitate a new type of control mechanism, in which the direction the mouse is moved indicates a command to the program. Figure 29.1 shows this application at run time.

Figure 29.1

The mouse vane application at run time.

"Mouse Vane" Mouse Direction Tester

Project name: MOUSEVAN.MAK
Constituent file: MOUSEVAN.FRM

Object Type	Property	Setting
Form	.Left	1035
	.Top	1200
	.Width	2850
	.Height	2400
	.Caption	Mouse Vane
Picture Box	.Name	Vane
Label	.Alignment	2 - Center
	.Caption	(blank)

Event Procedures

```
Sub Vane_MouseMove (Button As Integer, Shift As Integer,
➡X As Single, Y As Single)
Static LastX as integer
Static LastY as integer
If X > lastx Then xaxis = 1
If X < lastx Then xaxis = -1
If Y > lasty Then yaxis = 1
If Y < lasty Then yaxis = -1
Label1.Caption = Str$(xaxis) + " " + Str$(yaxis)
Select Case True
    Case (xaxis = 1 And yaxis = 1)
        Vane.Picture =
        ➡LoadPicture("d:\vb3\icons\arrows\arw10se.ico")
    Case (xaxis = 1 And yaxis = -1)
        Vane.Picture =
        ➡LoadPicture("d:\vb3\icons\arrows\arw10ne.ico")
    Case (xaxis = -1 And yaxis = 1)
        Vane.Picture =
        ➡LoadPicture("d:\vb3\icons\arrows\arw10sw.ico")
    Case (xaxis = -1 And yaxis = -1)
        Vane.Picture =
        ➡LoadPicture("d:\vb3\icons\arrows\arw10nw.ico")
    Case (xaxis = 1 And yaxis = 0)
        Vane.Picture =
        ➡LoadPicture("d:\vb3\icons\arrows\arw07rt.ico")
```

```
    Case (xaxis = -1 And yaxis = 0)
        Vane.Picture =
        ➥LoadPicture("d:\vb3\icons\arrows\arw07lt.ico")
    Case (xaxis = 0 And yaxis = 1)
        Vane.Picture =
        ➥LoadPicture("d:\vb3\icons\arrows\arw07dn.ico")
    Case (xaxis = 0 And yaxis = -1)
        Vane.Picture =
        ➥LoadPicture("d:\vb3\icons\arrows\arw07up.ico")
End Select
lastx = X
lasty = Y
End Sub
```

Note: Depending on how you installed Visual Basic, the device and directory locations of the supplied icons may differ from those shown in the preceding code.

Here is a basic pseudocode for the preceding procedure:

*Procedure awaiting the mouse pointer to move
within the vane area:
Declare two variables to have their values maintained
when this procedure is exited.
If the pointer's current **x** coordinate is greater than
the previously registered **x** coordinate, then
register a movement to the right.
If the pointer's current **x** coordinate is less than
the previously registered **x** coordinate, then
register a movement to the left.
If the pointer's current **y** coordinate is greater than
the previously registered **y** coordinate, then
register a downward movement.
If the pointer's current **y** coordinate is less than
the previously registered **y** coordinate, then
register an upward movement.
Display the registers for both directions.*

Search for logical truth in the following cases:
*   In the case of rightward and downward movement,*
*   Show a southeasterly pointing arrow.*
*   In the case of rightward and downward movement,*
*   Show a northeasterly pointing arrow.*

*   .*

*   .*

*   .*

End of cases.
Register the current pointer coordinates as the old
* coordinates.*
End of procedure.

In this application, the `_MouseMove` event is not recognized until the pointer enters the area of the picture box called `Vane`. At that point, the values X and Y passed to the procedure by the VB interpreter are compared with two static variables, `lastx` and `lasty`. Variables `lastx` and `lasty` contain the previously recorded values of X and Y, which were stored in those variables before the procedure was last exited. These variables were declared `Static` at the beginning of the procedure so that their values could be maintained on its exit. If the current value of X is greater than that of `lastx`, the pointer must have moved to the right. Likewise, if the current value of Y is less than that of `lasty`, the pointer must have moved up.

The direction of the pointer's movement is stored in variables `xaxis` and `yaxis`. A negative value here refers to a lesser value on the coordinate scale of the axis; so an `xaxis` value of −1 refers to the left direction, and a `yaxis` value of −1 refers to an up direction. Positive values refer to right and down movements, respectively. Zero values refer to no change in the axis. It is relatively difficult for most people's hands to achieve a perfect zero-movement along either axis without making the arrow tip in some diagonal direction.

The `Select Case` clause loads an icon into picture box `Vane`, whose direction corresponds with the direction of movement of the mouse. Here, logical expressions beside each `Case` are reduced, and their logically reduced values are compared with logical truth for equality. Finally, after `End Select`, the current states of the `xaxis` and `yaxis` values are shown in `Label1`.

When Is a Move a Move?

Visual Basic has no real mechanism for testing whether the rollers in your mouse changed position; thus, it's really not strictly accurate to say that the _MouseMove event is recognized whenever the mouse moves. Windows recognizes whether your mouse rollers moved enough to merit a pointer movement, and responds by moving the mouse pointer. The pointer moves in increments of at least one pixel, depending on how fast the user moves the mouse. If the user moves the pointer very quickly over an object, the pointer may only be considered officially moved three or four times; if the mouse is moved more slowly, the event may be recognized a few dozen times.

Because the ratio of pixels-per-twip changes when screen resolution increases, it's quite likely that computers with higher screen resolutions may recognize the _MouseMove event more times. Because of these two variable factors—the speed in which the pointer is traveling and the resolution of the screen—the _MouseMove event procedure for an application probably should not be used for data-intensive events, such as saving an entry to disk, or the entry may be saved an inordinate number of times. You should reserve _MouseMove mostly for animation purposes— for processes that graphically help the user comprehend what's going on. Use the _Click and _Change event procedures and their counterparts for other controls—the one-time events should be used for data-intensive processes.

The Appearance of the Pointer

You can make the mouse pointer change its appearance when it enters the area of a graphic object. A special procedure or event is not needed to accomplish this; it can be done through a property setting.

.MousePointer   **Property**

Representation: Pointer appearance
Applies to: Check, combo, command, directory, drive, file, form, frame, image, label, list, option, picture, screen, scroll, text
Set by way of: Properties window, program instruction

The .MousePointer property for a graphic object is set to an integer value that represents the appearance of the mouse pointer whenever it enters the region of that object. When the mouse pointer exits the object's region, the shape of the pointer resumes either its default state or the state designated by the .MousePointer property of its parent object. The property can be set to any of the following values:

0	Default state as determined by Windows
1	Arrow: the standard Windows arrow
2	Cross: thin crosshairs
3	I-Beam: the text locator pointer
4	Icon: (not to be confused with an icon, despite its name) a square bullet
5	Size: a four-pointed arrow
6	Size NE SW: a two-pointed arrow directed northeast and southwest
7	Size NS: a two-pointed arrow directed north and south
8	Size NW SE: a two-pointed arrow directed northwest and southeast
9	Size WE: a two-pointed arrow directed east and west
10	Up Arrow
11	Wait: the Windows hourglass symbol
12	No Drop: the circle-with-a-slash symbol indicating a control movement violation.

Example

Suppose that your form has a picture box where you intend to use the mouse pointer to draw pixels. When the pointer enters the picture box area, you want to have its shape change to a crosshair, which is far more convenient for drawing purposes. The following fragment of the procedure changes the pointer's appearance:

```
Sub DrawArea_MouseMove (Button As Integer, Shift As Integer,
➥X As Single, Y As Single)
DrawArea.MousePointer = 2
  .
  .
  .
End Sub
```

Example

As previously mentioned, Microsoft supplies Visual Basic with a text file called CONSTANT.TXT. This file contains sets of constant declarations pertinent to several areas of VB programming. It also contains several standardized terms that can be used in place of numerals, such as the set of numerals used by the .MousePointer property. Here from CONSTANT.TXT is the set of constant declarations pertinent to .MousePointer:

```
' MousePointer
Global Const DEFAULT = 0        ' 0 - Default
Global Const ARROW = 1          ' 1 - Arrow
Global Const CROSSHAIR = 2      ' 2 - Cross
Global Const IBEAM = 3          ' 3 - I-Beam
Global Const ICON_POINTER = 4   ' 4 - Icon
Global Const SIZE_POINTER = 5   ' 5 - Size
Global Const SIZE_NE_SW = 6     ' 6 - Size NE SW
Global Const SIZE_N_S = 7       ' 7 - Size N S
Global Const SIZE_NW_SE = 8     ' 8 - Size NW SE
Global Const SIZE_W_E = 9       ' 9 - Size W E
Global Const UP_ARROW = 10      ' 10 - Up Arrow
Global Const HOURGLASS = 11     ' 11 - Hourglass
Global Const NO_DROP = 12       ' 12 - No drop
```

With these declarations added to the global declarations section of an application, the previous procedure can be amended to read as follows:

```
Sub DrawArea_MouseMove (Button As Integer, Shift As Integer,
➥X As Single, Y As Single)
DrawArea.MousePointer = CROSSHAIR
.
.
.
End Sub
```

Now, the meaning of the pointer-changing instruction is far more evident to the human reader, without affecting the functionality of the procedure.

Summary

Visual Basic maintains events that recognize when the mouse pointer is moved and when a mouse button is pressed. The _MouseMove event for an object is recognized whenever the pointer passes over the area that object inhabits. The _MouseDown and _MouseUp events for an object are recognized when a mouse button is pressed as the pointer is over the area occupied by that object. By using the .MousePointer property for a graphic object, you can set the appearance of the mouse pointer when it enters the area of that object.

Review Questions

1. With respect to the preceding `Sub Vane_MouseMove ()` event procedure, why is it so difficult for the user to keep the arrow from pointing in a diagonal direction?

2. The `_MouseMove` event is recognized only when the pointer enters the region of its preceding object. How can you make a procedure recognize when the pointer has exited an object?

CHAPTER 30

Dragging the Controls

In this chapter, you learn how Visual Basic interprets and executes events that involve *dragging*. You may have used a computer from which you could delete files by dragging them to a "trash can" icon. You accomplish this drag by clicking on the item to be deleted and holding down the index button of the mouse, dragging the pointer, with the index button still held down, to the trash can, and releasing the button. Visual Basic interprets such events in the following way: certain controls on a form classified as *targets* act as the receivers of images of other controls. The receiving of these images is interpreted as a *drag* event. You learn how to program such events in this chapter.

When designing a form, you move a control on the form being designed by dragging the control to its new position. When the application containing that form is run later, the user can drag a control on top of another—like a file icon being dragged on top of a trash can icon.

A drag operation copies an image from the control.

When an application is running, *to drag a control* (in the way Microsoft uses the term) is to click and hold down the index button over a control, and then carry either a duplicate image of that control's border or a *drag object* assigned to that control. A drag object follows the mouse pointer as it is dragged across the screen. The object on which the drag object "lands" is the *target* object. The object where the image originated is the *source.*

Let's examine this act in more detail. Visual Basic controls, in a form running in an application, are by nature fixed. The drag operation does not move the control itself from one place to another. Normally, if the user clicks and holds the mouse pointer over a control, nothing happens. If the user releases the button without moving the mouse, however, he or she can generate a _Click event. For the drag operation to be enabled for a control, its *drag mode* is set to 1. Now when the user clicks and holds the mouse pointer over the control, a hazy gray border appears around that control and follows the pointer as long as the index button is pressed.

For Visual Basic, all that has taken place so far is special effects without meaning. The drag event that initiates the execution of a code takes place while the drag object is over the target control; specifically, the drag event takes place from the point of view of the target. If a drag object is placed on top of a control that isn't expecting this image, the entire operation is ignored. In other words, if dragging event procedures haven't been programmed for the target control, that control won't accept the image.

The two drag events in the VB vocabulary are the _DragDrop event and the _DragOver event.

_DragDrop   Event

Action: Dragged icon release
Applies to: Check, combo, command, directory, drive, file, form, frame, grid, image, label, list, MDI, option, picture, scroll, text
Parameters: Index As Integer (control arrays only), Source As Control, X As Single, Y As Single

A control's _DragDrop event is recognized when the drag object attributed to another control—generally an icon—is dragged on top of it and the mouse button is released. The procedure for this event takes three parameters: Source as an object variable that represents the drag object, declared for type Control, and the X and Y coordinates of the mouse pointer at the time of the drop.

_DragOver   Event

Action: Dragged icon traversal
Applies to: Check, combo, command, directory, drive, file, form, frame, grid, image, label, list, option, MDI, picture, scroll, text
Parameters: Index As Integer (control arrays only), Source As Control, X As Single, Y As Single, State As Integer

A control's _DragOver event takes place when the drag object attributed to another control is dragged on top of it, regardless of whether the mouse button is released. The procedure for this event takes four parameters: the Source object variable that contains the properties of the drag object's native object, declared as type Control; the X and Y coordinates of the mouse pointer at the time of the drop; and an integer State that registers the state of progress of the drag operation. This integer is given any of the following values by the interpreter:

0	The pointer is entering the area of the target control.
1	The pointer is exiting the area of the target control.
2	The pointer is within the area of the target control.

The drag object for a control does not appear at run time by default; through a property, a control is informed of its drag capability.

In the description for the _DragOver event, notice the standard declaration of one of the parameters, As Control. In Visual Basic, whenever a procedure needs to know the identity or property characteristics of a graphic object *other than* the one that triggers the event, the control's characteristics can be declared as an *object variable*. In this instance, the interpreter automatically generates the object variable and passes it to the _DragOver event procedure as a parameter, declared As Control. Throughout the event procedure, the term Source refers to whatever graphic object the drag icon belongs to. Object variables are discussed in more detail in Chapter 32, "Object Variables."

One of the two ways Visual Basic allows a control to be dragged is by setting its .DragMode property at design time.

.DragMode   Property

Representation: Control pointer accessibility
Applies to: Check, combo, command, directory, drive, file, form, frame, grid, image, label, list, MDI, option, picture, scroll, text
Set by way of: Properties window, program instruction

The .DragMode property for a control is set to 1 to make that control automatically draggable at run time. The property defaults to 0; this means dragging can be enabled with source code, either one time only with the .Drag method, or through the remainder of the program with the instruction Control.DragMode = 1 until disabled with Control.DragMode = 0. Note that this property is a *flag* and not a Boolean true or false register, so .DragMode is not a property that is set to True (–1).

Example

You can put this process to the test with another example application. A test form containing two pictures from the Visual Basic icon library—a file folder and a filing cabinet drawer—is shown in figure 30.1.

Figure 30.1

The "Drag" test form.

The two controls shown here are picture boxes, which can be any size and operated like buttons. The two icons shown are \VB3\ICONS\OFFICE\ FOLDER02.ICO and \VB3\ICONS\OFFICE\FILES03A.ICO, respectively. Although referred to as *icons,* from the point of view of the Visual Basic interpreter, these are small picture boxes. If they were each half the size of the screen, they would operate in the same manner as picture boxes.

To place a picture box on a form:

1. Click the Picture Box button in the toolbox.

2. Move the pointer to the area of the form that will contain the picture box.

3. Click and hold the index button over one corner of the picture box area, drag the pointer to the opposite corner, and release the button. The picture box border appears on the form, surrounded by indicator nodes you can use to resize the box.

4. To assign a picture or icon to this picture box, leave the picture box indicated and choose the Picture property from the properties list in the VB main window. The settings list reads (none).

5. What is normally the down-arrow button for the settings list now contains ellipses. To choose a picture to fit in the box, click the ellipses button. A file selector box appears.

6. Visual Basic interprets PC Paintbrush (PCX), Windows metafile (WMF), and Windows icon (ICO) formats for picture boxes. The file list in the selector box shows the files with these three extensions. Choose a picture file from this list. The picture appears in the box, flush left against the top. You can crop it from the right and along the bottom.

Keeping the process described above in mind, here are the property settings for the test application.

"Drag Strip" Drag Tester

Project name: DRAGSTRP.MAK
Constituent file: DRAGSTRP.FRM

Object Type	Property	Setting
Form	.Width	4650
	.Height	2175
	.Name	DragStrip
	.Caption	Drag Strip
Picture box	.Name	Folder
	.Tag	Folder
	.Picture	FOLDER02.ICO
	.DragMode	1 - Automatic
	.BorderStyle	0 - None
Picture box	.Name	Cabinet
	.Tag	Cabinet
	.Picture	FILES03A.ICO
	.DragMode	1 - Automatic
	.BorderStyle	0 - None
Label	.Caption	(blank)
	.Alignment	1 - Right Justify

Notice that setting the .BorderStyle property of a picture box does not affect its purpose or operation, as that property does with forms.

The challenge is to make it feasible for a drag object from the folder icon to be dragged over the cabinet icon and have the cabinet "know" it. Setting the properties as listed previously automatically facilitates the dragging process for the folder icon. Now you need to program the event procedure for the cabinet receiving the folder, as follows:

Event Procedures

```
Sub Cabinet_DragDrop (Source As Control, X As Single,
➥Y As Single)
If Source.Tag = "Folder" Then
    Label1.Caption = "Folder received."
End If
End Sub
```

Here is the pseudocode for this procedure:

*Procedure awaiting something to be dragged
on top of the cabinet icon:
If the tag for that item is called
"Folder," then
Show on the form that the folder was received.
End of condition.
End of procedure.*

The three parameters passed here are automatically formed by the VB interpreter. `Source As Control` passes all the properties of the "dragged" object (except the object whose drag object was placed on top of the target object) to this procedure, as a composite parameter. `X` and `Y` refer to the pointer location at the time of the drop.

The procedure must determine what control was dragged on top of it, so it checks to see if the control's `.Tag` property is `Folder`. The `.Name` for this property is also `Folder`; however, the VB interpreter doesn't allow you to refer to `Source.Name` in this context. Because a control in one form can receive the image dragged from a control in another form in the same application, it is possible for the two controls to have the same name. The two control names are distinguished by their root form objects. This distinguishing element is dropped when the source is indirectly referred to using the `Source.` object. To avoid confusion, the `.Tag` property is used to refer to graphic objects by a name. For this reason, no two objects in an application can have the same tag.

> **Note:** Unlike the `.Name` property, the `.Tag` property is case-dependent; this means that uppercase and lowercase letters are treated differently.

The way the procedure currently works, the image created while dragging the folder to the cabinet is a hazy gray border frame that follows the pointer. Microsoft was thoughtful enough to supply users with icons that show everyday items in various states—for instance, open and closed folders and file drawers, and card files with cards that can be removed or inserted. You can use one of these icons to replace the generic-looking gray border.

.DragIcon   Property

Representation: Drag object file name
Applies to: Check, combo, command, directory, drive, file, frame, grid, image, label, list, option, picture, scroll, text
Set by way of: Properties window, program instruction

The `.DragIcon` property contains the file name of a picture or icon that Visual Basic uses as the drag object for a control. When dragging is enabled for a control—and the user clicks and holds the pointer over the control that has a `.DragIcon` property that has been set to an icon's file name—an image is shown. When the user clicks the source object, the drag object appears in black-and-white in place of the current pointer, as long as the index button is pressed. This drag object can then follow the pointer to the target object of the drag.

For the example project, you can set the property `Folder.DragIcon` to \VB3\ICONS\OFFICE\FOLDER01.ICO, which shows a closed folder as opposed to an open one. Now when the user clicks and holds over the open folder icon, the image of a closed folder follows the pointer.

Example

Similarly, you can use Microsoft's multiple-state icons to add a degree of animation to the form. Suppose that while the closed file folder is over the cabinet, one of its drawers opens. When the index button is released and the closed folder image disappears, the drawer closes. You can "open" the file drawer with the following procedure:

```
Sub Cabinet_DragOver (Source As Control, X As Single,
➥Y As Single, State As Integer)
If Source.Tag = "Folder" Then
    Cabinet.Picture = LoadPicture
    ➥("d:\vb3\icons\office\files03b.ico")
End If
End Sub
```

instead of using the conventional BASIC syntax that might look like this:

```
LOADPIC "FILES03B.ICO", CABINET
```

`LoadPicture()` acts as a function rather than a command and returns a "value" in the form of a picture as a property setting for `Cabinet.Picture`.

Example

The problem is that this animation is relatively untidy; the file drawer is open. The `LoadPicture()` function will need to close the drawer after the file is dropped onto it. You can amend the original `Sub Cabinet_DragDrop ()` procedure as follows:

```
Sub Cabinet_DragDrop (Source As Control, X As Single,
➥Y As Single)
If Source.Tag = "Folder" Then
    Cabinet.Picture = LoadPicture
    ➥("d:\vb3\icons\office\files03a.ico")
    Label1.Caption = "Folder received."
End If
End Sub
```

A line has been added to this procedure that makes the file drawer revert to its closed state, by loading the original closed cabinet icon back into the picture box.

Example

One more untidy element remains: suppose the closed folder icon passes over the file cabinet without being dropped into it. At the moment, the drawer would remain open. You can amend the _DragOver event routine so that the drawer closes whenever you choose to ignore it:

```
Sub Cabinet_DragOver (Source As Control, X As Single,
➥Y As Single, State As Integer)
If Source.Tag = "Folder" Then
    Cabinet.Picture = LoadPicture
    ➥("d:\vb3\icons\office\files03b.ico")
End If
If State = 1 Then
    Cabinet.Picture = LoadPicture
    ➥("d:\vb3\icons\office\files03a.ico")
End If
End Sub
```

Here is the pseudocode for this procedure:

*Procedure awaiting something to be dragged
on top of the cabinet icon:
If the tag for that certain something is called
"Folder," then
    Load the open cabinet icon as the cabinet image.
End of condition.
If the pointer has just left the cabinet area, then
    Reload the closed cabinet icon as this image.
End of condition.
End of procedure.*

A conditional clause has been added to this pseudocode that reloads the original closed cabinet icon whenever the pointer leaves the picture box, regardless of what form the pointer has at the moment. Variable State is supplied by the interpreter, and a value of 1 represents the state of having left the target object area.

Figures 30.2, 30.3, and 30.4 show the animation sequence that takes place when the user clicks the folder icon, drags the folder image over the cabinet icon, and drops the folder into the cabinet.

Figure 30.2

"Folder's" .*DragIcon* is selected.

Figure 30.3

The _*DragOver* event opens the file drawer.

Figure 30.4

The _*DragDrop* event closes the file drawer.

Lock and Key Example

By skillfully using the Visual Basic picture box, you may be able to invent your own type of control scheme. Over the last decade of graphical programming, inventive programmers have tried to concoct unique graphical mechanisms that are both foolproof and practical to facilitate critical functions, such as file or record deletion. You can imagine what trouble could be ahead for your user if you left a big, unguarded Erase button in the middle of your form.

Generally, you invoke a dialog box that offers some last-second warning, such as, Are you sure you want to delete this file? [Yes¦No]. If you've ever hit that big Erase button by mistake, you are undoubtedly grateful for the dialog box in current programs. Still, many programmers envision a more graceful method to guard against accidental deletion (or accidentally doing anything else, for that matter).

Figure 30.5 shows a modified DragStrip test application. The control on the right is a deletion icon that was created with the IconWorks application supplied with Visual Basic. Its `.Name` and `.Tag` are both `DeleteFile`. Its `.DragMode` is set to 0, and its `.BorderStyle` is set to 1. The border style for this control implies its inaccessibility: you cannot use this control if there is a border around it. To remove this border, first drag the key to the control, then unlock the control with the key.

Figure 30.5

The modified
DragStrip
application.

The key, which is on the left in figure 30.5, is Visual Basic icon SECUR06.ICO. Its `.DragIcon` is SECUR07.ICO, which floats above -06.ICO. Its `.Name` and `.Tag` are both, understandably, `Key`. Its `.DragMode` remains set at 1.

Example

In the following procedure, the code of the original DragStrip application is rewritten to accommodate this new form of locked control. At the moment, the `DeleteFile` control needs no `_DragOver` event procedure. `DeleteFile` first needs to detect whether the key is dragged on top of it.

```
Sub DeleteFile_DragDrop (Source As Control, X As Single,
➥Y As Single)
If Source.Tag = "Key" Then
    DeleteFile.BorderStyle = 0
    Label1.Caption = "Clear to delete file."
End If
End Sub
```

Here is the pseudocode for this procedure:

*Procedure awaiting something to be dragged
on top of the lock icon:
If the tag of the received icon is "Key," then
    Take off the border from the lock.
    Tell the form the user can now delete the file.
End of condition.
End of procedure.*

Notice that only the *clearance* to delete the file is given, and that the `.BorderStyle` for the `DeleteFile` control has been removed. Next, the following event procedure is added:

```
Sub DeleteFile_DblClick ()
If DeleteFile.BorderStyle = 0 Then
    Label1.Caption = "File is deleted."
    DeleteFile.BorderStyle = 1
End If
End Sub
```

Here is the pseudocode for this procedure:

Procedure awaiting someone to double-click
on this control.
If there is no border on this control, then
  Tell the form the file is deleted.
  Replace the border.
End of condition.
End of procedure.

Note that this procedure is only symbolic of a deletion; there are no erasure instructions here. The purpose of this application is merely to act as a model for a deletion control. You can assume that the deletion process takes place in roughly the same area of the source code that the deletion notification takes place. The `.BorderStyle` is also reset, and the control is now locked. The deletion cannot take place unless the user double-clicks the `DeleteFile` control and the control has no border (`.BorderStyle = 0`).

Obviously, no one would *accidentally* drag the key all the way to the deletion control and double-click it.

Example

Here's another way to disable deletion for read-only files. Suppose the key's `.DragMode` is set back to automatic (1) as before, and has a `.BorderStyle` of 0—this way you don't have a situation in which the user locks the key. A check box is placed in the form, representing whether the file in question has a "read-only" status. If it does, the user is not allowed to delete the file. Here's a procedure that prevents the entire key-dragging procedure from being executed whenever the lock border is on and the read-only box is checked:

```
Sub DeleteFile_DragOver (Source As Control, X As Single,
➥Y As Single, State As Integer)
If DeleteFile.BorderStyle = 1 And Check1.Value = 1 Then
    Source.Drag 0
End If
End Sub
```

This procedure uses the .Drag method to manually control the drag process.

.Drag   Method

Purpose: Manual dragging engagement
Syntax:

```
Control.Drag integer%
```

The .Drag method is used to manually start or stop the dragging process for a control, whether or not the .DragMode for that control is set. This is especially helpful if the control's .DragMode is set to 0 (manual) and, by default, cannot be dragged. The value of integer% can be any of the following:

0	Cancel dragging the specified control.
1	Initiate dragging the specified control, when the .Drag method appears in an event procedure for the antecedent control.
2	End dragging the control and signal a _DragDrop event for that control.

Moving Controls

A *move* operation relocates the control.

Here is a twist on the prevalidation process. Suppose the form is to contain controls that are completely inoperable until they are moved to a marked region. Remember, *dragging* a control is not the same as *moving* that control; VB shows an image being carried from the control during the drag operation, while the control remains stationary.

The best way to have the source code move the control is to have a conventional drag-and-drop operation first, and then relocate the control to the position of the drop. Figure 30.6 shows a vastly modified DragStrip application. Here, the DeleteFile control takes the place of the key icon and is the control that is moved. The place to which it is moved is a picture box that contains no picture, only a pastel-shaded .BackColor. The _DragDrop event belongs to this shaded region. Controls can be activated only when they are found in this region (let's call it the OKArea).

Figure 30.6

The shaded region
(*OKArea*) in which
controls can be
activated.

The method that makes moving controls possible is explained here:

.Move   **Method**

Purpose: Manual control repositioning
Syntax:

```
Control.Move left%[, top%[, width%[, height%]]]
```

The .Move method moves the designated control on a form to the coordinate location on that form specified by *left%* and *top%* parameters. Only the *left%* parameter needs to be specified to move the control horizontally to the new twip position *left%*. If *top%* is specified, the control is moved vertically as well. If *width%* or *height%* is specified, the control is resized after it is moved.

For this procedure to work, you must declare certain information concerning the home position of the control and the deletion capability of the control at the form level. For this example, the statement

```
Dim DelEnabled, stdx, stdy
```

appears in the general procedures area of the form. These variables represent the deletion capability and the home coordinates, respectively, of the DeleteFile icon. In the form's SubForm_Load() procedure, variables stdx and stdy are set to the .Left and .Top properties of the DeleteFile icon, respectively.

At design time, DeleteFile.DragMode is set to 1 (enabled), and OKArea.DragMode is left at 0 (disabled). OKArea is the picture box, and the crucial event procedures are attributed to that control. DeleteFile.DragIcon is set to the same image as DeleteFile.Picture. DeleteFile.Tag is set to "DeleteFile" as well. After you make these settings, the following is the new dropping procedure:

```
Sub OKArea_DragDrop (Source As Control, X As Single,
➥Y As Single)
If Source.Tag = "DeleteFile" Then
    Source.Move OKArea.Left + X - 256, OKArea.Top + Y - 256
    DelEnabled = 1
    Source.DragMode = 0
    Label1.Caption = "Clear to delete file."
End If
End Sub
```

Here is the pseudocode for this procedure:

Procedure awaiting the receipt of a control:
*If the dragged control's tag is **DeleteFile**, then*
    Move the control to its new coordinates, accounting
    for the offset making them relative to the
    location of OKArea, plus the offset for
    the distance between the corner and center of
    the moved control.
    Enable deletion.
    Turn off the "draggability" of this control.
    Tell the user it's OK to delete the file.
End of condition.
End of procedure.

The dropping coordinates X and Y, automatically declared at the start of this procedure, are calculated by the interpreter relative to the object OKArea, *not to the form*. The coordinates required for the .Move event are relative to the form; so to move the control to the coordinates passed to the procedure, you must first add the .Left and .Top coordinates of the OKArea object itself to X and Y.

Next, you need to make a correction to the way Visual Basic normally works. When an image is dragged into the OKArea, it is dragged by the middle of the icon; so when the image follows the pointer, the middle of the image is at the pointer's *hot spot*. When the pointer is in the OKArea, the upper left corner of the .DragIcon is above and to the left of the pointer position by about 256 twips. Yet, if you specify the current pointer position as the destination of the .Move event, the control is replotted at the current pointer position starting at the control's upper left corner, not the middle. To correct this problem for both x- and y-axes, 256 is subtracted from both coordinates so that the .Move event moves the middle of the control to the current pointer position, and not the corner of the control.

The double-click procedure now belongs to OKArea, as demonstrated by the following code:

```
Sub OKArea_DblClick ()
If DelEnabled = 1 Then
    Label1.Caption = "File is deleted."
    DeleteFile.Move stdx, stdy
    DeleteFile.DragMode = 1
    DelEnabled = 0
End If
End Sub
```

The .Move method is again invoked to return the control to its rightful place only if the form-level variable DelEnabled is set to 1. Figures 30.7, 30.8, and 30.9 show the three stages of the sequence.

Figure 30.7

Dragging the
DeleteFile icon into
the *OKArea*.

Figure 30.8

Letting go of
DeleteFile.

Figure 30.9

After double-
clicking on the
control, the file is
deleted.

Summary

In graphical procedures, dragging a control and moving a control are two different operations. During dragging, a drag object copied from the control follows the mouse pointer, although the control maintains its position. This drag object can consist of either the border of the control being dragged or an icon referenced by the .DragIcon property. The control to which the drag object belongs is the source; the destination control where the drag object lands is the target. By contrast, moving a control relocates it to a new position.

Controls on a form cannot be dragged by default; their .DragMode properties can be set to 1 to initiate automatic dragging. Otherwise, any control can be made draggable through an instruction in an event procedure for that control, using the .Drag method. While a control is draggable, events for clicking or double-clicking on that control are not recognized. Event procedures for dragging controls provide coordinate information that can be helpful in programming operations that actually move the control from one position on the form to another, using the .Move method.

Review Questions

1. What is the difference between a *drag* operation and a *move* operation?

2. Is the event procedure awaiting the _DragDrop event always considered the target of the drop?

3. Are the coordinates stated in a .Move operation expressed relative to the screen, the current form, or the control to which the event procedure belongs?

Review Exercises

Using some of the preceding procedures as models, write procedures that use test controls that operate in the following ways:

1. An icon represents a file. Dragging its image inside a picture box places a border around that icon.

2. An icon represents a process to delete a file. Dragging a box around the icon enables deletion. Double-clicking the icon with the box around it initiates deletion.

CHAPTER 31

Grids and Tables

A *record* is a
grouping of related
elements of data,
such as a person's
name and medical
history.

This chapter examines the grid control, which displays data in rows and columns
like a spreadsheet. The grid is the first control in the standard Visual Basic repertoire
provided through an extension control file—namely, GRID.VBX. You'll see the
differences between how data is displayed as a conventional form and how it is
displayed as a table.

The resulting list box, however, is not extremely functional. To ensure that each
field is equally spaced apart, as they are in columns, you need to assign a
proportionally spaced font as the list box's .FontName. You are also unable to
indicate a particular field within a record for a specific operation or query. A
concatenated list box is able to function as little more than a scroll.

A *dynamic
link library* is a
Windows program
that contains
routines that are
easily accessible
to other Windows
applications.

Visual Basic maintains a special project file, AUTOLOAD.MAK, that the interpreter loads into memory upon its own startup. AUTOLOAD.MAK is a blank
project; it does not contain any source code. Its entire purpose is to contain the
extension controls that you always want to inhabit the VB toolbox; for the VB
Standard Edition, AUTOLOAD.MAK contains both the grid and OLE client
controls.

1. From the File menu of the VB control window, select Add File. The usual
   dialog panel appears, and the file list displays the FRM, BAS, and VBX files
   in the current directory. Concentrate now on the VBX files.

2. If you want, you can narrow the list of files to custom controls only by
   clicking the down-arrow button in the list marked List Files of Type,
   and choosing the entry Custom Controls (*.VBX).

3. The file name of the grid control is GRID.VBX. Click on the file name of
   the custom control file, and click OK. The access button for the control is
   displayed in the VB toolbox.

Anatomy of the Grid

The grid control is supplied to the Visual Basic toolbox when you include the GRID.VBX file in the current project. The symbol for the grid control then appears in the toolbox. Figure 31.1 shows the grid control components.

Figure 31.1

Grid control components.

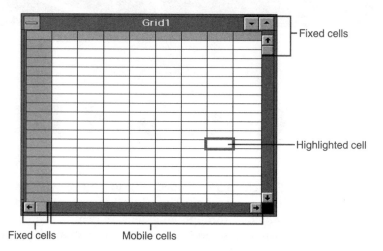

The grid may contain far more cells than are actually seen at any one time; a procedure can certainly assign textual contents to an unseen cell. The number of rows and columns in a grid, along with the rows and columns assigned for fixed cells, is set through property assignments exclusive to the grid.

.Rows, .Cols   **Properties**

Representation: Extent of cells
Applies to: Grid
Set by way of: Properties window, program instruction

.FixedRows, .FixedCols   **Properties**

Representation: Nonmobile cell amount
Applies to: Grid
Set by way of: Properties window, program instruction

The default state of an initialized grid control gives it a total of two columns and two rows. The fixed cells are counted as legitimate rows and columns; a two-by-two grid, in effect, starts with one cell, not four. A table of one item is somewhat pointless, so it is necessary to set the `.Rows` and `.Cols` properties at design time.

Example

It is, of course, possible to assign values to the minimum and maximum cell count of a grid at run time. Suppose a grid named `Loan` is being used to display the monthly payments for a 36-month prorated loan that is given ten different potential annual interest rates. Only one fixed row and one fixed column are necessary for labeling; counting fixed cells, the grid needs 37 columns and 11 rows. The `.Cols` and `.Rows` properties of the grid control set these parameters, as follows:

```
Loan.Cols = 37
Loan.Rows = 11
```

Assigning text to a cell may be somewhat confusing. The grid accepts data input to only one cell at any one time. The grid control maintains internal pointers to the location of the cell that may currently receive input. You manipulate those pointers through two property settings: `.Row` and `.Col`.

.Row, .Col   **Properties**

Representation: Cell pointer location
Applies to: Grid
Set by way of: Program instruction, user interaction

The `.Row` and `.Col` properties for a grid are set to the current internal pointer coordinates for that cell in the grid that is currently receiving data. The leftmost column in a grid is considered column 0, and the uppermost row is considered row 0. The cell at (0, 0) is generally a fixed cell anyway; the first addressable cell that appears in the upper left corner of the nonfixed data region of the grid is usually (1, 1). For this reason, the default settings of `.Row` and `.Col` are both 1.

> **Note:** Although the contents of the grid control appear like a spreadsheet, cells within a grid do not have addresses like "A2" or "P7."

Note the lack of an *s* at the end of these properties; be careful to distinguish between the `.Cols` and `.Col` properties. Remember that one is plural and the other is singular.

To give text to a cell, first set the grid's internal `.Row` and `.Col` pointers to the coordinates of the cell. Assigning text to the cell currently pointed to utilizes the same phraseology of instruction for a text box—string contents are assigned to the `.Text` property of the grid.

Example

Suppose you need to use a cell at location (13, 7) for a supplemental total field. The cell just to the left is to be used for a label for that field. The following instruction places the label into the grid:

```
Grid.Col = 12
Grid.Row = 7
Grid.Text = "Total:"
```

The field to the immediate right contains the total itself. Following is the routine:

```
Grid.Col = 13
Grid.Text = Str$(Total)
```

The cell pointer doesn't move after text has been printed to it, like after a carriage return has been pressed. Because of this, the pointer still registers (12, 7) after receiving the text `"Total:"`. The column pointer `.Col` is therefore moved one cell to the right before displaying the total itself. Like a text box, each cell in the grid receives alphanumeric string contents instead of values.

Example

Recall the loan payment grid example introduced earlier. The grid displays the payments made for a variable-rate 36-month loan. To assign reference cells for the month number to the uppermost fixed cell region, the row pointer `.Row` must first be set to row #0. Resetting the row pointer is accomplished with this instruction:

```
Loan.Row = 0
```

A loop clause then loads the label row for the x-axis of the table with reference labels for the month number in the payment schedule, starting with the *second* column, numbered 1:

```
For xlab% = 1 To 36
    Loan.Col = xlab%
    Loan.Text = Str$(xlab%)
Next xlab%
```

Assigning text to the current cell is similar to setting the contents of a text box, through an expression of assignment to the `.Text` property of the entire grid. This statement is in no way augmented with the coordinates of the cell receiving the text; that is set in advance with assignments to the .Row and .Col properties. The labels for the y-axis are set with a similar loop.

Assuming the results of all the calculations have been pre-loaded into a two-dimensional array payment(), here's how a two-tier loop clause assigns the contents of the body of the table:

```
For ycell% = 1 To 10
    Loan.Row = ycell%
    For xcell% = 1 To 36
        Loan.Col = xcell%
        Loan.Text = payment(xcell%, ycell%)
    Next xcell%
Next ycell%
```

Should the width of the column require expansion to fit the text assigned to it, you can adjust the width of that column with one of the following property settings:

.RowHeight(), .ColWidth()   **Properties**

Representation: Cell size
Applies to: Grid
Set by way of: Program instruction, user interaction

The .RowHeight() and .ColWidth() properties for a grid control are actually arrays whose length, in elements, is automatically set to the .Rows and .Cols, respectively, for the current grid. The elements for these array properties are set to the height and width in twips of the cells for their respective rows and columns. At run time, the user can change the settings for these properties by using the mouse pointer to slide the boundaries between rows and columns to new positions. This sliding does not trigger events for the grid.

There's no way to determine in advance the width of a column necessary to fit a particular string. You can use a "guessing" formula for estimating what the necessary length might be. Take the length of the string using the Len() function, and for an eight-point TrueType font, multiply that by 100 twips per character. Generally, the result is fairly close to the correct length.

Example

In the loan grid, you can change the width in twips of a column represented by variable `xwidth%` with the following instruction:

```
Loan.ColWidth(xcell%) = newwidth
```

It's interesting (and perhaps a bit confusing) to note that the `.ColWidth()` and `.RowHeight()` properties for a grid are maintained in arrays; whereas the `.Text` property with respect to a grid is merely a conduit for shuttling text into a cell. The contents of a cell cannot be tested with a conditional `If-Then` clause until the `.Row` and `.Col` properties for the grid are set to point to the cell being tested.

It's also interesting (and perhaps even more confusing) to point out that bit-mapped graphics, in either the .BMP or .ICO format, may be assigned to a cell by preloading the `.Row` and `.Col` properties and setting the `.Picture` property of the grid. The trouble is, the only property setting the grid allows is one that points to an existing `.Picture` property setting for another control in the same form—either a picture box or an image box. This strange behavior is discussed in greater detail in Chapter 42, "Picture and Image Boxes."

Normally, when text is assigned to a cell, it "leans" to the left side of that cell—what is normally called *left justification*. There are two properties that govern the alignment of text in the cells of a grid: `.ColAlignment()` and `.FixedAlignment()`.

.ColAlignment() **Property**

Representation: Weight of textual contents
Applies to: Grid
Set by way of: Properties window, program instruction

The `.ColAlignment()` property is an array whose individual elements apply, by number, to the columns in its antecedent grid object—specifically to their nonfixed cells. The settings for each element reflect the axis against which the textual contents of cells in each column are typeset. The property can be set to any of the following:

0	Left alignment (default)
1	Right alignment
2	Centered

You can set the alignment of a particular column through an instruction that uses the following syntax:

```
Grid.ColAlignment(column%) = setting%
```

.FixedAlignment()   **Property**

Representation: Weight of text in nonmovable cells
Applies to: Grid
Set by way of: Properties window, program instruction

The `.FixedAlignment()` property is an array whose individual elements apply, by number, to the columns in its antecedent grid object—specifically to their *fixed* cells. The settings for each element reflect the axis against which the textual contents of fixed cells in each column are typeset. Property settings are the same as those used for `.ColAlignment()`.

Putting the Grid to Work

Armed with this knowledge, you can now arm the MultiName test application with a single MDI form for the display of a multiple-name grid. Figure 31.2 shows how this grid looks alongside its single-name form companions in the MDI parent window.

Figure 31.2

A new child grid.

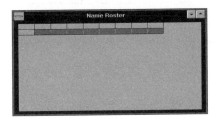

Multiple Name Display Application

Project name: MULTINAM.MAK
Constituent files: MULTINAM.FRM, NAMEFRM4.FRM, NAMTABLE.FRM, SELECTOR.FRM, MULTINAM.BAS

```
Option Base 1
Global TargetFile$, cancl As Integer, prmpt$, filename$,
➥pattern$
Type NameRecord
    LastName As String * 30
    FirstName As String * 20
    MidInit As String * 3
    CompanyName As String * 50
```

continues

Multiple Name Display Application Continued

```
        Address As String * 50
        City As String * 20
        State As String * 5
        Zip As String * 10
        MidProm As Integer
    End Type
    Global CurRecord As NameRecord
    Global Instance As Integer
    Global NameInstance(5) As New NameForm
```

The Type clause remains as it was earlier. Notice at the end of the global declarations the declaration of the Instance variable which keeps track of how many NameForms are currently active, and the declaration of the object variable array NameInstance(). The interpreter, when it executes this, recognizes five unloaded instances of forms taking the style defined by NameForm, each of which have the address name NameInstance().

NAMTABLE.FRM

Control Type	Property	Setting
Form	.Width	6264
	.Height	4056
	.Name	NameTable
	.BorderStyle	1 'Fixed Single
	.Caption	Name Roster
	.ControlBox	0 'False
	.MaxButton	0 'False
	.MDIChild	-1 'True
Grid	.Name	NameGrid
	.Cols	9
	.Width	5892
	.Height	3372

General Declarations

```
Dim MaxWidth (8) As integer, s$(8)
Dim TableRecord As NameRecord
```

Event Procedures

```
Sub Form_Load ()
NameTable.Show
NameGrid.Row = 0
NameGrid.Col = 1
```

```
NameGrid.Text = "Last Name"
NameGrid.Col = 2
NameGrid.Text = "First Name"
NameGrid.Col = 3
NameGrid.Text = "Mid.Init."
NameGrid.Col = 4
NameGrid.Text = "Company Name"
NameGrid.Col = 5
NameGrid.Text = "Address"
NameGrid.Col = 6
NameGrid.Text = "City"
NameGrid.Col = 7
NameGrid.Text = "State"
NameGrid.Col = 8
NameGrid.Text = "Zip"
NameGrid.Row = 1
Open "NAMES.NFM" For Random As #6 Len = 190
RecordNow = 1
If LOF(6) > 190 Then
    Do
        Get #6, RecordNow, TableRecord
        s$(1) = RTrim$(TableRecord.LastName)
        s$(2) = RTrim$(TableRecord.FirstName)
        s$(3) = RTrim$(CurRecord.MidInit)
        s$(4) = RTrim$(CurRecord.CompanyName)
        s$(5) = RTrim$(CurRecord.Address)
        s$(6) = RTrim$(CurRecord.City)
        s$(7) = RTrim$(CurRecord.State)
        s$(8) = RTrim$(CurRecord.Zip)
        NameGrid.Col = 0
        NameGrid.Text = RTrim$(Str$(RowNow))
        For RowPrint = 1 To 8
            NameGrid.Col = RowPrint
            NameGrid.Text = RTrim$(s$(RowPrint))
            If Len(s$(RowPrint)) * 100 > MaxWidth(RowPrint) Then
                MaxWidth(RowPrint) = Len(s$(RowPrint)) * 100
                NameGrid.ColWidth(RowPrint) = MaxWidth(RowPrint)
            End If
        Next RowPrint
        RecordNow = RecordNow + 1
    Loop Until TableRecord.FirstName = "~*End" Or
    ➥RecordNow > LOF(6) / 190
Else
    TableRecord.FirstName = "~*End"
    Put #6, 2, TableRecord
    TableRecord.MidProm = 0
    TableRecord.FirstName = ""
    Put #6, 1, TableRecord
End If
Close #6
End Sub
```

The following is the essence of this procedure, in a compressed form of pseudo-code:

Procedure that executes when this form is called.
Assign the column references to the first eight columns of row 0.
The row pointer now to 1.
Open the names file.
Assume you're counting the first record.
If it's apparent there's more than one record to be counted, then
*   Start the following loop:*
*   Get the next record from the names file.*
*   Assign the components of this record to eight array*
*   variables.*
*   Reset the column pointer to zero.*
*   Place the row number in the fixed row index column.*
*   Start counting columns from 1 to 8.*
*   Set the column pointer to the current count.*
*   Assuming 100 twips per character, adjust the maximum*
*   column width if necessary to fit the current*
*   contents.*
*   Count the next column.*
*   Increment the record number.*
*   Continue until you've reached the final record.*
Otherwise,
*   Place the false final record placekeeper into the file.*
End of condition.
Close the names file.
End of procedure.

The first part of this procedure loads the column references into the fixed row #0. Again, this can be done most efficiently by setting the cell pointer, assigning text to that cell, setting the pointer again, assigning text to the next cell, and so on. It's about as efficient as using the `.AddItem` method for filling a list box; the process is easy, but at times it's not simple.

After the row references are filled, the procedure starts a random-access load process. Each record is loaded into memory and displayed in sequence, so theoretically this procedure uses the sequential-access model. This loading process was taken from the `Sub LoadFile ()` procedure in the original NameForm application; there, it was necessary to place the `Get #` instruction in a `Do-Loop` clause to eventually reach the final record in the set. At this location in the code, the procedure isn't loading records into memory and ignoring all but the last (actually the next-to-last) one. In this case, the procedure loads the record variable into memory and assigns its components to a temporary array variable s$().

Other Grid Properties

A procedure manually sets the visible area of the grid by specifying the coordinates of the upper-leftmost column in its data area. For a grid with one fixed row and one fixed column, this would be cell (1, 1). Two properties are available for this purpose: the .TopRow and .LeftCol properties.

.TopRow, .LeftCol   Properties

Representation: First visible data cell
Applies to: Grid
Set by way of: Program instruction

The .TopRow and .LeftCol properties for a grid may be set in a procedure to the coordinates of the uppermost and leftmost visible cell, respectively, in the grid. These properties do not affect the positioning of fixed cells in the grid, nor do they affect the position of the current cell pointers .Row and .Col.

In addition to many of the visual effects properties normally available to a graphic object, the grid needs a special property to determine whether borderlines are to appear between the cells.

.GridLines   Property

Representation: Intermediate borderlines
Applies to: Grid
Set by way of: Properties window, program instruction

The .GridLines property for a grid control is set to a true or false value that denotes whether hazy borderlines are to appear between each cell in the grid, both in the fixed area and the mobile area.

Finally, one of the event terms native to a grid control represents the cell pointer location's being changed, whether by the user or by a program instruction:

_RowColChange   Event

Action: Cell pointer movement
Applies to: Grid
Parameters: None

The _RowColChange event for a grid is triggered whenever the current cell pointer is moved to a new location, whether through user interaction or by a procedure manually setting the .Row or .Col property of the grid.

If the procedure were to use the grid control for the entry and editing of names—which is entirely possible—the event procedure here that would record the entry of a field into a record would most likely be Sub NameGrid_RowColChange ().

Summary

The purpose of the grid control is to make it possible to display tabular data, or to display several records in individual rows. The grid control is supplied to the Visual Basic environment by way of a dynamic link library file, GRID.VBX. A grid may consist of fixed cells, generally reserved for displaying reference or index fields. These fields remain where they are while other data cells are scrolled.

Use the .Rows and .Cols properties to set the total number of rows and columns in a grid. Among those, the total number of fixed rows along the upper side, and fixed columns along the left side, are set using the .FixedRows and .FixedCols properties, respectively. At any point in time, a single cell within the grid is specially indicated as the one that receives text, whether from the program or the user. The .Row and .Col properties jointly maintain the coordinates of this cell pointer.

Once the pointer is set to the cell that receives text, text is assigned to that cell in the same way that text is assigned to a text field—by using the .Text property in an equation. The .RowHeight() and .ColWidth() array properties are used to adjust the size of cells to fit their contents. The .ColAlignment() and .FixedAlignment() array properties are used to position text within a cell. The _RowColChange event is triggered whenever the cell pointer for a grid is changed.

Review Questions

1. When a grid contains one fixed column, adjusting the column width of the second column in the nonfixed data cells area is accomplished through the use of what property term?

2. When a grid control is displayed with one fixed row and one fixed column, and the user starts typing text *first* without indicating a cell beforehand, and without the program having tinkered with the `.Row` or `.Col` property, where does that text go?

3. Can the user enter text into a nonvisible cell?

CHAPTER 32

Object Variables

In this chapter, you study the methods, events, and properties that relate to addressing, organizing, and manipulating graphic objects *in general*, in contrast to the control-exclusive instructions you've become more accustomed to using. In Visual Basic 3, graphic elements such as a form, a graphic object, and even the screen itself can be referred to through the use of object variables. The VB interpreter maintains a set of reserved object variables for itself, although it has modified the `Dim` statement—as you saw in Chapter 20, "The Window as Document"—so that you can refer to graphic objects *indirectly*, not just by their `.Name`.

The `.Tag` property—which was introduced in Chapter 17, "Control Identification and Contents"—may not seem to be very useful in the context of Visual Basic. Each graphic object already has one name, and you may be wondering why it also needs a pseudonym.

The reason for a second name is this: there will be times when you'd like to have a routine that *compares* one control to another, just as if that control were a variable of a specified data type. Visual Basic does recognize the data type `Control` for graphic objects inhabiting a form, so you can compare controls by using mathematical expressions. However, object-oriented syntax does not allow you to refer to objects *subjectively*. In other words, the control name of an object cannot be used as the subject of a comparison.

The solution to this is to create a second name for a control, when necessary, to act as its subjective name.

The purpose for the `.Tag` property is not at all self-explanatory. Assume the VB application you're writing is a children's game, in which the child picks up "toy" symbols on the screen with the mouse and drops them into a box. These symbols are represented by VB icons. An event procedure is programmed to detect whenever a symbol is dropped into the box; but the way the interpreter works, the event is based around the box that the symbol is being dropped into, not the symbol that is being moved. With that in mind, the objective is to have the event procedure determine which toy entered the box. The box is the object of the event procedure; however, the toy is the subject.

Example

To ensure you're able to identify the subject, you need to assign .Tag property settings to each icon either at design time or within the Sub Form_Load () or Sub Main () procedure. Here's the event procedure:

```
Sub BigRedBox_DragDrop (Source As Control, x As Single,
➥y As Single)
Select Case Source.Tag
    Case "Bear"
        Bear1.Picture = LoadPicture("C:\vb3\icons\mine\
        ➥hapybear.ico")
        Source.Parent.Message.Text = "Thank you."
    Case "Rocket"
        Rocket1.Picture = LoadPicture("C:\vb3\icons\mine\
        ➥blastoff.ico")
        Source.Parent.Message.Text = "We have liftoff."
    .
    .
    .
End Select
End Sub
```

The properties of a graphic object can be passed to a procedure through a variable declared *As Control*.

The _DragDrop event occurs whenever a graphic object or control with drag capability is dragged and dropped on top of the antecedent object. The icons being dragged, from the interpreter's point of view, are picture boxes whose contents can be established by means of the LoadPicture() function.

The key element of this procedure is on the first line, at the declaration Source As Control. Up to now, you've declared variables As Integer or As Double; in this instance, however, As Control refers to a *structural* form of declaration, not to a numeric form. The toy being dragged into the box is a control; and here it may actually be declared as such using the term As Control. When this happens, all the property data associated with the control—size, position, and contents—are passed along with it.

With that in mind, here's the procedure written as pseudocode:

Procedure awaiting a control to be dragged into the box:

Check to see what the tag of the source control is.
  In case its tag is "Bear"
    Load the happy bear picture into the control.
    Tell the parent form of the source control
     "Thank you."
  In case its tag is "Rocket"
    Load the rocket into the control.
    Tell the parent form of the source control
     "We have liftoff."

      .
      .
      .

End of cases.
End of procedure.

Addressing the *Parent.* object is one way to find out where a passed graphic object came from.

The choice of the term `Source` for the control data structure was arbitrary in this case, in the same way the choice of a variable name is arbitrary. In this procedure, all the properties that belong to the source control are copied and absorbed, in a sense, by the term `Source`. So if `Object1.Tag = "Bear"` and the bear is the toy that was dragged, once the drop occurs and this procedure executes, `Source.Tag = "Bear"`.

The term `Parent.` in this procedure acts like a property for the sake of `Source.`, but it acts like an object from the point of view of `Message`. `Message` is a control that can have a `.Text` property of its own.

Parent.   Reserved object variable

Representation: Source of passed object
Applies to: All controls
Syntax:

```
Source.Parent.Property
```

The `Parent.` object variable is used to refer back to the parent form of a control whose constituent properties have already been passed to a procedure. This property passing takes place by way of declaring the data structure at the beginning of the procedure, in the form `Source As Control`. Once a graphic object is passed to the procedure as data, the control that was passed may be referred to by way of the indirect reference `Source.`, regardless of the type of control that was passed. `Source.` can then be used to refer to all the properties allotted to the passed control. The properties of the form containing this control are therefore addressable from within the procedure as properties of the `Parent.` object variable.

In order to send a message back to the form to which the `Source.` control originally belonged, that form may be addressed within the procedure as `Parent.`, whatever the `.Name` of the form may be. In this instance, `Message.` is an arbitrary name for a text box belonging to the parent form. You don't need to know the `.Name` of the form, yet you do need to know the `.Name` of the object within that form in order to address it directly. So, the conglomerate reference `Source.Parent.Message.Text` refers to the text within a text box that is definitely called `Message`, residing in the parent form of whatever control was dragged into the box.

> **Note:** The term `Source` is used commonly as a reflexive reference, although it is an object variable rather than a Visual Basic keyword. Any other variable name can be used in its place except in cases where VB event procedures use the `Source` declarative in their headers—for instance, drag-and-drop events.

Putting Several Name Tags on the Same Item

The `.Tag` property may be most useful within MDI applications, in which you can have multiple instances in memory of the same child form. While activated and within the MDI parent workspace, each instance of an MDI child form can have its own exclusive `.Tag` property setting. This is one way a duplicate form can be exclusively identified without relying entirely on an instance variable.

Example

This example uses the MultiName application as an example. In the global declarations section is a declaration for a unit variable `Instance` that will keep track, at all times, of how many NameForms currently inhabit the workspace. When the user calls up a new name, `Instance` is incremented, and this number is passed to a form-level variable `ActiveInstance`, which is declared as follows:

NAMEFRM4.FRM

General Declarations

```
Dim RecordNo As Integer, MaxRecord As Integer
Dim sortarray() As Integer
Dim ActiveInstance As Integer
```

Because parameters can't be passed to a form module once it is initiated, a global variable is necessary to act as the "baton," providing an exclusive instance number to each MDI child invoked within the parent workspace. For now, this is the only means of identification exclusive to the running child; using the `.Tag` property, however, a far more versatile method can be created by invoking NameForm's `Sub Form_Load ()` procedure to read as follows:

```
Sub Form_Load ()
ActiveInstance = Instance
NameInstance(ActiveInstance).Tag = "Name" +
➥LTrim$(Str$(ActiveInstance))
filename$ = "NAMES.NFM"
LoadFile
End Sub
```

The first instruction is the "handoff," which receives the instance number from the global variable. This number is then taken and assigned to the exclusive `.Tag` property of the child form. The digits are added to the end of the word `Name`, resulting in tags such as `Name1` and `Name3`. Later in this application's development, if a graphic object's contents are being passed to a procedure by way of passing the entire object `As Control`, the syntax `Source.Tag` can be used to determine which child form instance is doing the passing.

Giving Focus to an Object

Graphic objects that have the focus have their own indirect references.

There will be occasions where the user will click a button that directs the application to acquire data from whatever control is currently active, or has the focus. In such situations, the `ActiveControl` and `ActiveForm` objects represent the active control and form, respectively.

ActiveControl.   **Reserved object variable**

Representation: Object bearing focus
Applies to: Form, MDI form, screen
Syntax:

> `Parent.ActiveControl`

The `ActiveControl.` object, when used in conjunction with the universal reference `Screen.`, refers back to whatever control currently is active or has the focus, on any form. The same object, when used in conjunction with a reference to a form, refers back to whatever control within that form would be given the focus on the control level, if that form is active or if that form were made active.

ActiveForm.   **Reserved object variable**

Representation: Form bearing focus
Applies to: MDI form, screen
Syntax:

> *Parent*.ActiveForm

The ActiveForm. object, when used in conjunction with Screen., refers back to the currently active form. When used in conjunction with a reference to an MDI parent form, the object refers back to the currently active instance of an MDI child form.

Example

Suppose you add a Copy button to one of the NameForms. Clicking it would copy the contents of the text field currently under the cursor—the control with the focus—to the system clipboard. The procedure needs to be able to determine what text box control contains the text to be copied. Here's how the procedure might appear:

```
Sub Copy_Click ()
copy$ = Screen.ActiveControl.Text
Clipboard.SetText copy$
End Sub
```

Here, ActiveControl. refers back to whatever control currently has the cursor. For the sake of .Text, ActiveControl. is the object. To be a reflexive reference, however, .ActiveControl must act as the property of something. Therefore, like .Parent in an earlier example, .ActiveControl is an object acting as a property. The VB interpreter has assigned it as the exclusive property of everything referred to by the object Screen., which is the necessary object in order for .ActiveControl to fulfill its role as property. This is because there can be only one active control on the Windows screen at any time.

The source or parent of all controls with the focus is referred to with the *Screen.* object.

In the preceding examples, you saw references to the all-encompassing Screen. object variable. If an application's workspace can be considered the parent, the Screen. object can be considered the "grandparent." Its purpose is to act as the primary platform on which reflexive references to active forms may be attached.

Screen.   **Reserved object variable**

Representation: Application display area

The `Screen.` object refers to the universal (screen-encompassing) coordinate system. It is used whenever a property of the whole screen, such as `.ActiveControl,` is invoked.

Indirect References

In Visual Basic, as in everyday life, some general graphic object-related tasks are best performed—more to the point, they are more efficiently performed—when these objects are not being referred to specifically. Say, for instance, you want to make all your text fields line up against the left margin of a form, regardless of where they were placed at design time. To create a process model for such a procedure that works for almost any form containing a set of text fields, it's good to have a single object variable referring to each text field indirectly, in turn. Object variables are good excuses for having your VB procedures "daydream" on the job.

Passing a graphic object to a procedure through a variable such as `Source` that has been declared `As Control` presents a very versatile system for referring to graphic objects indirectly, by stripping them of their identity. Passing a graphic object to a procedure also presents the programmer with a dilemma, with controls having been stripped of their identity. What are they? How will a procedure refer to the properties that are exclusive to a particular type of control without knowing what that control is, and whether a property is really available for that object?

For any test you impose on a property, you use an expression. For instance, in the instruction `If Sasquatch.Text = "Overblown" Then...End If,` the phrase `Sasquatch.Text = "Overblown"` is an expression. The `.Name` property of a graphic object is not available for such expressions, so you can't have an instruction that begins, `If Source.Name = 'Sasquatch...'.` There is, however, a way to acquire the `.Name` property of a graphic object passed `As Control`, through an expression operator reserved for cases of object variables: the `Is` operator.

Using the `Is` operator, it's possible to determine the name of a graphic object `Source` passed to a procedure `As Control` by means of an instruction with the syntax `If Source Is Name Then....`

A control's type is not a *property* of that control; in other words, you can't assign to a variable the results of `Mover.Type` and come up with `Scroll Bar`. Suppose you want to gather the textual contents of a graphic object, so you may want to refer to `Source.Text`; but what if the object is really a label? You'd need the `.Caption` property instead.

The TypeOf function is used for validating the control type of an unknown graphic object.

TypeOf   Function

Purpose: Control type determination
Syntax:

```
TypeOf Object Is type
```

The TypeOf function is used within an expression to return a true/false value, signifying whether the stated *Object*—referred to using an object variable name—is representative of a particular object *type* recognized by the interpreter. The object type terms recognized by the Standard Edition of Visual Basic are as follows:

CheckBox	ComboBox	CommandButton	DirListBox
DriveListBox	FileListBox	Frame	Grid
HScrollBar	Image	Label	Line
ListBox	Menu	OptionButton	PictureBox
Shape	TextBox	Timer	VScrollBar

Custom controls added to the VB toolbox may utilize their own type terms.

Note: Although TypeOf is officially a function, it does not accept parentheses as standard VB syntax would dictate.

Example

With regard to the problem posed earlier, the following routine determines whether a graphic object is a text box or a label, and acts on that finding:

```
If TypeOf Textual Is TextBox Then
    signal$ = Textual.Text
ElseIf TypeOf Textual Is Label Then
    signal$ = Textual.Caption
End If
```

The syntax of this function is highly legible; there's certainly no doubt about the meaning of the first line in the preceding example. What's unusual is that all the other VB instructions aren't phrased quite as linguistically. This instruction could arguably violate the laws of object-oriented syntax.

Object variables
may refer to
generic graphic
objects or to a
specific object
type.

When referring to graphic objects indirectly, sometimes you will need a procedure to be able to determine whether two or more indirect references refer to the same graphic object. In such instances, the Is operator is available for comparisons of equality between two object variables with the following example syntax:

```
If object1 Is object2 Then...
```

Arbitrary Object Variables

The next example illustrates the use of the Set statement.

Set   **Statement**

Purpose: Establishment of indirect representation
Syntax 1:

```
Set objectvar = [parentref!]objectref
```

Syntax 2:

```
Set objectvar = New objectname
```

The Set statement, using Syntax 1, attributes the object variable *objectvar* to the stated existent graphic object *objectref*. The reference *objectref* to this existent object may be placed by way of the .Name property for that object, or by way of yet another object variable. Once invoked, any reference to *objectvar* applies to the same graphic object as does *objectref*. The object variable *objectvar* may be set later to refer to some other graphic object, or disengaged by setting its reference to Nothing. Any object variable referred to by the Set statement must first have been formally declared using the Dim, Global, or Static statement, as described in Chapter 20, "The Window as Document."

If the parent object of *objectref* is not currently active (if it doesn't have the focus on the form level), to attribute the reference for the graphic object to the particular parent object to which it belongs, that parent's object reference *parentref* must be stated first, followed by the child control reference *objectref*. The two references are separated from one another with an exclamation mark.

Using Syntax 2, the Set statement attributes the object variable *objectvar* to a new instance of a predesigned object whose .Name property was set to *objectname* at design time. Invoking this syntax of the Set statement brings this New instance of the graphic object into existence. The parent of *objectname* must be currently active, or have the focus on the form level.

> **Note:** Syntax 2 of the `Set` statement worked successfully only in cases of declaring new instances of forms, but not new constituent controls. It is apparently Microsoft's intent to declare new instances of controls within a form using Syntax 2.

Example

Start by initializing a new project. Place a text box within Form1 of this project—it doesn't matter where. Currently, this graphic object has a `.Name` of `Text1` as well as a `.Text` property set to `Text1`. Next, add the following line to the general declarations area of Form1:

```
Dim TextCopy As Control
```

Now run the program; all we need it to do is dimension the object variable `TextCopy` as a generic `Control` variable. Next, break it—don't stop it, but press the break button in the toolbar or select Break from the Run menu. For this demonstration to work, you need the Debug window's command-line interpreter, which can respond to your direct commands. Type into the Debug window the following command:

```
Set TextCopy = Form1!Text1
```

If everything is going well thus far, the VB interpreter should not respond to this command—and no news is good news. You know that the `.Name` of this text box is `Text1`. Type the following command, however, and you'll see that there are now other ways to refer to this control:

```
TextCopy.Text = "Wow!  It works!"
```

Your message between the quotation marks should immediately appear within the text box `Text1`, even though the name itself appears nowhere in the command. You've just successfully invoked an object variable.

Now, to experiment further with this concept, change the only line in the entire VB application to read as follows:

```
Dim TextCopy As TextBox
```

Next, repeat the remainder of the steps. You should notice no difference in what happens.

Example

So what's the difference between declaring an object variable as a text box and declaring one as a control? Specifying the text box type seems to be more specific as far as the source code is concerned, but doesn't appear to add any efficiency to the code. This extension to the demonstration should answer some of these questions. Someplace on Form1, add a vertical scroll bar. Next, edit the general declarations section to read as follows:

```
Dim Whapjaw As Control
Dim TextCopy As TextBox
Dim ScrollCopy As VScrollBar
```

There are two specific object variable references here, and one generic one. When you run the application now, break it, and type the following into the Debug window:

```
Set Whapjaw = Text1
```

you get no response, which is good. When you enter the following into the Debug window:

```
Whapjaw.Text = "When in the course..."
```

you should see an echo in the text box Text1. Now, try typing the following in the Debug window:

```
Set Whapjaw = VScroll1
```

Follow it with the following two instructions:

```
Whapjaw.Max = 50
Whapjaw.Value = 25
```

The .Min minimum value for the scroll bar should already be 0; so the scroll box should now appear in the middle of the bar. Notice what's been accomplished; in the course of five instructions, the same object variable refers to two totally different types of controls. Notice, however, you've been using the one object variable that was declared As Control. Try the same succession of steps in the Debug window with either TextCopy or ScrollCopy. At some time, you'll find the VB interpreter responds with a "Type mismatch error" panel. The restriction placed on the other two object variables allows them to refer to only one type of graphic object.

Example

Finally, just as the value of a unit variable can be set to the value of another unit variable, as in valence = v1, the components of an object variable can be assigned to another object variable. The following instructions typed into the Debug window prove this:

```
Set TextCopy = Form1!Text1
Set Whapjaw = TextCopy
```

The second instruction is key here; it sets the object reference equivalent to another object reference. You can now address the .Text property of Whapjaw (not the .Max property).

Perhaps you might be able in your mind to apply this demonstration to broader tasks. Suppose you have a set of general modules containing procedures that generate results regardless of what form the inputs or outputs are in. You may use the Global statement within general procedures to declare object variable names; the results of these general procedures may be assigned to the properties of these object variables. Within the Sub Form_Load () procedures of your form modules, then, you can place Set statements equating the object variables referred to in the general procedures, to the .Name properties of the real controls in your form modules. This enables you to create fully functional *libraries* that you can easily use in your applications.

> **Note:** To disengage an object variable reference and release the memory apportioned to it, use the Set statement with the syntax Set *objectvar* = Nothing. The Nothing keyword releases the object variable back to the state it was in before the initial Set statement was executed.

Summary

A control appearing on a form can be assigned a .Tag property, which acts as its alias. Controls can be passed in the same manner as normal data (as parameters to procedures), as long as the control name is declared within the parentheses of the procedure's opening Sub statement as having data type Control. The form that contains the control passed as a parameter to the procedure can be addressed reflexively using the object/property hybrid term Parent.

The .ActiveControl and .ActiveForm can be addressed indirectly by using those terms. All properties and settings apply to these indirect references just as they would to their direct-reference antecedent objects. .ActiveControl and .ActiveForm relate back to the Screen. universal object.

You can use the Set statement to make a declared object variable refer to a specific control, or to a new instance of an existing form. Object variables can therefore be used by general procedure modules; form modules can then Set these object variables to refer to specific controls. The TypeOf function can be used later to verify that a declared object variable refers to a specified type of control.

Review Questions

Using object-oriented syntax, write references for the following properties:

1. A reflexive reference to the textual contents of the active control.

2. A reflexive reference to a text box called Status passed as a parameter to a procedure.

3. A reflexive reference to a text box called Status appearing within the active form.

4. A reflexive reference to a text box called Status appearing in the same form as that which contains the control that was passed to the current procedure.

Part VI

Arithmetic Functions

CHAPTER 33

Classification

Time now to turn your attention from the visually practical to the logically cerebral. This chapter reviews what a Visual Basic function is and what it does. Before you start examining these functions in detail, you see how their return values can be classified as variable types.

Function is used in the preceding paragraph to refer to the role of mathematics in the modern world, and not the role of terms or instructions in Visual Basic. As defined in Chapter 3, "Grammar and Linguistics," a Visual Basic function is a more fundamental, less esoteric thing. A *function* is an arithmetic operation performed on a value, variable, or expression, having a result that is returned in a single variable.

> A *function* is an arithmetic operation performed on a value, variable, or expression.

♦ An arithmetic comparison between two values, having a result that is expressed logically as a binary state

♦ One or more values or variables arithmetically joined by functions or functional operators

♦ An assignment of value to a variable through another value, variable, or expression

> An *expression* is a mathematical comparison or combination of values.

A Visual Basic function is a term that is said to perform an operation on a set of values or textual contents. It is sometimes said to *yield* a result, which is stored within a variable that uses the function. In all Visual Basic instructions that include intrinsic functions, the function is stated within the right side of an equation. This equation acts as an *expression of assignment*, because the solution of the equation is a result that is placed within a single variable. This variable is the only term on the left side of the equation. This expression takes on the following form:

```
variable = function(parameters)
```

Example

```
a# = Sqr(2)
```

Some Visual Basic functions are not mathematical; in fact, a great many of them concern the manipulation of text. They operate in the same manner, because textual assignments can be formulated like equations. A text function can be distinguished easily from a value function, because a text function always contains the $ character before its parentheses; for example

```
c$ = Chr$(65)
```

Example

Often, a function contains more than one parameter, in which case these parameters are separated by commas as delimiters, as in the following example:

```
n$ = right$("Mr. Scott", 5)
```

> **Note:** The dollar sign (`$`) within string functions is optional.

Redeclaration

You now have been refamiliarized with all the fundamental terms necessary to discuss Visual Basic functions. Before going on with Part VI, "Arithmetic Functions," you should learn about a series of statements you could use from time to time to make variable type distinction a little easier when you're creating your formulas:

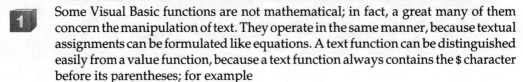

DefCur, DefDbl, DefInt, DefLng, DefSng, DefStr, and DefVar   **Statements**

Purpose: Alphabetic variable restriction
Syntax:

```
DefCur range[, range[, range. . . ]]
DefDbl range[, range[, range. . . ]]
DefInt range[, range[, range. . . ]]
DefLng range[, range[, range. . . ]]
DefSng range[, range[, range. . . ]]
DefStr range[, range[, range. . . ]]
DefVar range[, range[, range. . . ]]
```

Cur	Currency
Dbl	Double-precision floating-point
Int	Standard integer
Lng	Long integer
Sng	Single-precision floating-point
Str	Alphanumeric string
Var	Variant

> **Caution:** Remember that unless declared otherwise (by formal statement or `Def`*type* statement), a variable defaults to single-precision floating-point type.

Example

Many programmers, in the interest of memory conservation, override the `Variant` default variable type with the following statement, placed within the declarations area of a Visual Basic application:

```
DefInt a-z
```

Some programmers like to reserve a letter or two for strings only, with such a statement as this:

```
DefStr z
```

Pinning Down the Variants

The `Variant` data type replaces the single-precision floating-point type as the default for implicitly declared variables. A `Variant` variable may take on any form depending on the value or contents assigned to it; but if your `Variant` is a string, and you're attempting to convert it to a string with the `Str$()` function, obviously you'll have a problem—namely, a type mismatch error. You'll need one of the following functions to determine what type of contents have been assigned to your variant:

IsNumeric(), IsEmpty(), and IsNull()   **Functions**

Purpose: Variant content determination
Syntax:

```
boolean% = IsNumeric(variant)
boolean% = IsEmpty(variant)
boolean% = IsNull(variant)
```

VarType()   **Function**

Purpose: Variant type acquisition
Syntax:

```
type% = VarType(variant)
```

0	Empty
1	Null
2	Integer
3	Long
4	Single
5	Double
6	Currency
7	Date
8	String

Caution: The VarType() function generates a Type Mismatch error whenever a composite variable is supplied as its parameter.

Summary

A function in Visual Basic is a mathematical operation performed on a set of values or alphanumeric strings, the result of which is returned within or assigned to a single variable. This variable is the sole element of the left side of the equation. The function exists somewhere within the right side of the equation, perhaps as part of a mathematical expression. A Visual Basic intrinsic function always has a set of parentheses for enclosing input parameters.

Review Questions

1. What is the conceptual difference between a function of arithmetic and a function of Visual Basic?

2. Would the instruction `DefInt A-Z` reserve single letters for use in integer variables?

3. Why are parentheses used in this book—even empty ones—to distinguish Visual Basic functions?

CHAPTER 34

Conversion

In this chapter, you learn the intrinsic Visual Basic functions that take a single parameter of one type or form and convert it to a value or string of another type or form. These functions generally are the simplest BASIC functions.

At times, you might need to round a value within a floating-point variable to the nearest whole number, or perhaps you need to remove its fractional value altogether. Here are two functions for that purpose: Int() and Fix().

Int()   Function

Purpose: Numeric truncation
Syntax:

```
solution% = Int(expression)
```

The Int() function rounds the logically simplified value of *expression* downward to the nearest integer or whole number. The result of this rounding is returned in the variable *solution%*.

Fix() Function

Purpose: Numeric rounding
Syntax:

```
solution% = Fix(expression)
```

The `Fix()` function removes any fractional value from the logically simplified value of *expression*, leaving an integer or whole number value. This value is returned in the variable *solution%*.

Example

Here is a "conversation" with the Visual Basic Debug window (command-line interpreter), which should help you distinguish the difference (although there is little) between the `Int()` and `Fix()` functions. Responses made by the Debug window are shown in boldface.

```
a=4.9999
?int(a)
 4
?fix(a)
 4
a=-4.9999
?int(a)
-5
?fix(a)
-4
```

For a positive value of variable a, the `Int()` and `Fix()` functions return the same value. For a negative value of a, however, the results of the two functions differ by 1. This difference occurs because `Int()` rounds the value down to the nearest whole number (a downward direction increases a negative value). In contrast, `Fix()` simply removes the fractional value without performing any true arithmetic on the variable.

Example

A common use for the `Int()` function is to make values more manageable and tangible. Suppose that you have a loop clause that is executed as many times as there are miles between two points. The distance between those two points is found algebraically, and it is almost certain to contain a fractional value. A loop clause cannot be executed 8.26 times or a time and a half; a loop clause can have only a whole number of iterations. This whole number can be derived by rounding the distance using the Int() function, as follows:

```
distance# = Sqr(Abs((x2 - x1) ^ 2) + Abs((y2 - y1) ^ 2))
d% = Int(distance#)
For clomp = 1 to d%

    .

    .

    .

Next clomp
```

Here, the loop clause is executed Int(distance#) times, without any fraction of a loop to worry about. Actually, Visual Basic loop clauses ignore fractional values if the Step value is assumed to be 1 anyway. This way, however, variable d% can be addressed within the clause.

String Conversions

In an earlier chapter of this book, you wrote an application that, among other things, could convert a base 10 value to a base 16 value. Actually, a Visual Basic intrinsic function can convert for you. If you had known about this function in the beginning, you probably would not have learned as much about logic, would you? In any event, here are Visual Basic's base conversion string functions, Hex$() and Oct$().

Hex$()   **Function**

Purpose: Hexadecimal translation
Syntax:

```
solution$ = Hex$(num_expression)
```

The Hex$() function solves for the nonfractional value of *num_expression*, rounds that number down to the nearest integer, and finds the hexadecimal (base 16) value of the number. This number is returned as a string, especially because it might contain the digits *A* through *F* (10 through 15).

Oct$()   Function

Purpose: Octal conversion
Syntax:

```
solution$ = Oct$(num_expression)
```

The Oct$() function solves for the nonfractional value of *num_expression*, rounds that number down to the nearest integer, and finds the octal (base 8) value of the number. Although the solution contains only digits *0* through *7*, it is returned within a string variable *solution$*.

Example

A conversation with the Debug window CLI shows the preceding functions in action:

```
num=1495
?Hex$(num)
5D7
?Oct$(num)
2727
```

ASCII Conversion

As you discovered in an earlier chapter, Visual Basic (as well as Windows, DOS, and the BIOS itself) recognizes alphanumeric characters as numeric patterns. The patterns form a code that is called *ASCII* (pronounced *AS-key*) after the name of the standards document that defines it; however, Windows doesn't adhere to this code 100 percent. Nonetheless, Visual Basic does maintain functions that convert a character to an ASCII (ANSI, really) value and vice versa. These functions are explained more fully in the following sections.

Asc() **Function**

Purpose: ANSI character number acquisition
Syntax:

```
solution% = Asc(char$)
```

In this syntax, *char$* is a single character. If this character is written literally, it must appear within quotation marks.

The Asc() function obtains the ASCII (actually, the ANSI) code value for the character designated as *char$*. This value is returned within the variable *solution%*.

Chr$() **Function**

Purpose: ANSI character acquisition
Syntax:

```
solution$ = Chr$(expression)
```

In this syntax, *expression* can be simplified logically to a legitimate ASCII code value.

The Chr$() function accepts the whole-number value of *expression* and looks up the ASCII (ANSI) code equivalent character for that value. This character is returned as the single-character contents of *solution$*.

Example

Suppose that you have a program that maintains a large database of clients' names. A scroll bar in your program's main form represents the position of the currently displayed record alphabetically, with respect to the entire client database. You determine, however, that it would be a time-saver for the program if you split the database into 26 files organized alphabetically. Each file would be apportioned a particular letter of the alphabet, and only records containing surnames that begin with that letter would be stored there. You want this fact to be transparent to the user, however, so you want the scroll bar to tell the program which data file to look under for the current record.

For this example, the scroll bar is called `Scroller`, and the text box that contains the letter being pointed to is `Display`. The value of property `Scroller.Value` is represented by the scroll box—what Macintosh users call the *thumb*. In the ASCII code, the capital letter *A* is represented as number *65*, and the other capital letters through to *Z* are represented up to number *90*. When you're designing the form, you set the `.Min` property for `Scroller` to *65* and the `.Max` property to *90*. Now `Scroller.Value` registers only a valid capital letter. Here's the procedure for determining which letter is being "dialed" when the user operates the scroll bar:

```
Sub Scroller_Change ()
Display.Caption = Chr$(Scroller.Value)
    .
    .
    .
End Sub
```

The preceding procedure is waiting for a `_Change` in the position of the scroll box in `Scroller`. When that happens, the contents of the text box `Display` change to show the letter represented by the scroll box position. This letter is determined using the `Chr$()` function to convert `Scroller.Value`—which can only be a whole number between *65* and *90*, thanks to the `.Min` and `.Max` settings you made at design time.

Example

You may remember that you used the `Asc()` function in Chapter 28, "The Keyboard," to determine which key the user pressed and what instructions to execute as a response. Here once again is the procedure that included the function:

```
Sub HScroll1_KeyPress (KeyAscii As Integer)
Select Case KeyAscii
    Case Asc("0")
        If HScroll1.Min <= HScroll1.Value -
        ➥HScroll1.LargeChange Then
            HScroll1.Value = HScroll1.Value -
            ➥HScroll1.LargeChange
        End If
    Case Asc("-")
        If HScroll1.Min <= HScroll1.Value -
        ➥HScroll1.SmallChange Then
            HScroll1.Value = HScroll1.Value -
            ➥HScroll1.SmallChange
        End If
```

```
    Case Asc("=")
        If HScroll1.Max >= HScroll1.Value +
        ➡HScroll1.SmallChange Then
            HScroll1.Value = HScroll1.Value +
            ➡HScroll1.SmallChange
        End If
    Case Asc("\")
        If HScroll1.Max >= HScroll1.Value +
        ➡HScroll1.LargeChange Then
            HScroll1.Value = HScroll1.Value +
            ➡HScroll1.LargeChange
        End If
End Select
Label1.Caption = Str$(HScroll1.Value)
End Sub
```

Because you didn't use the ASCII values for the keys being polled, you invoked `Asc()` functions for the control keys.

Often you need to convert a numeric value to string contents and vice versa. Two functions for those purposes are `Val()` and `Str$()`.

Val()   Function

Purpose: String-to-value conversion
Syntax:

```
solution = Val(string$)
```

In this syntax, *string$* can be an expression that concatenates several strings. The `Val()` function converts the first set of digits with number-delimiting characters in *string$* to a value placed within the variable *solution*. The first alphabetic character encountered within a string cancels the conversion process. A totally alphabetic character, therefore, is converted to *0*. The contents of *string$* are unaffected by this conversion. The first set of nonspace characters in *string$* must be a set of digits, or any characters that the Visual Basic interpreter normally uses to distinguish fractional numbers. Decimal points are recognized as such characters.

Str$()   **Function**

Purpose: Value-to-string conversion
Syntax:

```
solution$ = Str$(value)
```

The Str$() function converts the digits contained within *value* into an alphanumeric string, which is placed within the variable *solution$*. The value of the variable *value* is unaffected by this conversion.

Example

As you've learned, certain object properties are recognized as strings and others are recognized as values, without any distinguishing characters such as $ to help you out. With that fact in mind, a result value of an equation often is placed within a text box on a form. Text boxes can have only alphanumeric contents; they do not interpret values directly. The following conversion comes from the two-dimensional distance converter program from Chapter 6, "Arithmetic Formulas."

```
Sub Go_Click ()
x1 = Val(Box_x1.Text)
x2 = Val(Box_x2.Text)
y1 = Val(Box_y1.Text)
y2 = Val(Box_y2.Text)
d# = Sqr(Abs((x2 - x1) ^ 2) + Abs((y2 - y1) ^ 2))
Distance.Text = Str$(d#)
End Sub
```

Here, the derived distance value must be converted into an alphanumeric string using Str$() before that solution can be displayed within the text box Distance.

Finally, here are some functions that convert the contents of values within a variable from one type to another.

CCur(), CDbl(), CInt(), CLng(), CSng(), and CVar()

Functions

Purpose: Variable content conversion
Syntax:

```
solution = Ctype(expression)
```

In this syntax, *type* is the abbreviation for the variable type being converted to, as introduced in Chapter 33, "Arithmetic Formulas."

The `Ctype()` functions solve for the logically reduced value of *expression* and then convert that expression to the specified variable type, even if that type requires more bytes than are necessary to represent the value. The result must be assigned to a variable having a type that is equivalent to the type being converted to.

> **Note:** The `CInt()` function is especially convenient for use in certain rounding operations. During conversion, the `CInt()` function rounds the logically reduced value of the expression between the parentheses to the nearest even number. The result of a value truncated by `CInt()` and divided by 2 is always an integer; this result makes `CInt()` useful in search operations where an item being searched for falls either before or after the currently indicated item in the list. The next item to be scanned divides the list evenly by 2; thus, `CInt()` is used instead of `Int()` to define the current pointer position.

Summary

You can round or truncate values to whole-number values using the `Int()` and `Fix()` functions. To convert base 10 numbers to base 16 and base 8, you can use the functions `Hex$()` and `Oct$()`, respectively. Using `Asc()`, you can obtain the ASCII code value for a character; likewise, using `Chr$()`, you can obtain a character from its ASCII code value. Using `Val()`, you can convert string contents to a numeric value; likewise, using `Str$()`, you can convert a value into a string. You also can convert a value's contents and reassign them to a variable of a new type using the `Ctype()` functions.

Review Questions

Using the functions introduced in this chapter and without the aid of the computer, estimate the solutions to the following expressions:

1. `Int(3.1415927)`

2. `Asc("A")`

3. `Chr$(Asc("z"))`

4. `Int(Asc("A"))`

5. `Val("1600 Pennsylvania Avenue")`

CHAPTER 35

Practical Math

In this chapter, you learn the intrinsic Visual Basic functions that concern algebraic, trigonometric, and logarithmic calculations.

Two functions that involve the sign of the numeric value (whether the value is positive or negative) are Abs() and Sgn().

Abs()   Function

Purpose: Absolute value acquisition
Syntax:

```
solution = Abs(expression)
```

The Abs() function returns the absolute value of the result of *expression*, within the variable *solution*. This value is equivalent to the value of the original expression, unsigned.

Sgn()   Function

Purpose: Value sign acquisition
Syntax:

```
solution% = Sgn(expression)
```

The Sgn() function returns a value that represents the sign of the logically reduced value of *expression*, within the variable *solution%*. This representative value can be any of the following:

−1	if *expression* is negative
0	if *expression* = 0
1	if *expression* is positive

Example

For this example, you need to think figuratively because explaining the specifics would take forever. The concepts of Abs() and Sgn() are so simple that, at first, you might not think that you need such functions. After all, if you know that a = -42, do you need Sgn(a) = -1 to tell you that you have a negative number on your hands?

As a Visual Basic programmer, you learn that these functions become far more valuable in complex situations. Suppose that you're writing a charting program that displays the progress of trading an issue of stock on the New York Stock Exchange. For each day of trading, a vertical bar is plotted along an x-y graph, showing the range between the issue's high and low trading value for the day. The bar can be wide or narrow, but the width by itself doesn't show the viewer the general trend, which is whether the overall trading value is lower or higher than it was during the previous trading session.

The closing value for each day is held within the array closing(), and the day being plotted is traced within the loop variable day. Naturally, today's bar is bar number day, and yesterday's is number day - 1. The difference in the values over a two-day period is determined by the following expression:

```
trend = closing(day) - closing(day - 1)
```

For this example, you want a green bar to represent a gaining day and a red bar to represent a losing day. You can set the color of the bar with the following clause:

```
Select Case Sgn(trend)
    Case -1
        colr = 4    'Red
    Case 1
        colr = 2    'Green
    Case 0
        colr = 0    'Black
End Select
```

In the preceding clause, Sgn(trend) can yield only one of three values, all of which are covered here. The value rendered matches in sign only the sign of the value of trend.

If each trading period is represented by a pixel on the graph, you use the following expression to find the length of the bar between the high and low value on the day:

```
range = Abs(high(day) - low(day))
```

Here `high(day)` and `low(day)` are arrays that store the high and low trading values.

More Math Functions

In this section, you learn about the more basic mathematic intrinsic functions, starting with the square root function term, `Sqr()`.

Sqr()   **Function**

Purpose: Square root acquisition
Syntax:

```
solution = Sqr(expression)
```

The `Sqr()` function returns the square root of the logically reduced value of *expression*, within the variable *solution*.

Example

By now, you're familiar with the two-dimensional distance-finding formula:

```
d# = Sqr(((x2 - x1) ^ 2) + ((y2 - y1) ^ 2))
```

Visual Basic offers you four functions that relate to trigonometry: `Sin()`, `Cos()`, `Tan()`, and `Atn()`.

Sin(), Cos(), Tan(), and Atn()   **Functions**

Purpose: Trigonometric operations
Syntax:

```
solution = Sin(expression)
solution = Cos(expression)
solution = Tan(expression)
solution = Atn(expression)
```

These four functions return the sine, cosine, tangent, and arctangent, respectively, of the logically reduced value of *expression*. This value is returned in the variable *solution* as a unit of *radians*, which are divisions of a circular arc.

Example

Because people tend to think in terms of degrees, you must convert degrees to radians—which Visual Basic uses to determine sines and cosines—before you can evaluate the trigonometric expression. The following conversation with the Visual Basic CLI shows how you can make this conversion:

```
pi=3.1415927
deg = 90
?sin(deg*(pi/180))
  1
```

Finally, Visual Basic offers you two functions regarding logarithms: Log() and Exp().

Log() and Exp()   Functions

Purpose: Logarithmic operations
Syntax:

```
solution = Log(expression)
solution = Exp(expression)
```

The Log() function returns the natural logarithm of the logically reduced value of *expression*, within the variable *solution*. Likewise, the function Exp() returns the base of natural logarithm *e* raised to the power of the logically reduced value of *expression*, within the variable *solution*.

Example

You can determine the base 10 logarithm for a value (in other words, answer the question, "10 raised to what power equals this value?") by dividing the natural logarithm of 10 by the natural logarithm of the value in question, using the following function procedure:

```
Function Base10Log (value As Double)
Base10Log(value) = Log(value) / Log(10)
End Function
```

Summary

Using Abs(), you can obtain the absolute value of an expression; likewise, using Sgn(), you can obtain the sign of that expression. To obtain the square root of an expression, you use Sqr(). Visual Basic's trigonometric functions are Sin(), Cos(),

Tan(), and Atn(). To find the natural logarithm of an expression, you use Log().
Likewise, you can obtain the number to which natural logarithmic base *e* is raised
to equal an expression's value by using Exp().

Review Questions

Given x = 6 and y = 9, solve for the following:

1. Abs(x - y)

2. Sgn(x - y)

3. Sgn(Abs(x - y))

CHAPTER 36

String Functions

In this chapter, you study how Visual Basic terms fashioned to resemble arithmetic functions actually operate on the contents of alphanumeric strings or string variables. You use Visual Basic string functions, for instance, to alter or adjust the contents of strings so that they can be displayed better or stored within a record, or so that you can extract certain fragments of information from that record.

When a function operates on a value stored within a variable, the contents of that variable are represented in a reserved region of the computer's memory. The location of this region may change from time to time. Microsoft Windows must find the most convenient location for this region for the present time, with regard to such factors as how many other applications are inhabiting the environment and how much data memory these applications require to operate.

When a function operates on the alphanumeric contents of a string variable, those contents are represented as a reserved region of the computer's memory. As you learned in previous chapters, each character of a string is represented as a pattern of bits. The code for this pattern is ASCII. ASCII is a more logical pattern than, for instance, Morse code. It is more logical because the equivalent code number for any given character can easily be determined arithmetically using binary logic rather than arbitrary guesswork.

Each character of an alphanumeric string is stored within one byte. Each byte of a string generally is stored in memory beside the other, in sequence. The region of memory containing the string has left and right bounds, which the Visual Basic interpreter can manipulate to some degree. You may remember that variable values with different types (integer, double-precision floating-point, and so on) are stored within regions of memory with differing bounds. In other words, a double-precision value can be stored within eight bytes, whereas an integer can be stored within two. To convert a double-precision value to an integer, from the interpreter's point of view, is a process of moving the bounds and repositioning the value within those bounds, after shaving away the bytes that contain the fractional portion of the value. Likewise, shaving away the trailing spaces from a string such as

```
"Sheffield[space][space][space][space][space]"
```

is accomplished by the interpreter's moving the bounds for the stored element of data. Thus, the mechanisms for storing values and storing textual contents do not actually differ much from each other.

The difference in the way a string is contained from the way a value is contained is that you have more control over the byte containment process with respect to strings. When you informally declare a variable as equaling a value, as in pi = 3.1415927, you create a four-byte containment region. You can make it an eight-byte region by converting the value to double-precision using CDbl(), but there is not much point in doing so unless you add a more detailed fraction to the value. When you informally declare a string variable as containing specific contents, as in ship$ = "Sheffield", you create a nine-byte containment region. To make it into a 14-byte region, you can write an equation such as

```
ship$ = ship$ + "[space][space][space][space][space]"
```

Likewise, you can change the upper bounds of the string by adding text to the beginning, as in ship$ = "HMS[space]" + ship$. (Note that the term [space] here substitutes for one character.)

Now you have an 18-byte region, although at first the trailing spaces may not appear to be of much use. However, suppose that you're storing data to disk in the form of records containing vital information about, for instance, British Naval vessels of the Falklands War. A record in a random-access file is defined to be a precise number of characters long. Somewhere within each record is a specific 18-character region containing the name of a vessel. If the name of the vessel contains fewer characters than the name of the region, the trailing spaces are necessary to separate the vessel's datum (item of data) from the next item in the record. This way, the name of the ship's captain doesn't bleed into the name of the vessel.

The type of control you have over the string containment process can at first be likened to the type of control a person has over the contents of the IRS Form 1040 each April. When you realize that there is logic behind the mechanism, however, you can more easily supply the logic for that mechanism. Therefore, once you have determined that the storage mechanism for string variables involves code, you can better understand the logic behind manipulating those codes. A coded value from 0 to 255 is stored within each byte of a string. Suppose you were to treat this value as a value by encoding vital information in sequence as characters and storing that data as a string rather than as an integer or, more wastefully yet, as a single-precision variable.

> **Tip:** To save memory, store some numbers as strings. If three low-value numbers are used to describe the state of some operation within the program, you can give the values for each state a character code. The characters can then be concatenated (joined) and stored as a single string—as in `status$ = fuel$ + coolant$ + battery$`. What might have required six (or, informally declared, 12) bytes to represent now takes only three.

For the preceding tip, you must program the mechanism for storing the code as a procedure. If you use this mechanism for encoding an entire array of thousands of items, the memory you save may begin to be measured in kilobytes.

Perhaps the most important function relating to controlling a string variable in this manner is the `Len()` function.

Len()   Function

Purpose: String length acquisition
Syntax:

```
value% = Len(string_exp$)
```

In this syntax, *string_exp$* is any expression joining one or more strings of alphanumeric text.

The `Len()` function returns the number of characters stored within the expressed string, in the numeric variable *value%*.

Example

Here's the `Len()` function at work, as demonstrated through a conversation with the Visual Basic Debug window CLI:

```
ship$="Sheffield"
?len(ship$)
 9
```

The function simply counts the number of characters in the string.

Naturally, because `Len()` is a function like any other intrinsic Visual Basic function, its result can be assigned to a variable, as shown by the following:

```
ship$="Sheffield"
ln=len(ship$)
?ln
 9
```

Example

To *pad* a string is to fill it at the end with spaces or null characters to make it fit a given storage space.

Suppose that a string array variable nam$() contains a list of surnames. The string space allocated for each datum in the array is only as long as the name contained within the string. The name *Enrik* is stored within a five-character string, for instance, whereas *Magnusson* is stored within a nine-character string. A record stored to disk contains a 25-character field for surnames called n$(), regardless of how long each surname is. When the length of each surname is less than 25, the right side of the string is to be padded with space characters. Here's a routine that supplies the padding:

```
For nam% = 1 to UBound(name$, 1)
    ln% = Len(name$(nam%))
    pad% = 25 - ln%
    n$(nam%) = name$(nam%) + Space$(pad%)
Next nam%
```

Here's the preceding procedure translated into pseudocode:

*Start counting from 1 to the number of names
 in the array.
   Assign the length of the name currently
   counted to this variable.
   Subtract this length from 25.
   Place this many spaces at the end of the name
   before storing it.
Count the next name.*

The loop clause uses the variable nam% to keep count as iterations proceed from 1 to the number of items in the array nam$(), as determined by the function UBound(). The length of each name in the array is found by the Len() function on the second line. This length is subtracted from 25—the length of each field to be stored to disk—to derive the number of spaces to be added to the end of the nam$(nam%) before it is added to n$(nam%). The Space$() function adds a specific number of spaces to the end of nam$(nam%).

Space$()   **Function**

Purpose: Multiple space invocation
Syntax:

```
string$ = Space$(number%)
```

The Space$ function returns a series of *number%* space characters, within string variable *string$*.

The Len() function is best used when invoked in a procedure that contains the other major string functions in the Visual Basic vocabulary.

Left$() and Right$()   Functions

Purpose: String segment portioning
Syntax:

```
substring$ = Left$(string$, number%)
substring$ = Right$(string$, number%)
```

The Left$() function extracts the first *number%* characters in sequence from the larger string *string$* and assigns those characters as contents of the smaller string variable *substring$*. Likewise, the Right$() function extracts the last *number%* characters of a string in sequence from the larger string *string$* and assigns those characters as contents of the smaller string variable *substring$*. In both functions, if *number%* is larger than the length of *string$*, the entirety of *string$* is returned in *substring$* without any characters added to either side of the string.

Example

Here you can see the Right$() function at work with the aid of the Visual Basic CLI:

```
ship$="Sheffield"
?right$(ship$,5)
field
```

Here, the Right$() function counts the first five characters from the right of ship$ toward the left and extracts those characters; however, the returned extracted characters are displayed from left to right and not backward, as in *dleif*.

It's important to note that you can substitute the .Text property of a text box and the .Caption property of a label or other graphic object that uses labels for *string_exp$* in any of these functions. The Visual Basic interpreter treats the stated properties of graphic objects as if they were string variables, for the sake of these functions.

Example

The previously introduced procedure did not consider cases in which a person's surname is longer than 25 characters. Certainly, the 25-character name is a rare case;

but if the surname exceeds 25 characters, you must trim the longer name down to the first 25 characters. Here's how to determine and execute the trimming:

```
For nam% = 1 to UBound(nam$, 1)
    ln% = Len(nam$(nam%))
    If ln% <= 25 Then
        pad% = 25 - ln%
        n$(nam%) = nam$(nam%) + Space$(pad%)
    Else
        n$(nam%) = Left$(nam$(nam%), 25)
    End If
Next nam%
```

An If-Then-Else clause divides the naming operations into a true side and a false side. The true side is executed when the length of nam$(nam%) is less than or equal to 25; the false side is executed when the surname is too long to fit in the record. In such a case, the function Left$() extracts the leftmost 25 characters from nam$(nam%) and places them within n$(nam%). (Note that the word *name* is not used as a variable in these procedures because Name is a reserved keyword in Visual Basic.)

When you use the preceding procedure to store people's names to disk as a table, the padding of spaces attached to the names that are shorter than 25 letters allows each name to fit neatly into the slot or field created for each name. The procedure that retrieves these names knows where to look to retrieve a particular name in the sequence because each stored field has a fixed beginning and ending byte location, regardless of the size of the data stored within the field. When the data is retrieved, however, you must strip the trailing spaces from each name so that you don't have to mail envelopes with names that appear like the following:

```
Lester          C. Thurow
Robert          B. Reich
Milton          Friedman
```

Thankfully, Visual Basic gives you functions for automatically removing whatever spaces with which you may have padded each name, namely, the LTrim$() and RTrim$() functions.

LTrim$() and RTrim$()   **Functions**

Purpose: Space trimming
Syntax:

```
string$ = LTrim$(string_exp$)
string$ = RTrim$(string_exp$)
```

In this syntax, *string_exp$* is any logical expression containing one or more concatenated strings or string variables.

The LTrim$() function removes all spaces from the left side of the expressed string. Likewise, the RTrim$() function removes all spaces from the right side of the expressed string.

Example

After you retrieve the padded names you stored to disk earlier, you can use RTrim$() to remove any trailing spaces from each name, as follows:

```
For nam% = 1 to UBound(n$, 1)
    nam$(nam%) = RTrim$(n$(nam%))
Next nam%
```

Notice that you don't have to use any arithmetic here to remove the spaces from the end of the name. The Visual Basic interpreter knows, when given the directive by RTrim$(), to search for any trailing spaces and purge them.

You use the LSet and RSet pair of statements to justify text within strings that contain spaces as padding so that the padding can be bunched up on one side of the strings or the other.

LSet and RSet   Statements

Purpose: Content justification
Syntax:

```
LSet field$ = entry$
RSet field$ = entry$
```

The LSet and RSet statements assign the textual contents already assigned to *entry$* to a string full of spaces: *field$*. The length of *field$* is not changed; instead, spaces within *field$* are replaced by the contents of *entry$*. The LSet statement enters *entry$* within *field$* starting at the leftmost character of *field$*, thus creating a left-justified field. Likewise, the RSet statement enters *entry$* within *field$* starting at the rightmost character of *field$*, creating a right-justified field. If *entry$* contains more characters than *field$* contains, only the leftmost characters of *entry$* appear in *field$* for both statements. The length of *field$* remains the same.

The *String$()*, *LCase$()*, and *UCase$()* Functions

Earlier in this chapter, you learned about Space$() as a function for placing a certain number of spaces into a string variable, generally as padding. A related function, derived from earlier in BASIC's history, is String$().

String$()   Function

Purpose: Multiple character invocation
Syntax 1:

```
word$ = String$(number%, char$)
```

Syntax 2:

```
word$ = String$(number%, ascii_char%)
```

The String$() function issues a designated *number%* of repeated characters as the string variable *word$*. Under Syntax 1, the single character to be repeated is expressed as *char$*, between quotation marks. Under Syntax 2, the single character to be repeated is expressed as the ASCII code equivalent of the character that is expressed as *ascii_char%*.

Example

Assume that you're designing a printout for a price sheet for your retail store. Your price sheet will show retail prices line by line for items you sell. After the name of each item, you want a series of asterisks linking the item to its price. You don't know in advance how long the item name might be, nor how many characters constitute the price. Here's a routine that determines how many asterisks you need to use between the item name and its price, for a line that is 66 characters long:

```
For nam% = 1 To UBound(item$, 1)
    li% = Len(item$(nam%))
    prce$(nam%) = "$" + Str$(price(nam%))
    lp% = Len(prce$(nam%))
    numast = 66 - li% - lp%
    PriceList.Print item$(nam%); String$(numast, "*");
    ➥prce$(nam%)
Next nam%
```

Following is pseudocode for this procedure:

> *Count from the first to the last item*
> *in the array.*
>> *Acquire the length of the current item*
>> *in characters.*
>> *Make the price string equal to "$" joined*
>> *with the alphanumeric form of the price*
>> *of the current item.*
>> *Acquire the length of this new price string.*
>> *The number of asterisks between these two*
>> *strings will be 66 minus the length of*
>> *both strings.*
>> *Print to the price list the current item's*
>> *name, the number of asterisks required, and*
>> *the current price.*
> *Count the next item.*

The lengths of the item name string and price string are assigned to variables `li%` and `lp%`, respectively. Variable `prce$` is created here by concatenating a dollar sign with the string-converted form of the price value. Visual Basic requires the names of string variables to be different from the names of value variables, so the *i* was removed from *price* in `prce$`. Naturally, the string must be created before its length is obtained. You use variable `numast` to determine the number of asterisks necessary to fill the space between the item name and the price so that both appear flush left and right on the price list. The `.Print` method then prints three items in succession, the second being a string of asterisks formed by the function `String$(numast, "*")`.

`String$()` is one example of what in old BASIC was called a *command function,* the term for a function that performs the role of a command. The interpreter is told to produce a row of characters of a specified type. Two similar functions that qualify as command functions by the old definition are `LCase$()` and `UCase$()`.

LCase$() and UCase$()   **Functions**

Purpose: String case conversion
Syntax:

```
string$ = LCase$(string_exp$)
string$ = UCase$(string_exp$)
```

The `LCase$()` function converts all alphabetic characters appearing within the expressed string or string concatenation *string_exp$* to lowercase letters. Likewise, the `UCase$()` function converts all alphabetic characters appearing within the expressed string or string concatenation *string_exp$* to uppercase letters.

Example

A conversation with the Visual Basic CLI demonstrates the use of both case-conversion functions:

```
ship$="Sheffield"
ship$=Ucase$(ship$)
?ship$
SHEFFIELD
ship$=Lcase$(ship$)
?ship$
sheffield
```

In the Midst of Strings

Up to now, you've been working with functions that concentrate on either the left or right side of the string, or the whole string. At some point in your programming career, you might need to know whether the user entered a particular string of characters someplace within the middle of a large text box. The InStr() function determines not only whether that text was entered, but where it appears.

InStr()   Function

Purpose: String clip search
Syntax:

```
position& = InStr([first_char&, ]string_exp1$,
➥string_exp2$[, compare%])
```

The InStr() function initiates a search for the string or string concatenation expressed by *string_exp2$*, within the larger *string_exp1$*. The length of *string_exp2$* must be less than 65,536 characters. If the search turns up a match, the number of the character in the larger string where the first character of the smaller string appears is returned as long integer variable *position&*. The first character of the larger string is considered character number 1. If the smaller string does not appear exactly within the larger string, or if *string_exp2$* is larger than *string_exp1$*, the function returns a null value (0).

If the long integer *first_char&* is passed as a parameter, the search begins with that character position of the larger string. The value of *first_char&* can be no larger than 65,535. The value of *compare%*, when passed as a parameter, specifies whether the textual comparison is case sensitive. A parameter of 0 specifies case sensitivity, so upper- and lowercase letters are distinguished from one another. A parameter of 1 specifies case insensitivity. If *compare%* is not expressed, text comparison uses either a case-sensitive method or whatever method has been specified by the Option Compare statement.

> **Note:** Even though *first_char&* is a four-byte long integer, the Visual Basic interpreter can only search a string that has fewer than 65,536 characters. It might seem that, because 65,536 characters require only two bytes for representation, this isn't the case; Visual Basic interprets two-byte integer values using one extra sign bit for positive and negative values. Thus, with two bytes, Visual Basic can count only from –32,768 to 32,767. To count higher, Visual Basic requires the next class of variable, a four-byte integer.

Example

As an example of the InStr() function, suppose that you have an application that manages text, and one of the procedures in your general module is a textual search-and-replace operation. An object variable Textor is declared to refer to whatever control in your main form contains the main body of text. When the user selects the text search function from the application's main menu, a dialog box pops up requesting the text to be searched for within the body of a document whose object variable is called Document, as well as the text with which it is to be replaced. This dialog panel has a .Name of Replacer. Its _Click event procedure can be made to invoke the search-and-replace procedure, which is written as follows:

```
Sub SrchRplc (Document As Control)
srch$ = SearchText.Text
rplc$ = ReplaceText.Text
If Len(srch$) = 0 Or Len(rplc$) = 0 Then
    Replacer.Hide
    Exit Sub
End If
trgt$ = Document.Text
pos = InStr(trgt$, srch$)
If pos = 0 Then
    MsgBox "Text not found.", 0, ""
    Exit Sub
End If
Document.SelStart = pos - 1
Document.SelLength = Len(srch$)
Document.SelText = rplc$
Replacer.Hide
End Sub
```

Following is pseudocode for this procedure:

Search-and-replace procedure:
Acquire the text to search for from a text box in the
dialog panel.
Acquire the text it is to be replaced with from the
other text box.
If the length of either specimen of text is 0, then
This must be a "pocket cancel," so take this
dialog box off the screen, and
Exit this procedure.
End of condition.
Take the text from the document.
Find the place where the search text begins within
the target text.
If the search text is not there, then
Notify the user.
Get out of this procedure.
End of condition.
Otherwise, start to indicate the beginning of the
search text in the document.
Extend the selector for the length of the search text.
Replace the selected text with the replacement string.
Remove this dialog panel from the screen.
End of procedure.

This procedure first assigns the text being searched for to the variable srch$. If the user did not type anything into this box (If Len(srch$) = 0), there's no point in searching for nothing. The dialog box is hidden, and the procedure is exited.

For the sake of this example, the entire document is assigned to variable trgt$. Now the crucial InStr() function is invoked, searching for the first instance of srch$ within trgt$, starting with character number 1 and proceeding one character at a time. Variable pos should contain the location of the first character where srch$ was located within trgt$; but if pos = 0, evidently the search string doesn't exist within the target, and a message box is displayed to that effect.

When the procedure finds a match for srch$ within trgt$, the found text is selected automatically as a property .SelText of the text box, and it is replaced by making that property equal to the replacement string rplc$. The text indication properties are covered in depth in Chapter 40, "Textual Properties."

This example demonstrates how search-and-replace functions work when you know precisely what text you're searching for. Assume, however, that you need a procedure that searches for an element of text based on its construction rather than its contents. Suppose that you're looking for a ZIP code—not a specific one, just any ZIP code. You know a ZIP code is at least five digits appearing next to one another. You can't use InStr() to search for unknown text, so you need the help of the Mid$() function.

Mid$()   Function

Purpose: String portion acquisition
Syntax:

> *substring$* = Mid$(*string$*, *start_pos&*, *number%*)

The Mid$() function extracts a *number%* of characters from a string in sequence from the larger string *string$*, starting at character position *start_pos&* counting from the left of *string$*. The extracted characters then are assigned to the smaller string variable *substring$*.

Example

The following procedure looks for anything resembling a ZIP code:

```
Sub ZipFind (Document As Control)
total = Len(Document.Text)
trgt$ = Document.Text
For pos = 1 To total - 4
    If Mid$(trgt$, pos, 1) > Chr$(48) And Mid$(trgt$, pos, 1)
    ➥< Chr$(57) Then
        zipfind = zipfind + 1
        If zipfind = 5 Then
            Document.SelStart = pos - 5
            Document.SelLength = 5
            zp$ = Document.SelText
            MsgBox "Possible ZIP code " + zp$ +
            ➥" found at position " + Str$(pos - 5), 0, ""
        End If
    Else
        zipfind = 0
    End If
Next pos
End Sub
```

Pseudocode for the this procedure is as follows:

ZIP code-finding procedure:
Find the length of the entire document.
Call the text of this document the target string.
Count from the first to the fourth from the last
 character in the document.
 If the character at this position is a digit, then
 Add one to the potentiality that this is a
 ZIP code.
 If this potentiality equals five digits, then
 Indicate the text at this point.
 Indicate five characters from this point.
 Place the indicated text in a string
 variable.
 Tell the user this may be a ZIP code, and
 where it was found.
 End of condition.
 Otherwise,
 Strike any hope of this being a ZIP code.
 End of condition.
Count the next character.
End of procedure.

This procedure belongs to the main form, not to a dialog box. First, the length of the text typed into Document is obtained and assigned to variable total. The text itself is assigned to trgt$. The loop clause keeps a count of characters called pos, starting with the first character and ending with the fifth from the end—because ZIP codes are five characters long. Within the loop clause is a conditional clause using Mid$(), which tests to see if the specified single character Mid$(trgt$, pos, 1) has an ASCII value between 48 and 57—which makes that character a digit. If it is indeed a digit, one is added to an independent counter variable zipfind.

When zipfind = 5, the procedure has found five digits in a row. The digits then are extracted from behind the current count position pos - 5 and displayed in an appropriate message box. If the procedure does not find enough digits in sequence, zipfind is reset to 0.

In Visual Basic, you also can use Mid$ as a statement, which in effect reverses the order of the transaction in the Mid$() function.

Mid$ **Statement**

Purpose: String portion insertion
Syntax:

```
Mid$(string$, start_pos&[, number&]) = substring$
```

The `Mid$` statement replaces the text currently assigned to *string$*, starting at cursor position *start_pos&* counting from the left, with the text contained within *substring$*. If *number&* is expressed, that number of characters is removed from *string$* and replaced with the first *number&* characters from the left of *substring$*.

As previously mentioned, you use the `Option Compare` statement to specify the text comparison method for a module.

Option Compare   **Statement**

Purpose: Text comparison process restrictions
Syntax:

```
Option Compare {Binary ¦ Text}
```

You use the `Option Compare` statement within the *declarations section* of a module to specify the type of textual comparison to be used by the instructions within that module. The instruction `Option Compare Binary` compares characters with one another for numerical value; thus, the comparison is case sensitive. The instruction `Option Compare Text`, in contrast, compares characters for textual content only; thus, the comparison is case insensitive. When this statement is omitted, the interpreter uses binary-mode comparisons.

Summary

A string variable is stored in memory with each byte representing a character of the string. Unlike the storage techniques given a numeral value, string contents in memory are given left and right bounds that you can manipulate by changing the contents of the string. Using the `Len()` function, you can find the length of a string in memory.

To create a sequence of spaces, you use the command function `Space$()`. Similarly, you can create a sequence of any single character using `String$()`. To trim leading and trailing spaces from a string, you use the `LTrim$()` and `RTrim$()` functions, respectively. You also can enter a smaller string into a larger string full of spaces. You can justify that larger string's contents using the `LSet` and `RSet` statements. Also, you can convert any string's alphabetic characters to upper- or lowercase using `UCase$()` and `LCase$()`, respectively.

Using `Left$()` and `Right$()`, respectively, you can extract and assign the leftmost and rightmost portions of any string to another string variable. Similarly, you can extract and assign several characters from the middle of any string to another string variable using the `Mid$()` function. You also can replace some characters within the middle of any string with a sequence of characters from another string by using the `Mid$` statement. Using the `InStr()` function, you can obtain the character position of the first instance of a smaller string within a larger string.

Review Questions

Assume that `srch$` is assigned the following string contents. Without using your computer, determine the result of the following functions:

```
When in the course of human events
```

1. `Left$(srch$, 4)`

2. `Right$(srch$, 7)`

3. `Mid$(srch$, 4, 1)`

4. `Mid$(srch$, 9, 4)`

Suppose that you invoke the following instruction:

```
Mid$(srch$, 6) = "in, of, and around"
```

5. What are the current contents of `srch$`?

CHAPTER 37

Time and Date

In this chapter, you briefly tour the timekeeping system of Microsoft Windows and see how Visual Basic uses it. This chapter is not a discussion of the timer control, which was introduced in Chapter 27, "The Timer." Instead, this chapter covers the actual system clock of your computer, the timekeeping resources of the Windows environment, and the different time formats used by Windows and Visual Basic.

Your computer system maintains a constantly running clock, and Microsoft Windows constantly reinterprets the value held in that clock. The result is a time and date that are stored as a large double-precision number. This number is updated with each passing millisecond. This data is supplied in turn to Visual Basic, where it can be referenced in a program as though the time and date were global variables.

The most important time-related internal variable Visual Basic uses is called Now, which is a double-precision, floating-point value. If you see this value written out, it is always fractional. The numbers to the left of this value's decimal point represent the number of days that have passed since 31 December, 1899. The numbers to the right of the decimal point represent the number of milliseconds that have ticked off since midnight on this day. The date and time presented together in this format can be reinterpreted by Visual Basic later as a *signature* for the date and time that have just passed.

The *time signature* is the double-precision value format maintained within the variant *Now*.

Now appears to be a simple written date and time. If you ask the Debug window to Print Now, it responds with something like 3/10/94 04:48:34 AM because the current value of Now is stored in an internal Variant variable; you don't have to declare this variable As Variant for Now to be interpreted as one. Among variants, Now is considered to have a variant type (determined using the VarType() function) of 7, which is a numeral reserved for values that can be translated into time and date formats. The format of Now is called a *time signature* format; the real value of Now represents the fundamental time variable of the entire Visual Basic environment.

The functions that extract date-related information from the Now signature variable, as well as other variants, are Day(), Weekday(), Month(), and Year().

Day(), Weekday(), Month(), and Year()   **Functions**

Purpose: Date component representation
Syntax:

```
variable% = Day(signature)
variable% = Weekday(signature)
variable% = Month(signature)
variable% = Year(signature)
```

Each function in this set accepts a double-precision value as its parameter, with the format of numbers in this value matching that of the signature format used by the internal variable Now. The function Day() returns the day of the month for the specified date. Likewise, Month() returns the month of the year, and Year() returns the current year. Weekday() returns the day number of the week, where 1 is Sunday.

In the same vein as the date-related functions are the functions that extract time-related information from a signature variable: Hour(), Minute(), and Second().

Hour(), Minute(), and Second()   **Functions**

Purpose: Time component representation
Syntax:

```
variable% = Hour(signature)
variable% = Minute(signature)
variable% = Second(signature)
```

Each function in this set accepts a double-precision value as its parameter, with the format of numbers in this value matching the signature format used by the internal variable Now. The function Hour() returns the hour for the specified time in 24-hour format. Likewise, Minute() returns the minute for the specified time, and Second() returns the second for that time.

Example

This part of the manuscript was written February 1, 1994. The following dialog took place with the Visual Basic Debug window on that day. Responses from the CLI are in boldface.

```
?day(now)
 1
?month(now)
 2
?year(now)
 1994
?now
2/1/94 09:32:52 PM
c#=now
?c#
34366.8973842593
```

Notice how difficult it would be to extract *2/1/94* mentally from the number *34366*. Notice also that the Visual Basic interpreter now treats the Now variable like a variant and automatically gives it formatting that makes it legible. To see what Now really looks like, you must first assign its value to a double-precision variable—in this example, c#.

Example

Following is more of the dialog presented in the preceding example, in which the time-related functions are invoked:

```
?hour(now)
 9
?minute(now)
 32
?second(now)
 52
```

For the cases you inevitably face in which you try to decipher such figures as the date of 40 days before D day or the date of three weeks after Thanksgiving or two hours and 15 minutes following the scheduled ETA, the Visual Basic interpreter provides two date and time arithmetic functions: DateSerial() and TimeSerial().

DateSerial() and TimeSerial()   **Functions**

Purpose: Date/time arithmetic
Syntax:

```
variant7 = DateSerial(year, month, day)
variant7 = TimeSerial(hour, minute, second)
```

The DateSerial() function evaluates the three parameters it is given, logically reduces each of them in conjunction with one another, and returns a date within a type 7 (date) variant variable. Similarly, TimeSerial() evaluates the three parameters passed to it, logically reduces them with comparison to one another, and returns a time within a type 7 variant variable. In this manner, you can determine relative dates and times using arithmetic.

Example

When they're joined with one another, the results of both DateSerial() and TimeSerial() functions jointly make up a date and time in the same reformatted style given to the signature variable Now. Thus, the following equation assigns to the variable once a value representing the time of the previous discussion with the Visual Basic Debug window CLI:

```
once = DateSerial(1994, 2, 1) + TimeSerial(4, 51, 38)
```

Because once has not been formally declared, it too is a variant like Now. You can formally declare once As Variant or As Double if you prefer once to reflect the "raw" native value of a time signature.

Example

Suppose that you need to know what date it will be 60 days from a certain date. The following discussion with the Visual Basic CLI poses this question:

```
?dateserial(1994,2,1)+dateserial(0,0,60)
3/3/94
```

Whereas Now deals with milliseconds, the internal variable *Timer* deals with hundredths of a second.

Notice that in the serial form of the date added to "today's" date, values of zero are assigned to the day and month parameters. These zeros tell the interpreter that you're not dealing with how many years and months have passed, just days. The 60 as the final parameter adds 60 days to the date represented by DateSerial(1994,2,1).

Another internal variable that is similar to Now—although it does not deal with the Visual Basic time signature—is the internal variable Timer. This counter is set continually by the interpreter to the number of seconds that have elapsed since midnight, according to the time kept internally by the computer. This number is expressed as a single-precision, floating-point value, estimated to 1/100 of a second.

Example

You can use Timer in much the same way you use Now, in timing situations in which fractions of a second are not critical. The following example shows how you can determine how many seconds elapsed during the execution of a routine:

```
StartTime = Timer
 .
 .
 .
EndTime = Timer
Elapsed = EndTime - StartTime
e$ = "Total elapsed time: " + Elapsed
TimeDisplay.Text = e$
```

The ellipses in this example substitute for the routine being timed. Notice how both variables StartTime and EndTime are set to the value of the same internal variable Timer. The two variables have different values, however, because the Visual Basic interpreter automatically updates Timer to reflect the number of seconds that have elapsed since 12:00 a.m. With StartTime subtracted from EndTime, the result is a single-precision value denoting the number of seconds elapsed between the execution of the first assignment instruction and the execution of the second one.

Note: In Chapter 27, "The Timer," you experiment with the timer control, which is available from the Visual Basic toolbox. The Timer internal variable, despite its name, has nothing to do with this control.

Times and Dates as Text

The Visual Basic interpreter maintains two internal string variables for printing the current date and time: Date$ and Time$. The internal variable Date$ is always 10 characters long and is continually maintained automatically so that its contents always reflect the current system date. This date is returned in the format *mm-dd-yyyy*. Likewise, Time$ always reflects the current system time, which is returned in the format *hh:mm:ss*.

Example

You can change the contents of `Date$` and `Time$` (unlike `Now`) by directly assigning them new strings that are interpretable as valid dates and times, respectively. As a result, you manually reset the system date and time. Here's how you can reset them from the Debug window CLI:

```
date$="9/30/91"
time$="6:33:45"
```

> **Note:** You can use slash marks in the `Date$` assignment in place of dashes; Visual Basic accepts either. Also, you can abbreviate the current year to the final two digits.

The reverse of these functions is to take string data in the proper formats and convert the data to signature value format, which is the purpose of the `DateValue()` and `TimeValue()` functions.

DateValue() and TimeValue()   Functions

Purpose: Date/time numeralization
Syntax:

```
variant7 = DateValue(Date$)
variant7 = TimeValue(Time$)
```

The function `DateValue()` accepts a validly interpretable date string and converts it to a variant type 7 date. These contents follow the visible time signature format used by the internal variable `Now`. It represents the number of days that have passed since 30 December, 1899. Acceptable date formats are *dd-mm-yyyy*, *dd-mm-yy*, *dd/mm/yyyy*, and *dd/mm/yy*. The function `TimeValue()` converts a validly interpretable time string to a variant type 7 date. The format of this value also follows the visible format used by `Now`.

Example

Suppose that you've loaded data into memory from two files. Their headers have different dates, and you need to know the number of days between the save dates of these files. The headers are in string format, although their date contents follow one of the four formats supported by Visual Basic. You can use the following function procedure to find the number of days between save dates:

```
Function diff_dates (dat1$, dat2$)
dv1 = DateValue(dat1$)
dv2 = DateValue(dat2$)
diff_dates = dv2 - dv1
End Function
```

Here's this procedure written in pseudocode:

Function for solving the difference between two dates:
  Solve for the value of date #1.
  Solve for the value of date #2.
  Subtract the date value of #1 from #2, leaving the
   number of days between the two dates.
End of function.

How Dated Are Your Variants?

Because date and time formats are *subtypes* of the umbrella category `Variant`, any double-precision value in the time signature format cannot be assigned to a variant and suddenly become a date and time. To tell a variant that its current value should be treated as a date (`VarType 7`) requires the use of a specific conversion function: `CVDate()`.

CVDate()   **Function**

Purpose: Variant conversion to date
Syntax:

```
signature = CVDate(value#)
```

The `CVDate()` function returns a converted date/time value using the `value#` parameter, within the type 7 variant `signature`. The variable type of `value#` must be a numeric type, although it can be any numeric type.

If you're unsure whether a particular value can be interpreted legally as a date using the format maintained by `VarType 7`, the `IsDate()` function is available to you.

IsDate()   Function

Purpose: Time signature format determination
Syntax:

```
boolean% = IsDate(parameter)
```

The IsDate() function returns a True/False value to variable *boolean%*, reflecting whether the specified *parameter* can be interpreted legally as a VarType 7 date. A string or value with such a format can be assigned directly to an undeclared variable, and the interpreter responds by giving the variant type 7 automatically. In this instance, *parameter* can be either a numeric value or a string; the function is incapable of generating errors based on this parameter type. Straight numeral values, however, most likely return a value of False.

Summary

The Visual Basic interpreter maintains one key internal variable: Now. Now uses the time signature format to represent a date and time. This format is stored within a variant with the reserved type 7. You can use other Visual Basic functions to extract date and time interval information from this key variable or from any other variable with the same format. The internal variable Timer returns the number of seconds elapsed since midnight.

You can use the DateSerial() and TimeSerial() functions in arithmetic to add dates and times to or subtract them from other dates and times. You also can use the DateValue() and TimeValue() functions to convert legitimate values into type 7 variants. One variant from each of the functions can be joined to form a time signature. The CVDate() function converts a value directly into a time signature format. Finally, you can use the IsDate() function to check whether a string or variant value can be interpreted as a legitimate date/time combination using the time signature format.

Review Questions

From the following sets of input parameters for the functions discussed in this chapter, determine which functions accept parameters in each format.

1. 1992, 2, 9

2. 15, 12, 49

3. 15:12:49

4. Time$

CHAPTER 38

The Random Number Generator

In this chapter, you experiment with one of the most intriguing features of this or any other high-level programming language, the feature that appears to act on its own: the interpreter's generator for random numbers. As a Visual Basic programmer, you use randomization to set up conditions for experiments and to create the random element for tests, simulations, and games.

After reading about the logical processes of computing thus far in this book, you might think that no process within a computer could possibly take the random element into account. In fact, no computer—or interpreter or compiler, for that matter—contains a true random number generator. Rather than skip to the next chapter, however, you should note that a logical function in Visual Basic appears to generate random numbers with no specific inputs or parameters passed to it: the Rnd() function, which is one of the oldest functions in the BASIC language.

Rnd()   **Function**

Purpose: Random number generation
Syntax:

    number# = Rnd[(process#)]

In this syntax, *process#* is any double-precision floating-point number, the sign of which, when *process#* is expressed, is crucial to the generation process.

The Rnd() function returns what appears to be a random double-precision floating-point number between 0 and 1. The value of *process#* affects the random number generation process. A particular "random" number is generated for each *process#* value passed to the function, if *process#* < 0. A particular sequence of random numbers might exist in an application for each number generation, in which case the same sequence is generated each time the application is executed. The next number in this sequence can be generated if *process#* > 0 or if *process#* is omitted. The previous random number is regenerated if *process#* = 0.

The random number generation process in Visual Basic is actually dependent on the current value yielded by the Timer function. The result is a sequence of numbers that appear to be random. After running applications that use random numbers repeatedly, however, you might notice that the same sequence of randomization appears each time. Getting the same "random" numbers might get frustrating for the programmer trying to maintain a constant level of difficulty for a blackjack game.

This repeated-sequence problem is solved easily through the invocation of the `Randomize` statement.

Randomize   Statement

Purpose: Random generator reseeding
Syntax:

```
Randomize[(seed%)]
```

The `Randomize` statement *reseeds* the random number generator for an application. In other words, it changes some of the constants in the random generation algorithm so that a different sequence of random numbers can be generated, thus eliminating the possibility of number prediction. If *seed%* is expressed, a particular sequence of random numbers referred to by *seed%* is initiated. If *seed%* is omitted, a "random" seed is initiated, the choice of which seed value is based on the current state of the random number generator itself.

Example

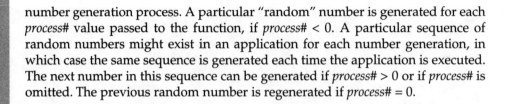
You can see that the generator really does appear to pick numbers out of a hat, as demonstrated by the following conversation with the CLI appearing in the Visual Basic Debug window. Responses appear in boldface.

```
?rnd(1)
 .7055475
?rnd(1)
 .533424
?rnd(1)
  .5795186

?rnd(1)
 .2895625
?rnd(1)
 .301948
```

Each time the Rnd() function is invoked, a different response is generated. It is possible, however, that a program which invoked the random number generator five times would, throughout several executions, generate the same *sequence* of "random" numbers each time, unless the Randomize statement appears somewhere toward the beginning of the program, perhaps in Sub Form_Load () or Sub Main ().

As a test, start Visual Basic, run the empty project, break it, and enter ?rnd(1) five times into the Debug window, without typing Randomize first. Your results should be exactly the same five values you see in the preceding example. Perhaps there is no clearer demonstration of the need to randomize the randomizer.

Example

The following function returns a random integer value between 0 and 15:

```
rnum = Int(Rnd * 15) + 1
```

The value returned by Rnd() (or Rnd without parentheses, if you prefer) is always between 0 and 1. Thus, if you multiply the value by 15, the result is always between 0 and 14. Making this result into an integer and adding 1 allows the interpreter to pick a number between 1 and 15.

Example

You can use a similar function to pick a capital letter between *A* and *Z*:

```
letr = Int(Rnd * 26) + 65
letr$ = Chr$(letr)
```

The ASCII code value for character *A* is 65. The 26 uppercase letters in the alphabet fall in the ASCII code from 65 to 90, in sequence. After you pick a number from 0 to 25, the result is added to 65 to obtain an uppercase letter from the ASCII code, which is assigned to string variable letr$.

Example

At some time, a game programmer uses the random number generator to shuffle cards. If you assume the standard deck contains 52 cards (54 if you count jokers), it is easy to pick a single card out of the deck using the function Int(Rnd * 52) + 1 (not counting card number 0). The shuffling process, however, from the point of view of the computer, picks 52 random cards from this deck successively. You can't say For card = 1 to 52 and have the randomizing process merely repeat itself because it's probable that the interpreter could pick the same card more than once. The shuffled deck can have only one instance of each card; each time that card is picked for the new deck, some indicator must remain to prevent the card from being picked again. Consider the following procedure:

```
Randomize
For plac = 1 To 52
choose:
    extract = Int(Rnd(1) * 52) + 1
    If slot(extract) = 1 Then GoTo choose
    card(plac) = extract
    slot(extract) = 1
Next plac
```

Here is this procedure translated into pseudocode:

Reseed the random number generator.
Start counting card places from 1 to 52.
   Pick a card between 1 and 52.
   If this number has been chosen before, then go back
   and pick another card.
   Otherwise, assign this card number to the deck.
   Record this card as having been chosen once.
Count the next card.

Here you assume that each card number is representative of a particular card; for instance, card number 1 can be the ace of spades.

Summary

Random number generation is accomplished in Visual Basic using the Rnd() function. A set sequence of random numbers exists virtually for each application, although you can replace that sequence with another sequence by using the Randomize statement. Each random number generated by the Visual Basic interpreter has a value between 0 and 1; this value can be multiplied and made into an integer, resulting in the appearance of the computer picking a whole number from a specified range.

Review Questions

1. In the expression Rnd(1) * 72, the function randomizes a number between 0 and what number?

2. Why are the parentheses in the Rnd() function optional?

3. Can the Randomize seed for the random number generator be a random number?

Part VII

Text

CHAPTER 39

Conventional Output

In this chapter, you examine the Visual Basic statements, functions, and properties that concern text production. In Visual Basic, the most well-known of BASIC instructions—PRINT—makes its appearance as the .Print method. Microsoft uses a character descriptor code among nearly all its Windows applications that describes for the application or interpreter the output format for an alphanumeric string. You study this code later in this chapter, and you also study some examples utilizing the code in .Print methods with the Format$() function.

.Print   Method

Purpose: Text display
Syntax:

```
[Object.]Print [expression1{;¦,} expression2{;¦,}
    . . . expressionn[{;¦,}]
```

in which each expression consists of any valid, logically interpretable mathematical or string expression.

The .Print method displays the logically reduced form of each expression in its expression list. If Object. is specified, the recipient of the printed text is either the stated graphic object, such as Form1, or an output device, such as Printer. If the interpreter allows Object. to be omitted, printing is directed to the form window to which the procedure containing the .Print method belongs. The recipient Object. cannot be omitted from the instruction if the .Print method appears in the context of a general module. If the recipient Object. belongs to a form other than the one containing the .Print method, the form name is specified before the object name, with both names separated from each other by a period.

A mathematical expression—in the case of an expression supplied as a parameter—is made up of one or more values or variables combined arithmetically using operator symbols such as + or function terms such as Int(). A string expression is made up of one or more elements of text, whether they are alphanumeric phrases, string variables, or string functions such as Right$(). Multiple-element string expressions can be concatenated using the + operator. Text that is to be printed literally must appear in double quotation marks, as in "Hello". You can print double quotation marks themselves by using the function Chr$(34), the function itself appearing outside any quotation marks. Likewise, you can express other special characters not appearing on the keyboard by using the Chr$() function.

The semicolon and comma as delimiters have specific uses with respect to the .Print method. Each expression in the list is separated from the others by one of these delimiters. If two expressions are separated from each other by a semicolon, the text of both expressions is printed next to each other (side by side). If two expressions are separated from each other by a comma, the interpreter inserts a tabulation character at the end of the first expression before printing the start of the second. A tabulation is equivalent to 14 *columns* or, to borrow a term from typography, 14 *ens*, in which an *en* is the average width of a letter in the currently chosen font.

The Visual Basic interpreter recognizes a virtual cursor for the graphic objects that receive text using the .Print method. This cursor's coordinate position is registered within properties of the graphic object, called .CurrentX and .CurrentY. Whenever a .Print method has completed execution, it by default leaves the virtual cursor at the beginning (by default, the left side) of the line immediately following the one just printed. If the .Print method is closed with a semicolon, the cursor position is set at the immediate end of the text just printed, without the interpreter executing a *carriage return* to the next line. If the .Print method is closed with a comma, the cursor is tabulated to the next 14-column stop and remains there without the interpreter executing a *line feed* to the next line.

If the .Print method appears on a line by itself, a carriage return with a line feed is generated. In other words, the "print head" is set to the far left by the carriage return and one line down by the line feed—like what happens when you press the Return key on an electric typewriter. The virtual cursor's position is set at the beginning of the next line below the previously printed one.

Print seems like a simple enough instruction until you try to explain it to somebody. Part of the reason the instruction is so complex today is that functionality has been added to it over time since 1964. Remember, when BASIC was first compiled on a college mainframe, the PRINT command was the language's only instruction for direct visual output. In other words, PRINT did all the display work for BASIC, before the advent of point-addressable graphics. On many systems, the only display device for the computer was the printer.

Imagine an old Digital Equipment DECwriter. It was, for the most part, a typewriter attached to a computer. It did include a full typewriter keyboard. For many terminal systems, the DECwriter was the input/output device. For this reason, the PRINT command in BASIC and the WRITE command in FORTRAN developed a typewriter-like mode of operation, keeping track of such things as carriage position, tab stops, and line feeds. A carriage return was—and still is—a character in the ASCII code.

Visual Basic maintains three categories of objects, which are distinguished from each other by their capability to receive text. The first category is a graphic object to be used specifically as a control. You assign text to such control devices by setting their .Caption properties as equivalent to that text, as in the following instruction:

> Graphic objects containing noneditable text have their contents set with the *.Caption* property.

```
Command1.Caption = "Cancel"
```

The user cannot edit the text on-screen that is assigned as a .Caption.

The second category of object is the text box, which generally is used as an explicitly marked area or field for the entry or display of text. You assign text to this category by setting its .Text property equivalent to that text. Conversely, you can acquire text from a text box by assigning its .Text property to a string variable, as in the following instruction:

> Text boxes or other graphic objects with editable text have their contents set with the *.Text* property.

```
name$ = Surname.Text
```

The primary difference between the operation of a text box and a captioned control, therefore, is that the text box is a *receptacle* for user-entered text, thus making text exchange in the source code a two-way process. Text is *acquired* from a text box as easily as it can be assigned to it, by merely reversing the order of items in the equation.

The type of object that can take advantage of the .Print method can best be thought of as a *terminal*, like the old DECwriter. In essence, each time you create a new form or picture box, you're creating a new terminal. Microsoft Windows thinks of such objects this way, as well; in fact, making the single terminal that is your computer's BIOS into multiple virtual terminals is the primary purpose of Microsoft Windows. The textual rules of each terminal you create within the Windows environment are still based in large part on the way old terminals like the DECwriter used to work.

In the Visual Basic scheme of things, the Debug window—the object name of which is Debug.—is the last remnant of the old terminal communication device for conversing with the BASIC command-line interpreter. You can use the Debug. device as an output device when all else fails.

The following example shows a statement that you can use if a benchmark program "errors out":

```
Debug.Print "Error after";iter;"iterations",stag;"stage."
```

The semicolons here have the interpreter print the value of the stated variables beside the text. Because they are values, the interpreter knows to add spaces between the text and values, so including an extra space in the quotation marks isn't necessary here. The comma after each literal expression (text appearing in quotation marks) has the interpreter "press Tab"—in other words, tabulate to the next tab stop on the line.

Another way to space elements of text from each other is through the use of functions. One of the oldest BASIC functions for such purposes is Tab().

Tab()   Function

Purpose: Text cursor tabulation
Syntax:

```
Tab(column%)
```

The Tab() function moves the text cursor within a picture box or other "virtual terminal" control to the specified *column%*. A column at any one time is equivalent to roughly the average width of every character in the type style and size being used, which is often the width of the lowercase letter *n*.

Spc()   Function

Purpose: Text cursor spacing
Syntax:

```
Spc(spaces%)
```

The Spc() function moves the text cursor within a picture box or other "virtual terminal" control for a specified number of *spaces%* to the right. A space in this instance is the width of the space character for the type style and size being used.

Example

The difference between the Tab() function and the Spc() function becomes evident when you print using proportionally spaced fonts. Following are two instructions containing text to be printed within the same text box, using a proportionally spaced font. Figure 39.1 shows the results of the following instructions:

```
Picture1.Print "Zappa"; tab(45); "Frank"
Picture1.Print "Zappa"; spc(45); "Frank"
```

One more terminal-control command from the old days making its appearance as a Visual Basic method is .Cls.

Figure 39.1

Tab() and *Spc()*
Example.

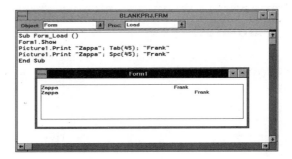

.Cls   **Method**

Purpose: Picture area clearing
Syntax:

```
[Object.]Cls
```

The .Cls method clears the specified graphic object of any printed or plotted contents, textual or graphic. If *Object.* is not specified, the form in which the *.Cls* procedure appears is cleared.

Example

Nothing is simpler than clearing the contents of a picture box:

```
Picture1.Cls
```

Formatting Textual Output

As mentioned earlier in this chapter, Microsoft has developed a text descriptor language for describing the appearance, display, or printing format of an element of text. Microsoft uses this language or some derivative of it in most of its Windows applications, including Visual Basic. This format descriptor code used to be prevalent in the old PRINT USING statement, which assigned an appearance format to the text of a value or numeric variable that followed the word USING. This term doesn't appear in Visual Basic; in its place is a separate function—not a statement—that states the appearance format for a specified value. This function is Format$().

Format$()   Function

Purpose: Value-to-string character conversion
Syntax:

```
string$ = Format$(value[, {"formattype$"¦descriptor$}])
```

In this syntax, descriptor$ is a series of placeholder and directive characters, written in as many as three groups using the following syntax:

```
descriptorpos[;descriptorneg[;descriptorzero]]
```

The Format$() function converts a numeric value to an alphanumeric string, in the same manner as the Str$() function. If no other parameter is specified, the Format$() function stops here; otherwise, it applies an appearance format to this value. This format can be one of the general type names formattype$ recognized by the interpreter, or it can be a series of placeholder characters descriptor$ arranged using Microsoft's number format descriptor code. If descriptor$ is to be stated outright in the function, it must appear in quotation marks; otherwise, you can assign the descriptor in advance to a string variable using an equation.

A placeholder in this instance is a character that does one of the following:

◆ Symbolizes the type of character that can appear in the position of the placeholder

◆ Instructs the interpreter to treat the placeholder characters that follow with special or different respect

Visual Basic recognizes any of the following characters as valid placeholders:

Character	Stands for
0	Representative of a digit. A digit must appear in the character position represented by the 0 placeholder, whether or not the numeric value being converted has an actual value for this given place.
#	Representative of a digit. A digit might appear in the character position represented by the # placeholder if the numeric value being converted has an actual value for this given place.
.	Representative of the decimal point—the period. Denotes the point in the character formatting where a decimal point appears.
%	Directive for percentages. It tells the interpreter to convert the given value into a percentage, by multiplying that value by 100.
,	Representative of the thousands separator—the comma. Denotes the point in the whole number side of the character formatting where a value that exceeds a multiple of a thousand, or one thousand to some power, has its place marked with a comma.
E+	Directive for scientific notation. For extremely large values, it directs the interpreter to display the value as a fraction no greater than 10, multiplied by a power of 10.
:	Representative of the time separator—the colon. Denotes the point in the character formatting where hours are separated from minutes or minutes from seconds.
/	Representative of the date separator. Denotes the point in the character formatting where the month is separated from the day or the day from the year.
-, +, $, (,), space	Literal characters. These characters, when included in a descriptor string, are displayed as-is in their representative positions.
\	Directive for literal display. It directs the interpreter to display the next character in the descriptor string, whether or not that character might also be considered a placeholder or directive character.

continues

Character	Stands for
`"s$"`	Directive for literal display. It directs the interpreter to display the characters in the quotation marks, whether or not those characters might also be considered placeholders or directive characters. To assign a quotation mark to *descriptor$*, use the function `Chr$(34)` in its place—for instance:
	<p style="text-align:center">`c$ = Chr$(34) + "Hello" + Chr$(34)`</p>
`*`	Directive for fill character display. It directs the interpreter to display the character following the `*` directive (which can be an asterisk itself) in place of any space or empty character.
`C`	Directive for time signature conversion. It directs the interpreter to convert the given value to the time signature format used by `Now`.

You can use semicolons as partitions in descriptor strings to have the interpreter convert negative or zero values differently than it converts positive values.

If *formattype$* is supplied as a parameter in place of *descriptor$*, the Visual Basic interpreter recognizes any of the following terms as being representative of standardized display formats:

Format Type	Directive
`Currency`	Display value with thousands separator comma if necessary, two decimal places at all times, negative values enclosed in parentheses.
`Fixed`	Display at least one whole number digit and two decimal digits.
`General Number`	Display value as-is without special formatting.
`Percent`	Display value as a percentage by multiplying it by 100 and adding the `%` symbol.
`Scientific`	Display value using standard scientific notation, using the syntax *multiplier*`E+`*power_of_10*.
`Standard`	Display value with thousands separator comma if necessary, and as many as, but no more than, two places to the right of the decimal point.

Format Type	Directive
True/False, Yes/No, On/Off	Display Boolean value with appropriate term.

Instances of *formattype$* must appear in quotation marks.

> **Caution:** Regardless of the advertised uniformity of Microsoft's descriptor languages between applications, characters such as the fractional directive and the "unknown placeholder," which appear in Microsoft Excel, are not recognized by the Visual Basic interpreter.

Examples

Several characters act as number formatters in Microsoft's code. Following are some of these format descriptors in action, using the Visual Basic Debug window CLI as a guide. Responses from the interpreter appear in boldface.

```
number=12.95
text$=format$(number, "0000.00")
print text$
0012.95
```

Each zero in the descriptor saves an absolute place in the text string for a digit, whether a value exists for the place of that digit. The preceding descriptor definitely displays a four-digit whole number, two-digit fractional-number value. The period in the descriptor reserves the place for the decimal point.

```
text$=format$(number, "####.##")
print text$
12.95
```

The use of the pound sign (#) in a descriptor holds a place for a digit in the converted text, unless no value exists for that digit.

```
text$=format$(number,"Currency")
?text$
$12.95
```

Spelling out a format type can be easier than always resorting to character placeholders.

```
text$=format$(number, "$####.##")
print text$
$12.95
```

A dollar sign in the descriptor places a dollar sign in the text at that place.

```
text$=format$(number, "$#000.00")
print text$
$012.95
```

You can mix zero placeholders and pound sign placeholders in a descriptor, although the results can be confusing.

```
text$=format$(number, "*******$#######.##")
print text$
*******$12.95
```

You can use asterisks and other symbolic characters as leading or trailing characters in a descriptor.

```
text$=format$(number, "###%")
print text$
1295%
```

```
text$=format$(number,"###.##%")
print text$
1295.%
```

```
text$=format$(number,"Percent")
?text$
1295.00%
```

The percentage sign used in a descriptor places a percentage sign in the converted text; however, the value before the percentage sign is then multiplied by 100.

```
number=1563534
text$=format$(number, "###,###,###,###")
?text$
1,563,534
```

You can use commas as delimiters for every thousandth place in a base 10 value.

```
text$=format$(number,"Scientific")
?text$
1.56E+06
```

In the preceding example, you get an idea of how the Visual Basic interpreter relates scientific notation. The response stands for 1.56 times 10 to the sixth power.

You may remember from Chapter 37, "Time and Date," how the internal variable Now maintains the current system time and date in a single-precision, floating-point number. You can extract the current month, day, and date from this internal variable using combinations of ms, ds, and ys. When two of each appear together, digital displays are returned.

```
?format$(now,"dd mmmm yyyy")
1 February 1994
```

Four ms together spell out the month, and four ys together display the entire year.

```
?format$(now,"dd/mm/yy")
2/1/94
```

For the benefit of those people who are accustomed to writing the day, month, and year in that order, you can use Format$() to reformat Now for whatever format is more suitable.

```
?format$(now,"dd mmm yy")
1 Feb 94

?format$(now,"mmm dd yyyy")
Feb 1 1994

?format$(now,"dddd, dd mmm yy")
Tuesday, 1 Feb 94
```

You can format dates in countless other ways.

```
?format$(now,"hh:mm:ss")
04:47:20
```

You can use combinations of hs, ms, and ss for expressing time. The Visual Basic interpreter somehow knows to distinguish the mm of time from the mm of date.

```
?format$(now,"h:m:s")
4:47:36
```

Single characters here display the time with leading zeros removed. Note here that a single m results in a single-digit minute readout when it is less than 10 minutes past the hour.

```
?format$(now,"h:mm:ss AM/PM")
4:48:42 AM

?format$(now,"hh:mm:ss a/p")
04:49:05 a
```

The preceding two examples express a.m. and p.m.

Example

```
desc$=chr$(34)+"The time is now "+chr$(34)+"C"
?format$(now,desc$)
The time is now 12/10/92 04:48:53 PM
```

Although largely undocumented, the directive character C tells the interpreter to convert the value to the time signature format. Notice also how Chr$(34) places quotation marks within the descriptor screen so that The time is now is displayed as literal characters.

```
?format$(now,"dd mm yy_____hh:mm:ss A/P")
10 12 92_____04:52:51 P
```

In the preceding example, the underscore character is a lead-in character. You can combine dates and times on the same line.

```
number=-15.5
?format$(number, "##.##;(##.##)")
(15.5)
```

The semicolon here separates the format for negative values from the format for positive values. Here you're telling the interpreter to display negative values in parentheses.

Example

```
fmt$="##.##;(##.##);"+chr$(34)+"Zero"+chr$(34)
?fmt$
##.##;(##.##);"Zero"
number=0
?format$(number,fmt$)
Zero
```

Here again you see an example of using Chr$(34) to place quotation marks in the descriptor string. The second semicolon in the descriptor specifies the appearance format for a zero value. In this case, the descriptor string fmt$ contains the text string "Zero". Now the Format$() function spells out *Zero* whenever the value is zero; otherwise, the value appears in accountants' format.

Summary

In Visual Basic, .Print manifests itself as a method, which dispatches text to a specific graphic object or output device. The .Print method can print multiple items in sequence, separated by delimiters having functions that were derived from the earliest use of the PRINT command in old BASIC for typewriter-type terminals.

Visual Basic maintains three categories of text-receiving graphic objects. The first is the command control object, which receives its text by assignment to the property .Caption. The second is the interactive text box, which receives its text by assignment to the property .Text. The third is the virtual terminal, which is the conventional primary output area for textual processes and interaction. This area receives its text from the .Print method. Virtual terminal display areas are handled as if they were typewriter pages with carriage returns and tab stops.

Microsoft uses a format descriptor code for describing the textual appearance of numbers and values. A measure of this code is supported by Visual Basic, through the Format$() function.

Review Questions

What Format$() descriptor can you use to display the following text, given the values listed?

1. *value* = .15, *text$* = "15%"

2. *value* = 365.5, *text$* = "****365.50"

3. *value* = Now, *text$* = "5 PM"

4. *value* = 0, *text$* = "Unchanged"

5. *value* = Now, *text$* = "by 8:00 PM tonight at the earliest."

CHAPTER 40

Text Properties

In this chapter, you briefly examine the properties of text that belongs to graphic objects. You then further investigate the notion of the *virtual cursor* that accompanies all objects that the Visual Basic interpreter sees as *virtual terminals*. Finally, you experiment with two methods for judging how much space text to be printed consumes in a graphic object.

Font Characteristics

The Visual Basic program uses the screen font and printer font generation system supplied to it as a resource by Microsoft Windows. Some Windows users prefer to use third-party print manager programs such as Adobe Type Manager, in which case their screen and printer fonts should appear significantly more clear and have more detailed characteristics such as true italicization. In any event, Visual Basic supports only the most general characteristics of a font or type style as supported by the standard font generation system of Windows.

FontName   **Property**

Representation: Character style attribute
Applies to: Check, combo, command, directory, drive, file, form, frame, grid, label, list, option, picture, printer, text
Set by way of: Properties window, program instruction

The `.FontName` property for a graphic object is set to the precise text of a name from the list of fonts currently maintained by Microsoft Windows. When this property is set, the font used for printing or assigning text to a form, graphic object, or the printer is referred to by this name.

FontSize   **Property**

Representation: Character size attribute
Applies to: Check, combo, command, directory, drive, file, form, frame, grid, label, list, option, picture, printer, text
Set by way of: Properties window, program instruction

The `.FontSize` property for a graphic object is set to the approximate point size available for a font that has its current `.FontName` supported by Windows and that is currently the chosen `.FontName` for printing or assigning text.

When a font is chosen for a textual label appearing in a form, you can set its alignment through the `.Alignment` property.

Alignment   **Property**

Representation: Contained text weight
Applies to: Check, label, option, text
Set by way of: Properties window, program instruction

The `.Alignment` property for a label or text box is set to an integer that describes how the text in that control is aligned. The property can be set to any of the following values:

    0   Left justification (default)

    1   Right justification

    2   Centered

For a check box or option dot control, the `.Alignment` property reflects the side of the control that the button occupies. When set to 0, the button appears on the far left side of the control with the text label to its immediate right; when set to 1, the button appears on the far right with the text on its left.

Tailoring Text to Fit Controls, and Vice Versa

When you place text within a label, the length and size of the text might leave extra space at the bottom of the label. On the other hand, too much text assigned to the `.Caption` property might make the text fall beneath the lowermost boundaries of the control. For both possible cases, properties enable you to give the interpreter permission to resize the label if necessary.

AutoSize   **Property**

Representation: Space conservation permission
Applies to: Label, picture
Set by way of: Properties window, program instruction

The .AutoSize property for a picture or label is set to a True/False value. This value reflects whether permission is granted for the control's lowermost boundary in the form to be *reduced* to fit the contents assigned to that control.

WordWrap   **Property**

Representation: Auxiliary space creation permission
Applies to: Label
Set by way of: Properties window, program instruction

The .WordWrap property for a label is set to a True/False value. This value reflects whether permission is granted for the control's lowermost boundary to be *expanded* to fit the contents assigned to the label's .Caption property.

> **Note:** The naming of the .WordWrap property is quite confusing. The term *word wrap* is used in other categories of applications to mean something entirely different. Also, notice that picture box contents cannot be expanded automatically to fit their contents, although they can be reduced.

True/False Font Properties

After a font name is chosen for a graphic object or device, five True/False properties describing the appearance of that font can be addressed.

.FontBold, .FontItalic, .FontStrikethru,   **Properties**
.FontTransparent, and .FontUnderline

Representation: Character styles
Applies to: Check, combo, command, directory, drive, file, form, frame, grid, label, option, picture, printer, text
Set by way of: Properties window, program instruction

The .Fontx properties for a graphic object are set to True/False values reflecting the state of the font represented by *x*. For controls whose contents are set by way of properties, setting the .Fontx properties at run time immediately changes the on-screen appearance of the fonts in those controls. For virtual terminal controls (form, printer, and picture box), setting these properties at run time changes the way text to be printed appears, although the appearance of text already printed remains the same.

If you set the .FontTransparent property to False, each character to be displayed or printed carries with it a surrounding block background of an assigned .BackColor. If you set the .FontStrikethru property to True, each character to be displayed or printed has a slash mark or other mark through it (only if this characteristic is available for the chosen font). By default, the .FontBold and .FontTransparent properties for a new graphic object are set to True; the .FontItalic, .FontStrikethru, and .FontUnderline properties are set to False.

The Technique of Text Trapping

In Chapter 36, "String Functions," you learned about a procedure that allows you to extract an element of text being searched for in a paragraph contained in a multiline text box. Here is a small application that puts the model for that procedure to work. Its objective is to demonstrate the properties for a text box that govern the indication of individual elements of text. Figure 40.1 shows this application's main window.

Figure 40.1

The TestText application.

"Test Text" Textual Indication Demonstration

Project name: TESTTEXT.MAK
Constituent files: SEARCHER.FRM, TESTTEXT.FRM, SRCHRPLC.FRM

TESTTEXT.FRM

Control Type	Property	Setting
Form	.BorderStyle	1 'Fixed Single
	.Caption	TestText
	.Height	5388
	.Name	TestText
	.Width	7680
Button	.Caption	Replace
	.Height	465
	.Name	Replace
	.Width	2115
Button	.Caption	Search
	.Height	465
	.Name	Search
	.Width	2115
Text Box	.Height	3315
	.Left	450
	.MultiLine	-1 'True
	.Name	BigTextBox
	.Top	750
	.Width	6615
Label	.Caption	Paragraph:
	.Left	450
	.Top	300

Event Procedures

```
Sub Form_Load ()
Load Searcher
Load Replacer

Sub Search_Click ()
Searcher.Show
End Sub

Sub Replace_Click ()
Replacer.Show
End Sub
```

These are the only two event procedures you need for this form module; their purpose is to bring two dialog panels into the workspace.

SEARCHER.FRM

Control Type	Property	Setting
Form	.Caption	Search
	.Height	1692
	.Name	Searcher
	.Width	7284
Button	.Cancel	-1 'True
	.Caption	Cancel
	.Height	315
	.Left	5400
	.Name	Cancel
	.TabIndex	0
	.Top	750
	.Width	1515
Button	.Caption	Start
	.Default	-1 'True
	.Height	315
	.Left	3750
	.Name	Start
	.TabIndex	3
	.Top	750
	.Width	1515

Control Type	Property	Setting
Text Box	.Height	315
	.Left	1200
	.Name	SearchText
	.Top	300
	.Width	5715
Label	.Alignment	1 'Right Justify
	.Caption	Search For:
	.Left	150
	.Top	150

Event Procedures

```
Sub Start_Click ()
srch$ = SearchText.Text
If Len(srch$) = 0 Then
    Searcher.Hide
    Exit Sub
End If
trgt$ = TestText.BigTextBox.Text
pos = InStr(trgt$, srch$)
If pos = 0 Then
    MsgBox "Text not found.", 0, ""
    Exit Sub
End If
TestText.BigTextBox.SelStart = pos - 1
TestText.BigTextBox.SelLength = Len(srch$)
found$ = TestText.BigTextBox.SelText
Searcher.Hide
MsgBox "Search string '" + found$ + "' found at position" +
➥Str$(pos) + "."
End Sub
```

When the text being searched for (represented by srch$) is found within the target trgt$, the pointer position at the time InStr() finds the text is one space beyond the first character of the found text segment. For this reason, the .SelStart property of the text box is set to pos - 1, or one behind the location found by InStr(). The selection is extended by setting the .SelLength property to the number of characters in the search string. The imprint of the found text is then "lifted" from the main body of the text and assigned to the string variable found$.

In this next example, the search-and-replace panel shows how this text extraction process can be taken one step further.

SRCHRPLC.FRM

Control Type	Property	Setting
Form	.Caption	Replace
	.Height	2436
	.Name	Replacer
	.Width	7284
Button	.Cancel	-1 'True
	.Caption	Cancel
	.Height	315
	.Left	5400
	.Name	Cancel
	.TabIndex	3
	.Top	1500
	.Width	1515
Button	.Caption	Start
	.Default	-1 'True
	.Height	315
	.Left	3750
	.Name	Start
	.TabIndex	4
	.Top	1500
	.Width	1515
Text Box	.Height	315
	.Left	1200
	.Name	ReplaceText
	.TabIndex	1
	.Top	900
	.Width	5715
Text Box	.Height	315
	.Left	1200
	.Name	SearchText
	.TabIndex	0
	.Top	300
	.Width	5715

Control Type	Property	Setting
Label	.Alignment	1 'Right Justify
	.Caption	Replace With:
	.Left	150
	.Top	750
Label	.Alignment	1 'Right Justify
	.Caption	Search For:
	.Left	150
	.Top	150

Event Procedures

```
Sub Start_Click ()
srch$ = SearchText.Text
rplc$ = ReplaceText.Text
If Len(srch$) = 0 Or Len(rplc$) = 0 Then
    Replacer.Hide
    Exit Sub
End If
trgt$ = TestText.BigTextBox.Text
pos = InStr(trgt$, srch$)
If pos = 0 Then
    MsgBox "Text not found.", 0, ""
    Exit Sub
End If
TestText.BigTextBox.SelStart = pos - 1
TestText.BigTextBox.SelLength = Len(srch$)
TestText.BigTextBox.SelText = rplc$
Replacer.Hide
End Sub
```

Notice how much this procedure resembles the search-only procedure presented earlier. The major difference here is the second-to-last instruction. Because the contents of the Replace With text field are assigned to string variable rplc$, rather than setting a string variable to be equivalent to the found text, the area of the found text itself is set as equivalent to the replacement string. Regardless of any length differences between the indicated found text and the replacement text, the replacement text substitutes for the found text entirely, through the simple invocation of one instruction.

Here's how all this is accomplished: the VB interpreter always maintains an internal location of a cursor for a text box object. You can set the cursor's location by assigning an index to it, and then use the index to select and extract a region of text using property settings.

.SelStart   Property

Representation: Text indication starting location
Applies to: Combo, text
Set by way of: Program instruction, user interaction

The .SelStart property is set to a value that designates where the cursor appears in the text in a text box. This is where extraction from this body of text begins. Each character of text in the box has its own index number, starting with character 1 at the beginning of the text. Setting the value of .SelStart places the cursor to the right of the indexed character; setting it to 0 places it at the beginning of the text. The cursor position is also called the *insertion point*.

.SelLength   Property

Representation: Number of indicated characters
Applies to: Combo, text
Set by way of: Program instruction, user interaction

The .SelLength property is set to the number of characters being extracted to the right of the cursor position .SelStart. This selection is always highlighted if the .HideSelection property for the text box is set to false.

.SelText   Property

Representation: Indicated text
Applies to: Combo, text
Set by way of: Program instruction, user interaction

The .SelText property is set to the contents of the text being indicated in the text box. Setting the .SelStart and .SelLength properties of a text box automatically sets the .SelText property to the characters starting at position .SelStart and extending for .SelLength characters. Setting the .SelText property manually replaces the indicated text with the contents of the property itself, or inserts that text at the current cursor location if no text is indicated.

When a text box operates at run time, and the mouse is used to indicate a region of text, that region is always highlighted with whatever color is chosen for indicated text in the Windows Control Panel. By default, when you move the mouse to another control, this highlighting immediately disappears. When you use property settings such as `.SelStart` and `.SelLength` to extract a region of text, by default this extraction is not highlighted. This can be changed by altering the `.HideSelection` property for the text box.

.HideSelection   Property

Representation: Text indication continuation
Applies to: Text
Set by way of: Properties window

The `.HideSelection` for a text or combo box is set to a True/False value and specifies if selected text remains highlighted when the control loses focus. By default, this property is set to True.

Making It All Fit

Suppose you want an element of text, which you plan to print to a picture box, to take up all the space it can in that box. Visual Basic gives you two methods for discerning the width and height of text for the given `.FontName` and `.FontSize` for a picture box or form, *before* the text is printed there.

.TextHeight and .TextWidth   Methods

Purpose: Textual size acquisition
Syntax:

```
value% = [Object.]TextHeight(string$)
value% = [Object.]TextWidth(string$)
```

The `.TextHeight` and `.TextWidth` methods are invoked like functions, except they are expressed using object-oriented syntax. These methods return the height and width, respectively, of the text expressed in *string$* as it might appear in the specified *Object* when printed using the `.Print` method. These values are returned in the integer *value%* as if the methods were functions. These methods work only with virtual terminal objects such as a picture box or form, or the printer device. If *Object* is not specified, the form containing the currently executing procedure is assumed.

Suppose you have a dialog panel in which a user is asked to enter a password. You don't want the characters the user enters to be displayed as characters; instead, for privacy purposes, you'd prefer that asterisks or some other characters take their place. Yet you'd rather not write a machine-language routine to intercept keypresses before characters reach the text box. To solve this dilemma, Visual Basic provides the .PasswordChar property:

.PasswordChar   Property

Representation: Place substitution character
Applies to: Text
Set by way of: Properties window, program instruction

The .PasswordChar property for a text box is set to a single alphanumeric character that the Visual Basic interpreter displays in the text box whenever a key is pressed. This prevents other viewers from detecting what the user is typing. When set to a null value, characters are entered into the text box as their keys are pressed.

Selection and the Grid

Now turn your attention back to the grid control. Indicating cells in a grid is similar to indicating text in a text box. There are properties which are native to the grid control that pertain to cell indication; and compared with the indication properties for a text box, they are actually rather easy to understand.

.SelStartRow, .SelEndRow,   Properties
.SelStartCol, and .SelEndCol

Representation: Corners of cell selection block
Applies to: Grid
Set by way of: Program instruction, user interaction

The .Selx properties for a grid control are set to the cell row and column numbers reflecting the beginnings and endings of a rectangular block of indicated cells. The .SelStartRow and .SelEndRow properties are set to the starting and ending row numbers of the indicated block, respectively. Likewise, the .SelStartCol and .SelEndCol properties are set to the starting and ending column numbers of the indicated block, respectively. Setting these properties to nonzero values starts the cell indication process manually. When the user clicks and holds the index button over a grid, these properties are set in the process.

.CellSelected   Property

Representation: Pointer indication status
Applies to: Grid
Set by way of: Program instruction, user interaction

The `.CellSelected` property for a grid is set to a True/False value, denoting whether the current `.Row` and `.Col` property settings place the cell pointer in an indicated region of cells.

By default, indicated grid cells are automatically highlighted; however, this can be adjusted.

.HighLight   Property

Representation: Indicated cell coloration permission
Applies to: Grid
Set by way of: Properties window, program instruction

The `.HighLight` property for a grid control is set to a True/False value, denoting whether the grid automatically highlights indicated cells. By default, this property is set to True.

Finally, because there may be occasions when the act of indicating cells in a grid should trigger a reevaluation of their contents, an event is provided so that a procedure can be written for such purposes.

_SelChange   Event

Action: Cell indication activation
Applies to: Grid
Parameters: None

The `_SelChange` event for a grid control is triggered whenever a cell indication process begins, whether by user interaction with the grid, or by setting one of the `.Sel`*x* properties for the grid.

Now that you have indicated cells, what do you do with them? There must be some way of extracting all the contents of indicated cells at once into an evaluable string variable, maintaining the identity of the string while keeping borders in place between the cells. Here is a string property that holds the contents of all the indicated cells, and, using ANSI character codes, maintains boundaries between the cell contents in the same string:

.Clip   **Property**

Representation: Collective contents of indicated cells
Applies to: Grid
Set by way of: Program instruction

The .Clip property for a grid control is set automatically by the Visual Basic interpreter to the textual contents of each cell in the indicated region of the grid. The property "reads" from left-to-right and then top-to-bottom. A tab character represented by Chr$(9) separates the contents of cells sharing the same row. Once the "read" has reached the end of the row, the next row below it is read into the property starting with the extreme left cell. This carriage return of sorts is represented in the .Clip property by an ANSI carriage return character, Chr$(13).

The upshot of separating cell contents with ANSI characters is that the .Clip property setting can be assigned to the Windows system clipboard at any time (you see how to do that later). The clipboard contents can then be pasted into any Windows application—especially a word processor or spreadsheet that imports raw text—and the contents will be perfectly formatted in rows and columns. (Isn't progress exciting?)

Summary

The Visual Basic interpreter borrows its resources for font and type style control from Microsoft Windows. The settings for the .FontName and .FontSize properties are supplied to the interpreter by Windows as resources. The bold, italic, strikethrough, transparency, and underline styles for any Windows font, if they are available, can be set using VB properties that have settings that are Boolean values.

The position of the cursor in text appearing in a text box can be set using the .SelStart property. If text is to be extracted from this cursor position forward, the number of characters to be extracted can be expressed as the .SelLength property. The extracted text thus becomes the .SelText property.

The predicted width and height of text to be printed in a form or picture box can be obtained using the .TextWidth and .TextHeight methods. These methods are expressed in an equation like functions, although with object-oriented syntax.

The .SelStartRow, .SelEndRow, .SelStartCol, and .SelEndCol properties govern the four corners of a rectangle representing a range of indicated cells in the grid. Like the selection properties for a text box, these properties can be set by user interaction with the grid, or by direct property settings in the source code.

Review Questions

Suppose the contents of a text box Prophecy are as follows:

```
Whosoever would accept jade pendants
➥who has first heard source code growing in a cliff?
```

1. What is the result of the function Instr(Prophecy.Text, "jade")?

2. What are the contents of Prophecy.SelText if Prophecy.SelStart equals 21 and Prophecy.SelLength equals 5?

3. Suppose you want to change the text in the text box Prophecy to a passage from the *Tao te Ching* as translated into English by Witter Bynner. You want to replace source code with stone. What are the three instructions necessary to make the replacement?

CHAPTER 41

The Printer and Sound Output

In this chapter, you begin to direct Visual Basic output to the `Printer.` device. This device has a few properties and methods that are specific to the printer.

Like a form or a picture box, Visual Basic considers the printer to be a *virtual terminal*, which receives text using the `.Print` method in the manner of an old TTY or DECwriter terminal printer. To print to the printer from any procedure appearing within any module, address the printer as follows:

```
Printer.Print "This is an example line of text."
```

The VB interpreter attributes a few extra characteristics to the printer. Each application is distributed its own printing process, beginning at page one. The current page number is stored within a property that is specific to the printer.

.Page   Property

Representation: Current printer page
Applies to: Printer
Set by way of: Course of program execution

The `Printer.Page` property is set to the current page number maintained by the VB interpreter for an application. Each time an application starts running, the `.Page` property is set to 1. The interpreter assumes a single document is being created for this application at any one time. Each time a page is finished printing, the `.Page` property is incremented.

.NewPage   Method

Purpose: Printer page eject signal
Syntax:

```
Printer.NewPage
```

The `.NewPage` method is invoked to eject the page being printed. This ejection signal is held within the Windows Print Manager until it dispatches that signal to the printer at an appropriate time. The `.Page` property for the application's internal document is automatically incremented.

To state that the end of a document has been reached, the `.EndDoc` method is called.

.EndDoc   Method

Purpose: Printer document ejection
Syntax:

```
Printer.EndDoc
```

The `.EndDoc` method is invoked to signal the completion of the application's internal document and to send the ejection signal for the last page to the Windows Print Manager. The `.Page` property for the application's internal document is automatically reset to 1.

Font Selection

A font installed in Microsoft Windows is intended to have the same general style and appearance on-screen as it does on the printer. Nonetheless, Visual Basic maintains two separate lists of fonts, one for the screen and one for the printer. Both lists have two properties associated with them: the `.Fonts` and `.FontCount` properties.

.Fonts()   Property

Representation: Installed typestyles
Applies to: Printer, screen
Set by way of: Windows resource

The .Fonts() property behaves as an array that contains the name of each installed Printer or Screen font in Microsoft Windows, in whatever order the current Windows font maintenance system has set for that list. This property array is likely to be different for each computer system.

.FontCount   **Property**

Representation: Installed typestyle amount
Applies to: Printer, screen
Set by way of: Windows resource

The .FontCount property contains the current number of Printer and Screen fonts installed in Microsoft Windows. This property also is likely to be different for each computer system.

Example

The following test routine sets the current printer font to the last font installed in Windows:

```
lastfont = Printer.FontCount
Printer.FontName = Printer.Fonts(lastfont)
```

The number of fonts installed is returned in the variable lastfont, used as an array pointer to the last font in the list, .Fonts(lastfont).

Sound

With the exception of the multimedia extensions, the Beep statement is the only sound-based option within Visual Basic.

Beep   **Statement**

Purpose: Internal sound activation
Syntax:

```
Beep
```

The Beep statement causes a *beep* noise to be sounded. This statement takes no parameters.

The Windows Application Program Interface can be programmed for beeps of different frequencies and intervals, although the API vocabulary is not a regular part of the VB vocabulary.

Summary

The Visual Basic interpreter maintains an internal printed document for each application. It therefore maintains a page count for that document as the property `Printer.Page`, which is incremented each time the page is ejected using the `Printer.NewPage` method. The `Printer.Page` property is reset to 1 each time the document is closed using the `Printer.EndDoc` method.

Microsoft Windows maintains two font lists for both the `Screen.` and `Printer.` devices. The lists are both addressable as property arrays, using the `.Fonts()` property. The number of fonts currently installed in the particular Windows environment where the interpreter is running is returned using the `.FontCount` property.

`Beep` makes the computer beep.

Review Questions

1. What is the property term that refers to the first printer font installed in Microsoft Windows?

2. If Microsoft Windows is supposed to facilitate a what-you-see-is-what-you-get text composition environment—where what you see on-screen closely corresponds to what's going to be printed—why does Visual Basic maintain two different lists of names for fonts belonging to the screen and the printer?

Part VIII

Bitmapped Graphics

CHAPTER 42

Picture and Image Boxes

In this chapter, you are reintroduced to the picture box—which has played a small role in the applications produced to this point—and learn about the image box. The difference between a picture box and an image box is that an image box cannot be classified as a parent object, and an image box cannot receive text through the `.Print` method.

Also in this chapter, you study the operation of picture boxes when they are used to display graphic images rather than just text. You see what properties are used to point the graphic contents of a picture box to a stored image file.

It's difficult to explain why there are such intentional ambiguities in our use of language. The difference between a picture box and an image box isn't intuitive. Both picture and image boxes are drawn on the form in much the same way, and their contents can be set to picture files, icon files, or Windows metafiles.

The first serious difference between the two controls is the fact that an image box cannot be classified as a parent control. That is, other controls cannot "belong" to an image. This is like comparing wall paneling to wallpaper. Wall paneling is not really part of the wall; it can be removed and attached someplace else. By contrast, wallpaper, once pasted, becomes an integral part of the wall. When you attach a picture box to a form, you've attached to it in many respects a panel. Controls can be attached to this panel; when you move the panel, controls move with it. On the other hand, an image becomes glued, in a sense, to the form to which it's attached. Like the `.Picture` property of a form, an image box can be part of the form's background—the wallpaper—although controls cannot be attached to an image box.

The other primary difference is that a picture box is the recipient of graphics methods, such as pixel drawing and the .Print method. As explained before, a picture box acts as something of a "virtual terminal." Like an old-style graphics terminal, each picture box has associated with it an internal cursor that points to the last point plotted to the picture box, or to the point that may be plotted next. In much the same way that the Visual Basic interpreter maintains a .SelStart property containing the cursor position for a text box, two properties are maintained for a form or picture box containing the current cursor coordinates: the .CurrentX and .CurrentY properties.

.CurrentX and .CurrentY   Properties

Representation: Virtual terminal pointer coordinates
Applies to: Form, picture, printer
Set by way of: Program instruction

The .CurrentX and .CurrentY properties for a virtual terminal graphic object are set by the current coordinates of the cursor for that object. By default, these coordinates are expressed graphically as twips, unless the .ScaleMode property for the object is set otherwise. The settings for these properties are relative to the current coordinate scale for the graphic object or device.

Once a control is loaded into the workspace, the .CurrentX and .CurrentY settings for that control are set to zero. Invoking methods for printing text to that control or drawing raster-oriented graphics to that control moves the cursor coordinates referred to by this property pair.

Each time a .Print method is invoked, the .CurrentX property for the object receiving the text is increased by a certain number of twips (or whatever units are in use at the time). At the end of the .Print method instruction, assuming there are no trailing delimiters, the cursor moves to the next line, at the same time increasing the .CurrentY property of the object. By default, the .CurrentX property is then reset to 0.

The Printer. object also is considered a virtual terminal control that has its own plotting cursor associated with it. While printing to the printer, the VB interpreter maintains .CurrentX and .CurrentY properties for the printer's internal "cursor." These cursor coordinates are not expressed in rows and columns, but in graphic coordinates according to the coordinate scale currently set for the printer.

Example

The following routine prints the printer's current coordinate scale to the printer:

```
Printer.Print "Current .ScaleLeft ="; Printer.ScaleLeft
Printer.Print "Current .ScaleTop ="; Printer.ScaleTop
```

```
Printer.Print "Current .ScaleWidth ="; Printer.ScaleWidth
Printer.Print "Current .ScaleHeight ="; Printer.ScaleHeight
Printer.EndDoc
```

A *twip*, when printed on most printers, consumes about 1/72 of a square inch.

For a laser printer that emulates a Hewlett-Packard LaserJet II+, the default .ScaleWidth property setting is 11520 and the default .ScaleHeight is 15120. Divided by 80 columns per page, you find that Printer.CurrentX is increased by 144 *printer twips* for each character printed. Likewise, divided by 60 lines per page, you find that Printer.CurrentY is increased by 252 printer twips each time a carriage return or line feed is generated. The printer's internal scale can be manually reset by altering the .ScaleWidth and .ScaleHeight properties for the Printer. object.

The "cursor" position for the printer is maintained in the Printer.CurrentX and Printer.CurrentY properties. The settings for these properties are expressed in *printer twips,* which correlate to the current scale set for the printer. This scale can be altered using the Printer.ScaleHeight and Printer.ScaleWidth properties.

When a picture box is used to display graphics from a file, the graphic image is considered to be the background for the picture box. When an image box is used to display graphics from a file (and this is crucial), the graphic image is considered to be the background for the *form*. Any text to be printed to a picture box using the .Print method appears "in front of" the image; if Windows screens were three-dimensional, the text would be more *toward* you than the background. Placing an image in a picture box does not affect the values of .CurrentX and .CurrentY for that control. When you use the .Cls method to clear a control of its method-drawn graphics or printed text, the background image from the graphics file remains intact.

The property that lists the file name for a background graphics file is the .Picture property.

.Picture   Property

Representation: Graphics background
Applies to: Form, image, picture

The .Picture property is set to the file name of the image that appears as the background for the antecedent picture box object. This file name may have a BMP (Windows bitmap), ICO (standard icon), or WMF (Windows metafile) extension. The picture is aligned with the top left corner of the picture box. If the image is wider or taller than the picture box, the image is said to *hang* beyond the right and bottom edges of the box, respectively.

To set the graphics file for a picture, a form, or an image box at design time, do the following:

1. Indicate the control that will receive the graphics file.

2. Choose that control's Picture property from the Properties window. The property settings bar reads (picture), and the drop-down arrow button beside the settings field becomes an ellipsis (...) button.

3. To choose a file name for this picture, click the ellipsis button. A file selector panel appears, containing a list of BMP bit-map files, ICO icon files, and WMF metafiles.

4. Choose a file name from the list presented and click the OK button. The image file chosen is loaded immediately into the control, and is displayed on the form as design continues.

> **Note:** The file selector panel also displays DIB files, which are not really images but serve as palettes. Visual Basic is capable of processing 256-color images. The colors that can be generated by most VGA graphics systems range in the hundreds of thousands, however, so .DIB files have been provided to help optimize the choice of colors that are interpreted.

When you attribute a graphics file to a picture box or to a form that is too small to fit the size of the graphics file, the overlapping portion on the right or bottom edges remains unseen. Likewise, if a graphics file is too small for the control to which it belongs, by default a margin is left along the right and bottom edges in the control. When you set the .AutoSize property of a picture box, it automatically *expands* to fit a graphics file that is larger than the box itself.

By contrast, when you attribute a graphics file to an image box, the sides of that box either shrink or expand to fit the graphics file, like the way some picture areas in desktop publishing programs shrink or stretch to fit contents assigned to them.

To load an image file into a picture box at run time, you use the LoadPicture() function.

LoadPicture()   Function

Purpose: Graphics file acquisition
Syntax:

```
[VirTerm.]Picture = LoadPicture("filename$")
```

in which *filename$* refers to a file with the extension BMP (Windows bitmap), ICO (standard icon), or WMF (Windows metafile).

The LoadPicture() function loads the specified image file into the virtual terminal control designated by *VirTerm*.

One of the interesting features exclusive to an image box is the fact that its graphics contents can be *stretched*—made bigger—to fit the boundaries of the image box, rather than have the boundaries shrink or stretch to fit the graphics. You set this mode of display with the .Stretch property.

.Stretch   Property

Representation: Permission to automatically resize contents
Applies to: Image
Set by way of: Properties window, program instruction

The .Stretch property for an image box is set to a True/False value denoting whether the interpreter is given permission to stretch (or shrink) the graphics contents of an image box to fit the existing boundaries of that control.

Figure 42.1 demonstrates how handy the .Stretch property can be. This picture displays two forms, with an image box in each form. The form on the right shows expanded image boxes containing exactly the same contents as the form on the left, although the right form has its .Stretch property set to true.

Figure 42.1

An image box
before and after
stretching.

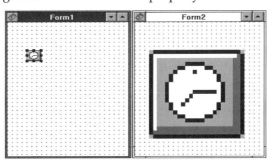

Persistent Bitmaps

The image contained in a picture box is maintained in memory as a separate view of the control's contents, called a *persistent bitmap*. Whereas the .Picture property refers exclusively to the background for a control, the .Image property refers directly to whatever graphics contents belong to the control at the time. When text or graphics are added to a picture box by way of methods, the resulting image becomes part of the .Image property for that control.

.Image   Property

Representation: Graphical contents
Applies to: Form, picture
Set by way of: Program execution

The .Image property for a form or picture box is always set to the graphical contents of that control. This property is set indirectly through the use of methods to add graphics to that control.

> **Note:** Text plotted to a picture box is not recognized as text, but as graphics. It therefore cannot be evaluated alphanumerically.

After the image in the picture box has been altered, its .Image property contents can be saved to disk using the SavePicture statement.

SavePicture   Statement

Purpose: Image content saving
Syntax:

```
SavePicture [Object.]property, filename$
```

in which *filename$* refers to a file with the extension BMP (Windows bitmap), ICO (standard icon), or WMF (Windows metafile).

The SavePicture statement saves to disk either the .Picture or .Image currently residing in the designated picture box *Object*, using the given *filename$*. The term *property* is set either to the word Image or to a direct reference to the *Object* and its .Picture property. If Image is specified, then regardless of the file name or extension expressed, the image is saved as a Windows bitmap file, which is given a BMP extension. If *Object*.Picture is specified, the picture is saved in its current format in the control, which can be a Windows bitmap, a standard icon, or a metafile.

Example

In the first DragStrip test application in Chapter 30, "Dragging Controls," the image of a folder was dragged by the mouse into the area of a picture box, which had the image of a file cabinet loaded into it. As the folder image crossed the boundaries of the picture box, another image was loaded into the box, making the file cabinet appear to open:

```
Sub Cabinet_DragOver (Source As Control, X As Single,
➥Y As Single, State As Integer)
If Source.Tag = "Folder" Then
    Cabinet.Picture = LoadPicture
    ➥("c:\vb3\icons\office\files03b.ico")
End If
If State = 1 Then
    Cabinet.Picture = LoadPicture
    ➥("c:\vb3\icons\office\files03a.ico")
End If
End Sub
```

When the pointer crossed over the image back into the regular form area, the original file cabinet image was reloaded into the picture box. The LoadPicture() function can be invoked any number of times during an application's run time for a single picture box.

As you saw in the discussion on MDI forms, the control area of that form is a picture box, which is by default aligned along the top edge. You can change this alignment through the setting of the .Align property.

.Align   Property

Representation: Automatic picture alignment
Applies to: Picture
Set by way of: Properties window

The .Align property setting for a picture box represents its automatic placement in a standard form or MDI form. The setting denotes whether the picture box should, by default, be stretched for the breadth of the form to which it belongs, as well as whether it is to be positioned along the upper or lower edges by default. With .Align set to a non-zero value, the interpreter repositions the picture box at design time as specified. Settings for this property may be as follows:

0   Picture box may appear anywhere as positioned (this is the default for a standard form).

1   Picture box is stretched to fit the .Width of the form, and is positioned along the upper edge (this is the default for an MDI form).

2   Picture box is stretched to fit the .Width of the form, and is positioned along the lower edge.

Summary

A picture box is different from an image box in that a picture box is a legal parent control, and that other controls can be assigned to it like a frame. An image box contains an image that belongs to the form that the image box is in.

The background image currently loaded into a picture or image box object is registered by its file name, appearing as the `.Picture` property for that object. An image can be loaded into a picture box at design time by setting this `.Picture` property. An image can be loaded into a picture box at run time using the `LoadPicture()` function; likewise, an altered image can be saved from a picture box to disk using the `SavePicture` statement.

Review Questions

1. After printing the words "Hello World" to the picture box `Biehl`, what is the value of `Biehl.CurrentX`?

2. Suppose you placed a semicolon to the right of the quotation mark closing the line. What would be the value of `Biehl.CurrentX` then?

3. What is the difference, in Visual Basic terms, between an image and a picture?

4. Why is `LoadPicture()` a function and `SavePicture` a statement?

CHAPTER 43

Plotting

In this chapter, you learn how to use the Visual Basic plotting mechanism to draw images directly into forms and picture boxes. For every form and picture box in a VB application, the interpreter maintains a *virtual pen* that makes particular elements of the drawing process simulate using a plotter device, giving the appearance of drawing with ink on paper. The VB interpreter knows how to move this pen from place to place, change pen colors, and draw a few basic shapes. First, however, you look at the origins of the Visual Basic coordinate system.

Coordinate Systems

The microcomputers of the late 1970s and early 1980s used their own fixed-screen coordinate systems. The coordinate systems of the first microcomputer BASIC implementations used parameter pairs to address individual pixels or pixel blocks on-screen. The block at the top left corner of the screen was generally addressed as (0, 0). Because, back then, people dealt with relatively low-resolution screens for output, the bottom right block was generally some value like (128, 64). Line-plotting statements, such as the ones pioneered by AppleSoft BASIC, used two pairs of these x- and y-axis coordinates as beginning and end points. More advanced BASICs used circle-plotting statements that used either two pairs of coordinates representing the "corners" of the circle-plotting area, or one pair representing the center and a third value for the radius of the circle. BASIC interpreters were considered advanced if they could draw circles this way.

Actually, the concept of addressing points on the screen or cursor locations with parameter pairs was quite advanced for the mid-1970s, because most minicomputer and mainframe computer programmers didn't have such tools on their own systems. Arguably, the major advances in programming languages premiered on home computers like the Apple II, the TRS-80, and the Atari 400/800 long before the big computer companies of today considered such innovations to have any purpose beyond the recreational.

One major reason parameter pairs were so innovative is as follows: At times, programmers wanted to plot data to just one rectangular region of the screen. On character-based minicomputers, plotting to the screen always began in the top left corner. The screen-plotting mechanism was as graphically complex as typing a picture of something on your portable typewriter; text and graphic blocks were "typed" to the screen. To get something to appear in the middle of the screen—this was like typing something in the middle of a piece of paper—the programmer had to invoke carriage returns for several lines and then tab several spaces to the right. These lines and spaces could be programmed in advance as y- and x-axis offset coordinates, respectively. Now, the PRINT command could return the carriage the number of lines in the offset variable OY, and the TAB() function could space the cursor to the right for the number of spaces in the offset variable OX.

Whereas the environment of character-based minicomputers existed in a virtual IBM Selectric II typewriter, the environment of such pioneering graphic computers as Apple's and Atari's was Cartesian geometric space, which gave programmers and mathematicians much more freedom of expression. The technique they used was to have OX and OY serve as offset intervals from the *origin* point (0, 0). These offsets allowed for the creation of a *virtual origin* of a semi-independent plotting region of the screen. By plotting to a point such as (75 + OX, 25 + OY), a point (75, 25) virtually exists in the programmer's mind relative to this semi-independent region. The programmer could then comfortably ignore OX and OY for now, and concentrate on the region as if it were itself a screen.

Later interpreters, using BASIC as well as other languages, allowed for the declaration of these independent regions without the use of offset variables in the plotting statement. No one is sure who gets the credit for first naming these declarable regions *windows*. So it was, arguably, that windows were created for the convenience of the programmer rather than the user.

Windows Inside Windows

Visual Basic maintains a coordinate system for the Screen. object, although this system is not intended for direct plotting. In other words, you can't draw a line from the absolute top left corner of the screen to the bottom right corner unless you find a way to expand the drawing area of a form so that it covers the entire screen, and then plot to that form as if it were the screen. In Visual Basic, screen coordinates are reserved for the positioning of forms. Each form then has its own coordinate system. As you've seen, graphic objects are positioned relative to the coordinates of the form rather than to those of the screen. Picture boxes, as you learned in the previous chapter, have their own coordinate systems, which are independent from the form.

The coordinate system Visual Basic uses is extraordinarily versatile. The "blocks" it uses, by default, are actually smaller in geometric configuration space than pixels themselves. The screen coordinate system is, thus, independent of the screen. Each point along this system is considered a *twip*. A twip is a plotting point, as interpreted in memory by Microsoft Windows, in a relative coordinate system that exists independently from the physical pixel-based coordinate system of the screen.

In all graphical computers, each unit in the coordinate system is represented in memory by a certain number of bits. Usually, the combination of bits for a pixel represents, using binary coding, the color of the pixel at that point. This is true for most VGA graphics systems. Memory in these systems is specially apportioned for the VGA card itself, so that the motherboard's main memory can be used for other purposes. In the main memory, Windows maintains a representation of the screen that has a greater resolution than the actual screen. Visual Basic is capable of allocating segments of main memory for itself to maintain images that have a greater resolution than the screen. This way, if the graphics hardware of the computer changes and the screen drivers are advanced to go with it, the screen representation can be rescaled to fit the new screen without drastically altering the VB program.

The Color Scheme

In Visual Basic, as with every graphical computer devised to date, when you plot a point of a particular color to a specified location, you change the bitwise pattern of the portion of memory that corresponds to that point. The new pattern then represents the new color of that point. Visual Basic maintains a variety of methods for determining which color is to be plotted. As you might have guessed, the system Visual Basic uses is far more complex than choosing a color for a box on your Apple II.

Using the same philosophy that says the programmer should have more points available for plotting than there are pixels, Visual Basic makes it possible for the programmer to have more color *values* available than there may be colors. Generally, Windows screen drivers mix existing colors to form patterns that represent in-between colors. These patterns are formed with multiple pixels, in the hope that your eye will perform the role of color blender. As a result, you cannot possibly plot a point to the screen using any one of 16,777,216 colors, although the RGB() function acts as if you can.

RGB()   **Function**

Purpose: Color value representation
Syntax:

```
color& = RGB(red%, green%, blue%)
```

in which *red%*, *green%*, and *blue%* are integers with the range 0 to 255, representing the intensity of each primary color in the mixture.

The RGB() function returns a single long integer value that is a mathematical combination of the three input parameters and represents, for the Visual Basic interpreter, a specific color-mixture value. Each parameter represents the amount of its optical primary color used in the mixture. The greater the parameter value, the brighter the primary color for the mixture.

This function comes in handy because it's doubtful you'd want to look up a particular color from a table of 16,777,216 choices. When blending colors optically, using light rather than pigment, the three primary colors are red, blue, and *green*. For some people, mixing colors in this manner may be a bit foreign at first. Optically, a full blend of red and green forms *yellow*. Using the RGB() function, the brightest yellow obtainable would be represented as RGB(255, 255, 0), in which the 0 stands for no blue. White would be represented as RGB(255, 255, 255), and a medium gray would be RGB(128, 128, 128).

At first, it might appear that such color blending makes available to the programmer every color imaginable; but this is not true. No optical cathode ray tube has yet been able to generate a true emerald green or leaf green, a warm gray, or a cobalt blue. Conceivably, you do have every color in the rainbow available to you, but keep in mind that browns are not in the rainbow. You could use pattern blending to try to simulate brown; however, what you really get is a warm but dark form of red, with red pixels against black ones—using, for instance, RGB(45, 10, 0). The green can be used to dull the brightness of the red. Too much green, however, generates yellow specks in the mixture. If you try to simulate burnt sienna or raw umber, you will most likely fail.

If you're familiar with programming using the BASIC interpreter that came with your version of DOS, or if you've used Microsoft QuickBASIC, you've probably become accustomed to the CGA color registers for plotting to the fixed coordinate system of DOS' character-based screen. Visual Basic provides a function that simulates these registers for those who have them already ingrained in their brains. It is the QBColor() function.

QBColor()   **Function**

Purpose: CGA color simulation
Syntax:

```
color& = QBColor(register%)
```

The QBColor() function returns a long integer value that represents, for the Visual Basic interpreter, a color mixture roughly equivalent to the value of the color register% used in Microsoft QuickBASIC for plotting to the CGA screen. The parameter register% can take any of the values in table 43.1. In this table, the values are shown next to their RGB() functional equivalents.

Table 43.1. QuickBASIC and RGB color conversion chart.

QB Color Value	QB Color	RGB Color
0	Black	RGB(0, 0, 0)
1	Blue	RGB(0, 0, 191)
2	Green	RGB(0, 191, 0)
3	Dark Cyan	RGB(0, 191, 191)
4	Red	RGB(191, 0, 0)
5	Magenta	RGB(191, 0, 191)
6	Dark Yellow	RGB(191, 191, 0)
7	Page White	RGB(191, 191, 191)
8	Gray	RGB(64, 64, 64)
9	Bright Blue	RGB(0, 0, 255)
10	Bright Green	RGB(0, 255, 0)
11	Bright Cyan	RGB(0, 255, 255)
12	Bright Red	RGB(255, 0, 0)
13	Bright Magenta	RGB(255, 0, 255)
14	Bright Yellow	RGB(255, 255, 0)
15	Bright White	RGB(255, 255, 255)

In most computer systems, plotting to or *setting* a point to a certain color changes the bitwise value of the location in memory that corresponds directly to the specified point. This setting in memory is what changes the color of the pixel on-screen. In Visual Basic, the coordinate systems are entirely relative. Setting a specified twip changes the bitwise value of the location in memory that corresponds to the twip. The point on the screen that corresponds to the twip coordinates, however, is determined relatively, not directly, with internal offsets as well as a variable coordinate scale.

The .PSet method is used to set a twip to a certain color.

.PSet   Method

Purpose: Pixel color value setting
Syntax:

```
[Object.]PSet [Step](twipx!, twipy!)[, color&]
```

The .PSet method sets the color value of a coordinate point represented by the coordinates (*twipx!*, *twipy!*). If the point is currently visible on-screen, the pixel relative to that point along the current twip coordinate system will have its color value set. If the point is not visible on-screen, the point in memory is set anyway, and the change (if any) is reflected on-screen when that point is made visible.

If *Object.* is specified, the method sets the point value relative to the coordinates of the specified object. Otherwise, the coordinate system of the form that contains the method is assumed. If *color&* is specified, the .PSet method sets the color value of the point to any long integer value in the range 0 to 16,777,215, representing a color or color pattern recognized by Microsoft Windows. The value of *color&* can be represented by the function RGB() or QBColor(). To *reset* a point—to give it the background color value—the property term .BackColor can be used as *color&*. If *color&* is not specified, the .PSet method sets the point's color value to the value of the .ForeColor property of the specified object.

If Step is in the method, the VB interpreter considers the coordinate system expressed in (*twipx!*, *twipy!*) to be relative to the last point plotted, or to (0, 0) if no point has been plotted. The last point plotted in a graphic object can be obtained through the .CurrentX and .CurrentY properties for that object.

The width and height of the point plotted with .PSet can be set in advance with the .DrawWidth property of the object receiving the point. The point can be plotted as an invisible point—existent although unseen—by setting the .DrawStyle of the object to 5.

The coordinate system used in Visual Basic graphics methods is the twip coordinate system, which is manually scalable by the programmer. If you can imagine the screen as a grid full of pixels, overlay in your mind a finer, more detailed grid that represents twips. Pixels are the little dots that make pictures or letters on your screen. A pixel is thus a small filled area of light. A twip, by contrast, is an intersection point between two logically interpreted axis lines. Figure 43.1 shows the conceptual difference between the pixel system and the twip system.

Figure 43.1

The two coordinate systems of Visual Basic.

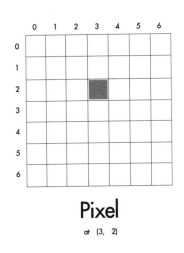

Pixel

at (3, 2)

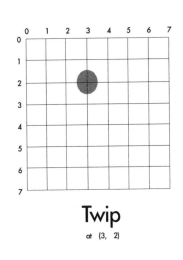

Twip

at (3, 2)

If you play board games, perhaps you'll better understand the pixels versus twips dilemma by imagining that each point plotted by a Visual Basic graphics method is a chesspiece. The pixel coordinate system would be like chess, in which the piece occupies the center of a space or square. The twip coordinate system, by contrast, is like Chinese checkers, in which each piece sits on the intersection between lines along the board. Instead of occupying a space, the Chinese checker piece occupies a point.

A *twip* is plotted along an intersection point in memory, whereas a *pixel* is plotted in a fixed space.

This analogy is important because an intersection point does not constitute a measurable area. There is therefore no unit of spatial measurement called a twip, whereas a pixel consumes space and therefore can be used as an area measurement. When a method such as .PSet is used to set the color value of a twip coordinate, the pixel—or even *pixels*—nearest that twip coordinate is set to the new color. If the .DrawWidth of each point or line in a picture box or form is set to greater than 1, then as figure 43.2 shows, a block of pixels having an approximate center that is at or near the twip coordinates is set to the new color.

Figure 43.2

Plotting a block of pixels along a twip.

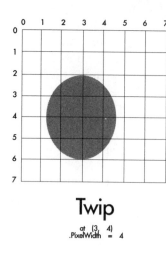

Twip

at (3, 4)
.PixelWidth = 4

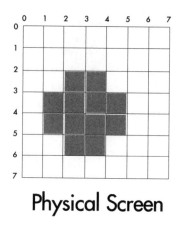

Physical Screen

Plotting Lines

The following routine plots a dotted diagonal line to the object `Picture1.`:

```
For plt = 0 To 50 Step 5
    Picture1.PSet (plt, plt)
Next plt
```

There are 11 dots in this line because the interpreter counts from 0 to 50 by fives, starting with 0. Here, the value of variable `plt` represents both the x- and y-axis values for the `.PSet` method. So, for each iteration of the loop clause, the plot point is spaced as many twips down as to the right. Twips are considered by Visual Basic to be relatively square. Depending on the screen driver and graphics hardware you're currently using, pixels on the screen should be square as well—in other words, a block of pixels `plt` wide and `plt` high should appear symmetrical.

Example

Suppose the diagonal dotted line is to extend from some unknown point where plotting has taken place previously. You could use the `Step` extension to have the virtual pen jump to a location relative to the previous plot coordinates, as follows:

```
For dot = 1 to 11
    Picture1.PSet Step (5, 5)
Next dot
```

This routine produces a dotted line identical in form to the one generated by the routine before it, although its plot position starts at the point returnable as (`Picture1.CurrentX, Picture1.CurrentY`). In other words, it starts at the last point that received a plot, or at (`0, 0`) if no plotting has taken place. With each iteration, the `.PSet` method steps the pen five spaces to the right and five spaces down. You can express 5 both times as a constant, because each `Step` takes place relative to the point previously plotted. The method uses `.CurrentX` and `.CurrentY` (although not explicitly) as offsets for the relative coordinate system—modern equivalents of the `OX` and `OY` variables from the historical example earlier in this chapter.

There is, thankfully, a more direct method for drawing a line: using the `.Line` method.

.Line   Method

Purpose: Geometric line plotting
Syntax:

```
[Object.]Line [[Step](twipx1!, twipy1!)]
➡ -[Step](twipx2!, twipy2!)[, color&][, B][F]
```

The `.Line` method sets the color value of a linear series of all addressable twips represented in memory, extending from the coordinates (`twipx1!, twipy1!`) to (`twipx2!, twipy2!`). The two coordinate pairs are always separated by a hyphen. The color value for each twip in the series is set, regardless of whether it is visible at present. If any or all of the specified twips are invisible or obstructed by some other graphic object, their color values are set anyway, and the change (if any) is reflected on-screen when those twips are made visible.

If `Object.` is specified, the method sets the twip values relative to the coordinates of the specified object. Otherwise, the coordinate system of the form containing the method is assumed. The form the line takes is returnable through the properties `.DrawStyle` and `.DrawWidth`, in which `.DrawStyle` represents the type of hatching used in the line (if any) and `.DrawWidth` represents the relative width of the line drawn.

If the first coordinate pair is omitted, the interpreter assumes that the line should extend from the last plotted point to the coordinates specified by the second pair, which cannot be omitted. The hyphen remains in the method instruction, nonetheless. The last point plotted in a graphic object can be obtained through the `.CurrentX` and `.CurrentY` properties for that object. If no points have been plotted for that object, initial coordinates of (`0, 0`) are assumed.

If Step is included before the first pair of coordinates, those coordinates are assumed to be relative to the last point plotted before the instruction was executed, as represented in .CurrentX and .CurrentY. If Step is included before the second pair of coordinates, those coordinates are assumed to be relative to the first pair of coordinates.

If *color&* is specified, the .Line method sets the color values of the twips in the series to any long integer value in the range 0 to 16,777,215, representing a color or color pattern recognized by Microsoft Windows. The value of *color&* can be represented by the function RGB() or QBColor(). To *reset* the points in a linear series—to give them the background color value—the property term .BackColor can be used as *color&*. If *color&* is not specified, the .Line method sets the series' color value to the value of the .ForeColor property of the specified object.

If B is included toward the end of the .Line method, the instruction does not just draw a line, but it draws a box with opposite corners that are expressed as the two pairs of coordinates. In other words, the box extends from point (twipx1!, twipy1!) to (twipx2!, twipy1!), to (twipx2!, twipy2!), to (twipx1!, twipy2!), and back to (twipx1!, twipy1!). Only coordinate sets 1 and 2 need to be specified. If F is included beside B, the box is filled with the color used to plot the box itself. If F is not included beside B, the box is filled with the color and pattern obtainable through the .FillColor and .FillStyle properties, which may be different from the color used to plot the box. By default, the filling color and pattern are transparent. If B or BF is included and *color&* is omitted, the comma used as a delimiter for *color&* remains, as in ,,BF.

If you specify a B *alone* in the .Line method, you have transformed the method into a box-drawing method. The graphic object receiving the box has a .FillColor and .FillStyle currently set to the independent color and style reserved for closed shapes produced by graphics methods. If you specify BF in the .Line method—the F stands for *filled*—you are telling the interpreter to *ignore* the current .FillColor and .FillStyle for the object receiving the box and to fill the box solidly with whatever color was used to draw the box, whether it was taken from the .ForeColor property or stated as the optional *color&* parameter.

Line Thickness and Fill

The preceding discussion mentioned four properties, each of which may affect the outcome of the .Line method: the .DrawStyle property, the .DrawWidth property, the .FillColor property, and the .FillStyle property.

.DrawStyle   **Property**

Representation: Plot dashing assignment
Applies to: Form, picture, printer
Set by way of: Properties window, program instruction

The .DrawStyle property for a virtual terminal object is set to a value that represents the style of line to be produced by the next method, which draws a series of points to the object. This property can take any of the following values:

0	_____	(Solid, resting half in, half outside the area of the box—the default)
1	_ _ _	(Dash)
2	. . . .	(Dot)
3	_ . _ .	(Dash-dot)
4	_ . . _	(Dash-dot-dot)
5		(Invisible)
6	_____	(Solid, although entirely inside the area of the box)

.DrawWidth   **Property**

Representation: Plot width assignment
Applies to: Form, picture, printer
Set by way of: Properties window, program instruction

The .DrawWidth property is set to the width, in pixels, of any lines or points to be plotted to the antecedent object using graphics methods.

.FillColor   **Property**

Representation: Closed plot solid color
Applies to: Form, picture, printer
Set by way of: Properties window, program instruction

The .FillColor property is set to the RGB color to be reserved for all closed shapes produced with graphics methods. The default value for .FillColor is 0 (black).

.FillStyle   Property

Representation: Closed plot pattern assignment
Applies to: Form, picture, printer
Set by way of: Properties window, program instruction

The .FillStyle property is set to the fill pattern to be reserved for all closed shapes produced with graphics methods. The value of .FillStyle can take any of the values depicted in figure 43.3. The default setting for .FillStyle is 1, for transparency.

Figure 43.3

The settings for
.FillStyle.

Example

Following is the routine used to generate the form in figure 43.3:

```
Sub Form_Load ()
Form1.Show
offsetx = 250
offsety = 250
For reg = 0 To 7
    Form1.FillStyle = reg
    Form1.Line (offsetx, 300 * (reg + 1) + offsety)
    ➥ - (offsetx + 500, 300 * (reg + 1) + offsety + 250), , B
    Form1.CurrentY = 300 * (reg + 1) + offsety
    Form1.Print reg
Next reg
End Sub
```

Here is the preceding procedure translated into pseudocode:

*Show **Form1**, although it's empty at the moment.*
Set two offset variables for the x- and y-axes to 250,
 so that you can have left and top margins.

Start counting from 0 to 7.
    Set the .FillStyle to the current count value.
    *Draw a box spaced out **offsetx** twips from the left,*
    500 twips long and 250 twips high, starting at
    (300 times the number of boxes drawn) twips down
    *from the top margin **offsety**, leaving a space of*
    50 twips between boxes.
    Set the y-axis value of the virtual pen so that
    it's aligned with the top of the box just plotted.
    Print the current count value.
Count the next value.
End of procedure.

The preceding procedure can be modified to show all the available color registers that can be obtained by using the function QBColor():

```
Sub Form_Load ()
Form1.Show
offsetx = 250
offsety = 250
For reg = 0 To 15
    Form1.Line (offsetx, 300 * (reg + 1) + offsety)
      -(offsetx + 500, 300 * (reg + 1) + offsety + 250),
      QBColor(reg), BF
    Form1.CurrentY = 300 * (reg + 1) + offsety
    clr& = Form1.Point(offsetx, 300 * (reg + 1) + offsety)
    Form1.Print clr&, Hex$(clr&)
Next reg
End Sub
```

In this procedure, the vacancy between the two adjacent commas in the .Line method of the previous procedure is filled with QBColor(reg). By specifying this color directly, you tell the interpreter to overlook the .ForeColor it would normally use for drawing this object; however, .ForeColor is not changed. By including the F after the B, you tell the interpreter to also overlook the .FillColor and .FillStyle normally reserved for closed shapes, and to instead use the specified color to solidly fill the object.

So that you can see the RGB color registers as decimal and hexadecimal numbers, these numbers are printed next to their respective boxes using the Form1.Print method. The RGB color was obtained from the box area through the use of the .Point method, which detects the color of any designated point.

.Point   Method

Purpose: Color value acquisition
Syntax:

```
color& = [Object.]Point(twipx!, twipy!)
```

The .Point method acts like a function in that it returns the RGB color value of the pixel nearest the specified twip coordinates, in the long integer *color&*. The method is specified, however, using object-oriented syntax. If Object. is included in the instruction, the coordinate system of the specified object is used. Otherwise, the system of the form currently containing the instruction is assumed.

Use the .Line method whenever you want to draw a box; there is no .Box method in Visual Basic, although there are BOX statements in other versions of BASIC. In a similarly odd manner, you must invoke the .Circle method to draw an arc or a curved line.

.Circle   Method

Purpose: Ellipse plotting
Syntax:

```
[Object.]Circle [Step](twipx!, twipy!), radius![, color&]
➥[, ang_start!, ang_end!][, aspect!]
```

The .Circle method plots a series of points in a curve, all of which geometrically converge around a center point specified as (*twipx!*, *twipy!*). By default, these points take the form of a circle; however, by specifying the latter three optional parameters, you can plot an arc or ellipse instead.

Unless *aspect!* is specified, each point in the series is plotted at a distance of *radius!* twips from the center coordinates. If *color&* is specified, the series is plotted in the specified color. The RGB() and QBColor() functions can be used to determine the value of *color&*. If *color&* is omitted, the series is plotted using the color set as the .ForeColor property setting of the object receiving the plot.

If *ang_start!* and *ang_end!* are specified, plotting of the circle begins at a point that forms an angle *ang_start!* radians relative to the center point and extends to a point that forms an angle *ang_end* radians relative to the center point. The radian range specifiable for these parameters is (–2 * Pi) – (2 * Pi). If neither parameter is specified, the curve is plotted as a closed shape, as either a circle or an ellipse. As such, the shape is filled with a pattern and color specified as the current values of the .FillStyle and .FillColor properties. By default, the fill style for an object is transparent (1) and the fill color is black (0).

The value of *aspect!*, when specified, represents the ratio of height to width for the series, for use in plotting noncircular arcs or ellipses. A 4:1 ratio of height to width is represented as an *aspect!* of 4, which forms a tall ellipse. Conversely, a 1:4 ratio is represented as an *aspect!* of .25, which forms a short ellipse. If *aspect!* is specified, the value of *radius!* becomes half the length of the *major axis* of the ellipse—being the widest obtainable diameter of the ellipse.

If Step is included with the .Circle method, the coordinate pair following Step is interpreted as relative to the last point plotted, or to (0, 0) if no point has previously been plotted. The last point plotted in a graphic object is returnable in the properties .CurrentX and .CurrentY.

Example

The QBColor() function test procedure can be converted to plot ellipses rather than boxes, as follows:

```
Sub Form_Load ()
Form1.Show
Form1.FillStyle = 0
offsetx = 250
offsety = 250
For reg = 0 To 15
    Form1.FillColor = QBColor(reg)
    Form1.Circle (offsetx + 250, 300 * (reg + 1) + offsety
    ➡+ 125), 250, QBColor(reg), , , .5
    Form1.CurrentY = 300 * (reg + 1) + offsety
    Form1.CurrentX = Form1.CurrentX + 300
    clr& = Form1.Point(offsetx + 250, 300 * (reg + 1)
    ➡+ offsety + 125)
    Form1.Print clr&, Hex$(clr&)
Next reg
End Sub
```

Here, the coordinate pair from the old .Line method was modified so that plotting takes place around the center. No angles were specified in the .Circle instruction, so the shape is closed and is filled solid because the Form1.FillStyle is set to 0 (solid). The aspect ratio is .5, so the ellipse is half as high as it is wide.

Because plotting ends at the bottom of the ellipse, .CurrentX had to be spaced out a little to make room for the text. The .Point method now obtains the color value from the center of the ellipse rather than from the top right corner of the box. Figure 43.4 is an example of what you should see.

Figure 43.4

The QuickBASIC-style watercolor paintbox.

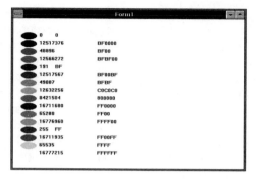

Summary

The Visual Basic coordinate system is based on a grid of twips. A twip point is really an intersection point on the coordinate grid; therefore, the system uses true Cartesian geometric coordinates. The twip coordinate system is separate from the pixel coordinate system. The pixel or pixels set with bitmapped graphics are the pixel(s) that are the closest to the twips addressed by the statement.

Visual Basic supports all of Windows' 16,777,216 logical colors, although graphics hardware still doesn't support that many colors. Instead of specifying a color register from the more than 16 million available, you can use the RGB() and QBColor() functions as substitutes for color numbers. These functions provide access to VGA color mixtures and CGA color register numbers, respectively.

The .PSet method is used to plot a point to a form, a picture box, or the printer. The .Line method is used to plot a line or series of points; however, it can also be used to plot filled and unfilled boxes. Unless otherwise specified in the instruction itself, the .Line method relies on the .DrawStyle, .DrawWidth, .FillColor, and .FillStyle properties for the graphic object that receives the plot to determine the appearance of the plotted line or shape.

You can obtain the color of the pixel nearest any specified twip location by using the .Point method. You can draw a circle, ellipse, or unclosed arc by using the .Circle method. If starting and ending angles are specified using this method, an arc is plotted; otherwise, a shape is plotted having a .FillStyle and .FillColor that both rely on the property settings for the object receiving the shape.

Review Questions

1. Does the `.PSet` method affect the values of properties `.CurrentX` and `.CurrentY`?

2. Does the `.Point` method affect the values of properties `.CurrentX` and `.CurrentY`?

3. Assume you've plotted a line to a picture box using the `.Line` method, which uses the twip coordinate system. As a result, the image in the picture box contains a line between two points. If you use the `.Move` method to magnify that image, making the line *bigger*, does the line become *thicker* or merely *broader*?

Review Exercises

1. Write a procedure that draws a circle gradually, as if it is being drawn with a compass and pen. Use the `.Circle` method and specify the start and end angles of the arc being drawn. **Hint:** Use a loop clause that counts the current value of the end angle.

2. Write a procedure that continually resets the `.FillColor` property for a picture box so that it gradually fades from white to black.

CHAPTER 44

Image Integrity and Scaling

In this chapter, you study the properties that direct the Visual Basic interpreter to maintain the image integrity of a form or picture box. You also learn how to resize a picture box while it is running, and how to make its coordinate system rescale itself to meet the current box size.

Integrity Properties

When the contents of a picture box are overlapped by another form, the portions that you no longer see may be retained in memory, although they may be lost—by default, they are lost. You can have the Visual Basic interpreter reserve a region of memory to maintain the graphics integrity of controls that may overlap; keep in mind, however, that this may consume valuable memory and Windows resources.

.AutoRedraw   **Property**

Representation: Image reserve permission
Applies to: Form, picture
Set by way of: Properties window

The `.AutoRedraw` property for a form or picture box is set to a True/False value that denotes whether the interpreter is to maintain a persistent bitmap of the specified image in memory. If the property is set to true, whenever another object is moved by process or user-directed motion to an area that partially or totally overlaps the antecedent object of the property, the graphic portion of that object is retained in memory. When the portion is no longer obstructed, the interpreter automatically replots the graphic contents to the object. If the property is set to False, whenever another object is moved to an area that obstructs the antecedent object, the obstructed portion is, in effect, erased from the object. However, when the object is no longer obstructed, the _Paint event is generated, and a _Paint event procedure may be invoked to refresh or repair the contents of the obstructed object.

A *persistent bitmap* is retained in memory for all virtual terminal graphics controls.

Whenever a persistent bitmap in memory is changed by the overlapping of controls on one another, the _Paint event for that control is generated.

_Paint   Event

Action: Reacquisition of reserve image
Applies to: Form, picture
Parameters: Index As Integer (control arrays only)

The _Paint event for a form or picture box is recognized when the .AutoRedraw property for that object is set to False (0), and the once-obstructed (partially or totally) antecedent object is partly or totally freed from obstruction. This allows the program to redraw the object manually, thus conserving memory for other purposes.

When a Visual Basic application is busy processing mathematical functions, it may choose, for time conservation purposes, to put off any regular updates that should be made to the contents of a graphic object. At times, you may need to shift the VB interpreter's attention for a moment to updating a specific object, if only to tidy up things. The .Refresh method is provided for such a purpose.

.Refresh   Method

Purpose: Forced update of object contents
Syntax:

    Object.Refresh

The .Refresh method tells the interpreter to suspend mathematical processes temporarily, long enough to update the contents of the specified *Object*. These contents may have been recipients of graphical or text-changing instructions, but the interpreter may have put off execution of these instructions to conserve time. If no such updates await the specified object, nothing happens.

Rescaling

As discussed earlier, the twip coordinate system is precise and, at the same time, somewhat confusing. Other optional coordinate systems are available for any graphic object, which you can select with the .ScaleMode property setting.

.ScaleMode   **Property**

Representation: Coordinate system choice
Applies to: Form, picture, printer

The .ScaleMode property for a virtual terminal graphic object is set to one of eight integer values that represent the type of coordinate system used for the antecedent object. This value can be one of the following:

0   User-defined. This setting takes place automatically when the programmer sets the scale for the antecedent object to a variable value.

1   Twip coordinate system (default).

2   *Points,* approximately 72 points per inch on a 14-inch-diagonal monitor.

3   Pixel coordinate system, determined using the current screen resolution of Microsoft Windows.

4   Twelve-pitch character-based system, representing 12 characters to the inch horizontally and six lines to the inch, when printed to a standard printer device.

5   *Inches,* again assuming a 14-inch-diagonal monitor.

6   Millimeters.

7   Centimeters.

Mode 2 is especially helpful when you are creating a page layout application. Mode 3 is for those who are more comfortable with pixel-to-pixel plotting. Mode 4 works best with picture boxes that will contain only text, and for the Printer. object. Modes 5 through 7 are helpful when you plot images to the screen that will be represented on paper using more definite and common units of measurement.

Four properties are available to the programmer for defining a particular coordinate scale for an object: the .ScaleLeft, .ScaleTop, .ScaleWidth, and .ScaleHeight properties.

.ScaleLeft, .ScaleTop, .ScaleWidth, and .ScaleHeight   **Properties**

Representation: Variable geometric coordinate establishment
Applies to: Form, MDI, picture, printer
Set by way of: Properties window, program instruction

The `.ScaleLeft` and `.ScaleTop` properties are set to the coordinate pair, representing the point at the top left corner of the antecedent object. The `.ScaleWidth` property represents the number of x-axis divisions in the coordinate scale of the antecedent object. Likewise, the `.ScaleHeight` property represents the number of y-axis divisions in the coordinate scale of the antecedent object.

These properties can be alternatively set with the `.Scale` method.

.Scale   **Method**

Purpose: Variable coordinate system establishment
Syntax:

> `[Object.]Scale [(origx!, origy!)-(extx!, exty!)]`

The `.Scale` method sets the coordinate pair for the top left corner of the antecedent object to `(origx!, origy!)` and the coordinate pair for the bottom right corner of the object to `(extx!, exty!)`. If both pairs of coordinates are omitted, the scale for the object is reset to the default twip coordinate scale.

To demonstrate rescaling at work, here is an application that generates a moving star pattern, like those you see in science fiction movies (only slower). The form itself can be set to any size; it is vital that you place a timer control somewhere within the form, to give the user time to resize the form while it's running. By setting the scale properties for the form, the star pattern will stretch or be squashed to fit the new form size after each resizing.

"Stars" Resizable Starfield Generator

Project name: STARS.MAK
Constituent file: STARS.FRM

General Declarations

```
Dim xoom(50), yoom(50), Rangle(50), Zang(50), lax(50), lay(50),
➡Voom(50), Hypo(50), Lum(50), Brite(50)
Dim rbrite As Integer, gbrite As Integer
Dim Bang As Integer
```

Event Procedures

```
Sub Form_Load ()
Randomize
Timer1.Interval = 20
ViewScreen.ScaleMode = 3
ViewScreen.Scale (0, 0)-(320, 200)
ViewScreen.Show
starbloom
End Sub
```

Here, the single form's .Name is ViewScreen. The interval for the timer control is set to 20 milliseconds (which is very fast; you may need to set this to a higher value if your computer is slower). The screen now is replotted every half-second. The scale is set to pixelline, using virtual 320×200 coordinates.

General Procedures

```
Sub starbloom ()
For bloom = 0 To 50
  Rangle(bloom) = Int(Rnd(1) * 359)
  Zang(bloom) = Int(Rnd(1) * 50)
  Lum(bloom) = Int(Rnd(1) * 255) + 1
  Brite(bloom) = Lum(bloom)
  Voom(bloom) = Zang(bloom) / Lum(bloom)
  Hypo(bloom) = Int(Rnd(1) * 5)
Next bloom
End Sub
```

The procedure Sub starbloom () is invoked to generate the parameters for the first 15 stars. The stars all start out in the center of the form and zoom out toward you. The angle of their trajectory is described by Rangle(bloom). The amount of stable visible speed for each star is described by Zang(bloom), and the visible speed increase as the star comes "closer" to you is described by Voom(bloom). Lum(bloom) is the stable color of each star, and Brite(bloom) is the visible color of the star as it comes closer to you. Hypo(bloom) is a speed multiplication factor that can give the star an extra shove toward you, for the illusion of perspective.

Event Procedures

```
Sub Timer1_Timer ()
For Bang = 0 To 50
    If (lax(Bang) > 0 And lax(Bang) < 319) And (lay(Bang) > 0
    ➥And lay(Bang) < 199) Then
        ViewScreen.PSet (lax(Bang), lay(Bang)), RGB(0, 0, 0)
    End If
    xoom(Bang) = 160 - Sin(Rangle(Bang)) * (Hypo(Bang) *
    ➥(Zang(Bang) * Voom(Bang)))
```

```
      yoom(Bang) = 100 - Cos(Rangle(Bang)) * (Hypo(Bang) *
      ➥(Zang(Bang) * Voom(Bang)))
      If (xoom(Bang) > 0 And xoom(Bang) < 319) And (yoom(Bang) > 0
      ➥And yoom(Bang) < 199) Then
          ViewScreen.PSet (xoom(Bang), yoom(Bang)),
          ➥RGB(Brite(Bang), Brite(Bang), Brite(Bang))
      Else
          Revive Bang
      End If
      lax(Bang) = xoom(Bang)
      lay(Bang) = yoom(Bang)
      Zang(Bang) = Zang(Bang) + .3
      Hypo(Bang) = Hypo(Bang) + 1
      Brite(Bang) = Brite(Bang) + 1
      If Brite(Bang) > 255 Then Brite(Bang) = 255
Next Bang
End Sub
```

By now, you may have become accustomed to trigonometrically extracting (x, y) coordinates from angle and radius values. The coordinate pair here is (Xoom(Bang), Yoom(Bang)). The "old" plot values are stored in (Lax(Bang), Lay(Bang)), and the zooming factors are increased to make the next plot for each star appear closer to you. Brite(Bang) is also increased to make the star brighter with each plot.

General Procedures

```
Sub Revive (Bang As Integer)
  Rangle(Bang) = Int(Rnd(1) * 359)
  Zang(Bang) = Int(Rnd(1) * 100)
  Lum(Bang) = Int(Rnd(1) * 255) + 1
  Brite(Bang) = Lum(Bang)
  Voom(Bang) = Zang(Bang) / Lum(Bang)
  Hypo(Bang) = Int(Rnd(1) * 5)
End Sub
```

The following procedure is used to create a new star each time one wanders off the edge of the form.

Event Procedures

```
Sub Form_Resize ()
ViewScreen.Cls
ViewScreen.ScaleHeight = 200
ViewScreen.ScaleWidth = 320
End Sub
```

Here is the crucial rescaling procedure in its entirety. Each time the `_Resize` event is allowed to occur, the screen is cleared and the scale of the image is reset to 320 units across and 200 units down.

Finally, although Microsoft has made a valiant effort to fix the proportion between twips and inches for all graphics systems, there still is a degree of variation among graphics systems. Because of this, Visual Basic has two properties that may help you adjust your own coordinate system where necessary: the `.TwipsPerPixelX` and `.TwipsPerPixelY` properties.

.TwipsPerPixelX and .TwipsPerPixelY   **Properties**

Representation: Coordinate scale conversion factor
Applies to: Screen, printer
Set by way of: Windows resource

The `.TwipsPerPixelX` and `.TwipsPerPixelY` properties for the `Screen` and `Printer` objects are set by Windows to the approximate whole number of twips per plotted pixel.

Summary

You can use the `.AutoSize` property to tell the Visual Basic interpreter whether to resize a picture box or label to fit oversized contents. You can use the `.AutoRedraw` property to tell the interpreter whether to automatically replot the contents of a bitmapped object after it is cleared from obstruction. If this property is set to false, the contents of the cleared object can still be redrawn manually through the `_Paint` event procedure for that object.

You can select a special coordinate scale for a *virtual terminal* graphic object by setting the `.ScaleMode` property for that object. When an object is rescalable, its top left corner coordinates can be described as (`Picture1.ScaleLeft`, `Picture1.ScaleTop`).

The number of x-axis divisions for an object can be set using .ScaleWidth. Likewise, the number of y-axis divisions for an object can be set using .ScaleHeight. All four of the scale properties can be set simultaneously with the .Scale method.

Review Questions

1. What is the functional difference between making a picture box's contents larger with the .Move method and making the contents larger with the .Scale method?

2. What output device would benefit most from setting the .ScaleMode property to 4?

3. In Cartesian coordinate geometry, a line on a graph that has a y-axis value that increases is a line pointing *upward* from your point of view—assuming the graph is turned "right-side up." In all of Visual Basic's coordinate systems for the screen, a line that has a y-axis value that increases is a line pointing *downward*. The most likely reason for this is one of engineering; speculate on what that reason might be.

Part IX

Error Trapping and Debugging

CHAPTER 45

Registering Errors

In this chapter, you examine the error-trapping mechanism of Visual Basic. Normally, when an error occurs during the processing of a program, the interpreter alerts the user with an alert box, and the process may shut down. As the programmer, you might want to include methods for taking corrective steps to solve manageable problems before the process shuts down. In such cases, Visual Basic offers you error traps, which send execution of the program to a specific routine. You learn how to invoke these routines in this chapter.

One of the common definitions that most requires altering when translated into the realm of computing is that of the word *error*. An error in computing is not necessarily an error in judgment or even a syntax error. An error in Visual Basic is VB's way of telling the program that some invalid condition was reached—for example, trying to read a data file that does not exist.

An error in Visual Basic is VB's way of telling the program that some invalid condition was reached.

The graphical control system of Windows is designed to be almost foolproof; a user still can crash a program using the conventional Windows controls, however. Graphical processes may cause errors to occur. For instance, in the STARS.MAK application programmed for Chapter 44, an error was generated when, for some reason, the coordinates for a star jumped from the maximum x-value of 320 to 1900. The source of the error might not be corrected, but some programming patchwork apparently fixed the problem.

Errors are a natural part of programming; in fact, they're necessary. Without errors, it's nearly impossible for you to know what course of action to take when you're developing a program. A flurry of errors might help you know when a particular course of action is unworkable. If you program an application from an idea in your head, and the program compiles correctly the first time without generating any errors, you are usually pleasantly surprised. When you first see errors being generated by your programs, you know that the process of programming actually is coming along rather smoothly.

In earlier editions of BASIC, programmers generally had to program error-trapping routines that waited for the user to make an error, such as responding to the numeric INPUT command WHAT IS YOUR CURRENT AGE IN YEARS? with an alphanumeric phrase rather than a numeric one. The Microsoft Windows system of user input is such that user-generated errors are minimized; the function Val(Text1.Text), which extracts a numeral value from a text box, for instance, can ignore alphanumeric characters and search only for numbers. In a way, this function is a major advance for computing. On the other hand, it now takes a deliberate process on the part of the programmer to determine whether letters really were entered into a numeric field by accident.

Still, errors are generated, for the most part, by faults in the source code. You should let these faults occur. Covering them with an error trap that ignores the fault can lead to a processing catastrophe later in the program. Perhaps it is best to add error-trapping routines to the code of the program last, after you find that the application's source code is foolproof.

Error-Trapping Routines

Here's how an error-trapping routine works: A statement is placed within a procedure, setting branching to a particularly labeled line whenever an interpreter-recognized error occurs. When that happens, processing is not stopped in the normal manner; instead, execution branches immediately to the statement following the error label in the procedure, regardless of what instruction caused the error. The On Error statement baits the proverbial trap.

On Error {GoTo | Resume}   **Statement**

Purpose: Intraprocedural error trapping
Syntax:

```
On [Local ]Error {GoTo label¦Resume Next¦GoTo 0}
```

The On Error branch statement sets an error trap that, when invoked for the first time within an application, forces execution of the current procedure to jump to a specified line label whenever any error occurs that normally would suspend or interrupt the normal process of execution. As long as the procedure continues to execute without trouble, branching to the label immediately takes place when an error occurs.

The phrase On Error GoTo 0 terminates an error trap and allows the Visual Basic interpreter to suspend execution again in the case of a serious error. The phrase On

`Error Resume Next` enables you to tell the interpreter to ignore any errors that might come along and to resume execution with the next instruction following the one that caused the error.

The keyword `Local` is provided as an option for users of other Microsoft BASIC compilers. Its invocation within a Visual Basic error trap has no effect, however, because all Visual Basic error traps exist on the local level.

The instruction that takes the program out of the error trap routine and back into the main body of the program is the `Resume` statement.

Resume   Statement

Purpose: Error-trap routine termination
Syntax:

```
Resume {[0] ¦ Next ¦ label}
```

The `Resume` statement is reserved for the end of error-trap routines within a procedure. Invoked on a line by itself or accompanied by a `0`, this statement sends execution back to the statement that caused the error which sprang the trap. The formerly erroneous statement is then reexecuted to see whether it generates the same error a second time.

The phrase `Resume Next` sends execution back to the statement immediately following the one that caused the error. The phrase `Resume label` sends execution back to the statement immediately following the specified `label`.

Example

Because the controls and instructions of Visual Basic are more versatile than they once were, programing error-trapping routines is less necessary now than at any time in the past. Besides, branching can take place only to labels within the procedure that contained the error. Still, an error trap might be necessary for such potential errors as trying to find a specific file name on disk and not finding it, as shown in the following procedure fragment:

```
Sub FileFind (filepath$)
    On Error GoTo NoFile
    Selector.Show 1
    Open targetfile$ For Input As #1
        .
        .
        .
NoFile:
```

```
    If Err <> 53 Then
        msg$ = Error$(Err)
        MsgBox (msg$, 16)
        Stop
    Else
        msg$ = "File " + targetfile$ + " not found."
        MsgBox (msg$, 16)
        Resume Next
    End If
    .

    .

    .
Exit Sub
```

Following is pseudocode for the error trap-routine, starting at the line marked by the label `NoFile:`.

> *If the error is not a file-not-found error, then*
>   *Tell the user what the error actually is.*
>   *Place this error message in a message box.*
>   *Stop the program.*
> *Otherwise,*
>   *Tell the user what file wasn't found.*
>   *Tell the user using in a message box.*
>   *Resume the program where it left off.*
> *End of condition.*

Suppose that the file selector box invoked by the instruction `Selector.Show 1` can return a nonexistent file name to the routine that invoked it. If such a file name appears, instead of stopping execution altogether, a branch is made to the line `NoFile`. At this time, the internal variable `Err` is polled to see whether the error number generated is error 53 (file not found).

The interpreter sets the internal variable `Err` to the value of the last error that occurred during processing of the program. If no error has occurred, `Err = 0`. You can set this variable to any value for use in simulating error conditions when you're testing the applicability of error-trapping routines. Setting the value of `Err` manually, however, does not result in the automatic generation of an error.

If the error that triggered the execution of the preceding fragment is any number other than 53, an error message is generated to that effect, and execution is forced to stop via the `Stop` statement. If `Err` is 53, the name of the file that wasn't found is added to the message box before it is displayed. The `Resume Next` reverse branch statement allows execution to continue, however, with the line following the one that caused the error.

The preceding fragment introduced you to a number of error-related instructions. When an error occurs, the user sees a message relating the nature of the error; however, such dialogs mean nothing to the interpreter. The Error$() function conveys the bad news to the interpreter.

Error$()   Function

Purpose: Error description acquisition
Syntax:

```
string$ = Error$(ercode%)
```

In this syntax, *ercode%* is an integer value corresponding to a valid error code. You can use internal variable Err as *ercode%*.

The Error$() function returns a text string describing the error code that is passed to the function, within the string variable *string$*.

Wanting to generate an error might seem odd, but suppose that you're testing an error-trap routine and you're incapable of generating a real erroneous instruction on purpose. In such situations, you're provided with a means to generate a false erroneous instruction—by using the Error statement.

Error   Statement

Purpose: Error simulation
Syntax:

```
Error ercode%
```

In this syntax, *ercode%* is an integer value that corresponds to a valid error code. You can use internal variable Err as *ercode%*.

The Error statement forces the Visual Basic interpreter into acting as though the error specified by *ercode%* has occurred. This statement is particularly useful when you test the applicability of error-trapping routines.

Thus far in this book, you haven't seen examples of line numbering in the old-fashioned BASIC style, with the exception of one puzzle that had to do with subroutines. Visual Basic, however, does recognize line numbering within a procedure, although using line numbering tends to be hazardous. In this multiprocedural system, I strongly advise against it.

If you do use line numbering, Visual Basic makes available to you, for purposes of error-trapping, an internal variable Erl. This internal variable is set by the interpreter to the number of the line that last generated the error, assuming you use the old BASIC method of numbering lines—which is supported by Visual Basic as an option. If an application doesn't have line numbers, this variable is useless.

Summary

An error is a fault in program processing that suspends or terminates execution. Despite the negative connotation of the term, errors help you determine whether the logical structure of a procedure being developed is workable. Suspension or termination of a program's execution can be intercepted with a procedural error trap. The error-trap branch is baited using the phrase On Error GoTo. Within this error-trap routine, you can use the internal variable Err to determine what error occurred, and you can use Error$(Err) to generate a system-defined error message. The Resume statement terminates an error-trapping routine. A bug is a failure on the part of the program to operate in the way it was intended, although it may be operating in the way it was designed.

Review Questions

1. Does the instruction Form1.Line xbeg, ybeg, xend, yend generate a bug or an error?

2. Does the instruction circ = 2 * pi / r, which calculates the circumference of a circle, generate a bug or an error?

CHAPTER 46

Debugging Techniques

In this chapter, you examine programming conditions in which even the most advanced error traps may not be of much help.

Errors are relatively nice because you can use error-trapping routines to trap them, tame them, and release them. Bugs are not as nice. Generally, bugs cause things to go wrong with the program, although from the interpreter's point of view, everything is proceeding fine.

A *bug* is an error that cannot be detected by the interpreter.

A program bug, technically speaking, is not an error. A bug can lead to the generation of errors, but the interpreter really cannot track the presence of a bug. A *bug* in computing is the result of any process that fails to perform in the manner for which it was intended or designed; it cannot be detected automatically by the interpreter or compiler, and, thus by its nature, allows logical program execution to continue along a potentially disastrous course.

While I was testing Visual Basic for this book, I programmed an application wherein I could plot a point to the screen using a mouse pointer I programmed manually, and a device that I called the compass would echo the direction in which I was moving the pointer. While I was developing this project, my program contained a few bugs that were difficult to find. For days, whenever I plotted a point, my compass control registered that point as being located 180 degrees in the opposite direction from where it actually was. From the computer's point of view, nothing was going wrong. It was doing exactly what it was told to do. Bugs are not necessarily examples of instructions being misexecuted. Often they happen because the interpreter followed instructions to the letter.

I discovered the source of the bug in my program by using the Debug window, which you've used elsewhere in this book. This window's Immediate panel is in fact a command-line interpreter (CLI). Using the CLI, you can break an operation in progress and quiz the interpreter about the status of the program and its individual variables.

You invoke the Debug window automatically during an application's run time by selecting Break from the Run menu, by clicking on the toolbar's Break button, or by pressing Ctrl-Break on the keyboard. (On some keyboards, the Break key doubles as the Pause key.) Someplace in one of the code windows now, a specially highlighted line denotes the Visual Basic instruction that is about to be executed. If you want only this instruction to be executed, you can single-step your way through the program by pressing the F8 key. After the program executes just this one instruction, execution is suspended again, and the hazy box moves down one line.

A *breakpoint* immediately suspends the program when it is reached, before the statement line is executed.

After you suspend the program's execution by pressing Ctrl-Break, you can set the *breakpoint* for this routine by indicating the instruction line to receive the breakpoint and pressing the F9 key. A breakpoint is an instruction line that forces the execution of the program to be suspended temporarily just preceding execution of that line.

Figure 46.1 shows an example of a breakpoint.

Figure 46.1

An example of a breakpoint.

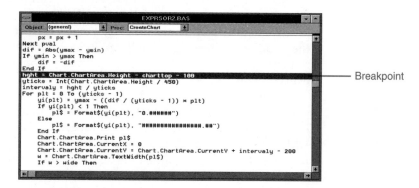

Breakpoint

To set the breakpoint for an instruction line, do the following: While the application is in suspension, indicate the instruction line to receive the breakpoint by placing the cursor within that line and pressing the F9 key, or by selecting Toggle Breakpoint from the Debug menu. The interpreter indicates this line with the colors for breakpoint instructions you've chosen from the Visual Basic Project Options window.

With the breakpoint having suspended the application, you now can use the Immediate panel to quiz the current state of the program. Although it is not a well-known fact, you can use the Immediate panel to execute small programs. As in the old BASIC interpreters, you can use colons to separate instructions typed to a single line within the CLI. You then can enter a small loop clause to a line, like the one used to determine what was wrong with the point values of the stars in the STARS.MAK project in Chapter 44:

```
for b=1 to 50:?xoom(b),yoom(b):next b
```

Here, you can use abbreviated syntax and lowercase letters; the ? stands in place of the `Print` command. The Immediate panel enables you to pack as many instructions as you can on one line, as long as you separate them with a colon.

You also can use the Immediate panel of the Debug window to resume execution at any procedure heading by typing that heading as an instruction line, as though it were a procedure call in the program. Using the CLI, you can type the name of the `SUB` procedure into the Debug window. You also can render it an expression that passes control to a `FUNCTION` procedure, or a `GOTO` or `GOSUB` statement that picks up execution at a specific line. You can use any of these alternatives as "hooks" so that you can begin a program, for the sake of testing, in the middle. After the procedure that contains the hook completes execution, however, control is passed back to the Debug window, which is identified by the Visual Basic interpreter as though it is the calling body of a program. Execution ceases as though the interpreter processed an `END` statement.

Another way to pass control to a specific statement is through the source code window that contains the statement. When the application is in break mode (the control window's title bar reads `break`), the instruction to be executed next appears in one of the source code windows, highlighted with the color for `Next Statement Background` as listed in the **Environment** command on the **Options** menu. You can highlight the instruction line within the procedure that you want to have executed next by placing the cursor on that line and selecting Set **N**ext Statement from the control window's **D**ebug menu. The instruction you highlight must appear within the same window as the instruction the interpreter was about to execute before the break; otherwise, the interpreter does not know which instruction to execute.

Bugs are nontrappable because the interpreter cannot recognize them.

No debugging system is automatic, in the same way no spelling checker for your word processor can spot every possible error. For a spelling checker to correct all errors, it must know the context in which the word you intended to spell should appear. One of the most commonly misspelled words, for instance, is *you're*. It seems correct from *your* vantage point, but in the sentence "*Your* going too far," or "Why, *your* much thinner than you were," you can plainly see the two misspelled words. A spelling checker cannot know that these words are incorrect because the misspelled words are words nonetheless.

Similarly, for Visual Basic to spot a mathematical operator bug, it would have to estimate what geometry you intended for your program. From your point of view, you made an error; from the interpreter's viewpoint, everything is proceeding smoothly. This subtlety is what differentiates a bug from an error in computing; if things do not proceed smoothly, a formal error is generated and possibly can be trapped.

Using Watch Expressions

One of the debugging features programmers greatly appreciate in Microsoft's "professional" programming environments is the *watch expressions*. These mathematical expressions are as complex as a hierarchical Boolean comparison or as simple as a single variable. The current status of these watch expressions is displayed within the Watch panel, which is the upper portion of the Debug window (you may not have seen it up to now because it requires watch expressions to make it visible).

With the Visual Basic watch system, you also can have the interpreter break the program's execution whenever a certain mathematical condition evaluates true or when it becomes false. This condition is written as an expression of comparison, just as if it were appearing beside If in an If-Then clause; you don't have to include the If, however. Your Visual Basic application never "sees" the break expression, so the expression never really knows it's being watched. The interpreter evaluates all watch expressions separately; they never really affect the execution of the application, except perhaps to slow it down—the degree of speed reduction is hardly noticeable on faster computers.

Figure 46.2 shows the Debug window with the watch system engaged, keeping track of certain variables and expressions pertaining to EXPRESOR.BAS, the calculator application introduced in Chapter 4, "The Development Process." Notice that some of the watch expressions are simply variables unto themselves; remember, the Visual Basic interpreter evaluates single variables as whole expressions.

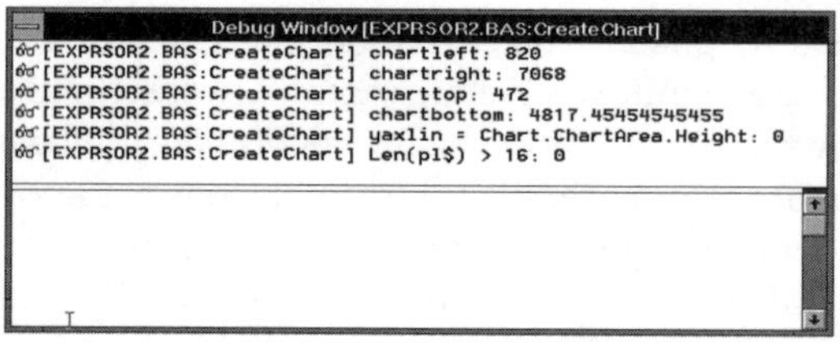

Figure 46.2

The Watch panel makes itself known.

When you manually break a Visual Basic application by pressing Ctrl-Break, by selecting Break from the Run menu, or by pressing the Break button in the toolbar, the interpreter switches into its watch display mode and reevaluates the watch expressions you've told it to monitor for you. The status and result of those expressions then are displayed within the Watch panel.

You can, however, have the interpreter break the application for you, conditionally, at any point during run time. Suppose that you use some sort of a *progressive value* someplace in your Visual Basic application—for instance, a loop that counts from 1 to 1000 or an axis coordinate value for a control being dragged over the form. You want to stop the program at a specific point in the progression and poll the Immediate panel for the contents of specific variables. To do so, you can place an expression in the watchpoint list, stating the mathematical condition that must exist for the program to break.

You can use either of two ways to enter a watchpoint into your current Visual Basic application. Following is the conventional method:

1. From the control window **Debug** menu, select **A**dd Watch. A dialog box appears, as shown in figure 46.3.

Figure 46.3

The watchpoint control panel.

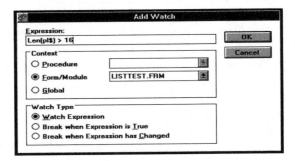

2. Within this dialog is a text box marked `Expression`, within which you can enter a Visual Basic expression, using the standard Visual Basic syntax for expressions. This expression triggers execution to be suspended. You don't have to write `If` before the expression—just the variable, a mathematical operator, and something to compare it to. If you want the interpreter to simply watch the value or contents of a variable for you, you can state this variable on the text line by itself. Otherwise, you also can state any rationally interpretable and logically reducible Visual Basic expression that contains any number of mathematical and Boolean operators, as well as parentheses.

3. Within the frame marked `Context` are two drop-down lists, which currently register the names of the module and the procedure whose code editing window is currently active in the Visual Basic interpreter workspace. Because local variables across multiple procedures can share names with one another, designating the context of the watch expression here is necessary to prevent the interpreter from becoming confused.

4. Within the frame marked `Watch Type` is a list of three conditions inside an options set. The first item, marked `Watch Expression`, is the default setting; the interpreter doesn't break the application, regardless of the outcome of the evaluation. For the other two options, the interpreter breaks if the expression proves true for the second option or false for the third. In both these cases, you should enter an actual expression, complete with operator, into the watch line because the interpreter breaks when the evaluation results in –1 or 0.

5. Click the OK button. The watchpoint is entered into the Debug window.

Alternatively, while the interpreter is in break mode, you can highlight an expression within the source code and select Instant Watch from the **Debug** menu. The expression that you highlight appears within a dialog panel. Click the Add Watch button, and the familiar dialog panel in figure 46.3 appears. The Expression line already is filled in for you; however, at this point, you can edit it to read something else. Click the OK button, and the expression is added to the Watch panel of the Debug window. This process enables you to enter into the Watch panel a line that already appears in the source code, without your having to retype it.

A watch expression you enter into the Debug window is marked with a "pair of eyeglasses" icon, followed by a line of information with the following syntax:

```
[MODULE[:Procedure]] watch: {status¦<Not In Context>}
```

The context of the *watch* variable or expression appears at the beginning of this line, and the current *status* of the evaluation appears at the end of the line, unless the variable doesn't officially "exist" at the point of execution. (Even in break mode, the interpreter does not let you accidentally enter into the watch line an expression containing a variable that doesn't exist.)

So What Is Debugging?

The majority of the programming process is an effort in debugging. Oftentimes, programming books treat debugging as though it were some sort of after-the-job-is-done cleanup process. Debugging actually is part of the everyday business of making your application work.

An error in many instances is merely a misstatement—a grammatical glitch. The Visual Basic interpreter knows such a glitch when it sees one and stops execution, unless you have the application trap the error and make the corrections itself. In some cases—such as the "error" that's generated if you've reached the end of a data file and there's no more data to read, or if the user chooses a file name that doesn't exist—there's nothing erroneous about error-generation.

A bug occurs when the interpreter follows its orders, and in so doing causes wrong things to happen. The watch system enables you to run your application like a videotape recorder: in slow motion or "frame by frame." In so doing, you can "magnify" the symbols the application uses that may be the culprit. Whatever you think the purpose of a Visual Basic application may be, its real purpose is to maintain a series of values represented in memory by symbols. A bug, therefore, is caused by some misrepresentation of this symbology. It therefore follows that the watch system and the conversational Debug window can reveal the cause of any bugs, unless you change the course of the application beforehand and correct yourself even before you know you need to do so.

Summary

A bug is an error in symbology that leads to a serious malfunctioning during the course of your Visual Basic application. The Visual Basic interpreter does not recognize the presence of bugs; the only way you can correct any malady an application might have is if you can recognize what that malady is. The interpreter gives you two main tools for the eradication of bugs in the application: the command-line interpreter in the Immediate panel of the Debug window and the watch expression system. The watch system displays the status of given symbols and the results of given expressions while the application is in break mode.

Review Questions

1. Although a bug in a program can lead to the generation of error messages, why can't error-trapping routines fix the bug?

2. Although Windows 3.1 is capable of spotting bugs before they happen (or so Microsoft claims), why can't Visual Basic spot bugs in the source code before they occur?

Part X

Physical Data

CHAPTER 47

Sequential Access

In this chapter, you examine the mechanism used by the BASIC programming language for storing user-created data to disk as files. This mechanism has changed little since the early 1970s, even with its inclusion in Visual Basic. You see how DOS file names are assigned to Visual Basic as ordinal numbers, which serve to represent data *channels*. These channels are opened and closed like the locks on a dam. When the channels are opened, data flows through the *stream*. In this chapter, you learn how to "turn the locks" and manage the stream.

Most applications you will ever use create stored files for one purpose or another. BASIC programs themselves are files; a Visual Basic program can consist of several files. Yet up to this point, this book hasn't discussed how the Visual Basic application produces files outside of itself, in the manner and format specified within the program. It may seem unusual at first, but originally, BASIC could not be programmed to produce files for the user other than its own source code file. The reason was not lack of foresight on the part of its designers, but that operating systems used by relatively inexpensive computers of the mid-1960s stored memory on rotating drums, so the one program running at the time was the file. Only in the 1970s when BASIC started to be used on computers that had memory that was more *solid-state*—reliant more on electrical currents than on centrifugal force—was a BASIC program capable of being instructed to produce files.

A *database* is data stored structurally as records of related entries.

All applications that produce and use their own data files—regardless of the language they're programmed in—are said to have their own *database*. A well-structured database includes a small portion of data that describes how the rest of the data relates to each other. The mechanics of BASIC data files were invented, for the most part, in 1970, at about the same time E. F. Codd was developing the concepts of modern databases for IBM. Because BASIC couldn't wait for Dr. Codd, the data file storage mechanism chosen for the language was somewhat blind to the structure and relationships between the elements of data being stored.

A *channel* is a logical device that maintains the flow of data between the interpreter and an output device.

In a sense, the data storage and retrieval mechanism for BASIC-produced files is little more than a verbally commanded tape recorder. For a sequential-access file (the subject of this chapter), each element of data is stored to disk in a stream, one datum after the other. This stream is referred to as a *channel*, which is a throwback term to the first file-maintaining small systems of the 1970s. A channel is a logically interpreted device (in other words, not a tangible, physical entity) for maintaining the flow of data between the interpreter and an output device or storage unit.

Here's how the sequential-access mechanism works: a channel is opened with the Open statement, and this channel is rendered an ordinal number—for instance, #1. Each element of data is "printed" to this channel, one datum after the other, using the statement Print #1. No data concerning the physical makeup or construction of the file is included with this data. A bunch of raw numbers simply is printed to magnetic media, with the same technical consideration given to them that a typewriter gives the individual letters it types on a page.

A sequential-access data file is always read in the same way it was written—beginning-to-end, one datum after the other. When the file is created, the first 1000 elements may be names of people, the second 1000 may be their addresses, the third may be their cities of origin, and so on. You can store these elements in this order by using the Print # statement. For the recalled data elements to retain the same meaning and purpose in the program after they are loaded back into memory from disk, each element must be reloaded in exactly the same order in which it was saved. In this instance, the 1000 names are reloaded first, followed by the 1000 addresses, and then the 1000 cities. A program could not open the file and have it immediately pick out just the addresses. In fact, if you want just the addresses, after you open the file using the Open statement, you need to read the 1000 names anyway to get to the 1000 addresses.

Storing data in this manner may seem archaic—and for many programmers, it is. Assume, however, that you're writing a program that maintains several array variables to describe the main portion of data in memory—for instance, a vector-plotted drawing like you find in a CAD program. In such cases, the data is pertinent only in its entirety; half the number of vector plots in a drawing would result, no doubt, in a senseless drawing. In cases where dumping the entire image of data from memory to disk in one lump is more convenient, sequential-access techniques prove to be convenient. In cases in which an individual item of data is important by itself—for instance, somebody's address in a list—sequential access is rather cumbersome. *Random-access* data storage is less cumbersome, although it is far more complex. Discussion of that technique is reserved for Chapter 48, "Random and Binary Access."

Example

Here's how an array of 1000 items is stored to disk using sequential access:

```
Open "array.fil" For Output As #1
For stor = 1 To 1000
    Print #1, item(stor)
Next stor
Close #1
```

Following is the pseudocode for the preceding procedure:

*Open a storage file for the arrays generated
 thus far, make this an output file for sequential
 access, and give this file channel 1.
Count from 1 to 1000, the maximum number of units in
 the array.
    Store the array value for this count to disk,
    using channel 1.
Count the next item.
Close the channel.*

Here, you see the modern incarnation of the old BASIC ordinal file system. A channel is opened and given ordinal number 1. The Open statement links #1 with the file name array.fil. As a result, anything that is sent through the channel using Print #1 is written to that file. When the array is depleted, the channel is closed.

The Open statement is the primary instruction behind all data file access operations.

Open   **Statement**

Purpose: Data pointer initiation
Syntax:

```
Open filename$ [For mode] [Access restriction] [locktype]
➥As [#]channel% [Len = bytelength%]
```

The Open statement initiates a channel for the transfer of data between the Visual Basic interpreter and a physically stored file. The DOS file name of this file is specified as *filename$* and can contain the complete file storage path. The channel number associated with this file is expressed as *channel%* and can be any integer between 1 and 255. The choice of numbers here is completely arbitrary; a lower numbered channel need not be opened before a higher number is chosen. After you use the Open statement to assign a channel number to a file name, any data transfer instruction that refers to this number affects the file attributed to the number by the Open statement. A pound sign before the channel number is optional to maintain syntax compatibility with earlier versions of BASIC.

The term represented by *mode* specifies the type of data transfer being established. This term can be stated as any of the following:

Statement	*Explanation*
Sequential access	
Output	Opens a channel for sequential data output to the specified file, starting at the beginning of the file. If the file does not exist at the time of the Open statement's execution, the file is created; otherwise, it is overwritten.
Append	Opens a channel for sequential data output to the specified file, beginning at the point just following the last datum entered into the existing file. If the file does not exist at the time of the Open statement's execution, the file is created; however, with Append, an existing file is never overwritten.
Input	Opens a channel for sequential data input to the specified file, in the order the data was output, starting with the beginning of the file.
Random access	
Random	Opens a channel for data exchange using random-access mode. In this mode, data can be written to or read from a file at any specifiable point, at any time. Random is the default mode for channel initiation, and is assumed if *mode* is omitted from the Open statement.
Binary access	
Binary	Opens a channel for data exchange using binary file mode. In this mode, individual bytes of data—for instance, pixels in an image or characters in a document—can be written to or read from a file at any specifiable point at any time.

The optional parameter *restriction,* which follows Access, can include either or both of the terms Read and Write, specifying any extra restrictions to be placed on file access, especially with regard to running the Visual Basic application over a network. The optional term *locktype* that follows specifies any access restrictions for clients attempting to open the same data file already opened by another client in the network. You can state the term *locktype* as Shared to allow any other client access to the open data file, Lock Read to prevent every other client from reading the data file while it's open, or Lock Write to prevent every other client from writing to the data file while it's open. These two terms are especially—and in many ways exclusively—helpful in networking environments, for use in "steering" a data file so that all clients in the network can obtain access to the most current version of the file, and no single client can override the changes made to that file by another client.

The term Len = *bytelength*% is used in random-access mode to establish the fixed character length, in bytes, of each element of data being exchanged between the interpreter and the data file. Random access uses fixed field lengths to establish the beginning and end of a data item within a file; by default, this length is set to 128 bytes. Sequential access, by contrast, relies on the program to know the sequence in which each item was stored to the file and the field length of each item in the sequence. The methodology is that if the program knows in advance the precise contents of a file being recalled from disk—as it must with sequential access—it must know, as a result, the byte length of each item in that file. The term Len = *bytelength*% is used optionally in sequential-access mode to establish the length of the internal memory buffer being used to house characters being exchanged between the interpreter and data file. By default, this length is set to 512 bytes.

Obviously, Open is an extremely complex statement, and it will probably require all of this chapter and the following two chapters to explore every permutation of Open. By stark contrast, the statement's counterpart on the reverse side of the channel control operation—Close—is extremely simple.

Close   Statement

Purpose: Data pointer termination
Syntax:

```
Close [#]channel1%[, channel2%, . . . channeln%]
```

The Close statement terminates access to the data files that have names that were attributed by the Open statement to the channel% numbers listed. Any read or write instructions after Close that pertain to the channel numbers stated just previously within `Close` generate errors. Access to files using those numbers can only be reinstated using an `Open` instruction. `Close` cancels any association between the stated numbers and the file names attributed to them by the `Open` instruction, so you can use the numbers again for other file names. Pound signs are optional before each channel number. If no channel numbers are specified, all open channels are closed.

In Windows, data that is stored to a file might not actually make it to disk, but instead might go to an in-between region. This *buffer zone*, as it is actually called, is retained in memory until it is full. At this time, only the buffer is stored to disk in one lump, unless the `Close` statement is executed. At `Close`, the entire buffer is stored to disk whether or not it is full.

Example

Suppose that you have data in memory that contains the names of the 50 states, along with each state's governor's name, total population, total land mass measurement, and official state bird. Here's one way you can save all that data to disk using a sequential-access technique:

```
Open "50states.dta" For Output As #2
For state = 1 To 50
    Print #2, name$(state)
Next state
For state = 1 To 50
    Print #2, pop(state)
Next state
For state = 1 To 50
    Print #2, mass(state)
Next state
For state = 1 To 50
    Print #2, bird$(state)
Next state
Close #2
```

At some later date, when you've just started running the program and memory is clear, you can use the following routine to load all that data back into memory:

```
Open "50states.dta" For Input As #3
For state = 1 To 50
    Input #3, name$(state)
Next state
```

```
For state = 1 To 50
    Input #3, pop(state)
Next state
For state = 1 To 50
    Input #3, mass(state)
Next state
For state = 1 To 50
    Input #3, bird$(state)
Next state
Close #3
```

Your choice of numbers for both Open statements is not extremely important, if that choice remains constant throughout the data exchange process and doesn't conflict with any other existing open channel number. What must remain identical in both instances is the order in which data is stored and retrieved from the file.

The preceding two routines were written more for ease of reading by human beings than for ease of interpretation by Visual Basic. The Output routine stores each list of 50 in sequence, in its entirety, before storing the next list. One good reason, perhaps, for dividing this sequence into individual loops is so that functions specific to the variables being stored can be placed easily and isolated. For instance, the preceding routines contain two numeric array variables. If these variables are being retrieved from text box fields in a form, however, the text from those boxes must be converted into numeric variables before it can be stored as values. You convert the routines as follows:

```
Open "50states.dta" For Output As #2
For state = 1 To 50
    Print #2, name$(state)
Next state
For state = 1 To 50
    pop = Val(pop$(state))
    Print #2, pop
Next state
For state = 1 To 50
    mass = Val(mass$(state))
    Print #2, mass
Next state
For state = 1 To 50
    Print #2, bird$(state)
Next state
Close #2
```

```
Open "50states.dta" For Input As #3
For state = 1 To 50
    Input #3, name$(state)
Next state
For state = 1 To 50
    Input #3, pop
    pop$(state) = Str$(pop)
Next state
For state = 1 To 50
    Input #3, mass
    mass$(state) = Str$(mass)
Next state
For state = 1 To 50
    Input #3, bird$(state)
Next state
Close #3
```

Notice that in both of the preceding routines, when you wrote the numeric values to disk and read them from the disk, you did not need to specify the variable as an array. The values in the Input routine were first restored to simple numeric variables and then assigned to string arrays. Visual Basic does not keep track of the variable name associated with the data stored to disk, only the variable type. You can use a variable with a different name to restore data that was stored to disk. It is essential, however, that the variable you use is declared, either explicitly or informally, to be the same type as the one you used to store the data to disk.

The reason for this necessity is as follows: each variable type has a different number of bytes reserved for storage in memory. When you use the Print # statement (explained in detail later in this chapter), the contents of the data are printed digit by digit to a *text file*, in the same manner used by the .Print method for a *virtual terminal* graphic object. So, instead of saving an image of data to disk as it appears in memory, Print # saves the textual equivalent of that data. You can go into that file with a text editor such as Notepad, and the file appears with precisely the same contents it would have if the data were printed to a graphic object.

When it reads this file back into memory, the Visual Basic interpreter does not know what it sees at the moment. The only clue it has about what each character represents is the variable type of the Input # statement for the variable that is supposed to hold the converted value in memory. The interpreter determines the beginning and end of each printed element in the file by looking for its surrounding space characters. In the midst of an opening and closing space is an alphanumeric string that is extracted into memory. The interpreter then performs its own covert form of the `Val()` function to convert this string back to a value, if the variable type expressed in `Input #` is numeric. The results of this translation do not correspond with the data as it was printed to the file, if the variable type expressed in `Input #` is not the same as it was in `Print #`. The interpreter then uses the wrong number of bytes to store the value conversion.

The two data storage and retrieval instructions are `Print #` and `Input #`.

Print #   Statement

Purpose: Data transmission to device
Syntax:

```
Print #channel%, expression1[{;¦,} expression2]
➥[. . . {;¦,} expressionn]
```

In this syntax, each *expression* either can be logically reduced to a numeric value or expressed as an alphanumeric concatenation of one or more elements of text.

The `Print #` statement prints the text of the values or contents of each expression in the list to a text file that acts as the data file attributed to the integer *channel%*. This channel number must have been opened previously with the `Open` statement for `Output` or `Append` and attributed to a specific file name found within the `Open` statement. `Print #` prints text to a file with this file name. The form of this text is exactly as it would appear if you had used the `.Print` method to print to a graphic object or to the printer.

If a semicolon appears before an expression, the expression is printed immediately to the file at the present character pointer position—thus canceling any carriage return or line feed before printing begins. If a comma appears before an expression, the expression is printed to the file at the beginning of the next print zone. Because no text font is assumed for printing to a disk file—because you're not dealing with images or appearance specifically—a print zone begins every 14 characters.

For each open channel, the interpreter maintains the current character position within the file until it is closed when the `Close` statement is executed. Multiple `Print #` statements executed in sequence for the same channel number have their results appear within the file associated with that channel, in the same sequence.

Input #   Statement

Purpose: Data acquisition from device
Syntax:

```
Input #channel%, variable1[, variable2, . . . variablen]
```

The Input # statement reads data from a textual data file whose *channel%* number was previously opened for Input by the Open statement and whose file name was previously specified within the Open statement. The pound sign is required to distinguish the Input # statement from the old BASIC Input statement, although that particular statement is no longer supported by Visual Basic. Each textual element from the file is assigned to the variables in the Input # instruction's list, in sequence. If the variable being assigned a datum from the file is a numeric variable, the interpreter automatically attempts to convert the text string associated with that variable to a numeric value before assigning a value to the variable.

Caution: A pound sign must precede the *channel%* number in the Print # statement so that the interpreter can better distinguish this statement from the .Print method.

Example

Now that you know more about the nature of printing to a sequential-access file, you can modify the two Print # and Input # routines for greater efficiency, as follows:

```
Open "50states.dta" For Output As #2
For state = 1 To 50
    Print #2, name$(state);
    pop = Val(pop$(state))
    mass = Val(mass$(state))
    Print #2, pop, mass,
    Print #2, bird$(state)
Next state
Close #2
```

```
Open "50states.dta" For Input As #3
For state = 1 To 50
    Input #3, name$(state); pop, mass, bird$(state)
    pop$(state) = Str$(pop)
    mass$(state) = Str$(mass)
Next state
Close #3
```

A *record* is a logical grouping of related elements of data within a data file or database.

In both cases, you're using single loops to govern both the storage mechanism and the retrieval mechanism. In so doing, each item of information is interleaved into the others so that the data entries for each state appear on the same "line" within the text file. You can officially consider this grouping of related elements to be a *record*.

Example

The previous examples assume that the program knows in advance how many records of related data will be entered into application memory. Suppose that you extend the program, however, so that the application stores information about the individual counties or boroughs in each state. You really don't want to have to create 50 different array variables for the states. Instead, it is more convenient for you to create two-dimensional array variables, of which the first dimension represents a state and the second dimension represents a county. You then let the data file decide for you, after the data is loaded into memory, how many counties each state has. Following are the storage and retrieval routines you might write for storing each county or borough's name, land area, and county seat:

```
Open "counties.dta" For Output As #4
For state = 1 To 50
    Print #4, counties(state)
    For lc = 1 To counties(state)
        Print #4, cname$(state, lc), mass(state, lc),
        ➡cseat$(state, lc)
    Next lc
Next state

Open "counties.dta" For Input As #5
For state = 1 To 50
    Input #5, counties(state)
    For lc = 1 To counties(state)
        Input #5, cname$(state, lc), mass(state, lc),
        ➡cseat$(state, lc)
    Next lc
Next state
```

In the preceding pair of routines, each state has a variable called `counties()` apportioned to it. This variable keeps count of the number of counties or boroughs in the state. By looking at the `Print #4` routine, you can see that the number of counties per state is stored to disk first. Following that is a list of as many names, land masses, and bastions of power as there are counties in the state currently being counted.

Because the `lc` loop counts only to the number of counties registered to be in the current state and then stops, you can be certain that in the similar `Input #5` routine, the loading loop "knows" in advance how many counties to load in memory before it initiates the loop. This number is always the first number in a county *cluster*. After the cluster is loaded, the file pointer automatically points to the next number of counties. Because of the identical way you've structured the saving and loading routines, you also can guarantee that `Input #5`, `counties(state)` always picks up the number of counties for the current state, and not a county name by mistake.

One of the dangers of using this method of storage is that, when the sequential-access loader is reading character files into memory, it treats commas and semicolons as delimiters. You can easily store the sequence of characters *Washington, D.C.* to disk using `Print #`, but the comma after the *n* causes the interpreter to think *Washington* is the entire data field. What's worse, *D.C.* is likely to become the start of the next data field, and chances are that the District of Columbia itself shows up as a ZIP code, and all the fields to follow are one datum off.

In a strange way, the cause of this problem is also the solution to it, as you learn in the section explaining `Write #`.

Write #   Statement

Purpose: Text transmission to disk
Syntax:

```
Write #channel%, expression1[, expression2 . . , expressionn]
```

In this syntax, each *expression* either can be logically reduced to a numeric value or expressed as an alphanumeric concatenation of one or more elements of text.

The `Write #` statement prints the text of the values or contents of each expression in the list to a text file that acts as the data file attributed to the integer *channel%*. This channel number must have been previously opened with the `Open` statement for `Output` or `Append` and attributed to a specific file name found within the `Open` statement. `Write #` prints text to a file with this file name. This text is in the form of an *ASCII-delimited* data file as used by the *mail merge* feature of many word processors. All elements are separated from each other by commas, and all alphanumeric strings are enclosed within quotation marks. Commas and any punctuation other than quotation marks themselves that are intended to appear within a string are enclosed within the quotation marks.

> **Caution:** A pound sign must precede the *channel%* number in the Write # statement. You use commas within the Write # statement only to separate data items; they do not affect the "printing" position of that data in the text file generated by the interpreter. You cannot use semicolons as delimiters within Write #.

Sequential Data as Pages

When you're outputting character-based data to the printer, you can set the coordinate system for the Printer. object for characters rather than graphic points (Printer.Scalemode = 4). You then have a general understanding of the .Height and .Width of the printed page, with regard to character spacing. A stored sequential-access file is, in essence, a printed page, although Visual Basic maintains no height property for that page. Visual Basic does, however, maintain an optional column width, which can be reset by means of a statement, but not a property.

Width #   Statement

Purpose: Textual data file formatting
Syntax:

    Width #channel%, columns%

The Width # statement sets the "printing" width of a sequential-access file whose channel% is currently open by means of the Open statement. The setting is made to a specified number of columns% from 0 to 255. After the interpreter has stored columns% number of characters to an open file, it automatically generates a carriage return and line feed character. "Printing"—or storage of entries to the file—then begins on the following line. If columns% is zero, no lines are assumed, and text is presumed to wrap around without carriage returns until its termination.

Assuming Width # is set to a reasonable amount, you then have access to the Line Input # statement.

Line Input # Statement

Purpose: Formatted text transmission from device
Syntax:

```
Line Input #channel%, string$
```

The Line Input # statement reads a line of text from a sequential-access file and stores it in memory within the variable *string$*. A line of text, in this instance, is defined as a continuous stream of characters that end with a carriage return. This character is assumed to be the end-of-line character. If no such break occurs in the file, or if Width # was not used to specify the line width of the sequential data file, you can use Line Input # to assign the entire textual contents of the data file to string variable *string$*.

Summary

All applications that use data in one form or another operate a database. A database management system maintains the categorical and relational information about elements of data. Visual Basic opens channels for data and maintains their through-put and positioning in a file.

The appearance of a Visual Basic stored data file is a page, although one that seems to be "printed" to disk. In fact, the statement Print # is the primary statement for printing a sequential-access record to disk. You open a channel using the Open statement. If the access mode is specified as Output, using sequential access, you can "print" data to this file or "write" to this file with more descriptive delimiters using Write #.

Review Questions

1. What is the operational difference between the Print # statement and the Write # statement?

2. What is the operational difference between the Input # statement and the Line Input # statement?

3. Why is printing to the screen or printer accomplished with the .Print method, and printing to a file accomplished with the Print # statement?

Review Exercises

1. Suppose that you're writing an astronomy program in which the user catalogs the celestial objects she happens to view with her telescope. Write a routine that stores to disk all the objects the user has cataloged thus far, along with their celestial catalog names and observed magnitudes and brightness.

2. Suppose that the astronomer sees planets, stars, galaxies, or other celestial phenomena. Given the fact that the description criteria for each category is different, but you don't have it all on-hand at the moment, write a routine that saves a sequential-access file for all objects observed in the skies thus far. Have the saving and loading routines differentiate between the celestial objects so that each time a new type of object is sighted, the individual content and structure of the object is chosen and utilized by the program.

CHAPTER 48

Random and Binary Access

In this chapter, you witness another method of storing and retrieving data as files in Visual Basic—the random-access method. This method involves the storage of related data elements as records and the retrieval of each record by number, although not necessarily in sequence. You can pull one record out of a file at random, which is where the access method gets its name. You also see the binary-access method in action, in which data is stored and retrieved byte by byte into memory rather than datum by datum.

In the real world of file storage, people do not open up a cabinet and read word for word the contents of every file that falls before the one they are looking for. If that were so, people with last names beginning with Z would probably receive their tax refunds last. Random-access file storage should perhaps be called *rational access* because each element of data has its own recognized place or location within the file, and you can call the element at any time by specifying that location.

Programmers actually use the term *random access* often in their lives, especially with regard to memory—as in random-access memory or RAM. In random-access memory, you can address, acquire, and store a byte of data by referring to its location—or in terms of memory, its address. When you're programming in assembly language, data is addressed by its byte location, and often for arithmetic operations, certain elements of data are copied into *registers*, which on paper appear to be variables.

Normally in BASIC, a variable refers to a location in memory where the data resides or, in the case of an alphanumeric string, begins to reside. In many versions of BASIC, you can address this memory location directly using the VARPTR statement; Visual Basic does not and cannot support this statement, however, because

Microsoft Windows frequently shifts the location of the data frames for an application in memory without notifying any of those applications. Microsoft employs what can best be called a "Data Relocation Program" for segments of data in which the data has grown too large for the segment.

The invocation of a Visual Basic variable is an example of random access, technically speaking. Such an invocation is merely an indirect way of referring to an element of memory by its address—except for the fact that in Windows, that address keeps changing. Notice that in the sequential data access technique, you actually employ random access anyway. You use sequential access to place all the data that had been stored on disk into *memory*, and from there you can access any element of it randomly. The subscript of the array into which you loaded the data serves as the address of that element—so you have random access whether you want it or not.

In the random-access data storage and retrieval technique, you're merely being more up-front about what technique you use to address data. The access takes place from the disk or stored file rather than from memory; you use the `Put #` and `Get #` statements rather than `Print #` and `Input #` to retrieve and store, respectively, an element of data by its address. You, therefore, directly address the disk rather than the memory and save the VB application a bit of work.

Following is the `Put #` statement, which you use to write data to a random-access file, described in detail.

Put #   Statement

Purpose: Data storage to device
Syntax:

```
Put #channel%, [location&], variable
```

The `Put #` statement writes the contents of the specified *variable* to a random-access data file, previously opened with the statement `Open...As Random` or `Open...As Binary`, and whose *channel%* number is designated by that `Open` statement. You cannot replace the term *variable* with an expression or a value. In the instance of the `Put #` statement, only a variable can be explicitly stated. You can include only one variable; the VB interpreter does not recognize lists of variables for this statement.

When you're using the random-access technique, if *location&* is stated, the *variable* contents are assumed to be written to the element position in the list numbered *location&* from the beginning of the file. If an element already exists at that position, it is replaced with the contents of *variable*. If *location&* is not stated, the comma that holds the place where *location&* would have been stated must remain to distinguish its purpose in this statement from that of *variable*.

The Visual Basic interpreter maintains a file pointer for each data file opened with the Open statement. This pointer registers the location where the next data element is written. In random access, if *location&* is omitted, writing takes place to the location currently being pointed to by the file pointer. After writing to a random- or binary-access file takes place, the file pointer registers the location just following the preceding write. If a Put # statement writes to some *location&* in the middle of an existing file, therefore, after the write the file pointer increments itself to the next location in the middle of that file. In other words, the default location of the file pointer when *location&* is not specified is not at the end of a random-access file in Visual Basic.

If the value of *location&* is beyond the value where any data has been written to the file, the contents of the data at locations previous to *location&* might be erroneous. It is legal, however, to specify a storage *location&* that is far greater than the number of elements in the file.

The length in stored bytes of each element is, by default, 128 bytes. You can respecify this length with the Len = *length%* portion of the Open statement for that file. This length is considered the field length of each element in the file. Each field can be from 1 to 32,767 bytes in length, and all fields within a random-access file have identical lengths. This many bytes are written to the file each time Put # is executed, regardless of the byte length of the specified *variable*. An alphanumeric string cannot be longer than the number of bytes in the field length minus two, to account for a string descriptor value. Each time Put # is executed, the number of bytes in the field length is added to that pointer to maintain that pointer's current absolute location.

When you're using the binary-access technique—when you open the data file using Open...As Binary—the value of *location&*, when specified, represents the absolute byte number within the open file. This byte number acts as an absolute address. Elements of a binary-access file do not have identical lengths; the Put # statement therefore writes exactly as many bytes to the binary-access file as are used to store the specified *variable* in memory. If *location&* is not specified, writing takes place at the next byte address in the sequence.

> **Caution:** The binary-access method does not write descriptors to a file, to specify the beginning and end of a variable's contents or value. You therefore can accidentally (or purposefully) write bytes as data in the midst of a previously stored element, thus invalidating that element. You therefore should use binary access only for nonrecord data, such as long textual documents and bitmapped images.

Figure 48.1 shows the differences between random-access and binary-access storage. In the upper panel, a random-access file has been opened with a field length of 16, specified within the Open statement by Len = 16 at the end. Two variables are stored to this file using Put #. The first is a double-precision floating-point variable consuming eight bytes of memory, and the second is the string form of the file name CUOMO1.DTA, which is 10 characters long. With the random-access file, the eight-byte value is stored within a 16-byte field, leaving an excess of eight bytes. The 10-character string then is stored within another 16-byte field, with two characters included as a string descriptor, leaving an excess of four bytes.

Figure 48.1

The two addressable data storage schemes.

In the lower panel of figure 48.1, a binary-access file has been opened, and such files have no fixed field lengths. Here, the same two variables are stored to the file using the same Put # statement. The eight-byte value is stored to eight bytes of the file, leaving the file pointer at the next byte. The ASCII value of the 10 characters in CUOM01.DTA are stored immediately following the eight-byte value. The file pointer then rests at the byte just following the *A*.

Keep these two panels in mind as you read about the Get # statement, which reloads variables from a data file into memory.

Get #   Statement

Purpose: Data retrieval from device
Syntax:

```
Get #channel%, [location&], variable
```

The Get # statement reads the contents of the specified *variable* from a random-access data file, previously opened with the statement Open...As Random or Open...As Binary, and whose *channel%* number is designated by that Open statement. You cannot replace the term *variable* with an expression or a value. In the instance of the Get # statement, you can explicitly state only a single variable by itself, not a list of variables.

When you're using the random-access technique, if *location&* is stated, the *variable* contents are assumed to be read from the element position in the list numbered *location&* from the beginning of the file. If *location&* is omitted and a comma holds the empty space where *location&* would have appeared, reading takes place at the location currently being pointed to by the file pointer. After reading from a random- or binary-access file takes place, the file pointer registers the location just following the preceding read. If a Get # statement reads from some *location&* in the middle of an existing file, therefore, after the read the file pointer increments itself to the next location in the middle of that file.

If the value of *location&* is beyond the location where any data has been written to the file, any value read from that nonexistent position is zero, and any string read from that position is null. Legally, however, you can specify a storage *location&* that is far greater than the number of elements in the file.

When you're using the binary-access technique to load a value into memory, the Get # statement reads exactly as many bytes to the binary-access file as are used to represent the specified value *variable* when it is loaded into memory. When you're loading an alphanumeric string and assigning its contents to a string variable in memory using binary access, the number of characters loaded into memory is exactly the number of characters currently belonging to that string variable. In other words, if contents have yet to be assigned to a string variable and its official contents are null (*string$* = ""), a Get # statement does not load any characters into the specified string variable.

If *location&* is not specified, reading takes place at the next byte address in the sequence.

> **Caution:** If the variable type stated within Get # is different from the type you used when storing that variable to the binary-access file using Put # earlier, the value or contents of the Get # variable is erroneous. It is, therefore, important that the instruction pattern of the binary-access loading routine be somewhat similar to that of the binary storage routine.

A *field* is any container for an element or item of data.

In some of the preceding descriptions, this book introduced the concept of *fields*, or regions of data. A field is any container for an element or item of data, whether it be any of the following three things:

A graphic object for the display of that datum

A region of memory reserved for that datum

A region of a file reserved for that datum

One of the primary differences between the sequential- and random-access techniques is that random access is *bidirectional*—you can read to and write from the same channel. With sequential access, the mode Output or Input is specified first, setting the direction of the data stream in advance. With random access, there is no data stream; the file pointer is positioned wherever you want, and data is either sent to or acquired from that position. The file pointer then moves over one element, so it knows that a sequence exists. In random access, however, the sequence of data elements in a file does not govern how that data is accessed.

Suppose that an application has an on-screen form that contains fields for data about one of the 50 states. To acquire this data, the user types the two-letter postal abbreviation for a state into a field marked Postal Abbr., which is a text box. The user then clicks a button marked Reference, and the application is then directed to acquire the rest of the data for that state from the file. In memory is a string array variable that acts as a sort of directory; within each element of the array is a postal abbreviation. If the abbreviation typed matches an abbreviation in the array, the array subscript value for that abbreviation is used to acquire the record of that state from a file.

Example

Here's how the procedure for determining which record is loaded might appear:

```
Sub StateFind ()
pa$ = PostalAbbr.Text
For state = 1 to 50
    If postal$(state) = pa$ Then Exit For
Next state
Acquire state
Exit Sub
```

First, the contents of the postal abbreviation field are copied to string variable pa$. The loop clause then compares these contents to those within the array postal$(state) and continues to execute this comparison as long as the contents are not equivalent to each other. When they become equivalent, the loop is exited and control is passed to Sub Acquire (), a procedure that loads data about the state into memory. Assume that earlier in the program the following instruction was executed:

```
Open "50STATES.DTA" For Random As #1 Len = 48
```

As you move from procedure to procedure, channel #1 is still open. You can address the file for channel #1 using Sub Acquire () as follows:

```
Sub Acquire (state As Integer)
locat = (state - 1) * 4
Get #1, locat, name$(state)
StateName.Text = name$(state)
Get #1, , pop
pop$(state) = Str$(pop)
Population.Text = pop$(state)
Get #1, , mass
mass$(state) = Str$(mass)
LandMass.Text = mass$(state)
Get #1, , bird$(state)
Bird.Text = bird$(state)
End Sub
```

The first order of business is to determine where the record for this state starts. The way the example works thus far, each record contains four fields. When the first state's record (Alabama's, if you're proceeding alphabetically) was saved to the file 50STATES.DTA, the file pointer started at location 0. After all four elements of that record were saved, the pointer was at location 4, waiting for the next record to be saved. The pointer position is, therefore, at a location four times the value of the state being saved minus 4. The formula `locat = (state - 1) * 4` thus returns the proper file pointer location for the state being loaded into memory.

You load the first element of the record into the string array variable `name$()` using `Get #` and specify the starting file pointer location `locat` directly. From then on, each time you load an element, the pointer location is incremented automatically, so you don't need to specify a pointer location variable again for the rest of the loading procedure. In the preceding procedure, after you load each element into its appropriate string array variable, the text of that element also is displayed within the form on-screen.

Records versus Data

If you're comparing the terms this book uses to discuss random access with the terms in the manuals that were supplied with your copy of Visual Basic, you may be confused at the moment, and with good reason. To dispel the confusion, here's an explanation: the term *record* is used universally to describe a grouping of related elements of data. This technical definition of record is subscribed to worldwide, especially by programmers of database management systems. Microsoft uses the term *record* only with respect to Visual Basic to describe an element of data being written to or read from a file—or what is still sometimes called a *datum*.

Example

Here's how a Type clause might appear within the global module of the 50 States program:

```
Type StateData
    name As String * 24
    pop As Long
    mass As Long
    bird As String * 16
End Type
Global StateRecord as StateData
```

When you declare a string as in String * 24, you set the length of the declared string. Formal data records using "user-defined" composite variable types might not include strings of variable length because a formal random-access record must have a fixed length for it to be recognized as a record. You cannot invoke array variables within a Type clause; but in the case of the revised 50 States program, you no longer need array variables because the record arrays are now kept on disk rather than in memory. The active record number still is kept in variable state; however, the value of state is now also the value of the current file pointer location, assuming record number 0 is a null record.

Assume now that, someplace in the application, you invoke the following instructions:

```
RecLength = Len(StateData)
Open "50STATES.DTA" For Random As #1 Len = RecLength
```

Normally, the Len() function returns the length of a string variable; here, however, it also can return the byte length of a composite variable. In this case, RecLength is now 48, and that value is now assigned as the length of the formal records accessed through channel #1. The storage routine for a state's data can now appear as follows:

```
StateRecord.name = StateName.Text
StateRecord.pop = Val(Population.Text)
StateRecord.mass = Val(LandMass.Text)
StateRecord.bird = Bird.Text
Put #1, state, StateRecord
```

The preceding is the entire storage routine. The contents of the currently displayed form are transferred to constituent variables invoked as properties of an object StateRecord. You can use object-oriented syntax to address these variables because they were previously included within a Type clause that attributed them to StateRecord as if that were an object. The values and contents of these variables having been set, StateRecord now contains a complete record for the state. It is stored to disk at location number state; translation from state number to location number does not need to take place.

You can now modify Sub Acquire () to work in the reverse:

```
Sub Acquire (state As Integer)
Get #1, state, StateRecord
StateName.Text = name
Population.Text = Str$(pop)
LandMass.Text = Str$(mass)
Bird.Text = bird
End Sub
```

After StateRecord is loaded into memory, the contents and values of its four constituent variables follow.

Summary

After you use the Open statement to open a file in random-access mode, data elements may be stored at random and retrieved from a designated file at any time and from any location within the boundaries of the file. Random access is bidirectional, whereas sequential access is unidirectional—either Input or Output/Append. Opening a file in Binary access mode allows for the storage and retrieval of individual bytes from a file, rather than elements of data in the form of variables.

You use the Put # statement to write the value or contents of a single variable to a random-access file, either at a specified location within the file or at the point just following the last recorded writing to that file. You use the Get # statement to retrieve data from a random-access file, from a specified location or just after the last location read from or written to.

A data element within a random-access file has a fixed field length, specified within the Open...As Random statement using the optional Len term. If Len is not included in the Open statement, the field length is set to 128 bytes. A record is a collection of related data elements. An entire record can be stored within this single field, as long as the constituent variables within that record have fixed field lengths themselves. The constituent variables of a record can be specified within a Type clause in the global module of a Visual Basic application.

Review Questions

1. What is the maximum length of an alphanumeric string within a random-access data element?

2. In the formal database model, if you can consider a set of records defined by a Type clause as a table, what can you consider a variable within the clause?

3. What is the value returned by Len(Precinct) if the Type clause is expressed as follows?

```
Type Precinct
    name As String * 36
    seat As String * 25
    latitude As Single
    longitude As Single
    PopRegistered As Long
End Type
```

CHAPTER 49

Data File Attributes

In this chapter, you learn the functions that you can use to retrieve data *about* a data file, or, in other words, functions that return the attributes of that file. Later, you learn an alternate method for retrieving individual bytes from a stored data file in either sequential- or binary-access mode. The chapter closes with a look at the system clipboard and the methods that send data to and retrieve data from this logical device.

As you've seen in the previous two chapters, the Visual Basic interpreter maintains a file pointer for each open data channel. This pointer is a value in memory—not a variable—which registers the current location where an element of data would be read from a file or would be stored to a file. Because Visual Basic does not see stored data files as formal structures with stored field lengths, attributes, and relations, practically the only control the programmer has over the data-transfer process is through this file pointer.

Perhaps the simplest file pointer control function to comprehend is the one that tells you whether you've reached the end of the file.

EOF()   **Function**

Purpose: Data file end determination
Syntax:

```
variable% = EOF(channel%)
```

The EOF() function returns whether the file pointer for a specified `channel%` is currently within its boundaries. If the file pointer has reached the end of the file, EOF() returns a Boolean value of True (–1). If there are still more data elements or bytes to be read within an open data file, EOF() returns False (0). The function works only on files that have a `channel%` opened previously with the Open statement, and are currently considered open by the interpreter.

Example

One common use of the EOF() function is in loading the contents of a sequential-access file into array variables in memory, when the number of data elements in the file has not been determined. The following example routine loads the contents of a sequential-access file of any length into an array variable, assuming that variable has been dimensioned for a high enough value:

```
Open "test.fil" For Input As #1
While EOF(1) = False
    Input #1, item(test)
    test = test + 1
Wend
```

You could have used a For-Next loop in the preceding routine, but only if you knew ahead of time or could specify indirectly in a variable the number of elements in the data file—because you'd have to count from 1 to *something*%. Here variable test is incremented manually, and the While-Wend loop executes until the end-of-file register is set to true.

The Visual Basic interpreter maintains values for the last location written to or read from a data file, as well as the *next* location. These are not to be confused with each other.

Loc() Function

Purpose: Returns location of file data pointer
Syntax:

```
location& = Loc(channel%)
```

The Loc() function returns the location of the previous storage to or retrieval from an open data file, the *channel*% number of which is specified between the parentheses. For random-access files, the Loc() function returns the number of the previous data element or record, in which 1 is the number of the first element in the file. For sequential-access files, Loc() returns a rounded value equivalent to the current byte location of the data pointer—not the element or record location—divided by 128. For binary-access files, Loc() returns the location of the byte previously written to or read from the data file. The pound sign before *channel*% is omitted for this function.

Seek()   **Function**

Purpose: Data pointer position acquisition
Syntax:

```
location& = Seek(channel%)
```

The `Seek()` function returns the location of the file pointer within an open data file, the `channel%` number of which is specified between the parentheses. This pointer location is where the next read or write operation will take place. For random-access files, `Seek()` returns the number to be given the next data element written to or read from the data file. For sequential- and binary-access files, `Seek()` returns the byte location where the next character of data will be written to or read from the data file. The pound sign before `channel%` is omitted for this function.

Example

Suppose your application maintains a random-access data file. A record of related data elements within this file is grouped informally—in other words, without the aid of the `Type` clause. A cluster of individual elements (each with a small, fixed data length) make up a record. You may have a procedure that at some time needs to know whether the current file pointer is in the midst of a record or at the beginning of one. You can use the following routine fragment to determine this state:

```
lc = Seek(1)
If lc / reclength = Int(lc / reclength) Then
    Rem Beginning of Record
    .
    .
    .
Else
    Rem Midst of Record
    .
    .
    .
End If
```

The total number of data elements in a complete random-access data file *must* be a multiple of the number of data elements in a complete record in that file. It therefore follows that if the record length does not evenly divide into the element location of the file pointer, the pointer must not be at the beginning of a new record.

You can use the `Seek #` statement, which is related to the `Seek()` function, to manually set the current location of the file pointer.

Seek #   Statement

Purpose: Data pointer position directive
Syntax:

```
Seek [#]channel%, location&
```

The Seek # statement sets the pointer location for a data file, where the next read or write operation will take place, to a specified *location&*. The data file is specified by its designated *channel%*, which was given to that file when it was opened using the Open statement. The value of *location&* can be specified as greater than the actual current length of the file. In such cases, the interpreter generates null values for all locations between the final location and the stated *location&*.

For random-access files, the value of *location&* is set to the data element number where a variable is to be written when Put # is invoked next, or to the data element number where it is to be read when Get # is invoked next. For sequential- and binary-access files, the value of *location&* is set to the byte address of the next character to be written to or read from the data file. The pound sign before the *channel%* number is optional.

Example

Perhaps the most common use for the Seek # statement is to set the current file pointer to element #1 of a file, as with the following instruction:

```
Seek #1, 1
```

Data Process Control

A *buffer* is an area of memory where data is temporarily stored.

When storing information to a data file, that data usually waits within a data *buffer* before it actually is sent to disk. A buffer is a holding area in memory consisting of a fixed number of bytes, reserved for data that are to be sent to some device—often a disk file—at some later time, generally when the buffer is full.

The purpose of a buffer here is to speed writing operations to a file, because writing to an address in memory is much faster than writing to a single location on a disk, and writing several data elements to a single location on a disk *once* is much faster than writing several data elements to *several* locations on that disk at different times. In sequential access, specifying the Len = option in the Open statement sets the size of this buffer in memory; by default, it is set to 512 bytes, or half of a kilobyte.

Each open channel has its own memory buffer. Part of what the Close instruction does is flush the memory buffer set aside for the stated channel number. Until the

`Close` instruction is executed, the image of the data file that the VB interpreter sees may not be equivalent to the image of the data file on the disk. Updates of the physical file on-disk take place only when the buffer is full; after each update, the buffer is emptied. *Caching* in microcomputer hardware is similar to buffering in software, in that hard-coded registers are reserved for holding data that are to be transferred to another device. Because transferring data all at once is always faster than transferring one unit at a time, processing is noticeably expedited.

The only danger in batch-storing is that, in the event of a fatal error or a system crash, the logical image of the data in memory is lost and the nonupdated physical image of the data remains. You can use the `Reset` statement at the end of a program, during an error-trapping routine, or before loading a new document file into memory to shut down data transfer officially and to make the physical data image equivalent to the logical image.

Reset   Statement

Purpose: Data transfer process clearance
Syntax:

```
Reset
```

The `Reset` statement shuts down all data-transfer processes by flushing the contents of all open data buffers to their apportioned `Open` files and closing all open channels without having to invoke `Close` statements for those channels.

Visual Basic's other general file maintenance functions are the `LOF()`, `FreeFile`, and `FileAttr()` functions.

LOF()   Function

Purpose: Data file length acquisition
Syntax:

```
length% = LOF(channel%)
```

The `LOF()` function returns the length in bytes of the open file whose `channel%` appears between the parentheses. The pound sign before `channel%` is omitted for this function.

FreeFile Function

Purpose: Free channel acquisition
Syntax:

```
channel% = FreeFile
```

The FreeFile function returns the lowest-valued available unopened channel number, in the variable *channel%*. You can then use this variable in an Open statement that may follow. The FreeFile function requires no parentheses.

FileAttr() Function

Purpose: Data file type acquisition
Syntax:

```
setting% = FileAttr(channel%, attribute%)
```

When *attribute%* is stated as 1, the FileAttr() function returns a value that describes the data file access mode assigned to the specified data channel. This value can be any of the following:

1	Sequential Input
2	Sequential Output
4	Random
8	Sequential Append
32	Binary

When *attribute%* is stated as 2, the FileAttr() function returns a value representing the file's handle or access number attributed to it by the Microsoft Windows environment. You can use this handle in conjunction with instructions to the Windows Application Program Interface.

Unformatted Data Input

Visual Basic maintains one function (not a statement) for the acquisition of data from any file that may not necessarily be in one of the three regular VB formats. You can use the Input$() function to acquire characters from a regular text file and later convert those characters into usable data.

Input$()   **Function**

Purpose: Raw data acquisition
Syntax:

```
string$ = Input$(numchars%, [#]channel%)
```

The `Input$()` function is used to acquire raw data from a file, the data elements of which, if any, are not distinguished from each other in any way that Visual Basic immediately recognizes. After the data is acquired, it is up to the VB application to interpret the data and find a purpose for them.

The function retrieves *numchars%* number of alphanumeric characters from a data file which has a *channel%* number apportioned to it by the `Open` statement for sequential `Input` or `Binary` access. It moves the current file pointer to the byte following the last one read by `Input$()`. The function retrieves the string and assigns it to the string variable *string$*. Each byte in the retrieved string is treated as an alphanumeric character that can be converted to a value between 0 and 255 with the `Asc()` function. This function is not available for files opened for `Random` access. The pound sign before *channel%* is optional for this function.

Example

Suppose you have a file selector box that contains a preview line, which shows the first 85 characters of a text file currently being highlighted within the file directory box. The following routine displays the first line:

```
If Right$(File1.FileName, 4) = ".TXT" Then
    Open File1.Filename For Input As #64
    pview$ = Input$(85, #64)
    Preview.Text = pview$
    Close #64
Else
    Preview.Text = ""
End If
```

Following is this routine written as pseudocode:

*If the file currently being highlighted is a
text file, then
    Open that file as a data file, give it channel
    number 64, and pretend it is a sequential-access
    input file.
    Retrieve the first 85 characters from channel #64.
    Place those characters within the preview text box.
    Close the channel, because you need no more
    characters.*

Otherwise,
Clear the preview text box, because you're not reading
a conventional text file.
End of condition.

System Clipboard Management

You've seen the methods for facilitating cut-and-paste operations several times throughout this book. From the point of view of managing the system clipboard, this process might best be called "set-and-get" rather than "cut-and-paste." The Cut and Paste facility in Windows has expanded to handle data in differing formats—raw text, rich text, object graphics, and bitmaps—without users having to set these formats themselves.

You'll probably appreciate this even more now as a programmer, especially because it is your job to maintain the format of the data going into and out of the system clipboard. Microsoft Windows recognizes certain integer values as representative of clipboard data formats; these values are in turn recognized by Visual Basic. They are listed in table 49.1.

Table 49.1. Windows' clipboard data formats.

Data Type	Const Name	Value
Text	CF_TEXT	1
Standard bitmap	CF_BITMAP	2
Windows metafile	CF_METAFILE	3
Device-independent bitmap	CF_DIB	8
Image color palette	CF_PALETTE	9
Dynamic link	CF_LINK	48,896 (&HBF00)

The *device-independent bitmap* format uses scalable bitmaps, with more color capacity than most video drivers are capable of handling.

A *standard bitmap* is an image represented photographically, in which pixels are represented binarily as on/off states. The original Windows icons for versions 1 and 2 used the default black-and-white format for the standard bitmap, which is now called the *device-dependent bitmap*. With Windows 3 came the *device-independent bitmap* format, which was easily scalable for many different output devices and which also used an RGB lookup table to produce colors. A DIB bitmap can have more colors than your screen can display—the format is ready for some of the new 32,000-color Windows video drivers being produced. The standard color palette of an image of any format is represented by data format 9.

A Windows metafile is a combined element of object-oriented graphics, produced by lines proceeding in specifiable vectors, along with filled shapes and colored areas. The new edition of Microsoft Draw being shipped with some Windows applications enables the user to produce metafile images for importing into the main application. Metafiles are described logically by instruction rather than by numeric representation. In other words, the metafile tells Windows how to draw the image rather than what to draw.

The dynamic link format is reserved for pasting data to an application, although a link is still retained to the application that created the cut data in the first place. Visual Basic reserves six methods for controlling the contents of the system clipboard: `.SetText`, `.SetData`, `.GetText()`, `.GetData()`, `.GetFormat()`, and `.Clear`.

.SetText   **Method**

Purpose: Clipboard text placement
Syntax:

```
Clipboard.SetText string$[, format%]
```

The `.SetText` method places the text currently referred to as *string$* on the system clipboard. By default, this text is assumed to be of data format 1 unless specified as &HBF00, in which case the text is assumed to be part of a dynamic link operation.

.SetData   **Method**

Purpose: Clipboard data placement
Syntax:

```
Clipboard.SetData Object.{Image ¦ Picture}[, format%]
```

The `.SetData` method assigns to the system clipboard the `.Picture` (bitmap on the form) or `.Image` (bitmap in memory) referred to using object-oriented syntax. By default, the image is assumed to be a standard bitmap of data format 2; however, formats 3 and 8 are also supported.

.GetText()   Method

Purpose: Text acquisition from clipboard
Syntax:

```
string$ = Clipboard.GetText (format%)
```

The .GetText method acts like a function, in that it returns the current textual contents of the system clipboard within *string$*. If *format%* is specified as either type 1 or &HBF00 (dynamic link), the contents of the clipboard are returned to *string$* whether or not that format was intended for those contents.

.GetData()   Method

Purpose: Data acquisition from the clipboard
Syntax:

```
Object.Picture = Clipboard.GetData (format%)
```

The .GetData method acts like a function in that it returns the .Image or .Picture contents of the system clipboard and assigns those contents as the .Picture property of the specified Object. If format% is stated as data format 2, 3, or 8, the contents of the clipboard are assigned to the .Picture property, regardless of whether that data was designed to be image data.

.GetFormat()   Method

Purpose: Clipboard content type acquisition
Syntax:

```
boolean% = Clipboard.GetFormat (format%)
```

The .GetFormat method acts like a function in that it returns in the integer variable *boolean%* a true/false value that indicates whether the data currently residing on the system clipboard is of the specified *format%*.

.Clear   Method

Purpose: Clipboard content clearance
Syntax:

```
Clipboard.Clear
```

The .Clear method clears the current contents of the system clipboard.

Example

In the Expressor application, a clipboard method is used to place on the clipboard the number currently in the readout:

```
Sub EditCut_Click ()
Clipboard.SetText readout.Caption
End Sub
```

At any time, an instruction can be invoked that takes the text currently indicated by the user in a large text box and copies it to the system clipboard:

```
Clipboard.SetText Text1.SelText
```

Now, if you want to make this operation an Edit Cut operation rather than an Edit Copy operation, you might want to add the following instruction:

```
Text1.SelText = ""
```

Later, if you want this clipped text inserted at the current cursor location, you can do the following:

```
Text1.SelText = Clipboard.GetText()
```

Notice that the parentheses are left in the Get operations but omitted in the Set operations.

Summary

The EOF() function is used as a flag to determine whether the final element of a data file has been read. The Loc() function is used to return the file pointer location of the element that has just been read, whereas the Seek() function is used to return the file pointer location of the element that is about to be read. The Seek # statement is used to position that pointer to a specific location. The file pointer location for a sequential- or binary-access file is a byte address in the data file, whereas the location for a random-access file is a data element number, regardless of the length of that element.

The LOF() function is used to return the length in bytes of an open file. The FreeFile function is used to return the first available unopened file channel. The FileAttr() function is used, for the most part, to determine the file-access mode attributed to an open channel.

The Input$() function is used for files that appear to be opened for sequential or binary access, for acquiring a specified number of characters from any file, whether or not it is a formal Visual Basic data file. This function bypasses the standard access techniques for sequential and binary access.

The Microsoft Windows system clipboard maintains one text format, three image formats, and a special format reserved for dynamic linking. The .SetText and .SetData methods for the Clipboard. object are used to acquire data from an object and place it on the system clipboard. Likewise, the .GetText and .GetData methods are used to place data from the clipboard on a qualifying object. The .GetFormat method is used to acquire the format number of the data currently maintained by the system clipboard. The .Clear method is reserved specifically for use with the Clipboard. object; it is used, naturally, to clear the clipboard of its contents.

Review Questions

Assume a text file is made up of the following:

```
We hold these truths to be self-evident: that all men
➡are created equal...
```

This file has been opened and given a channel number with the following instruction:

```
Open "CONSTITU.DTA" For Input As #5 Len = 512
```

1. What is the current value returned by LOF(5)?

2. What are the contents of c$ after invoking the instruction
c$ = Input$(7, #5)?

3. After invoking the preceding instruction, what is the value returned by Loc(5)?

4. What is the current value returned by Seek(5)?

5. Suppose the instruction Seek #5, 32 is executed. What are the contents of c$ now?

6. What are the contents of c$ after executing the instruction
c$ = Input$(7, #1)?

CHAPTER 50

Formal Records

In this chapter, you see the latest update of the NameForm application that you have continually amended throughout the book to make the application serve its promised purpose. You use random-access techniques to make the application store its data not to arrays in memory as it has been doing, but to a physical data file on disk.

Making NameForm Work

The stand-alone version of NameForm Mark IV is shown in figure 50.1.

Figure 50.1

NameForm
Mark IV.

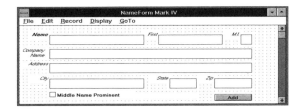

NameForm Mark IV Mailing List Manager

Project name: NAMEFRM4.MAK
Constituent files: NAMEFRM4.BAS, NAMEFRM4.FRM, SELECTOR.FRM

NAMEFRM4.FRM

Object Type	Property	Setting
Form	.Width	8655
	.Height	3750
	.Name	NameForm
	.Caption	NameForm Mark IV

Menu	Control Name	Caption
	File	&File
	FileOpen	----&Open
	FileSort	----&Sort
	hyphen1	-----
	FileSaveMerge	----Save as &Mail Merge
	FileTrim	----&Trim
	Edit	&Edit
	EditCopy	----Cop&y
	EditClear	----Clea&r
	Record	&Record
	RecordInsert	----&Insert
	RecordDelete	----&Delete
	Display	&Display
	DisplayFirst	----&First Name First
	DisplayLast	----&Last Name First
	GoToRecord	&GoTo

Object Type	Property	Setting
Text box	.Name	LastName
	.Caption	(blank)
Text box	.Name	FirstName
	.Caption	(blank)
Text box	.Name	MidInit
	.Caption	(blank)

Object Type	Property	Setting
Text box	.Name .Caption	CompanyName (blank)
Text box	.Name .Caption	Address (blank)
Text box	.Name .Caption	City (blank)
Text box	.Name .Caption	State (blank)
Text box	.Name .Caption	Zip (blank)
Label	.Caption .FontItalic .Alignment	Name True 1 - Right Justify
Label	.Caption .FontBold .FontItalic .Alignment	First False True 1 - Right Justify
Label	.Caption	M.I.
Label	.Caption	Company Name
Label	.Caption	False
Label	.Caption	City
Label	.Caption	State
Label	.Caption	Zip
Label	.Name .Caption .Alignment	Register (blank) 1 - Right Justify
Scroll bar	.Name .Min .Max .LargeChange .Value	RecordShown 1 1 10 1

continues

NAMEFRM4.FRM Continued

Object Type	Property	Setting
Check box	.Name	MidName
	.Caption	Middle Name Prominent
	.Value	0
Button	.Name	Add
	.Caption	Add
	.Enabled	False

NAMEFRM4.GBL—Global Module

```
Option Base 1
Global TargetFile$, cancl As Integer, prmpt$, filename$,
➡pattern$
Type NameRecord
    LastName As String * 30
    FirstName As String * 20
    MidInit As String * 3
    CompanyName As String * 50
    Address As String * 50
    City As String * 20
    State As String * 5
     Zip As String * 10
    MidProm As Integer
End Type
Global CurRecord As NameRecord
```

The first `Global` statement here contains variables that you use for SELECTOR.FRM, the file selector box you created in Chapter 23, "Managing List Boxes." In the type clause is the new record format for each name to be stored in the random-access file. `NameRecord` acts as the formal record type, whereas `CurRecord` acts as the "object" for all the attributes listed in the type clause. Notice the fixed length of all variables declared as type `String` in the `Type` clause.

Declarations Section

```
Dim RecordNo As Integer, MaxRecord As Integer
Dim sortarray() As Integer
```

Variable `RecordNo` holds the current record number in the sequence stored to disk. `MaxRecord` contains the highest record number in the file. Previously, you dimensioned array variables for 1000 units each; by keeping all the records in a random-access file, memory doesn't have to maintain the record image. Array sortarray() keeps the image of the data table in memory so that it can be sorted alphabetically later.

Event Procedures

```
Sub Form_Load ()
filename$ = "NAMES.NFM"
LoadFile
End Sub
```

The default file to be scanned from disk is called NAMES.NFM. You're not loading this file into memory; you're simply loading individual records into the form one at a time. You use the NFM extension for NameForm files. This file is opened but not loaded. Note the distinction.

General Procedures

```
Sub LoadFile ()
Open filename$ For Random As #1 Len = 190
If LOF(1) > 190 Then
    Do
        Get #1, MaxRecord + 1, CurRecord
        MaxRecord = MaxRecord + 1
    Loop Until CurRecord.FirstName = "~*End" Or MaxRecord >
    ➥LOF(1) / 190
Else
    CurRecord.FirstName = "~*End"
    Put #1, 2, CurRecord
    CurRecord.MidProm = 0
    CurRecord.FirstName = ""
    Put #1, 1, CurRecord
    MaxRecord = 1
End If
titl$ = "NameForm Mark IV - [" + UCase$(filename$) + "]"
NameForm.Caption = titl$
RecordNo = 1
RecordShown.Max = MaxRecord
RecordShown.Value = 1
If RecordNo < MaxRecord Then
    Add.Enabled = 0
Else
    Add.Enabled = -1
End If
ShowRecord
End Sub
```

This is a crucial procedure, so take a look at it in pseudocode:

*Start of the **LoadFile** procedure:*

*Open a file having the name that the user selected
from SELECTOR.FRM a moment ago, or whatever some
other procedure is passing as a default name. You
call this a random-access file having a length of 190
bytes per record. If the file doesn't exist yet,
create it.*

*If there appears to be more than one record in this
file, then*

   Repeat the following until told to stop:

      *See if you can grab the record that resides at
      a location one higher than the one you know so
      far to be the highest location.*

      Add 1 to that highest location tally.

   *Repeat the preceding instructions until you reach a
   dummy record marked ~*End or until the maximum
   record tally appears to be beyond that which is
   logically feasible for this record, given its
   limited length.*

Otherwise, because this is obviously a new file,

   Create a dummy first name ~*End.

   *Save this dummy first name to the physical end of
   the file, which is record #2.*

   Clear the middle-name-prominence register.

   Clear the dummy first name field.

   *Save this clean-slate record as the first record
   of this new file.*

   *Set the logical maximum record number in memory
   to 1.*

End of condition.

*Create a new title for this form, containing the
current file name of the open file.*

Assign this title to the title bar of the form.

Call this the first record number in the file.

*Set the scroll bar so that its maximum registerable
value is exactly that kept by the logical maximum
record tally.*

Set the scroll bar slider value to 1.

*If the current record number is less than the maximum
number, then*

   Disable the Add button.

> *Otherwise,*
> > *Enable the Add button.*
> *End of condition.*
> *Branch to the procedure that shows the current record.*
> *End of procedure.*

The `Open` statement is found as the first instruction of `SubLoadFile ()`. The instruction is here rather than in `Form_Load` because there may be more than one occasion during the run time of the program when a data file is opened. It is best to make your code reusable whenever possible—that's the purpose of modularization.

This procedure used to be part of `Sub Form_Load ()` until it was cut and pasted here. The Add button, which you didn't see in the earlier chapters, is another afterthought. The original incarnation of NameForm had 1000 blank records stored in memory. You could add a record at any location at any time. With Mark IV, `MaxRecord` stored only the number of records that had been entered into the file, taking into account that the last record in the file would always be a blank record; after filling it in, the next record could be created and made blank. But there is no way the application can know for sure whether a record is "filled in" completely unless the record is told. So, the Add button was added.

The initial presence of the Add button in the form created a problem: Just what does Add mean? You already have a menu selection for inserting a record in the midst of a file and scooting the other records one position to the right. To add is therefore not to insert. Add can therefore only mean that the currently displayed record must be added to the end of the file. If the scroll bar doesn't show that the file pointer is at the end of the file, however, what purpose does the button serve? The Add button should be disabled if you're not looking at the final record in the file, thus the presence in `Sub LoadFile ()` of the `If RecordNo < MaxRecord Then...` conditional clause.

Now when `Sub LoadFile ()` is first called by `Sub Form_Load ()`, for the first time in the program's history, the file pointer is at the end of the file NAMES.NFM, because the only record officially in the file is blank. The Add button is therefore enabled. However, `Sub LoadFile ()` is called throughout the execution of the application, in which case there may be occasions where the button should be disabled by setting its `.Enabled` property to 0.

Placing the End in the Middle

When you save a Visual Basic record to a disk-based data file, you can imagine the process being similar to carving that record in a marble wall. To delete the record carved on the face of the wall, you could deface the record by carving the entire marble face down until all that's left is a blank record. The face on which the record is carved, however, does not go away. You cannot delete a random-access data record and its field in Visual Basic.

When the user of the NameForm application deletes a record by selecting Delete from the Record drop-down menu (the procedure for that selection follows later), the contents of all the records following the deleted one are extracted using Get #1 and rewritten at a location one below the previous location. The record that previously existed one ahead of the deleted record now inhabits the deleted record's space. Variable MaxRecord is decremented by one, so for the moment it looks like there is one fewer record in the table. Suppose, however, that the user at some later time reloads the data table. The table appears to contain just as many records as it did before the deletion. This is because the record at the end of the file—the one that should have been axed because its contents moved one location down in sequence—never really goes away.

Now, the way many formal database tables are structured once they are stored to disk, there are often several bytes of structural information at the beginning regarding the lengths of each record and the mathematical relations between them. No structural information about the data is at the beginning of the NameForm data file, because this information would constitute a record itself. This record would rest at position 1, which would make the first real record rest at position 2. Explaining to the interpreter that the first record is number 2 in a series takes more arithmetic; and the more unnecessary arithmetic you can avoid, the better.

Instead, the application writes a false record—one whose .FirstName is ~*End and which contains nothing else—at a record location just one past the value of MaxRecord. When assessing the length of a data table, you could invoke a formula that takes the number of bytes in the record—LOF(1)—and divides that figure by the length of each record—190. This formula was invoked as a precautionary measure within the Do-Loop clause in Sub LoadFile() a while back. The result of this formula is the number of physical records within the file. This takes into account, however, all the defaced or deleted records hanging at the end of the file that you don't want any more. By having a dummy ~*End record just after the last logical record in the file, any process that assesses the number of records within the open file, such as sorting, will know to not look at or beyond the record marked with ~*End. No defaced record will therefore ever be accidentally loaded into the NameForm form.

Physical records are stored to disk; logical records are manipulated in memory.

Variable RecordNo is used as a pointer to the current record number, or the number of the record that should be displayed. The way you'll use RecordNo in the future, the variable will be set to the record number to be displayed first. Immediately, that record is loaded into the record variable CurRecord. For now, RecordNo should point to record number 1, the first in the sequence. The .Max property of the scroll bar is set so that it cannot scroll past the maximum record number MaxRecord; subsequently, the .Value of the scroll bar is set to 1, again representing the first record. The Add button conditional clause then appears here, enabling the button if the currently shown record is the last in the sequence. The current record can be the first and the last, of course, if there's only one record in the file.

From here, control is passed to the ShowRecord procedure:

```
Sub ShowRecord ()
Get #1, RecordNo, CurRecord
Reg$ = "Record #" + Str$(RecordNo) + " of " + Str$(MaxRecord)
Register.Caption = Reg$
LastName.Text = RTrim$(CurRecord.LastName)
FirstName.Text = RTrim$(CurRecord.FirstName)
MidInit.Text = RTrim$(CurRecord.MidInit)
CompanyName.Text = RTrim$(CurRecord.CompanyName)
Address.Text = RTrim$(CurRecord.Address)
City.Text = RTrim$(CurRecord.City)
State.Text = RTrim$(CurRecord.State)
Zip.Text = RTrim$(CurRecord.Zip)
MidName.Value = CurRecord.MidProm
End Sub
```

The first instruction in this sequence is the crucial Get #1 statement, which retrieves the record numbered RecordNo in the sequence to the record variable CurRecord. At the bottom of the form is a label called Register that now shows not only the current record number, but also the total number of records in the file. The nine elements of the record variable CurRecord are each assigned to text box and check box objects within the form. Notice here how record components and graphic objects can share the same name.

Notice for each alphanumeric component of CurRecord assigned to a .Text box, you used the function RTrim$(). Remember in the Type clause how you declared certain component variables As String with asterisks denoting the fixed length of each string. When a string of characters shorter than this fixed length is assigned to one of these variables, the interpreter fills the rest of the space with space characters. These characters become part of the record. So when that record is redisplayed, those space characters become part of the display. This isn't noticeable at first until you try to edit the name and find that the cursor can be positioned far beyond the end of each element that is redisplayed. This really becomes visible when you select Display and the envelope form of the current record has lots of extra space in it. Therefore, RTrim$() is used to trim the rightmost spaces from each textual element being placed in a text box—which is the primary purpose of the RTrim$() function.

The one check box added to the main form, marked Middle Name Prominent, is reserved especially for people like F. Lee Bailey, H. Ross Perot, C. Everett Koop, and J. Fred Muggs who prefer to spell out their middle names and abbreviate their first names. In such instances, you can swap the first and middle names, as in Lee F. Bailey, and set the check box. When copying the name and vital information to Envelope$, the program then knows to swap the first and middle names.

```
Sub Address_Change ()
```

```
CurRecord.Address = Address.Text
End Sub

Sub City_Change ()
CurRecord.City = City.Text
End Sub

Sub CompanyName_Change ()
CurRecord.CompanyName = CompanyName.Text
End Sub

Sub LastName_Change ()
CurRecord.LastName = LastName.Text
End Sub

Sub FirstName_Change ()
CurRecord.FirstName = FirstName.Text
End Sub

Sub MidInit_Change ()
CurRecord.MidInit = MidInit.Text
End Sub

Sub State_Change ()
CurRecord.State = State.Text
End Sub

Sub Zip_Change ()
CurRecord.Zip = Zip.Text
End Sub
```

Each of these procedures is executed after the text box values in the form change. This can happen when a character is typed in the box; so if you're entering a seven-letter surname in graphic object LastName, the value of component variable CurRecord.LastName would change seven times. There's also this new procedure to consider:

```
Sub MidName_Click ()
CurRecord.MidProm = MidName.Value
End Sub
```

This changes the only value variable in the record variable CurRecord.

```
Sub Add_Click ()
Put #1, RecordNo, CurRecord
RecordNo = RecordNo + 1
MaxRecord = MaxRecord + 1
ClearForm
CurRecord.FirstName = "~*End"
Put #1, MaxRecord + 1, CurRecord
RecordShown.Max = RecordShown.Max + 1
RecordShown.Value = RecordNo
If RecordNo = MaxRecord Then
    CurRecord.FirstName = ""
    Put #1, RecordNo, CurRecord
End If
ShowRecord
End Sub
```

If the Add button is enabled, you must be entering the last record in the sequence. After clicking this button, the first Put # statement places the record CurRecord at the current RecordNo location. Because this is at the end of the file (otherwise you wouldn't have clicked this button), RecordNo, MaxRecord, and RecordShown.Max (the maximum scroll value) are each incremented. The record just added replaces—or more descriptively, overwrites—the dummy ~*End record. The next order of business is to add a new dummy record to the location just following the logical end of the file. The scroll bar is then manually moved to the end of the file at RecordNo, which was just incremented.

Toward the end, Sub Add_Click () places a call to Sub ClearForm():

```
Sub ClearForm ()
```

```
FirstName.Text = ""
LastName.Text = ""
MidInit.Text = ""
CompanyName.Text = ""
Address.Text = ""
City.Text = ""
State.Text = ""
Zip.Text = ""
MidName.Value = 0
End Sub
```

The operation of this procedure is nearly as self-evident as its purpose. All the text boxes are set to null values and the check box is unchecked.

Event Procedures

```
Sub RecordShown_Change ()
Put #1, RecordNo, CurRecord
RecordNo = RecordShown.Value
If RecordNo < MaxRecord Then
    Add.Enabled = 0
Else
    Add.Enabled = -1
End If
ShowRecord
End Sub
```

The other way a record is officially stored to a file is by changing the value of the scroll box. Remember that the data file now acts in place of memory, so if you cleared the form or replaced its contents before you stored the current contents to disk, the record just typed would be lost. For that matter, no records with nonblank contents would even exist for the data file, because every time the scroll bar was moved, the record's contents would be overwritten before the record could be saved. The displayed record could only be overwritten by an existing one, which must be blank anyway because a nonblank record could not be saved. The solution to the problem is to save the record to disk each time a scroll bar change is registered, before the current record numbers are updated.

After the Put #1 statement is executed, the new record number is obtained from the current value of the scroll bar. Again, the .Enabled property of the Add button is determined by whether the last record in the sequence is chosen.

In keeping with a new tradition started by Microsoft, menu selections have names that are concatenations of the menu category and command—for instance, FileOpen. There are a few exceptions here, such as when a control name would be too long or would be the same as a Visual Basic reserved word. Here are some of the menu procedures for NameForm Mark IV:

```
Sub FileOpen_Click ()
prmpt$ = "Choose a file to open:"
pattern$ = "*.nfm"
Selector.Show 1
filename$ = targetfile$
If cancl = 1 Then Exit Sub
cancl = 0
Close #1
LoadFile
End Sub
```

This procedure executes if the user selects Open from the File menu. The way this particular program works, a file is opened but it is not saved, because records are saved to an open file along the way. To create a new file, you open that file as if it already existed. Thus, you don't need a New selection within the NameForm Mark IV menu.

This procedure basically operates the file selector box. The way SELECTOR.FRM works now, a special prompt can be passed to it through the global variable prmpt$, and the default file extension for your files—in this case, *.NFM—can be passed to the selector through the global variable pattern$. After the Selector's modal dialog completes execution, it returns two global variables—targetfile$ (the name of the chosen file) and cancl—to the main form. If the value of cancl is 1, the user clicked the Selector's Cancel button, so the file-opening operation aborts. If the user clicked OK, the existing random-access file closes and the call is made to procedure Sub LoadFile (), which was listed earlier.

```
Sub FileSaveMerge_Click ()
prmpt$ = "Name of mail merge file:"
pattern$ = "*.mrg"
Selector.Show 1
If cancl = 1 Then Exit Sub
filename$ = targetfile$
Open filename$ For Output As #2
For ConvRec = 1 To MaxRecord
    Get #1, ConvRec, CurRecord
    Write #2, RTrim$(CurRecord.LastName),
    RTrim$(CurRecord.FirstName), RTrim$(CurRecord.MidInit),
    RTrim$(CurRecord.CompanyName), RTrim$(CurRecord.Address),
    RTrim$(CurRecord.City), RTrim$(CurRecord.State),
    RTrim$(CurRecord.Zip), CurRecord.MidProm
Next ConvRec
Close #2
ShowRecord
End Sub
```

As discussed in Chapter 47, "Sequential Access," Visual Basic maintains an alternate command for saving sequential-access data elements to a file that can be interpretable by word processors with mail merge features. Selecting Save as Mail Merge from the File menu enables the user to create a second file that mirrors the current one, although its format is a sequential mail merge file rather than a VB random-access file.

The Selector is used again to obtain the file name. This time, the user is still allowed to enter in the Filename: box a name that does not yet exist in the directory. If the chosen file does exist, in this case invoking Open #2...As Output overrides its existing contents entirely. Both channels #1 and #2 are now open simultaneously, so you can Get data from one file and Write it to the other. The immediate problem with this is that record variables declared with a Type clause cannot be addressed within sequential-access statements. It therefore follows that every component variable to CurRecord must be written to the sequential file individually, although they can be expressed within a list, unlike with the Put # statement.

In FileSaveMerge_Click (), a loop clause is initiated from the beginning to the last record in a random-access file. Within the loop, a record is obtained, and its constituent variables are trimmed of their trailing spaces and then written to channel #2 using Write #. Notice that the value of RecordNo wasn't affected.

```
Sub GoToRecord_Click ()
recno$ = InputBox$("Go to which record number?", "Go To. . .")
If recno$ <> "" Then
RecordNo = Val(recno$)
RecordShown.Value = RecordNo
ShowRecord
End If
End Sub
```

Selecting the GoTo category is an alternate method for changing the currently displayed record number. Using this procedure, you can easily type the new number into an input box. This value is then assigned to RecordNo; the program manually updates the scroll bar and calls ShowRecord, which brings this new record to the screen.

```
Sub EditCopy_Click ()
c$ = Envelope$(RecordNo, 1)
Clipboard.SetText c$
End Sub
```

One other useful purpose for this program is for copying a single name to the clipboard so that you can paste it into another application—for instance, a word processor, perhaps for the top of business correspondence. Selecting Copy from the Edit menu places the text of the current record in the clipboard, first by placing a call to the new Function procedure:

General Procedures

```
Function Envelope$ (rec As Integer, order As Integer)
Get #1, rec, CurRecord
If Asc(Left$(CurRecord.MidInit, 1)) <> 0 Then
    Separator$ = " " + RTrim$(CurRecord.MidInit) + " "
Else
    Separator$ = " "
End If
```

```
If order = 1 Then
    If MidName.Value = 0 Then
        FullName$ = RTrim$(CurRecord.FirstName) +
        ➡Separator$ + RTrim$(CurRecord.LastName)
    Else
        FullName$ = RTrim$(CurRecord.MidInit) + " " +
        ➡RTrim$(CurRecord.FirstName) + " " +
        ➡RTrim$(CurRecord.LastName)
    End If
Else
    If MidName.Value = 0 Then
        FullName$ = RTrim$(CurRecord.LastName) +
        ➡", " + RTrim$(CurRecord.FirstName) +
        ➡Separator$
    Else
        FullName$ = RTrim$(CurRecord.LastName) +
        ➡", " + Separator$ +
          RTrim$(CurRecord.FirstName)
    End If
End If
WorkPlace$ = RTrim$(CurRecord.CompanyName)
StreetAddress$ = RTrim$(CurRecord.Address)
Residence$ = RTrim$(CurRecord.City) + ", " +
➡RTrim$(CurRecord.State) + "  " +
➡RTrim$(CurRecord.Zip)
Next_Line$ = Chr$(13) + Chr$(10)
Envelope$ = FullName$ + Next_Line$ + WorkPlace$ +
➡Next_Line$ + StreetAddress$ + Next_Line$ + Residence$
End Function
```

Here's the preceding procedure written in pseudocode:

*Function for generating a name for the
 envelope:
Get from channel 1 the specified record number, and
 call that the current record.
If the middle initial field has a real character in it, then
    Make the separator string that middle initial
    sandwiched between two spaces.
Otherwise,
    Make the separator string just a space.
End of condition.*

If the last name order is to fall last, then
    If the middle name prominence check box is
    not checked, then
        The full name is a concatenation of the
        first name, the separator, and the
        last name in that order.
    Otherwise,
        The full name is a concatenation of the
        middle initial, a space, the first name,
        another space, and the last name in that order.
    End of this condition.
However, if the last name comes first,
    If the middle name prominence check box is
    not checked, then
        The full name is a concatenation of the
        last name, a comma and space, the first
        name, and the separator in that order.
    Otherwise,
        The full name is a concatenation of the
        last name, a comma and space, the
        separator, and the first name in that
        order.
    End of this condition.
End of the major condition.
Acquire the workplace from the appropriate field.
Acquire the address from the appropriate field.
The residence is a concatenation of the city, a
comma and space, the state, two spaces, and the
ZIP code.
The "next line" string is a carriage return and
line feed joined together.
The full envelope string is a concatenation of the
full name, "next line," the workplace, "next
line," the street address, "next line," and the
residence.
End of function.

The `Envelope$()` function creates a long, concatenated string made up of the contents of all the fields of a designated record `rec`, combined as they might appear typed on an envelope. This record `rec` may be the current record or one not currently shown. You may remember the general structure of this function from seeing its forebear `Sub ShowEnvelope ()` in NameForm Mark I.

The first conditional clause checks to determine the contents of the Middle Name field. In many cases, this field is left blank. If it is blank, its numeric value is considered 0, which is the terminating character for alphanumeric strings for some Windows and Visual Basic functions. So, if you add a 0 to the middle of the long, concatenated string, Windows might mistake that string as ending in the middle. Thus the string Separator$ was created, which has meaningful, nonzero contents even if the middle name field is left blank.

One of the parameters this function takes is order, which determines whether the last name is to come first (0) with a comma separating it and the first name, or whether the last name is to fall last (1). Another conditional clause has been added so that F. Lee Bailey's feelings won't be hurt by receiving mail addressed to Lee F. Bailey. If MidProm.Value is set to 1 in the form (if it's checked), the clause puts Separator$ in the middle of the name; otherwise, it puts Separator$ at the beginning of the name. The conditional clause surrounding that one places the last name last or first, depending on the value of order.

The carriage-return (Chr$(13)) and line-feed (Chr$(10)) characters are used here so that the person's name and address don't appear all on one line when pasted to the other application. After you tack the rest of the fields onto the end, the result is Envelope$, which is passed back to the calling body of the application.

Event Procedures

```
Sub DisplayFirst_Click ()
c$ = Envelope$(RecordNo, 1)
MsgBox c$, 0, "Preview"
End Sub


Sub DisplayLast_Click ()
c$ = Envelope$(RecordNo, 0)
MsgBox c$, 0, "Preview"
End Sub
```

There are now two different Display preview selections, depending on whether you want to see the first or last name first. Selecting the Display category allows the user to preview the currently displayed record pointed to by RecordNo as it would appear typed on an envelope, before it's copied to the clipboard. The 0 in the MsgBox instruction means you need nothing else within the message box but an OK button.

```
Sub EditClear_Click ()
ClearForm
End Sub
```

You can manually call the procedure for clearing the current form by selecting Clear from the Edit menu. Remember that the event procedures for each text box, such as Sub Address_Change (), execute whenever the contents of the form change as a result of any action, even if that action is made by the program and not the user. Therefore, clearing the form causes all the _Change event procedures to execute in turn. So by clearing the screen, you clear the current record.

```
Sub RecordDelete_Click ()
If RecordNo < MaxRecord Then
    For mve = RecordNo To MaxRecord
        Get #1, mve + 1, CurRecord
        Put #1, mve, CurRecord
    Next mve
End If
ClearForm
If RecordNo = MaxRecord Then
    RecordNo = RecordNo - 1
End If
If MaxRecord > 1 Then
    MaxRecord = MaxRecord - 1
    RecordShown.Max = RecordShown.Max - 1
Else
    Put #1, 1, CurRecord
End If
ShowRecord
End Sub
```

Finally, there are the relatively ingenious procedures for deleting a record from a data file and inserting a record into the middle of it. In random access, you can Get # and Put # records using the same open channel. With sequential access, by contrast, an accessed file is locked into either being read or written to. The For-Next loop clause counts every record numbered between the current RecordNo and the last logical MaxRecord and keeps that count within variable mve. The loop then takes the record just ahead of the counter location using Get #1 and uses it to overwrite the record at the current location using Put #1. Remember, this includes the dummy ~*End record. At the first iteration of this loop, the current record saved to disk is overwritten by the record that follows it in the sequence. Temporarily, there are two copies of the same record next to each other, until the next iteration of the loop, when the record that follows overrides the older copy.

At the last iteration of the loop, there are temporarily two copies of the final physical record. Because this is the dummy ~*End record, there's no problem. The final conditional clause makes the current record blank only if there's only one record in the file anyway, and that's the one that was deleted. Otherwise, the maximum logical record tally and current record number are both decremented.

```
Sub RecordInsert_Click ()
For mve = MaxRecord + 1 To RecordNo Step -1
    Get #1, mve, CurRecord
    Put #1, mve + 1, CurRecord
Next mve
ClearForm
Put #1, RecordNo, CurRecord
MaxRecord = MaxRecord + 1
RecordShown.Max = RecordShown.Max + 1
End Sub
```

The user selects Insert from the Record menu when she wants to place a new record—at the moment, one that hasn't been typed—at the location currently registered by the scroll bar. Remember, when the user types data, it's automatically considered part of the current record, and not some future record. If you programmed an insertion routine to add a record having contents that appeared within the form, at the point currently indicated by the scroll bar you would have two copies of the same record. When the current record is moved to make way for the new one, the current form contents represent the record that was moved. If the current form contents also represent the record that is being inserted, you have two copies of the same record.

For this procedure, you have a loop clause that is to some extent the reverse of the one you programmed for the Delete routine. Here variable mve counts backward from the absolute last record in the file (including the dummy record) to the current record number. The record pointed to by mve is then acquired from the file using Get #1, and then is copied to the location just following the current location using Put #1. On the first iteration of this loop, one record is added to the end of the file: a copy of the final record. After the loop clause is completed, the form is cleared and stored as the current record. You have therefore made space, literally, for a new record.

```
Sub FileTrim_Click ()
Open "~temp.fil" For Random As #2 Len = 190
plc = 1
tmp = RecordNo
Do
    Get #1, plc, CurRecord
    Put #2, plc, CurRecord
Loop Until CurRecord.FirstName = "~*End"
Close #2, #1
Kill filename$
Name "~temp.fil" As filename$
Open filename$ For Random As #1 Len = 190
RecordNo = tmp
ShowRecord
End Sub
```

Finally, this procedure was added as the only way to get rid of the trailing blank or dummy records from a data file containing numerous deletions. A second shadow file is opened called ~temp.fil and is given channel #2. Each record from #1 is copied to #2 in exactly the same location, until the dummy ~*End is reached and the Do-Loop clause ceases. At that time, both channels #1 and #2 are closed; the file once belonging to #2 now has exactly as many records as it should, without any blank trailing records.

Next, the old #1 data file is deleted from the disk using the Kill instruction. The Name instruction then renames ~temp.fil to whatever file name was being used previously, and then that file name is reopened as #1. Channel #1 now points to a new file; after this procedure is exited, however, the rest of the application doesn't know the difference.

A Procedure of Sorts

An algorithm is a repetitious process that models a real-world function.

The Sub FileSort_Click () event procedure is used to sort the records the user has entered into the NameForm so far. This sort is by last name, in ascending alphabetical order. The procedure incorporates what is called an algorithm, which is a repetitious mathematical process that, by its very repetition, manages to accomplish its goal.

```
Sub FileSort_Click ()
Dim j As Integer, k As Integer, l As Integer, t As Integer,
➥seed As Integer
ReDim sortarray(MaxRecord)
tmp = RecordNo
RecordNo = MaxRecord
If Asc(Left$(LastName.Text, 1)) > 0 Then
    Put #1, RecordNo, CurRecord
End If
For seed = 1 To MaxRecord -1
    sortarray(seed) = seed
Next seed
Do
    l = l + 1
    If l = MaxRecord Then Exit Do
    j = l
    For k = j + 1 To MaxRecord - 1
        If Envelope$(k, 0) <= Envelope$(j, 0) Then
            j = k
        End If
    Next k
```

```
    If l <> j Then
        t = sortarray(j)
        sortarray(j) = sortarray(l)
        sortarray(l) = t
    End If
Loop
Open "~temp.fil" For Random As #2 Len = 190
For replac = 1 To MaxRecord - 1
    Get #1, sortarray(replac), CurRecord
    Put #2, replac, CurRecord
Next replac
Close #2, #1
Kill filename$
Name "~temp.fil" As filename$
Open filename$ For Random As #1 Len = 190
RecordNo = sortarray(tmp)
ShowRecord
End Sub
```

The name of the algorithm incorporated here is BubbleSort, and it is actually one of the simpler sorting algorithms devised. This doesn't make it necessarily quicker than the others, just simpler. BubbleSort starts with the first element in the array. It considers this—represented by variable l—the element to currently sort. The only real job BubbleSort has is to find the lowest-valued element from the remainder of the array. So a comparison location variable j is created, and its initial value is set to the value of l. Variable k is used in a loop clause that counts from the element of the array just following j to the last element: 100.

The loop clause counts to see if any value is lower than that currently held within the unit() array at position j. If there is, j is set to the location of that lowest value; however, the loop isn't exited yet. Instead, it continues to the end to see if there's an even lower value. The result of this loop is that j contains the address of the lowest value in the remainder of the array. Note how the mechanism works here: Before the For-Next begins, the value of j is set to the value of l. Within the loop, if the conditional clause finds there's a lower value in the kth unit than there is in the jth unit, j is made equal to k. After the loop clause, j is tested to see if it still equals k—in other words, to see if the conditional clause was activated. If the two values are no longer equivalent, the conditional clause must have found a lower value, now pointed to by j. This value is swapped with the one to which l currently points; so the lowest possible comparison address contains the lowest possible value. Variable l is then incremented, and all the elements behind l are considered sorted. The comparison process then continues with the new element pointed to by l. You can say l acts as a sort of zipper.

The result of the swap between the array elements at locations l and j is that element j must now contain a higher value than it did. As the sorting process continues, the values that l has not touched toward the end of the array tend to grow higher in value. The higher values are said to bubble toward the high end, which is how this sort algorithm gets its name.

Visual Basic is quite kind in the way it allows you to evaluate the "value" of such things as words and even sentences. The "value" of such alphanumeric strings, in this case, is the relative position of each string in the alphabet. This value isn't really representable numerically, but if a$ = "Aaron" and b$ = "Zenith", the expression a$ < b$ would evaluate logically to be true (–1), because *Aaron* falls below *Zenith* alphabetically.

The result of this form of alphabetic expression is that you can add the `BubbleSort` routine to the `NameForm` application without much reorganization. I have created an array variable `sortarray()` that contains the number of each record in the current data file, listed in the order in which each record appears in the sorted data file. At the beginning of the procedure, `sortarray()` is seeded with an integer value equal to its own subscript; thus `sortarray(1)` = 1, `sortarray(2)` = 2, and so on. You never load every data record from the file into memory all at once. Instead, you invoke the comparison

```
If Envelope$(k, 0) <= Envelope$(j, 0)
```

which places two calls to the procedure `Function Envelope$()`. This way, only two records need to be loaded into memory at any one time.

The mechanism of the sort proceeds as if it were sorting numbers, although the comparison is made between the contents of the two `Envelope$` strings. The 0 parameter here causes `Function Envelope$()` to return a concatenation of all the elements of the form, with the last name of the person placed first, followed by the first name and middle initial (or middle initial and first name if the box is so checked). The swap is performed not between the names, but between the numbers that represent them within `sortarray()`. After the `Do-Loop` clause is completed, `sortarray()` acts as a list of all the name swaps that will take place now within the physical data file.

You may remember from the procedure `Sub FileTrim ()` how a second data file was created using the `Open` statement, and only the meaningful records were copied into that file. Both files were then closed. Then the original file was deleted, the newly created file was given the file name of the old file, and the new file was reopened. After the procedure was exited, the rest of the application would never know a switch had taken place. A similar process is found at the end of `Sub FileSort_Click ()`. This time, the file ~temp.fil is created and given channel #2. The loop being counted by variable `replac` goes through the `sortarray()` list and retrieves from the existing record the data file found at the current place within the array list. So, if `sortarray(1)` = 23, the first record retrieved will be the twenty-third.

Each record is then written to the second data file in sequence, with the result being that the second file is a sorted form of the first one. Both files are then closed with the `Close` statement, and the first file is deleted. The second file is then given the name of the first one. The file that was being viewed at the time `Sub FileSort_Click()` was called is retrieved from its new position in the `sortarray()` and is given to procedure `Sub ShowRecord ()` for redisplay.

Algorithmic Logic

It might seem at first that the sorting algorithm demonstrated here models nothing resembling a real-world process that you know of. Yet for any process that you perform regularly and repetitively that you think you can do in your sleep, your mind has probably worked out a standard operating procedure that makes the process simple enough that you don't have to think much about it. This may be a matter more for psychologists than programmers, but it is likely that if you were to write this process, it would be mathematical.

When a repetitive real-world process becomes so mathematical as to be logically encodable, what code is necessarily the right code? Efficiency in computing depends on the coordination of those elements we choose to call efficient. Raw ingenuity has proved here that the most efficient way of working can easily become the least efficient if another process with which it works in conjunction slows it down. Suppose these sort elements represented records in a random-access data file, and instead of I/O calls to the screen, you placed calls to that file. The `QuickSort` algorithm is known in programming to be the fastest and most reliable process; still, it can make the most calls to a disk device during the data retrieval process. If the drive is slow, it could make the fastest algorithm slower than the slowest, in terms of raw performance. The interrelationship of efficient processes does not necessarily result in an efficient process.

Summary

This is the second time in this book that you've seen the `NameForm` form module listed in full; this time, you've seen a more mature form of the program. It is one thing to program a working Visual Basic application, but the point at which the programmer decides the job of programming an application is complete may be purely arbitrary. There are always more new ideas that can be implemented in code. Perhaps this is why in the realm of commercial software there are so many packaged applications with skyrocketing version numbers.

Review Questions

1. When a record is "erased" from a random-access data file, how many fewer records are there now than there were before?

2. Why is it inconvenient to place a data file descriptor at the beginning of a random-access data file, even though such construction makes sense for a normal database?

3. Why is there no Save button or menu selection in the NameForm application?

ASCII/ANSI Code Chart

The following table lists the values that represent alphanumeric characters for the Visual Basic interpreter. The table shows the basis of the character code of the American National Standards Institute (ANSI). This code has been adapted by Microsoft for use with Microsoft Windows, so it contains some elements of the all-encompassing ANSI code as well as some elements of ASCII (American Standard Code for Information Interchange) on which the ANSI code is partly based. This table assumes you have installed the English code table for your copy of MS-DOS.

Character	Hex Code	ANSI Code
Backspace	&H08	8
Tab	&H09	9
Line feed	&H0A	10
Carriage return	&H0D	13
Space	&H20	32
!	&H21	33
"	&H22	34
#	&H23	35
$	&H24	36

continues

Character	Hex Code	ANSI Code
%	&H25	37
&	&H26	38
'	&H27	39
(	&H28	40
)	&H29	41
*	&H2A	42
+	&H2B	43
,	&H2C	44
-	&H2D	45
.	&H2E	46
/	&H2F	47
0	&H30	48
1	&H31	49
2	&H32	50
3	&H33	51
4	&H34	52
5	&H35	53
6	&H36	54
7	&H37	55
8	&H38	56
9	&H39	57
:	&H3A	58
;	&H3B	59
<	&H3C	60
=	&H3D	61
>	&H3E	62
?	&H3F	63

Character	Hex Code	ANSI Code
@	&H40	64
A	&H41	65
B	&H42	66
C	&H43	67
D	&H44	68
E	&H45	69
F	&H46	70
G	&H47	71
H	&H48	72
I	&H49	73
J	&H4A	74
K	&H4B	75
L	&H4C	76
M	&H4D	77
N	&H4E	78
O	&H4F	79
P	&H50	80
Q	&H51	81
R	&H52	82
S	&H53	83
T	&H54	84
U	&H55	85
V	&H56	86
W	&H57	87
X	&H58	88
Y	&H59	89
Z	&H5A	90

continues

Character	Hex Code	ANSI Code
[	&H5B	91
\	&H5C	92
]	&H5D	93
^	&H5E	94
_	&H5F	95
`	&H60	96
a	&H61	97
b	&H62	98
c	&H63	99
d	&H64	100
e	&H65	101
f	&H66	102
g	&H67	103
h	&H68	104
i	&H69	105
j	&H6A	106
k	&H6B	107
l	&H6C	108
m	&H6D	109
n	&H6E	110
o	&H6F	111
p	&H70	112
q	&H71	113
r	&H72	114
s	&H73	115
t	&H74	116
u	&H75	117

Character	Hex Code	ANSI Code
v	&H76	118
w	&H77	119
x	&H78	120
y	&H79	121
z	&H7A	122
{	&H7B	123
|	&H7C	124
}	&H7D	125
~	&H7E	126
'	&H91	145
,	&H92	146
"	&H93	147
"	&H94	148
°	&H95	149
–	&H96	150
—	&H97	151
Space	&HA0	160
¡	&HA1	161
¢	&HA2	162
£	&HA3	163
⊗	&HA4	164
¥	&HA5	165
¦	&HA6	166
§	&HA7	167
¨	&HA8	168
©	&HA9	169
ª	&HAA	170

continues

603

Character	Hex Code	ANSI Code
«	&HAB	171
¬	&HAC	172
-	&HAD	173
®	&HAE	174
‾	&HAF	175
°	&HB0	176
±	&HB1	177
²	&HB2	178
³	&HB3	179
´	&HB4	180
µ	&HB5	181
¶	&HB6	182
•	&HB7	183
¹	&HB8	184
‾	&HB9	185
º	&HBA	186
»	&HBB	187
¼	&HBC	188
½	&HBD	189
¾	&HBE	190
¿	&HBF	191
À	&HC0	192
Á	&HC1	193
Â	&HC2	194
Ã	&HC3	195
Ä	&HC4	196
Å	&HC5	197

Character	Hex Code	ANSI Code
Æ	&HC6	198
Ç	&HC7	199
È	&HC8	200
É	&HC9	201
Ê	&HCA	202
Ë	&HCB	203
Ì	&HCC	204
Í	&HCD	205
Î	&HCE	206
Ï	&HCF	207
Ð	&HD0	208
Ñ	&HD1	209
Ò	&HD2	210
Ó	&HD3	211
Ô	&HD4	212
Õ	&HD5	213
Ö	&HD6	214
×	&HD7	215
Ø	&HD8	216
Ù	&HD9	217
Ú	&HDA	218
Û	&HDB	219
Ü	&HDC	220
Ý	&HDD	221
Þ	&HDE	222
ß	&HDF	223
à	&HE0	224

continues

Character	Hex Code	ANSI Code
á	&HE1	225
â	&HE2	226
ã	&HE3	227
ä	&HE4	228
å	&HE5	229
æ	&HE6	230
ç	&HE7	231
è	&HE8	232
é	&HE9	233
ê	&HEA	234
ë	&HEB	235
ì	&HEC	236
í	&HED	237
î	&HEE	238
ï	&HEF	239
ð	&HF0	240
ñ	&HF1	241
ò	&HF2	242
ó	&HF3	243
ô	&HF4	244
õ	&HF5	245
ö	&HF6	246
÷	&HF7	247
ø	&HF8	248
ù	&HF9	249
ú	&HFA	250
û	&HFB	251

Character	Hex Code	ANSI Code
ü	&HFC	252
ý	&HFD	253
þ	&HFE	254
ÿ	&HFF	255

The _KeyPress event is recognized whenever a standard ANSI character—not including function keys or control keys—is pressed once on the keyboard. The returned value will be one of those listed in the preceding table. By contrast, a key code is recognized continually by the _KeyUp and _KeyDown events *while* a key on your keyboard is being pressed. This key may be one of those in the preceding ANSI table, although it may also be a key that is not represented by the ANSI code, such as the Ctrl key or Print Screen. These other keys are listed within the CONSTANT.TXT file supplied with your copy of Visual Basic as declarations of constants that can be attached to the global module of your VB application.

Answers to Review Questions

The following is a listing of answers to the Review Questions provided at the end of each chapter. You can obtain answers to Review Exercises through the disk offer. See the disk offer page at the back of this book for more information.

Chapter 1 Answers

1. Because BASIC is designed to more closely approximate the language used by people, whereas a low-level language is designed to more closely approximate the logic of the computer.

2. An instruction.

3. Machine language.

4. MS-DOS, or whatever acts as your computer's operating system.

5. A computer does not receive information; it can't be informed of anything because information implies the presence of a reasoning capability that the computer does not have. The instruction does, however, inform the human reader that a symbolic reference or variable called "a" is used to represent the numeral value "6." It also tells the person to think of "a" as being equal to "6"—to replace *a* for 6 in his mind. The BASIC language thus performs a dual purpose: it informs the human reader while it instructs the computer. This is another reason why we consider BASIC a high-level language.

Chapter 2 Answers

1. A project.

2. Buttons.

3. An underscore character (_).

4. _Click; in other words, the term following the underscore character.

5. The title bar, where you'll find the term [design] if the application is being constructed or written, [run] if it's currently running, or [break] if the program is currently in suspension.

6. Design mode.

7. FRM, the extension given to form modules.

Chapter 3 Answers

1. f = 6

2. Int(a + b + c)

3. good = 1

4. 3

5. A subroutine.

Chapter 4 Answers

1. Whenever you press a calculator key from 1 through 9, that digit appears in the display, moving any other digits before it to the left. The 0 key works in a similar manner, except that if the display already reads 0, no digits are added. Because there is an exception, the 0 key is excluded from the control array. It could have been included, although you would need to add a special conditional statement to the procedure, such as Select Case 0, that would determine whether the key pressed is the 0 key. The period or point key is not handled like a digit, so it should remain outside the control array.

2. In standard calculator notation, or *algebraic notation*, the user enters the mathematical function *before* entering the value to which that function pertains. As a result, when entering the expression *5 + 8 - 6*, the addition of *8* to *5* takes place when the user presses the *minus* key just before pressing *6*. This makes algebraic notation a confusing procedure to implement. In Reverse Polish Notation, the preceding expression would be entered as *5 Enter 8 Enter 6 -*. The function takes place when the user presses the function key. This makes it possible in Visual Basic for a procedure to be executed on pressing a command button that acts as the function key.

Chapter 5 Answers

1. A value.

2. A statement.

3. A statement or expression of assignment.

4. 32

5. The sign of a value in memory consumes one bit, thus reducing its maximum absolute numeric value by a power of two. If one bit isn't being used to store the sign of the value, it can be used to store a digit, thus increasing the capacity of that value by a power of two. Furthermore, if you divide the number of representable values in half, resulting in the negative side and the positive side; you would be forgetting 0, a value that is neither negative nor positive. The number of representable values in a byte is always an even number, but 0 is one value and 1 is an odd number. It must therefore take space from one side or the other, negative or positive; computer designers chose the positive side. This is why a byte can represent -256 but not $+256$.

Chapter 6 Answers

1.   **A.** $x = 47.2$
     B. $x = 3.333333$
     C. $x = 48$

2.   **A.** $v = (3.1415927 / 3) * r ^\wedge 2 * h$
     B. $P = F / (1 + i) ^\wedge n$

Chapter 7 Answers

1. −1

2. −1

3. 0

4. −1

5. −1

6. 0

7. 0

8. The sixth power.

9. Zero.

10. No, because any number to the zeroth power is 1, and 1 divides into every integral (whole) number evenly.

Chapter 8 Answers

1. Ardwight

2. 94201

3. WallaceArdwight (notice that no space separates the two words)

4. 5151 Back o' the Bay Way

5. Oakland, CA 94201

6. Wallace T. Ardwight
   5151 Back o' the Bay Way
   Oakland, CA 94201

7. Wallace T. Ardwight

   Oakland, CA 94201

8. Mr. or Ms. Wallace T. Ardwight

Chapter 9 Answers

1. Nebraska.

2. A bishop.

3. 400

4. `Dim Aspen() As Double`

Chapter 10 Answers

1. 0. Without formal declaration, the scope of `c` is local to the procedure.

2. 5. The `Dim` statement in the general declarations section makes `c` a module-level variable.

3. 0. Variable `c` is still equal to 5 in the procedure, even after it has been exited; however, outside of the procedure, `c` is officially undeclared.

4. Yes. The components of a composite variable are not limited to one type.

5. No. The only variables whose contents affect those of the composite variable are those listed in the `Type` clause for that composite variable. Some other variable can be used to assign a value to a component of a composite variable, but that borrowing doesn't tie the independent variable to the composite.

Chapter 11 Answers

1. `Let`

2. `'Convert 9-digit to 5`

3. `Left$("75059-0612", 5)`

Chapter 12 Answers

1. 15

2. 3

3. `"Go"`

4. 0

5. `""`

Chapter 13 Answers

1. For-Next

2. Do-Loop Until

3. Do While-Loop

Chapter 14 Answers

1. The interpreter "errors out"; naturally, it generates a Return without GoSub error.

2. Any form of Do-Loop constructs using While c < 4 as a qualifier, or a While c < 4. . . Wend loop.

3. Any form of Do-Loop constructs using Until c = 4 as a qualifier.

Chapter 15 Answers

1. The End Sub statement closes a procedure, whereas the Exit Sub statement forces an exit from that procedure before its End Sub statement is executed.

2. End by itself ends the entire program; no other statement does that.

3. The global module.

4. Sub Form_Load ().

5. Either Form2.Show or Load Form2.

6. After the interpreter clears and resets the workspace, absolutely nothing. No instructions are executed whatsoever. The project rests in limbo.

7.

Procedure or Region Name	Location
Global declarations	general module 1
Sub main ()	general module 1
Sub blowed_up_good ()	general module 1
Function angle_over (angle, circle)	general module 1
Declarations section	Form1 module
Sub Form_Load ()	Form1 module

Procedure or Region Name	Location
Sub Command1_Click ()	Form1 module
Sub main ()	Form1 module
Sub main ()	general module 2
Declarations section	Form2 module
Sub Form_Load ()	Form2 module

Chapter 16 Answers

1. A function in computing combines arithmetic functions to derive a single value; a statement changes the operative state of the program without returning a value. Because all instructions in Visual Basic are arithmetic operations in some form, the instruction that calls the Function routine must be mathematical as well. Because this instruction is stated in the form of an equation—and the equation contains an obvious result value location—the instruction fulfills all the requirements of a function in computing. Thus, a call to a procedure that returns a value is a function. All function procedures in computing—whether they are written in Visual Basic or assembly language—must be called by some body of the source code, so all functions are in turn *function calls*.

2. The Call statement places a call to a procedure that is not considered a function, because no value is returned. Values are passed to this Sub procedure, however, and those values are declared at the beginning of the Sub procedure in parentheses. Throughout this book, functions and function calls are specified with parentheses, as in Len(), even when no parameters are stated. Programmers do this to distinguish the role of the instruction as a function or function call. If you left parentheses around the Sub (nonfunction) procedure call, you would be violating the syntax of functions. By *including* parentheses in the Call syntax, you are specifying parameters using standard syntax not for the name of the Sub procedure, but for the word Call itself.

Chapter 17 Answers

1. The current setting of their .Index properties, because they are control arrays.

2. Their .Name properties, because the VB interpreter uses the form's own unique .Name property to distinguish between the graphic objects in multiple forms.

3. The _Click event procedure. The giveaway here is the use of the button. If there was no button on the form, perhaps the _Change event procedure might be used.

4. The .Name property is not available to any Visual Basic source code instructions; you simply cannot address it. You could make the setting of the .Tag property for each control equivalent to the setting of the .Name property, because .Tag is not only addressable in the source code, it is changeable by instruction.

Chapter 18 Answers

1. Black

2. Blue

3. .Text

4. Surname.Text

5. Group(1).TabIndex

6. BobTheBear.Tag

Chapter 19 Answers

1. No. If the form has not yet been loaded using the Load statement, the .Show method performs that duty on behalf of Load.

2. Yes. Unload only takes the form out of the workspace and out of memory.

3. In object-oriented methodology, an object is referred to as such only if it has the memory constructs associated with it that make the item *object*-ive. Those constructs do not exist when the object is not in memory. Object-oriented syntax thus cannot be used to refer to a nonexistent object. Load and Unload are both nonobject-oriented because the forms and graphic elements to which they refer do not yet exist in memory, and so do not have objective constructs associated with them.

4. 2

5. 1

6. 0

7. 3

Chapter 20 Answers

1. `Dim NewDoc As New Doc1`
`NewDoc.Show`

in which `NewDoc` can be replaced with any arbitrary object variable name.

2. `Dim NewBarom As New Barometer`
`NewBarom.Show`

in which `NewBarom` can be replaced with any arbitrary object variable name. There is no variation in the syntax of instructions that brings standard forms and MDI child forms onto the screen. What affects each form's ultimate destination is whether its `.MDIChild` property is set to `True`. In answer 2, `Barometer.MDIChild` should be `False`, whereas in answer 1, `Doc1.MDIChild` should be `True`.

3. None. The private workspace of an MDI parent form is considered a void, and not a platform for controls. Thus, no events take place here.

Chapter 21 Answers

1. An input panel.

2. Modal.

3. Because the program, by displaying a file selector panel, needs a file name for its process to continue, it is generally safer to suspend any other inputs to the program until such a file name is delivered.

Chapter 22 Answers

1. A menu bar cannot be positioned on a form using a pointer; thus, you should not use a pointer graphically to invoke a menu bar in a form.

2. A dialog box follows the selection of this menu command.

3. Yes. They are still considered independent objects, although they are referenced using the same procedure.

4. No. A control is made part of a frame by creating it within the frame area. If it is created outside the frame, the VB interpreter always considers it to be outside the frame.

5. Visually it can, but logically a control cannot "half-belong" to a frame.

6. The general procedures area of the form that contained the removed button and now contains the menu command.

Chapter 23 Answers

1. Alaska is state #49 and Hawaii is state #50, regardless of the `.Sorted` state of the list.

2. Guam is the 11th item in the list, because it has yet to be loaded into memory, and you're accounting for the State of Columbia.

Chapter 24 Answers

1. Textual, generally into a text field. The `.Pattern` property must be *intentionally* set to a file search pattern. This pattern is not the result of clicking list boxes; it should be typed by the user.

2. No. The `_Change` event is triggered when a list entry is chosen, not when the list's scroll bars are operated. With standard scroll bars drawn onto a form using the VB toolbox, the `_Change` event *is* generated when the user operates the slider control or clicks any area of the bar.

3. Common dialog boxes are used to gain the information needed to open and save files and print information.

Chapter 25 Answers

1. No. The minimum setting for `.BorderWidth` is 1.

2. Yes, because coordinate settings for a form can be negative (extending beyond the top and left edges of the form), and are also not bounded by the right and bottom edges. Of course, this may mean the control isn't actually visible, although the interpreter does consider it present.

Chapter 26 Answers

1. Directly in the middle of the scroll bar.

2. The `Integer` type, or an integer represented by the `%` symbol.

3. The scroll box is placed at the bottom (or far right) of the scroll area, and the value represented by the scroll bar is set to its `.Max` property setting, regardless of the fact that the incrementation to its value is less than its `.LargeChange` property setting.

Chapter 27 Answers

1. About 1:05.536.

2.   **A.** `_Timer`
        B. `Timer`
        C. `Timer()`

Chapter 28 Answers

1. The scan code values are not functionally additive. The BIOS doesn't think in decimal numbers anyway, so if there is any summing of the two, the result is Boolean rather than decimal.

2. Most likely the first key pressed out of a sequence, no matter how closely together the sequence is pressed, is the first key scanned; however, the lower BIOS values take precedence.

3. You have to read this question carefully to be able to answer it logically. If you understand the problem logically, you understand something about the art and theory of programming. Mechanically speaking, one key takes precedence over the other. The faster the computer scans, the more adept

it is at determining which key comes first—or rather, *appearing* to determine which key comes first. The BIOS code at its lowest level scans for only one key at a time. It does not consider which comes first because it never deals with two values at the lowest level. Thus the computer's quick reflexes have nothing to do with which key takes precedence over the other.

4. By virtue of the scanning sequence, yes, one key higher up in the sequence has "authority" over another. This is not, however, a hierarchy by virtue of one key's assumed importance over another—just its sequence.

Chapter 29 Answers

1. The way this particular procedure is written, the only way a nondiagonal arrow could appear is if the movement of the mouse along either axis is absolute zero. In other words, you'd have to move the mouse perfectly straight to get the arrow to point in a nondiagonal direction.

2. The `Sub Form_MouseMove ()` event procedure is triggered whenever the pointer enters the background area of the form. If a control is blocking the background area, that control might be the one that receives `_MouseMove` events. It therefore follows that if the `_MouseMove` event for a form is recognized, the pointer must have exited the area of any other control—unless, of course, the pointer falls outside the form.

Chapter 30 Answers

1. A drag operation leaves the dragged control where it is, and carries a *copy* of the control. A move operation actually relocates the control to a new location.

2. Yes. The procedure responds only to drops into the region it inhabits, thus making it the target.

3. Coordinates are relative to the control, and must be offset by means of additive arithmetic if they are to be made relative to the form or the screen.

Chapter 31 Answers

1. `.ColWidth(2)`. Remember, the fixed column is the first actual column in the grid, but it is numbered 0.

2. `Cell (1, 1)`.

3. Technically speaking, no. The user can place the cursor in a cell and then scroll the grid so that the cursor becomes invisible. When he begins typing text, however, the cell receiving the text becomes visible.

Chapter 32 Answers

1. `Screen.ActiveControl.Text`

2. `Source.Status.Text`

3. `Screen.ActiveForm.Status.Text`

4. `Source.Parent.Status.Text`

Chapter 33 Answers

1. A function of arithmetic is any operation that can be expressed symbolically and that changes the state or value of something. In trigonometry, for instance, a "true" function is any operation that can be solved logically as a single value for any one unit of time. A graph of such a function, therefore, may only show one point plotted for any vertical line along the graph. A Visual Basic function is representative of a low-level process in the interpreter. It represents an arithmetic function and logically "returns" an explicit value. It *simulates* an arithmetic function, although it may not calculate that function specifically.

2. Not in Visual Basic, as this instruction might in some other dialects of BASIC. In Visual Basic, the instruction reserves all variables of single or multiple letters beginning with the letters *A* through *Z* as being integer variables by default, unless stated otherwise.

3. Because the `Timer` control, the `_Timer` event, and the `Timer()` function, for instance, can be confused with each other if not for the extra punctuation provided in this book.

Chapter 34 Answers

1. 3

2. 65

3. `"z"`

4. 65

5. 1600

Chapter 35 Answers

1. 3

2. -1

3. 1

Chapter 36 Answers

1. `"When"`

2. `" events"`

3. `"n"`

4. `"the "`

5. "When in, of, and around the course of human events"

Chapter 37 Answers

1. `DateSerial()`

2. `TimeSerial()`

3. `TimeValue()`

4. `TimeValue()`

Chapter 38 Answers

1. Between 0 and 1. The multiplication by 72 takes place after the randomization rather than during the randomization.

2. Most of the time, you use the function as if it were written `Rnd(0)`. Omitting the parentheses along with the "dummy parameter" makes using this function a bit easier.

3. Yes, as long as that number is rounded to a short (two-byte) integer expression.

Chapter 39 Answers

1. `"##%"`

2. `"****000.00"`

3. `"h AM/PM"`

4. `"##.##;(##.##);Unchanged"`

5. `Chr$(34) + "by " + Chr$(34) + "h:mm AM/PM" + Chr$(34) + " tonight at`
   `➡the earliest." + Chr$(34)`

Chapter 40 Answers

1. 20

2. pt ja

3. ```
   Prophecy.SelStart = 58
   Prophecy.SelLength = 11
   Prophecy.SelText = "stone"
   ```

Chapter 41 Answers

1. `Printer.Fonts(1)`

2. Many laser printers have internal fonts and font cartridges that have no corresponding fonts in Windows. Some Windows laser printer drivers therefore use "best-guess estimate" fonts to represent those in the printer. These estimate fonts have different names and metrics than the real printer fonts, so it's important you keep the lists separate.

Chapter 42 Answers

1. 0. After printing the line, the interpreter executes a carriage return with line feed, resetting the `.CurrentX` value to 0.

2. 53. The semicolon stops the interpreter from resetting `.CurrentX`. If you were to print anything else using the `.Print` method, it would appear just to the right of the exclamation point.
   ```

3. A Visual Basic image is the bitmap in memory that represents, point by point, what you see on the screen. By comparison, a VB picture is a more abstract concept that describes not only what you see, but also the file format in which it is presented.

4. When a graphics file's contents are loaded into an object, the graphic object is the recipient. Its content properties are immediately set to the contents of the graphics file; so those contents are represented almost as if they were a value; or as a *function* that appears to substitute for a value. By contrast, when a picture or image is saved to disk, the file is the recipient. A file is not an object, so object-oriented syntax does not apply. For this reason, you have to rely on the older style of BASIC syntax and phrase the instruction as a "command." The statement form is used here.

Chapter 43 Answers

1. Yes, because the .PSet method makes a direct plot to the object.

2. No, because the .Point method does not plot to the object, but simply makes a request of that object.

3. Yes, the line does become thicker. Geometrically speaking, because the .Line method plots between two intersection points, it might seem that stretching those points has nothing to do with the thickness of the line between them. Yet once the point is plotted, the *image* of the picture box is set as a bitmap; the .Move method magnifies that bitmap, not its underlying coordinate system.

Chapter 44 Answers

1. The .Move method does not affect the internal coordinate system for that image; .Scale does affect that system.

2. The printer, because a .ScaleMode of four selects elite pitch type, or 12 characters to the inch. Because an inch on your screen cannot be reasonably estimated by your program, although an inch on your printer *can* be estimated, the printer benefits most by this .ScaleMode setting.

3. All cathode ray tube scanning systems start at the top left corner of the screen, scan a line toward the right, and then skip to the line below starting at the left side—the way you're reading the lines in this book now. From an engineering standpoint, to place the origin point at the bottom and proceed upward would be backward.

Chapter 45 Answers

1. An error, because this is not the proper syntax for the `.Line` method. Two sets of parentheses are missing.

2. A bug, because the division operator in the instruction should be a multiplication operator, but the interpreter has no way of knowing the programmer's original intentions.

Chapter 46 Answers

1. Because Visual Basic has no way to test that the logic in your program is appropriate.

2. Windows 3.1 tests those calls an application makes to the Windows API before they are executed. If the call is improperly phrased, contains erroneous data, or could cause Windows to crash, Windows 3.1 apprehends the culprit and immediately claims a General Protection Fault. This is not bug correction, but error trapping. Incorrect phraseology, if the VB interpreter let it go, would certainly cause bugs to happen. Filtering out the errors is a process similar to using your word processor's spell checker: it cleans up your typos, but doesn't make you a better writer.

Chapter 47 Answers

1. The `Print #` statement creates text on disk that has the same format as if the same text were printed to the screen or printer using the `.Print` method. The `Write #` statement, by contrast, places all data entries in quotation marks and separates each entry with a comma, so that applications with "mail-merge" features can import this data.

2. The `Input #` statement retrieves data entries from disk that are saved using the `Print #` statement. These entries have the same length after the `Input #` is executed as they have after the `Print #` is executed. The `Line Input #` statement inputs a string of characters—rather than an explicit entry—that is terminated by a carriage return.

3. The screen, its constituent graphic objects, and the printer all have properties and can be expressed using object-oriented syntax. A data file is governed not by Windows but by DOS, and has no properties, so you must express instructions regarding files using the older style of BASIC syntax.

Chapter 48 Answers

1. 32,765 bytes, which is the maximum length of the actual element minus two for the descriptor.

2. A field.

3. 73 bytes.

Chapter 49 Answers

1. 74

2. "We hold"

3. 7

4. 8

5. "We hold". The Seek statement does not affect the contents of a string variable.

6. " these " with spaces around the word. The Input$ function starts inputting characters beginning at the current Seek() position.

Chapter 50 Answers

1. None. There is a blank record in place of the erased one. NameForm Mark IV has a procedure for covering blank records with the contents of the record immediately following it.

2. The interpreter considers the header a formal record, making the first real record #2 in the count rather than #1.

3. Each record is considered saved once the user enters it or corrects it. The random-access data file is modified periodically by the program.

Complete Source Code Listings of Major Applications

In this appendix are the complete listings for the final and working states of the major applications covered in this book. The FRM listings are presented in Visual Basics *alternative* ASCII text format for forms. To generate graphic objects, you may either refer to these listings and draw the objects onto your forms and enter the procedure listings into module windows as you normally would; or you may instead enter the contents of each listing as you see them here into a text editor, and save the file with the usual FRM extension. You don't need to import text-based FRM files; the interpreter recognizes them automatically and enters them into the workspace with no problem. The BAS listings are best typed directly into a module window. If you prefer, you may use a text editor instead, save the source code as a TXT file, and enroll that file as a BAS module by selecting **Add** File from the **File** menu of the VB interpreters main window. The GBL listings are for global variable declarations only, and are stored in ASCII format anyway. You may enter them with a text editor or through a VB module window. The Menu Design listing shows the contents of the VB interpreters Menu Design Window at the forms design time.

The Expressor—Textually-Assisting Calculator

Project Files:

EXPRESOR.FRM
EXPRESOR.GBL

EXPRESOR.FRM

```
VERSION 2.00
Begin Form Panel
    BackColor       =   &H00FF8080&
    Caption         =   "Expressor"
    ClientHeight    =   4272
    ClientLeft      =   2364
    ClientTop       =   1656
    ClientWidth     =   5340
    ForeColor       =   &H00808080&
    Height          =   4740
    Icon            =   EXPRESOR.FRX:0000
    Left            =   2292
    LinkMode        =   1   'Source
    LinkTopic       =   "Form1"
    ScaleHeight     =   4272
    ScaleWidth      =   5340
    Top             =   1260
    Width           =   5484
    Begin CommandButton EditCut
        BackColor       =   &H00400000&
        Caption         =   "Cut"
        Height          =   375
        Left            =   4680
        TabIndex        =   9
        Top             =   240
        Width           =   495
    End
    Begin TextBox Param
        BackColor       =   &H00FFFF00&
        Height          =   285
        Index           =   0
```

```
          Left            =      3240
          TabIndex        =      10
          Text            =      "0"
          Top             =      720
          Width           =      1335
       End
       Begin CommandButton StoreBank
          BackColor       =      &H00400000&
          Caption         =      "<<"
          Height          =      255
          Index           =      0
          Left            =      4680
          TabIndex        =      11
          Top             =      720
          Width           =      495
       End
       Begin TextBox Param
          BackColor       =      &H00FFFF00&
          Height          =      285
          Index           =      1
          Left            =      3240
          TabIndex        =      29
          Text            =      "0"
          Top             =      1080
          Width           =      1335
       End
       Begin CommandButton StoreBank
          BackColor       =      &H00400000&
          Caption         =      "<<"
          Height          =      255
          Index           =      1
          Left            =      4680
          TabIndex        =      25
          Top             =      1080
          Width           =      495
       End
       Begin TextBox Param
          BackColor       =      &H00FFFF00&
          Height          =      285
          Index           =      2
          Left            =      3240
          TabIndex        =      30
```

```
                        Text            =    "0"
                        Top             =    1440
                        Width           =    1335
                     End
                     Begin CommandButton StoreBank
                        BackColor       =    &H00400000&
                        Caption         =    "<<"
                        Height          =    255
                        Index           =    2
                        Left            =    4680
                        TabIndex        =    26
                        Top             =    1440
                        Width           =    495
                     End
                     Begin TextBox Param
                        BackColor       =    &H00FFFF00&
                        Height          =    285
                        Index           =    3
                        Left            =    3240
                        TabIndex        =    31
                        Text            =    "0"
                        Top             =    1800
                        Width           =    1335
                     End
                     Begin CommandButton StoreBank
                        BackColor       =    &H00400000&
                        Caption         =    "<<"
                        Height          =    255
                        Index           =    3
                        Left            =    4680
                        TabIndex        =    27
                        Top             =    1800
                        Width           =    495
                     End
                     Begin TextBox Param
                        BackColor       =    &H00FFFF00&
                        Height          =    285
                        Index           =    4
                        Left            =    3240
                        TabIndex        =    32
                        Text            =    "0"
                        Top             =    2160
```

```
        Width           =    1335
   End
   Begin CommandButton StoreBank
        BackColor       =    &H00400000&
        Caption         =    "<<"
        Height          =    255
        Index           =    4
        Left            =    4680
        TabIndex        =    28
        Top             =    2160
        Width           =    495
   End
   Begin ComboBox CalcList
        BackColor       =    &H00C00000&
        ForeColor       =    &H00FFFFFF&
        Height          =    300
        Left            =    240
        Style           =    2    'Dropdown List
        TabIndex        =    4
        Top             =    2640
        Width           =    2895
   End
   Begin CommandButton ButtonPos
        BackColor       =    &H00400000&
        Caption         =    "7"
        FontBold        =    -1   'True
        FontItalic      =    0    'False
        FontName        =    "Courier New"
        FontSize        =    9.6
        FontStrikethru  =    0    'False
        FontUnderline   =    0    'False
        Height          =    375
        Index           =    7
        Left            =    3360
        TabIndex        =    22
        Top             =    2640
        Width           =    375
   End
   Begin CommandButton ButtonPos
        BackColor       =    &H00400000&
        Caption         =    "8"
        FontBold        =    -1   'True
        FontItalic      =    0    'False
```

```
         FontName        =   "Courier New"
         FontSize        =   9.6
         FontStrikethru  =   0    'False
         FontUnderline   =   0    'False
         Height          =   375
         Index           =   8
         Left            =   3720
         TabIndex        =   23
         Top             =   2640
         Width           =   375
      End
      Begin CommandButton ButtonPos
         BackColor       =   &H00400000&
         Caption         =   "9"
         FontBold        =   -1   'True
         FontItalic      =   0    'False
         FontName        =   "Courier New"
         FontSize        =   9.6
         FontStrikethru  =   0    'False
         FontUnderline   =   0    'False
         Height          =   375
         Index           =   9
         Left            =   4080
         TabIndex        =   24
         Top             =   2640
         Width           =   375
      End
      Begin CommandButton Percent
         BackColor       =   &H00400000&
         Caption         =   "%"
         Height          =   255
         Left            =   4560
         TabIndex        =   8
         Top             =   2640
         Width           =   615
      End
      Begin CommandButton DividedBy
         BackColor       =   &H00400000&
         Caption         =   "/"
         Height          =   255
         Left            =   4560
         TabIndex        =   15
```

```
    Top            =    2880
    Width          =    615
End
Begin CommandButton ButtonPos
    BackColor      =    &H00400000&
    Caption        =    "4"
    FontBold       =    -1    'True
    FontItalic     =    0     'False
    FontName       =    "Courier New"
    FontSize       =    9.6
    FontStrikethru =    0     'False
    FontUnderline  =    0     'False
    Height         =    375
    Index          =    4
    Left           =    3360
    TabIndex       =    19
    Top            =    3000
    Width          =    375
End
Begin CommandButton ButtonPos
    BackColor      =    &H00400000&
    Caption        =    "5"
    FontBold       =    -1    'True
    FontItalic     =    0     'False
    FontName       =    "Courier New"
    FontSize       =    9.6
    FontStrikethru =    0     'False
    FontUnderline  =    0     'False
    Height         =    375
    Index          =    5
    Left           =    3720
    TabIndex       =    20
    Top            =    3000
    Width          =    375
End
Begin CommandButton ButtonPos
    BackColor      =    &H00400000&
    Caption        =    "6"
    FontBold       =    -1    'True
    FontItalic     =    0     'False
    FontName       =    "Courier New"
    FontSize       =    9.6
```

```
                    FontStrikethru  =   0    'False
                    FontUnderline   =   0    'False
                    Height          =   375
                    Index           =   6
                    Left            =   4080
                    TabIndex        =   21
                    Top             =   3000
                    Width           =   375
                 End
                 Begin CommandButton ClearEntry
                    BackColor       =   &H00400000&
                    Caption         =   "CE"
                    Height          =   615
                    Left            =   2760
                    TabIndex        =   6
                    Top             =   3120
                    Width           =   375
                 End
                 Begin CommandButton Times
                    BackColor       =   &H00400000&
                    Caption         =   "X"
                    Height          =   255
                    Left            =   4560
                    TabIndex        =   14
                    Top             =   3120
                    Width           =   615
                 End
                 Begin CommandButton ButtonPos
                    BackColor       =   &H00400000&
                    Caption         =   "1"
                    FontBold        =   -1   'True
                    FontItalic      =   0    'False
                    FontName        =   "Courier New"
                    FontSize        =   9.6
                    FontStrikethru  =   0    'False
                    FontUnderline   =   0    'False
                    Height          =   375
                    Index           =   1
                    Left            =   3360
                    TabIndex        =   1
                    Top             =   3360
                    Width           =   375
```

```
      End
      Begin CommandButton ButtonPos
         BackColor       =    &H00400000&
         Caption         =    "2"
         FontBold        =    -1    'True
         FontItalic      =    0     'False
         FontName        =    "Courier New"
         FontSize        =    9.6
         FontStrikethru  =    0     'False
         FontUnderline   =    0     'False
         Height          =    375
         Index           =    2
         Left            =    3720
         TabIndex        =    17
         Top             =    3360
         Width           =    375
      End
      Begin CommandButton ButtonPos
         BackColor       =    &H00400000&
         Caption         =    "3"
         FontBold        =    -1    'True
         FontItalic      =    0     'False
         FontName        =    "Courier New"
         FontSize        =    9.6
         FontStrikethru  =    0     'False
         FontUnderline   =    0     'False
         Height          =    375
         Index           =    3
         Left            =    4080
         TabIndex        =    18
         Top             =    3360
         Width           =    375
      End
      Begin CommandButton Minus
         BackColor       =    &H00400000&
         Caption         =    "-"
         Height          =    255
         Left            =    4560
         TabIndex        =    13
         Top             =    3360
         Width           =    615
      End
```

```
Begin CommandButton Enter
   BackColor       =    &H00400000&
   Caption         =    "Enter"
   Height          =    495
   Left            =    4560
   TabIndex        =    12
   Top             =    3600
   Width           =    615
End
Begin CommandButton ApplyFormula
   BackColor       =    &H00400000&
   Caption         =    "Apply Formula"
   Height          =    375
   Left            =    240
   TabIndex        =    16
   Top             =    3720
   Width           =    2415
End
Begin CommandButton ClearAll
   BackColor       =    &H00400000&
   Caption         =    "C"
   Height          =    375
   Left            =    2760
   TabIndex        =    7
   Top             =    3720
   Width           =    375
End
Begin CommandButton Button0
   BackColor       =    &H00400000&
   Caption         =    "0"
   FontBold        =    -1   'True
   FontItalic      =    0    'False
   FontName        =    "Courier New"
   FontSize        =    9.6
   FontStrikethru  =    0    'False
   FontUnderline   =    0    'False
   Height          =    375
   Index           =    9
   Left            =    3360
   TabIndex        =    2
   Top             =    3720
   Width           =    735
End
```

```
Begin CommandButton ButtonPoint
    BackColor       =   &H00400000&
    Caption         =   "."
    FontBold        =   -1  'True
    FontItalic      =   0   'False
    FontName        =   "Courier New"
    FontSize        =   9.6
    FontStrikethru  =   0   'False
    FontUnderline   =   0   'False
    Height          =   375
    Index           =   10
    Left            =   4080
    TabIndex        =   3
    Top             =   3720
    Width           =   375
End
Begin Label Readout
    Alignment       =   1   'Right Justify
    BackColor       =   &H00FF0000&
    Caption         =   "0"
    FontBold        =   -1  'True
    FontItalic      =   0   'False
    FontName        =   "Courier New"
    FontSize        =   12
    FontStrikethru  =   0   'False
    FontUnderline   =   0   'False
    ForeColor       =   &H00FFFFFF&
    Height          =   372
    Left            =   240
    TabIndex        =   0
    Top             =   240
    Width           =   4332
End
Begin Label ParamText
    Alignment       =   1   'Right Justify
    BackColor       =   &H00FFFFFF&
    ForeColor       =   &H00FF0000&
    Height          =   252
    Index           =   0
    Left            =   240
    TabIndex        =   5
    Top             =   720
```

```
         Width            =   2892
      End
      Begin Label ParamText
         Alignment        =   1   'Right Justify
         BackColor        =   &H00FFFFFF&
         ForeColor        =   &H00FF0000&
         Height           =   252
         Index            =   1
         Left             =   240
         TabIndex         =   33
         Top              =   1080
         Width            =   2892
      End
      Begin Label ParamText
         Alignment        =   1   'Right Justify
         BackColor        =   &H00FFFFFF&
         ForeColor        =   &H00FF0000&
         Height           =   252
         Index            =   2
         Left             =   240
         TabIndex         =   34
         Top              =   1440
         Width            =   2892
      End
      Begin Label ParamText
         Alignment        =   1   'Right Justify
         BackColor        =   &H00FFFFFF&
         ForeColor        =   &H00FF0000&
         Height           =   252
         Index            =   3
         Left             =   240
         TabIndex         =   35
         Top              =   1800
         Width            =   2892
      End
      Begin Label ParamText
         Alignment        =   1   'Right Justify
         BackColor        =   &H00FFFFFF&
         ForeColor        =   &H00FF0000&
         Height           =   252
         Index            =   4
         Left             =   240
         TabIndex         =   36
```

```
        Top             =   2160
        Width           =   2892
    End
End
Dim label$(15, 4), p(4)
Dim solution As Single
Const PI = 3.1415927
Const GRAV = 6.6732E-11!

Sub ApplyFormula_Click ()
For in = 0 To 4
p(in) = Val(param(in).Text)
Next in
ndx = CalcList.ListIndex
Select Case ndx
    Case 0
        solution = surf_area_rccyl(p(0), p(1))
    Case 1
        solution = volume_rccyl(p(0), p(1))
    Case 2
        solution = zone_sphere(p(0), p(1))
    Case 3
        solution = force_att(p(0), p(1), p(2), p(3))
    Case 4
        solution = dopp_shift(p(0), p(1), p(2), p(3))
    Case Else
        Exit Sub
End Select
Readout.Caption = Str$(solution)
End Sub

Sub assess_readout ()
readout_value = Val(Readout.Caption)
End Sub

Sub Button0_Click (Index As Integer)
If ready > 0 Then
    If ready < 20 Then
        Readout.Caption = Readout.Caption + "0"
        ready = ready + 1
    End If
End If
assess_readout
```

```
    End Sub

    Sub ButtonPoint_Click (Index As Integer)
    Static point_lock As Integer
    If point_lock = 0 And ready < 20 Then
        Readout.Caption = Readout.Caption + "."
        point_lock = 1
        ready = ready + 1
    End If
    assess_readout
    End Sub

    Sub ButtonPos_Click (Index As Integer)
    If ready > 0 Then
        If ready < 20 Then
            Readout.Caption = Readout.Caption + Right$(Str$(Index),
    1)
            ready = ready + 1
        End If
    Else
        Readout.Caption = Right$(Str$(Index), 1)
        ready = 1
    End If
    assess_readout
    End Sub

    Sub CalcList_Click ()
    For n = 0 To 4
        ParamText(n).Caption = label$(CalcList.ListIndex, n)
    Next n
    Clear_Params
    End Sub

    Sub Clear_Params ()
    For pl = 0 To 4
    param(pl).Text = ""
    Next pl
    ClearAll_Click
    End Sub

    Sub ClearAll_Click ()
    Readout.Caption = "0"
```

```
readout_value = 0
combine_value = 0
ready = 0
End Sub

Sub ClearEntry_Click ()
Readout.Caption = "0"
readout_value = 0
ready = 0
End Sub

Sub DividedBy_Click ()
assess_readout
If readout_value <> 0 And combine_value <> 0 Then
    readout_value = readout_value / combine_value
End If
combine_value = readout_value
Readout.Caption = Str$(readout_value)
ready = 0
End Sub

Function dopp_shift (vo, vs, fo, c)
dopp_shift = ((c + vo) / (c - vs)) * fo
End Function

Sub EditCut_Click ()
Clipboard.SetText Readout.Caption
End Sub

Sub Enter_Click ()
assess_readout
readout_value = readout_value + combine_value
combine_value = readout_value
Readout.Caption = Str$(readout_value)
ready = 0
End Sub

Function force_att (rme, mb, r, y)
force_att = -GRAV * ((rme * mb) / ((r + y) ^ 2))
End Function

Sub Form_Load ()
```

```
CalcList.AddItem "Surface Area of RC Cylinder"
CalcList.AddItem "Volume of RC Cylinder"
CalcList.AddItem "Zone Area of Sphere"
CalcList.AddItem "Force of Earth/Body Attraction"
CalcList.AddItem "Doppler Shift Transmitted Freq."
label$(0, 0) = "Radius of right circular cylinder"
label$(0, 1) = "Height of cylinder"
label$(1, 0) = "Radius of right circular cylinder"
label$(1, 1) = "Height of cylinder"
label$(2, 0) = "Radius of sphere"
label$(2, 1) = "Height of zone"
label$(3, 0) = "Mass of Earth"
label$(3, 1) = "Mass of body in Earth's grav. field"
label$(3, 2) = "Radius of Earth"
label$(3, 3) = "Distance of body above Earth's surface"
label$(4, 0) = "Observer velocity"
label$(4, 1) = "Source velocity"
label$(4, 2) = "Observed frequency"
label$(4, 3) = "Velocity of wave"
End Sub

Sub Minus_Click ()
assess_readout
readout_value = readout_value - combine_value
combine_value = readout_value
Readout.Caption = Str$(readout_value)
ready = 0
End Sub

Sub Percent_Click ()
readout_value = readout_value / 100
Readout.Caption = Str$(readout_value)
ready = 0
End Sub

Sub StoreBank_Click (Index As Integer)
param(Index).Text = Readout.Caption
ready = 0
End Sub

Function surf_area_rccyl (r, h)
surf_area_rccyl = (2 * PI) * r * h
```

```
End Function

Sub Times_Click ()
assess_readout
readout_value = readout_value * combine_value
combine_value = readout_value
Readout.Caption = Str$(readout_value)
ready = 0
End Sub

Function volume_rccyl (r, h)
volume_rccyl = PI * (r ^ 2) * h
End Function

Function zone_sphere (r, h)
zone_sphere = 2 * PI * r * h
End Function
```

The Selector—Alternative File Selector Dialog

Project File:

SELECTOR.FRM

SELECTOR.FRM

```
VERSION 2.00
Begin Form Selector
   BorderStyle    =    3   'Fixed Double
   ClientHeight   =    3588
   ClientLeft     =    2016
   ClientTop      =    1932
   ClientWidth    =    5796
   Height         =    4056
   Left           =    1944
   LinkMode       =    1   'Source
   LinkTopic      =    "Form2"
   ScaleHeight    =    3588
   ScaleWidth     =    5796
```

```
Top              =     1536
Width            =     5940
Begin CommandButton Cancel
    Cancel       =     -1   'True
    Caption      =     "Cancel"
    Height       =     315
    Left         =     4200
    TabIndex     =     6
    Top          =     3000
    Width        =     1365
End
Begin CommandButton OK
    Caption      =     "OK"
    Default      =     -1   'True
    Height       =     315
    Left         =     2700
    TabIndex     =     5
    Top          =     3000
    Width        =     1365
End
Begin FileListBox File1
    Height       =     1752
    Left         =     2700
    TabIndex     =     2
    Top          =     1056
    Width        =     2568
End
Begin DirListBox Dir1
    Height       =     1815
    Left         =     300
    TabIndex     =     1
    Top          =     1050
    Width        =     2115
End
Begin TextBox Filename
    Height       =     315
    Left         =     2700
    TabIndex     =     4
    Top          =     450
    Width        =     2565
End
Begin DriveListBox Drive1
```

```
                Height      =    288
                Left        =    300
                TabIndex    =    0
                Top         =    456
                Width       =    2112
             End
             Begin Label Prompt
                Caption     =    "Filename:"
                Height      =    165
                Left        =    2700
                TabIndex    =    3
                Top         =    150
                Width       =    2565
             End
          End
       End

       Sub Cancel_Click ()
       cancl = True
       TargetFile$ = ""
       Unload Selector
       End Sub

       Sub Dir1_Change ()
       File1.Path = Dir1.Path
       File1_Click
       End Sub

       Sub Drive1_Change ()
       Dir1.Path = Drive1.Drive
       ChDrive Drive1.Drive
       End Sub

       Sub File1_Click ()
       Filename.Text = File1.Filename
       End Sub

       Sub File1_DblClick ()
       OK_Click
       End Sub

       Sub Form_Load ()
       File1.pattern = pattern$
```

```
Filename.Text = File1.pattern
cancl = 0
If prmpt$ = "" Then
    Prompt.Caption = "Filename:"
Else
    Prompt.Caption = prmpt$
End If
End Sub

Sub OK_Click ()
pth$ = Dir1.Path
If File1.Filename = "" Then
    fil$ = Filename.Text
Else
    fil$ = File1.Filename
End If
If Right$(pth$, 1) = "\" Then
    Filename.Text = pth$ + fil$
Else
    Filename.Text = pth$ + "\" + fil$
End If
TargetFile$ = Filename.Text
Unload Selector
End Sub
```

Index

Symbols

- subtraction operator, 76
(pound sign), 457
$ (dollar sign), 458
  as string identifier, 261
  indicating strings, 100
% (percent sign) indicating
  integers, 100
&H prefix, 96
" " (double quote marks)
  indicating null strings, 159
* multiplication operator, 76
+ addition operator, 76
/ division operator, 76
< (less than) operator, 88
<= (less than or equal)
  operator, 88
<> (not equal to) operator, 88
= (equals) operator, 88
> (greater than) operator, 88
>= (greater than or equal)
  operator, 88

A

Abs() function, 411-413
absolute value acquisition, 411
accessing immediate pane, 67
accidental deletion, 357-360
Action property, 303
active form, 225
ActiveControl object, 383
ActiveForm object, 384
Add File command (File menu), 249,
  365
Add Module command (File menu),
  185

AddItem property, 282
addition operator, 76
addressing
  directories, 297-298
  arrays, 157
algebraic calculations, 411
algorithms, 597
aliases for graphics objects,
  204-206
alignment
  fonts, 464
  picture boxes, 491
allocating array space, 116
alphanumeric strings, *see* strings
Alphanumeric-type variables, 70
ANSI (American National Standards Institute), 101, 599-607
answers to review questions,
  609-626
Append statement, 540
appending graphics objects to
  forms, 28-30
application workspace (MDI
  parent forms), 247
applications, 12
  building, 52
  developing, 51-62
  Expressor, 53-56
  libraries, 185
  MDI, 183
  modules, 123
  NameForm Mark IV, 575-581
  programs, 41
  see also programs
arbitrary object variables, 387-390
arithmetic
  binary number system, 86
  date, 436-437

operations, 96
operators, 76
time, 436-437
see also formulas; math
operations
Arrange method, 253
arrays, 111-119
addressing with loop clauses, 157
allocating space, 116
bounds, 117-118
capacity, 111
control arrays, 159-160, 277
creating, 278-279
indexing, 206-207
dimensioning, 112-114
dynamic arrays, 115
lower-bounds address
numbers, 117
passing to procedures, 181
regulating, 115-116
two-dimensional, 113-114
Asc() function, 290, 405
ASCII (American Standard Code
for Information Interchange),
101, 599-607
code chart, 599-607
conversion, 404-409
KeyDown events, 332
ASCII-delimited data files, 548
assignment expressions, 72
assignment operators, 40
asterisks in descriptors, 458
Atn() function, 413
attributes
data files, 563-574
fonts, 463-464
AUTOLOAD.MAK, 365
AutoRedraw property, 511
axes (tables), 113

B

Babbage, Charles, 93
BackColor property, 226
background graphics, 487-488
BackStyle property, 312
base 10 logarithms, 414
base 16 numbers, 94
BASIC, 13
beep, 481-482
binary digits, *see* bits

binary evaluations, 39
binary numbers, 93-95, 86
binary operators, 76
binary statement, 540
binary states, 39
bitmaps
device-dependent, 570
device-independent, 570
persistent bitmaps, 489-491
standard bitmap, 570
bits, 69, 85-86
Bohr, Niels, 102
bold text, 307, 465
Boole, George, 93
Boolean logic, 85-87
Boolean operators, 90-93, 148
border styles (forms), 237
BorderColor property, 312
BorderStyle property, 236, 312
BorderWidth property, 313-314
bounds (arrays), 117-118
boxes (forms), 236
panel comparison, 257-261
branching, 167-172
GoTo statement, 169-173
manual jump mechanism, 168-169
sequential, 175-176
subroutines, 173-175
Break command (Run menu), 388
break state (projects), 24
breakpoints, 190, 528
breaks, manual, 530
buffer zones, 542
buffers, 566
bugs, 527
building
applications, 52
programs, 56-61
buttons, 25
indicator nodes, 31
keyboard events, 335-336
bytes, 69
bits, 69
strings, 99, 417

C

caching, 567
Cancel property, 336
Caption property (graphics
objects), 209

carriage return, 450
Cartesian coordinates, 79
Cartesian Coordinates Calculator, 80-81
case conversion, 425-426
CCur() function, 409
CDbl() function, 409
cell totals (grids), 368
cells (grids), 474-476
CGA color simulation, 497-498
Change event
    graphics objects, 212
    list boxes, 302
channels, 538
    memory buffer, 566
characters, 101
    placeholders, 454-456
    styles, 465-466
    substitution characters, 474
Check box control, 27
Checked property, 273
child windows, 245
Chr$() function, 108, 405-407
circle, 311
clauses
    conditional, 143-154
    conditional branches, 148
    conditional execution clauses, 91
    constructing, 143-146
    If-Then statements, 144-145
        Boolean logical operators, 148
        expressions, 148
        list boxes, 146
        number boxes, 147
        option buttons, 146
    loop clauses, 46, 155-165
        addressing arrays, 157
        data extraction, 164
        Do Loop clause, 162-164
        embedding, 160
        Expressor, 158-160
        plotting data over time, 157-158
        testing, 160-162
        While-Wend clause, 163
    nesting, 46
    nesting instructions, 144
    Select-Case statement, 148-153
        capacity, 151
        equality-only restriction, 152-153

    string variables, 151-152
    subroutines, 45
clearing Clipboard, 572-574
CLI (command-line interpreter), 67, 79, 528
    see also immediate pane
Click event (graphics objects), 207
Clipboard, 570-573
    GetData() method, 572
    GetText() method, 572
    clearing, 572-574
    contents, 572
    data placement, 571
    text placement, 571
CLng() function, 409
clock, 433
    see also time
clock control (forms), 239-240
Close statement, 541
Cls method, 453
clusters, 548
Col property, 367
ColAlignment() property, 370
color
    cells (grids), 475
    CGA color simulation, 497-498
    controls (forms), 225-227
    conversion chart, 497
    lines, 503
    plotting, 495-499
    setting points, 498
Color dialog box, 303
color schemes, 495-499
color values, 495, 498, 506
Cols property, 366
column width, 370
Columns property, 292
ColWidth() property, 369
Combo box control, 27
combo boxes, 282-291
comma delimiter, 450
Command button control, 26
command instructions, 212-214
command-line interpreter, *see* CLI
commands
    Edit menu
        Copy, 278
        Paste, 130, 278
    File menu
        Add File, 249, 365
        Add Module, 185

Index

Make EXE File, 34
New Form, 52
New Module, 185
New Project, 67
Save As, 185
Save Project, 33
menus, 267-268
  designing, 269-273
  grouping controls, 274-279
Options menu (Project), 187, 246
PEEK, 327
Run menu (Break), 388
Window menu (Menu Design), 270
common dialog boxes, 303-307
Common dialog control, 28
common option dot set, 274
comparing controls, 379
comparison operators, 40, 87-89
compilers, 15
complex logical comparisons, 92-93
composite variables, 130-133
compound instructions, 38
concatenation
  strings, 102-103
  string expressions, 450
conditional branches, 148
conditional clauses, 143-154
  see also clauses
conditional execution clauses, 91
conserving memory, 71-72
Const statement, 128
CONSTANT.TXT, 129-130, 347
constants, 128-130
constructing clauses, 143-146
control area (MDI parent forms),
    247-248
control arrays, 57-58, 159-160, 277
  creating, 278-279
  indexing, 206-207
  initiating, 57
control boxes (forms), 233
control characters, 108
control names (forms), 233
control programs, 17
ControlBox property, 234
controls, 21, 29
  comparing, 379
  control arrays, 57-58
  dragging, 349-364
  forms
    color, 225-227

monitoring focus, 224-225
positioning/sizing, 218-220
temporary, 221-222
frames, 275
grid control, 365-377
grids
  cell totals, 368
  column width, 370
  properties, 366-377
  reference cells, 368-369
grouping
  forms, 274-277
  source code, 277-279
indicator nodes, 278
list boxes, 281-295
  multiple choice selections, 291-
  294
  storing choices, 293-294
menus, 267-273
moving, 360-363
overlapping, 220
scroll bars, 317-322
targets, 349
see also graphics objects
conversational programs, 47-49
conversion, 401-410
  ASCII, 404-409
  binary numbers to decimal, 94
  octal numbers, 404
  radians to degrees, 414
  string conversion
    string-to-value, 407
    value-to-string, 408
    variable content, 409
  string conversions, 403-404
converting number systems, 95-96
coordinate position of cursor, 450
coordinate systems, 493-494
  geometric coordinate establish-
    ment, 514
  integer values, 513
  scaling, 513-517
  selecting, 513
  variable, 514
coordinates, 486
Copies property, 306
Copy command (Edit menu), 278
Cos() function, 413
CPU (central processing unit), 13
CSng() function, 409
Currency format, 456

Currency-type variables, 70
.CurrentX setting, 486
.CurrentY setting, 486
cursor
  coordinate position, 450
  insertion point, 472
  virtual cursor, 463
CVar() function, 409
CVDate() function, 439

D

data, 16
  see also strings
data buffer, 566
data channels, 537
Data control tool, 28
data extraction, 164
data files
  ASCII-delimited, 548
  attributes, 563-574
  length, 567
  pointers
    file pointers, 555, 564
    position, 565-566
  text, 549
data pointer
  data files, 566
  initiation, 539
  terminating, 541
data types, 397-398
databases, 12, 537
  record-keeping system, 103-109
date
  arithmetic, 436-437
  as text, 437-439
  format, 459
DateSerial() function, 436-437
DateValue() function, 438-439
datum, 108
Day() function, 434
DblClick event (graphics objects),
    207-209
Debug window, 451
  invoking during run time, 528
debugging, 532
decimal numbers, 93
  converting to binary, 94
  versus binary, 94-95
declaring
  composite variables, 132-133
  object variables, 388-389

string length, 560
  variables, 65-69, 121-134
DECwriter, 451
Default property, 336
degrees, converting to radians, 414
deleting records in NameForm,
    582
delimiters, 77, 450
design state
  graphics objects, 230
  projects, 24
designing forms
  color, 225-227
  controls, 218-222
  monitoring focus, 224-225
  tabs, 222-223
  twip coordinate system, 217-218
developing applications, 51-62
device-dependent bitmaps, 570
device-independent bitmaps, 570
diagnostic routines, 175
dialog boxes
  Color, 303
  common dialog boxes, 303-307
  File, 304-305
  Font, 307
  Font Type, 303
  Open File, 303
  Print, 303, 305-306
  Save As, 303
dialog panels, 259-261
Dim statement, 112-113, 115,
    250-252
dimensioning arrays, 112-114
directories, 297-298
Directory list box control, 27
disabling deletion of read-only
    files, 359-360
disk operating system, *see* DOS
disks, printing text to, 548
display formats, 456-461
displaying
  dialog panels, 259-261
  graphics in picture boxes, 487
distributing p-code files, 34
division operator, 76
Do Loop clause, 162-164
DoEvents statement, 188-189
dollar sign ($), 458
DOS (disk operating system), 18
dotted lines, 501, 503

double-precision floating-point
    numbers (random), 441
Double-precision-type variables, 70
Drag method, 360
DragDrop event, 350
dragging controls, 349-356
    accidental deletion, 357-360
    moving, 360-363
DragIcon property, 354
DragMode event, 351
DragOver event, 350-351, 356, 358
DRAGSTRP.MAK, 353
drawing lines, 309
Drive list box control, 27
Drive property, 297
DropDown event, 291
dynamic arrays, 115

E

edit box, 210
Edit menu commands
    Copy, 278
    Paste, 130, 278
editing graphics objects, 209-211
ejecting printer pages, 480
ellipses, 506-507
embedding loop clauses, 160
Enabled property, 272
encapsulated pseudocode (EP), 170
End statement, 189-191
EOF() function, 563-564
equations, 67, 75, 199-200
Erase statement, 115
Error statement, 525
Error$() function, 525
error-trapping routines, 522-526
ErrorCancel property, 303
errors, 521-522, 525
    see also bugs
event-driven programming, 29
events
    Change, 302
    DragDrop, 350
    DragMode, 351
    DragOver, 350-351, 356, 358
    DropDown, 291
    graphics objects
        Change event, 212
        Click event, 207
        DblClick event, 207-209

keyboard, 327-337
    button assignments, 335-336
    graphics controls, 333-335
    KeyDown event, 329-332
    KeyDown, 328
    KeyDown event, 329-332
    KeyPress, 331
    KeyUp, 328
mouse pointer, 339-348
    appearance, 345-347
    tracking movement, 341-345
    MouseDown, 340
    MouseMove, 341, 345
    MouseUp, 340
    object events, 207-209
    PatternChange, 302
    RowColChange, 376
    Timer, 324
    timer, 323-326
events (graphics objects), 139
Exit statement, 191
Exp() function, 414
exponential operator, 76
EXPRESOR.FRM, 628-643
expressions, 39-40, 66, 450
    assignment operators, 40
    comparison operators, 40
    constants, 128-130
    delimiters, 77
    operators, 40
    string expressions, 450
    unary operators, 40
    watch expressions, 530-532
expressions of assignment, 67
Expressor, 53-56
    global module, 126-127
    list boxes, 284
    loop clauses, 158-160
    procedure calls, 198
extension modules, 22, 41

F

fields, 210
File dialog box, 304-305
File menu commands
    Add File, 249, 365
    Add Module, 185
    Make EXE File, 34
    New Form, 52
    New Module, 185
    New Project, 67

Save As, 185
Save Project, 33
file pointers (data files), 555
    location, 564
    position, 565
file selector boxes, 52, 299-302
`FileAttr()` function, 568
filed state (graphics objects), 230
`FileName` property, 298, 304
files
    CONSTANT.TXT, 129-130, 347
    data files, 548
    distributing p-code files, 34
    graphics, 488
    GRID.VBX, 28, 365
    metafiles, 315
    NameForm, 587
    ordinal file system, 539
    read-only files, 359-360
    saving, 33-34
    trash can icon, 349
Files list box control, 27
fills (lines), 502-507
`Filter` property, 304
`Fix()` function, 402-403
`Fixed` format, 456
`FixedAlignment()` property, 371
`FixedCols` property, 366
`FixedRows` property, 366
floating-point numbers, 69
    double-precision, 441
focus (object variables), 383-385
Font dialog box, 307
font properties, 307
Font Type dialog box, 303
fonts, 307, 463-464
    printers, 480-481
    size, 464
    style, 463
`For-Next` loops, 46, 160-162
`For-Next` statement, 156
`ForeColor` property, 226
Form module, 22, 41, 186-187
`Format$()` function, 449, 454
formats
    dates, 459
    display, 456-461
    time, 459
formatting
    ouput, 454-461
    text in data files, 549

forms
    active form, 225
    as graphics objects, 229-243
    border styles, 237
    boxes, 236
    clock control, 239-240
    control boxes, 233
    control names, 233
    designing, 217-228
        color, 225-227
        controls, 218-222
        monitoring focus, 224-225
        tabs, 222-223
        twip coordinate system,
        217-218
    frames, 275
    graphics objects, 28-30
    grouping controls, 274-277
    implicit loads, 232
    list boxes, 283-284
    loading, 231-232
    location, 229-231
    maximize/minimize buttons
        (Windows), 234
    MDI parent forms, 246-253
    operating state, 240-242
    picture boxes, 352
    scroll box, 234
    shapes/lines, 309-314
    text searches, 238
    time-display, 325
    type 3 windows, 237
    window types, 236
    workspace, 229
    see also programs
formulas, 75-83
    binary operators, 76
    equations, 75
    operators, 76
    parentheses in, 77-82
    precedence of operators, 76-77
    seeding, 68
fractional value storage, 69
Frame control, 26
frames
    controls, 275
    forms, 275
    procedures, 23
`FreeFile()` function, 568
`FromPage` property, 306
`Function` statement, 182-183

functions, 44-45, 137, 395-399
  Abs(), 411-413
  Asc(), 290, 405
  Atn(), 413
  CCur(), 409
  CDbl(), 409
  Chr$(), 108, 405-407
  CLng(), 409
  Convert$(), 95
  Cos(), 413
  CSng(), 409
  CVar(), 409
  CVDate(), 439
  DateSerial(), 436-437
  DateValue(), 438-439
  Day(), 434
  EOF(), 563-564
  Error$(), 525
  Exp(), 414
  FileAttr(), 568
  Fix(), 402-403
  Format$(), 454
  FreeFile(), 568
  Hex$(), 403
  Hour(), 434-435
  Input$(), 569-570
  InputBox$(), 261
  Int(), 401
  intrinsic functions, 40-41
  IsDate(), 440
  IsEmpty(), 398
  IsNull(), 398
  IsNumeric(), 398
  LBound(), 117
  LoadPicture(), 355, 380
  Loc(), 564
  LOF(), 567
  Log(), 414
  mathematical calculations,
    411-415
  Minute(), 434-435
  Month(), 434
  MsgBox, 258
  multiple parameters, 396-397
  Oct$(), 404
  QBColor(), 497-498
  redeclaration, 396-397
  RGB(), 496
  Rnd(), 441-442
  Second(), 434-435
  Seek(), 565

  Sgn(), 411-413
  Sin(), 413
  Spc(), 452-453
  Sqr(), 413
  Str$(), 81, 397, 408
  string functions, 417-432
    InStr(), 426-429
    LCase$(), 425-426
    Left$(), 421-422
    Len(), 419-420
    LTrim$(), 422-423
    Mid$(), 429-430
    Right$(), 421-422
    RTrim$(), 422-423
    Space$(), 420-421
    String$(), 424-425
    UCase$(), 425-426
  Tab(), 452
  Tan(), 413
  testing, 91-92
  text functions, 396
  TimeSerial(), 436-437
  TimeValue(), 438-439
  TypeOf, 386
  UBound(), 117
  user-defined, 181
  Val(), 81, 407
  Variant data type, 397-398
  VarType(), 398
  Weekday(), 434
  Year(), 434

G

general declarations sections
  (modules), 124
general modules, 22, 41
General Number format, 456
geometric coordinate
  establishment, 514
geometric line plotting, 501
Get # statement, 556
global constants, 129-130
global scope, 125, 197
Global statement, 126
global variables, 55-56
  passing parameters, 197
GoSub statement, 174-175
GoTo statement, 169-173
graphical environments, 18
graphical objects, 207-209
graphical program, 47-49

graphics
  background, 487-488
  displaying in picture boxes, 487
  files, 488
  metafiles, 315
  object graphics, 314-315
  OLE, 315
  raster-oriented graphics, 314
  resizing, 489
  stretching, 489
graphic controls of keyboard events,
    333-335
graphics objects, 25-30, 138,
    203-204
  aliases, 204-206
  appending to forms, 28-30
  buttons, 25
  design state, 230
  editing, 209-211
  events, 139
    Change event, 212
    Click event, 207
    DblClick event, 207-209
  filed state, 230
  forms as, 229-243
  methods, 138
  processing command instructions,
      212-214
  properties, 30-33, 138, 203-204
    Caption, 209
    Index, 206-207
    MultiLine, 213-214
    Name, 203-204
    name, 31-33
    ScrollBars, 214
    Tag, 205-206
    Text, 210
  toolbox, 26-28
  unloaded state, 230
  see also controls
grid control, 28, 365-377
GRID.VBX, 28, 365
GridLines property, 375
grids (controls), 474-476
  cell contents, 476
  cell totals, 368
  color, 475
  column width, 370
  pointer, 475
  properties, 375
  reference cells, 368-369

grouping controls
  forms, 274-277
  source code, 277-279

H

Height property, 219
Hewlett Packard notation, 59
Hex$ () function, 403
hexadecimal &H prefix, 96
hexadecimal numbers, 94
  translating, 403
Hide method, 232
high-level programming
    languages, 13
Horizontal scroll bar control, 27
hot spot (pointer), 362
Hour() function, 434-435

I

ICO files, 352
Icon property, 242
icons
  files (Windows), 352
  multiple-state icons, 355-357
If-Then statements, 89-90,
    144-148
  Boolean logical operators, 148
  expressions, 148
  list boxes, 146
  number boxes, 147
  option buttons, 146
Image box control, 28
image boxes, 485-489
image reserve, 511
immediate pane, 67
  see also CLI
implicit loads (forms), 232
incrementing variables, 155
Indefinite-type variables, 70
Index property (graphics objects),
    206-207
indexing control arrays, 206-207
indicator nodes (buttons), 31, 278
indirect references to object
    variables, 385-387
information, 15
initiating control arrays, 57
input
  panels, 261-262
  unformatted, 568
Input # statement, 546

Input statement, 540
Input$() function, 569-570
InputBox$() function, 261
insertion point, 472
InStr() function, 426-429
instructions, 13
  branching, 167-172
    GoTo statement, 169-173
    manual jump mechanism, 168-169
    sequential, 175-176
    subroutines, 173-175
  compound instructions, 38
  nesting, 46
  phrases, 37
Int() function, 401
Integer-type variables, 70
integers, 113
  color values, 496
  trailing zeros, 72
  values in coordinate systems, 513
integrity, 511-512
intermediate code, 14
  see also p-code
interpreters, 14-15
Interval property, 324-326
intrinsic functions, 40-41
  see also keywords
intuit, 13
Investigation of the Laws of Thought, 93
invoking Debug window during run time, 528
IsDate() function, 440
IsEmpty() function, 398
IsNull() function, 398
IsNumeric() function, 398
italic text, 307, 465

J–K

justification, 423-424

Kasparov, Gerry, 12
keyboard
  events, 327-337
    button assignments, 335-336
    graphics controls, 333-335
    KeyDown event, 329-332
  scan codes, 329
KeyDown event, 328-332
KeyPress event, 331
KeyUp event, 328

keywords, 41
  see also intrinsic functions
kilobyte (K), 71

L

Label control, 26
labels, 168
languages, 13
  BASIC, 13
  clauses
    conditional, 143-154
    conditional branches, 148
    conditional execution clauses, 91
    constructing, 143-146
    If-Then statements, 144-148
    loop clauses, 46, 155-165
    nesting, 46
    nesting instructions, 144
    Select-Case statement, 148-153
    subroutines, 45
  high-level programming languages, 13
  low-level programming languages, 13
LargeChange property, 318
LBound() function, 117
LCase$() function, 425-426
left justification, 370
Left property, 218
Left$() function, 421-422
LeftCol property, 375
Len() function, 419-420
libraries, 185
line control, 27
line feeds, 450
Line Input # statement, 550
line numbering, 525
line objects, 310
lines, 309-314
  fills, 502-507
  plotting, 500-507
  width, 503
List box control, 27
list boxes, 281-295
  addressing directories, 297-298
  Change event, 302
  combo box comparison, 282-291
  file selector box, 299-302
  If-Then statements, 146

multiple choice selections,
291-294
rectangles, 314
storing choices, 293-294
List() property, 285
ListCount property, 285
ListIndex property, 286
listing projects, 51
listings, *see* source code listings
LISTTEST.MAK, 288
Load statement, 231
loading
forms, 231-232
graphics files, 488
LoadPicture() function, 355, 380
Loc() function, 564
local context (procedures), 43
local scope (variables), 44, 123-126,
197
locked controls, 357-360
LOF() function, 567
Log() function, 414
logarithmic calculations, 411
logarithmic operations, 414
logarithms, 414
logic
Boolean logic, 85-87
Boolean operators, 90-93
comparison operators, 87-89
If-Then statements, 89-90
number systems, 93-96
Long integer-type variables, 70
loop clauses, 46, 155-165
addressing arrays, 157
data extraction, 164
Do Loop clause, 162-164
embedding, 160
Expressor, 158-160
For-Next loops, 46
plotting data over time, 157-158
testing, 160-162
While-Wend clause, 163
low-level programming languages,
13
lower-bounds address numbers
(arrays), 117
LSet statement, 423-424
LTrim$() function, 422-423

M

Make EXE File (File menu), 34
manage lists, 287
mathematic functions, 411-415
Max property, 306, 318
MaxButton property, 234
maximize/minimize buttons
(windows), 234
MDI (Multiple Document Inter-
face), 183, 245-255
MDIChild property, 249
megabyte (M), 71
memory, 554
bytes, 69
conserving, 71-72
kilobyte (K), 71
megabyte (M), 71
Menu Design command (Window
menu), 270
Menu Design window, 269-271
menus, 267-273
message boxes, 109
metafiles (Windows), 315, 352
methods, 138
Arrange, 253
Cls, 453
Drag, 360
Hide, 232
Move, 361, 363
Print, 449
Show, 231
ZOrder, 220
Mid$ statement, 431
Mid$() function, 429-430
Min property, 306, 318
MinButton property, 235
Minute() function, 434, 435
modeless windows, 261
modular scope, 125, 197
modules, 41, 45, 123, 179-194
DoEvents statement, 188-189
End statement, 189-191
extension modules, 41
Form module, 186-187
form modules, 41
general declarations sections,
124
general modules, 41
origins, 179-183

sequence, 183-186
Sub Main () procedure, 187-188
modulo arithmetic, 96
monitoring control focus, 224-225
Month() function, 434
mouse pointer, 339-348
    appearance, 345-347
    hot spot, 362
    tracking movement, 341-345
MouseDown event, 340
MouseMove event, 341, 345
MousePointer property, 345
MouseUp event, 340
MOUSEVAN.MAK, 342-343
Move method, 361, 363
moving controls, 360-363
MS-DOS, 18
MsgBox function/statement, 258
MultiLine property (graphics
        objects), 213-214
MULTINAM.MAK, 371-372
MultiName application (Tag
        property), 382-383
Multiple Name Display Applica-
        tion, 371-375
multiple-state icons, 355-357
multiplication operator, 76
MultiSelect property, 292

N

Name property, 31-33, 203-204, 354
Name-Only Record-Entry System,
        Mark II, 319
NAMEFM2B.MAK, 124
NameForm
    creating files, 587
    deleting records, 582
    sorting records, 594-597
NameForm Mark IV, 575-581
NAMEFORM.MAK, 104-107
NAMEFRM2.MAK, 319
NAMEFRM4.FRM, 382, 576-578
NAMEFRM4.GBL, 578
name controls (forms), 233
naming fonts, 307
NAMTABLE.FRM, 372
nesting, 46
nesting instructions, 144
von Neumann, John, 93

New Form command (File
        menu), 52
New Module command (File
        menu), 185
New Project command (File
        menu), 67
null strings, 159
number boxes, 147
number systems, 93-96
    &H prefix, 96
    binary numbers, 93
    binary versus decimal, 94-95
    conversion procedure, 95-96
    decimal numbers, 93
numbering program lines, 525

O

object code, 14
object events, 207-209
object graphics, 314-315
object properties settings, 139
object variables, 379-391
    arbitrary, 387-390
    declaring, 388-389
    focus, 383-385
    indirect references, 385-387
    multiple Tags, 382-383
    Parent, 381-382
    Tag property, 380-382
    terminating references, 390
objects
    ActiveControl object, 383
    ActiveForm object, 384
    graphics objects, 25-30, 203-204
        aliases, 204-206
        buttons, 25
        design state, 230
        editing, 209-211
        events, 139, 207-209, 212
        filed state, 230
        forms as, 229-243
        methods, 138
        properties, 30-33, 138, 203-214
        unloaded state, 230
    Screen object, 385
    updating, 512
Oct$() function, 404
octal number conversion, 404
OLE (Object Linking and Embed-
        ding), 315

OLE Client control, 28
On Error statement, 522
On...GoSub statement, 176
On...GoTo statement, 176
Open File dialog box, 303
open statement, 539
operating state (forms), 240-242
operational elements (programs), 56
operators, 40, 76
  arithmetic, 76
  assignment operators, 40
  binary operators, 76
  Boolean operators, 90-93
  comparison operators, 40,
    88-89
  precedence, 76-77
  unary operators, 40
  XOR operator, 92
Option Base statement, 118
option buttons, 274
Option Compare statement, 431
Option dot control, 27
Option Explicit statement, 122
option sets (Windows), 274
Options menu commands
  Project, 187, 246
order of module execution,
  183-186
ordinal file system, 539
output
  display format, 456-461
  formatting, 454-461
  length, 472
  placeholders, 454-456
  text size, 473-474
Output statement, 540
ovals, 311
overlapping controls, 220

P

p-code, 14-15, 34
pachinko machine, 86
paging area, 234
panels/box comparison, 257-261
parameter pairs, 494
  see also coordinate systems
parameters, 43, 58
  functions, 396-397
  passing, 195-200

  procedures, 43-44
  Sub procedures, 181
parent forms, 246-253
Parent object variable, 381-382
parent windows, 245
parentheses in formulas, 77-82
passing arrays to procedures, 181
passing control, 529
passing parameters, 195-200
password requests, 262
Paste command (Edit menu), 130,
  278
Path property, 298, 301
Pattern property, 298
PatternChange event, 302
patterns in lines, 504
PC DOS, 18
  see also DOS
PC Paintbrush files, 352
PCX files, 352
PEEK command, 327
Percent format, 456
persistent bitmaps, 489-491
phrases, 37
Picture box control, 26
picture boxes, 485-489
  alignment, 491
  bitmaps, 489-491
  graphics, 487-488
  on forms, 352
  redrawing, 512
  refreshing, 511
  saving contents, 490-491
pixels, 498
placeholders, 454-456, 458
plotting
  coordinate systems, 493-494
  ellipses, 506-507
  lines, 500-504
  virtual origin, 494
plotting data over time, 157-158
pointer (mouse), 339-348
  appearance, 345-347
  hot spot, 362
  tracking movement, 341-345
pointers
  coordinates, 486
  data files, 564-565
  data pointer termination, 541
  file pointers (data files), 555
  grids, 475

polling data, 205
polling for keys, 327
positioning
    controls (forms), 218-220
    scroll bar, 317-321
pound sign (#), 457
precedence (operators), 76-77
precision types (variables), 69-71
Print method, 449
Print # statement, 545
Print dialog box, 303, 305-306
printer twips, 487
printers
    coordinates, 486
    current page, 479
    ejecting pages, 480
    fonts, 480-481
    virtual terminals, 479
printing
    carriage returns, 450
    DECwriter, 451
    line feeds, 450
    text to disk, 548
procedural algebra, 49
procedure declarations, 42
procedure window, 23
procedures, 23, 41, 173
    frames, 23
    local context, 43
    parameters, 43-44
    passing arrays, 181
    passing parameters, 195-200
    routines, 45
    Sub Form_Load (), 320, 390
    Sub LoadFile (), 375
    Sub Main (), 187-188
    Sub procedures, 43
processing command instructions,
    212-214
programming
    event-driven, 29
    objective, 11-12
    structured, 121-122
programs, 11-19, 41
    AUTOLOAD.MAK, 365
    binary evaluations, 39
    binary states, 39
    branching, 167-172
        GoTo statement, 169-173
        manual jump mechanism,
        168-169
    sequential, 175-176
    subroutines, 173-175
breakpoints, 190
building, 56-61
compilers, 15
compound instructions, 38
control, 17
controls, 21
databases, 12
DRAGSTRP.MAK, 353
expressions, 39-40
    assignment operators, 40
    comparison operators, 40
    operators, 40
    unary operators, 40
functions, 44-45, 137
high-level programming lan-
    guages, 13
instructions, 13
interpreters, 14-15
intrinsic functions, 40-41
keywords, 41
labels, 168
languages, 13
LISTTEST.MAK, 288
low-level programming lan-
    guages, 13
modules, 41, 45, 179-194
    DoEvents statement, 188-189
    End statement, 189-191
    Form module, 186-187
    origins, 179-183
    sequence, 183-186
    Sub Main () procedure,
    187-188
MOUSEVAN.MAK, 342-343
MULTINAM.MAK, 371-372
NAMEFRM2.MAK, 319
NAMEFRM4.FRM, 382, 576-578
NAMEFRM4.GBL, 578
NAMTABLE.FRM, 372
operational elements, 56
p-code, 14
phrases, 37
procedures, 23, 41
purposeful elements, 56
readout, 56
record-keeping system, 103-109
remarks, 139-141
routines, 45, 172

SCROLKEY.MAK, 330-331, 334-335
SELECTOR.MAK, 299-300
sequence, 13
source code, 13
startup form, 186
statements, 38, 39, 137
subprograms, 180
syntax, 37-39
timer, 323-326
user programs, 17
variables, 16, 37, 49, 65-73
  conserving memory, 71-72
  declaring, 65-69
  global variables, 55-56
  local scope, 44
  precision types, 69-71
  string variables, 71
  variant, 71
  see also applications; functions; projects; statements
Project command (Options menu), 187, 246
Project window, 22
projects, 21-25
  break state, 24
  design state, 24
  extension module, 22
  form modules, 22
  general module, 22
  listing, 51
  NAMEFM2B.MAK, 124
  NAMEFORM.MAK, 104-107
  run state, 24
  saving, 33-34
  toolbar, 24
  see also programs
properties, 30-33, 138
  Action, 303
  AddItem, 282
  BackColor, 226
  BackStyle, 312
  BorderColor, 312
  BorderStyle, 236, 312
  BorderWidth, 313-314
  Cancel, 336
  Checked, 273
  Col, 367
  ColAlignment(), 370
  Cols, 366
  Columns, 292

  ColWidth(), 369
  ControlBox, 234
  Copies, 306
  Default, 336
  DragIcon, 354
  Drive, 297
  Enabled, 272
  ErrorCancel, 303
  FileName, 298, 304
  Filter, 304
  FixedAlignment(), 371
  FixedCols, 366
  FixedRows, 366
  fonts, 307
  ForeColor, 226
  FromPage, 306
  graphics objects, 203-204
    Caption, 209
    Index, 206-207
    MultiLine, 213-214
    Name, 203-204
    ScrollBars, 214
    Tag, 205-206
    Text, 210
  grid control, 366
  GridLines, 375
  grids, 375
  Height, 219
  Icon, 242
  Interval, 324-326
  LargeChange, 318
  Left, 218
  LeftCol, 375
  List(), 285
  ListCount, 285
  ListIndex, 286
  Max, 306, 318
  MaxButton, 234
  MDIChild, 249
  Min, 306, 318
  MinButton, 235
  MousePointer, 345
  MultiSelect, 292
  Name, 354
  name, 31-33
  Path, 298, 301
  Pattern, 298
  RemoveItem, 283
  Row, 367
  RowHeight(), 369
  Rows, 366

Selected(), 293
settings, 52
Shape, 310
SmallChange, 318
Sorted, 287
Style, 282
TabIndex, 222
TabStop, 223
Tag, 354, 379-383
Top, 219
ToPage, 306
TopRow, 375
Value, 276
Visible, 273
Width, 219
WindowList, 273
WindowState, 240
X1, 310
X2, 310
Y1, 310
Y2, 310
Properties window, 22
Put # statement, 554

Q-R

QBColor() function, 497-498

radians, converting to degrees, 414
random number generator, 441-445
Random statement, 540
random-access, 538, 553
Randomize statement, 442-444
raster-oriented graphics, 314
read-only files, 359-360
readout, 56
real-number values, 150
rearranging windows, 253-254
record-keeping system, 103-109
records (NameForm), 559
    deleting, 582
    sorting, 594-597
rectangles, 311
redeclaring functions, 396-397
ReDim statement, 116
redrawing, 511-512
reference cells (grids), 368-369
references (object variables),
    385-387
registers, 553
regulating arrays, 115-116
Rem statements, 140-141

remarks (programs), 139-141
RemoveItem property, 283
requesting passwords, 262
rescaling coordinate systems,
    513-517
reseeding random number
    generator, 442
Reset statement, 567
resizing graphics, 489
restore button (windows), 234
resuming execution, 529
retrieving data, 556
Reverse Polish notation, 59
RGB() function, 496
Right$() function, 421-422
Rnd() function, 441, 442
rounded rectangles, 311
rounded squares, 311
rounding, 402-403
routines, 172
    error-trapping, 522-526
    subroutines, 45
Row property, 367
RowColChange event, 376
RowHeight() property, 369
Rows property, 366
RSet statement, 423-424
RTrim$() function, 422-423
run state (projects), 24

S

Save As command (File menu), 185
Save As dialog box, 303
Save Project command (File menu),
    33
saving
    picture box contents, 490-491
    projects, 33-34
scaling coordinate system, 517
scan codes (keyboard), 329
Scientific format, 456
scope (variables), 123-128, 197
Screen object, 385, 494-495
SCROLKEY.MAK, 330-331,
    334-335
scroll bars, 317-322
scroll box (forms), 234
scroll boxes, 233
ScrollBars property (graphics
    objects), 214